THE DEVELOPMENT OF
MODERN FRANCE
(1870–1939)

FRANCE
UNDER THE REPUBLIC
The Development of Modern France
(1870-1939)

by

D. W. BROGAN

GREENWOOD PRESS, PUBLISHERS
WESTPORT, CONNECTICUT

Library of Congress Cataloging in Publication Data

Brogan, Sir Denis William, 1900-1974.
    France under the republic.

    Published in England under title: The development of
modern France.
        Reprint of the 1940 ed. published by Harper, New York.
        1. France--History--Third Republic, 1870-1940.
    2. France--Politics and government--1870-1940.
    I. Title.
    DC335.B75 1974   944.081   74-11934
    ISBN 0-8371-7718-9

This book is published in
England under the title
THE DEVELOPMENT OF
MODERN FRANCE

Originally published in 1940 by Harper & Brothers
Publishers, New York and London

Reprinted in 1974 by Greenwood Press,
a division of Williamhouse-Regency Inc.

Library of Congress Catalog Card Number 74-11934

ISBN 0-8371-7718-9

Printed in the United States of America

PREFACE

THE object of this book is to provide an account of modern French history from the fall of the Second Empire to the outbreak of the present war. It is designed for the general public. As the history of the Third Republic has only recently begun to be studied in a scholarly fashion, many important questions are still unsettled and it has been necessary to omit discussion of the evidence for the views taken here and to drop any apparatus of notes or bibliography. As the story approaches the present day, the traps in the way of the narrator increase in number and in complexity. The writing of very recent history must involve the use of materials which it is almost impossible to control. I have tried to reduce to a minimum the amount of guesswork at the cost of reducing to a mere narrative a very complex story. The last year has, indeed, been sketched only in the baldest outline. It should be said, however, that all of this book was planned and nearly all of it written before the outbreak of the present war. I have not attempted to alter the judgments passed on individuals and events in deference to any supposed need for reducing modern history in war-time to the level of a royal biography. It should be said, too, that the account of the origin of the last war, of the conduct of the last war, and of the nature of the peace settlement was largely written and entirely planned some years ago. The views here expressed on German diplomacy, military methods and geo-political position were formed long before the last reputable friends of the Third Reich were silenced by the event.

There is one feature of the plan of this book which, even apart from the faults in execution, may be adversely criticized. For here the 'development' of France is described only in its community aspects. There is what will seem to many an old-fashioned emphasis on political history. That the result is a distorted and unjust picture of modern France will be at once admitted. At no time since the reign of Louis XIV has the genius of individual Frenchmen and Frenchwomen been more brilliantly displayed, or in a greater variety of fields, than in this period. A history of modern France which finds space for the Duc de Broglie, historian and politician, but not for his grandson, the great physicist; for Calmette the journalist and not for his brother, the great pathologist; for Raymond Poincaré and not for his cousin, Henri Poincaré, the great mathematician: which has room for Zola

vii

but not for his school-fellow Cézanne, for Senator Antonin Proust and not for his kinsman Marcel, obviously cannot pretend to give anything like a complete picture of French activity in this period. Pasteur, Debussy, Degas, Pierre Curie, Mallarmé, Bergson, the two Charcots, Alexis Carrel, André Citroën, Blériot, Père de Foucauld, Saint Theresa of Lisieux, Madame de Noailles, Sarah Bernhardt, Gaston Paris, Littré, Le Corbusier, a handful of names taken almost at random reveals the variety of talents or of genius that modern France has bred or provided a home for. But to assess the importance of these leaders in so many fields is beyond my knowledge and abilities, and I have chosen to ignore those brilliant but private careers, and concentrate on the institutions and events affecting the political unit called France, a unit much more easy to describe than the indefinable thing called 'French civilization'.

Whatever merits this book may have it owes largely to the many Frenchmen and Frenchwomen of all classes who have submitted to questioning, who have helped to form the picture which has grown up in my mind of the recent past of the nation to which our Western civilization owes most. Of that Western civilization (of which with all its faults we are unescapably the children) France has been, since the time of the *Chanson de Roland*, the main sword and the main shield. So it is to-day.

Note. I have not attempted to preserve French capitalization in proper names of persons or of institutions. In English the oddity outweighs the attractions of pedantic accuracy.

CONTENTS

CONTENTS

BOOK I

THE BIRTH OF THE REPUBLIC

Fluctuat nec mergitur.

Motto of Paris.

CHAPTER I

THE FALL OF AN EMPIRE

I

IN December 1848, ten months after the revolution that had expelled the junior line of the House of Bourbon from the French throne, Louis Napoleon Bonaparte, nephew of Napoleon I and grandson of Josephine, was elected President of the Second French Republic by an overwhelming majority. Three years later by the *coup d'état* of December 2nd, 1851, he dissolved Parliament by armed force and made himself a dictator, a drastic solution of the problem of his relations with the Assembly that the French people, in a plebiscite, overwhelmingly ratified. A year later, another plebiscite ratified the assumption of the imperial crown under the title of Napoleon III. The new Emperor was detested by the adherents of the fallen legitimate monarchy of the elder line of the Bourbons, by the adherents of the constitutional monarchy of the younger line, by the devotees of the Republic. In this band of opponents were some of the greatest names in contemporary France: Victor Hugo, the greatest living poet, who remained in obstinate exile; Adolphe Thiers, the most famous of French historians, who was also one of the most famous of French politicians; Alexis de Tocqueville, theorist and practitioner of popular government, and a host of others. But the French peasant and the French shopkeeper of the small town, as well as many in all classes in the great cities, were indifferent to the vitriolic poetry of Victor Hugo or the dignified hostility of M. Thiers. The new Emperor (who had promised peace) gave two great wars, neither very popular but both successfully glorious; he made an ally of England and humiliated Russia and Austria. He was the chief maker of united Italy and patron of revived Rumania. Paris was modernized and made more splendid if not more beautiful. It became the pleasure capital of the world; and rapid economic development made it one of the business capitals, too. The Imperial Court, if sometimes vulgar, was magnificent in a fashion unknown in London, Vienna, or St. Petersburg. The Empress, the beautiful Spaniard, Eugénie de Montijo, set the fashions in ladies' dress, as her husband did in politics. There was an heir, an attractive boy, and, though opposition grew in France it was deeply divided, ranging as it did from the great Royalist lawyer, Berryer, to such dangerous demagogues as the young Republican advocate, Gambetta, whose manners, morals and political principles terrified the right-minded.

By 1870, the Emperor was getting old and was already ill. He had been compelled to withdraw the French troops who were trying to set up the Archduke Maximilian on the throne of Mexico. His brilliant protégé, Herr von Bismarck of Prussia, had, under imperial patronage, attacked Austria, and when the 'Six Weeks' War' was over, the Prussian Prime Minister not only turned himself into Chancellor of a North German Confederation without asking Napoleon's leave, he refused to give any compensation for thus upsetting the balance of power. When in 1867 the King of Holland was prepared to sell his Grand Duchy of Luxemburg to France, Bismarck vetoed the sale. It was a great blow, and by the standards of that age had to be revenged, but Napoleon III was weary, and when the Opposition won a great many seats at the general election of 1869, he took the last steps in a long-drawn-out process. He resigned himself to the position of a constitutional monarch like Queen Victoria and accepted as Prime Minister, Émile Ollivier.

The willingness of M. Ollivier to serve Napoleon III and the willingness of Napoleon III to be served by him did them both credit, for not only had M. Ollivier been a leader of the Opposition, but his father had been arrested by the Emperor's police when Napoloen was seizing dictatorial power in 1851. The more violent members of the Opposition denounced Ollivier as a traitor, but he was approved of by M. Thiers and the sight of a former Republican in the uniform of a Minister of the Empire was not without its lesson for practical politicians. Of course, there was violent Socialism rampant among the Paris workers and in the great steel works of the President of the Corps Législatif at Le Creusot. But an attempted revolution, provoked by the killing of a journalist by a ne'er-do-well cousin of the Emperor, failed miserably, despite the provocation to revolt of the nobleman who, dropping all his titles, had become the most popular journalist of the Paris working-men. It would take a great deal more than the eloquence of Maître Gambetta, the pen of Henri Rochefort, or the conspiratorial gangs of Auguste Blanqui to overthrow a power so strongly based on a strong army, a resolute police force and popular acquiescence.

The Emperor had asked the people of France to express approval or disapproval of the move towards liberal institutions. The plebiscite was violently attacked and the Opposition did their best to show that the country was not taken in by this trick. The result was more gratifying than the Emperor dared hope and far worse than the Opposition had feared. Over seven million Frenchmen approved of the imperial régime in its new dress, while the number of opponents was only a little greater than in 1851 and 1852. The million and a half of irreconcilables were helpless in face of this vote. The Emperor had a new grant of authority. The Opposition clung to the crumb of comfort that over 50,000 soldiers had voted 'no' and other Frenchmen were puzzled that only 350,000 soldiers voted in all. Where were the remaining 150,000 that were assumed to be in the most formidable army in the world? But these critics and these wondering statisticians could not hide from themselves that the Second Empire, eighteen years after its violent birth, seemed to have undergone a new birth of freedom, and that government of the people, by the people, for the people, in a republican form at least, was far enough off in France, if France was to have the last word in her own destiny. The plebiscite was France's Sadowa, Ollivier had declared, and it was also an indication that the French Government realized that peace had her victories no less renowned than war, a belief whose sincerity had been shown by the decision to reduce the annual contingent of conscripts for the army by 10,000. It was a gesture towards that era of disarmament of which the Emperor dreamed.

II

On July 5th, Lord Granville, who was about to become British Secretary of State for Foreign Affairs, talked over the general situation with Hammond, the veteran Under-Secretary. The report made to the successor of Lord Clarendon was highly reassuring to him both as a Foreign Secretary and as a member of the pacific Cabinet of Mr. Gladstone. Never had the Under-Secretary known so great a lull in foreign affairs. The new Minister would not, as far as could be seen, have any important business to deal with. That evening Granville, like the rest of the world, learned that a diplomatic mine had been exploded; and although it was not quite certain who had laid it, there was no doubt what country and Government was shaken by the explosion. Prince Leopold of Hohenzollern-Sigmaringen had accepted the offer of the vacant throne of Spain.

In 1868, Queen Isabella II had by the extravagance of her life, the looseness of her morals and the absurdity of her politics, worn out the patience of the ruling class in Spain, the generals, and she had been deposed and had gone into exile with her son.[1] Marshal Serrano and Marshal Prim, convinced that a Spanish Republic was impossible, began to look around for a prince who could be induced to mount the not very stable throne. The fall of Isabella was a blow to the policy of Napoleon III, for he had taken a kindly interest in her fortunes: and his Empress was even more involved in the politics of her native land. But even had Napoleon been completely indifferent to

---

[1] Later Alfonso XII, father of ex-King Alfonso XIII.

Isabella, the question of who should rule Spain was traditionally of tremendous importance to the ruler of France. The greatest danger run by France in the past had come, it was believed, from the union in one family of the thrones of Spain and of the old German Empire. Since the establishment of the Bourbons at Madrid in 1700, that danger of an enemy on the north-east and also on the south-west frontiers of France had ceased to be a nightmare. Spain had only two neighbours, Portugal and France. Of all the great powers, France alone had a natural interest in Spain and, in 1870, no Frenchman doubted these simple geographical truths. But it was learned on July 3rd that the rulers of Spain were about to propose to the Spanish Cortes (which would do as it was told) the candidacy of Prince Leopold of Hohenzollern-Sigmaringen, a member of that family which, above all others, it was to the interest of France to keep away from her back door, since the recently victorious armies of this house lay so uncomfortably close to her front door.

It is true that the young Prince was not a near kinsman of the King of Prussia, being a cadet of the elder line which had stayed at home in pleasant Swabia while the junior line sought greater fortune in the dreary plains of Brandenburg. But the senior line had been willingly absorbed by the junior, had ceded the little ancestral principality to Prussia and had been recognized as part of the Royal House. The princes were all loyal Prussians, and this much more than set off the indubitable but unimportant fact that they were more closely connected by blood and marriage with the Emperor of the French than with the King of Prussia.[1] The young Prince had some claim to being a suitable candidate for the Spanish throne. He was a Catholic, like the rest of his branch, and he had married a Portuguese princess. But although he was a cousin of the Emperor of the French and connected with the dynasty of Spain's other neighbour, he was first and last a Prussian prince. It was one thing to put his brother Charles, with the approval of Napoleon III, on the throne of Rumania,[2] or to offer Leopold the throne of Greece, but no French Government could look on calmly while a Prussian officer was made ruler in Madrid. This fact was perfectly well known to the two chief actors, Marshal Prim and Count von Bismarck, for though it may be doubtful when the Chancellor of the North German Confederation first took a hand in the plot, by the spring of 1870 he was one of its moving spirits.

From Bismarck's point of view, the 'Hohenzollern candidacy', as the world soon learned to call it, had everything in its favour. If all went well, if the new King were elected and France was thus presented with a *fait accompli*, Napoleon III would have to submit—or to in-

---

[1] The Prince had a Murat grandmother on his father's side and a Beauharnais grandmother on his mother's side.
[2] Leopold was the grandfather of King Carol II of Rumania.

6

furiate Spanish pride by denying the right of the Cortes to elect whom it chose. If he did submit, then there was a dutiful Prussian in Madrid to give the French cause to look to their southern frontier. However little King Leopold could do, it would be better than nothing when that inevitable day came, the day of reckoning between the great power of the present and the great power of the future.

The unification of North Germany under Prussia had been carried out with the benevolent assistance of Napoleon III. He believed in national unity, in the policy of 'great agglomerations'. He also expected to be in a position to impose his own terms after a long and exhausting struggle between Prussia and Austria. But in six weeks Prussia had completely defeated Austria, and France was too late to intervene. Peace was made with only the most formal participation of Napoleon III. To a simple-minded imperialist soldier like Colonel du Barail, this ignoring of the Government of the 'great nation' was impudent. And other servants of the Emperor felt the same: 'It is France that has been beaten at Sadowa,' said Marshal Randan.

The enemies of the Empire were quick to rub in this truth. Many of them, on the Left, rejoiced in the Prussian victory. Many of them agreed with what that anti-clerical Bonapartist, Edmond About, had written in 1860, that France would welcome the union of Germany under Prussia. Only 'the princes and the junkers' would not help Prussia to this high destiny. Protestant and enlightened Prussia was admired by the enemies of the Church in France. What Sainte-Beuve had called the 'vague and lyrical' view of Germany that Madame de Staël had helped to spread in France was far from dead. Even after Sadowa, George Sand had refused to believe the warning of the veteran revolutionary Barbès who wrote to her that 'it is really barbarism which is ready to throw itself on us'. Germany was the land whose scholars had freed Renan from his faith and which had inflamed the heart of young Edgar Quinet even before he knew much German. And, in any case, not only were the Germans a philosophical and anti-clerical people, they were also harmless. Parisians had seen what a small German court was like in the famous comic opera 'The Grand Duchess'. Who could be afraid of the army of Gerolstein and of General Boum? Too many people confused Gerolstein with Prussia and Count von Bismarck (a great admirer of the comic opera) with General Boum. The sense in which Germany, like the Grand Duchess, loved military men was not well understood in France.

Spain was not Gerolstein, and the sudden revelation that the elaborate preparations for putting Prince Leopold on the Spanish throne had almost been completed was too much for the temper of the French ruling classes and for their political enemies of the same education. So when on July 6th the Duc de Gramont made a strong speech to the Chamber announcing that France could not look on 'while a neighbour-

7

ing people obliges us to permit a foreign power, by placing one of its princes on the throne of Charles V, to disturb to our detriment the present equilibrium in Europe and to place the interests and honour of France in peril', there was general approval of his firm attitude. He was indeed only representing the views of such organs of respectable opinion as the *Temps*, and it was an organ of the partisans of divine right, the *Gazette de France*, which had first published the news. The Imperial Government, which had allowed itself to be tricked once by Bismarck, could not afford to do so twice.

The speech of the Duc de Gramont was the first of the French mistakes in the crisis. Suspecting, rightly but without proofs that could be made public, that the Hohenzollern candidacy was a move of the Chancellor's against France, the French Government took up the challenge, anxious to make public its views and to prevent the Opposition in France from accusing it of slackness. A prudent commentator, the young Albert Sorel, pointed out that the proper move was to approach Madrid, to point out to Serrano and Prim that the candidacy was intolerable to France, and get them to withdraw the proposal. Once Prussia was directly involved, France would have to deal with a great power, not with disunited and corrupt Spain; with Bismarck, and not with the current military saviours of the Spanish people.

Bismarck's policy was simple; he wanted, if possible, to get the Prince made King of Spain. It was true the secret of the intrigue had leaked out, but the Cortes had been summoned for July 20th and whatever France was to do would have to be done quickly. If it was too late to face her with an accomplished fact, then the war which Bismarck wished for was at hand, a war in which, if all went well, Spain would be an ally and at the worst France could be given the appearance of attacking Prussia gratuitously—before the military reforms in France had produced any serious results, before France had managed to secure any allies, and before any attempt to sow discord between North and South Germany had any chance of success.

There were two obstacles to the success of this policy, the King and the Queen of Prussia. King William was old and sincerely anxious to avoid another war. His ingenious Minister had already involved him in two aggressive and glorious conflicts, and the King had been fearful when the acceptance of the Spanish crown had first been suggested. He had swallowed the casuistical explanation that his consent to the acceptance was purely the act of the head of the House of Hohenzollern and in no way involved the Prussian state, but the morsel had been hard to swallow and lay heavy on the royal stomach.. The King's conscience might be aroused, and the one person likely to arouse it was Queen Augusta, who detested Bismarck, who was detested by him— and who was, alas!, on excellent terms with Count Benedetti, the French Ambassador.

8

The sudden explosion of the mine found its chief engineer away at his estate in Pomerania; the King was taking a cure at Ems; the Queen was close at hand at Coblence; and Count Benedetti near the Queen at Wildbad. One other important actor was in his remote castle of Sigmaringen, an hour from any railroad. Prince Karl Anton was rejoicing in the great destiny of his son. 'Our house is at a turning-point of history,' he wrote to his daughter, Princess Marie of Belgium.[1] '. . . Fate is knocking at our door, our children and our children's children would not only be astonished but could also reproach us with not having asked it to come in.' Full of these grandiloquent ideas, the Prince was not likely to help King William in his dilemma, for although the King had never liked the candidacy he felt himself bound by the consent that he had given. He would be delighted if the acceptance were withdrawn, but he would not order either Prince Leopold or his father to withdraw it.

If the French Ministers had made a mistake in meeting Bismarck half-way by demanding satisfaction from Prussia, not from Spain, by making it evident that their aim was to persuade or coerce Berlin, not Madrid or Sigmaringen, they showed some sense in their choice of means. They attacked King William, first of all by impressing the danger of the situation on the Prussian ambassador, Werther, who was all the more susceptible since Bismarck had hidden the intrigue from him. Werther was worried and innocent and he was about to visit the King at Ems. And interrupting the cure of Benedetti at Wildbad, they ordered that resourceful diplomat to visit the King, with whom he was on excellent terms—and on the way Benedetti visited the Queen, with whom he was on even better terms.

The sudden storm that had sprung up alarmed all the Cabinets of Europe. Their first view was that even if the French reaction had been unnecessarily violent, the candidacy, and especially its secret negoti-ation, justified a stiff attitude. The Kings and Ministers were all informed of the French view, and they in turn made known their attitude to the Prussian Government, which did not care, and to the Prussian King, who did. King William was anxious and the attitude of his Queen, who saw in the crisis another example of Bismarck's diabolic arts, added to his worries. It was Werther's report of the anger shown in Paris that induced the King to make the first dangerous move, from Bismarck's point of view. King William wrote to Prince Karl Anton asking what he proposed to do in the emergency; thus re-opening the whole question and running the risk of involving Prussia, or rather Bismarck's scheme, in disaster, the disaster of a withdrawal of the candidacy in face of French pressure. The time-bomb had exploded, but it was not yet quite certain who was to be injured by its splinters.

[1] Mother of King Albert I,

9

From Varzin, Bismarck kept an eye on the men whose folly or wisdom, weakness or strength, could upset his admirable plans. His representative in Berlin, Herr von Thile, kept on denying any knowledge of the question. It was entirely a matter for the Hohenzollern princes to settle with the representatives of the Spanish people; it was not the business of Berlin or Paris. His agents in Ems watched the King, who soon became conscious that his imperious servant was displeased with him and yet the King was not ready to be a mere tool in his minister's hands. The German press, carefully worked by Bismarck's agents, began to show signs of irritation, but the real press storm was in Paris.

In Paris, the editors and politicians were hysterical. Prussia must not only be thwarted, she must appear to be thwarted. The impudent comedy of pretending that Bismarck was outside the whole affair must be shown up. The Government was under constant pressure to be strong, firm, noisy. After its first blunder, it was not given time to recover. It had before it the demand of *Le Public* that, as Prim had behaved like a Spaniard and Bismarck like a Prussian, 'we must know whether Messrs. Ollivier and de Gramont have behaved like Frenchmen'. That clever weathercock, Edmond About, was now convinced that the honour of France was at stake, and it became clear that only war would satisfy him. An even more representative journalist, Émile de Girardin, in the next week did all in his power to make war certain.

The Emperor, it is true, wanted peace. He told the representative of the King of Italy that if the candidacy was withdrawn, no matter how, France would be satisfied. Ollivier was for peace, if not at any price, at any price that gave France the substance of her demands. The reports of the Prefects showed how far the provinces were from sharing the hysteria of Paris, or of that part of Paris which was represented in newspaper offices and on the smart streets. War would be accepted if necessary, but the necessity had to be proved to the peasants and small traders, who had three times voted for the Emperor because he promised peace at home and abroad. M. Thiers, whose reputation as a prophet had been made by his gloomy but accurate prophecies of what the brilliant foreign policy of the Empire involved, had warned the Chamber, over a year before, against any war with Prussia except in circumstances in which intolerable aggression would force France to fight and when she might have 'the world as witness, as friend, and perhaps as auxiliary'.

But the Chamber was not very ready to listen to reason. The Imperialist majority was discontented by the mildness and apparent weakness of Ollivier. It looked, in order to discover the Emperor's wishes, less to his Minister than to such bellicose orators as Clément Duvernois. Under such pressure, Ollivier and Gramont weakened; they had not only to thwart the Prussian plot, not only to defeat Prussia in the eyes of the world, but to give that defeat a character which would produce a parliamentary victory. If the Cortes had been sitting, there might have been a *fait accompli*, in face of which Napoleon III might possibly have taken the advice of his cousin, Prince Napoleon, and, refusing to recognize King Leopold, let the Spanish people get rid of him. If the French Chamber had not been sitting there might have been no war, for the Cabinet and the Emperor would not have been under constant pressure. Not all the pressure came from Parliament. Napoleon was at Saint-Cloud, surrounded by courtiers, by soldiers, by ladies, and most of these were enemies of the Liberal Empire, sure that anything short of a complete diplomatic victory would weaken the Empire still further, and that a war with Prussia (which, of course, would be victorious) would ensure a peaceful end of the reign of Napoleon III and a glorious beginning for the reign of Napoleon IV. The Empress was of this school, not content with half-measures, ambitious for her son and, like a good Spanish Catholic, detesting the very word Liberal and the party of Prim.

The third man in whose hands the destiny of France lay was the Duc de Gramont. Superficially brilliant, cosmopolitan,[1] he had been a great social success as Ambassador in Vienna, and he took too seriously the anti-Prussian talk of the Austrian court circles, and too seriously his own popularity. Austria would have liked, that is to say the military party would have liked, to avenge Sadowa, but they were not ready for a risky war, and the hopes that had been based on the recent visit of the Archduke Albrecht to Paris were baseless. Even. more baseless were hopes of Italian aid. France could only offer Italy one thing, the free occupation of Rome, and a Catholic minis- try like Ollivier's could not promise that. Whatever King Victor Emmanuel might want to do, the Italian politicians, less perhaps than the politicians of any other nation, were disposed to let their policy be affected by mere gratitude. Thanks to the distrust aroused by the secret way in which the affair had been managed, the sympathies of Europe were at the beginning with France, and, had Gramont been competent, they could have been kept with France. But France had no allies. Even if Austrian policy had been bolder, Russia would have vetoed active intervention, and the price of Italian aid was too great. The belief that the small German states were anxious to throw off the Prussian yoke, a view held by General Ducrot, the commander of the Strasbourg garrison, was nonsense. There was some discontent in South Germany; Würtemberg especially gave Bismarck a little to worry about; but in face of France, of an aggressive France, all Germany would unite. This, indeed, was Bismarck's main calculation of benefit from a war; fighting a common enemy, North and South Germany would achieve a spiritual unity, which was still only embryonic.

[1] He married a Miss MacKinnon.

The French diplomatic offensive, launched with the despatch of Benedetti to Ems, was made on a wide front. Strat, Rumanian agent in Paris, was told that the conduct of Prince Karl Anton was not going to result in planting one son in Madrid, but might very well result in the ejection of another son from Bucarest. M. Strat got to Sigmaringen on the evening of July 11th with this disconcerting message; but more important, there arrived late that night a special messenger from Ems, Colonel Strantz, sent by King William to induce Karl Anton to withdraw his son's acceptance. The French had won. King William's conscience had overborne his Minister's entreaties and, despite the wrigglings of the disillusioned father, the renunciation was inevitable.

The news was sent in an unciphered telegram to Madrid and to the Spanish Ambassador in Paris, so that the French Government might learn their good fortune indirectly. For it was most important that the fiction of the innocence of Prussia should be maintained. King William rejoiced. 'A stone has been lifted from my heart,' he wrote to the Queen, 'but be silent about this toward everyone, in order that the news may not come first from us.' The news lifted stones from some hearts in Paris, too. Napoleon III told General Bourbaki that peace was secure. It was, he said, as if an island had suddenly arisen in the Channel over whose ownership there had been a danger of war between England and France. The island had sunk and the danger was over.

The impression outside France and among wise people inside it was that a real diplomatic success had been won. This view was represented in a *Punch* cartoon, and it was the opinion of a good authority, Bismarck himself. The Chancellor knew that he had lost the first battle, but he was not ready to admit that the campaign was over. For the moment he had to change tactics. In the newspaper war, in the declarations in the Chamber, there had been foolish things said. The German people was to be instructed by the Bismarckian press that its honour and security were endangered by this French arrogance, all over a matter with which the Prussian Government had nothing to do! It was not yet certain that Bismarck would not have his war, but it would have to be an offensive war; a much less attractive proposition than a defensive war, but not altogether worthless all the same.

Bismarck was saved all need for further worry by the folly of Napoleon, Gramont and Ollivier. The withdrawal was not enough, so the Paris press now asserted. After all, it was not the Prince who had withdrawn, but his father, and there was much Parisian wit expended on 'Papa Anthony's letter'. Who knew if the Prince might not suddenly turn up in Madrid as his brother had done in Bucarest? In any case, Prussia should be made to admit her share in the conspiracy. There must be an end once and for all to this project of encircling France. The unfortunate Benedetti was instructed to get an approval of the renunciation from the King which was going to be difficult enough. He was then told to get a promise that the King would forbid any renewal of the candidacy, and Werther was told to ask his master for a personal letter to the Emperor expressive of good-will, but almost necessarily involving a confession of ill-doing! The letter was the joint folly of Gramont and Ollivier, the demand for a royal promise of 'never again' was the joint folly of Napoleon and Gramont. From these two attempts to show that Prussia had seen the light came the war. When the first news of the renunciation arrived, a Paris newspaper had announced it as 'Prussia climbs down'. It was now proposed to make Prussia admit it.

It was on the thirteenth day of July that Count Benedetti, already alarmed at having been given room 13 in his hotel, obeyed his instructions and, accosting the King on the promenade, tried in vain to get him to give an undertaking to prohibit a renewal of the candidacy. William had gone as far as to authorize Benedetti to telegraph to Paris that he approved of the renunciation. Further he would not go and, as the exchanges grew warm, he broke off the conversation. But Benedetti's instructions were formal; he was to try again, and he asked for a fresh audience. But the King, tired, irritated and afraid of his angry Minister, who was now at Berlin threatening resignation, sent an aide-de-camp to say that he could not see Count Benedetti. The refusal was perfectly courteous and need have meant no more than that the King preferred to have these negotiations transferred to Berlin, where Count Benedetti could try his arts on Count Bismarck. This message was repeated in a more severe form when the King received the news of Werther's acceptance of the proposal that he should write to Napoleon. There was definitely to be an end of this kind of thing and Benedetti was told so. And this decision was communicated to Bismarck in Berlin in a fairly long telegram which the Chancellor was authorized to publish—if he thought fit.

That night Bismarck had as his dinner-guests, the Minister of War, General von Roon, and the Chief of the General Staff, General von Moltke. All the efforts of the soldiers for four years past had been directed to preparing the army to fight France. The failure of Bismarck's diplomatic campaign had depressed them, and the first impression made by the telegram from Ems depressed them even further. Here was new French insolence unpunished! But Bismarck was busy on the literary effort of which he was for the rest of his life most proud. Cutting the telegram down to a brief message but interpolating nothing, he produced a message which suggested that the King had brutally refused to receive the Ambassador, with the consequent implication that the snub was deliberately intended to suspend, if not to break off, diplomatic relations. What had been 'a drum beat of a parley was now a flourish of trumpets', said Moltke. 'The old

God still lives and will not let us perish in shame', said the pious Roon. 'It will be a red rag to the Gallic bull', said Bismarck. The communiqué was at once sent to the press and to all Prussian embassies and legations. The humiliation of the French Ambassador would be published to all the world and what would the French do then? They would, of course, fight.

Ollivier, Gramont and the Emperor were now mere flotsam in the sea of anger that raged in Paris. In vain they thought of appealing to a European congress. The power was out of their hands. Thiers, who had tried to warn Napoleon of his danger, might have been strong enough to have resisted successfully, but the Emperor had snubbed him. On the fifteenth of July the Chamber voted war credits, after a debate in which the tough little man, speaking wisdom, was howled down by an assembly whose temper was represented by Birotteau's, 'When one has been insulted there's no need of reflection'. It was an appropriate confession of political bankruptcy, but no worse than the declaration of Ollivier that he and his colleagues accepted their responsibilities with a light heart. King William, when he had been induced to agree to the candidacy, had done so, he declared sincerely, with a heavy heart. But Ollivier, as he boasted in one of his numerous apologias, was an optimist. In the furious debate, the text of the famous despatch was never produced, and even supporters of the war, like Gambetta, and of the régime, like Buffet, wanted more information. Leboeuf talked of the military dangers of delay, and Gramont of the diplomatic combinations with Austria and Italy that he hinted he was negotiating, and the deputies followed him down the slope.

Bismarck had his war in an even better form than he had hoped for. For France appeared not merely as the aggressor, but as a frivolous aggressor, and when the foresighted Chancellor was able to produce from his portfolio schemes for a joint Franco-Prussian partition of Belgium obligingly written out by Benedetti, the picture of France as the villain of the piece was complete. Soon Carlyle was able to draw, for the benefit of the British public, a contrast between 'noble, patient, deep, pious and solid Germany' and 'vapouring, vainglorious, gesticulating, quarrelsome, restless and over-sensitive France'. In America President Grant was ready to tell the French chargé d'affaires that American sentiment was on Germany's side. And in Germany itself, the unity Bismarck had counted on was at once manifest. For all these follies and their results there could only be one remedy, victory. With the re-enforcement of a good many police agents, mobs were parading central Paris shouting 'To Berlin' and singing the long-forbidden *Marseillaise*. There was the answer to M. Thiers.

Allons, enfants de la patrie,
Le jour de gloire est arrivé.

III

France and most of the world awaited the news of early and brilliant victory with easy confidence. Even Germans who were rightly confident in ultimate victory, feared some sudden stroke. The German lands that lay in the way of a French invasion were full of memories of the first Napoleon, and the Germans, who feared no Austerlitz or Jena, were not altogether sure that there would not be an Ulm. In London, the great editor of *The Times*, Delane, was strongly in favour of the Germans but highly sceptical of their chances. 'I would lay my last shilling on Casquette against Pumpernickel.' Naturally, in France herself, hopes ran high and most of the enemies of the Empire believed, with varying emotions, that the Emperor's authority would be strengthened by the imminent victory. Gambetta went off on a holiday to Switzerland in full expectation of good news, for he was too simple a patriot to wish for bad news that would weaken the Empire. A cautious Orleanist, Cuvillier-Fleury, relied on the genius (and the strength) of France, seeing clearly that no other genius or strength was available. Even the sceptical Taine preserved his modified optimism through the first weeks. That France should be beaten by mere Germans, by the hastily-trained militia that they called an army, was out of the question for all whose minds were not poisoned by political rancour—or enlightened by real knowledge of the formidable power which had risen across the Rhine.

Despite the lesson of Sadowa, there were still those who thought, as Drouyn de Lhuys had thought in 1866, that gamekeepers were all that was needed to sweep away the Prussian levies. Cham, the most popular caricaturist of the time, showed a Zouave battering at the King of Prussia's door with the butt-end of his rifle, and the legend below ran: 'A new Ambassador whom he can't shut out.' The most famous of French journalists, Émile de Girardin, constant to the policy of bellicosity that had helped to make a peaceful settlement impossible, was a noisy discounter of easy victory. When singers at the Opéra admitted that they did not know the words of Alfred de Musset's famous song 'We have had your German Rhine', Girardin shouted from his box, 'It will take longer then to learn it than to take it.' [1]

Yet there have been few wars in which the odds were more decisively on one side—and that side not the French. The uncle of Napoleon III is reported to have said that God was on the side of the biggest battalions, and the biggest battalions in this war were the German. Even had other things been equal, the numerical superiority of the German Army would have been decisive. Moltke had calculated on putting 330,000 men in the field if Bavaria and Würtemberg did not join the

---

[1] In French a pun, 'Il faudra donc plus de temps pour l'apprendre que pour le prendre'.

North, 360,000 if they did; and he put the maximum French strength at the beginning of the campaign at 300,000. In fact, the French strength when the campaign opened was under 270,000, and from that inferiority flowed all the disasters, since so great a numerical inferiority ensured that French mistakes would be fatal and German mistakes reparable.

The numerical weakness of the French Army was caused by its very nature. It was a professional force raised with as much regard for the security of the régime and for the political advantages of popularity as for military efficiency in a narrow sense. France had, it was true, conscription, but conscription of a kind well described by Marshal Gouvion Saint-Cyr as 'the blood tax'. All Frenchmen might be called on to serve—if France insisted on using all the healthy men who came of military age each year. But she did not, and so most of the annual 'contingent' was exempted. By means of a lottery the necessary number of recruits, nominally 100,000, was chosen from the total of the annual 'class', and these who drew 'bad numbers' had to serve, unless they found someone to take their place. This meant in effect that poor men with bad numbers served; richer men bought substitutes.

The consequences of this system were far-reaching. If all Frenchmen had had to serve, as all Prussians had, the period of service would have had to be comparatively short and the discipline and treatment of the troops would have had to make allowances for the temporary character of the military service of the rank and file. But with a system that exempted all the middle- and upper-classes and only caught a portion of the working-classes and small peasants, it was easy and tempting to treat the recruit as a professional soldier with no civilian future. It was possible to impose the comparatively long term of seven years' service and to treat the private soldier as a very rough diamond whom it would be a pity to spoil by excessive polishing. The recruit was sent away from his native district, to be enrolled in units without any local attachments; he thus acquired, it was held, true soldierly spirit; henceforward the regiment was his home. Once in the Army the recruit was encouraged to stay in it, not by good conditions or reasonable pay, but by a system of bonuses on re-enlistment; the more old soldiers who could be induced to rejoin, the more efficient the army—such was the theory. This theory had two valid political arguments to make it palatable to the régime. The more re-enlistments, the more 'good' numbers at the annual army lottery—and the 'blood tax' was very unpopular with the peasants who were its chief victims, for the poor men of the towns very often failed to pass the medical examination. The more re-enlistments, the more isolated from the country the soldier was, and the less likely to be tainted by politically dangerous thoughts.

Under this system, an army of professional long-service soldiers was created which was used with a freedom that a short-service force, more intimately connected with the country, might not have endured. Between 1820 and 1869, an era of comparative peace, 300,000 Frenchmen died on military service in China, Africa, Spain, Italy, the Crimea, Mexico. So lavish an expenditure of lives was possible only as long as the victims were looked on as a mere part of the whole nation, set apart for disease, death and glory.

The military drawback to this system was obvious. It limited the numerical strength of the Army in war to what the country would stand in peace. Moreover, the cost of this professional force was great, since the bonuses paid on re-enlistment were a heavy item in the budget. Once out of the Army or given long leave, the ex-soldier bitterly resented being recalled to the colours, since he had reason to feel that his country was dealing hardly with him. He had been unlucky once; was he to be doubly unlucky, to be called back to the colours when war broke out, while men who had escaped service altogether were immune? In any case, the military standards set up by a professional army were not easily met by the ex-soldier softened by peaceful avocations. The officers did not think it possible to make good fighting soldiers out of men who were not under the colours when war broke out. All schemes for the inclusion in the active army of reservists, or troops partly-trained in peace-time, broke down in face of the scepticism of the War Office. Only after the great Prussian victory over Austria in 1866 did the French military authorities begin seriously to think of adding to the peace strength a proportion of reservists.

This change had long been advocated by the most intelligent critic of the French military system, Napoleon III. He knew Germany well; he had served in the Swiss Army, and he had tried and failed to convince the Army, of which he was the nominal chief, that there was a great deal to be learned from the neighbours of France. It was politically impossible to increase the regular annual contingent; so, if the numerical military strength was to be increased, the prejudice against reservists would have to be abandoned. A reform was instituted that had not had time to bear much fruit by 1870. The term of service was cut down to five years followed by four in the reserve, and when the war broke out there were 60,000 men in this regular reserve.

This was very inadequate when compared with the vast reserves built up by the Prussian system, and the Emperor and some of his advisers were in favour of adopting the central feature of that system, universal service. Even with the Prussian modification that allowed the middle-class recruit to serve one year instead of three (and that in special conditions), the French bourgeoisie were bitterly hostile to any such suggestion. Thiers had declared thirty years before (and he had not changed his position) that conscription for the educated classes was out of the question. The peasant or worker was no worse off in the Army than on his farm or in his workshop, but to force the sons of the middle-classes to serve would be tyranny in guise of a false equality. The bourgeoisie did enough in providing most of the officers. If the Republicans asked for universal service, they also asked at the same time for the replacement of the regular army by a militia. Whatever the military merits of this policy, it would weaken the Imperial Government, which is why it was advocated by Jules Simon and rejected by Napoleon III. But something had to be done, and Marshal Niel, Napoleon's reforming War Minister, produced a scheme for creating a 'mobile National Guard'. This scheme originally called for a serious military training of the young unmarried men enrolled in the National Guard. Had it been carried out it would have provided a large reserve of locally organized and reasonably well-prepared militiamen. But the period of training was cut down from months to days, and after Niel's death even this amputated scheme was killed. When the war broke out, the 'mobiles' existed only on paper. Except in Paris, it was simply a list of young men who might, when war came and if the struggle lasted long enough, be turned into soldiers.

The numerical superiority of the German armies could not be countered by a Government depending as much on popularity with the bourgeoisie and peasants as the Government of Napoleon III. If the Germans were to be beaten it could only be by other means. One advantage of a professional army, or so it was alleged, was superiority in technical efficiency. There was apparent justification for this view. The French Army, as even Moltke admitted when he visited France in 1867, was smart. It was smart in uniform and smart in drill. Cavalry and artillery in particular were proud of the speed and accuracy with which they performed complicated evolutions. The famous cavalry school at Saumur was above all a school for making fine horsemen, not for making efficient cavalry officers. The cavalry officer's duty was to lead his troopers in elaborate but highly unrealistic drill formations in peace and in heroic and useless charges in battle.

The officers of the artillery had, of course, a more serious military education at the École Polytechnique than was given at Saint-Cyr or Saumur. But that education was narrowly technical and the French artillery in 1870 had forgotten most of the teaching and practice of the greatest of gunners. Apart from an excessive devotion to smartness and to shining harness, the French artillery was noted for the speed with which it unlimbered and opened fire, and this virtuosity was over-prized. Instead of massing guns in the old Napoleonic fashion and blasting a way for the infantry, the French artillery was anxious to make it as difficult as possible for the enemy to find the proper range.

Had the contest otherwise been equal, this might not have mattered, but the equipment of the French artillery was terribly inferior to that of the Germans. The latter had adopted a breech-loading steel gun of the famous Krupp firm. This gun was both more accurate and of far greater range than the French bronze muzzle-loader; and artillery duels in the war of 1870 were farcical, since the Germans could fire from a range far beyond French powers of reply. Again, Napoleon III, himself a gunner, had seen the importance of the new artillery, and there were in existence in 1870 two types of breech-loading gun made under his orders. But they were only models; they were not ready for issue to the Army and few people knew how they should be used. The clumsy handling of the Prussian artillery in 1866 which, in any case, was then only partially equipped with the new cannon, actually led most French officers to accept the Austrian boast that their artillery had been better than that of the victors, an illusion against which the French attaché in Berlin, Colonel Stoffel, vainly protested. Next to numerical inferiority, the inability of the French artillery to fire as far as the German guns was the main cause of French disaster.

One cause of the Prussian victories in 1866 *had* been given its due weight by the French Army; the breech-loading 'needle' rifle had completely demonstrated its superiority over the muzzle-loader. It was not only that the breech-loader could be fired faster and at greater ranges than the older type of rifle, but it could be easily loaded by men kneeling, standing, sitting, lying down, a change that would have had great effect on infantry tactics if the makers of drill-books had been ready to adjust their sacred rites to reality. But even the Prussians, with their experience of 1864 and 1866, had hesitated to scrap their infantry regulations of 1847, and the French were not ready to see that the day of the massed column of Wagram was over—especially as it was no longer backed by the massed guns of Wagram. But the French infantry was given a new rifle. The 'chassepot' was, in fact, much better than the needle gun. The chassepot was not the only new weapon of French might; the French Army and public were asked to give their confidence to an entirely new instrument of war, the 'mitrailleuse', the ancestor of the modern queen of battles, the machine-gun. The mitrailleuse was not a true machine-gun, that is to say, it was not an automatic weapon. It consisted of twenty-five rifle-barrels bound together, loaded and fired simultaneously. It was mounted on a gun-carriage like a field-gun, and so was less mobile and much more easily spotted and knocked-out by artillery fire than a modern machine-gun. But, for all its faults, it was a formidable weapon; if it did not kill its tens of thousands where the rifle killed its thousands, it inspired a healthy fear that was almost as good. For fear of the discovery of the secret of this new weapon, it was manufactured, under the direct patronage of the Emperor, at Meudon, and it was not exhibited to the

Army until war broke out. Artillery officers were sent to Meudon to learn how to handle it, but when war came many of these officers were in command of ordinary batteries, and many officers and men who had never seen this odd-looking weapon had to learn all about it on the spot!

Outnumbered, hopelessly inferior in artillery and superior to its probable enemy only in infantry equipment, the French Army did not make up for its material weaknesses by moral or intellectual strength. The professional troops had many admirable qualities, but they also had many grave faults. Stoffel in Berlin, alarmed by the inability of his countrymen to see the danger they were in, described the contrast between Prussia, where every able-bodied man was called on to serve, and France, whose army was 'an agglomeration of the poorest and most ignorant Frenchmen, to whom the more fortunate classes entrust the task of fighting for them'. Largely illiterate and often drunken, brave and enduring, full of confidence in their military prowess, these much-abused soldiers deserved better leaders than they got.

The French officers of this period, however, were admirable from the point of view of courage, and took seriously the military duties imposed on them by the current standards. Unfortunately these standards were not nearly high enough. The comfort and even the decency of the rank-and-file were disregarded and, since the law of 1832 gave every officer a proprietary title to his rank, the favourite reading of the regimental officer, according to General Thoumas, was the Army List. Computations of future automatic promotion was the only intellectual effort of most officers. Taine, who was an inspector of the entrants to Saint-Cyr, the great military school, noted how few young officers 'read or think for themselves. All their family and social connections keep them from it.' In the two learned arms of the artillery and engineers, the officers trained at the École Polytechnique were often of high intellectual merit, and the French Army had no difficulty in finding designers of the most modern weapons at least as competent as any the Germans had. But even the gunners and sappers were devoid of any training for the general problems of war; and the officers of the General Staff, quite ignorant of regimental life, were incapable of such elementary work as organizing mobilization or transport efficiently, much less of providing an intelligent guidance and assistance for their chiefs.

These chiefs had far more military experience than any Prussian officers. But von Verdy du Vernois in 1866, and many other officers in 1870, were to show that theoretical training was superior to mere experience on whose lessons no reflection had been expended. The type of Frederick the Great's army mule, which had made twenty campaigns and knew as much at the end as at the beginning, was

20

common in the higher ranks of the French Army. Indeed, their experience did them harm in some cases. The motto of the Algerian Army was 'débrouillez-vous' [1] and no irretrievable disasters had come from acting on it. A neglect of outpost duty and of scouting was an odd habit to contract from colonial wars, but it was contracted all the same. The officers who distinguished themselves in Africa and then in Mexico were commanders of small columns, and they rose to the top without ever learning how to handle big units or developing a higher sense of military duty than was involved in recklessly risking themselves in the front line and inspiring courage in all the troops within ear-shot. The Crimean and Italian wars did nothing to shake this attitude, for it was believed that the victories had been won by gallant attacks with the bayonet. MacMahon on the mined breach of the Malakoff Redoubt announcing 'Here I am and here I stay', or turning defeat into victory by mere phlegmatic courage at Magenta, was a specimen of the French Army at its best. At less than its best, there was still plenty of courage, but there was an unbridled appetite for promotion and reward, and a consequent unwillingness to collaborate that was very dangerous. The chief representative of this school was Marshal Bazaine, an excellent regimental officer, but a selfish and secretive general. His career in Mexico had been marked by glory and graft, and whereas other officers gained promotion, it was said, by service at the Imperial Court, acting in amateur plays with the ladies-in-waiting or playing the piano to amuse the Empress, Bazaine, it was believed, cultivated not only Napoleon III, but such enemies of the Empire as Jules Favre.

Pursuing the mirage of an alliance with Austria, the French plan of campaign was a rapid advance from the Rhine across South Germany, intimidating the South German states into neutrality, joining an Austrian Army in Franconia, and, in the more golden of the dreams of Saint-Cloud, being joined by an Italian force coming up from Innsbruck. The Prussians, held up by a covering force in Lorraine, would then be crushed by the Allies. This scheme was based on the card-castle of Gramont's diplomacy; but even had that castle been fit to resist a puff of wind, the march to Nuremberg would have required the genius of a Napoleon or a Marlborough. It got the equivalent of the talents of Mack or Soubise.

It was realized that, if they were given time, the German Confederates could put a bigger army in the field than France could muster, and it was decided not to give them time. The main advantage of the French professional system ought to have been the presence with the colours, when war came, of a larger number of men than those available in a short-service army. Well organized, the French Army ought, in the first two weeks of war, to have had an advantage in numbers; and

[1] 'Muddle-through.'

Marshal Lebœuf, the War Minister, proposed to use this advantage by sending troops to the front without waiting for the reservists. Such a scheme required careful working out; it got none. No detailed plans had been made in peace for the use of the railways in war and the moving of troops to the frontier was a miracle of improvisation. In fact, the French did gain a few days on the Germans, and had they pushed forward rapidly the German concentration in the Palatinate might 'have been seriously embarrassed. But the troops rushed to the front were not ready to advance. In the German Army, all units existed in peace-time, from the regiment to the army corps. In France, the highest peace-time unit was the regiment; all bigger formations only came into existence when war began, and generals and their staffs might be perfect strangers to each other and to the troops they were to command. Marshal Niel had drawn up a complete list of higher commanders, but that had been scrapped by Lebœuf; and the troops hustled to the front had to be hastily organized into brigades, divisions and corps in those precious days at the end of July when the last chance of victory—and of allies—was being lost, as an astounded world waited in vain for the rapid stroke against the slower Germans which had been universally anticipated. The expensive and brilliant Imperial Army only managed by August 1st to assemble 270,000 men in Lorraine and in Alsace, and the disorder of the preceding days had been fantastic.

Lebœuf, who had boasted that the Army was ready down to its gaiter buttons, found it was not even ready in such details. There had to be hasty decisions as to what kind of caps the troops would wear, and the brilliant shakos of the line and bearskins of the Guard were replaced by képis. The amount of cartridges carried by each man was suddenly altered by the Minister of War, and troops arrived without cooking utensils or, in some cases, without the minimum of engineering equipment. The supply service broke down; there was a shortage of bakers and bread; a great wagon camp at Châlons had only one exit and it took days to get the wagons out, and without transport the Army could not move. While troops were piling up in frontier camps, reservists were wandering over France looking for their regiments. Instead of waiting until a regiment had received and equipped its reservists and was at full strength, the regiment was sent off to the front at once, and the reservists, once the depot had equipped them, went off to find their units. These depots were not necessarily located near the areas from which the recruits came, and a reservist living in Alsace, and whose regiment was in Alsace, might have to go to Bayonne or Algiers to get his equipment and then return right across France to find his regiment—if he could. This was not easy for more important people than reservists. The case of the general who wired to the War Office 'Arrived at Belfort. Cannot find my brigade. Cannot find my divisional commander. Do not know where my regiments are. What shall I do?' was exceptional; but precious days were wasted in solving only slightly less absurd problems.

It is true that the mobilization of 1870 was far more efficient than that of 1859, whose slowness had so distressed Napoleon III; it is also true that the ingenuity displayed in doing hurriedly in July what should have been done at leisure years before was astonishing—but the results were fatal. The troops, eager for action, were wearied and discouraged by the disorder in which they found themselves. Their despatch to the front had been marked by disquieting scenes of drunkenness. A veteran who remembered the First Empire alarmed his neighbours by announcing that 'we are beaten', on no more evidence than the drunken disorder of the troops going to the front.

The last improvisation was that of the high command and the plan of campaign. Instead of three armies, one in Alsace, one in Lorraine, one in reserve, Napoleon III, at the last moment, assumed command of one united army strung out over the whole 200 miles of frontier with Lebœuf, the Minister of War, as his Chief of Staff. It was an unfortunate decision. Napoleon was an intelligent critic of military organization, but he was ill-prepared for high command. An important staff officer [1] had noticed with apprehension that the Emperor could only read a map with great difficulty and to this intellectual limitation he added the physical disability of a severe bladder complaint that made riding very difficult. A surgeon had to be in constant attendance to operate if the illness took a sudden turn for the worse.

The Emperor and Lebœuf were incapable of effectual control over the seven army corps in line [2] and these units were left isolated. Worse still was the effect on the morbidly ambitious Bazaine, who saw himself reduced from an army to a corps commander, and immediately lost all sense of responsibility for the welfare of any unit except his own.

On August 2nd the French Army moved; the frontier town of Saarbrücken was occupied after a trifling skirmish in which a communiqué (that would readily have been forgiven had it been the first of a series of victorious bulletins) dwelt with pride on the courage of the young Prince Imperial. The advance of Frossard's corps was, in fact, a meaningless move, but as happened frequently in this war, meaningless moves were just what the German General Staff was least prepared to counter. Moltke had the fault, so severely condemned by Napoleon I, of 'making pictures'; his plans provided for rational but not for irrational action by his opponents, and the news of Saarbrücken, received late, resulted in a confusion of orders issued to the advancing Germans. Had the French Army been ready, or had its leaders had any resolution, the German hesitation might have been exploited; but Napoleon III's brief will to action had already been killed by the news of the defeat, on August 4th, of the small force under Abel Douay

[1] Jarras.   [2] Canrobert's corps was assembling at Châlons.

stationed near the obsolete fortress of Wissembourg in Alsace and by the death of its commander. If Wissembourg was only a minor victory, it was, unlike Saarbrücken, a genuine minor victory; and it was at once followed by German major victories.

Alarmed by the news of Wissembourg, the French Army in Lorraine was thrown on to the defensive; and Frossard, abandoning Saarbrücken (but not burning the bridges over the Saar), took up a strong position. The advancing Prussians ran into the French 2nd Corps and the battle of Spicheren began. It was typical of all the battles of the first and decisive stage of the war. The Prussian troops were often very ill-directed from above. Not only was Moltke slow to readjust his plans to the eccentric movements of the French, but he was often given no information at all, for many hours at a time, by his subordinates in the field. They fought battles and engaged the fortunes of the whole Army without consulting the Great General Headquarters. The success of this loose, not to say anarchical, system blinded many foreigners and most Germans to its faults—with results dearly paid for, forty-four years later.

The subordinate commanders were trained to attack at almost any price; always to march to the sound of the guns, so that a minor encounter could rapidly develop into a great battle as all the German units within reach rushed to the fray. The advantages of this system were manifest. Confident of support, subordinates took responsibilities on their shoulders very readily and the German troops never had the depressing experience of realizing that not only did the rank-and-file not know what was being done and why, but that their leaders knew almost as little. On the other hand, the subordinate leaders could only see through the fog of war what was under their noses and that was not enough. So battle after battle was engaged in which the general numerical inferiority of the French was, for many hours, turned into a great local superiority. The Germans escaped the results of this state of affairs because no intelligent attempt was made by the French to exploit this temporary superiority, often more fully realized by the fighting troops than by the French generals. The Moltke system not only required for its success subordinates like Prince Frederick Charles and the Alvenslebens, but opponents like Frossard and Bazaine.

At Spicheren, attack after attack was launched on the French holding a strong position, and with strong reinforcements in easy reach. If Frossard's neighbours had supported him, the German advance guard would have been in Vandamme's position after Dresden and the war in Lorraine would have begun with a great French local success. But French corps commanders took a narrow view of their duties; the security of their neighbours was not their business, but that of the Commander-in-Chief, the Emperor. So Bazaine gave no help to Frossard and may have made the notorious comment: 'The schoolmaster is in the soup, let him stay there.' [1]   Whether he said this or not, Bazaine acted in the spirit of the words.   Frossard withdrew in good order and the Germans, hardly believing in their good fortune, not merely let him get away, but completely lost touch with the main French Army.

On the same day, a much more important battle had been fought and lost in Alsace.   MacMahon had taken up a strong position at Wörth within easy reach of the 5th Corps; General de Failly was, in a rather undetermined way, under the Marshal's orders—and also directly under the Emperor's orders.   At Wörth, the battle took the same course as at Spicheren except that MacMahon was outnumbered far more seriously than Frossard had been.   With his usual stubbornness MacMahon held on to his position and the Germans learned that a repetition of 1866 was not good enough.   Attacking French infantry, armed with the chassepot and aided by the mitrailleuses ('the damned coffee mills' as the Bavarian commander, von der Tann, called them), was very different from attacking ill-armed and moderately combative troops like the Austrians of 1866.   The future maker of the Japanese Army, Meckel, coming on to the battlefield, was not only startled by the rows of dead and dying that bore testimony to the efficacy of French fire, but shocked by the sight of German troops hiding in ditches and behind trees rather than return to the assault.   But the great numerical strength of the Germans told; MacMahon was outflanked and the attackers got to grips with their stubborn enemy.   An English spectator, Sir Charles Dilke, noted that the most desperate fighting was between two subject peoples, the Algerian Turcos of MacMahon and the Poles of the Prussian 5th Corps.   What might have been a retreat in good order became a rout, and Failly's troops came on the scene too late to do more than prudently retreat.

A heroic charge by the French cuirassiers at Reichshoffen did little more than create a great legend, of troopers plunging to death in the hop-fields with a futile courage worthy of the countrymen of the knights of Crécy and Agincourt.   Alsace was lost; the shattered troops were hurried off to the great camp at Châlons where they arrived dirty, hungry, demoralized.   There were thousands of stragglers, and for days the only thought of the survivors was to sleep and eat.   The first news of Wörth, or rather of Reichshoffen, had been received in Paris as a victory and the streets were gay with flags and full of cheering crowds. But the truth was not long hidden.   France learned with stupefaction that her armies had been defeated three times in three days.   The tactless phrase of the Emperor's message, 'all can yet be saved', revealed how much had been lost.

The news of the defeats, of course, ended any hope of alliances.

---

[1] 'Le pion est dans la marmelade, qu'il y reste.'   Frossard, the 'pion', was not merely a learned soldier, but had been Military Governor of the Prince Imperial.

France had to face her enemy alone. It was fitting, then, that the Ollivier Ministry should bear the first brunt of popular wrath. The Corps Législatif was summoned to meet on the ninth of August. In a dream-world to the last, Ollivier had planned to arrest the leaders of the Left, but such a *coup d'état* needed the presence of the Emperor in Paris and he was at the front. But this fantastic reply to Wörth and Spicheren was given no chance of life. The Left-wing parties realized that it meant that 'the armies of the Emperor had been beaten', and so did the Chamber. Ollivier and Gramont were overthrown and a new Ministry, headed by the Comte de Palikao, was formed. Palikao was the soldier who, as General de Montauban, had commanded the French corps in the Chinese war of 1860. He was energetic and reso-lute and he and his colleagues represented, far better than had Ollivier, the sentiments of the Imperialist majority. But that majority was already stricken by fear. The Opposition could only be defeated by victories in Lorraine.

The Republican deputies wanted a return to the great traditions of their spiritual ancestors. All powers were to be given to the Chamber and to a committee of that Chamber, while there was to be a universal arming of the people; in short, a recourse to the great legend of the Convention. Revolution was in the air, though not yet practicable. A premature effort by the irrepressible Blanquists failed miserably, for the Paris mob was fiercely patriotic and treated the Blanquists as Prussian agents. The direct command of the Army by the Emperor was discredited and the parties of the Left had their general at hand. Marshal Bazaine must be given the chance to save France that had been taken from him by Napoleon III and Lebœuf.

The Germans in Lorraine were still uncertain as to what the French had done after Spicheren; and Moltke assumed that they were in rapid retreat. It would have been the wisest course to fall back on a position where the Army of Lorraine could join the remnants of MacMahon's Army of Alsace, but the political pressure from Paris was too strong. A stand must be made, and the job of holding the Germans was entrusted to Bazaine, who was made Commander-in-Chief on August 12th. The new Commander-in-Chief, from the beginning, displayed that astonishing indifference to the fate of his Army which led, in the not very long run, to suspicions of treason. It is true that Bazaine's position was difficult. The Emperor was still with him and he could not be wholly disregarded. Military policy was more and more coloured by political events at Paris; the best military decisions being overruled because they might unchain the revolution. The Germans, confident that the enemy was in full retreat, rushed ahead, and at Borny ran into an army not in retreat but ready to resist. The battle reinforced the lesson of Wörth. The chassepot again worked wonders; the harassed French troops were full of fight and, at the end of bloody assaults, held the battle-field with a gratifying feeling of victory. Their tactical success was real, but Borny, though it seemed to justify the appointment of Bazaine, was really a defeat. The French Army *should* have been in full retreat, and the day lost in beating back the Germans was never recovered. The Germans again assumed that the French would do what they should have done and marched in hot pursuit of the fleeing enemy. But Bazaine was not fleeing. He had got his army under the walls of Metz and the job of getting them beyond the city was too much for his staff. There was no direct railway line with the other great fortress of Verdun and, though the Emperor was at last safely shipped off, the streets of the fortress were crowded with troops and the temptation to rest a little and straighten things out was too much for the Marshal. Metz, it is true, was an obsolete fortress; the conversion of it into a modern entrenched camp had just been begun when war broke out, but it was the sort of city of refuge likely to appeal to a general in a dilemma.

It was on August 16th that the Germans discovered where the French Army was, by their usual method of running into it. Inferior in numbers, the Germans again and again launched desperate and futile attacks on French infantry in the comfortable position of having only to shoot their enemy down. If French corps commanders observed a cold neutrality towards one another, matters were not always better in the German camp, and the Commander of the German 1st Army, Steinmetz, was on bad terms both with his superiors and inferiors. His ardour involved another attack on a superior French force which, though surprised, had plenty of time to react while still much stronger than its opponent. But Bazaine had become obsessed with the danger of being cut off from Metz, so obsessed that he strengthened his left, which was in no danger, and left his right to fend for itself. The great battle of Vionville-Mars-la-Tour was thus a German defeat on the Vionville side which did not matter, and a French defeat on the Mars-la-Tour side which did. To neither event did Bazaine contribute more than his initial blunders and his refusal to do anything to remedy them. He behaved in the next two days like a brave regimental officer with no higher responsibilities. He was bruised by a shell splinter while directing the fire of a battery; he was nearly captured by German cavalry. He disappeared for hours: and his immediate subordinates, who had realized with horror his complete nullity, entertained the hope that he had been killed or made a prisoner and that the Army would now be commanded by Bourbaki or Canrobert.

The tactics of the battles were still the same. The German infantry and the French (when the latter was given a chance to do so) showed the most stubborn courage in fruitless assaults against the enemy lines. Suffering frightful losses, both sides became demoralized. Bismarck

and the King were horrified to find themselves in a panic-stricken mass
of troops reduced to a mob by the chassepot and the mitrailleuse. On
both sides the cavalry had failed miserably as scouts, but the German
cavalry was slightly less carelessly led than the French. There was no
German equivalent of the surprise of Forton's division while the horses
were being watered. Under the critical eyes of General Philip Sheridan, cavalry was used in masses of shock troops, in charges of troopers
against troopers, and of less brilliant attacks of armoured horsemen
against infantry and artillery. At Rezonville, the cuirassiers of the
French Guard were piled up in masses of horses and men in front of
the German troops they had not been able to reach. It was the last
great effort of the mounted swordsman or lancer; futile and heroic.
Only one of these efforts had any military results, the great 'death-ride'
of von Bredow's squadrons at Vionville. That held up the French
advance at a critical moment; it, unlike the other charges, was magnificent and it was war.

The second battle, Gravelotte-Saint-Privat, completed the strategical
defeat of the French. Never using his troops in any articulated way,
refusing necessary artillery aid to the unfortunate Canrobert whose
corps, rushed up from Châlons, had no entrenching tools, resisting all
the pleas of his own devoted staff officers to advance against a shattered
and smaller army, Marshal Bazaine in the two great battles showed
less sense of his duty and of the opportunities of the battle than did the
rank-and-file. The Germans, at least, knew their own minds; they
learned more quickly than their opponents the tactical lessons of the
war. They began to use their artillery superiority skilfully, blasting
the French infantry out of its positions before attempting to throw in
their own infantry. And the French guns, badly outclassed in any case,
were stupidly used or not used. The Germans had more guns and
better guns and used them all; the French had fewer guns and inferior
guns and let many of them stand idle. Even the asserted superiority
of long-service troops was not put to the test, for the crack French
corps, the Guard, for which the line regiments had been drained of
their best recruits, was kept idle and only used in driblets and too late.

By the evening of August 18th, the main French Army was penned
up under the walls of Metz. The results of the fortnight since the
German advance had begun were decisive and were summed up a
generation later by Colonel Foch in his lectures to the students of the
War School. 'The defeated French Army was thrown back into Metz.
Its final destruction was merely a question of time. Before the 18th
it had shown itself, whether by the feebleness of its leaders or of its
resources, incapable of any manœuvre to defeat the enemy, make good
its retreat to the interior of the country, or of rallying the still available
forces. How could it henceforward hope for better results in face of
a victorious enemy, in command of the lines of communication?'

French forces were, by this disaster, reduced to the garrisons of various old and ill-equipped fortresses, Strasbourg, Belfort, Toul, to the Army of Metz and to the Army of Châlons. The last was the only available field force; and all the arguments that had made it wise for the Army of Metz to fall back on MacMahon, told with redoubled force in favour of keeping the Army of Châlons intact. Its morale was badly shattered. The Emperor had come to Châlons where his forlorn state was bad for discipline and where the elaborate Imperial travelling household was the subject of mockery. The Paris 'mobiles' had been sent to Châlons after a drunken and ill-disciplined departure from the capital which made their procession to the station look more like a carnival parade than a military move. At Châlons, they were forced to do endless fatigues, partly because the camp was in a dirty and chaotic condition and partly because there was nothing else for them to do, no proper arms and equipment for the raw recruits, whose discipline, slight at best, broke down. They filled the drinking dens and brothels of the camp, and in despair were sent back to Paris. The only sensible thing suggested had been the incorporation of the mobiles, in groups of a hundred, in the regular regiments, where they would have been fairly easily absorbed. As it was, MacMahon found his Army reduced to regular troops collected from the wreck of the Army of Alsace, reservists from the depots, troops from Africa and some admirable battalions of marines. With these troops of mixed quality he was ordered to advance to the relief of Metz.

It was an absurd project, only justifiable on narrow political grounds. If the Army and the Emperor fell back on Paris, as all military prudence commanded, the régime would collapse. The Empress Regent and Palikao forbade this, and MacMahon marched forward, hesitating and trying to turn back, but driven on by imperative orders from Paris. The rashness of the march and the vacillations of the Marshal bewildered the Germans, whose first news of Mac-Mahon's movements came from the *Temps*. At once the German armies began to close in on the doomed French. At Beaumont, Failly's corps was badly surprised and showed, in sudden panics, the effect of demoralization consequent on defeat. The Marshal had little faith in his plan and gladly took refuge in the little fortified city of Sedan, where his harassed troops could rest. MacMahon did not realize that, already, the Germans had united their armies in front of him, and he was more concerned to shelter his troops than to take up a good position on the hills round the city.

On the morning of September 2nd the battle began. The Marshal was badly wounded; the Emperor, rouged lest the troops should see his deadly pallor, rode about under shell-fire in agony, but was not lucky enough to be hit. Ducrot, who had succeeded MacMahon, was all for an immediate retreat, but Wimpffen, who had just arrived from

Africa and who had Palikao's authority to take command, still hoped for a miracle. Some of the Army was ready for battle.

The marines, who had scandalized some of their comrades by their straggling on the march, showed admirable courage and constancy. Wimpffen hoped to force a way out, at any rate for the Emperor, and had Napoleon taken the chance and died at the head of a desperate sortie, his name might not have been dishonoured. But rightly convinced that the battle was lost and anxious not to be the cause of useless slaughter, the Emperor retired into Sedan. The superiority of the German artillery was felt far more at Sedan than in any previous battle. Moltke had his enemy securely held and he did not launch his infantry to vain attacks, when he could destroy the French will to resist by an artillery bombardment to which no real reply was possible. Surrounded on all sides, the French were under a constant cross-fire. The heroic combats of the marines at Bazeilles were worthy of the repute of French arms. The cavalry charges of the Chasseurs d'Afrique and cuirassiers covered the ground with gay uniforms, like a carpet, as one narrator put it, and the King of Prussia, looking down on this fruitless gallantry cried, 'Oh, the brave fellows'. But into Sedan the fugitives poured, filling the narrow streets with men and horses and baggage. An army paymaster had to crawl under the horses' bellies to get past. Napoleon ordered the hoisting of the white flag. Wimpffen, mad with rage, tried to resist, but the battle was over. Napoleon offered his own sword in surrender, but Moltke reasonably had to have the whole Army. Bismarck met at a wayside inn the man whom he had last seen in his glory in Paris in 1867; and Moltke, coldly inflexible, insisted on a complete surrender despite the vehement pleading of Wimpffen. The French losses were over 20,000, the German losses about 6,000, testimony to the superiority of the German guns. A few thousand troops managed to get away, but 80,000 prisoners, among them the Emperor and a Marshal of France, testified to the most complete and dramatic of German victories. Though not as important as the battles round Metz, Sedan was the crowning glory of Prussian arms and the end of the French Empire.

Although Paris and many other French towns have their street of the 4th of September, that date is not one which all French Republicans then or since have delighted to honour. The imminent collapse of the Empire had been discounted since the middle of August, and Lord Lyons, the British Ambassador, doubted if even a victory could save the régime. Despite the attempt at secrecy the news of Sedan spread, and by the evening of September 3rd the only question was what would replace the fallen Empire.

The Republican leaders were by no means all anxious to replace the Imperial Government at once. The burden laid on the successors of Napoleon III would be heavy and, perhaps, unbearable; moreover, the deputies feared a revolution. Let the Corps Législatif, the organ of universal suffrage, however tainted and corrupted, provide France with a temporary Government. Some of the Left were even ready to contemplate a triumvirate of Palikao, Trochu, the Military Governor of Paris, and Schneider, the President of the Chamber. But all these combinations broke down on two obstacles. The Imperialist deputies who were the overwhelming majority of the Chamber hesitated to pronounce the fatal word 'deposition' and wasted time in seeking plausible solutions that would not commit the future. And the Paris mob was in no mood for these tricks, any more than it had been in February, 1848. The Blanquists were active and, by September 4th, the only remaining question was whether the change would be made peacefully or not. The police might still resist. But there was no fight left in the Imperialists. Had Napoleon III been killed at Sedan, his heir might have had more friends, but the captivity of the Emperor tied the tongues of the majority and their delay ended the possibility of a pacific transition to a provisional régime. The impatient mob made an end of the protracted intrigues and negotiations, invaded the Chamber, and the Empire was over. Dr. Evans, an American court dentist, smuggled the Empress out of Paris; and at the Palais Bourbon, Jules Favre, accepting the popular acclamation of the Republic, cried, 'It is not here but at the Hôtel de Ville that we must proclaim it'.

France had made another revolution, or rather Paris had. The system that had resisted all attacks and which had, a few months before, been acclaimed by the vast majority of the French people, was overthrown without a shadow of resistance as a result of a great French defeat. Bismarck, more than any other man, founded the Third Republic.

The collapse of schemes for a regular transference of power made it necessary to find a new Government at once. There was now no thought of Palikao or Schneider. And since the revolution was the work of Paris, it was fitting that the new Government should be exclusively formed of deputies of Paris or of deputies who had been elected for Paris but had chosen to sit for other constituencies.

The 'Government of National Defence' ranged from such deeply conservative members of the Left as Ernest Picard to the bugbear of all respectable people, Rochefort, the scurrilous editor of the *Lanterne*, idol of the Paris mob. One reassuring gesture was made, the appointment of General Trochu as head of the Government. The Governor of Paris, as a critic of the old Army, inspired confidence in the new rulers of Paris, and his great gifts as a talker made him more of a match for his eloquent colleagues than, say, Moltke would have been. By assuming the Ministry of Foreign Affairs, Jules Favre took over what was at the moment the most important of the departments, for it was his place to determine the question of peace or war. By his famous circular of September 6th he decided for war, for he announced that even to get peace France would not surrender an 'inch of her territory or a stone of her fortresses'. Considered in cold blood, the circular to French diplomats was absurd. It shut off negotiation at once; it would have been wiser to have asked for Prussian terms and then to have appealed to the conscience of Europe and the pride of France. But such a course was impossible. In Paris all sections applauded the eloquent declaration and there were critics on the Left who would have liked to add 'not a dollar' to the list of things France would not give to the victors. Thiers defended the circular in terms that the outside world could understand: 'What would you have? The French Revolution, our mother, was born speech-making: you mustn't take what she says literally.'

There were plenty of people in France, and above all in Paris, who took it all very literally. Prussia might have one French Army on the way to Germany and the other shut up in Metz, but France had the Republic. Prussia had announced, as is the way with belligerents at the beginning of a war, that her quarrel was with the Emperor not with France; now the Emperor was gone, so what was there left to fight about? But even if Bismarck should prove perfidious, there was the Republic confronting him. Had not a schoolboy under the Empire, instead of writing Latin verses on the death of Prince Jerome in the general examination, described the Republic coming:

> Pâle encore, et des plis de sa blanche tunique
> Cachant son front voilé?

She was no longer pale or veiled, but faced the invaders 'terrible as an army with banners'. 'They won't dare to come now that we have *her*,' said a workman. And spectators all over Paris noted that September 4th was like a holiday. It was a beautiful day and holiday crowds watched the shopkeepers who had, a few days before, been so proud of the signs that announced that they were purveyors to the Imperial Court, climb up ladders and scrape off the incriminating legends. Others cheered as busts of the Emperor were thrown into the Seine, and far away, in Auvergne, young men climbed the mountain of Gergovia, where Cæsar had been repelled by the Gauls, and knocked down the monument that recorded the visit of the Imperial archæologist. It was very different in the wake of the advancing German armies, where the boy Maurice Barrès never forgot the drunken French troops going off to the front then returning a few days later, hungry and shattered—to be followed by the inexorable armies of the invaders. But all that was remote enough from the Paris that celebrated the newborn Republic and to which, in the next day or two, the great exiles, Victor Hugo, Louis Blanc and the rest, hurried to give their moral support. It was a brief delirium, but not all were victims of it. The youngest member of the Government knew that there was more to be done than make speeches and issue proclamations. While his colleagues were busy at the Hôtel de Ville, Léon Gambetta had taken possession of the Ministry of the Interior and, announcing his action to the provinces, made sure that the citadel of the political machine would be in safe hands, his own. The cautious Ernest Picard arrived at the Place Beauvau just too late.

In conjunction with Arago, the famous scientist who had been made Mayor of Paris, Gambetta nominated mayors for the twenty arrondissements of the city—and his colleagues learned of it for the first time by reading the notice in the official paper! To secure the machinery of local government was essential for the young Republic —and, from that point of view, it was unfortunate that the local elections had taken place on the day of Wörth and Spicheren, before the result of these battles had begun to weaken the Imperialist party. Although Gambetta had nominated the new mayors, he wished to strike while the iron was hot and have new municipal elections despite the opposition of his colleagues. They were in favour of postponing everything until peace was near, with or without further fighting, but Gambetta was resolved both to beat the Prussians and to give the Republic a chance to dig itself in: for he, like the rest of the Left, could not realize how completely, for the moment, Bonapartism was dead.

Gambetta was not blindly partisan; he made the engineer, Charles de Freycinet, a prefect, although he had been an Imperialist candidate; but the Republican zealots of the Lot and Tarn would have none of him. In general, however, Gambetta was mindful of his friends of Belleville days, of men like the very red Arthur Ranc and of other old associates, likely to be regarded by the prudent as specimens of the class described by Jules Vallès as 'réfractaires', 'fellows who have tried everything and who have not become anything; fellows who have studied in all the faculties: law, medicine, or history, and who have not got rank, degree or diploma'.

As Minister of the Interior, Gambetta was in charge of the National Guard and it was possible to arm the people against reaction as well as against the Prussians. That is to say, if there were any arms. Ranc, whom Gambetta had made Mayor of the ninth arrondissement, tells how a zealous citizen came to him to enroll, and on being told that he would get a rifle in two days' time burst out, 'We've still got to wait? So it's still just as it was under the Empire.' However, arms of a kind were got and the National Guard of Paris rose in number to 360,000 men—one of the decisive political factors of the next six months.

Politically, at any rate, the Republic was accepted and safe all over France within a few days of its proclamation. There might be differences of opinion about the kind of Republic. Prudence or pedantry kept a veteran of the cause like Jules Grévy in ostentatious

33

aloofness from a Republic created by a revolution, and the most famous French politician, Thiers, refused firmly to enter the Government of National Defence, although he was willing to serve it as long as it represented France, in however imperfect a form.

Only in one region was the change ignored. Inside Metz, Bazaine had set up what was equivalent to a military dictatorship. He refused to proclaim the Republic and was more and more preoccupied with the problem of 'restoring order' after peace was made. He had made a half-hearted sortie as MacMahon drew near, but he gave no sign that he had any hope of success or any plan except to stay in Metz as long as food held out—and then save France from 'anarchy' in collaboration with the Empress and with the consent of Bismarck. He indulged in cryptic negotiations with the Germans and sent off Bourbaki, under a German safe-conduct, to negotiate at Hastings with Eugénie. But the Empress soon realized that a restoration of her husband or her son by the consent of Prussia was unworthy and impossible. As long as France resisted, she would do nothing to hamper the work of the Government of National Defence.

Inside Metz, discontent grew. Civilians threw the bust of the Emperor out of the Hôtel de Ville and a local paper compared the conduct of the Marshal unfavourably with that of Beaurepaire, who had committed suicide at Verdun in 1792 rather than surrender that fortress to the Prussians.[1] Eager and angry officers talked of kidnapping Bazaine, and some of his immediate subordinates were bitter against him. But they were professional soldiers bound by hierarchical respect. Their honour was satisfied by an occasional bloody and futile sortie, and they settled down to the regular siege ritual of eating horses and dying of typhus, until the approach of starvation would justify surrender. For the cream of the Imperial Army of France could not, for a moment, believe it possible that an amateur Army and an illegitimate Government could succeed where the Emperor and his troops had failed. As long as Bazaine held out, 200,000 German troops were engaged, but he held out without hope of victory and merely from professional decorum—if not from dark and treasonable ambition. As far as the Army of Metz was concerned, the war was over bar the formalities.

[1] It is probable that Beaurepaire was murdered by townspeople who wanted to surrender, but the importance of a legend has no relation to its truth.

CHAPTER II

THE SIEGE OF PARIS

O N September 19th the German Armies completed their investment of Paris. For a few days the cable in the bed of the Seine remained undiscovered, but after September 25th the beleaguered city could communicate with the outside only by balloon and carrier pigeon. The folly that kept the 'Government of National Defence' in Paris was soon made evident. The Imperial Government, in its last days, had prepared for the imminent siege by sending agents of the ministries to Tours; the new Government accepted the decision of its predecessor and despatched delegates to Tours to deal with the provinces. But these delegates, Crémieux, Glais-Bizoin and Admiral Fourichon, were only delegates without independent authority, and they were old and worn-out men. Indeed, their age seems to have determined their departure as much as anything else. Younger members of the Government had to prove their courage by standing in the breach as their great ancestors had done. The Republican myth, the belief that the sacred name was the new sign in which France would conquer, compelled the Government to stay in the sacred city where the Convention in 1792 had defied the embattled kings. Every member of the Government had to act as if he were Danton. It was as deputies of Paris that the members of the Government of National Defence had been thrown into power; they could not desert their maker. And there was, too, in the Government and in the population of the city, a good deal of Parisian conceit. France was saved in 1793 because Paris was saved; France was conquered in 1814 and 1815 because Paris was conquered. It was the duty of the provinces to do all they could for the sovereign city; but Paris would save herself by her exertions, and France by her example.

Illusions were not confined to Paris. The Parisians thought that it would be impossible for the Germans to blockade effectively the vast circuit of their city, for the wall was 20 miles round and the forts of the entrenched camp would impose an even greater extension of their lines on the besiegers than that.[1] But the Germans, and many non-Germans, thought it would be materially and morally impossible for the frivolous capital to stand a siege. Moltke, like a good professional

[1] The German lines came to cover over 50 miles.

35

soldier, was convinced that the war was over. Most of the French professional soldiers were prisoners, and he had now only to deal with amateurs. He expected to be home and at peace by the end of October.

There were good military reasons for this optimism. The fortifications of Paris were out of date; in the thirty years since they had been built, the range of artillery had vastly increased and the reconstruction of the defence works had proceeded very slowly. In August, Thiers had been infuriated by the pedantry and slackness of the engineers. They in turn were held up by the legal difficulties of getting sites for new defence works; they added to their difficulties by the snobbery that made them prefer to begin elaborate permanent fortifications instead of temporary but efficient earthworks of the type that had served the Russians so well at Sebastopol.

The combat of September 19th seemed to justify the gloomiest French views. The important position of Chatillon had to be abandoned after a skirmish in which the Zouaves fled in ignominious panic. It is true that these Zouaves had nothing of the Zouave about them but the name and the uniform; they were raw recruits, but to a population brought up to regard the crack Zouave regiments with superstitious awe, the news was a cold douche. Of more permanent importance was the imposition on the defence of a mere retention of the permanent works; it was no longer possible to hold off the Germans and force them to extend their quarter of a million men over a vaster perimeter. Indeed, there were moments when it seemed doubtful if the permanent works could be held. On the second day of the siege, Parisian mobiles abandoned the key fort of Mont-Valérien, marching back into the city to the tune of the *Marseillaise*. But despite momentary panic and more permanent indiscipline, the Germans were not tempted to assault a city that they assumed would soon fall without any great activity on their side.

There was a moment when it seemed that it might fall at once, for on September 19th the Foreign Minister of the provisional government, Jules Favre, left the city under a safe-conduct to interview Bismarck in the great Rothschild château of Ferrières. Cut off from Europe, Favre had in Chaudordy, his representative at Tours, an excellent agent, but his own policy was imposed on him by his own illusions and the still more formidable illusions and passions of the Parisians. He wanted an armistice which would allow the election of a Constituent Assembly and the regularizing of the position of the Government, but 'if we must give up an inch of soil, no negotiations'. It was a repetition of the old declaration; but, whatever Favre or his colleagues in their hearts may have thought, an acceptance of Bismarck's terms was impossible. The American Minister, Elihu Washburne, wrote in his diary of September 22nd, 'the Prussians demanded territory, and no government could yield to such a demand and live a day in France'. If Prussia would not relent and Paris would not abase herself, the siege was inevitable.

In the last days of the Empire, preparations had been made for a siege. The Minister of Commerce, Clément Duvernois, had displayed great energy in collecting foodstuffs for Paris, and the sight of parks and squares full of cattle, the Halles full of civilian, and the unfinished Opéra full of military, stores comforted the citizens. But the results of these measures could not be fully estimated, for two reasons. No full and accurate statement of the amount of food actually in Paris was ever available. In the last month of the siege, Ernest Picard, the Minister of Finance, noted with gratification that the Government was 'surprised to find that there was still so much wheat and flour' in hand. More indefensible than the neglect to make and draw up a strict balance sheet of stores for the besieged Government, was the neglect, until December, to make an accurate census of the number of inhabitants. In September, Parisians had been advised to leave Paris if no good reason kept them there, but there was no attempt to force useless mouths to leave the city and, worse still, the inhabitants of the neighbouring towns and villages were encouraged to enter Paris to be safe from the invaders! It was, of course, impossible to determine how long an unknown number of inhabitants could be fed on an unknown quantity of wheat, meat and other foodstuffs. It was consequently impossible to answer accurately the fundamental question, how many days had the provinces got in which to rescue Paris? This mattered little as long as Metz resisted, for it was obviously desirable, at almost any risk, to deliver Paris before the troops besieging Metz were freed to protect the troops besieging Paris. But after October 28th the basic calculation of French strategy was the duration of the resistance of Paris; and had the armies of the provinces known that they could depend on the resistance of Paris into 1871, it would have been unnecessary to try so many forlorn hopes.

The statistical deficiencies of the defenders of Paris had other minor but not unimportant results. The food supply was controlled by the mayors of the twenty arrondissements of the city and, apart from the varying efficiency and honesty of the administrators, it was impossible to insist on rigid justice when the exact population of each district was unknown. So in the beleaguered city, there were startling discrepancies in the amount of food available in the different arrondissements, differences which did not add to the moral resources of the defence. These moral resources were further weakened by the refusal of the Government to ration everybody. The Blanquists demanded rationing on the ground that Paris was like a becalmed ship and an equal division of its limited resources was just and necessary. But such a drastic step was opposed by a Government which shunned any revolutionary

37

measures and was strongly influenced by the doctrines of classical economics. 'Rationing by dearness' was the slogan of Molinari, the great economist. For all their Jacobin airs, the lawyers who dominated the Government were timid souls. In the days before the siege began, Ernest Picard had strongly opposed raising the *octroi*, the municipal tax on foodstuffs entering Paris. Such a measure would encourage speculators to pour supplies into Paris which would be unfair to the owners of the existing stocks and it would seriously affect the revenue of the city which had to stand so much extra expense anyway! A temporary suspension was voted, but as it was only to apply to goods brought in by genuine refugees or citizens, it ensured that the *octroi* officials would inspect all importations, collect no revenue but impose enough delay to diminish seriously the amount of food that business men on the make would otherwise have poured into Paris. A Government like this was not likely to affront private property or the bellies of the rich by insisting on a share-out. It fell back on that device dear to all French Governments, the fixing of a legal price for certain foodstuffs without doing anything serious to ensure control of the supply. Butchers, forced to sell at this unprofitable price, simply shut up shop, thus creating vast queues at such shops as remained open. Food cards were reluctantly introduced and, even when the last days of the siege were at hand, the Government issued a proclamation denouncing rumours that bread was to be rationed. At last it came to that; and the greatest of privileges for a Frenchman, the right to ask for more bread, was taken away, too late to delay the surrender of the city.

The clue to the resistance of Paris was the food supply, but the only hope of the deliverance of Paris was in its garrison. That garrison was formidable in numbers. There was Vinoy's corps, which had moved too slowly to be caught at Sedan. There were some survivors of that battle itself. There were two good regular regiments which had been brought from Rome, there were 13,000 excellently disciplined sailors and marines. There were in the city, in the police, the fire-brigade and in other services many veteran soldiers of whom better use might have been made had they been employed to stiffen the new units.

The new units were 100,000 mobiles from the provinces, 15,000 mobiles of the city and the vast amorphous mass of the National Guard. Had the political position of the Government been stronger, a powerful army could have been created. But neither Trochu nor his colleagues were modern Carnots. Trochu was sceptical of the power of improvised troops and, though he had moments of optimism, was as much concerned with making an honourable as a successful resistance. His deep religious faith at times led him to believe that Sainte-Geneviève would deliver her city from the barbarians in the nineteenth century as she had in the fifth. His colleagues did not share this faith, but they had their own myths. Had not Ernest Picard declared that the revival of the National Guard would give France 500,000 trained soldiers in a week? There were other reasons why a rational use of the man-power of Paris was difficult. The National Guard of the working-class districts was deeply suspicious of its rulers and leaders. This suspicion had led to the introduction of the election of their officers by the mobiles. Were not the existing officers of that corps nominees of the dethroned tyrant? Was it not an insult to Paris that bearers of such hated names as Piétri and Baroche were high officers in the Garde Mobile? So in the first days of the siege, indeed while some of the Garde Mobile were actually fighting, its discipline was strained by an electoral campaign, and it was not until December that the Government took the political risk of abolishing election. In the 'sedentary National Guard', election was of course a sacred right. So three battalions of the Belleville Guard elected Flourens as their colonel and Belleville thought of its soldiers as defenders of the Republic and of the revolution, as much as of the country. They suspected that if they were submissive to the orders of the generals, they would be sacrificed by those enemies of the Republic. And the National Guard was the only defence of the authority of the Government. 'We were,' wrote Jules Ferry, 'a Government resting on moral force; we had nothing else at our disposal; what had we to maintain order and defend it against the party of anarchy? the National Guard and nothing else.' A Government of this type could not impose on its only support an amalgamation of the old and the new armies such as had accounted for the successes of the First Republic. In addition, the National Guard was the only obvious solution of the great unemployment problem. By paying the amateur soldiers a franc and a half a day,[1] the Government saved from destitution a mass of workers cut off from their normal employments by the siege. That watchdog of the Treasury, Picard, protested against such extravagance, adding that paying allowances straight to the wives meant weakening the authority of the husbands. Gambetta wanted to secure that, in return for these payments, real work was done. But although the defence needed great masses of labourers, it did not find it easy to get them. Until the last month of the siege, the National Guard confined itself to maintaining order, or creating disturbances inside Paris, and to guarding the walls; the active defence was left to the regulars, the sailors and the mobiles.

Even these units were not sufficiently amalgamated. The defence of the city was divided into nine sectors [2] and these did not always co-operate willingly or in time. Moreover, the War Office, with its mind on the really interesting problems of peace, for long refused to give the

[1] The pay was thus 1s. 3d. (thirty cents) a day for each man; a man with a wife and two children got 2s. 3½d. (fifty-five cents) a day.
[2] It is significant of the dearth of higher officers, that four of these sectors were commanded by admirals.

new regiments of the regular army a permanent organization lest vested interests should be created, a future economy purchased at a serious loss of efficiency. The provincial mobiles were in the main well-disciplined, but they were affected (or tainted) by the more politically-minded Parisian battalions[1] and by the survivors of Sedan who naturally placed no blind confidence in the high command.

The defenders of Paris, however, with few exceptions, contributed an asset far more important than their defects of temper, discipline and stolidity. They refused to recognize what all the world but they recognized, that the game was up. The great French talent for improvisation was fully drawn on. Cut off from normal supplies, Paris was provided with an army and a fairly well-equipped army. In some ways, it was better equipped than the Imperial Army had been. The breech-loading artillery which existed only in a model or two and in some blue prints, became a reality in Paris, despite inexpert manufacturers and a desperate shortage of trained artillery officers. The machinery for manufacturing mitrailleuses had been shifted to the provinces, but new machinery was improvised and the attitude of the Germans showed outside Paris, as it had outside Metz, that, for all its defects, the new weapon had a formidably depressing effect even on first-class troops. A flotilla of gunboats was put on the river, and following up a bright idea of Napoleon III, armoured trains were created to take advantage of the railway resources of the city.

All this technical ingenuity would have availed little had there not been courage behind it. There were still panics, and the new regiments were often only covered by the discipline of the few regulars, but the fighting force of the Parisians surprised the Germans and the world. Paris had men and courage, how were they to be used? Merely by holding out, Paris immobilized 250,000 Germans and that was a great deal, but it was not enough for the rôle in which the Parisians had cast themselves. They were to break the German lines and liberate France, and, when that proved impossible, they were to issue forth from the beleaguered city when the new provincial armies got within reach.

The deliverance of Paris by Paris, always impossible, had not been made easier by one of the few preparations for the siege that had been really thorough. Obsessed by the need of preventing a Prussian assault on the ramparts, all the roads round Paris had been elaborately made impassable and all the gates had been blocked up or narrowed. When it became evident that the invaders had no notion of assaulting the fortifications, these defences became an obstacle to the defenders, who wished to attack. The Germans fortified themselves all round Paris and the garrison repeatedly found that the temporary and local superiority in strength which it gained from its position in the centre of

---

[1] Paris affected the bodies as well as the minds of its defenders; there were 8,000 cases of venereal disease in the garrison.

the vast perimeter, could not be made effective fast enough to break through. Sortie after sortie failed, ending after initial success, with desperate combats in the great walled parks of suburban châteaux, Gros Bois and Malmaison, Ladoucette and Villiers.

These sorties, if useful in themselves in keeping the Germans on the alert, would, if no more than that, have been but bigger versions of the exploits of Sergeant Hoff. What he did by his nightly raids, Trochu could do less well on a bigger scale in his monthly sortie. But, as Trochu told his colleagues, he had a plan. It was not in origin his plan, but Ducrot's. That general, taken prisoner at Sedan, had escaped from his captors and was now Trochu's second-in-command. His plan was bold. Its object was not to achieve the impossible, to break up the besieging army by a sortie, but the more limited and practicable one of getting out of Paris the pick of the garrison. This army would be the nucleus of a provincial army of rescue. In his choice of a direction for this break-through, Ducrot showed originality. France had complete command of the sea, but apart from capturing German merchantmen was making no use of it. It was Ducrot's plan to use it; the escaping army was to march on Rouen by Pontoise; there its back would be to the river and its bases would be the Channel ports, from which the Germans could not cut it off. It would be in touch with the new armies of the north gathering round Amiens and the frontier fortresses, while the new armies on the Loire would be transported by rail and sea to lower Normandy. In fortified lines based on sea communications, it could resist all German attempts to repeat Sedan until it was ready to advance to the relief of the sedentary garrison of Paris. Once out of Paris, Ducrot proposed to play the part of Wellington in 1810 and make for a new Torres Vedras. Ducrot and Trochu were ready for the risky break-through when their plan was made obsolete by the decision of Léon Gambetta.

Although there is no evidence that he foresaw the consequences of letting the Government be shut up in Paris, Gambetta's temperament was too active and combative to let him rest content with the rôle of sending balloon messages to his nominal subordinates in the provinces. There were disquieting symptoms of disunion in the south; there were disquieting signs of independence at Tours. After many hesitations and changes, the Paris Government had finally decided against holding elections for a Constituent Assembly, but the delegates at Tours had disregarded the wishes of the Government in Paris. It was high time that someone more important than mere officials should represent the authority of Paris in the provinces, and, on October 9th, Gambetta arrived at Tours, a day after he had left Paris by balloon.

Henceforward all the general political and strategic decisions were imposed on France and on Paris by the will of the demagogue of thirty-two. In his passion for secrecy, Trochu had not confided his plan to the Government as a whole, and Gambetta was allowed to leave Paris without any knowledge of it. His friend, Arthur Ranc, who joined him a few days later, was told and he told Gambetta. But whether Gambetta's later professions of ignorance were deliberate lying or simply reflected the indifference with which he had heard Ranc's story, he paid no attention to the Trochu plan and adopted and forced on Trochu an entirely different strategy. In this scheme, there was no question of getting the best part of the Paris garrison out. The new provincial armies were to advance as fast and as directly as possible to the relief of Paris; when they got close enough, the Paris garrison, in a vast mass movement, was to issue forth and the two French armies would meet in the Forest of Fontainebleau. There was an historical parallel for this scheme. The leader of the Gaulish resistance to Cæsar, Vercingetorix, had shut himself up in Alesia awaiting deliverance at the hands of the new Gaulish armies which, in co-operation with his, would break the Roman lines of circumvallation. But attack from within and without had not shaken the grip of Cæsar on the Gaulish citadel, and Alesia had fallen. It was not an encouraging parallel, but then the Italian Gambetta was really a countryman of Cæsar and not of Vercingetorix.

There was an immediate argument for doing what could be done quickly. The greater part of German military resources was employed in the two great sieges of Metz and Paris. It was essential to deliver Paris before Metz fell, before the avalanche—to use Gambetta's metaphor—descended on the new armies gathering on the Loire.

Although he later gave the impression that he had created armies out of nothing, Gambetta found that a good deal had been done under great difficulties. The nominal War Minister, Le Flô, was in Paris and so was the greater part of the War Office staff. Le Fort, who was organizing the troops at Tours, did so less in the hope of being able to resist the Germans than to secure that, at an armistice, France should have a respectable military force in the field. Tours was a Bedlam of Catholic volunteers with the emblem of the Sacred Heart on their tunics; adventurers of all nations looking for jobs, rank or contracts; old officers recalled from retirement; newly-promoted officers of good Republican antecedents; the officials of the remnants of departments sent from Paris; the troops of the raw 15th Corps. The Ambassadors and Ministers of the powers had mostly left Paris and were dealing with M. de Chaudordy, the cool and competent diplomat who was running his branch of the Foreign Office much more competently than Favre was running the head office in Paris. And in the midst of them all, the aged delegates of the Government squabbled and procrastinated. The head of the War Office, Admiral Fourichon, had just resigned and Gambetta seized the office, as he had seized the Interior on September 4th. Within forty-eight hours of his arrival he had made himself Minister of War, presenting both Tours and Paris with an accomplished fact, and his dictatorship had begun. Two days before Gambetta arrived, the nascent army of the Loire under La Motte Rouge had been defeated and Orleans abandoned to the Bavarians under von der Tann. It was a bad beginning. Gambetta immediately removed La Motte Rouge, but how was he to replace him? Nearly all the professional French officers were now prisoners of war or besieged. Gambetta had to call on retired officers, men invalided out, men at the base whose experience had been gained as adjutants or as quartermasters. He had to appeal to the Navy: and soon Army Corps and smaller units were commanded by naval officers given temporary military rank. The names of these transplanted mariners were quickly famous, Jaurès and Jauréguiberry, Pallu de la Barrière, Penhoat, Pothuau, La Roncière, Saisset; in the provinces and in Paris sailors fought regiments, forts, and corps as they would, had they been given a chance, have fought their ships. But such resources were not enough. Gambetta and the brilliant civil engineer, Charles de Freycinet, whom he had made his executive agent, hoped for great things from the new Auxiliary Army which was to produce the brilliant young generals that the Republic needed. Gambetta thought of 1793, Freycinet of the more recent example of the American Civil War. Gambetta forgot that it was the Royal Army that provided most of the generals of the Republic, and Freycinet that nearly all the successful generals in America were professional soldiers.

The new Commander of the Army of the Loire, General d'Aurelle de Paladines, was a competent officer, a good trainer of troops but no thunderbolt of war. He was less pessimistic than Bourbaki, who had refused to command the mob that called itself the 'Army of the Loire', but the ignorant optimism of the young civilian under whose orders he was, irritated him. He thought that Gambetta trusted too much to mere numbers and did not realize how difficult it was to move ill-trained troops, much less fight and win battles with them. 'It would be dangerous to trust to the deceptive mirage of paper figures, and to take them for a reality,' he told Gambetta on the eve of the great advance which was designed to deliver Paris. And within three weeks of Gambetta's arrival, the fall of Metz had profoundly altered the situation for the worse. With the Army of Prince Frederick Charles hurrying to the west, the race was to the swift—and that race was halted while M. Thiers sought for a decent diplomatic end for the war in which enough honour had been saved to satisfy the survivor of the reign of Louis Philippe.

Thiers had gone on a mission to the Courts of Europe using all his prestige and power of argument to induce them to intervene on behalf of prostrate France. The only two countries that could or would do anything were Britain and Russia. Chaudordy had managed to induce Britain to take the lead in making the peace terms a matter of general European interest. Gladstone was deeply alarmed by the dangerous future created by the projected German annexation of Alsace-Lorraine; and Bismarck was equally alarmed at the prospect of this, or any other part of the peace, being discussed in a general assembly of the powers. But Thiers was irritated with England and, being warmly received at St. Petersburg, misunderstood the situation. 'The very flattering reception he was given,' wrote the chargé d'affaires, Gabriac, 'led him to conceive hopes that could not be realized, for that welcome was, unfortunately, almost entirely personal.' The Russian plan, which Thiers accepted, was to bring about direct negotiations between France and Germany and to secure a pass from Bismarck to permit Thiers to enter Paris to confer with the Government. Thiers insisted that Gambetta delay the offensive of the Army of the Loire while he went to Paris. Gambetta was full of fight, believing as he did that the war was far from lost and that peace and elections at this moment meant ruin for the infant Republic.

The old statesman left Tours on the 28th October. After a brief interview with Bismarck he entered Paris, bearing with him the dread news which the Government had refused to believe, the news of the fall of Metz and the judgment that the time had come to accept the inevitable. October 30th was a black day for Paris, since the furious population, ever ready to suspect treason, learnt at one stroke of the fall of Metz, of the unsuccessful fight at Le Bourget, and of the arrival of the old enemy of the Paris workers, ready to betray them to the Prussians with his perfidious proposals of an armistice.

On October 31st the explosion came. Round the Hôtel de Ville the crowds became more and more ugly. Jules Ferry was there and he sent for Jules Favre, who hastily left Thiers and went off to join his colleagues; Trochu was added to the hostages that the rash confidence of the Government put in the hands of what was now the insurgent party. There must be municipal elections at once, the Government must resign, any attempt to rescue its members would be the sign for their death. Such were the insurgent terms. The day wore on with the unfortunate Ministers more and more alarmed, but refusing to resign. The news of their situation spread fast, but no one seemed disposed to do anything to rescue them. Flourens, booted and spurred, walked among the ink-pots on the table, incarnation of the embattled National Guard of Belleville. The most Left-wing member of the Government, Dorian, tried to reason with the leaders of the *émeute;* the most Right-wing, Ernest Picard, who did not share the confidence of his colleagues in the good will of the Parisians, was busy planning a rescue that would not mean the death of the Ministers. There was perpetual disorder among the noisy crowds that filled the Hôtel de Ville; the courage of the Ministers baffled the mutineers, and time was given to appeal to battalions thought to be loyal, like that of the Folies Bergère club. A first raid rescued Trochu, Ferry, Arago and Pelletan, but Jules Simon, Jules Favre, General Le Flô and Garnier-Pagès were still captive. It was obvious that the revolt had not succeeded, but that increased the danger for the Ministers who were now hostages. The Hôtel de Ville was surrounded by loyal troops, and some mobiles, who had entered its kitchen by a tunnel that ran from a neighbouring barracks, opened the doors to the besieging troops, and Jules Ferry was in time to save his colleagues.

The leaders of this abortive revolution were not prosecuted. Told in stern tones not to do it again, their thunder was stolen by the announcement of a plebiscite asking the Parisians to express their approval of the Government of National Defence. The election of November 3rd gave an overwhelming majority to the Government and, as a gesture that may have concealed a half-surrender, it was announced that mayors and aldermen would be elected. Peace, for the moment, was made between Paris and its rulers, because all chance of peace between Paris and its besiegers was over.

It was the opinion of Thiers that, had it not been for the disastrous *émeute* of October 31st, he would have obtained an armistice from Bismarck which would have permitted the holding of a general election without the surrender of any French military advantages, such as they were. Thiers hoped, that is to say, that Bismarck would allow Paris to be supplied with food during the armistice. There seems little reason to believe that Bismarck would or could have granted an armistice without continuing to starve out Paris, or without the surrender of one of the forts; and the Paris workers, whatever the bourgeoisie thought, were still vehemently opposed to compromise. It was a little later that Trochu, replying to one of his colleagues who had said that the man in the street wanted peace, said, 'The people in some drawing-rooms want peace; the man in the street wants war'. Thiers was forced to admit his failure. 'The Empire ruined us; the Republic keeps us from saving ourselves.'

All the wisdom was on the side of Thiers, but on November 9th the battle of Coulmiers seemed for a moment to show the folly of wisdom, for what the professional soldiers of the Empire had failed to do, the raw recruits of the Army of the Loire had done; they had won an undisputed victory over the Germans. The French had a great superiority in numbers, but even so, to win at all was miraculous and the face of the war was transformed. Two days before the battle, Hatzfeld, Bismarck's aide-de-camp, had expressed his scorn of the new levies. Prince Frederick Charles at the head of the veteran troops from before Metz could 'march over the whole of France from north to south and from east to west, driving all these creatures before him and pillaging the country as he chooses'. The complacency of the

Germans gave way to something like panic, and the wiser heads realized how narrow an escape they had had. Prince Frederick Charles declared that, had Metz held out a day longer, he could not have got his troops up in time to save the army round Paris from having to raise the siege. If Metz had held out a day longer—or the advance on Orleans had been made, as Gambetta had wanted, on November 1st. For the moment, the prudence and pessimism of Thiers and Favre were at a discount; Gambetta and his armies must be given a chance to succeed where Thiers and his diplomacy had failed.

CHAPTER III

GAMBETTA'S WAR

THE despair of the rulers of France and the sublime self-confidence of the German generals were both deeply affected by the news of Coulmiers. For the Government in Paris, the victory meant the transfer of the effective authority from them to Gambetta. The strategy of the campaign was no longer controlled by Trochu and Ducrot; Paris was to be rescued by the provincial armies and the movements of its garrison must be co-ordinated with those of its potential rescuers. For the Germans, the new development was both surprising and dangerous. The German lines of communication stretched right across France, menaced from the troops in the east round Dijon and in the Vosges, from the troops in the north round the fortresses of French Flanders, and from the armies to the west and south if they should choose to move east.

The very amateurishness of the new French armies worried the Germans. Which of these hastily raised corps would turn out to be formidable? The normal calculations of the General Staff were out of place here. The greater part of France was still in French hands; and the commanders of the German wedge thrust into its heart found it impossible to decide where to strike, especially as every blow gave breathing space to the forces in other regions where the indomitable nation that did not know it was beaten could raise and train troops.

Yet Coulmiers and the battles that followed showed how limited was the French power of action. Had the Army of the Loire been a little better trained, the Bavarians would not merely have been defeated but destroyed. But, in attack, the new French troops were capable of only the simplest manœuvres and quite incapable of exploiting a victory. In going into action it was found necessary to deploy the troops long before the attack could be delivered, as a quick change from marching to battle order was too difficult for them. The country over which the Army of the Loire was forced to fight was particularly unsuitable for raw troops, as the great plain of the Beauce deprived them of cover. Shortage of officers and lack of the *esprit de corps* of old units made it seem advisable to keep the troops always together, which meant that they were not quartered in houses or farms, but forced to camp out in the fields or on the roads, a source of desperate hardship and loss as winter came.

47

The equipment of the new armies represented an administrative miracle, but the problem of arming the new armies was insoluble. Fortunately most of the regular arsenals were far away from invasion and they were utilized to their full capacity, but their output was insufficient. Arms were bought from America, from England, from Belgium, good weapons and bad. But even the good ones were not standardized. The troops of the Army of the Loire had fifteen different kinds of rifles and a constant source of ill-feeling was the difference between regiments that had chassepots or Remingtons or other modern types and the less lucky units that had to put up with muzzle-loaders. At critical moments troops were liable to panic as the deficiencies of their equipment were realized.

Like the garrison of Paris, the new corps were, in some ways, better off than the old had been, since they got some breech-loading field-guns and abandoned Lebœuf's bad fuses. The rapidity with which good batteries were put into the field and good gunners improvised illustrates the best side of the military administration. Freycinet, much more than Gambetta, was the author of these prodigies of technical improvisation. Yet Freycinet hesitated to take what might seem very obvious steps like imposing unified control on the railways, which might have made it easier to increase German embarrassment by rapid troop movements by rail. Both he and Gambetta had to allow for the novelty of their authority; the Government of National Defence at Tours, as at Paris, had to negotiate almost as much as it had to command.

Gambetta did not separate, in his own mind, defence of France from defence of the Republic. As Minister of the Interior he had turned over, as far as he could, the control of the local government to loyal Republicans, but in so many regions of France, loyal Republicans a few months ago had been scarce and not very well thought of by the average man and woman. The old political machine had collapsed and the new party in power was, as yet, short of prestige and of administrative experience.

Gambetta's troubles were, if anything, greater where the Republican party was strong. Lyons caused him serious difficulties, for in that old centre of socialist and republican agitation the Republic had been proclaimed a few hours before it had been proclaimed at Paris. The party leaders in Lyons were by no means ready to recognize, unconditionally, the authority of the Government of National Defence. They treated with it as equal to equal. The philosopher, Challemel-Lacour, whom Gambetta sent to Lyons as Prefect of the Rhône, was not recognized under that title by the municipality; he was merely the delegate of the Government of National Defence, and was often forced to play the part of an ambassador rather than of a ruler. The red flag floated over the Hôtel de Ville; the defence of Lyons and of the valley of the Rhône was treated as a private problem of the region;

regular officers were suspect and the self-styled 'Committee of Public Safety' offered the command to Garibaldi and to Cluseret. The latter had served in the Union Army during the American Civil War, so it was as a 'Republican general of the United States of America' that he was asked to 'come and help us to found the United States of Europe'.

A city thinking of the United States of Europe was naturally attractive to the most notorious practising revolutionary of the age, and by September 15th Michael Bakunin was in Lyons, where he founded a 'committee for the saving of France'. Already the ebullient Russian had decided that the way to save France was by 'an elemental, mighty, passionately energetic, anarchistic, destructive, unrestrained uprising of the popular masses'. But no French rising was elemental enough for Bakunin and his methods were 'too Kalmuck' for the French. By September 28th Lyons had lost its chance of inaugurating the new age and next day Bakunin was again on the road. But Lyons continued to give trouble, to fly the red flag, to hamper Gambetta. The murder or 'execution by popular justice' of Commandant Arnaud two months later showed that there was still revolutionary yeast at Lyons, but the danger from Gambetta's point of view was over.

In Marseilles, Cluseret on October 31st carried out a *coup d'état* with more success than Flourens was doing at the same time in Paris. Cluseret was aided by George Francis Train, the American Bakunin of this experiment, but within three days Gambetta was able to impose his authority through a new Prefect, Gent. There were risings and demonstrations all over the south, notably at Toulouse and at Saint-Étienne, and the notorious 'League of the South' bred fears for national unity, while the separatist language of southern soldiers scandalized a patriotic boy in Saint-Quentin [1] in the invaded north.

As the war continued, weariness naturally grew. Thiers on his journey to Paris at the end of October heard the ruined peasants ask for peace; and the enemies of the Dictator in the bitter December days commented bitterly on the telegram Gambetta had sent from Bourges to one of his friends. 'Things are getting better here very fast and a few days from now you will hear news of us. Fine cigars, keep cheerful.' It was easy, it was said, for the shabby lawyers whom accident had thrust into power to be cheerful. It was harder for the freezing troops on the Loire, or for the miserable recruits in the wretched training camps, or for the peasants and townspeople in the German lines paying now for the anger the unexpected French resistance aroused in the breasts of the much-tried German troops!

The patriotic fervour that made these sufferings endurable was not present in all Frenchmen. While Henri Regnault, whom his friends thought the hope of French painting, was serving under the walls of

[1] Gabriel Hanotaux.

Paris where he was to die, Paul Cézanne in German-free Provence was hiding from the police who had tried to drag him into the army. In Normandy, Gustave Flaubert, more pessimistic than ever since the despicable revolution of September 4th, drilled his militia company without much hope; and among people with a good deal to lose, the Gambetta policy of war to the bitter end was less and less popular. These sections of the country agreed with Thiers that the time had come to make the best of a bad job, but the more energetic Frenchmen agreed with the spirit of Ducrot's reply that political wisdom, as well as military honour, made it necessary for the present generation to suffer that the next generation might benefit by their heroism.

In besieged Paris, the grimmer days of the siege were at hand. Gallant efforts were made to keep up the spirits of the population. Theatrical performances were warmly patriotic, but the violent attacks on the fallen régime that had gratified public opinion in the days immediately after September 4th began to bore the public. For a few weeks it seemed as if the opportunity to recite the bitter verses of 'Les Châtiments'[1] almost compensated for Sedan. The delight of listening to these long-banned verses was not confined to old Republicans. Men whom no one had suspected of disaffection to the ex-Emperor were zealous in the good cause. An irritated officer[2] complained that whenever he went to the theatre to amuse himself he was sure to see a gloomy gentleman get up and 'rolling his eyes fiercely' recite,

L'enfant avait reçu deux balles dans la tête.[3]

yet 'whilst people grew sorrowful over the two stray bullets in the head of this hypothetical child, German shells were disembowelling real children a few hundred yards away'. Immediately after the fall of the Empire, a member of the Comédie Française had refused to take part in one of these performances 'in a theatre which a few weeks ago was so willing to be known as the home of the "Regular Actors of the Emperor" ', but what delicacy did for Edmond Got, boredom did for other people. The demand for new scandals about the Emperor and Empress diminished; in a city more and more wretched, the easy pleasures of abuse were not so comforting and medals of Napoleon III wearing the spiked helmet of the Prussians were less popular, as it seemed impossible to escape from the real spiked helmets of the besiegers. Even a lecture by Émile Legouvé on 'Moral nourishment during the siege' was more comforting than the publication of love-letters from Napoleon III to his mistress.

For a city whose physical as well as its spiritual lighting had been its pride, cutting off the gas supply at the end of November was a great blow, following as it did on the failure of the battles of the Marne on

[1] Celebrated poems against Napoleon III written by Victor Hugo in exile.
[2] Comte d'Hérisson.   [3] 'The child had received two bullets in its head.'

the previous days and on the recapture of Orleans by the Germans. The high hopes of Coulmiers were fading; Paris could not deliver herself, and the relieving army was in retreat. Food was becoming a serious worry; the supply of milk for children presented impossible problems and, though the rich could buy the animals from the zoo, compare the taste and price of zebra and bear, of camel and elephant, the poor were less happy. Prices soared so that at a charity bazaar, chickens were £1 [1] each, butter £1 [1] a pound, and eggs 1s. 3d. [2] each (the daily pay of a National Guardsman). Rats became edible and vendible, and the city that had been the envy of the world settled down to a bitter winter.

The strain of the siege was not only felt by the Parisians. The Germans had not counted on this stubborn resistance; the besieging troops, though better fed than the besieged, suffered from the very severe winter and from the constant strain. Bismarck was eager to end the siege—and the war—before the neutrals could interfere, and, backed by the War Minister, Roon, he wanted to bombard the city. He was full of scorn for the muddle-headed humanitarianism of the Prussian court ladies who thought a bombardment inhuman: for, in that age, the crushing of military resistance by the killing and maiming of women and children was opposed with a warmth and sincerity that we can hardly understand to-day.

The victor of Coulmiers, Aurelle de Paladines, was less impressed by his victory than almost anybody else. A veteran of the old army, he was conscious of the bad training and bad equipment of the new levies. Many of his men had the old muzzle-loading rifles; they were short of equipment; they carried cartridges in the haversacks along with their food, and biscuits on string over their shoulders. Their clothing and their shoes were very inadequate for the rain and hail that soon became snow. There was much to be said for digging in round Orleans and awaiting, in a prepared position, the German assault. But Gambetta was obsessed with the belief that Paris could not hold out beyond the fifteenth of December. 'Paris is hungry and needs us.' [3] An advance was begun and, at Beaune-la-Rolande, the Germans defeated a surprisingly vigorous attack. News had come of a sortie planned by Trochu [4] and all local considerations were sacrificed to the need of aiding the victorious army of Paris, for, mistaking a reference to the capture of Epinay-sur-Seine for Epinay-sur-Orge, Gambetta saw the two armies triumphantly meeting. But the sortie failed, and in any case the Army of the Loire not only did not advance but had to retreat. Gambetta did not lose heart: Aurelle was denounced almost as Bazaine had been, and peace moves were repressed. Moltke was again convinced that the war was over and

[1] $5.　　　[2] 30 cents.
[3] This slogan had the appeal of a jingle in French, 'Paris a faim et nous réclame'.
[4] The balloon was blown away to Norway, and Trochu's message came via Oslo.

could not understand why the French did not see this too, and in Paris the combative Ducrot, defeated and discredited by his part in the battle from which, despite his promise, he had returned alive though not victorious, thought that Moltke was right.

Gambetta now begun to discount the fall of Paris, and to prepare for a campaign against the Germans even when their field armies had been reinforced by the arrival of the Paris siege troops. German patience and morale were to be worn down by a war that would seem endless. The removal of the temporary capital from Tours to Bordeaux was a sign of the times; Gambetta's headquarters was no longer near Paris; indeed it was no longer in any fixed place, for only half of the remaining days of the war were spent by him in Bordeaux. He was now for ever on the move, encouraging, bullying, harassing lukewarm patriots and enemies of the 'Republic'.

The Army of the Loire had been cut in two in its retreat and its western half now had, in Chanzy, a general after Gambetta's own heart, a man full of hope and energy, conscious of the defects of his troops but willing to make the best of them. Chanzy knew how much heartening the infantry needed. He deplored the habit of the artillery of galloping off once the German guns had got their range. The very speed and skill with which these tactical moves were carried out was bad for the ill-armed, raw infantry who had to stand their ground. The sight of the general with his picturesque escort of Algerian cavalry in their flowing cloaks was comforting to the troops. In the north, another able and resourceful general had been thrown up by the war. Faidherbe had shown great initiative in the colonies and he showed equal initiative in his campaigns in Artois and Flanders. Indeed, almost to the end, he held his own against the Germans, showing prudence in brief moments of success; and when he succumbed at last at Saint-Quentin in January, he gave a very good account of himself.

The third general on whom Gambetta relied was Bourbaki. A former commander of the Imperial Guard and a convinced Imperialist, he was unlikely either to feel much optimism when faced with the amateur regiments of Gambetta's army or to have much confidence in the demagogue who had been so violent an enemy of the fallen régime. He saw difficulties all the time and there were difficulties everywhere, but Chanzy and Faidherbe showed that they were not insuperable. At a critical moment, when all depended on a last desperate effort, Bourbaki wired Gambetta, 'You think there is a well-organized army. I think I have often told you the contrary.' Forced to campaign in an abnormally severe winter, Bourbaki provoked Freycinet to ask why the snow and ice did not stop the Prussians too? It was not altogether a fair question, but it was not wholly unfair.

The spirit of Chanzy was very different. He was now face to face with one of the best of the German generals, Prince Frederick Charles,

Both the French and German troops suffered from the bitter cold. The invaders had often to clothe themselves in French uniforms, and were very far from being the well-equipped and overwhelmingly confident troops of August. But the state of the French was far worse. In retreat, the rickety fabric of discipline often broke down; there were thousands of stragglers; there were demoralizing failures of supplies and it was a tribute to the courage of the rank-and-file, and to the skill and resolution of Chanzy, that so desperate a resistance was made in the three days' battle of Le Mans (January 10th, 11th, 12th). But for all Chanzy's optimism, his army, after the retreat on Laval, was incapable of causing serious alarm to the Germans.

That task fell upon Bourbaki. Between Gambetta, Freycinet and the railway manager, Auguste de Serres, a plan was concocted which Bourbaki undertook to carry out in a spirit of duty rather than of hope. His army was to be transferred east as fast as possible by railway to menace the German lines of communication. In Burgundy, Garibaldi was still in the field, although suspect to many Frenchmen as a revolutionary charlatan, and Belfort, the only survivor of the great frontier fortresses, was still holding out under its bold governor, Denfert-Rochereau. A rapid raid on the German flank might have given a respite to Chanzy or Faidherbe, it might have relieved Belfort, it might even have made possible a successful sortie from Paris. But speed was impossible. Bourbaki was suspect to the Government and Serres accompanied him with an order of revocation in his pocket. The task of transporting over 100,000 men across country was too much for the railways and the miserable troops were frozen in the stationary trains, suffering almost as much as if they had marched. They got within the sound of the guns of Belfort, but all the attempts to break through the German lines failed. Bourbaki tried to commit suicide (and failed). His army now under Clinchant was cut off from its base and, excluded from the armistice, made the most disastrous marches of the war in frightful weather. Eighty thousand men, frozen, starving and in rags, crossed into Switzerland. At Saint-Quentin, at Le Mans, at Héricourt, the three main French armies had been defeated. Chanzy, Faidherbe, Bourbaki—all had failed to deliver Paris or seriously to endanger the German position. And Paris could not help herself; she was bombarded from January 5th; food supplies were at last coming to an end; sorties were now hopeless butchery.

On January 26th, the armistice terms agreed on by Bismarck and Jules Favre were accepted; the war was over except for the unfortunate Army of the East which was being driven into Switzerland. Whether the neglect to mention the Army was due to the folly of Jules Favre or the duplicity of Bismarck matters little; its complete destruction had only one important consequence, it made quite hopeless Gambetta's resistance to peace.

For the Dictator was still bent on war. 'Thanks to Paris,' he declared on January 31st, 'if we are resolute patriots, we have in hand all the necessary means to avenge it and free ourselves.' Chanzy was still ready to fight and, in Paris, there were plenty of fanatics ready to believe that in face of 'the flag of the democratic and social Republic, Bismarck will recoil in terror and the German Army will pass the Rhine in disorder'. But these illusions of La Villette were recognized for illusions in the rest of France. Bismarck had got what he wanted; he had imposed unconditional surrender on the politicians who claimed to represent France. These politicians had helped him by not sending Favre to London to the Congress that met in January to discuss the formulas needed to cover the repudiation by Russia of the treaty imposed on her by the victors in the Crimean War. There was now neither military nor diplomatic hope for France. In vain, Gambetta tried to resist. Bismarck had insisted on an Assembly which should have authority to make peace. Gambetta had attempted to exclude from it all Imperialist officials and leaders, but Bismarck had insisted on a free election and the older politicians were now in no mood to submit to any dictatorship. On February 6th, Gambetta resigned. Two days later, the elections overwhelmingly ratified the policy of peace.

The formal ending of the war was delayed until the signing of the Treaty of Frankfort (May 10th, 1871), but all but details were settled in the preliminary Treaty of Versailles. Thiers displayed his oratorical talents in his interviews with Bismarck and he obtained two concessions, the indemnity was reduced from £240,000,000 ($1,200,000,000) to £200,000,000 ($1,000,000,000) and, in exchange for the entry of the Prussian troops into Paris, Belfort, the still untaken fortress, was to remain French. France had lost over 150,000 lives and had suffered great material losses. But more permanent was the humiliation of the loss of the two frontier provinces, despite the protests of their deputies in the new National Assembly at Bordeaux. When the Mayor of Strasbourg died after making his protest, his end was suited to the national mood. As important as the ratification by the Assembly of these humiliating terms, was the recognition that an epoch was over. It was over two centuries since France had arisen on the ruins of Spain and of the Holy Roman Empire as the strongest power in Europe, a match for any state singly and for most combinations of states as well. Only six months before, that position was still apparently unshaken, but on January 18th, 1871, the German Empire had been proclaimed in that Palace of Versailles built by the great king whose proud motto had been 'Nec pluribus impar'.[1] That France was dead beyond hope of resurrection.

[1] 'Not unequal to several', the motto adopted by Louis XIV after his successful war against Holland, Spain and the old German Empire.

CHAPTER IV

THE COMMUNE

I

IN 1867, Victor Hugo wrote an introduction to a guide to Paris, published for visitors to the Exhibition. It was a hymn of praise to Paris. 'She goes her way alone, France follows, has to follow and is irritated thereby; later she calms down and applauds; it is one of the forms of our national life. . . . Paris decrees an event. France suddenly summoned, obeys.' The great romantic poet was then in exile, but he expressed, well enough, the spirit of Paris. Silenced and subdued by the Empire which was backed by the millions of rural voters, Paris bided her time and on the eve of the war was ready for a revolt or, if all went well, a revolution.

A new generation of workers had grown up that knew nothing, at first hand, of the bloody days of June, when the workers who had made the revolution of February 1848, learned that they had not made it for themselves. The revolution of September, like the revolutions of July 1830, and February 1848, had been taken over by the bourgeois politicians: and the brief reactions of the militant revolutionaries against this Government of lawyers and talkers failed, without bloodshed on October 31st and with bloodshed on January 22nd, when the demonstrating National Guards were shot down outside the Hôtel de Ville by the Breton mobiles inside it, mobiles who, it was believed, had fired at the command of Jules Ferry's deputy, Gustave Chaudey. It was in protest against the surrender of Paris that the National Guards had assembled on January 22nd, and their failure had been followed by the end of the siege. And, however necessary that submission to the will of Bismarck was, there were orators and journalists in plenty to declare (and simple souls in plenty to believe them) that there was still food in store, that there was still a fighting chance, that the Government of National Defence was not merely incompetent, but treacherous.

The resignation of Gambetta, the Conservative triumph at the elections, the sudden appearance of Thiers as the ruler of France, all irritated the Parisians. They thought of their resistance as heroic and reproached the provinces for not coming to the rescue of the city, but they realized that the majority in the new National Assembly was more inclined to blame the disasters of the war on Paris than to be grateful for its courage. The provinces were full of stories of the heroism of mobiles and sailors who had held the forts while the Parisian National Guard was idling in clubs and in the streets. And if the name of Thiers sounded gratefully in the ear of the provincial bourgeoisie, it had a very different sound in the ears of the Parisian workers, for whom Thiers was the man of the massacre of the Rue Transnonain, the most savage episode of the social war of the reign of Louis Philippe.[1] By its refusal to move to Paris, the Assembly showed its distrust of the capital, and this insult seemed to the Parisians fully to justify their worst fears for the Republic and the Revolution. While the newly-elected deputies were getting ready to sleep on camp-beds in the great halls of the Palace of Versailles, the armed Paris workers were being prepared for a new revolution or for resistance to an attempted counter-revolution.

In his negotiations with Bismarck, Jules Favre had secured the right of the National Guard to retain its arms and, though he later repented of this, he could not in fact have guaranteed the disarming of the workers. Indeed, it was in defence of their arms, not merely their rifles but their artillery, that the workers first moved, collecting the guns in great parks, to save them from the Prussians and the 'yokels' of Versailles. What did the squires of the Assembly and their peasant electors know or care for the honour of Paris? 'An assembly of country bumpkins' was how Gaston Crémieux described the new Parliament. The very claim of the Assembly to sovereignty was maddening. Felix Pyat asserted that, by consenting to the mutilation of France, the Assembly had committed suicide. When the Prussian troops entered Paris, they were received by black flags, by silent streets, by a public day of mourning. Women whose curiosity or business instincts brought them out into the streets through which the conquerors passed, were publicly whipped. Paris passed through her hours of deepest humiliation and the blame was only in part imputed to the Prussians.

II

The bitterness roused by the rise and fall of the Commune of 1871 has never quite abated, and it is still a matter of violent controversy whether a Parisian revolt was inevitable or whether, if inevitable, its defeat was certain. Even had the Assembly been sympathetic and tactful, the embittered—and armed—proletariat of Paris might not have accepted its authority. Whatever orthodox Republicans might say or think, the Paris worker (and the militant everywhere) was inclined to 'set the Republic above universal suffrage', and this dogma

[1] Now chiefly remembered because of Daumier's picture.

of the divine right of the Republic was reinforced by the anti-parliamentary bias of the Blanquists, who were the most active revolutionaries in Paris. In his newspaper, *La Patrie en Danger*, Blanqui had asked the workers to look at 'the fifteen or twenty samples of parliaments which have bored, perverted or laid waste the country for nearly a century, it is a heap of nullities and egoisms'.

The quarrel between the Assembly and Paris was not merely due to mutual suspicion and dislike based on abstract political and social differences. The Assembly, moved by its natural desire to get back to normality as soon as possible and blinded to the harshness and rashness of what it was doing by its hatred of Paris, passed two laws which not only showed how little the Assembly knew or cared for the disorganization of Paris after the ordeal of the siege, but were of immediate and disastrous consequences to scores of thousands of anti-revolutionary bourgeois. By a law published on March 10th, to go into effect on the 13th, commercial bills, whose maturity had been postponed by a moratorium, were to be paid seven months after they were normally due, which, since the first moratorium dated from August 13th, 1870, meant, in very many cases, at once. This measure threatened many honest and conservative shopkeepers and business men with ruin.[1] Another law repealed the moratorium on house rents. The Assembly, that is to say, threatened a great part of the population of Paris with bankruptcy or eviction or both. Having done this, it adjourned itself, to meet at Versailles on March 20th.

That Paris was in one of its combatant moods was obvious and, as long as it remained a centre of armed discontent, conservative people in general and business in particular would be uneasy. It was necessary, so Thiers thought, to show that the new Government was master before the Assembly met. The removal of the artillery from control of the National Guard was as essential in the eyes of the party of order as, in 1848, the suppression of the National Workshops had been. So, on the night of March 17th, the walls were placarded with a proclamation from Thiers, appealing to the patriotism and good sense of the people of Paris. 'Evilly-disposed men, under the pretext of resisting the Prussians have taken control of a part of the city . . . forcing you to mount guard under the orders of a secret committee . . . Parisians, . . . you will approve our recourse to force, for it is necessary, at all costs . . . that order, the very basis of your well-being, should be reborn.'

The immediate act of force thus announced was the seizure of 'the guns stolen from the State'. The most famous of the gun parks was on the Butte de Montmartre, still a half-built area, separated from Paris at its feet and only accessible by one decent road and a number

---

[1] It should be remembered that bills were, and are, far more commonly used by small business men in France than they are in England. 150,000 bills were at once protested.

of steep lanes. It was to Montmartre that General Lecomte climbed at the head of his squad of police and his larger body of very raw troops. The Butte was successfully surprised, the guns taken—but there were neither horses nor harness to haul them away, which in any case was a difficult enough job. The Montmartre of 1871 was abed in the early hours of the morning, but it had plenty of time to awake. Soon the streets were full of men and women; the weary, puzzled and hungry troops of the 88th regiment were surrounded; an attempt by Lecomte and his police to fire on the crowd and restore discipline among the troops failed; the young soldiers turned the butts of their rifles up and Lecomte was arrested. Later, another general, Clément Thomas, hated since his suppression of the workers in June 1848, was recognized, although in civilian clothes, crossing the Place Pigalle, and he, too, was arrested. On the same day, the attempt to seize guns at Belleville failed. M. Thiers had lost the first round in his war with Paris or the revolutionary sections of Paris.

The 'Chief of the Executive Power' was not the only representative of established order to suffer defeat that day. The Mayor of Montmartre, since the siege, had been a doctor just under forty, Georges Clemenceau. He had hoped to negotiate the peaceful surrender of the guns, so the arrival of Lecomte and his men had alarmed him and, now that the attack had failed, he was still more alarmed at the possible fate of the generals. But his authority was crumbling every minute. His deputy, Ferré, was openly hostile, and all the east end of Paris was now on the move; the ominous beat of the drums calling out the National Guard was silencing prudence. The two generals were doomed and were shot down by unknown National Guardsmen; women danced obscenely round their bodies. The Mayor, shattered by this revelation of his own impotence and popular savagery, burst into tears.[1]

In Paris, if there was any authority, it was now in the hands of that mysterious Committee denounced by Thiers. The Committee was not, in fact, an obscure body, although most of its members were unknown except to their fellow-workers. During the siege two authorities had grown up to rival the Government of National Defence: the mayors of the twenty arrondissements and the officers of the National Guard. After the siege, the delegates of the battalions of the National Guard continued to meet, and after some preliminary discussion, there was organized on March 3rd, the 'Republican Federation of the National Guard' with a Central Executive Committee.[2] The Central Committee was organized by arrondissements but, in fact, only the working-

---

[1] According to his biographer, M. Georges Suares, Clemenceau did not weep again until the victory of 1918.

[2] The Federation comprised 215 battalions out of 270. From the Federation came the name 'fédérés', usually translated into English as 'federals', thus leading to over-emphasis on the federalist ideas of some members of the National Guard.

class arrondissements really took part in the organization, just as only the working-class and lower-middle-class battalions joined the Federation.

The Central Committee, suddenly projected into the limelight, was not an organized revolutionary party. Its members were, apart from a few crooks and cranks, representatives of the Paris workers, and the Paris workers were still mostly not factory hands but skilled craftsmen working in small businesses like the bookbinder, Varlin, or lower middle-class employees like Jourde, the clerk in the Bank of France. Nor were they united by doctrine. The Government at Versailles and the world were ready to believe that the revolt of Paris was the work of that mysterious 'International' whose early congresses had alarmed the bourgeois public of the 1860's, providing raw material for the romantic imagination of Mr. Disraeli when he was writing *Lothair*, but which was, in fact, at death's door owing to the fight between Marx and Bakunin. But neither formally nor really had the International a leading rôle in the revolt, and although Marx came to its defence in the manifesto of the International,[1] it was not Marxism that was the animating creed of the Paris workers or their leaders. Only Vaillant knew anything of German socialism, and the men who were now thrown to the top were disciples of Proudhon or of Blanqui, or belated Jacobins like Delescluze, re-enacting '93—as they understood the history of the heroic year.

Their immediate objects were simple: to escape the effects of the Assembly's withdrawal of the moratorium; to save the Republic; and to save the autonomy of Paris and of the National Guard. They wished to overthrow the authority of the Commander-in-Chief appointed by Thiers, Aurelle de Paladines, and to secure that Paris would not be deprived of her local autonomy by the Assembly. None of these objects, it was held, was in itself revolutionary, and the Central Committee was not prepared to recognize that a revolution had begun; that it had to win or be destroyed. So the first day of triumph was wasted; such regular troops as did not desert or disband were allowed to withdraw from the city—and so were Thiers and his Ministers.

M. Thiers recognized when he was beaten; he had lost the first round, but he was not unduly depressed. He had, ever since 1848, held that the way to deal with a serious Parisian revolt was the method practised by Windischgrätz against Vienna in 1848. Get outside, assemble your forces and retake the capital. To this plan Thiers now clung, believing in it so firmly that he even ordered the evacuation of the key of the Paris fortifications, Mont-Valérien.

March 19th was a Sunday and, like September 4th, a fine day. The enthusiastic Yves Guyot wrote to a provincial paper run by a revolutionary friend of his [2] an enthusiastic description: 'A crowd on

---

[1] Now better known as *The Civil War in France*.   [2] Jules Guesde.

the quays, on the boulevards, women, children, men surprising themselves by their calm and order; and the Republicans breathing freely and saying, "Ah! it's the first time we have really felt ourselves to be living in a Republic". ' The Republic was, for the moment, in the somewhat surprised hands of the Central Committee, which rejoiced with the good people of Paris and summoned it to elect a municipality. It still tried to avoid breaking with legality altogether.

The retreating Government had left its authority, for what it was worth, to the mayors, and they were the link between Paris and Versailles. Most of the twenty mayors were Left-wingers and deputies like Clemenceau. Even the Right mayors were anxious to avoid a fight to a finish of the kind anticipated, without enough repulsion, by some of the more vehement members of the Assembly and, perhaps, by M. Thiers. The attempted compromise failed, as all subsequent compromises failed. The Blanquists were not ready to recognize the authority of the Assembly and insisted that the Central Committee must keep control of Paris, pending the election of the municipality; while the Government and the Assembly, although willing to make very inadequate adjustments of the laws on bills and rents, were angered at the pretensions of Paris to make terms with the only legal and sovereign body in France.

For a day or two there were hopes that the right-thinking elements in Paris would deliver the city from its usurpers. Admiral Saisset, who had earned popularity during the siege, was nominated Commander of the Department of the Seine and he had hopes that the large number of Parisians who had a good deal more to lose than their chains would rally to him. But before and after the siege, a very large proportion of the more prosperous inhabitants of Paris had left it for the country, so that the National Guard battalions of the richer quarters were much under strength. In any case, as Andrieux noted in Lyons, the members of the National Guard were prudent fathers of families not anxious to take too many risks in the restoration of order; they were very unlike modern storm troopers. A demonstration of the 'better elements' of Paris was dispersed in the Place Vendôme with the loss of fifteen lives, and there was more blood between the Assembly and Paris. Despite all protests from alarmed or prudent deputies, the election of the municipality went forward. On both sides compromise was more and more suspect; the Central Committee occupied the bourgeois quarters of Paris, while the Assembly disowned Saisset, who had made promises of concessions that were intolerable to the irritated majority. The mayors agreed with the Committee that the election would have to go on. In this atmosphere of quasi-legality, the people of Paris, on March 26th, elected a municipal council which was overwhelmingly revolutionary and which showed it by taking the august and terrifying name of 'the Commune of Paris'. For if the word 'commune' recalled to some historically minded people the revolt of the commonalty in the Middle Ages, it recalled to far more, the great Paris Commune of the Revolution that had dethroned Louis XVI, overawed the Convention, and whose fall had been the beginning of the end for the Jacobin republic. Against the Assembly which at any moment, it was feared, might proclaim the King or give the executive power to the Duc d'Aumale, Paris evoked the memory of 1792.

Without prevision, the capital of France had fallen into the hands of a revolutionary government, but it had not fallen into the hands of a revolutionary party. It was this lack of an organized revolutionary party that prevented the Central Committee from taking advantage of the panic that fell upon Versailles. Although Vinoy forced Thiers to authorize him to reoccupy Mont-Valérien, the position of the Government was dangerous. It had few troops, and the desertions and mutinies of March 18th had shown how unreliable those few were. There were some loyal units; the Foreign Legion was especially trustworthy; there were also a few Turcos;[1] but French soldiers, worn out by the war, were in no combative mood; least of all were they in a mood to fight their own countrymen. Despite the appeal of the Assembly, it had proved far harder in 1871 than in 1848 to rouse the provinces against Paris. To get a force together, Thiers had to ask Bismarck to accelerate the release from Germany of the prisoners of war of the old Imperial Army; these professionals were used to obeying orders and were not as war-weary as the remnants of Gambetta's levies.

While troops were being accumulated at Versailles, while the old historian of Napoleon I was visiting their camps, looking after their food, clothing, and drink, hurrying on the preparations for attack, showing up the slowness of the regular soldiers by hiring contractors to build a battery, the chances of victory for Paris were slipping away. As Lissagaray bitterly pointed out, the Commune started with many more advantages than most revolutions command; immunity from attack, for a short time at least; abundant arms and supplies; and a near-by enemy who could hardly have resisted a march of the National Guard on Versailles. But to attack was to admit a definitely revolutionary purpose, to abandon the pretence that only Parisian municipal rights were being fought for. The Blanquists had, it is true, no such prudery and, by decreeing the disestablishment of the Church and the abolition of conscription, Paris was in fact stepping outside the bounds of her authority. But the fiction of a contest over municipal autonomy, expressed in comic form by references to the 'Government of Seine and Oise'[2] and, more seriously, by appeals to the great cities of the provinces for aid, was observed until it was too late.

The refusal of the deputies of Paris, led by Louis Blanc, and the Mayors of Paris like Clemenceau, to collaborate with the Commune,

---

[1] Algerian native troops.   [2] Versailles is the capital of this department.

made a revolutionary policy even more necessary. But what kind of a revolution? Lenin declared that for a successful revolution it is necessary to have 'a high development of productive forces and the preparedness of the proletariat'. Paris had neither. There was no Parisian equivalent of the great Putilov works in the Petersburg of 1917, and no equivalent of Lenin and his party. War-weariness was not confined to the partisans of Versailles. One of the Commanders-in-Chief of the Commune, Cluseret, was later to say that he always asked for twice as many men as were necessary for any operation as the only way of getting the minimum. A nominal strength of 200,000 men produced about 40,000 combatants. Then the sectionalism that had made the defence of Paris difficult during the first siege, was even more marked during the second. The National Guardsmen were ready to defend their own quarters, but very reluctant to defend other sections. And the sections of Paris which were in danger were those nearest Versailles, the richest quarters, whose inhabitants were not anxious to keep out the assailants, while the most strongly *communard* areas in the north-east of the city were safe anyway, as that section of the fortifications of Paris was inside the German lines and the German troops were officially neutral. Lastly, there was never an uncontested authority in Paris. Although it had the sanction of popular election, the Commune had always to face the rival authority of the Central Committee, as the Government of National Defence had had to bargain with the National Guard. It is true that in its triumphant proclamation of March 19th, the Central Committee had boasted that it would not conserve the power that had fallen into its hands, but although its mandate had expired, the members of the Committee could not divest themselves of their feeling of responsibility for the fate of the Revolution, and the Committee was tempted to behave to the Commune as the great Commune had behaved to the Convention.

Thus it came about that Thiers was given a few days to recover from his expulsion of March 18th, days which he used profitably, while Paris enjoyed its recovered liberty and its assumption of its historical rôle. As Lissagaray put it, 'For the tenth time since 1789 the workers put France on the right track.' It remained to be seen whether France would stay on that track. For a moment there seemed to be hope that she would. All over the south there had been, during the war, a good deal of revolutionary feeling, most obvious at Lyons, but visible everywhere and taking form in federalist organizations like the 'League of the South'. The claim of Paris to autonomy and the appeal to outraged patriotism evoked sympathy in a region where Royalism and militant Catholicism were always at war with red Republicanism, militant anti-clericalism and Protestantism.

The war had not directly touched the south, and it seemed, for a moment, that that ebullient region would make up in civil conflict for what it had been spared in national war. But except at Marseilles, where Gaston Crémieux was the nominal leader of a local Commune which proclaimed that 'the Republicans of Paris and Marseilles wish that Paris and the Government that sits there should rule France politically and, at Marseilles, the citizens of Marseilles claim to administer themselves', there was no serious disturbance. Even at Marseilles, despite some bloodshed, the revolt was short-lived and futile. At Saint-Étienne, the Prefect was killed. At Toulouse, the officers of the National Guard demanded 'the dissolution of the Assembly . . . cause of all the difficulties, fruit of fear and of clerical corruption', but surrendered to legal authority without difficulty. At Narbonne, Digeon, who had been one of the leaders of the League of the South, found that his followers were not ready to resist two companies of Turcos. In short, in the south, all that words could do to save Paris and the Republic was done. In the rest of France, still under German occupation or only recently delivered from the menace of invasion, there were not even words, only a deep desire to get back to peace and order.

Paris and M. Thiers were left to fight it out. On April 2nd, the complacency of the Commune was shaken, for the Army of Versailles attacked and seized Courbevoie and shot the prisoners it took. The civil war had begun; Versailles was avenging Lecomte and Clément Thomas and, from that day on, both sides were provided with good emotional excuses for savagery. In Paris, the news of the attack was received with fury. The Executive Committee of the Commune announced that 'the Royalist conspirators have attacked. . . . The Chouans of Charette, the Vendeans of Cathelineau, the Bretons of Trochu, backed by policemen . . . have begun civil war'. [1]

The proclamation revealed a great deal of the illusions of Paris. The ignorant and brutal Catholic peasants, led by their squires, were attacking the sacred city of enlightenment and progress. The romantic Amazon of the Commune, Louise Michel, professed to have noticed the eyes of the Breton mobiles who had fired on the crowd on January 22nd, 'blue, looking at us with glints of steel', and although she hoped that, in time, these bandits would see the error of their ways, for the moment these victims of priest-craft were deadly enemies of Paris. The same point was made, with his usual vehement vulgarity, by Vermesch in his *Père Duchêne*.

It was outrageous that such yokels should dictate to Paris. Not until Paris and the other great cities had completed 'the Parisification of the whole of France' would there be justification for the 'voluntary abdication of Paris in favour of her children come to their majority'. So Blanqui had written and, to carry out Blanqui's programme, it was

---

[1] Charette and Cathelineau were famous leaders of the Royalists during the great Revolution and their descendants had distinguished themselves in 1870.

necessary not merely to repel the attacks of the yokels but to drive them off. So, on April 3rd, came the sortie. Three columns under Duval, Flourens and Eudes issued forth to try what the National Guard could do, now that it was no longer hampered and betrayed by people like Ducrot and Clément Thomas. The sortie, hardly organized at all, was a disastrous failure. Flourens was found in an inn and immediately shot. Duval was captured along with other Federals who surrendered on promise of their lives. The column of prisoners was met by General Vinoy, who asked who was their leader. Duval stepped forward and was executed on the spot. There was more blood between Paris and Versailles.

The defeat of the sortie produced the same effect on the authority of the Commune as was produced by defeats during the first siege on the authority of the Government of National Defence. The contempt for regular military authority was discredited and Cluseret was named Commander-in-Chief.

Cluseret had had a varied career in America and France;[1] and, despite his ostentatious cynicism, he brought a necessary minimum of authority into the military affairs of the Commune. The collapse of the sortie was an even greater disaster than it appeared at first sight, for it meant that Paris was cut off from the provinces; and this time there was no Gambetta organizing relieving armies. There was still agitation among the Left parties; there were further attempts at mediation organized by the 'Republican League for the Liberties of Paris' and by some Freemasons, but the resolution of Thiers was unshakable. He had fought these disturbers for a generation; he was now going to finish them off. How to do it, was not so easy to see, for Paris was being fed from the outside; only the Germans could have blockaded the city, and even had they been willing, Thiers dared not reduce Paris with too open German aid. The French Army would have to do what the Germans had not attempted, to force its way into Paris. This did not seem easy, especially to Thiers, who regarded himself as the creator of the fortifications and was torn between anger and pride as he contemplated their resisting powers. So while Thiers and his new Commander-in-Chief, MacMahon, were pondering on this problem, the Commune was given time to take stock and organize resistance.

The execution of Flourens and Duval had infuriated the Federals, and the Commune unanimously passed a decree setting up a system of hostages. If the Versaillese murdered Federal prisoners, the Commune would avenge them on the bodies of the prisoners most likely to be prized at Versailles. So the Archbishop of Paris and many other priests were arrested, a step which, it was believed, would cause second thoughts among the Catholic majority of the Assembly and which gratified the anti-clericalism of the Parisians. By arresting Bonjean,

[1] See p. 49.

President of the Supreme Court, the Commune not only expressed its hate of an ornament of the fallen Empire and the bourgeois legal system, it brought pressure to bear on the conscience of a member of the Versailles government whom it detested almost as much as it did Thiers—Dufaure, the Minister of Justice.

With the arrest of the hostages, there came to the front one of the most remarkable figures of the Commune, Raoul Rigault. Rigault was a formidable specimen of the middle-class revolutionary. What he loved few knew, what he hated was no secret. He had used a short period at the Prefecture of Police, after September 4th, to discover the secrets of the spy system of the Empire. He had pursued his researches at what was now known as the 'Ex-Prefecture' of Police under the Commune, and, in his last stage, as Procureur of the Commune, he saw himself as the heir of his heroes, the atheistic leaders of the great Commune, Chaumette and Hébert, the true revolutionaries who had been betrayed by that religious windbag, Robespierre. In more than his anxiety to represent the true revolutionary tradition, Rigault was historically minded, for he seemed more concerned with punishing treachery to the people in the past than with preventing it in the present. This type of belated revolutionary justice was not a purely private fad of Rigault's, but it was carried to pathological lengths by him.[1] Above all, he wanted to pay out Gustave Chaudey for having, it was asserted, ordered the mobiles to fire on January 22nd. So the eminent Republican was arrested and treated as an even more valuable prize than the Archbishop or the Judge.

Meantime, Paris was full of rumours of treason. Monks and nuns were, of course, more suspect than any other class, and when they could not be charged with dealings with Versailles, or even with treasonable dealings in the late war with the Prussians, the floors of their chapels were dug up and all the bones found were assumed to be of recent and scandalous origin. The nuns of Picpus were charged with torturing their rebellious sisters with horrible devices which the nuns said were supports for cripples, a defence that was scornfully laughed out of court by Rochefort and failed to take in the vigilant correspondent of *The* (London) *Times*. Ranking next to the priests and nuns as dangers, came the old police; their special art was entering Paris through the sewers, ready to emerge like so many Greeks in Troy from the man-holes. While a public too deeply impressed by Eugène Sue swallowed these fables, there were even more traitors in Paris than they suspected, traitors who pursued their trade very little bothered by Raoul Rigault. Thiers was in constant communication with Paris and had spies and allies in the service of the Commune, as well as a potential fifth column in the residents of the richer quarters of the west end. The

[1] The oddest example of this paying off of old scores was the arrest of a man denounced for having betrayed the Four Sergeants of La Rochelle in 1822!

walls of Paris might be impregnable if honestly and vigilantly guarded, but Thiers had reason to hope that they would not be both or either for long.

As the fate of the Commune seemed more certain, it lost the support of the lukewarm and of the elements merely disgruntled by the errors of the Assembly. Supplementary elections to replace resigned members increased the revolutionary temper of the Council of the Commune, which was now a revolutionary committee more than a regular, if ambitious, municipal government. The emblem of Paris was a ship and this particular ship was sinking and was losing its complement of rats. Inside Paris, life was still cheerful. There was no shortage of food, there were plays and concerts, including, of course, readings from *Les Châtiments*. It is true that the new rulers of Paris were rather puritanical. They raided the gambling games in the streets that had become a feature of Paris during the first siege and they were given to arresting all the customers found in certain cafés frequented by the higher class of prostitutes, much to the indignation of British journalists who found themselves, by accident, in one of the cafés during a raid. Despite its revolutionary character, the Commune did little to interfere with the normal economic life of the city. It granted, of course, long extensions of the moratoriums on rent and bills that the Assembly had foolishly stopped. It decreed the occupation by the workers of the abandoned workshops and it abolished night-work in bakeries, but with all the will in the world, it is hard to show much on the credit side in the way of positive socialist achievement. It is to one point that most Socialist criticism of the Commune has been directed. 'The hardest thing to understand', wrote Engels, 'is the holy awe with which they remained standing outside the gates of the Bank of France.' It is true that the dealings of the Commune with the Bank make odd reading if we think of the Commune as a socialist revolution. At the beginning of the first siege, the employees of the Bank were organized in three companies of the National Guard and, at the outbreak of the Commune, the Bank companies totalled about 500 men, a garrison for what might soon become a besieged fortress. That this fate was avoided was due to the self-regarding tact of the Bank and to the caution of Beslay, the elderly and well-meaning business man whom the Commune appointed to negotiate with it. The officials of the Bank were, of course, anxious to keep on good terms with the legal government at Versailles, which was likely to win, and which, in any case, controlled the branches of the Bank. On the other hand, the head offices were in Paris and the collapse of all hopes based on the resistance of the loyal National Guard battalions put the main assets of the Bank into great danger. So the Governor, within two days of the outbreak of the revolt, was sending bundles of notes off to Versailles and also sending off the plates from which the notes were printed. In Paris the

Bank had to meet the demands of the Commune. Fortunately, the Bank had a balance of 10,000,000 francs to the credit of the city, on which at first the Central Committee and then the Commune drew. But up to the end of March, the Versailles Government was still borrowing from the Bank and, even after the Commune had forbidden communication between the Bank officials and Versailles, the Court of Directors secretly continued to make advances to M. Thiers' Finance Minister, Pouyer-Quertier. This was odd enough, but at least the Commune did not know of this deceit. But Pouyer-Quertier knew of the loans to the Commune and, in cautious language, approved the decision of the Bank officers to buy immunity for the Bank, especially for the sacred private accounts. Not only were these not touched but they were kept secret.

This subsidizing of both sides in a civil war and the success of a private financial corporation in making bargains with a desperate revolutionary body have their comic side. Yet the arguments used by Beslay to justify his anxious watch over the solvency of the Bank were not without value. Any tampering with the formal immunity of the Bank would destroy credit, and many supporters of the Commune, or passive endurers of its rule, were small traders nervous about credit. The terror of the return of the assignats [1] was powerful. Who would sell food to the wives of the National Guards if there were any doubts of the soundness of the backing of the paper money in which they were paid? And an alternative policy of requisition was as unthinkable in the first as in the second siege. Beslay and Jourde were just as orthodox financiers as Picard and, although the advancing Versailles troops rushed to the rescue of the Bank as soon as they prudently could, it was never in real danger. Within a few days of the end of the Commune it was doing regular business with its branches. The dying Commune, ever old-fashioned, had been too busy with priests to bother with bankers.

With the complete collapse of the communal movement in the provinces and the assembly of a disciplined and well-equipped army at Versailles, the military prospects of the Commune grew dark. But until the abandonment of the fort at Issy on April 27th, the Parisians received no shock comparable to the failure of the sortie. Cluseret was in time to reoccupy the abandoned fort before the Versailles troops had summoned courage to seize it, but the news had spread and, as on October 31st, and January 22nd, the National Guard surrounded

---

[1] Paper money of the great Revolution which became worthless. The Bank hoped that its advances to the Commune would be acknowledged by the victors, but after a great deal of haggling, the Chamber took the view in 1879 that the Bank had only been protecting itself and, under the lead of M. Daniel Wilson, refused to be a party to any concessions to the money power. So the Bank was forced to face a loss of 7,000,000 francs (£280,000 or $1,400,000). By 1891, the necessary internal book-keeping was completed and the debt of the defunct Commune was carried on the books at one franc 'as a reminder'.

the Hôtel de Ville demanding some kind of satisfaction. They got two kinds: the arrest of Cluseret and the establishment of a 'Committee of Public Safety' which was to supervise the work of the departmental committees of the Commune and to be a kind of collective dictatorship. The idea of establishing such a committee had naturally appealed to the devotees of the old Jacobin tradition. On the other hand, it was the old Committee which had betrayed the great Commune in 1794; and the spiritual heirs of Hébert had no liking for this imitation of Robespierre. On May 1st, the Committee was set up despite the protests of men like Charles Longuet [1] who talked scornfully of mascots. The arrest of Cluseret, however soothing to the resentment of the Parisians at their military ill-fortune, was not very helpful either, since it was necessary to find a successor. The new leader was Rossel. Rossel had been a regular officer so embittered by his experiences at Metz and the treason, as he thought, of Bazaine, that he joined the Commune merely as a protest against the surrender to the Prussians. He had acquired, as Chief of Staff, an accurate knowledge of the military weaknesses of his new rulers. Of Huguenot origin, rigid and proud, Rossel had perhaps more ability than any of the other *communard* generals (he was an even more convincing talker than Trochu), but he was not well fitted to command so individualistic an agglomeration of soldiers as the garrison of Paris. He wished to insist on a high standard of duty from his subordinates and he did not regard any services or sufferings under the Empire as excusing neglect of duty in 1871. He wished to confine the Central Committee to the supply side of the army and to organize a well-disciplined and mobile force. Rossel soon found that he was almost as helpless as Cluseret had been, and, after the final fall of the fort of Issy, he announced the bad news in a contemptuous proclamation and resigned, asking to be arrested like his predecessor.

It was obvious that the Commune was soon going to be confined within the walls of Paris, and the bastions and forts were being heavily bombarded. Thiers was negotiating for the opening of a gate or gates to the besiegers: and suspicion of treason spread fast, even attacking the reputation of the new actual Commander-in-Chief, the Pole Dombrowski, a suspicion that only his gallant death in the last days of the Commune dissipated. The nominal Commander-in-Chief in the last agony was Delescluze, the veteran Jacobin, and his simple faith and courage were perhaps as useful as mere military knowledge could have been. But the organization of the defence was breaking down. The battalions guarding the walls were left unrelieved for long periods, with the natural result that long stretches of the walls were soon left unguarded. Desperation was reflected in gestures. Thiers' house was destroyed; the Vendôme column was pulled down as a protest

[1] Later son-in-law of Karl Marx and father of Jean Longuet.

against militarism;[1] and the expiatory chapels erected to the memory of Louis XVI and of General Bréa [2] were ordered to be razed.

On Sunday, May 16th, two popular performances took place in Paris: a concert for the benefit of war orphans and the trial of Cluseret. At the concert an officer, in asking the audience to come to next week's performance, mocked the boastings of Thiers who had promised to enter Paris the day before. Thiers was only twenty-four hours late, for at that moment the Versailles troops were entering through a gate opened by Ducatel, hero or traitor according to taste. Thiers and MacMahon watched with anxiety the entry of the troops, fearing that all was going too smoothly to be safe; but all was well. Through the unguarded gates the regulars poured. Dombrowski received the news with calm and sent off a despatch to the Committee of Public Safety. Interrupting the trial, Billioray read the fateful despatch to the Council of the Commune; Cluseret was hastily acquitted and, after an indecisive discussion, the Commune adjourned. It never met, formally, again.

It is possible that if the Versailles troops had rushed ahead that Sunday evening, they would have occupied most of Paris without difficulty. No serious preparations for a resistance within the city had been made, and a silly communiqué attempting to deny the entrance of the enemy was the only immediate contribution of the Committee of Public Safety. But the generals were afraid of ambushes, of the great artillery park at Montmartre; they knew from 1848 that a Paris workman behind a barricade was a formidable enemy and they were impressed by the atrocity stories of mined streets and unknown chemical methods of war. So the chance, if it was a chance, was lost and Paris began the 'bloody week'.

Once inside Paris, the Versailles troops found plenty of friends and, advancing within the ramparts, extended two great arms round the centre of Paris. Effective resistance was not possible west of a line through the Rue Royale and on the other bank, the Boulevard Saint-Michel. To the east of this line lay the heart of the revolt. Round the Panthéon on the left bank and in the smart shopping streets on the right the barricades were bombarded and stormed. In the Place Vendôme, renamed by the Blanquists 'Place of Pikes' and by the Commune 'International Place', was the Ministry of Justice as well as the fallen column. Only a few days before a hopeful citizen, after a good deal of trouble, had got the job of concierge from the Delegate of Justice, Protot. Now the Versailles artillery was firing there, and a gunner needing a support for the wheels of his gun, called out, 'Roll

---

[1] It had a statue of Napoleon I at the top. Courbet, the artist, was in charge of the destruction.
[2] Bréa had been assassinated in 1848 by a man called Nourri, who was still a prisoner in New Caledonia. The Commune amnestied him and promised to free him 'as soon as possible'. In the meantime they voted a pension for his mother.

over the old forty-eighter, he'll do '. Mounted on the body, the gun battered down the barricades and the hopes of the aspiring job-holder.

The bombardment had set fire to many houses and what it did not do, desperate *communards* did. From the terrace of Saint-Germain, horrified deputies and their friends saw Paris go up in flames. Adherents of the fallen cause rejoiced as the dome of the Tuileries fell in; that den of kings was gone. The advancing troops were confronted by a wall of smoke and fire and the countryside was covered with blackened papers from the burning Ministry of Finance. After the troops came the fire-brigades, in time to save the Louvre. On the left bank, Raoul Rigault wanted to retire into the Cité and go down fighting in the little island that had been the cradle of Paris, burning Nôtre Dame and the Palace of Justice before all was over. But the Cathedral was saved and the fire in the great Palais put out. Except for isolated barricades, all serious resistance was now confined to the working-class sections stretching east and north from the Louvre, on the right bank.

Formal military and political authority disappeared. In a proclamation, Delescluze had called on Paris to rise, rejoicing in the disappearance of military order with 'its gold-braided officers'. The Paris workers had nothing left to do but to die hard, as was their habit. Each section now fought for itself or did not fight. The famous Butte de Montmartre was captured, almost as easily as it had been on March 18th, and this time there was no recovery. While the troops advanced systematically and carefully, the *communards* fought desperately or slackly as the energy of their local leaders varied. Old Delescluze at least knew his part. He was dressed, as usual, as a sober bourgeois, top-hat, frock-coat and cane. He wore his sash of office inconspicuously, as he had always done, and seeking death with rather more persistence than Napoleon III had shown at Sedan, he climbed on a barricade and was shot down.

In the agony of the Commune, Raoul Rigault came into his own. There would be no more of the tender-heartedness that had saved the hostages up to now. Thiers had refused to make the bargain of exchanging the Archbishop and his colleagues against Blanqui, who had been arrested in the provinces on the eve of the Commune. He professed to believe that the old man was too formidable to be let loose in Paris and he professed to be shocked by a phrase in a letter of the Archbishop that referred to the shooting of prisoners by the Versailles troops. This charge, Thiers asserted with histrionic indignation, showed that the Archbishop was not a free agent. The priest sent to negotiate the release of the hostages found reasons for not returning to Paris, and the Committee of Fifteen of the Assembly approved the decision of Thiers. No doubt he would have liked to save the Archbishop, but what was one life when society was endangered? He might have said to Darboy as Ney did to the dying soldier, 'You are a victim of the fortune of war'.

The Archbishop and his companions had little hope. The priests asked their chief (who had been a learned theologian) whether they could hope to be classed as martyrs and he replied that they could, since they would be killed as representatives of the Church and not as individuals. There was a missionary among them and it was remarked that the see of Paris was as dangerous as the see of Corea.[1] President Bonjean, who, as befitted an eminent Gallican lawyer, had been strongly opposed to the Jesuits, made his peace with the Society in the face of death, receiving the last sacraments from a Jesuit hostage.

The leaders of the Commune were now a handful, but they had still some authority and they authorized Rigault to collect the hostages and remove them to La Roquette away from the advancing army. They were at Mazas, near the Gare de Lyon. The prisoners were put in railway delivery vans, for the fall of Montmartre had exposed all the flank of the Federal position. The time for vengeance was running short.

It was on May 23rd that Rigault arrived at Sainte-Pélagie and demanded the delivery to him of Chaudey and three policemen. They were executed on the spot, but one policeman got away and Rigault called out, 'Don't kill him, bring him back'. He was shot in due form. There was still fighting going on round the Panthéon and Rigault did his best to keep the fight alive. But as resistance collapsed, he took refuge in his lodgings in the Rue Gay-Lussac. His landlord was arrested, but Rigault came downstairs, gave himself up and was dragged out and shot, dying, so it is said, with the cry of 'Long live the Commune'. His body lay in the gutter, partly stripped by the women for whom the end of the Commune, like its beginning, was a carnival. Half-naked, the body of the Procureur of the Commune of Paris lay unrecognized until his mistress came and threw a covering over it.

There were still optimistic souls who thought there was a chance of an armistice, some even hoped for Prussian mediation, but the Central Committee wasted no time in vain negotiations. In the Town Hall of the eleventh arrondissement, Ferré took up the work of Rigault. A curious noble adventurer, Charles de Beaufort, was shot for treason or for rash words. The mob was clamouring for the blood of the hostages and they were brought down to the courtyard of La Roquette and shot. The Archbishop alone stood after the first volley, but he was soon finished off. 'It was a magnificent sight', wrote an eyewitness; 'these traitors stretched on the ground made one feel the strength of the Revolution, one felt that we were already doomed, we wanted to die in our turn, but to avenge ourselves first, we looked at our dead enemies and felt relieved. . . . When all was over, the Federals went off, each on his own business, pleased at having shot the

---

[1] Two of Darboy's immediate predecessors had met violent ends. Affre was killed while preaching peace on the barricades of 1848 and Sibour was murdered by a mad unfrocked priest in church in 1856.

71

deadly enemies of civilization, auxiliaries of all the monarchies and propagators of ignorance in every generation.'

On the left bank, the retreating Federals had brought with them the Dominicans of the College of Albert the Great, arrested in one of the panics of the early days of the Commune. They were put into a police station, then told to get out and get away. As they did, they were shot down like rabbits. Then there came the killing of Jecker, the shady Swiss banker, whose bogus claims had been the pretext for the invasion of Mexico by the army of Napoleon III. 'Leave that dung alone,' said Clavier to boys who had run up to the body. More priests, policemen, miscellaneous prisoners were taken from La Roquette and marched under the shouts of maddened crowds through the streets. In the Rue Haxo, they were taken into an interior court-yard and shot down by National Guards, completely out of hand. In the intervals could be heard the waltz tunes played on their accordeons by the German troops a few hundred yards away. One body, it was later noted, had seventy-two bayonet wounds in it. It was Friday; the Commune had less than two more days to live.

The last stage of the Commune was not a battle but a massacre. The number of combatants on the losing side grew smaller as the victors occupied district after district, but the slaughter did not stop. The victors were embittered by the shame of having to fight a fresh war against their own countrymen under the disdainful eyes of the Prussians. The sight of the city in flames was not soothing; and the troops had been fed on atrocity stories, of poisoning, of bayonets with fish-hook edges, of the *pétroleuses*, horrible, drunken women who burned the city of malice aforethought.

Despite promises from Thiers that only the law should punish, and orders from MacMahon that the lives of prisoners should be spared, the victors killed without mercy. As the army advanced, the conquered areas were cleaned-up by careful searches, and any man wearing a National Guard uniform, or wearing Army boots, or with a discoloured right shoulder that seemed to show the mark of a rifle stock, was arrested and brought before court-martials which condemned casually, without thought and without evidence. Woe betide a man who looked like a leading *communard*, like Vallès or like Billioray. These unfortunate doubles were shot without mercy and without proof. At least one luckless tourist, a Dutchman, was shot in this fashion. Leaders of the Commune, or even men who were merely notorious instigators of that 'bad spirit' of Paris which the victors regarded as the curse of France, were condemned after farcical trials, like the court-martial on Millière that ended with the death of that old enemy of Jules Favre on the steps of the Panthéon. From the rich quarters that had not resisted the Commune came volunteer hunters of the defeated and there were over three hundred thousand written denunciations. Women and children did not escape. That clever turncoat, Edmond About, wrote on the 25th, that the troops 'had to kill many women who threw petroleum into the cellars and then threw blazing tow on to it'. Startled spectators saw, with increasing horror, the streams of blood that ran without stopping from the barrack-gates and listened to the endless rattle of rifle-fire.   In a few days, the stink of imperfectly-buried bodies roused protests even in the most bourgeois organs.   The men caught on the barricades expected and received no quarter.   A young student, Paul Bourget, who was to be a great Conservative man of letters, saw, with horror, the regular troops beating out the brains of wounded *communards* with the butts of their rifles.

Despite the killings with and without the formalities of trial, there were prisoners.   They were marched, men and women (and among them many innocent bourgeois caught up in the great raids), to Versailles.   'A band of rascals' was the verdict of a young author who was to die the literary idol of the Left.   'They were repulsive, as you would imagine', wrote Anatole France.   The population of Versailles shared this view.   As the prisoners marched in, some bewildered (as were many of the women), some frightened, some proud (or insolent), smart ladies lined the streets to jeer, to strike the vanquished with their umbrellas, to behave as the gutter women had behaved in Paris with the added ingenuity of their better education.   In the Orangerie, in the camp of Satory, the prisoners were huddled together, kept in order under the muzzles of machine-guns, shown off to the fine ladies who wished to inspect this new zoo.

Order reigned in Paris and M. Thiers had at last conquered the rebellious city.   It was a pity, as Jules Simon was later to admit, that there were excesses, but 'men who see their blood flowing, who have advanced over the bodies of their comrades, cannot be merciful'.   All in all, the regular army lost less than a thousand dead, while a reasonable estimate of the dead on the defeated side cannot be less than 20,000. But the victors were avenging not the few hundred dead of Paris, but the much more numerous dead of Metz, Sedan, Le Mans.   No defeat at German hands was nearly as costly of French life as was the defeat of the Commune; and few victories have been more blindly rejoiced in. 'The repression of the Commune was vile', as a Catholic and Royalist writer, M. Georges Bernanos, has said.   A simple and frightened priest cried at the news of the deliverance of Paris, 'It is God's victory, the army without wishing it has done His work; it has conquered Paris for religion'.   It had in fact founded, if not a new religion, a new shrine, the 'wall of the Federals' in Père Lachaise, where the defeated remnants of the Commune had died fighting.   It was a wiser judgment that made the young Catholic officer, Albert de Mun, furious against the murderers of priests and the shamers of the nation, later wonder what it was in this bad cause that made so many simple men die so bravely, on the barricades or before the firing-parties.

That faith had few friends at the moment, at any rate few friends in high places. The deputy who had been elected at the head of the poll by the workers of Paris, Louis Blanc, attempted to disarm the Assembly by reminding it that a further revolt was out of the question because of the 'excess of evils that it [the Commune] had caused . . . and the proof now acquired of its impotence'. George Sand rebuked one of her correspondents who had seemed tainted with pity for the conquered. 'The true friends of progress are known by the indignation they vent against the infamous innovators of the Commune.' Even Tolain, the only member of the International who was a deputy, denied his brethren, and, although he was expelled from the dying society, that was no handicap to a politician in 1871.

A surprising number of the leaders of the Commune escaped death on the barricades, or before the firing-parties of law and order. Exiles were to be found as far apart as Glasgow and New York, but London and Switzerland got most of them. Others like Rochefort and Louise Michel were deported to New Caledonia, where Nouméa became what Lambessa had been under the Empire, the capital of the defeated party. Among the leaders who did not escape, Rossel got the most sympathy and his execution was a cause of sentimental grief to people in many countries who thought of him as a misguided patriot. Fewer were of the mind of John Richard Green, who kept his sympathy for the men who, like Delescluze, had believed in the cause for which they died.

When the full possibilities of destruction are realized, Paris got off easily, but though the Louvre and Nôtre Dame were safe, the Tuileries, the Hôtel de Ville, the Cour des Comptes and many other great monuments remained in ruin to remind the prosperous of the price of their victory and the poor of the fruitless anger of their defeat. On the first day of the Commune, the excited crowds had stood in reverent silence at the sight of an old man following a coffin to Père Lachaise. It was Victor Hugo following his son to the grave. And in the Commune died the old, confident, romantic Paris of which Hugo had been the product and the poet. 'Since 1789', wrote Louis Veuillot, 'France has had only one King, Paris.' That monarch was now dethroned, with far more bloodshed than had been necessary to secure the deposition and execution of the heir of thirty kings. For the Reign of Terror was far less bloody than the 'Bloody Week' and its blood thinly spread over a year. In the conflict between France and her arrogant capital, Paris was at last beaten. And if universal suffrage was to have its way, it was as necessary to dethrone Paris as to dethrone any Bonaparte or Bourbon. Thanks to M. Thiers it had been done. 'They had seemed to think', said MacMahon of the *communards*, 'that they were defending a sacred cause, the independence of Paris.' That sacred cause was dead, leaving to the workers of the world a legend.

BOOK II

THE REPUBLIC FILLS A GAP

Non, l'on n'a point vu d'âme à manier si dure,
Ni d'accommodement plus pénible à conclure:
En vain de tous côtés on l'a voulu tourner,
Hors de son sentiment on n'a pu l'entraîner;
Et jamais différend si bizarre, je pense,
N'avoit des ces Messieurs occupé la prudence.

Le Misanthrope.

CHAPTER I

THE NATIONAL ASSEMBLY

THE National Assembly, in whose hands the immediate problems and, perhaps, the destiny of France were placed, was a unique body, although it had points of resemblance with the Assembly of 1849 and with the 'horizon blue' Chamber of 1919, in that it represented those Catholic and Conservative forces which normally are so weak in French political life. It had been elected after a fantastically brief election campaign. There was only a week between the summoning of the Assembly and the election, and the brevity of the time was not compensated for by the activity of the party organizations which were, in fact, almost as disorganized as the Army or the administration.

It was only nine months since the Empire had triumphed in the plebiscite, but the Empire, for the moment at least, was hated and despised. Only the faithful island of Corsica sent deputies to represent the dynasty which had, for the moment, shrunk to the status of a clan. But if Republican fears of Bonapartism were baseless, their fears of the results of a completely free election were not, for the results astonished all parties. There was an overwhelming Right majority—and the members of that majority were, for the most part, Royalists. The country had turned away from the Republicans who had waged the disastrous war almost as decidedly as from the Imperialists who had made it. The nation, which was resolved on peace, had to turn to those sections of the community which were innocent of the recent disasters. That usually meant the local notables who had stood aloof from both Napoleon III and Gambetta, although many of the new Right members had added to their negative claim of political innocence, the positive asset of gallant service in the war. For the French gentry, excluded from politics by their own traditions almost as much as by principle, were admirably at home in one branch of the public service. They had flown to arms in the darkest days of the war, and had acquired a new claim on the trust of their villagers. But it was to express its distrust far more than to express its confidence that the French nation elected to represent it a majority of Catholic Monarchists.

As far as the question of the régime had been presented to the electors, this had been done by the Republicans, who asserted that a vote for the Right was a vote against the Republic. The Conservative candidates had, in the main, not stood as partisans of any Pretender, but, humanly enough, when the results became known, the victors were very willing to accept the challenge which the defeated party now gladly withdrew. The majority of the Assembly decided that it had been commissioned to make peace and the Monarchy, whereas the minority declared that it had been commissioned only to make peace. Both sides, in 1871, would have dismissed with scorn the idea that the Assembly had been elected to give permanent institutions to the Republic.

It would be unprofitable to try to guess all that the French people thought they were voting for in February 1871. They undoubtedly voted for peace and they undoubtedly voted for persons. The system of 'scrutin de liste', that is to say, the election of all the deputies of one department together, had been adopted, with a consequent confusion of the issue which only a rigid party system could have clarified; but there was, in 1871, hardly any party system at all. Names were symbols. Thus Paris returned at the head of the poll Louis Blanc, in exile until September 1870 since his brief period of power (or office) in 1848 ; he was a symbol of the 'Social Republic' and innocent of all the recent disasters, treasons and crimes. Twenty-two departments elected Thiers, who had been (it was believed) always right and who had, in fact, been very often right. But Thiers was more than a man, he was an emblem. In the usually left-wing department of the Côte d'Or, the Burgundian electors had chosen the list headed by Thiers against the list headed by Garibaldi. It was hard to decide whether they voted for the great Frenchman against the famous Italian, or merely for peace against war—or for 'order' against the dangers of radical Republicanism. In other areas there was even greater confusion. In the normally conservative Deux-Sèvres, a Republican candidate, Ricard, who was to die a Republican minister, appeared on *all* the lists, Right, Left and Centre. Defeated with Antonin Proust, on the Left, he scraped in at the bottom of the Right list whose most prominent member was the violent legitimist, the Marquis de Larochejaquelein whose devotion to 'Henri V' redeemed the apostasy of his father to Napoleon III. But not only was Ricard one of the notables of the department, he had been counsel for Larochejaquelein in a contested election case against the official Imperialist candidate in 1869. Indeed, all over France, Republicans, Orleanists and Legitimists had been thrown together in the past by their common hostility to Napoleon III.

The general confusion combined with the 'scrutin de liste' to produce very odd electoral combinations. Thus the Bouches du Rhône, home of extremes, chose Radicals like Pelletan and Gambetta, the most famous of its native sons, Thiers, the Papal Zouave and hereditary Royalist hero, General de Charette, the moderate Republican, Grévy, and that ghost of 1848, Ledru-Rollin!

When the Assembly met at Bordeaux it was not only disorganized but bewildered. Some members had been elected while they were in war prisons, not only without making any campaign, but without their knowledge. A majority were, to quote Arthur Meyer, mere political conscripts, but they had at hand a political veteran in Thiers and, in any case, his election by twenty-two departments imposed him on the amorphous body which was nominally sovereign. So on February 17th, he was elected 'Chief of the Executive Power of the French Republic'. The vagueness of the title and its ambiguity were not accidental, for the Assembly, under the hostile gaze of the Bordeaux mob, had to make many immediate decisions which left it no time to debate or decide the future of French institutions. It had to make peace, to get the Germans away from Paris, to begin the reconstruction of a country profoundly disorganized, if not vitally injured, by war, revolution and invasion. For the moment it was necessary to postpone party conflict. In this, Thiers and the majority of the Assembly were of one mind; and it was in this spirit that they concluded the 'Compact of Bordeaux'.

Thiers was to be the executive agent of an Assembly which was sovereign and, whatever the Left might assert, constituent. A time would come when the Assembly would give permanent institutions to France: and in these early and hopeful days, it seemed possible that in this, as in other matters, Thiers and the Assembly would work together. For Thiers had been the great apologist of constitutional monarchy; he had been one of the great Orleanist 'Burgraves' under the Second Empire, as he had been one of the most contemptuous critics of the Second Republic. He had even allowed his admiration for the sacred system of constitutional monarchy to lead him to toleration of the Empire, once it seemed set on the path of parliamentary supremacy. There seemed no reason why the Minister of Louis Philippe should not become the Minister of another king. It is true that there were suspicious signs. The important ministries in the cabinet formed by Thiers were given to Republicans like Jules Simon, Jules Favre and Ernest Picard, but his bland courtesy allowed all hopes to be plausibly held. This art of agreeing with all parties was one of the political trumps of the Chief of the Executive; in postponing all action on fundamental political questions, he was careful not to antagonize his old Orleanist friends or, indeed, his old Legitimist enemies. But for other ears he had other words. He repeatedly told Jules Simon that there could be no royal restoration; that if the Republic collapsed, the beneficiary would be the Empire.[1] And the Commune, in part provoked by the danger of a royal restoration, strengthened the hands of Thiers. For until the revolt was crushed, no monarchist decisions could be taken, and after it was crushed, why need they be? Thiers

[1] This was also the opinion of that acute diplomat, the British Ambassador, Lord Lyons.

had shown (if the demonstration was needed) that a Republican Government could crush a rebellion of the Left with all the rigour of an absolute monarch—if not with more. The collapse of the Commune, by destroying the radical parties for the time being, made it harder for the Right to find convenient scarecrows. The most violent leaders of the Revolution were dead, in jail, or in exile.

What could a king do that M. Thiers could not do as well or better? M. Thiers was by this time convinced that there was nothing. He had exchanged confidences with Bismarck in which the Chancellor, not perhaps with perfect candour, had made it plain what a nuisance a monarch could be even to a great minister. Why bother to bring in a Louis XIII or a Wilhelm I when the rôle of Richelieu or Bismarck could be played without them? Thiers, in fact, enjoyed himself as the sole executive authority in France. He had been out of office, except for a few humiliating hours in 1848, for thirty years; he had been reduced to writing history instead of making it; his turn had now come, and if he developed what the bitter Bonapartist pamphleteer, Paul de Cassagnac, called 'an itch for power', it was all very natural. When he passed in review the troops who had conquered Paris, the satisfaction of the little civilian sitting in a chair at Longchamps, where Kings and Emperors had preceded him on horseback, was obvious; and he himself has told us that 'at that moment I found the burden I carried not so heavy as usual'. Thiers had not forgotten the lesson of 1848, but there were Republics and Republics; Republics headed by windbags like Lamartine or doctrinaires like Louis Blanc—and Republics headed by practical men like Thiers. Thiers did not quite see himself as Napoleon, but there were some signs (it was suspected) that the historian of the Consulate saw in himself a new First (and sole) Consul. Crushing the Commune was his Marengo. There remained before him a fruitful reconstruction of France, and if the new Consul was inferior to the old in military capacity (as even Thiers would probably have admitted), he was far superior to him on the battlefield where the new war had to be fought. He was a great parliamentarian, a great politician, and he hoped to win in the Assembly his Austerlitz, his Jena.

It did not take the more acute Royalists long to realize that the Chief of the Executive was giving to them only kind words and to the Republicans the more substantial tokens of his esteem. Although occasionally forcing a compromise, like that which sent the Assembly to Versailles instead of to Paris (as Thiers wanted) or to Fontainebleau (which was the first thought of the majority), the Assembly had to tolerate a good deal from its nominal servant. Decentralization had been one of the themes of Royalist theory in opposition, but Thiers had no sympathy with such sentimentalities; he did not desire to weaken the central authority, above all when he was that authority. So when the majority wished to give the right of electing their mayors to all communes, Thiers was able to force them to limit this concession to communes with less than 20,000 population, in which rural and semi-rural areas the Right was convinced in any case that its strength lay.

A more important conflict occurred over the definition and title of the office held by Thiers. His friend, Rivet, wished to give him the title of 'President of the Republic' and a term of office of three years, thus defining the office and implicitly recognizing the existence of the Republic, a step which it was inconceivable that the Assembly would take while its hopes that the King would soon enjoy his own again were still so high. For with the failure of the Commune, the Royalists were now ready to restore the monarchy, as soon as they could decide on the person of the monarch. At first the task of replacing the Third Republic by the Third Restoration seemed even easier than that of replacing the Second Republic by the Second Empire. Both rival systems, Republic and Empire, were, it was believed, hopelessly discredited; but an Assembly chosen by universal suffrage, and therefore free from the defect of a too narrow base which had ruined the monarchies of Charles X and of Louis Philippe, was ready to proclaim the King. Or rather it was ready to proclaim a king.

There were two possible candidates, the Comte de Chambord and the Comte de Paris, the grandsons of Charles X and of Louis Philippe. Both these monarchs had died in exile, a fate due in part, it was believed, to their rivalry. The House of Orleans in 1830 had capitalized its liberalism and had stepped into the place of the senior line of the House of France. But the experience of the constitutional monarchy of Louis Philippe had not repeated the happy history of the corresponding substitution in England. France, even after 1792, wanted either a King who had more claims to the throne than those conferred by an Act of Parliament, or it wanted no King at all. And even if this lesson of the collapse of Louis Philippe in 1848 was not accepted by all the Orleanist party, the fact remained that a monarchist majority in the Assembly was possible only if the partisans of the two Pretenders united. The Orleanists were in a weak bargaining position, since they could not plead any principle binding them to perpetual loyalty to the heirs of Louis Philippe, while the Legitimists were bound, by the very basis of their creed, to support the claims of the heir of Charles X who was also the heir of Louis XVI, of Henry IV and of Saint-Louis. Happily a compromise seemed easy.

The posthumous birth of the son of the Duc de Berri, after his father's murder in 1820, had delighted the right-wing Royalists who hailed the baby prince as 'the miracle child'. To more practically-minded Royalists, the birth had not been so gratifying; for it had cut off from the succession the popular Duke of Orleans and had thus forced him, in 1830, to be a usurper instead of a legitimate heir. But Providence had redressed the balance, for the miracle child was childless; the heir of the Comte de Chambord was the Comte de Paris.[1] The solution of the problem of 1871 was obvious. Let the Comte de Chambord, now entering on his fifties, be King and then in due course let his younger kinsman succeed. As a necessary preliminary, let the two branches of the royal family make peace, publicly, to the delight of their supporters and to the confusion of the enemies of public order and of the Assembly. The 'fusion' of the two dynasties and claims in one united family and theory would unite the fervour of the Legitimists, a much more warm and combative political force than the prudent utilitarianism of the Orleanists, with what those same prudent Orleanists had in plenty, money, presentable modern doctrines and leaders of ability. La Vendée would be allied with the *Revue des Deux Mondes*, the Academy, the great banks and the great industrial companies.

What was potentially a great event encouraged the Royalists. After forty years of exile, the Comte de Chambord had revisited the country from which he had fled as a boy. He had passed hastily through Paris and had gone on to the great château from which he took his title.[2] The opportunity of sounding out public opinion, of getting to know the leaders of the majority, most of whom, inevitably, had never seen the Pretender, was open—and it was not taken. After a few days, the future King left France; and almost all his supporters were still in the dark as to his personality and projects. It is possible that many weary and disillusioned Frenchmen might have rallied round the person of 'Henri V' had he given them any chance to do so, but by his voluntary exile he forced them to see in him less a man than a name, a principle. What that principle involved was still little understood. The Legitimists had been in opposition as long as their King had been in exile, and faced with the usurping rule of Louis Philippe and still more of Napoleon III, they had, naturally if inconsistently, taken up a parliamentary, even a Liberal, attitude. Macaulay had noted the 'Jacobinical attacks' on the Government of Louis Philippe that came from the Legitimist leaders, Larochejaquelein and Berryer. Larochejaquelein had gone over to the Empire, but Berryer had been the ally of Thiers and the Orleanists in their opposition to

---

[1] To extremists of divine right, the Orleanist princes were not the next in succession, for they were only descended (in the male line) from the younger brother of Louis XIV, whereas the Spanish Bourbons were descended from Louis XIV himself through his grandson, Philip V of Spain. It is true that King Philip had renounced all claims to the French throne when he became King of Spain, but what were renunciations and treaties in face of the will of God? To these logical royalists, the heir of the Comte de Chambord was the father of that Don Carlos who was getting ready to wage a civil war in support of his claims to the Spanish throne, claims quite inconsistent with the doctrines advocated by his partisans in France. But the party of the 'Blancs d'Espagne' had not much more importance than the English Jacobites of to-day have.

[2] His formal title had been 'Duc de Bordeaux', but he was always known by the name of the château that in his infancy had been bought for him by a public subscription which had been collected by methods familiar to all readers of Paul-Louis Courier as typical of restoration tyranny. The bourgeoisie was full of readers of Paul-Louis Courier.

Napoleon III and in that dangerous company had moved far from the doctrines of Charles X.[1] It was natural to assume that Berryer's master had moved with the times. Even in 1830, the Royal Family and the Royalist party had not been united in support of the follies of Charles X. It was difficult to believe that, in 1871, the grandson of Charles X, exiled by the old King's folly, would have learned nothing and forgotten nothing. But this fantastic possibility began to seem less fantastic as the conduct of the Pretender was studied. His departure from France was interpreted as a snub to the Comte de Paris, who had taken the first step towards reconciliation by proposing to visit his cousin. The visit was to be put off, the Comte de Chambord announced, until after the issuing of a proclamation which would make known to France 'all his thought'. And the nature of this proclamation was known to the Royalist leaders and it filled them with despair. For the most startling part of the imminent declaration was the refusal of the Pretender to accept the tricolour which, save for an interval of fifteen years, had been the flag of France since 1789.

It was an absurd affront to the vast majority of the French people. The tricolour flag was theirs; it was the flag of Valmy and of Austerlitz; more than that, it was the flag of the recent disasters, of the shame of Sedan, of the glory of Belfort; to abandon it now, in its moment of distress, would have been odious. All of which things were obvious to almost everybody in France, even to those Royalists who detested the emblem of Revolution—and yet they meant nothing to the elderly, lame, and obstinate man whose life in exile had cut him off from the living forces in the land which he believed he was divinely designed to rule. To ask him to give up 'the flag of Henri IV, of Francis I, of Joan of Arc', was to attack his honour. With that flag he asserted (with imperfect regard for history) 'the unification of the nation was achieved, it is with it that your fathers, led by mine, conquered Alsace-Lorraine, whose fidelity will be the consolation of our misfortunes . . . I have received it as a sacred trust from the old King, my grandfather, dying in exile. . . . In the glorious folds of this stainless standard, I shall bring you order and liberty! Frenchmen! Henri V cannot abandon the flag of Henri IV!' In its own negative way, the manifesto was almost as much of a masterpiece as any proclamation of Napoleon. Its naïveté, in which the question of honour was assumed to concern only the exile and not the nation, gave reasonable grounds for doubts as to the sense in which Henri V would interpret 'order and liberty'. Its reference to Charles X reminded Frenchmen of the danger that the new King might follow in the footsteps of that spoiled boy who had changed from a frivolous and dissipated young

---

[1] Modern Royalists of the school of the 'Action Française', unwilling to abandon their claims on the fame of Berryer and still more unwilling to tolerate political Liberalism, have had to display great casuistic ability in staking out their claim to the great man.

man only to become a frivolous and bigoted old man. No one expected the Pretender to renounce his grandfather, but to have his legacy publicly and proudly accepted was too much. And the last straw was the reference to Henri IV, for there could be no doubt that had he returned to earth in 1871, the first person to abandon the flag of Henri IV would have been Henri IV. To the founder of the Bourbon dynasty, Paris had been well worth a Mass; to its modern representative, all France was not worth gaining at the expense of sacrificing private honour identified with a family flag.

The effects of the proclamation were all that the more prudent Legitimists had foreseen. The Republicans rejoiced. Thiers told Marcère that 'this event may definitely establish the Republic'. Laurentie, who had tried in vain to save the Pretender from his folly, lamented, 'We have just lost in twenty-four hours the fruits of twenty years of prudence'. Even the Legitimist organ, the absurdly named *Union*, hesitated for a day or two, but in deference to its principles rallied round. The extreme Catholic organ, the *Univers*, agreed with 'Henri V'. Louis Veuillot was off again on his endless and fruitless quest for a true Christian prince to redeem France.

The readers of the *Union* and the *Univers* were a small section of political France. To all other sections, the act of the Pretender was decisive. The Royalists in the Assembly refused 'to separate themselves from the flag which (France) has given herself, a flag made illustrious by the courage of her soldiers and which has become, in opposition to the bloody standard of anarchy, the flag of social order'. In private, many Royalists expressed themselves far more heatedly, The famous Bishop of Orleans, Mgr. Dupanloup, was deeply distressed by the manifesto. A typical bourgeois Orleanist like Vitet, exclaimed, 'O blood of Charles X', and other Orleanists, who had been indignant at the easy and unconditional submission of their leader to Legitimist pretensions, were now ready to withdraw from the bargain, or to move over to a conservative Republic. The one justification for rushing into union with the Legitimists would have been success. 'You take more trouble buying a horse', said M. de Lasteyrie. And the horse on which the Royalist assets were now put was not only literally lame and afflicted with a bad pedigree, but the odds against him had suddenly lengthened. For on July 2nd, the first batch of by-elections to the Chamber had been held.

There were nominally 768 seats in the Assembly, but there were only 630 members. Some who had been elected had resigned, while the numerous cases of members being elected for more than one department had made other vacancies, so that there were 112 places to be filled. And on July 2nd they were filled. Forty-six departments went to the polls, representing every part of France—and elected Republicans. Only in Paris, bled white by the Commune, did the Conservatives gain. Not only did France thus dramatically reverse her attitude of February, but in some regions she went further, for the Bonapartists had taken the field and, coyly hiding under various transparent guises, they had won substantial support. If the attitude of Thiers had been in doubt, it was so no longer. His old Royalist acquaintance and colleague, Falloux, reasonably asked whether it could be expected that a man who had hesitated to embark on the monarchist ship while it still had a favouring breeze behind it, would do so out of pure devotion, when a shipwreck was certain. And a shipwreck was certain unless the Comte de Chambord could be brought to see reason.

From July 1871 until the final disaster, all turned on the character of the Pretender. In some ways that character was admirable. 'Henri V' had many virtues that Henri IV lacked; he was deeply religious and he was chaste. Although displaying an unusual loyalty to his own partisans, he welcomed new converts with charity. He was far above his grandfather in public and private virtues, and if he resembled any of his immediate ancestry, it was his great-grandfather, the son of Louis XV, who had never reigned. But he had in the straitest sect of the Royalist religion been bred, if not a Pharisee, a high priest. He saw France, which he had known only as a child, as a sinner led astray from her true salvation by various wicked men. Those men had murdered his great-uncle, his father and various other members of his family. High in the roll of great malefactors ranked two princes: the Duke of Orleans, who had voted for the judicial murder of his sovereign and kinsman, Louis XVI, and his son, who had fought for the rebel Republic and had usurped the throne of Charles X. It was the will of God that the rightful King should have as *his* heir, the heir of these two men. But if the sins of Philippe Egalité and Louis Philippe were not to be visited on the Comte de Paris, it was his duty to expiate them by loyal submission to the head of the House of France. That submission had to be public and complete. For the taint of the Orleans blood had not been removed in more recent generations. The father of the Comte de Paris had, in his will, pledged his infant heir to the cause of the Revolution. His uncle, the Duc d'Aumale, had consented to election to the Assembly and had spoken tolerantly of the Republic.

Round the princes of Orleans clustered the great magnates who had failed in loyalty to the throne. There was the Duc de Broglie, son of one of the chief traitors of 1830, grandson of that Broglie who had contumaciously refused to emigrate with his fellow-nobles and had paid for his sin with his head. There was the Duc d'Audiffret-Pasquier, descendant of those great lawyer-aristocrats who had been among the makers of the Revolution and who was full of their spirit of conditional loyalty. There was the Duc Decazes, whose name was a challenge to the heir of Charles X, for had not the first Duke been the unworthy 'Liberal' minister of Louis XVIII, chief enemy of the Pretender's grandfather in those days when the Comte d'Artois, as heir-apparent to the throne, was striving to save his brother from the false gods of constitutional government? As has been said, the Pretender was not malignant or revengeful; he was careful to assure the politicians that he would not be King of a party; that he would not reserve his favours for the faithful remnant. He would imitate Louis XII and Henri IV. But can we wonder that his heart went out to the real Legitimists who had no thought of bargaining with their King?

The Royal agent in Paris was Dreux-Brézé, bearer of a name that reminded the average Frenchman of the most unpopular bishop of recent times, or of that master of ceremonies of 1789 who was shaken out of his courtier's complacency by the refusal of the rebellious Third Estate to do as the King bade them. A chief figure in the exile's court was a Blacas, ominous name to those who remembered how an earlier Blacas had helped to alienate a France, weary of Napoleon, from the restored King. The Pretender's dealings with Frenchmen during his exile had naturally been with the extreme Legitimist party which, in the nature of things, had been cut off from the development of modern French life. To this isolation a modern Royalist leader [1] has attributed much of the failure of the Pretender to see France as she really was. 'Having no communication with the spirit of France, this Prince, whose spirit was truly magnanimous but ill-fitted to the circumstances, believed that opportunity had several locks to be grasped. Now she has never more than one.'

To persuade the Pretender of this fact a series of envoys followed him into exile. The most violent Royalist of the leading generals, Ducrot, went to Antwerp. He told the Pretender that he was ready to do anything except 'to make a single regiment accept the white flag. This is impossible, quite impossible, to-day, to-morrow, for ever. . . . It might be forced on the Army, but it will never be accepted.' The Pretender was unshaken. He could not but believe that for France, as for him, there was something mystic in the white flag which had not known the shame and crimes that befouled the tricolour. There were, of course, many Frenchmen who agreed with him. In regions like La Vendée and Provence there were multitudes for whom the tricolour was then as odious as the Orange flag is to Ulster Catholics, or as the Stars and Stripes was for so long to unreconstructed rebels in the South.[2] But even the most famous representative of La Vendée, General de Charette, was ready to submit to the tricolour if the King adopted it; even the Royalist deputy of Nîmes, Numa Baragnon, though many or most of his supporters hated the flag of rebellion and

---

[1] M. Léon Daudet.
[2] Canon Dimnet has told of the distress of the Superior of the Seminary of Cambrai when, after the *Ralliement*, the tricolour was hoisted for the first time over the college.

heresy, knew that to most good Frenchmen the tricolour was as dear as it was to the detested Protestants and atheists of Languedoc. There were still many families outside the Royalist strongholds to whom the white flag was as sacred as the memory of M. de Charette shooting the revolutionary partridges was delightful, but they were everywhere a minority and a dwindling minority. A well-known Paris bookseller, who had been one of the Guards of Charles X, had preserved as a relic a fragment of the white flag given to the loyal soldiers who had escorted the King to Cherbourg in 1830. But M. Thibault's young son, Anatole, though staunchly Conservative at the moment, did not share that reverence, and what was true of the future Anatole France was true doubtless of other sons of Royalist families.

For the moment the restoration was impossible; the royal family was not united and the Pretender, if he could be so called, was impossible. The Head of the House of Orleans had withdrawn his claims; the Head of the House of France had made his supporters seem ridiculous; the memory of Sedan was too recent for any serious project of restoration of Napoleon III—and the Republic was in possession. It was not merely in possession, but, since the elections of July, in possession with a basis of popular support which it had lacked. And as the monarchical solution was for the moment out of the question, it was necessary to provide France with a form of government less ill-defined than that hitherto exercised by Thiers and the Assembly in uneasy partnership. The Rivet motion could no longer be merely stifled; if it was to be rejected, it could be rejected only in favour of an alternative.

To accept the motion as it stood would have been dangerous if not suicidal for the Monarchists. To create a presidency of the Republic for three years was to give the Republic a minimum lease of life which might make the restoration impossible. The Rivet motion was replaced by another which was defended before the Assembly by Vitet. This motion gave the 'Chief of the Executive Power' the title of 'President of the French Republic', and confirmed his powers 'under the authority of the National Assembly until it has completed its labours'. It provided that he could address the Assembly whenever he liked, after informing the President of the Assembly, and it gave him power to name and remove Ministers. 'The Cabinet and the Ministers are responsible to the Assembly. Every act of the President of the Republic must be signed by a Minister.' And, lastly, the 'President of the Republic is responsible to the Assembly'. The declaration, as Vitet said, did not establish the Republic; it merely recognized its existence *de facto*. Defective as the scheme was, it had the merit of reserving the constituent power of the Assembly. It was just this power that the Republicans now vehemently denied. Since the elections of July they were convinced that the country was with them; they feared that any system set up by this Assembly would be fatal to their cause which they had reason to hope would triumph completely in a new general election. Their denials of the constituent power were, of course, opposed by the Right, which quoted manifestoes of the previous autumn that committed the Left parties to regarding the Assembly (whose election was then thought to be imminent) as fully provided with constituent authority. But these debates were essentially barren and fruitless. Everybody knew that, if they could, the majority would make a monarchical constitution for France. Against the sole legal power in France, the only remedy of the Left would be revolt; and the Assembly might not altogether regret the opportunity to crush those radical Republican elements which had not been involved in the Commune and thus show the country that the Republican cause and civil war were one and indivisible.

There were two obstacles to the majority's plans, Thiers and the Comte de Chambord. The President had facetiously suggested that history would regard the Pretender as the American Washington, the true founder of the Republic. But if the Comte de Chambord was its founder, the bulwark of the Republic was its President. The last hopes of rallying him to the Royalist cause were vanishing. The average Republican had no fondness for the old Orleanist, the merciless enemy of the Commune, the incarnation of all the inflexible bourgeois ideas of the July monarchy. But they fully appreciated the service he was doing their cause by persuading multitudes of timid Frenchmen who might otherwise have taken refuge under a King or Emperor that, if the 'Red Republic' was as much of a nightmare as ever, the 'Republic of M. Thiers' was very different and quite tolerable. This was Thiers' own opinion. As he said with some naïveté, he would not 'betray the Government of which I have become the head'—at any rate as long as he was the head. And to a nation faced with all kinds of problems requiring at least as much the resolution to impose a solution as the intelligence to find the best solution, Thiers was still indispensable. At least so Europe and France thought: and the Assembly, whatever its own growing doubts, had to bow to this general belief. It was in vain that Falloux warned his old colleague that experts 'assert that for flattery Trouville beats Saint-Cloud'. The old President held his court at Trouville with at least as much authority as Napoleon III at Saint-Cloud. He inspected new guns, manipulated the press, incarnated in his neat little figure, the thrifty, industrious, unimaginative bourgeoisie whose money was redeeming the sacred soil of France from the invader. To exchange him for a mere politician was impossible. Only a king, who could set off the friendship of the sovereigns against the patronage extended by Bismarck to Thiers, could replace him.

The Republican triumph of July 2nd had diminished the Right majority very seriously; it now was necessary to get all possible votes together to carry any monarchical project; and that meant conciliating extreme right-wing fire-eaters. The Legitimists were merely concerned that the King should enjoy his own again on his own terms. They included deeply religious fanatics like Belcastel and a more numerous body of 'guardees',[1] equivalents of the October Club which had harassed the Tory leaders in the last years of Queen Anne. These fire-eating squires were for the most part novices in politics which they treated as a new kind of blood-sport.[2] Nearly everything in France since 1789 had gone wrong, they believed, and the more vocal members of the extreme Right could usually be goaded into saying as much by the skilful picadors of the Left.

On one question, above all others, the Left delighted to divide the Right and startle the nation into a further move away from the principles of the majority. With the empire of Napoleon III had fallen the temporal power of the Pope. On September 20th, 1870, the Italian Army had entered Rome and Pope Pius IX had constituted himself a prisoner in the Vatican. To keep the 'Savoyards' out of Rome had been the main principle of the French Conservatives since the Italian war of 1859. Rome must not become the capital of what they believed (misled by their own prejudices and by the fantastically incompetent politicians of the Vatican) to be a necessarily short-lived and absurd state. Whatever slight chance there had been of Italian intervention on the side of France in 1870, had been lost because the Italians had been refused permission to occupy Rome. And now the evil day had come and the Pope was calling on all the faithful of the world to aid him with prayers, with alms and with what secular arms they controlled, to deliver him from captivity.

A French warship was stationed off Cività Vecchia to receive the Pope should he choose to fly from the polluted city; a new French Ambassador was accredited to the Holy See and he talked of the recent events in a fashion that infuriated the Italians, but the extreme Right wanted more. The restoration of Henri V and of Pius IX were linked together in their minds and plans. Even a reasonably prudent bishop, like Saivet of Mende, dreamed dreams. The restoration of Henri V 'would be the signal for the fall of revolutionary Italy, of the reconstitution of the Papal States, of a breach between Prussia and Italy and of the moral triumph of France, pending her military triumph'. There were prayers to 'save France and the Holy See' and a great deal of loose language which made it hard for the Frenchman in the street to decide whether some of his 'natural leaders' did not think the overthrow of the secular authority of the Pope a more dreadful disaster than Sedan and the loss of Alsace-Lorraine.

---

[1] 'Chevau-légers.'
[2] M. Louis Teste computed the number of nobles in the original Assembly at 234, of whom 39 were Republicans. Many of these gentlemen, he adds, had ennobled themselves or were sons of men who had assumed the particule.

The Left fully exploited the political assets of the Roman question. Even under Napoleon III, the Government had discovered that the temporal troubles of the Pope disturbed the Conservative peasant elector much less than they did the clergy, or the upper bourgeoisie and noblesse. It was not always easy to make clear to the ignorant in what way the survival of the Pope as an Italian prince was necessary to the spiritual welfare of the Church. Even so good a churchman as the future Cardinal Meignan had wondered if the imposition of papal authority on unwilling subjects by foreign arms was not a luxury for the Church. But for the most part, even bishops like Dupanloup and lay-men like Broglie, who were hostile to most temporal activities of Pius IX, were sound on the temporal power. Yet whatever could be said for the policy of maintaining the political power of the Pope by French arms before 1870, France had other things to think about in 1871. If there were 'Savoyard' troops in Rome, there were Prussian troops in France. Four hundred thousand Frenchmen had just returned from a captivity somewhat more rigorous than that of the self-constituted prisoner of the Vatican and a defeated and humiliated country, which had discovered in 1870 that she had no friends in Europe, was now being asked (so the Left maintained) to make herself an extra enemy.

It was the aim of the Left to exaggerate the degree to which the Conservatives were active in their campaigns for the delivery of the Pope, to stress every folly of indiscreet devotees, to ignore the plaintive pleas of more responsible Catholics that all they were offering the Pope was sympathy. For the lesson of the election of 1871 had been learned. Whatever may have been the case before 1870, a reputation for belligerency was now fatal to parties and individuals all over France. As the war party, the Republicans had been destroyed in February 1871; they proposed to recover that lost ground by becoming the peace party and by pinning to their opponents the fatal label of war-mongers. There was to be no French crusade for the delivery of the Pope; there would have been none even had there been no Republican party at all, but the moderate Catholics were put into the impossible position of having to deny any warlike aims in Italy without seeming indifferent to the wrongs of the Pope. Everything they said to reassure the pacific majority of their supporters, and to disarm their opponents, gave fresh ammunition to the Ultramontane party of which the Legitimists were the core. Every concession made to Royalist and Catholic unity gave the Left its opportunity.

External events played into the hands of the Republicans. Bismarck quarrelled with the Pope; and friends of the Pope were, it was asserted, natural enemies of Bismarck. As the nightmare under which all Frenchmen lived was the threat of another German invasion, it was politically disastrous for the Right to seem to provoke Bismarck and that not for any French aim. It was bad enough that the Chancellor regarded with a frown the rapid recovery of France. That could not be avoided; but that his irritation should be increased by Catholic and monarchical agitation could be helped, and the agitators irritated their countrymen as much as they did Bismarck. For he now saw Catholic conspiracies against him everywhere. Inside the new Reich his triumphant career was being halted by the German Catholics and the German Catholics were encouraged in their resistance by Catholics everywhere, notably in France. And he feared that in alliance with the Catholics were the court party in Germany, the Conservative nobles and the women who had hampered him ever since 1866. If there was a Catholic restoration in France, the reverence of his master, the Emperor, for the sacred rights of all legitimate sovereigns whose territories were not immediately needed by Prussia, would become a French diplomatic asset. M. Thiers could only deal with Prince Bismarck; Henri V could go over his head to Wilhelm I. Already, the tactful, aristocratic French Ambassador in Berlin, M. de Goutaut-Biron, was *persona grata* at Court. Already, the German Ambassador in Paris, Count Harry von Arnim, was dangerously zealous for the restoration. As far as France was concerned, Bismarck was an anti-clerical Republican and, though it would be too much to say that the reputed ability of politicians to please Bismarck was a great asset in France, a reputation for annoying him was a great handicap.

Nor was the religious division in the ranks of the Conservatives purely tactical in origin. The feud between Liberal Catholics, suppressed both by the Pope and the Emperor and the Ultramontane party, always cherished by Pius IX and, for a time, supported by Napoleon III, had not been ended. The great Orleanist leaders were, for the most part, sound Catholics, but they were tainted with Gallicanism and, living in the world, they had fewer illusions about the religious state of France than had the country parsons who read the *Univers* and the country squires who read the *Union*.

The politician who was soon to become the leader of the Right, Duc Albert de Broglie, had testified to his faith by leaving the *Revue des Deux Mondes* when it patronized Renan. But as a scholar, as a man of the world, as the friend and ally of Montalembert, of Lacordaire, of Dupanloup, he realized that the days of enforced religious unity in France were over. He knew how lively was the fear of clerical rule, even among multitudes which had no hatred of the Church. He knew, too, that the naturally Conservative forces in France included many Protestants, Jews and still more Voltairians. To insist on all the claims of the Church to be found in the text-books of seminaries was to commit political suicide. In any case, the great Orleanist Liberals were not enamoured of the results of the policy of forced conformity which, in a century, had led from the Revocation of the Edict of Nantes to the Civil Constitution of the Clergy.

Whatever the Comte de Chambord and his friends might think, the fundamental principles of the Revolution were too deeply rooted in France to be pulled up even by a strong hand. The Conservatives had to rule and provide institutions for the France of the Encyclopædists as well as the France of St. Louis and Bossuet. And, much as they deplored the fate of the Pope, his loss of temporal power had at least saved them from the heavy task of defending or explaining away all aspects of the exercise of that temporal power which had been a burden before 1870. They must, then, avoid outraging the prejudices of the bourgeoisie, many of whom thought with Thiers that religion was indispensable for women and workers, but hardly compatible with the dignity of a man of education and property. It was important not to make the heathen rage unnecessarily and quite as important not to make them laugh.

Popular Catholicism in France in the nineteenth century was as hard to reduce to this sage self-control as popular Radicalism was disobedient to the precepts of M. Thiers. In an age in which it was asserted that miracles do not happen, most French Catholics asserted that they were still happening on an impressive scale. The old pilgrimages were revived and new ones started. If the circumstances surrounding the apparition at La Salette enabled the authorities to chill the early enthusiasm for the vision,[1] the same could not be said of Lourdes. The heirs of M. Homais were not merely surprised that such things could be in an age of enlightenment, they were profoundly irritated. And when pilgrims prayed for France and the Pope as well as for the alleviation of their own spiritual and physical ills, the devotional aspect was inextricably mixed with the political. To the multitudes who were irritated by any kind of pilgrimage, were added other multitudes who were irritated by the implication or assertion that France was suffering for her sins.

The Ultramontane party was not without its answer to the prudential appeals of the centre politicians. Of what use in resisting the rising tide of Radical fanaticism was the prudent, calculating policy of these eminent persons? They talked of their zeal for the 'moral order'. What meaning could you attach to so vague a phrase? The most famous of the right-wing bishops, Pie of Poitiers,[2] talked scornfully of these 'smart people who provide for everything except God': and his low opinion of them was shared by the famous Abbot of Solesmes, Dom Guéranger. Was it wise to throw cold water on the zeal of the undoubted partisans of Church and King just to win wavering support from the proud and self-satisfied 'Liberals'? A France which would not acknowledge her God would not loyally serve her King.

[1] It should be remembered that the reputed disbelief of the most famous of French priests, the Curé of Ars in the miracle of La Salette counted for a good deal.
[2] Pie himself had had to bow to facts and discourage certain devotions which would have given arms to the enemy.

Both Orleanists and Legitimists had a common enemy, while Thiers was still in office and increasingly suspect to the majority, increasingly hostile to their ideals. As long as the life of the country was overshadowed by the immediate results of the war, Thiers was indispensable, but with every fresh achievement, he made himself less so. The chief remaining asset of the President of the Republic was his claim to be the bulwark between the Conservative and the Red Republics. 'The Republic will be Conservative or it will not survive' was the theme of the President. But if the Left were very willing to use, to flatter, and, if necessary, to support Thiers against the Right, they had no intention of accepting his view of the Republic as a new Government of July with Thiers as Louis Philippe. This cleavage between the President and the Left was watched by the Right, which tried to force Thiers to break openly with the Left. That Thiers would not do, nor would he openly ally himself with the Left. The art of tightrope walking was brilliantly displayed, but the act could not last for ever. In his message of November 13th, 1872, Thiers had finally declared without any ambiguity for the Republic: 'It exists. It is the legal government of the country; to replace it would be a revolution and the most dangerous kind of revolution.' With Thiers the majority could not hope to restore the King.

That majority had now a leader. The Duc de Broglie, whom Thiers had sent as Ambassador to London, had taken his place in the Assembly to unite the majority in a firm policy of Conservatism. Broglie was the head of one of the most talented families in French or any other history. His ancestors and descendants have shone in almost every kind of activity. They have been Marshals of France, Prime Ministers, great physicists, eminent historians; only poets are lacking in the *fasti* of this great house. Duke Albert's father, Duke Victor, had been a friend and political ally of Thiers as Prime Minister under Louis Philippe. His mother was the daughter of Madame de Staël and Benjamin Constant, a Protestant background which Duke Albert's enemies on his own side remembered. Duke Albert had been brought up to be a statesman. 'From my earliest childhood,' he tells us in his *Memoirs*, 'I believed that I was destined for public life, and I had never stopped preparing myself for it.' But that career was first interrupted by the Revolution of 1848, then halted altogether by the Second Empire. It happened, then, that 'when that public life, for which I thought myself made, was at last opened to me in the gloomiest circumstances, it was too late; more than one weakening habit had been acquired'. Even without the long internal exile of the Second Empire, Broglie would have been greatly handicapped. He was not popular and he only once managed to be elected by universal suffrage. He had the stiffness, but not the impressiveness of the aristocrat, and he had something of the pedant in him too. He had himself described his ancestors as 'more upright than attractive, more convinced than convincing, more austere than likeable'. He and they would, indeed, have made very good Adamses had they lived in America; passable Russells had they lived in England. He was handicapped by his voice; an unfriendly critic [1] said that 'he spoke as other people gargled'. But Broglie, with all his faults and limitations, had great qualities as a leader; his strength as a debater covered many of the weaknesses of his manner, and the pride that made him a poor manager of men gave him admirable courage. As Gambetta said, Broglie 'had guts'.

From the end of 1872, the pretence of collaboration between the President and the Assembly wore rapidly thin. Thiers did not, however, lose hope. His self-satisfaction was immense; and the suggestion that the Assembly would force him out of office did not frighten him, since, like the Duke of Guise before his murder, he was convinced that 'they would not dare'. Where were they to find a successor?

For the moment, the second consideration did tie the hands of the majority. Many of the Orleanists wished to make the Duc d'Aumale, President. The most brilliant of the sons of Louis Philippe, he was distinguished as a soldier, as a man of letters, as a man of the world. His political views were Liberal; indeed, he was suspected of being a Republican. But the Legitimists would have none of him. An Orleanist prince of the blood in office might play the Monk for his nephew, the Comte de Paris, rather than for his distant kinsman the Comte de Chambord. He might even forget, so the malicious thought, to play the Monk at all. The Comte de Chambord agreed with his partisans.

There remained Marshal MacMahon. He was a man generally respected for his courage and his character, if not for his abilities. He was a sound Catholic, a good Legitimist (and the husband of a fanatical one), but he had served Napoleon III loyally, not as a courtier but as a candid soldier and administrator. In the Senate, and as Governor-General of Algeria, he had shown independence. He was no adventurer, but 'brave homme et homme brave'. MacMahon had, however, no political ambitions; he was reluctant to accept the great responsibility of the presidency, reluctant to set up as a rival to Thiers whom he respected and, perhaps, feared. But the moment to appeal to the Marshal had not yet come. The Assembly had first of all to elaborate the still rather sketchy organization of the Executive, and some decisive development was needed to rally the doubtful Centre that was discontented with Thiers, but was not enamoured of his enemies.

The death of Napoleon III on January 9th, 1873, as a result of an operation which was designed to fit him for an attempt to regain his lost throne by a military conspiracy, disorganized the renascent Imperialist party which had now no effective head, the Prince Imperial

[1] P. Bosq.

being still a minor and the Empress and the heir-presumptive, Prince Napoleon, being on their usual bad terms. The removal of the Emperor should have helped the Royalist cause with the numerous class of timid or worried citizens who only wanted a 'strong Government'. But the Comte de Chambord was again in the breach. The Pretender again refused to surrender his flag. Thiers, for the moment, was safe.

A parliamentary committee had been entrusted with drafting a law regulating the relations of the President with the Assembly and defining ministerial responsibility. Thiers saw in this project only a method of gagging him. The proposal laid before the Assembly by Broglie, indeed, allowed the President to address the Assembly, but only after a day's notice had been given, and, once he had spoken, the sitting was automatically suspended. This device reduced the most effective parliamentarian in France to a position similar to that of Louis XVI during the Revolution, except that the presidential veto was far less effective than that of the King had been. For the President could only ask for a new debate on urgent laws and impose a two months' delay before this second debate took place in the case of ordinary laws. All other fundamental questions of constitutional organization were left in the air; there could be no general system as long as the ambiguous relationship between Thiers and the majority subsisted.

The acceptance of the law of March 13th by Thiers continued the truce, but not for long. Despite the fury of the extreme Right, the majority was still making an effort to get along with the irritating little man, who, if not now indispensable, was still, it was thought, extremely useful. But the evacuation of French territory by the Germans was at hand and a dramatic confutation of the legend of Thiers as the guarantee of the conservative Republic was soon to be given.

In April the last struggle began. The Assembly, angered by the revolutionary attitude of the municipality of Lyons, took from the second city of France its right to have a mayor; as in Paris, the Prefect was to be the head of the municipality. The deposed mayor, Barodet, became overnight the martyr of the Left. The President of the Assembly, Grévy, piqued by a minor incident in a debate, resigned, and although given a chance to withdraw his resignation, he refused. The orthodox and eminently respectable Republican, Grévy, was replaced by an orthodox and equally respectable Royalist, Buffet, but Thiers had wanted Martel, so that the action of the Assembly was a revolt, if not yet a revolution.

There was a parliamentary vacancy in Paris; and the whole of the city, under the existing electoral system, would be called on to vote at the by-election. Thiers determined to give Paris a chance to show its gratitude to himself by letting them elect his Foreign Minister, Charles de Rémusat. The Left determined to rebuke Thiers and show *its* strength by running the ex-schoolmaster, Barodet, whose deposition had made him a symbolic figure of municipal liberty. The candidacy was, obviously, designed to remind the Parisian voters that if Thiers and his Minister had freed the sacred soil of France from German occupation, the President of the Republic had abandoned, had besieged, had dishonoured Paris, had been the cause of the death of thousands of her citizens and was still the gaoler of thousands more. Barodet got 180,000 votes, Rémusat 135,000. Even if the 26,000 votes given to the Bonapartist candidate, Stoffel,[1] had been given to Rémusat, he would still have been beaten. Paris had recovered from her momentary fit of Conservatism. Fear and dislike of the Parisian tradition of violent revolution was the common denominator of all the Conservatives of the Assembly, and Thiers had, by his own act, shown how vain were his hopes of dominating the Republican parties and modelling them on his lines. He could no longer claim to be an effective barrier defending both the Republic and the social order.

Other by-elections showed that the Left was still gaining and, where the Left did not triumph, it was the Bonapartists. On May 16th the Ministry was reconstructed on a Republican basis, but the President was doomed. Broglie launched the attack on May 23rd. The Conservatives of the Assembly, he said, should avoid imitating the Girondins. They should not perish in 'uniting the misfortune of being victims with the folly of being dupes'. Under the new law Thiers could not at once reply in person and his chief Minister, Dufaure, an ex-Orleanist lawyer, a Catholic, honest and resolute, tried to take the place of his chief.[2] He was quite unequal to his task, and Thiers had to step into the breach. As the law provided, he could not speak until next day, although he had been present at the debate in his private capacity as a member of the Assembly.

He was at the height of his form when he at last was free to defend himself. He pointed out that there was only one throne and there were three candidates for it, so there was only one solution, the Republic, which should be given good institutions. And, attacking Broglie, he turned against him the charge that Thiers was the protégé of the radicals. Broglie, he said, would be the protégé of a protector whom his father would have repulsed with horror. 'He will be the protégé of the Empire.'

The debate on the President's speech took place that afternoon in his absence. His Minister of the Interior, Casimir-Périer, was a belated convert to Republicanism, son of the famous Minister of Louis Philippe who had saved the monarchy of July by his rigorous repression of Republicanism, brother-in-law of the Duc d'Audiffret-Pasquier—and

---

[1] The former military attaché in Berlin.
[2] Elihu Washburne, the American Minister, said of Dufaure that he looked like 'a supervisor from one of the back towns of Jo Daviess County, Illinois'.

head of one of the greatest business interests in France, the great coal and iron company of Anzin. His presence at the side of Thiers was symbolical of the strength that the divided Monarchists had lost, but he could not shake the resolution of the majority to end the comedy. A small group of the Centre, led by Target, although declaring themselves reconciled to the Republic, voted against Thiers. He was beaten by sixteen votes, the exact strength of the Target group.

Thiers resigned at once, and the victors had an awkward moment to live through, for MacMahon had not realized that he would have to decide so soon. The Assembly accepted the resignation, the Left drowning with cries of 'no hypocrisy' an attempt of the President, Buffet, to pay a tribute to Thiers. The Left refusing to vote, Mac-Mahon was elected with only one vote cast in favour of Grévy to break the formal unanimity. It remained to persuade him to accept. MacMahon, like a good soldier, wanted a lead from above. He had gone to ask advice—of Thiers—but the ex-President told him coldly that he had often given him orders but never advice. After vigorous appeals from Buffet, the bewildered soldier consented; the anxious Assembly received the good news; and Thiers learned that no man is indispensable.

The overthrow of Thiers, when it came, came so easily that the victors were as surprised as they were delighted. There was no disturbance of the public peace; the whole parliamentary revolution was so easy to carry out that the Monarchists began to wonder whether a restoration would not have been just as easy—if there had been a possible Pretender at hand. But the Pretender was not at Versailles, but in that castle of Frohsdorff in Upper Austria where, *mutatis mutandis*, he lived like another sleeping beauty, with only the faint murmur of the real world to disturb his dreams. The time for a last attempt to awaken the Prince from his own illusions was at hand.

The election of MacMahon to the presidency cleared up many points. The new President of the Republic was that, and, politically speaking, nothing else. He was not a member of the Assembly, he was no orator, no politician, and he eagerly announced his complete submission to the Assembly that had elected him. The offices of President and of Prime Minister were effectually separated, thanks to the political naïveté and timidity of the President and the talents and character of Broglie. Broglie, like Dufaure before him, had only the title of Vice-President of the Council, but he was Prime Minister in all but name. He had overthrown his enemy, what was he going to do with his new authority? If it were at all possible, he would restore the monarchy. The more hopeful Royalist leaders had plausible reasons for wondering whether the Prime Minister had the necessary faith in the possibility of a speedy and easy restoration of Henri V to his throne. He had republished, in 1872, the posthumous tract of his

97

father on the government of France, an excellent exposition of Whig doctrine which noted that with three pretenders, 'unequal in their claims, in the eyes of reason and of history, but nearly equal in their chances of success', it might prove to be wise to prefer the 'government which divides the least'. And it was because the Republic was the government that divided Frenchmen the least that Thiers had been converted to it—or so he said. Even if there was only one effective candidate, as was the case at the moment, the elder Broglie had pointed out that he needed more than hereditary or historical claims. The Pretender 'must be a man of the wood from which one makes kings'. Would the Comte de Chambord at last turn out to be that man? The Prime Minister, in private, expressed his doubts. The Pretender must 'come half-way: will he? Will he take even one step? I have no reason to think so'.

If the Pretender had taken no steps, other people had. The Comte de Paris had at last been permitted to make his long-postponed visit to the head of the House of France. His reception had been correct, and had even been welcomed as an acceptance of the principle of Legitimacy. But the grandson of Louis Philippe had only accepted that principle while hoping that France would see her salvation in it. For him Legitimacy became active only when ratified by the will of the people; for the Comte de Chambord, the principle needed no popular ratification, since it was precedent to the existence of the French people and was the divinely appointed condition of their well-being. The agreement between the Princes was thus very far from complete, but to the outside world the action of the Comte de Paris seemed a submission, and this surrender without conditions was disapproved of even by so stout a Royalist as Falloux. It remained to make some bargain between the Assembly and the Pretender. It was no longer possible to postpone indefinitely the question of a new constitution. Thiers, by his own prestige, might be a substitute for institutions, MacMahon was not.

It was at this moment that the religious question was reopened in a form most damaging to the Royal and Conservative cause, because of the material it provided for Republican and anti-clerical propaganda, and most harmful, in the Assembly, because of the way that it under-lined the difference of temper and belief between the Orleanists and the Legitimists. It was the belief of many pious French Catholics that, for 200 years, it had been the will of God that a church or chapel should be erected in France wherein should be 'the image of the Sacred Heart, there to receive the homage of the King and all the Court'. In the agony of the war, the fulfilment of this divine command seemed urgent to many pious souls, and it was decided to erect on the heights of Montmartre a basilica of the Sacred Heart. The Archbishop of Paris had been won over to the idea and, to secure legal powers to build the church and acquire the site, he had appealed to the Government. The Government was still Thiers; the Minister, Jules Simon; but by the time the bill could be presented to the Assembly, Thiers had fallen. So instead of a concession made by free-thinking Ministers in a simple and inoffensive form, there was a project of law in the hands of Catholic Ministers who could be taxed with religious tepidity if their zeal seemed insufficient to the more fanatical, or indiscreet, or unworldly members of the Right.

The administrative baldness which was complained of in the bill drafted by Jules Simon was no longer enough. There should be some reference, said the lay sponsors of the project, to the 'divine protection and pity' which France had need of. The prudent Archbishop, Mgr. Guibert, a protégé of Thiers, was alarmed. The religious character of the building, he said, could be left to him. What he wanted was a simple law from the Assembly voted by the greatest possible majority. The Orleanists were decidedly of the Archbishop's opinion. They would ask from Cæsar the things that were Cæsar's and no more. But the prudence of Guibert and Broglie was not to the taste of the Legitimists. The most fanatical and most respected orator of the extreme Right, Belcastel, wished the Assembly to pay homage to the Sacred Heart in the words of the law itself. The Left attacked the proposition —and the devotion—while the Centre tried to put an end to this profane discussion of holy things. The moderates had their way; the non-committal law was voted as it stood, but the Left asserted, and a great part of the country believed, that the Assembly had vowed France to the Sacred Heart and decreed the erection of a church in expiation of national sin. M. de Chambord hastened to express his hearty approval of the most extreme party in one of those devastating open letters of which he had the secret. Another barrier was erected between the Royalist parties and the hesitant bourgeoisie. The new church had become a symbol, symbol of a faith and policy that alienated more and more Frenchmen.[1]

The law defining the powers of the President had entrusted to the Government the duty of proposing a constitutional scheme, and Dufaure had laid his plans before the Assembly. After the fall of Thiers, the duty fell to Broglie, who, refusing to do anything in the first weeks of his administration, agreed that the Assembly should begin to discuss the constitutional question a month after the end of the summer recess. For the monarchists it was now or never; by November they must have their restoration ready or abandon hope.

Thus began the siege of Frohsdorf. The Pretender was, or appeared to be, full of goodwill on the constitutional question; liberty of con-

---

[1] When the Republic was finally secure, there was set up in face of the Basilica, a statue of that Chevalier de la Barre whose torture and execution in the eighteenth century for alleged blasphemy was, to the Voltairian bourgeoisie, one of the greatest crimes of that dominant Church that they feared almost as much as they feared the Commune.

science, equality before the law, parliamentary government, all were guaranteed. There would be no charter granted by royal favour as in 1814, but a constitution drawn up by the King and the Assembly in collaboration. Except for the flag, he was on formally good terms with all sections of the majority. On that point he reserved the right to discuss the question directly with the army *after* he had been restored. He was confident that he would 'find a solution compatible with his honour' without any outside interference. It was in vain that the agents of the Government pointed out the danger of making the tri-colour the flag of rebellion. If the white flag was rejected, the King would go back to Frohsdorf. It was stalemate, but the accident of heredity had bound up with the prejudices of this honest and obstinate man the fate of great interests and powerful parties. The Right did not, could not, abandon hope. Emissary after emissary went off to Austria with no result, and the fatal day when the Assembly would have to do something was approaching.

The various sections of the Right met under the chairmanship of the fiery General Changarnier; a committee of nine representing the four Right groups was created to decide on a common front to be presented to the Assembly—and to the Pretender. The lively Duc d'Audiffret-Pasquier was all for insisting on a previous acceptance of the tricolour by the Comte de Chambord as a necessary condition of restoration. He saw himself as the heir of those 'politiques' of the religious wars 'rejecting the League and imposing on the King the conditions which the voice of the nation has the right to have accepted'. What had been good enough for Henri IV was quite good enough for Henri V. But the Legitimists were shocked and startled by this atti-tude. They refused to bandy conditions with their sovereign. They might regret his obstinacy and rejoice if others could break it down, but they could not take an active part in forcing the King to do what he did not want to do. So, when it was decided to make a last great effort and to send a deputation to Frohsdorf to inform the Pretender that, if he wished, he could be King—on conditions—no Legitimist would agree to be part of it. M. de Larcy refused to go at all. Lucien Brun agreed to go, but merely as a witness; the whole burden of negotiation had to be undertaken by someone less committed to passive obedience, to Chesnelong.

Chesnelong was in many ways an excellent choice. He was eloquent, honest and able. He was a Gascon with an almost Italian taste and talent for ingenious adaptations of the incompatible and the impossible into something the same yet different. He was a master of formulas and a believer in them. And in these skilful hands the fate of the monarchy was placed in the fateful interview of October 14th at Salzburg.

Chesnelong had never before seen the Pretender. He was attracted by the simplicity and candour of 'Henri V', but even his loyal eye could not find the Comtesse de Chambord attractive. She was deaf and dowdy; she might win the respect of the French people, but she would never win their love or dazzle them. Chesnelong, who had known the Empress Eugénie, could not think this plain, bigoted woman an asset.[1] But his business was with her husband, and in three interviews he described the political situation to the Pretender. The majority of the Assembly was ready to restore him and in a form that reconciled the principle of legitimacy with the authority of the Assembly. The law would assert that France was a 'national, hereditary and constitutional monarchy' and that the head of the House of France was King. The same law would declare that the public liberties were guaranteed; all details would be worked out by the King and the Assembly in collaboration.

Then came the flag. The Committee of Nine had had their hands strengthened by a message from MacMahon declaring that neither he nor the Army would consent to abandon the tricolour. This was true and of the greatest importance, but it helped to preserve the Pretender in his illusion that he had only the Army to deal with, that if he could win over the Army, the problem was solved—and he thought that he could win over the Army. So he listened politely to the eloquent and subtle Gascon, but his mind was made up. He took no interest in the various compromises suggested, that there should be a private flag for the King, that there should be a tricolour with the fleur de lys on it, most fantastic of all, that there should be a flag, white on one side and tricolour on the other! He could not control himself, and burst out, 'I shall never accept the tricolour flag.'—'Sir,' replied Chesnelong, 'allow me not to have heard that remark.'

Finally an agreement was reached; the tricolour would remain the legal flag until after the restoration; the King would not encourage the display of the white flag on his return and he would submit the whole question to the Assembly. It was a settlement that settled nothing. Chesnelong had failed, although he did not admit it to himself. For all his talent, he was not perhaps a good ambassador. He could not understand the fundamental obstinacy of the Pretender, petrified in his prejudices by the double disadvantage of a royal education and a life of exile. To Chesnelong the question was simple enough. His main passions were the Church and the stability and prosperity of France. He was a recent convert to the Legitimate monarchy; he had loyally accepted the Empire; to serve France and the Church [2] he had made and was willing to make many sacrifices of *amour propre*. Henri V, like Napoleon III, was only an agent. The parliamentary talent displayed

---

[1] Like James II of England, the Comte de Chambord had married a princess of Modena.

[2] Chesnelong's religious feelings were far deeper than those of many prominent defenders of the Church. As a boy at the *lycée* of Pau under Louis Philippe, he had been the only practising Catholic in the school!

in these monologues was irritating to the Pretender. He was not used to subjects who disputed, no matter how politely, with their master. Despite his formal acceptance of parliamentary government, it is very doubtful if he either liked or understood it. The Government of Napoleon III in the first quasi-dictatorial years of his reign, was more to his liking than the parliamentary Government of Louis Philippe, which was planned for him by Broglie, Audiffret-Pasquier and Chesnelong. He was not far from the opinion of the Royalist philosopher, Blanc de Saint-Bonnet, who told him that 'in abolishing public assemblies you do not deprive the country of anything useful and at one stroke you deprive the Revolution of its head'. A little later he was to express his disgust with 'sterile parliamentary conflicts from which the sovereign emerges, in most cases, powerless and weakened'. If he were restored, he would have to deal with these fluent, self-opinionated orators like Chesnelong. If he gave way to them now, what hope had he of resisting in the future? His grandfather had once said that he would rather be a day-labourer than a mere constitutional king like the King of England, and 'Henri V' was one of the few people alive who did not think the political opinions of Charles X worthless.

Chesnelong returned to Paris and, keeping the fatal outburst to himself, produced the agreement, satisfactory on the constitutional question, highly ambiguous on the question of the flag. What would the King do if (as was certain) the Assembly refused to abandon the tricolour? He would not abdicate to make room for the Comte de Paris; he would leave the throne to which he had been restored and return to Austria, reducing the whole restoration to farce. But as the Pretender cherished the illusion that even hardened parliamentarians could not resist the appeal of the King when once he was among them, the parliamentarians could not believe that, once on the throne, Henri V would be foolish enough to leave it.

Now that they were committed to a restoration, monarchist spirits rose. A kind of religious hallucination clouded the minds of many otherwise sensible people, and M. de Cumont saw nothing less than Providence in the resignation of Grévy and the fall of Thiers. They had behaved like Balaam's ass; they had promoted the good cause all unwittingly. But Cumont's belief that God was at work did not make him willing to give in to the Pretender over the flag. The parliamentarians, with their taste for compromise and ingenious political carpentry, were almost as illusion-ridden as Chambord himself!

The country knew that some great event was preparing behind the screen; despite the reassurances of the royal manifestoes, the peasants feared that the restoration of the King meant the old régime of tithes and feudalism. Writing from a deeply Catholic part of France, Berthelot told Renan that 'the return of Henri V is the greatest chimera that could possibly have entered the heads of intriguing politicians.

Anything is possible in this country except that. The peasant will rise, note this well, in thirty or forty departments, because he really fears (I don't ask whether he is right or not) that the common lands which he got in '93 will be taken away from him.' In the towns the hostility to the restoration was even greater, but the majority were ready to risk all that. They believed that France would submit to a strong government imposed from above. The Army was well in hand. Bourbaki, who commanded at Lyons, was ready to put down any rebellion, and would then resign, being too good a Bonapartist to serve 'Henri V'. Magne, the Finance Minister, too, thought himself bound by his past to the cause of 'Napoleon IV', but General du Barail, the Minister of War, although he would have preferred the Prince Imperial, would stand by his colleagues. A minor general, who publicly protested against the approaching restoration, was dismissed. Léon Say, the ex-Orleanist, gloomily told the American Minister that the restoration was certain. On October 18th, Audiffret-Pasquier in his vehement fashion said that 'the campaign is begun, we shall carry it on until it triumphs . . . in three weeks, the national, hereditary, and constitutional monarchy will be established'.

The one hope of the Republicans and the Bonapartists was the Pretender. Chesnelong still kept his secret; in his own mind he was justified, since the outburst of the Pretender had not been meant for the public. But with every day that passed, the majority was more and more converted to the view that the flag question was all but settled. In Austria, the Pretender was irritated and then alarmed. In Paris, the politicians, so he thought, were manœuvring him into a position in which he could not defend himself. An indiscreet communiqué of the Right Centre, which suggested that there were no serious differences between the views of 'Henri V' and the majority, was the last straw. The Comte de Chambord wrote to Chesnelong, absolving him of all charges of duplicity, but making his position clear. He would not 'become the Legitimate King of the revolution'. He insisted on his flag. A Bonapartist journal, *Liberté*, got wind of the letter, and on October 27th the secret was out. In vain the desperate Royalists attempted to evade admitting the authenticity of the letter, in vain they attempted to get the royal representative in Paris to hold it up. The King's orders were final; his paper, the *Union*, published the letter and the restoration was dead. At the most, only eighty members of the Assembly would have voted for the restoration with the white flag. 'Henri V' had made, not by cowardice but by pride and dignity, the great refusal.

The majority were discredited and humiliated, but had they brought 'Henri V' back he could hardly have lasted more than a few weeks; he would have insisted on his flag, and when that was refused would have gone off, in his own opinion like another Regulus, to

Austria. Ridicule does not always kill, even in France, but the Assembly might have died of that farcical conclusion!

It was still possible to save something from the wreck. The constitutional question had to be decided, and the temporary solution of a term of seven years for the Marshal-President was decided on. The term was a compromise, for the original project had been for a term of ten years. Even in the shorter term much might happen. The Comte de Chambord might die, thought some; the Prince Imperial would have come of age, thought others. In any case, the executive citadel would be held by a staunch Conservative, no matter what electoral disasters followed the dissolution of the Assembly.

The majority, got together with difficulty to make the Monarchy, made the Septennate, minus the zealots of Legitimacy, but plus some doubtful Republicans and Bonapartists. As Ernoul put it, 'After the hopes which the country has conceived and the disappointment which it is undergoing, we owe it something'. But the Septennate was a blow which the Legitimists could not receive in silence. In their hearts many of them must have blamed the King, but in public they could not, so their anger was increasingly turned against those moderate politicians who, they managed to persuade themselves, had magnified the flag question by their clumsiness and, it was soon asserted and perhaps believed, had done so deliberately. The Orleanists had played in 1873 their rôle of 1830; they were worse than the Republicans or Bonapartists; they were hypocrites as well as traitors. The standards prepared for the procession, the harness with the royal arms for the joyous entry of 'Henri V' into his good city of Paris, the rumoured inspection of the stables of the Louvre by one of the Frohsdorf court which had persuaded Beulé, the Minister of the Interior, that all was well; all these petty details of the great event that had been discounted were present in the memory of the disillusioned partisans to irritate them further. One last episode came to give romance and a further reason for anger to the defeated cause and to its devotees.

On November 10th, a lame man arrived at a small private house in Versailles, where the Assembly was debating the Septennate in the palace from which his great ancestor, Louis XIV, had ruled France, and, for a time, most of Europe by his simple will, 'De par le roi'. What suddenly brought the Comte de Chambord back to France when all was lost may never be known.[1] He was, after all, as M. Daniel Halévy reminds us, a disciple of Chateaubriand and an admirer of the elder Dumas. He would cut the Gordian knot of political intrigue, he would appeal to the traditional loyalty of M. de MacMahon, to the gratitude due from the descendant of the Irish refugee gentleman to the descendant of Louis XIV. Together they would appear before

[1] We may compare it with the belated arrival in 1715 of the Old Pretender. It is not the only point of resemblance between the two distant kinsmen.

the garrison which would surely welcome the King and his flag? Although the parallel would not have pleased 'Henri V', he was to act Napoleon I in 1815, and MacMahon was to act Ney. This was a new return from Elba.

The fantastic scheme had not even the honour of a direct refusal from MacMahon. The projected interview never took place. The astounded President would not come to see the Pretender, and it was, so the Pretender thought, out of the question for the King to visit the President. A suggested accidental meeting fell through, but it did not matter. At the suggestion that the troops would give up the tricolour the Marshal had exclaimed, so it was said, 'The chassepots will go off of themselves'. But in any case, MacMahon felt himself bound in honour to obey the authority of the Assembly. Had it restored the King, he would willingly have put 'Henri V' in his rightful place, for he agreed with his zealous wife that 'We have no right to be here'. But he would not play the part of Monk. The Pretender was as incapable of understanding the Marshal's sense of honour as the Assembly was of understanding the King's. M. de Roux has suggested that the Comte de Chambord would never have attempted to seduce MacMahon from his loyalty to Napoleon III who, although a usurper, was a monarch, and one who had made MacMahon a duke and a marshal. But this loyalty to an Assembly was incomprehensible, and no palliation for disloyalty. 'I thought to have found a Constable of France; I found a chief of police', [1] said 'Henri V'.

The secret of the stay of the Pretender at Versailles was well kept during the week that followed the refusal of MacMahon to aid the romantic scheme, and the vote of the Septennate which marked the final refusal of the politicians to give France her chance of salvation in the hereditary and undiminished monarchy of the heir of forty Kings. When it was all over, the secret was revealed, and his partisans flocked to see their chief. But although he had a legal right to stay in France, next day he left for ever that country to which his blood bound him, but which for him on the throne or as a private gentleman could never have been anything but exile. Frohsdorf and his dreams were home.

---

[1] Constable was the highest military rank under the old monarchy.

CHAPTER II

THE CONSTITUTION OF 1875

THE importance of the failure of the restoration is almost entirely negative. From the first the project of restoration diverted the majority of the Assembly from its real work, alienated it from the nation and encouraged it in more and more fantastic schemes. It threw together in uneasy alliance Orleanists and Legitimists, separating the former from their true allies, the right-wing Republican bourgeoisie. The peasantry, seeing their natural leaders increasingly involved in intrigues which meant nothing to the vast majority of Frenchmen, lost faith in such errant guides. Thiers and his friends were driven to the Left and even the meagre compensation of a united right-wing party was denied. The increasingly embittered Legitimists were ready for any means of revenge on their allies. In vain the Orleanist historian, Thureau-Dangin, reminded them in 1874 of the results of the follies of their 'ultra' ancestors under the restored monarchy of 1815. The wise words of M. de Villèle found no echo in the hot hearts and heads of the 'Guardees', and the more moderate Royalists could not be brought to realize that they had far more in common with Léon Say and Casimir-Périer than with Belcastel or La Rochette. To avoid disturbance during the critical summer, silence had been imposed on France. Even the evacuation of France by the Germans had not been celebrated, since that might have given a chance to the friends of the Republic to celebrate its virtues in celebrating the great achievement of Thiers. No attempt had been made to win public opinion; all had been made dependent on elaborate diplomatic negotiations in the Assembly and at Frohsdorf. The doubtful Broglie, the hesitant *Journal des Débats*, had followed the more confident politicians and newspapers to a farcical conclusion. It was the devoted Legitimist, Lucien Brun, who best summed up the adventure: 'So we have been dreaming a dream then and it is over.' The dream was over, but in that dream, the French Conservatives had expended much of their strength and most of their prestige. It was a prodigality that was to cost them and France dear.

It was Gambetta's paper, *La République Française*, that was best to describe the constitutional activities of the Assembly after the collapse of the restoration: 'We are entering the Republic backwards.'

Firmly pretending not to see where they were going, the Government and the majority, bit by bit, created the institutions under which France still lives.

In this ungrateful task they were helped by the Republicans. Denying the constituent power of the Assembly, the Radicals helped to strengthen the resolution of the majority to use it. The orthodox Republican tradition made it clear what kind of Government (if promises were kept) a Left National Assembly would adopt. There would be no President; good Republicans now agreed with Grévy's views of 1848. Not merely should there not be a President elected by the people directly, there should be no permanent President at all. The whole executive should be immediately under the control of the Assembly. There would be only one Chamber. The Assembly of the past, to whose glories all sections of the Radicals laid claim, the Convention, had been a single Chamber. A Second Chamber was an insult to the freedom of universal suffrage since it was designed to limit the sovereignty of the people as expressed in their delegates in the popularly elected House.

These doctrines were well known to the Right, who were thus induced to give France a constitution with a President and an Upper House. It would have to be a Republic (the word was still abhorrent), but it would have as much of the monarchical spirit united to its democratic body as possible.

There was a President in existence it is true, but he had been elected as a person; he was not yet a mere incumbent of an office, but he was there. An Upper House, however, had to be created. M. de Broglie produced a scheme that revealed very clearly how oligarchical, ingenious and wrong-headed were his ideas. It was marked by that naïve belief in the natural authority of the 'notables' of France which, since 1848, had had less and less plausibility to commend it. Edgar Quinet noted in the Broglie Ministry the persistence of the spirit of coterie that was the great weakness of the Orleanist leaders. They were a small, distinguished, unpopular circle, dukes and great business magnates, academicians and directors of the sage, weighty and almost impotent journals. Their preoccupation with institutions was a matter for ridicule. What political institutions had achieved anything in France since 1789? France had had nine or ten constitutions; none of them had survived the man or men whose ideas or ambitions they represented. Yet the men who had designed or influenced them, Mirabeau, Condorcet, Siéyès, Bonaparte, Benjamin Constant, Tocqueville, Lamartine, were men of talent or of genius, and some of them had had (what the Broglie Government so conspicuously lacked) popularity. A scheme coming from this source would probably have no more life than the 'Additional Act' of 1815 had. The grandson of Benjamin Constant was as misguided as his ancestor. The plan for a

'Grand Council', which the Prime Minister submitted to an indifferent Assembly, was an ingenious piece of political carpentry, but in the France of 1874 it had no foundations. It was to have three classes of members, one of members sitting in their own right, Cardinals, Marshals, Presidents of the Supreme Courts; a second class nominated by the President; and a third elected by a special panel. It was in the choice of this panel, even more than in the choice of members *ex officio*, that the isolation of Broglie from his country was revealed. He recognized (as the old régime had done) the aristocratic claims of the judges; members of that numerous body were electors of right. But for the representatives of the barristers and solicitors, only the heads of the local bars were electors. Those important and representative institutions, the *conseils de prud'hommes*, the amateur courts of industrial arbitration which had been one of the happiest inventions of Napoleon I, were not mentioned at all—perhaps because they had been invented by Napoleon I. The whole scheme would have been an able project to submit to the States General of 1789 as the joint work of an earlier Broglie and an earlier Pasquier. It was the scheme of a 'duc et pair' who had forgotten that the Parliament of Paris was dead, but it did not receive the honour of a discussion; the extreme Right joined the Left to defeat the Duke on a point of procedure. It was May 16th; just a year since the beginning of the crisis that ended the rule of Thiers.

Whatever the faults of the Broglie scheme it was, at any rate, a serious plan for the future government of France, but, now hopelessly divided, the Assembly was in no condition to accept or discuss elaborate plans for a constitution. And, M. Daniel Halévy suggests, with much plausibility, it was only fear that gave Left and Right the necessary shock, fear of what both Left and Right hated more than they hated each other, the Empire. In the Nièvre, the peasants had triumphantly elected a former equerry of Napoleon III, the Baron de Bourgoing. The Right learned (what they ought to have learned long before) that there was only one dynasty that still had a real hold on the imaginations of the mass of the French people. If there was going to be a monarch in France it would be the young and attractive Prince Imperial. And the Left, hitherto confident in its inevitable triumph, was startled. Universal suffrage, divine though it was, had been disastrously fickle in the past. Fear and often hate of the rural population which supported the tyrant had been marked among the intellectuals, the rebels of the Second Empire. Were the peasants, after betraying their betters by electing a Monarchist Assembly in 1871, going to do even worse and make possible the restoration of the Empire? Some of the Left were panic-stricken; all were irritated and alarmed. The Republicans knew well that the Empire was more formidable and had greater sources of strength than had the Royal cause. 'Henri V' might have been a mere transitory phantom had he come to the throne, but

'Napoleon IV', once in power, would be far harder to dislodge. Rouher and all the veterans of autocracy would see to that. After all, it was only four years since France had been overwhelmingly Bonapartist.

One excuse of the majority for not bowing to realities and formally establishing the Republic had been the assertion that to do so would be to promote the re-establishment of the Empire. But the refusal to proclaim the Republic was apparently having the same result. The Left had refused to recognize the constituent power of the Assembly, confident that new elections would give them an overwhelming victory. The Royalists were absurdly incompetent in electioneering tactics. They lost touch with their electors almost as soon as elected; after that, it was said, the electors saw only the dust of their carriage-wheels. But the official candidates of the Empire had been masters of tactics; they knew whom to flatter, how to cajole, how to avoid the degradation of bribery without offering to the electors only the repulsive austerity of general principles. The Empire and more rural roads; the Empire and a return to the days when phylloxera did not ruin the vines; these were good election points. Napoleon III was dead, but all the good that the peasants thought he had done was not interred with his bones.

To give France permanent institutions was a way to bar the road to 'Napoleon IV'. No one had much faith in the permanence of the permanent institutions, but even if imperfect and short-lived, they were better than nothing, for France had only the powers of the Marshal President as a substitute for a constitution. And to ask France to postpone any final decision until the Marshal's term expired in 1880 was absurd. The country wanted some political structure to live in. It would not be content, to borrow an image from the *Siècle*, to go on living in a tent.

On the Right the hostility of the 'chevau-légers' could be discounted. Their day was over, except for mischief. On the Left there were great names which were an emotional and doctrinal asset, but which were also a great deal of a nuisance. The younger leaders of the Republican party were tired of hearing, again, what Louis Blanc had said in 1848 or Victor Hugo in 1851. These great men of the dead past were formally alive but, as M. Krakowski puts it, they had been sent to the Panthéon in their lifetime. Their active day was over. The constitution would be the work of disillusioned Royalists, and of Conservative Republicans allowed to do their necessary but unimpressive best with the aid of the votes, if not the voices of the sections on their flanks.

All interest was concentrated on the affirmation or rejection of the word 'Republic'; France had the thing; should she still be denied the name? On January 30th, a lawyer who knew his own mind and who had been converted by realities carried the day. France, according to

M. Wallon, wished to know under what régime she was to live. She must escape from the provisional. The occasion was the debate on the law for the election of the President. Wallon's amendment ran simply, 'The President of the Republic is elected by the plurality of votes cast by the Senate and Chamber of Deputies united in a National Assembly'. What could be more innocuous? There *was* a President. Some method of providing for his successor must be found and the junction of the future Senate to the future Chamber made the election as conservative as was possible in the circumstances. And if the name 'Republic' was enacted into law, that was merely a recognition of the facts. By providing for a regular succession to the Marshal, it ended the personal and temporary character given to the executive. It did not 'definitely' establish the Republic. What was definitive? But it ended the rule of the provisional.

Seven hundred and five members voted and the Wallon amendment was carried by one vote. The Target group, whose shift to the Right had overthrown Thiers, had shifted to the Left. The monarchist Assembly had established the Republic and M. de Cumont's allusion to Balaam's ass was justified at last, in a sense that its author would have deplored.

From January 30th onwards, the Republican majority grew rapidly. Only the first step had counted; the Assembly had taken the plunge and the rest of the constitutional laws were voted easily by increasing majorities. They were, indeed, voted too easily. Both sides in the Assembly had been hypnotized by the question of the régime. That decided, there was little energy left for discussing the details of the powers of the Senate, the method of amending the Constitution, the nature of the Executive. There had to be a Senate; the majority and the Marshal insisted on that, and the young Republicans, who saw the promised land in sight, had to disregard the solemn warnings of their venerable elders. MacMahon made a great concession when he abandoned his claim to nominate the first life Senators of the new Upper House. The seventy-five life Senators were to be elected by the dying Assembly. This, it was thought, would at least secure a handsome representation of the majority in the future Upper House.

In any case, the Conservatives looked to the composition of the Senate with some confidence, whatever doubts they may have had of its utility. It was to be elected by electoral colleges in each department consisting of the deputies, the councillors of the arrondissements and cantons and an equal number of delegates from each commune, large and small. The greatest city and the tiniest village in a department were equal. This last provision, thought the Right, would be some compensation for the disappearance of any extra voting strength for the biggest taxpayers—a detail of the dead Broglie scheme. For, it was thought, the gentry and the local notables could control their peasants, and the Senate would thus be a barrier to the tide of universal suffrage which would, it was realized, swamp the new Chamber of Deputies with Republicans.

In the election of the deputies there were a few precautions that it had been possible to take. There was to be a second ballot if no candidate got a majority in the first. It was hoped that this would compensate the Right for their inferior discipline in face of the organized Radicals. And the Assembly took comfort, too, in the decision (powerfully influenced by a speech of Gambetta's on the opposite side) to abolish *scrutin de liste*, the election of groups of deputies by the whole department, in favour of single-member constituencies. The passionate plea of the great demagogue for the existing system convinced the majority that they were right to abolish it. A party with a united doctrine, with great national leaders, could hope to sweep whole departments, could hope to elect carpet-baggers. But the Right had no doctrine, only a barren preaching of resistance. Its strength, it was thought, was the sum of the individual influence and popularity of the local notabilities. These could more easily be brought to bear in a narrow field.

It would be taking the details of the constitutional laws more seriously than the Assembly took them to devote time to discussing the views of Cézanne on the Senate or of Laboulaye on the Presidency.[1] As the pertinacious Bonapartist, Raoul Duval, pointed out, both sides were swallowing their principles. The acceptance by the Republicans not only of a Senate, but of the granting to that Chamber the power, on the request of the President, to dissolve the Chamber, was almost a greater defiance of sound Republican doctrine than was the creation of a Second Chamber itself. Yet it was a provision that had its uses, for previous Republican assemblies, not being legally dissoluble by anybody, had had to be 'purged', as happened more than once during the Revolution, or to be swept away by armed force as in 1851. The right of dissolution might be monarchical, but it was a convenient safety-valve in the event of a conflict between the directly-elected Chamber and the two indirectly-elected authorities. It made possible an appeal to their common master, the electorate, or, as it was more mystically put, to 'universal suffrage'.

The Assembly, once it had put its hand to the plough, was in a hurry. It only took a month to enact the main body of the Constitution; and the supplementary laws were enacted after a committee stage of only twelve days. The text of the fundamental laws, brief, ambiguous and clumsily drafted, shows both the haste and the indifference of the makers of the only French constitution since the Revolution which has

---

[1] Laboulaye, who was supposed to be an expert on American matters, absurdly argued that the President in the French system was being given more power than the President of the United States had.

outlived its makers. France was no longer living in a tent, but in a ramshackle hut, hastily knocked together, devoid of such necessities as declarations of rights or preambles of principles. And in that ramshackle hut, dilapidated by the wear and tear of over two generations of use, France still lives. 'In France,' said a wise man, 'nothing lasts so long as what is only temporary.'

One last important political act remained to the moribund Assembly. It had to elect the seventy-five life Senators. Having a majority in the Assembly, the Conservatives, if they had united, could have secured that all the seats fell to them. It only needed tact and unity. But tact was not displayed in dealing with the all-important Left Centre, and this group prepared to deal with Gambetta rather than with Broglie and Buffet. And Gambetta was preparing a stroke of malicious genius. He was making a bargain with the leader of the extreme Right, M. de la Rochette, who had told Jules Simon that he was ready for a deal. The secret of the conspiracy was well kept: and it was not until the voting began that the flabbergasted Right saw how it had been tricked. The most eminent leaders of the quondam majority were beaten and obscure Legitimists elected, with those veterans and casualties of political war that the triumphant Left thought ready for the political Invalides. At the end, a few of the Legitimists lost their nerve in face of the astonished and indignant Right. They broke ranks and four moderates were elected, among them Bishop Dupanloup. But the result of the first choice of life Senators was farcical. It was farcical by the obscurity and unimportance of most of the new life Senators:[1] it was farcical because of its political results. An Assembly with a normal Right majority elected fifty Left Senators out of seventy-five. Nine of the extreme Right were chosen.

This result achieved, some of the Legitimists had the grace to be a little ashamed of the bargain they had made with Jules Simon and Gambetta. Unable to blame either Charles X or Henri V for the disasters of their cause, the Legitimists had revenged themselves on their tepid allies. And the *Union* revealed the kind of triumph that the elections were for it. 'We have seventy-five immovable senators, of whom the Duc Decazes is not one, and this negative merit is not to be despised.' It was the last consolation for the 'Guardees'.

The ordinary senatorial elections gave a substantial majority to the Right, a majority which, but for the Simon-Gambetta-La Rochette coup, would have been overwhelming. The Legitimists gained 2 elected seats out of 224; the Bonapartists gained 39!

Like the French officers at Waterloo, the Conservatives advanced to the battle of the general election without fear and without hope. Their official leader was Buffet, honest, able, politically incompetent, and

---

[1] No one, no matter how distinguished, was elected who was not a member of the Assembly.

with a talent for repelling popularity that surpassed Broglie's. Buffet, like Broglie before him, clung to the faint hope of conciliating the Right. He neglected to conciliate the Left Centre whose alliance with the Right Centre had made possible the new Constitution. It is just conceivable that a campaign based on the union of the sections symbolized by the two brothers-in-law, Casimir-Périer and Audiffret-Pasquier, might have been successful or, at any rate, reduced what was to be a débâcle to a mere defeat. It was still possible to say that France was 'Left Centre'; that in Dufaure, even in moderate members of the Left like Jules Simon, were the natural allies of the defeated Orleanists who had made the constitution. After all, one of their own princes, Joinville, had voted for the Republican constitution; another, Aumale, was deeply suspect to all good Royalists.

The results were a devastating commentary on the policy of 'no enemies on the Right and no friends on the Left'. On the first ballot, the Republicans got a clear majority of the whole Chamber. On the second, their numbers rose to 340 out of 533. The Right had less than 200 members, only 30 of them Legitimists and nearly half of them Bonapartists. Gambetta had been a candidate in four districts and was elected in all. Buffet was a candidate in four districts and was defeated in all. He was offered a 'safe' seat and replied, 'If I stand for it, it will cease to be safe'.

The new system was at last in operation. 'What can come of this mixture of two kinds of fraud, each seeking to deceive the other? . . . Everything depends on origins. What a poisoned seed! What can it produce?' So the angry Edgar Quinet had written of the new constitution, deceived again in a long lifetime of political day-dreaming. But the young men of the triumphant party did not share the apprehensions of the boring veteran of 1848. They had the Republic.

CHAPTER III

RECOVERY

I

IT is possible that in his estimate of what France could pay and remain solvent, and pay in a reasonably quick time, Bismarck was misled by the gloomy view of French finances, that was natural if one took seriously the opposition criticisms of the budget system of the Imperial régime. Extravagance, lack of proper accounting, improvident mortgaging of the future which had been the main sins attributed to the financiers of Napoleon III had, indeed, existed; not only were real reforms made in the last period of the Empire, but the rapid growth in the national wealth that marked this period would have made the criticisms of Léon Say, Jules Favre, Joseph Magnin and the rest excessive, even had they been quite devoid of party bias and party exaggeration.

France was not merely solvent in 1870; she was solvent in 1871, after the great losses of the war and with the prospect of paying an indemnity of an unprecedented amount weighing on her credit. It was the fundamental solvency of French economy which made possible the rapid recovery of French credit and more than anything else convinced a doubting world that, despite the war and the Commune, the days of French greatness were not over. As soon as it was obvious that there was a securely established central Government, there poured in from the traditional woollen-socks of the peasants and from the notaries' strong-boxes of the bourgeoisie, abundant savings whose owners were ready to serve their country at a reasonable rate of interest. The first loan floated by Thiers was issued on what proved to be over-generous terms, but it was most important that it should not fail. With the collapse of the Empire, whose credit had remained good up to the last, regular borrowing had become very difficult; and the nightmare of the financial officials, the issue of unsecured banknotes, the dreaded 'assignats' of the Revolution, was narrowly avoided, largely thanks to the technical skill and resolution of O'Quin and of the much respected old imperial Finance Minister, Magne.

By the time of the armistice, the position was desperate. The holders of the main securities, the *rentes* and railroad shares, had suffered very great losses. Apart from the multifarious expenses of supplying the troops besieging Paris, the German army of occupation was costing £50,000 ($250,000) a day, and France had undertaken to pay the whole indemnity of £200,000,000 ($1,000,000,000) by March 2nd, 1874! It was very excusable, therefore, in Thiers to paint too rosy a picture of the public finances and, at the same time, to offer most generous terms (roughly 6·25 per cent.) for the loan of June 1871. He asked for two milliards (£80,000,000; $400,000,000): he got five milliards, but the demonstration of public confidence was well worth the apparent extravagance of the terms and the lesson was learned, for re-conquered Paris was able to borrow on a good deal better terms, and it was evident that French public credit could stand the strain of raising the indemnity.

The National Assembly, in financial as in other matters, was animated with the best intentions and with, in this case, fairly intelligent intentions. In some of its minor taxes, it is true, it displayed its extraordinary lack of political sense. Largely composed of country-gentlemen, it doubled the price of licences for shooting game, a measure not only profoundly unpopular, but one which did not even raise much revenue, as the falling off of sales of gunpowder, a State monopoly, wiped out the gain from the dearer licences. A bold attempt was made to deal with one of the great sources of tax evasion, the permission given to wine growers to distill spirits for their own use; the amount allowed was now limited to twenty gallons.[1] But no fundamental reform in the elaborate tax system was possible without an attempt being made to increase the revenue from direct taxes, without, that is to say, introducing some form of income tax.

In this, as in many other fields of gover. ment activity, the Assembly was greatly influenced by English precedent. But whatever chance this revolutionary proposal might have had was killed by the violent opposition of Thiers. An opponent of the tax compared it to the hated 'taille' of the old régime and Thiers heartily agreed. Even worse than the compulsory service of sons of the bourgeoisie in the army, was the inspection of their private affairs which an income tax involved. Thiers admitted that there was much in the history of the Revolution to strike horror, but there were things that aroused 'a feeling of satisfaction and esteem'. There had been a Reign of Terror, but there had been no prying into the most holy recesses of private life, that is into the business secrets and the income of the citizen.

It was not only an income tax that Thiers opposed with this sacred anger, but a turnover tax which some manufacturers wanted in preference to the favourite project of the President, import duties on raw materials. Thiers had disliked the low-tariff policy of the Empire almost as much as he had its sentimental foreign policy. In power at

---

[1] On the eve of the elections, the courage of the Assembly failed and the 'bouilleurs de cru' were given a freer hand again. They have kept it.

last, he proposed to cut through the Gordian knot of the commercial treaties that had tied France's hands and, rashly bold, he proposed a tariff system which had to be hurriedly withdrawn in the face of opposition from the other parties to the treaties.[1]

In his positive action, Thiers was baffled; in his negative action he was successful. The prying fiscality of the English system was avoided; and, with a few additional revenues like the match monopoly created to avoid difficulties in collection of duty, France had to face a severe financial strain with the resources of the Napoleonic system, a system which had the merit of age and habit, if not the merit of flexibility or of abstract fiscal justice. But with all its faults, it provided the money that made it possible to liquidate the war charges, to pay somewhat meagre compensation to those who had suffered from the worst disasters of the invasion—and to pay the ransom demanded by the invader still encamped on the sacred soil of France.

To this task, Thiers devoted all his diplomatic as well as his financial talents. He was resolved on a policy of 'fulfilment', on an avoidance of all vain repining; on the sacrifice of all the easy chances of ostentatiously patriotic indignation and resentment which would give the Germans an excuse for staying on in France and certainly make harder his ambition of persuading them to leave before the appointed day—if the money to buy them off could be found before then. In his ambition, Thiers had two very useful assistants. One was his representative at the headquarters of the Army of Occupation, the Comte de Saint-Vallier, a very resourceful diplomat. The other was the Commander-in-Chief of that army, General von Manteuffel. Manteuffel was almost as great an admirer of Thiers as was Thiers himself. He once begged Saint-Vallier to tell Thiers of his 'veneration, I might say adoration for this great citizen, patriot, character, in a word for this great man'. Thiers naturally did everything he could to keep Manteuffel in this frame of mind.

It was not always easy. Not only was the German Ambassador, Count Harry von Arnim, hostile to Thiers, to the Republic and to France, but there were other Germans who thought that the rapid revival of the lately prostrate enemy was ominous for the future, and it was necessary to persuade them that their fears were groundless, and that once France was evacuated, a real period of peace and mutual esteem could be looked for, that the preachers of revenge had no serious following, that 'real patriots want peace, while leaving to a distant future the decision of our destinies'. So Thiers and his agents vigorously repressed the administrators who did not protect German troops from popular anger; managed, as tactfully as possible, to combine courtesy visits on the Kaiser's birthday with regard for the feelings

---

[1] One item in the new tariffs that amused a depressed nation was a very high duty on laxatives.

of the local population; accounted for the hostility of the wives of officers of the German troops by their natural sense of inferiority in feminine elegance to Frenchwomen; explained away rash speeches by Gambetta and Radical triumphs like the election of Barodet in Paris. Thiers, Saint-Vallier and Gontaut-Biron in Berlin had the reward of their tact and self-control. By the early summer of 1873, the great task was completed and its chief architect overthrown.

II

Of all the reforms to make, all the reconstructions to be put in hand, one united the most diverse sections of the Assembly and the Nation. 'Give us back our legions', Audiffret-Pasquier had cried from the tribune of Bordeaux in his philippic against the fallen Emperor. One French institution above all had a claim on all the energy, courage and wealth of the defeated and humiliated nation: the Army.

The reconstruction of the French Army was less a work of innovation than of imitation, as was freely admitted at the time. To create on French soil as close an imitation of the Prussian Army as possible was the aim of the Assembly and of most of the military chiefs.[1] The first point of imitation was also the most important. All sections of the Assembly were agreed that the 'blood tax' had to be paid by all classes. Had the Assembly had its way, the comparatively simple system of three years' service in the active army and a much longer period in the various reserve organizations would have been followed.

There were two obstacles to this solution; there was the general professional view, still held despite 1870, that although you could train a competent soldier in two years or less, that was too short a time to make regiments where officers and men were sewn to each other, as the Duc d'Aumale put it. This was not only the view of the soldiers (and the Assembly tended to follow, in military matters, its numerous military members), but, much more important, it was the view of M. Thiers. That indomitable survivor of the age of Louis Philippe was, indeed, far more rigorous in his standards than were the soldiers, for, unlike them, he had no use at all for the new-fangled Prussian idea of universal service. He had opposed this dangerous doctrine when it was advocated in 1848, and he had not really changed his mind since 1848. 'I don't want', he wrote to Saint-Vallier, 'a compulsory service that will inflame all heads and put a rifle on the shoulder of every Socialist; I want a professional army, coherent, disciplined, capable of making us respected abroad and at home, very limited in number, but superior in quality.'

---

[1] The oddest example of imitation of German methods was furnished by the law laying down scales of compensation payments for damage done by troops on manœuvres. The scales used by the German Army of Occupation were taken over by the French.

Thiers saw and allowed for the momentary madness of the nation and the Assembly. 'Universal compulsory service was the only thing, they said, to bring back to France the power she had lost.' This was 'the opinion of everybody, except some very few men of unusual good sense'. The men of very good sense were few indeed; perhaps they were only one man, but that man was full of energy, talked of himself as a new Carnot and was indispensable, for the moment, to the Assembly. So playing his trump card, his threat of resignation, Thiers drove a bargain.

The President would accept universal service in return for making the period of service of the backbone of the army a minimum of five years. For Thiers, five years was not nearly enough, he wanted seven or eight, but he knew when he was beaten. But if a high proportion of the army was to serve five years, the rest of it must serve for a very short period, six months in fact. Otherwise the financial burden of keeping five classes under arms would be ruinous. But how were the men of five years' service to be distinguished from those of six months? It would have been possible to choose the long-service men by their special aptitude for arms or, alternatively, restrict the short service privilege to those whose quickness marked them out as natural soldiers requiring little training. But such choices would have been too offensive to the new spirit of equality; and the old system of lot was revived. There were again good and bad numbers, although no number was now as good as that which had brought complete exemption under the Empire. This inequality had bad results. Obsessed by the view that it took a long time to make a real soldier, the Army authorities did not count the short-service men as real effectives, either while they were in the Army or when they had passed to the reserves. They were a kind of amateur reserve to be used for less serious work.

The new French Army did not, in fact, draw on the whole male population of military age to furnish the first-line; there were still large numbers of citizens exempt from the heaviest burden of citizenship, although now (and it was an important difference) this privilege was not to be bought. But, as Trochu pointed out, the inequality of service was sure to kill the new scheme. It was hardly instituted when a movement for doing away with the privilege was started, a movement that not only led to an alteration of the law in 1877, but, long before that, had gained much of its object by administrative means, as War Ministers increasingly cut down the nominal five years and raised the nominal six months until the difference between the two classes was slight.[1]

This was the most substantial but not the only inequality of the new

---

[1] A week before his death, Thiers told Jules Simon that he was resolved to speak against any tampering with the sacred five years, if he was to die while doing so.

law. Imitating the Prussian system, men of education were allowed to 'volunteer', on paying for their own equipment (at a cost of £60: $300), and on showing proof of exceptional education they served only a year and were trained to be reserve officers. This breach of equality with its flavour of privilege bought for cash did not seriously affect the numbers of the army, but it made the new law suspect. A still more unpopular feature of the law was the complete exemption given to future priests, ministers, rabbis and schoolmasters, whether lay or clerical. The Left at this stage did not propose to make combatants of the clergy, but it insisted that they should at least serve as stretcher-bearers. The majority was not to be shaken. Excluding the mass of the clergy from the Army, it created on the other hand, a service of peace-time chaplains, a change very little to the taste of the Minister of War,[1] but characteristic of the majority who were deeply concerned with the rôle of the Army as an educational force, hoping as they did, that the bourgeois soldiers would win over their proletarian comrades to sound ideas, and that the chaplains would make of the Army a moralizing force in a country that needed moral reinforcement very badly.

One consequence of the horror of voluntary enlistments, of buying recruits with cash or privileges, was the almost complete disappearance of the old professional soldier so common under the Empire. General du Barail regretted this; a handful of these veterans were good for the spirit of a regiment. Not many were needed, 'just enough to serve as models to the young soldiers, keep up the military spirit, the traditions, to tell cheerful soldierly stories in the barrack-room, sing the old songs on the roads'. A more serious loss was the disappearance of the old type of non-commissioned officer. No longer tempted to re-enlist by high pay or a bonus, there was no reason why the sergeants should stay on in the Army and, in six years, the number of veteran non-commissioned officers was halved. Only when the prudish refusal to make the service financially attractive was abandoned was the lost ground slowly and imperfectly recovered.

In other ways, the reform was not as thorough as it might have been. The War Office had still a deep respect for the rights of seniority; and one reason for the organization of fourth battalions in 1875 [2] was to provide jobs for superfluous captains, and something of the same spirit was behind the law limiting the normal tenure of command of an Army Corps to three years. The social position of officers was safeguarded by giving the War Minister a veto on their marriage, and the rank of officer was given to officials of semi-civilian auxiliary services, in part because it increased their matrimonial status and thus compensated for low pay. Despite a realistic doctrine of fire based on the experience of 1870, many relics of the old days survived. The pro-

[1] General du Barail. [2] See p. 122.

posal to issue entrenching tools to a third of each battalion was vetoed as crippling to the offensive spirit which was deemed to be the great asset of the French Army. So the old sappers with their white leather aprons and ornamental hatchets were preserved, and two were allotted to each company. In the cavalry, distinctions between heavy, medium and light cavalry, meaningless since the disappearance of shock tactics, were preserved. And 10,000 military bandsmen were kept to encourage the martial spirit. After all, everybody had read in *Les Châtiments* how the Old Guard had advanced at Waterloo—

> ... à pas lents, musique en tête, sans fureur.

One part of the Prussian system which the French Army was not yet ready to imitate was the territorial location of regiments. To recruit each regiment from one area meant, it was boldly asserted, endangering national unity, creating not a French Army, but an army of Burgundians, Bretons, etc. The real reason was probably a desire not to tie officers to one, possibly unpleasant, garrison-town. There was even a proposal to give every regiment a turn in Paris, and the proposal of Cézanne, to establish Alpine regiments to match those in the Italian Army, was turned down on the ground that service in these units would soon be looked on as a punishment! The history of the *Chasseurs Alpins*, when these regiments were at last founded, showed how baseless this fear was.

In some ways, the new army was remarkably like the old. The short-service troops and the Territorial Army were the equivalent of the mobiles; only the full-time troops, either in the Army or in the reserve, were taken into account. They were the 'true army', wrote General du Barail. There remained a dangerous scepticism of the value of reserve formations, a belief that all would be settled in the first weeks of war (as in 1870). A belief was expressed on the eve of 1914 by a competent military critic, that despite the millions of men in reserve who had passed through the Army, only a few hundred thousand men would be put into the field at the beginning.

The new Army was, in most ways, vastly superior to the old. Its officers worked hard, read and thought hard; the spit-and-polish tradition of the showy Imperial Army died, not all at once, but it died. Yet the lesson of 1870 that numbers are, if not all, more than half the battle was not learned. A War Minister of this period, General Charreton, expressed the dominant view. 'With our national character so impressionable, so ardent in exploiting a first success, so easily discouraged at the first defeat, we ought to devote ourselves to winning the first success.' In 1914, fortunately for France, General Charreton's view of his countrymen was proved wrong. But the hold of that view on the minds of the dominant school of French officers was expensive if not disastrous, for it was vain to think that the lesson which was not obvious to the men who had been beaten in Alsace and under Metz by armies full of reservists, would be appreciated by their successors who had no personal memories to set against the fashionable theory.

III

The labours of the Assembly, the retreat of the Conservatives within the lines of the Conservative Republic, took place under the suspicious eye of Prince Bismarck. The rapid recovery of French credit, and the internal calm of the conquered nation, were alarming to so perspicacious a statesman as the Chancellor, who knew, better than anyone else, the great risk he had taken in humiliating and mutilating France in 1871. He knew, too, that it was inevitable that Germany should replace France as the object of general European suspicion; a nation of such military prowess, ruled by such a successful master of politics as himself, placed in the centre of the Continent, was bound to be regarded with suspicion and, perhaps, with fear by the other states. From France they had nothing to fear now; from Germany they might have much.

The victorious Prussian soldiers began to talk of putting an end to the danger of a French war of revenge by a preventive campaign. France was rapidly recovering her strength, but she was still no match for her conqueror. Determined, as France was believed to be, on a war of revenge, it was surely only prudent to defeat her finally before she could become really dangerous again? These calculations were made, were heard and were adversely commented on in all the European capitals. Bismarck was not afraid of France alone; but he was afraid of a France allied with Russia or Austria. All his art was devoted to keeping on good terms with both his neighbours, linked in a common fear of the Revolution of which France was supposed to be the centre. But it was hard to persuade anyone that the France of the National Assembly was the tool of that International over whose dread designs so much sleep was needlessly lost. But if the France of M. de Broglie was not a centre of Red Revolution, she might be considered a centre of Black Counter-Revolution. To represent France as the champion of the Pope was, from Bismarck's point of view, a good move. It effectually separated Italy from her 'Latin sister'. It made English sympathy more easy to win for the enemy of Giant Pope than for his supposed champion. It drew the Tsar closer to Germany, for the Catholic Poles were his chief internal worry. Even in Catholic Austria, the claims and complaints of Pius IX were coldly received.

The Roman menace was not real enough to cement so unnatural a combination of all the great powers against a weak nation, especially on behalf of a nation suspected to be too strong for her neighbour's peace of mind. A recovery of France was essential to the balance of power in Europe, and a permanent reduction of France to impotence involved serious dangers for all the states which had reason to fear a dominant Germany. For this reason, if for no other, the plan of a preventive war was impossible. It could only be talked about, not carried out. The French Foreign Minister, the Duc Decazes, knew this and acted on it to score a superficially brilliant victory over Bismarck. The talk of war or of further coercion of France had alarmed the English Government, so Queen Victoria wrote a friendly if unnecessary letter of warning to the far from bellicose old Emperor. Relations between France and Italy improved; relations between Germany and Russia became less good. The diplomatic situation was altering to Germany's disadvantage when the 'war scare' of 1875 startled Europe.

Its origins were simple enough. French army reforms [1] seemed to nervous (and possibly inspired) German journalists important enough to justify a violent press campaign of which the highlight was an article in the Berlin *Post* entitled 'Is War in Sight?'. There were rumours of extensive French purchases of horses in Germany, and an embargo was put on the export of horses from the Empire. But France had no intention of making war and Bismarck had no intention of pushing matters too far. Had the French Government been content with the mutual explanations that followed, the scare might have been completely forgotten. But Decazes was partly afraid, partly anxious to put Germany in the wrong. His attempts to persuade the other great powers that Bismarck had sinister intentions against France and Belgium were not at once successful. Even the *Post* article did not frighten the other capitals as much as it was asserted to have frightened Paris. But rash remarks by a German Foreign Office official to the French Ambassador in Berlin provided new evidence of German designs. The British Government at last began to move; the British public began to share its rulers' anxiety after an alarmist article had appeared in *The Times*; and the Russian Chancellor, Prince Gorchakov, was at last ready to give some sign of his displeasure with his hated rival, Bismarck. The Tsar and his Minister were due to visit Berlin and, although the Tsar was not alarmed, the conjunction of Russian and British efforts to keep the peace which Bismarck denied was threatened, infuriating the German Chancellor. Decazes had the satisfaction of representing France as a harmless victim saved from the wolf by her great and good friends in London and St. Petersburg, and Bismarck had strong personal reasons for wishing to revenge himself on Gorchakov.

The immediate results of the scare were not important, but in the long run it had an important effect on French foreign policy. Thiers had always hoped to find in Russia the counter-weight to Germany. He had based his diplomatic campaign of 1870 on the erroneous belief that Russia could be induced to help France. Whereas some people in

[1] The creation of fourth battalions. See p. 119.

France, like Gambetta, hankered after an alliance with Austria, and others on the Left wished to cultivate England, Thiers had clung to his Russian dream. Decazes seemed to have proved Thiers right; Russia had saved France. Henceforward an alliance with Russia appealed to the French imagination for two different reasons. For some it was the only chance of undoing the crime of 1871; for others, Russian support was the only safeguard of France against a sudden attack by Germany. A new invasion was a nightmare for millions of Frenchmen, and the mythical projected attack of 1875 revived all the fears bred by 1870-1. Whether to revenge the disasters of the war of 1870, or merely to prevent their repetition, Russian aid was henceforward deemed to be necessary.

BOOK III

THE REPUBLICANS TAKE OVER THE REPUBLIC

Le peuple souverain s'avance.
Le Chant du Départ.

CHAPTER I

THE SIXTEENTH OF MAY

I

THE defeat of Buffet and the imminent replacement of the old leaders of the National Assembly by the untried and formidable Republican majority, were inevitably a source of distress for the soldier whom the defeated party had made head of the State. MacMahon took seriously the commission that he held from the National Assembly; it was his duty to avert or, if no more was possible, to postpone the arrival in power of the dangerous Radicals and, above all of their leader, Gambetta. The tribune had talked in a famous speech of the 'new levels' of society which were now becoming politically conscious and powerful. He was their mouthpiece, but MacMahon was unwilling to listen. The Marshal had, it is true, some regard for Gambetta; while a prisoner of war in Germany, he had not permitted his officers to sneer at the amateur armies raised by the Dictator, but since then Gambetta had been erected into a scarecrow by the Right and, to some extent, by himself. But the Marshal failed to realize that the tribune of Belleville was, as he claimed, not by nature a leader of the opposition, but a man of government. If the Empire had lasted, Gambetta might have been a minister of 'Napoleon IV' and he might well have been a minister of MacMahon.

Despite all Gambetta's overtures, the Marshal was unshakable. He refused to receive Gambetta, partly because of his general distrust, partly, it is said, because he learned that Gambetta was on close terms of friendship with his own sister-in-law, the Comtesse de Beaumont, and MacMahon shared the view of his wife that her sister's catholicity of taste in social and political matters was highly unbecoming.

A defence of his action that MacMahon later made, revealed how deep was his incomprehension of the situation. For the President believed that he showed his impartiality by refusing to have anything to do with either the Comte de Chambord or Gambetta, with the elderly obstinate heir of the dead past and the plastic representative of the living future. As leader, Gambetta had only one possible rival, Thiers, but as MacMahon said, he could not make Thiers Prime Minister, he could only retire in his favour. So, failing Thiers, he called on Dufaure to form a ministry. Dufaure had been born in 1798, during the Directory; the Third Republic was the seventh form of government he had lived under, but he had been indelibly marked by the reign of Louis Philippe. He wore 'the frock-coat, the eloquence, and the Gallicanism of 1830', says M. Hanotaux. His colleagues were as little representative of the new levels as he, and it was characteristic that the occupant of the Ministry of the Interior was Ricard, one of the few Republicans who had been beaten at the elections.[1] But to MacMahon, Dufaure represented the limit of concession, that position on the edge of the political fortress beyond which he would not retreat.

On the mined rampart of the Malakoff, in 1856, General de MacMahon had refused to be withdrawn. 'Here I am; here I stay.' The Elysée was the new Malakoff from whose walls the garrison looked out on the enemy. For, as M. de Marcère, one of the leading Catholic Republicans, complained, the Elysée, as far as the Republic was concerned, was 'an armed camp'. It was an armed camp which MacMahon would not abandon, for that would mean 'legalizing the Convention', since he thought the Senate would fall with the Presidency. It was unlikely that the alarmed Conservatives would find any Republican leader less alarming than Dufaure, but they showed little disposition to foster that union of the centre parties which had made the Constitution. They treated Dufaure and Marcère like prodigal sons who had yet to make their peace with their father and, in the meantime, were fittingly left to the husks and the swine of Republicanism.

It was in the Senate, with its narrow Conservative majority, that the Right fought its campaign: in that Senate which represented in personnel and in temper the dead National Assembly, so unlike the unruly Chamber 300 yards away at the other end of the Palace of Versailles. Broglie was there to display his pride and talents by warning the ministers of the danger of taking the first step. Where would it all end? Where would the resistance of the Right end? asked Dufaure. He remembered—as, oddly enough, the Duc de Broglie did not—the lessons of 1830 and 1848.

There were grounds enough for fear on both sides. The personnel of the administration was still Conservative and, although Dufaure was ready to replace such political officials as prefects by Republicans, he was not willing to purge the whole administrative and still less the whole judicial system. Yet that was what the victors wanted, and the defeated feared. For the vanquished Conservative bourgeoisie, a purge of the administration was a blow to pride and purse, and ominous of the exclusion of their sons from the profits of politics. For the Republicans, the sight of Royalists and, still worse, of Bonapartists, in office was irritating; it was the reward of political sin as well as the exclusion

---

[1] At Niort, by a Bonapartist.

from power and profit of the heirs of the martyrs of 1851. It was not enough that the future was bright; the present had to be illuminated too, although it was still possible for Gambetta to announce, without being laughed to shame, that the real difficulty of a Republican Minister of the Interior was 'to find trustworthy Republicans who are willing to take jobs. They are so little affected by the love of jobs that even under a Government of their choice, of their wishes, it is the hardest thing in the world to get them to accept them'. This iron resolution was breaking down faster than Dufaure's purge went on. If the days of the battle-cry of 1924, 'all the jobs and quick about it', had not yet come, they were coming.

Intensely interesting as the question of jobs was to present and future job-holders, it was not so close to the heart of the average elector. For him there was one burning question; the Church. It was the Church that had been beaten in the elections. And that defeat had to have results. The administrative favours and exceptions which had been enjoyed under the 'moral order' were now to be cut off, but there was a marked difference between what even sincere Catholics, like Dufaure and Marcère, thought were favours and what even a liberal bishop, like Dupanloup, thought were rights. Dufaure, for example, took administrative steps against some fiscal methods of the clergy, steps which irritated some zealots; and, like a good Gallican, he refused to permit the registration of a papal bull which had referred to a possible division of the vast diocese of Lyons. Pope Pius IX must be reminded that the Concordat reserved all these questions to the French State. It was no more than had been done under all previous French Governments, but it was ominous. It was no wonder that the uncompromising Bishop of Poitiers [1] was soon to appeal to MacMahon as a new Clovis, or that Dupanloup compared him to the saviours of the people spoken of in Holy Writ. But the legitimist Pie had little hope of any good coming from a Republic, whereas Dupanloup, for all his fears, still clung to the belief that much could be saved. So on May 16th, 1876, there appeared the first number of his paper, *La Défense Sociale et Réligieuse*.

Aaron was to hold up the arms of Moses in his fight against the forces of evil. It is difficult, as M. Daniel Halévy has reminded us, to realize what a great figure Dupanloup was in his lifetime, a modern Bossuet and Fénelon. He is now so forgotten that his name is more likely to suggest an obscene song than the great cleric who reconciled Talleyrand to the Church, resisted what he thought the mistakes of Pius IX, and now was active in forcing MacMahon to play the part of a new Napoleon III, instead of being content to play the part of Soult to the Guizot of Dufaure or even of Gambetta.

Two topics put the Government into difficulties at once. The

[1] Pie.

policy of 'no enemies on the Left' was being born, and the Republicans were forced by the pressure of their militant supporters to propose an amnesty for the *communards* who were still in exile, or in prison, and to demand the cessation of prosecutions for offences committed during the Commune or, at any rate, the transfer of the trials from military to civil courts. It was difficult to commend such a policy to Dufaure, who had been, next to Thiers, the chief enemy of the Commune. But this was not the only cause of disunion between the Ministry and the majority. The burning question of lay funerals was hotter than ever. The Catholics were, for the most part, still resolved that the State should stigmatize as deplorable the growing habit of omitting religious ceremony at funerals. The majority were equally resolved that it was intolerable that citizens who, as members of the Legion of Honour, were entitled to certain honours after death, should be denied them. Marcère's compromise, which proposed to abolish funeral honours in the case of civilians and retain the regulations untouched in the case of soldiers, pleased neither those who, like Monseigneur Dupanloup, were determined that the French State should publicly profess religious views, nor those who, like Jules Ferry, asserted that the State must be lay, be neutral. The day when the State was to be lay, but not neutral, had not yet come. The fate of the lights of heaven was, so it was asserted, a private matter; the Republic was not yet identified with a campaign for their extinction.

If the amnesty and the war for or against the Church were politically the most exciting themes, they were not the only themes that underlined, or seemed to underline, the differences between the Right and the Left. Gambetta had been elected chairman of the budget committee of the Chamber, and in that capacity he had declared for a bold attack on the question of income tax. Such words alarmed not only the Right, but many good Republicans, who were only moderately reassured by the reply of the Minister of Finance, Léon Say, that any 'general recasting of the tax system was an alarming chimera'. It was certainly a chimera but, had there been more political sagacity on the Right, it need not have been alarming.[1]

Republican unity was, except on the surface and where the régime was concerned, superficial. Gambetta had discovered this when, at the beginning of the first session of the new Parliament, he had tried to institute a 'full meeting of the Left' as a party caucus. Significantly for the future, the Republican Senators had declined to forget that they were Senators or to remember that they were merely mandatories of the great Republican party. Even more significant for the future, the Republicans in the Chamber had refused to regard themselves as one big party, of which Gambetta was the leader. The deputies did not

---

[1] Income tax took fifty years to arrive; the complete recasting of the tax system is still a subject of pious resolution by party congresses.

like the idea of one party and one leader, and their objection was given plausible general grounds by Jules Ferry. 'To remain united, truly united, united without any humbug, the real way is to remain distinct. That is not a way of dividing the party, it is a way of strengthening it by sorting it out. Discipline, without which the parliamentary system is only chance and anarchy, is only learned and is only consolidated in separate and limited groups, in homogeneous gatherings; the compromises between the extremes being possible only through the action of the middle sections.' Jules Ferry was to learn the limited value of this flexible discipline, but he undoubtedly spoke for the majority. The Chamber of Deputies was not going to be an English Parliament, and Gambetta was not going to be given the chance of playing the part of a Gladstone or Disraeli.

But Ferry had given the clue to the policy which alone could have saved Dufaure, the union of the Centres, excluding both extreme Right and Left. For that union there was needed, on both sides, moderation and prudence. There was not enough of it on the Left; there was even less on the Right, which used its senatorial majority to defeat Dufaure. Regarding it as the duty of the Cabinet to be a link between the two Chambers, Dufaure had defended before the Senate an amnesty bill which he had vainly opposed before the Chamber. The Conservatives, in their clever, frivolous way, were thus able to vote against Dufaure with an air of saving him from his friends. But the old man was not deceived and he resigned.

The first effort to govern with the consent of both Houses and of the President had failed. The new Prime Minister was Jules Simon, once famous for a cruel attack on MacMahon, but really distrusted by the President as one of the authors of the revolution of the 4th of September. MacMahon had not altogether pardoned Simon, but that astute politician had allowed it to be understood that the Marshal's control of the Army would not be interfered with. As for the Chamber, Simon was a masterly walker on tight-ropes. His adroitness in conciliating the Catholics had led Dupanloup to say that the non-Catholic politician would be a Cardinal before he would. And in his first speech to the Chamber, the Prime Minister, while affirming his unshakable Republicanism, had equally insisted on his firm Conservatism.

The crisis came over the old bugbear, 'the Roman Question'. Pius IX was as convinced as ever that the triumph of the revolution in Rome was only temporary, and he still looked to the Catholic states to aid him, in some undefined way, to free himself from the tyranny of the usurper. He had been irritated by the raising of the French representative at the Italian Court from the rank of minister to that of ambassador, and he was still further irritated by a holiday taken by Jules Simon in Italy, during which the Prime Minister accepted the order of SS. Maurice and Lazarus from the Italian Government.

These demonstrations that the French Government was less sympathetic with the wrongs of the Holy See than was proper in the rulers of the Eldest Daughter of the Church were annoying, but there was worse to come. A bill was introduced into the Italian Parliament making it an offence for ecclesiastics to publish writings threatening the security of the State, a general ban which might well cover the not infrequent protests of the Pope against the loss of the temporal power. Pius IX protested, and he appealed to the Catholics of the world to bring pressure to bear on their Governments to put a stop to the Mancini Bill.

As usual, the militant French Catholics rushed into battle. A deputation called on the Foreign Minister, the Duc Decazes, and demanded assurance that the independence of the Holy See would not be further invaded. A monster petition was organized in which the President was asked to 'employ all the means in his power to ensure respect for the independence of the Holy Father, protect his administration, and assure to the Catholics of France the indispensable enjoyment of a liberty dearer than any other, that of their conscience and faith'. This was to play directly into the hands of the Left. The old grievance that the chance of the Italian alliance in 1870 had been sacrificed to save the temporal power was given renewed plausibility. The Empress Eugénie and her son, the Prince Imperial (who was the godson of the Pope), had visited Pius IX—reminding France of the reputed Catholic intransigence of 'the Spanish woman' which, it was believed, had cost France so dear. 'All the means in his power' was a vague term which the Left promptly translated into 'war'.

The Eastern crisis, which was soon to end in the Russo-Turkish war, was alarming observers. Who could be certain that a great European war would be avoided? Who, on the Left, could doubt that Pius IX looked forward to a general convulsion in which the impious and rickety Kingdom of Italy would collapse? As the *Petit Parisien* put it: 'at an hour when France has greater need than ever of peace and calm, a party rises up and asks the Government to send our children to the slaughter-house'. The vast majority of Catholics had no such intention, but the temporal power of the papacy had been for so long their chief public preoccupation that it was difficult to disown the interpretations of the Left without seeming to take less seriously than did Pius IX, the crime of which the Kingdom of Italy was the fruit. Nor did all Catholics do much to refute the charges made by the Left. The Bishop of Nevers, worthy successor of Monseigneur de Dreux-Brézé, wrote an open letter to MacMahon informing him that he should 'free the France of Charlemagne and Saint-Louis from all connivance in that revolution in which they do not recognize their child'.

As if this was not enough, the bishop took on himself to circularize the mayors of his diocese to the same effect, a breach of administrative decorum that Jules Simon was, of course, forced to rebuke. The indignation of the Left was doubtless mixed with pleasure at the sight of the old enemy choosing to fight on such bad ground, for the grievances of Pope Pius IX were not of a kind to evoke much sympathy among neutrals. He was not a prisoner as the man in the street understood the word, and Jules Simon was able, indeed, forced to say as much, to the indignation of the Catholic zealots. The Right politicians knew how foolish it would be to fight on the question of the temporal power, and a resolution was passed by the Chamber, and reluctantly accepted by Jules Simon, condemning the 'ultramontane activities'. The Marshal bided his time and the Left was suspicious of the Prime Minister, who, they thought, had not been zealous enough in repelling the assault of the clericals on the independence of French policy, and they became still more suspicious when they read in Dupanloup's paper, *La Défense Réligieuse et Sociale*, that Jules Simon had given guarantees to the Catholics on taking office, and if he did not keep his word, 'we know well by what means we can force him to come round'. It was a most indiscreet boast, which had slipped into the paper, so the editor later said, without his noticing it. But it represented what many Catholics were saying, and though the Prime Minister tore the paper to pieces in front of the Chamber, he now could not appear to weaken in face of the clerical menace. In any case, the Marshal had decided to strike, and on May 16th, taking advantage of two minor points of difference over a new press law and a law making public the sessions of municipal councils, he sent the Prime Minister a letter to which the only possible answer was a resignation. The crisis of the Sixteenth of May had begun.

II

The new Prime Minister was the Duc de Broglie. He was the obvious choice, for he was the leader of the Opposition, yet he was not really fitted for the task he undertook. As in the crisis of the abortive restoration, he lacked faith, and he was too clear-sighted not to recognize the odds against which he was fighting. Watching the smart crowds round the Arc de Triomphe, he remarked to a colleague that these people were better fitted 'for a *coup d'état* than for the effort which we are going to ask of them'. And that colleague, M. de Meaux, complained that the French Conservatives were waiting for a saviour from heaven to do their work for them. They were, indeed, waiting for several saviours. The old feuds were only superficially healed. The Legitimists were suspicious of the motives of MacMahon and Broglie and demanded an assurance that the Marshal would not be a candidate for re-election in 1880. The Orleanists, or some of them, were not resigned to their failure to make the Duc d'Aumale President, and they knew that both the duke and his nephew, the Comte de Paris, disapproved of the undertaking. The Bonapartists had now the most attractive chief in the young Prince Imperial, although they had to put up with the alleged Republicanism of the heir-presumptive, Prince Napoleon, who was a deputy. The politicians and publicists who were above all Catholics were angered by the unwillingness of the ministers to fight openly on the religious ground. Louis Veuillot allowed one of his contributors to declare that the battle-cry ought to be 'clericalism, there is salvation'. What with the attacks of Paul de Cassagnac on the Duc Decazes, the open suspicion with which the Legitimists regarded Broglie and the internal feud in the Bonaparte family, the forces of order were not conspicuously orderly.

Very different were the tactics of the Left. Under Gambetta's lead, all the opponents of the new Ministry and all the friends of the old were united. After some resistance, M. de Marcère and his friends of the Left Centre joined the Left bloc and the Committee which had been appointed to decide on a united front policy. Thiers, Dufaure, Bardoux, Marcère, Casimir-Périer, Léon Renault, Gambetta, Clemenceau, Louis Blanc, every shade of opinion in the majority was represented, and it was resolved that no deputy who voted for the decisive resolution against the Broglie Cabinet would be opposed at the imminent election, even though this policy meant refusing to oppose Prince Napoleon! That there would have to be an election was obvious; otherwise the Broglie Ministry could not last. The only doubtful point was whether the Senate would grant the President's demand for a dissolution. If it was right to refuse such a demand at all, there was much to be said for refusing it in 1877. The Chamber had still half its life to run; it had not been unmanageable in deeds, although violent enough in words. The fall of the Simon Ministry was not due to a difference of opinion between the Ministry and the Chamber, but to their agreement. The acceptance of a right of dissolution given to the President and Senate had been a grave breach of Republican tradition. It was unfortunate that it was to be exercised so soon and in circumstances so likely to confirm all Republican suspicions of that monarchical relic.

More important than these long-term constitutional considerations were the very reasonable doubts of many Conservatives as to the success of the dissolution, and it was 'with death in their hearts' that some Centre Senators voted for the dissolution. Some of them, despite all appeals to party loyalty, refused, among them the President of the Senate, the Duc d'Audiffret-Pasquier. By a narrow majority the dissolution was voted, and the President and the Senate appealed to the country to disown a majority in the Chamber whose programme had hardly been outlined, much less put into effect. The electors were asked to change their minds because of future evils, not because of present discontents.

The folly of 'the Sixteenth of May' seems so clear to-day that it is hard to do justice to its authors. Brunet might appeal to posterity for admiration of the authors of this legal *coup d'état*, but the time has not yet come when they are thought justified. As Père Lecanuet suggests, their chief fault was being beaten, but to engage a battle in which defeat is likely is a fault. But it should be remembered that the Right was both frightened and proud. It was frightened as it saw its assets dwindling. In 1878 there would be the municipal elections, so important for the senatorial elections of 1879: and, by bad luck, the third of the Senate to be renewed in the first election was strongly Conservative. Of seventy-five seats to be contested, two-thirds were held by members of the Right. Thus the narrow Right majority could not in all probability be increased and would in all likelihood be destroyed. Then, in 1880, would come the election of a new Chamber which, in conjunction with the republicanized Senate, would elect MacMahon's successor.

It was all very well to play for time, to wait until the Left had frightened the country, but what if that did not happen until all the machinery of government was in the hands of men who, it was sincerely believed, were anxious to carry out the Belleville programme of 1869. That many parts of this programme would be still pious aspirations in 1939 was unforeseen by a defeated party without sufficient cynicism to take French party manifestoes with the necessary quantity of salt: a quantity that varies, but is always more than a pinch. Then the difference in popular support between the two parties was not fairly represented by the election figures. An overwhelming majority in the Chamber represented only 51 per cent. of the votes cast. To Veuillot, the Republic was a mere electoral accident; and it was surely not beyond the power of a resolute government to turn the 49 per cent. of votes won by the Right in 1876 into a majority in 1877?

The dangers of the future appalled the timid and corrupted the judgment of the normally prudent, as had the dreadful thought of the dangers of the election of 1852. Then the Conservatives agreed with the Bishop of Chartres that by the *coup d'état* 'we have avoided the 2nd of May, 1852, which opened a frightful abyss before France'. Now, it was to be hoped, they would agree with Paul de Cassagnac that it was not a question of fighting 'for one kind of government or another, it is a matter of life and death for society'. Were there not signs of the times? A few weeks before the dismissal of Jules Simon, Rochefort had founded *La Lanterne*, Rochefort the *communard*! And the exiles like Brousse in a manifesto told the workers: 'You must prepare yourselves to pass from words to deeds, from the ballot-box to the barricades, from the vote to the insurrection.' Would not this be enough to frighten the timid middle-classes? Gambetta was resolved that it should not be enough.

The campaign of the Left, like that of the Right, was designed to frighten, and the Left had two scarecrows to the Right's one. There was the menace to peace arising from the Roman question. A victory for Broglie would be a slap in the face for Italy and for Germany. France, isolated at the moment of a great European crisis, was in no mood to run any risks to oblige the Pope. It was in vain that Mac-Mahon asserted that he and his ministers sought only peace. There were many alive who could remember Napoleon III making the same promise. Next to the danger of war, there was the danger of clerical rule. France did not want to be ruled by priests, asserted the Left, and the Right showed how true this was by the anxiety they displayed to impose discretion on the clergy. So the nation was treated to the comic spectacle of the Minister of Cults in a Conservative and Catholic Government forbidding public prayers for the success of that Government!

France is a country where historical precedent plays a great part in politics, and the precedent for 1877 was obvious enough; it was 1830, when the foolish King Charles X had dissolved the Chamber, had seen his opponents triumph and had resorted to a policy of repression which had led to his overthrow by such defenders of liberty as M. Thiers—and the father of the Duc de Broglie. The Left maliciously pointed out that MacMahon asked for trust in words almost identical with the fatal proclamation of July 1830. Already, in the great debate ended by the dissolution, Gambetta had stressed the parallel with the crisis that led to the 'three glorious days of July'. 'I dare to assert that as in 1830 they were 221 when they went off and came back 270, so, in 1877, we go off 363, and we will return 400 strong.' To achieve this, discipline and industry were needed.

The Republican press was taken in hand. *La République Française* was the *National* of the new campaign, but Émile de Girardin, John Lemoinne, Edmond About were powerful auxiliaries. There were special sheets, like the *Père Gérard*, designed to reach the peasants, written in simple language. The occasional indiscreet left-winger who talked in a way to frighten the timid was silenced or denounced as a Bonapartist agent, for it was the tactics of the Left to see in the Broglie Ministry only a precursor of the Empire. Not even the Empire of 1870, but, as Girardin pointed out, the Empire of 1852. The violence of such Bonapartists as Paul de Cassagnac and Cunéo d'Ornano was some justification for this charge. The new prefects and other officials hastily appointed by the Minister of the Interior, M. de Fortou, were largely Bonapartists, as was natural since his chief agent at the Ministry was M. de Saint-Paul, who was devoted to the Imperial cause. This was inevitable, for the notables, as Tocqueville had pointed out a generation before, were unpopular; other things being equal, the electors would rather vote against them than for them. Thus the only real political machine available was that of the fallen Empire, and many of its favourite dodges, like the special white posters reserved to the 'official candidates', were lavishly employed, but without the resolution and contempt for criticism that had marked the great days of Rouher. Even had the occasion for attempting a reaction been better chosen, had the country been really frightened by the dangers of radicalism, really convinced that there was no difference between the Gambetta of 1877 and the Gambetta of 1869, the lack of a positive programme would in any case have condemned the Ministry, if not to defeat, to a barren victory. The fiery Royalist Bishop of Poitiers, Monseigneur Pie, was right when he commented pessimistically: 'We know enough [of politics] to be able to say that a *coup d'état* (and that is what the 16th of May is) isn't directed against someone or something, but for something incarnate in someone. Otherwise, the *coup d'état* is only a sword stroke in water.'

In vain that the Government attempted to make MacMahon a symbol. The honest, but not very able or resourceful, soldier was paraded about the country like a mascot. His reception was seldom warm and he was lucky when he had not to undergo the ordeal of organized hostility like that prepared at Tours by M. Daniel Wilson, or the dreadful drive through Bordeaux with boys dropping into his carriage from lamp-posts to insult him! Official visits and reviews, manifestoes and Army orders, did little to exalt his prestige. The emptiness and banality of the Government's programme was as irritating to observers as the bad political judgment displayed in the whole affair. His rage at the Sixteenth of May made Flaubert forget his old detestation of the Fourth of September. The whole business provided more materials for his abundant repertory of human stupidity. Had the Government had the courage of the convictions of Louis Veuillot, had it fought for the supremacy of the Church by the aid of the secular arm, had it disdained the prudential counsels of the Orleanists, it would not have done much worse, and would have gone down with dignity. But the old error of the 'moral order' was repeated. The Government of the Duc de Broglie appeared, in fact, as the Government of M. Joseph Prudhomme.

> Il est grave: il est maire et père de famille.
> Son faux col engloutit son oreille. Ses yeux
> Dans un rêve sans fin flottent, insoucieux,
> Et le printemps en fleur sur ses pantoufles brille.

Many voters, who had no more use for the unkempt makers of verses than had M. Prudhomme, were yet as bored as Verlaine with the identification of the safety of society with the narrowest interests of the middle-classes—and doubtful if they were, in any case, in real danger from the triumph of a coalition where Louis Blanc was offset by M. Thiers, Gambetta by M. de Marcère, Clemenceau by M. Léon Say.

The Government did its best to make up for its weakness by displays of vigour. The noisy southerner at the Ministry of the Interior was anxious to show that he was a new Morny. Indeed, there were critics who said that M. de Fortou was so busy trying to look like Morny that he had no time to act like him. He had not, of course, the resources at the command of his predecessor. The Government had not the courage to put the country under martial law, and the regular law did not allow the silencing of all hostile criticism such as had been practised in December 1851. It was not possible in 1877 to clap all dangerous critics in jail. It is true that the law was strained to the utmost to hamper the opposition. The legal rights of newspaper sellers were, for instance, attacked with a disregard for formal constitutional doctrine that recalls an American city boss anxious to save his clients from dangerous thoughts, more than a Government presided over by an eminent academic Liberal like Broglie. One of the electoral moves of the Government was to flood the country with pictures of the Marshal on horseback, and several wits found it was dangerous to remark that 'He has an intelligent eye—I mean the horse'. But it was not only minor members of the Republican coalition who were arrested. Gambetta was charged with insulting the President and condemned to fine and imprisonment—a vain gesture, for, of course, he appealed and was still at liberty when the election day came, with all the advantages and none of the disadvantages of martyrdom.

An event which was not in itself very surprising raised the hopes of the Government. The rôle of Thiers in making the opposition less terrible to the timid had been very important. The old man was determined to have his revenge for his overthrow in 1873: and fortune gave him both his enemies at one time as prey. His revenge over Broglie and MacMahon would be complete; he would help to defeat the one and drive the other out of the Presidency, where he proposed to replace the Marshal. Gambetta's share was to be the offices of Prime Minister and Foreign Minister. Thiers would 'present him to Europe'. From Gambetta's point of view, this had obvious advantages; and those advantages were not merely personal. Gambetta was afraid that Mac-Mahon, after the defeat of Broglie, would attempt to create another Centre Government, a move which, if it succeeded, would make the victory less than complete. But, he wrote to Arthur Ranc, 'thanks to the animosity of M. Thiers, to his influence over the section of the Left which might weaken, there is really nothing to worry about, from which you will see how much, apart from other and excellent reasons, it was desirable to run Thiers for the Presidency'. On September 3rd, Gambetta was thunderstruck and the Government delighted to hear that Thiers had died suddenly. Fears and hopes were alike groundless.

In death Thiers still hurt Broglie and MacMahon, for his widow would not agree to the terms on which the Government offered a State funeral and the private funeral was a great demonstration of Republican unity. The body of the man of the Rue Transnonain and the 'Bloody Week' was carried through the working-class districts of Paris with the greatest of honour, for the hatred of the Paris workers for their old oppressor was subdued this day in face of a common enemy. Gambetta was delighted at the 'spectacle of a million men animated by the same devotion to justice and the Republic, some forgetting their bitter memories of civil war, others silencing their fears'. With glory, Thiers was buried in that cemetery of Père Lachaise where the Commune had died.

There was still a danger that the death of Thiers would hurt the Republican cause: for, with Thiers, died the most obvious guarantee against the complete triumph of Gambetta. Gambetta knew this—as did his colleagues—and in default of Thiers, the most reassuring of the Republican leaders, Jules Grévy, was nominated as candidate to succeed Thiers in his Parisian constituency—and, it was given to understand, was destined to succeed MacMahon in the Elysée. M. de Broglie might exercise his aristocratic wit at the expense of Grévy of whom Europe knew nothing, but the French voters knew how far the Republic of M. Grévy, like the Republic of M. Thiers, was from meaning red ruin and the breaking-up of laws.

It is possible that had Broglie dissolved at once, he would have done better, but by October the unity of the Republicans was complete, while the hastily assembled Right coalition was barely held together. The campaign, too, took on more and more a Bonapartist appearance. Fortou was, or professed to be, full of confidence. His illusions were common to all those who regretted the Empire, to those who agreed with what Émile Ollivier had written in 1874, 'if they knew at Paris how easily they could bring all these windbags to heel'. But alas! the good old days were over and, despite police prosecutions, the windbags continued to talk of the danger to Republican institutions, to peace, to freedom, of the clerical menace, of the dangers of what a candidate at Parthenay brutally called 'a Government of priests and a new Sedan', brutal for the dead Emperor—and for the living Marshal! There were replies. The red ghost was made to walk and there were local scarecrows. On the eve of the election, the Republican Mayor and candidate at Arles was attacked in a pamphlet *Citizen Tardieu and the finances of the Town of Arles*. But all was in vain. Gambetta, indeed, was proved wrong; the Government gained about fifty seats, but in the new Chamber, as in the old, there was an overwhelming Republican majority—and the Republicans had polled 52 per cent. of the votes.

What was now to be done? Fortou characteristically lost heart at once and wanted to resign, but Broglie was made of sterner stuff than the pseudo-Morny and the Government met the new Chamber. By that time, Fortou had recovered his wind and reproached the Republicans with not realizing that they were beaten! Broglie was his arrogant, decisive self. But he had, and could have, no reply to the reproaches of Léon Renault, 'The grievance that all France has against him [Broglie] is that he has put the country in a state in which there is to-day no longer a Conservative interest, a Conservative idea which does not feel itself threatened and compromised by him and on his account'. And Gambetta, sincerely enough, made the same reproach of wasting valuable French assets when he talked of 'that mounting wave of democracy which it was your business to control, to enlighten, and to direct'.[1] How completely Broglie had failed in that duty was shown by the local elections, which took place between the first and second ballots of the parliamentary elections, for not only did another series of local government bodies go over to the Left, ensuring a Republican majority in the Senate in 1879, but Broglie was himself defeated for election to the council of the Department of the Eure, his own bailiwick in Conservative Normandy.

There were still bold and foolish spirits who talked of further resistance. The Bonapartist Cardinal de Bonnechose was all for martial law and a plebiscite, but although the Left was alarmed by rumours of military conspiracy, and found in Labordère an officer who denounced the suspected *coup d'état*, there was no danger. It is true that the Marshal, in one of his manifestoes, had talked of pursuing his policy 'to the very end'; and the officials who had staked their careers on his success were faintly hopeful that the end was not a mere election defeat. But not only would another dissolution be likely to produce the same results; it was improbable that the Senate, not enthusiastic for the Marshal's policy when it had first been tried, would agree to a new election. After vain attempts to get Pouyer-Quertier to take over the job of liquidating the adventure, MacMahon fell back on a business cabinet, headed by a soldier, General de Rochebouët, a Cabinet whose political members were known chiefly as unsuccessful candidates. These evasions only postponed the evil day. In one of his most famous phrases, Gambetta had announced that the President would have 'to give in or get out'; he gave in and sent for Dufaure; the adventure of 'the Sixteenth of May' was over.

It was a parody of the most inexcusable adventure in modern French politics, the Hundred Days, with Broglie as a more guilty Ney, punished (and with him his whole party) more effectually than a firing-party could have done it, but with a severity not excessive for the offence. For not only had the administrative machinery been scandalously abused in a vain attempt to win a doubtful victory, an important piece of constitutional machinery had been utilized without real justification

---

[1] Gambetta began his reply to the ingenious defence by Broglie with 'Kindly spare us these ingenuities', a close parallel with Campbell-Bannerman's famous rebuke to that other aristocratic and incompetent politician, Balfour. Campbell-Bannerman was a close student of French politics.

and so had been destroyed. There has never since been a dissolution of the Chamber: and the conviction of the newly-elected deputy, that he has four years in which to indulge his personal views with no risk of having to justify himself to his electors, has been of the greatest importance in French political practice. That conviction of immunity the deputy owes to M. le Duc de Magenta and to M. le Duc de Broglie. Since 1877 dukes have played no important rôle in French politics.

M. Dufaure had been the Marshal's first Prime Minister after the Republican triumph of 1876; he was again Prime Minister after the Republican triumph of 1877. It was not merely because M. Dufaure was now in his eightieth year that things were different, he was no longer the Marshal's Minister, he was the Prime Minister accepted by the President of the Republic at the hands of the triumphant majority, a majority more confident and more bitter than it had been in 1876. Then, it had been fearful of the unknown power of the Senate and the President; it had suffered the worst and had survived the ordeal triumphantly. And there was in the Republican ranks a great gap; Thiers was dead, Thiers who had said that 'the Republic would be Conservative or would disappear'. In his place was Gambetta, half the age of Dufaure.

The first fruits of victory were taken from the defeated Right. The Republicans were furious at the revival of the hated official candidacies of the Empire, and there were some who wanted to invalidate the elections of all the deputies who had accepted the white posters that marked the official candidate under M. de Broglie as under Napoleon III. The Chamber was complete master of the election returns, not only legally but by custom; there was no tradition of fairness to bind the hands of the victors, much less a judicial procedure like that which had recently been adopted in Britain. The victors, if they did not abuse their powers, used them to the uttermost; seventy-two deputies were unseated, and although some of them got back, the tradition was established or re-inforced, that pressure, clerical or official, on behalf of a candidate of an unsuccessful party was corruption of the judgment of 'universal suffrage'. No pressure, governmental or private, by prefects or by schoolmasters, by masonic lodges or by other organs of organized Republicanism and 'laicity' was anything but a legitimate aid to the voter as long as it helped candidates approved of by the majority of the new Chamber. For many years to come, France was faced with the odd political phenomenon that corruption always came from the Right. No 'Republican' deputy was ever unseated, however warmly his election had been recommended by the officers of the Central Government.

III

Despite this purge of the Chamber, politics in 1878 were at slack-water. For 1878 was the year of the great 'Exposition Internationale'. The Exhibition was to be a demonstration, as George Augustus Sala, the famous London journalist put it, of 'Paris herself again'. In 1867 Paris had been glorified in the great exhibition of that year, despite such clouds as the execution of the imperial protégé of Napoleon III in Mexico. Things had changed since 1867. There were no foreign sovereigns visiting Paris in 1878, except the Shah. However, there was the Prince of Wales, already .familiar as a private visitor to the city, and there were many thousands of tourists, who came not to gape at the ruins of the Commune, but at a city largely restored to its old glory, with the completed Opéra in addition, if without the great Palace of the Tuileries. It was a wonderful demonstration of French vitality; and while the show was on, burning political questions were kept in the background. The victorious Left even voted £20,000 ($100,000) to the defeated Marshal to enable him to act as host to the distinguished visitors, and MacMahon, with his amiable courtesy, showed that there was something to be said for having a nobleman at the head of the State on show occasions. There were, of course, indications of the collapse of the old order. There was that 'festival of the people', which, care-fully arranged for June 30th to avoid the dangerous memories of July 14th, was yet celebrated by the playing of the long-forbidden *Marseillaise* by the band of the Republican Guard. This dire innova-tion was made only by special permission, but it was a sign of the times. There were others; the by-elections to the Chamber showed a continued move to the Left. As a commentator put it,[1] 'Being in a Republic, the electors thought that to control the business of a Republic, one ought to choose Republicans'. There were votes for new school buildings, votes on a scale that alarmed the timid Conservatives whose objections to these 'palace schools' were perhaps reasonable, but whose fond hope that those objections would be shared by the parents of the children who were to be housed in this new luxury was only another example of the political folly of the former ruling classes. It was already the dogma of the majority of French voters that, as M. Bardoux put it, 'The man who does not love the schools is not patriotic'. M. Naquet proposed to re-establish divorce abolished since the fall of Napoleon I, and the crowds admired the great statue of Liberty that was destined to be a present from the great Republic of the old world to the great Republic of the new. When 1878 was over, there would be stirring times!

In October there was another series of local elections and the Left again triumphed. On January 5th, the Senatorial Elections came.

[1] J.-J. Weiss.

Of 82 seats, the Left won 66. It had now a majority of 50 in the Upper House—and of the 16 new Conservatives, 13 were Legitimists from the West! The Orleanists were destroyed as a party; on one side, there was the handful of zealots for the King and the white flag; on the other the mass of voters won over to the Republic, the tricolour—and what? There were soon to be indications.

The military law limited the tenure of office of Army Corps commanders to three years, but MacMahon had been able to secure their reappointment and all the great commands were in the hands of the old generals of the Empire or of Royalists, including in that class His Royal Highness the Duc d'Aumale. Gambetta had attacked this evasion of the law, this tenderness for soldiers whose services, as he hinted very broadly, could well be spared. But command of the Army was the last prerogative to which the Marshal clung, and he refused to accept changes in the higher commands. He had again either to 'give in or get out'. He got out. He resigned and was succeeded on January 29th by Jules Grévy; Dufaure had refused to be a candidate and so had Gambetta. Grévy, after all, had been presented to the country as the heir of Thiers; he was old, respectable, drab and reassuring. He was also, and this was not disliked by many rising politicians, a determined if not open enemy of M. Gambetta. So the Presidency of the Republic lost a little more of its prestige. Thiers, a great man, and MacMahon, a fine figurehead, had both been forced out of office by Parliament. Their successor was merely politically eminent. He would add very little to the intrinsic powers of his office, nor did he aim to, for he announced in his first message that he would not set his personal views against those of the representatives of the people. 'Sincerely submissive to the great law of parliamentary government, I shall never begin a contest with the national will expressed by its constitutional organs.' The new President still knew his place.

CHAPTER II

GRÉVY, GAMBETTA, FERRY

I

WITH the accession of Grévy to the Presidency, the stage seemed set for a more important change, the accession of Gambetta to the office of Prime Minister. Gambetta had been the leader of the resistance to MacMahon, the organizer of victory in 1877. Only Thiers could have competed with him for public attention, either in France or in Europe, where he was classed with Bismarck, Gladstone, Disraeli. But Grévy was obstinate, cunning and, at this stage of his long life, was not yet so much a victim of vanity as to be vulnerable. He was not going to begin his Presidency overshadowed by Gambetta. Not only had he this personal reason for disliking the over-mighty leader, he had a genuine suspicion of the great demagogue. Grévy was a lawyer of a very different kind from the flamboyant orator who had upset the tribunals of Napoleon III. He was a cautious family lawyer, his client was France—and the Republic—and he was not going to let them be led off on adventures.

It was in vain that Gambetta had tried to live down his reputation for wildness, for rashness. Grévy, like MacMahon, was unconvinced. Ludovic Halévy, watching this attempted evolution, compared Gambetta to a light lady who never forgets her first love—and Gambetta's first love was Belleville. All the fiery rhetoric which had delighted the revolutionary proletariat of Red Paris, ten years before, now arose to plague its author. This Gambetta felt was very unjust. Even under the Empire he had not been a preacher of opposition for its own sake. He had never forgotten that a Government has its rights and duties as well as its temptations and crimes. He saw no reason, now that the Republic was in control, why Republicans should continue to regard the Government, any Government, as a dangerous dog to be kept on as short a chain as possible. He hoped to win over to the new régime some of its old enemies, to make of the Republic the heir not only of its own glories, but of all French glories. Perhaps his recent Italian origin blinded him to the fierce partisanship of the French, to their refusal to make friends when they could so easily make enemies. His attempts to live in a more decorous fashion, to abandon the Bohemian habits of his youth, did nut convert his old enemies and angered his old friends. He might be presentable enough for the Prince of Wales, but not for M. Buffet, and, on the other hand, the man whose trousers at last met his waistcoat, who delighted in society, whose dinner-parties were smart as well as important, could hardly be a sound Republican in the eyes of Camille Pelletan whose own general grubbiness and rudeness were to be, for a generation, proof that he, at least, was immune from the seductions of the old order. His old friends began to look askance at his new friends. Those able young men, of whom Joseph Reinach was the spokesman, with their English doctrines exalting party discipline, a predetermined programme and, above all, the authority of the party leader, were they to be the marshals of the new Emperor? Grévy, Clemenceau and scores of less famous but equally resolute members of the new ruling class were determined that the new republic should be more like the old Polish Republic than like the contemporary English constitutional monarchy. The Republic did not mean merely the substitution of a non-hereditary ruler for an Emperor or King. The Republican deputies and senators and the leaders of the local political machines in the provinces were to be the new *Schlachta* of this western Poland.

In the centre of the Republican mass, Gambetta's *Union Républicaine* became not the great united Republican party dreamed of, but the personal following of Gambetta. On its right and left were vigilant groups whose Republican orthodoxy could not be questioned and which, especially the Left, were not above clandestine alliance with the Right whose fighting force came from the extreme Bonapartists. Thus Grévy, blandly protesting that he did not want to use up Gambetta too soon, was able to form a 'replastered' Ministry, that is a Ministry whose chief, Waddington, had been in the previous Ministry, a precedent that was to become part of parliamentary custom. That Grévy could do this, could take this dignified, able, but unpopular semi-Englishman as Prime Minister, showed that the Presidency, even in his hands, was not a mere formal office—and how, from the beginning, the French parliamentary system in Republican hands was not going to be the copy of the English system that had been intended. What Victoria could not do in the next year, Grévy did with ease.[1]

But even Grévy could not deprive Gambetta of authority; and instead of the open power of the premiership, the tribune had the hidden power that came from holding two offices, the presidency of the Chamber and the chairmanship of its finance Committee, at that time the only permanent committee of the Chamber and consequently even more important than it is to-day. Gambetta could not be neglected,

[1] The way in which Victoria had to take Gladstone in 1880, despite her intense dislike of him, was noted by Gambetta's friends. To them, Waddington, Freycinet and the rest were mere Granvilles and Hartingtons.

but his power was dearly bought, for it was soon attacked as a 'hidden power'; its reality was recognized, indeed exaggerated, but the reputation of being an occult dictator was increasingly harmful. Gambetta was blamed for what the new Republican Government did not do, for Waddington's refusal to give a general amnesty to the *communards*, for instance. He was not thanked for what was done; for the symbolic triumph of the Republic revealed in the adoption of the *Marseillaise* as the national anthem, in the return of Parliament to Paris, in the choice of the Fourteenth of July as the national holiday and, more practically, in such important measures as the re-organization of the Council of State which insured that Republican administrations would not find too many legal obstacles to their activities in the decisions of the great administrative court. The enemies of Waddington were not united, for the extreme Left hesitated to unite with Gambetta's men, but the administration was too feeble to stand even when backed by fear of Gambetta. It fell—and Grévy replaced Waddington by Freycinet; it was a 'replastering of the replastering'.

The new Prime Minister was Gambetta's old ally of the National Defence, the old Imperialist candidate. He was able, he was eloquent, and he was weak. The Chamber was in no danger of finding a master in him and had no more eloquent exponent of the excellence of doing nothing in particular. Had there been no more vigorous personality in the Government than its chief, it might have collapsed ignominiously. But there was such a personality and there was a policy which could be followed with political profit by the Government. It could 'deliver the University' from the grip of the Church.

The University was the name given by Napoleon I to his organization of all levels of French public education from the highest to the lowest. All were controlled by the Minister of Public Instruction and his inspectors; local authorities had little financial or other authority over any part of the system.

Although there were many lay private schools, the good ones among them were usually boarding houses and cramming establishments associated with the State schools, and the bad were simple refuges for dull boys whom unsympathetic masters had driven from public establishments (whose financial stability did not depend on numbers) to private establishments (whose financial stability did). The real competition came from Church schools, from the secondary schools primarily designed to train future priests, the 'petits séminaires' of which Dupanloup's Saint Nicholas du Chardonnet was the exemplar, or colleges run by priests but largely staffed by lay masters like the Collège Stanislas in Paris, or the schools of the great religious orders, like the Jesuits. These clerical schools won patronage by their readiness to adjust fees, by their willingness to adjust programmes, but above all, because they gave efficiently the formal education demanded by the State educational system and, in addition, gave far more attention to the non-intellectual sides of education than a State system, now officially neutral, which had, in the not too distant past, encouraged religious hypocrisy and which left the education, as apart from the instruction of the boys, to a depressed class of ushers.[1] Then the secondary schools recruited their pupils mainly from bourgeois families, and the professors of 'the University' had a reputation for radicalism that did not prepossess the timid parent in their favour. The 'redness' of the University was not very profound, but under the Empire most professors had been Republicans, suspect to the authorities in Church and State. Eminent churchmen who had themselves been members of the University before taking orders (and there were more of these than is always realized), usually took a kindly view of the activities of their former colleagues, but the average priest and average bishop regarded the University as dangerous.

For them the Falloux law of 1850, allowing anybody who had certain minimal qualifications to open a school, was a charter of liberty. It allowed Catholic parents to send their boys to schools which would prepare them for both success in this life and salvation in the next. The result was an astonishing growth in schools run by priests, especially by members of religious orders. Even after the fall of the Empire the tide flowed the same way. In Lyons, for instance, while lay. private schools decayed, the religious schools grew faster than the State secondary schools. In the first generation of the Republic, the number of pupils in the Church secondary more than doubled and was greater than the number in the State *lycée*—and this in a politically Republican city.

Such a development was both startling and infuriating to the Republicans. It meant that the bourgeoisie was, in greater and greater degree, given an education which denied some of the optimistic views of human nature held by Republicans and emphasized supernatural views which denied that heaven was about us here if we looked for it in the proper way. No Frenchman, Catholic or Agnostic, thought that it did not matter what a people believed. What both parties too often forgot is that people do not always believe what they are taught. Education at the Collège Stanislas did not prevent Anatole France from being a bitter enemy of the Church; it may indeed have helped to develop his anti-clericalism. Education at the State *lycée* of Clermont-Ferrand did not either keep Paul Bourget in the Church or prevent him from returning to it. In the next generation, when State education was more openly agnostic, the grandsons of two notables of the régime, Renan and Jules Favre, were to become leading apologists of the old faith, although neither Psichari nor Maritain had been influenced by an early Catholic bending of the twig.

---

[1] The professors in a *lycée* had almost exclusively teaching duties; the supervision of the boys, especially of the boarders, was left to an inferior caste of 'répétiteurs'.

The vitality of the Church, revealed in the growth of monasteries, of convents, of schools, of centres of advanced study like the new Catholic Institute in Paris, of hospitals, of lay charitable organizations like the Society of Saint Vincent de Paul, was startling in a country where it was almost impossible for others to build up powerful organizations without State patronage. The decay of lay private schools was only an example of a general law; co-operative manufacturing societies, for all the optimistic propaganda with which they were surrounded, only kept going through getting State contracts on special terms. Selling co-operatives were sickly plants compared with those of England and Belgium. Trade-unions, though legal, were poor and short-lived. Rich Frenchmen were slow-givers to public objects; what the State did not do was not done. To all this sterility of private action there was one exception, one institution which was as capable as any private organization in America or England, of supplementing or competing with State action, there was the Church. It could even induce the stay-at-home Frenchman and Frenchwoman to emigrate. A great colonial empire was being formed, but it was not being peopled by Frenchmen. But, all over the world, in every climate, in the Arctic and in the Tropics were to be found, in perpetual exile, French missionaries, men and women. Can we wonder that the rulers of the Republic should be both startled and indignant at the survival and growth of activities which were not only not helped by the State, but frowned on by it?

The real driving force in the Freycinet Government was the Minister of Public Instruction, Jules Ferry. Ferry was a tenacious Lorrainer whose severe features and long whiskers gave him an air of a French Matthew Arnold. He had married into one of the new Republican dynasties [1] and, what is more, had disdained the common hypocrisy of a marriage ceremony in church, an act of candour almost as offensive to the feelings of polite society as a civil funeral. Ferry was, in fact, a man of strong views and strong character and his views and character made him an admirable instrument of the Republican policy of 'laicity'.

There were many nominal Catholics whose supernatural faith was very weak indeed and there were many 'priest-eaters' whose anti-clerical views had no deeper roots than local jealousies and personal resentments. But there were many on both sides whose whole philosophy of life was involved and among these was Ferry. He was not a vulgar priest-baiter of the pornographic type commoner then than now in French polemical speech and writing, but he was hostile to most or all of the claims of the Catholic Church. He was not indeed

[1] He married Eugénie Rissler, member of an important Alsatian family, whose aunts were, respectively, Madame Charras, Madame Floquet, Madame Scheurer-Kestner, all names dear to the Republican party. His brother Charles was the son-in-law of Allain-Targé, one of Gambetta's closest collaborators.

one of those anti-clericals whose zeal Littré had reproved, those whose 'compel them to go out' was merely the converse of the Catholic 'compel them to come in'. But if he could truthfully deny that he favoured the separation of Church and State, he was frank enough in his desire to secure that the next generation of Frenchmen, especially the next generation of his own class, the bourgeoisie, should be saved from clerical influence during their impressionable years. It was only of the Jesuits that he openly declared that 'it is from them that we wish to tear away the soul of the youth of France', but his concentration on the Jesuits was largely tactical. He would have been far from pleased if he had thought that the secular clergy could have stepped immediately and effectively into the place of the ·Society.

In choosing to begin his attack on the clerical educational system by an offensive against the Jesuits, Ferry was well advised. The Society had, as the event proved, plenty of sincere friends in those classes of society where it was well known, but those classes were, in any case, almost entirely hostile to the Republic; they were not friends whom a Republican Government had any political reason to conciliate. Among the workers and the petty bourgeoisie of the towns the traditional hostility against the Society, as the enemy of progress and of the liberties won by the Revolution, was very deep. It was often as fanatical as anti-semitism was to become, and many an honest shop-keeper or minor official was as convinced of the reality of the Jesuit conspiracy as others were of the Jewish conspiracy.[1] The very success of the Jesuits among the upper classes made it peculiarly vulnerable and perhaps made it harder for the rulers of the Society to realize how little its friends could do to save it.

In attacking the Society, Ferry not merely appealed to a great existing body of bitterly hostile enemies of the Jesuits, he hoped to appeal to a great body of men who were not unfriendly to the Church but who were, at best, indifferent to the fate of the great order. It was a common and, possibly, a sincere protestation of some supporters of Ferry that they really thought that the expulsion of the Jesuits or of the other orders was all for the good of the Church, a protestation which Catholics naturally thought added the insult of hypocrisy to the injury of persecution. Yet there were undoubtedly Republicans, often very hostile to the Church, who still clung sincerely enough to an Erastian Gallicanism which wished to preserve the union of Church and State for the advantage of the State—and who nourished vague hopes of fostering such doctrines among the secular clergy by a mixture

---

[1] Even so learned a politician as Louis Blanc was not above delighting his audiences with lively scandal about the Society. Had not the Jesuits poisoned their enemy Clement XIV? The Pope had died horribly, his bones peeled like the bark of a tree, his hair stuck to the velvet pillow. 'The Jesuits were avenged.' Need we wonder that this thrilling story caused a 'profound sensation' among the audience?

of promises and threats.[1]   No sincere Catholic, not even so Republican a Catholic as Eugène Lamy, could stomach this doctrine, but there were Catholics, not all of them lay, who were no very warm friends of the Jesuits, or who were anxious that the general interests of the Church of France should not suffer by too close an association of the other orders and the secular clergy with the threatened Society. Ferry played up to this sentiment by the famous Article Seven of his bill on the reform of higher education.   'No one', the Article ran, 'is to be allowed to teach in State or private schools, nor to direct a teaching establishment of any kind if he belongs to an unauthorized religious order.'   This Article hit, of course, at other orders too; the Dominicans and the Marists were teaching but unauthorized orders.   But it was the Jesuit teachers against whom the might of the French State was to be directed; for, as the event showed, the Government was ready to let the lesser fish escape through the net.

It was Article Seven that united this fissiparous Republican majority.   In the Chamber, the Government's victory was easy.   In the Senate, the Right and Centre were still strong and the burden of the defence of the right of Frenchmen, even of Jesuits, to teach, was assumed by Jules Simon, whose task of insisting on the inconsistency of this proscription with the Liberal doctrines preached by the Republicans, was easy enough.   Freycinet's reply was politically cogent; no Government that abandoned Article Seven could live for a day in the Chamber; if the Senate forced the Government's hands by rejection of the clause, other means would have to be found.   By a narrow majority, the Senate took the risk.   The answer was to act without a special law; two decrees were issued, one giving the Society of Jesus three months to dissolve itself, the other giving three months to the remaining unauthorized orders to apply for authorization.[2]

The decrees were duly executed; the Jesuits did not dissolve as ordered but waited to be expelled.   In Paris, the priests expelled by the deputy-turned-policeman, the Prefect Andrieux, left their houses on the arms of distinguished pupils.   The spectacle of venerable men going into exile surrounded by the affectionate regret of a large number of gentlemen in frock-coats and top-hats was less moving than the simpler-minded Catholics imagined it would be, for the Paris crowds disliked the gentlemen for being friends of the Jesuits and the Jesuits for being friends of the gentlemen.   Two hundred magistrates resigned their posts rather than take part in the expulsions,[3] and their names

---

[1] Paul Bert, the French equivalent of T. H. Huxley, gave a good sample of this doctrine in replying to the theological faculties of Paris when he became Minister of Public Instruction in 1881.   He insisted that the Catholic faculty of Theology in its teaching should respect 'the fundamental laws which govern the relations of the Catholic Church and the State', while the Protestant faculty was congratulated for having shown that 'religious science and sincere convictions are not incompatible with a broadminded liberalism'.

[2] With prudent regard for the feeling of parents, the Jesuit schools were somewhat inconsistently given a little longer to dissolve than the other houses of the Society.

[3] Among them M. Pierre de la Gorce, who thus found the leisure to turn historian.

were inscribed by the Catholics in a 'Golden Book', but more important was the welcome opportunity thus given to the Government to
republicanize the legal system still further. Protests were not confined to magistrates. As the war against the orders continued, it was
found necessary to defend the authority of the State by suspending
one of the most eminent Catholic members of 'the University', Ollé-
Laprune, the eminent philosopher of the École Normale Supérieure,
but this attack on the famous mother house of 'the University' was
resented even by sound Republicans and by the student body whose
most brilliant member, Jean Jaurès, headed the movement of protest.
Neither Catholic indignation nor ironical surprise at seeing the Republic imitating the administrative methods of the Empire had any effect
on the main Ferry reforms. In his war to free education from clerical
control, indeed from religious influence, Ferry was representative of his
party and that party was preferred by the average Frenchman to any
alternative open to him.

In the eyes of the University one of the great crimes of the Second
Empire had been the abolition, in the early tyrannical years, of the
class of philosophy. Like the prohibition of wearing a beard and the
rules laying down the number of buttons on the waistcoat of a *lycée*
master, it had been inspired by suspicion of the soundness of the
teaching body. Like all the other prohibitions, it had not survived
the early years of the alliance between Emperor and Pope, but under
the Third Republic formal philosophical teaching was necessary for
the inoculation of a common philosophy of life and thought in the new
ruling class. There were critics of this system; unwilling and not very
successful pupils like Maurice Barrès, who regarded Kant as being as
much a Germanic conqueror as Moltke, and better-informed critics,
like Gaston Paris, who observed of philosophy as taught in the *lycées*, 'by
the very fact that it is above [the heads of the pupils] it has the serious
drawback of making them believe that they know everything without
their having learned anything'. It was remarkable enough, that at a
time when hatred of all things German made it dangerous for a musician
like Chabrier to be too enthusiastic a propagandist for German music,
it should have been possible for educational administrators like Lecha-
pelier to make of Kant the main intellectual food of boys of eighteen
and nineteen—as far as they could digest it. That it was possible
showed how deeply resolved the new rulers of France were to remake
the national tradition in their own fashion. Both sides believed, too,
firmly, that they could not exist together. It was this belief that made
Dupanloup resign from the French Academy when Littré was elected,
for that noble man and great scholar was an enemy of supernatural
religion. Dupanloup knew that Littré was no more an atheist than
thousands of the upper classes in France were, but the public admission
of such a man to the Academy shocked him as the election of Brad-

laugh to Parliament, a few years later, shocked so many people in Britain.

If the Littré affair was to many gloomy Catholics a sign of the times, so, to many apprehensive Republicans, was the alienation from the old Republican anti-clerical faith of so many bourgeois families. The grandson of an old Bordeaux anti-clerical and Republican was brought up by nuns and religious, and what happened to François Mauriac happened to many others. French Catholicism, round whose death-bed so many spectators had been clustered since 1789, was an unconscionable time dying. Among the young Republicans there was a general belief that, until France escaped from the relics of her Catholic past, she could not hope to equal the progressive nations of the world: the English, the Americans, the Germans. These had had the inestimable advantage of the Reformation which France had missed, but while individuals like Taine and Renouvier might dally with the idea of adopting a non-dogmatic Protestantism, it was not much easier for Frenchmen to become real Protestants in the nineteenth century than in the sixteenth.

II

It is not altogether the fault of Ferry's enemies that his educational policy is remembered too exclusively as an incident in the war against the Church. For his friends then—and since—in celebrating the triumph of 'free, compulsory and lay education', have always laid most stress on its laicity. This was natural enough. The relation between the schoolmaster and the priest had never been easy. Under the old régime he was the servant of the priest; and the clerical party attempted, as long as it had the power, to make him if not the servant at least the auxiliary of the parish priest. Under the Empire, at least while the Government and the clergy were still on good terms, he was often forced to hypocritical religious observances. More Frenchmen than Bouvard and Pecuchet had been impressed—and repelled—by this control of the teachers by the clergy. Yet the teacher's position, even when he was docile, was not secure, for as far as they could the clergy tried to induce communes to bring in members of the teaching orders of brothers and sisters who could undercut the lay master who might be married and who had not taken a vow of poverty. And, from the clerical point of view, a brother was preferable to the most pious lay master, for who knew how genuine or lasting the piety might be?

In general, the communes were not very enthusiastic about replacing the lay masters by brothers, but nuns were very generally welcome. Thus when the Republicans came into power in 1877, there were four times as many lay masters as teaching brothers, but nearly twice as many nuns as lay schoolmistresses in the State elementary schools. The Republicans were ready, from the beginning, to put an end to the employment of members of religious orders in the schools, whatever might be the wishes of the local authorities, but it was impossible, offhand, to replace nearly 10,000 brothers and nearly 40,000 nuns. So it was not until 1886 that the entry of new brothers and nuns into the State schools was forbidden, and, as late as 1914, there were still schools staffed by religious orders.

The fundamental reform was the insistence on the possession of a teacher's certificate by all teachers and the provision of a normal way of securing it, not open to nuns or brothers. One of the most reasonable grievances of the lay schoolmaster or schoolmistress had lain in the fact that the members of religious orders could teach on the mere production of a 'letter of obedience' issued by the local bishop. Freppel, Bishop of Angers, might assert that a 'letter of obedience' was as good or better than a State certificate, but it was an astonishing anomaly that entrance to a profession paid by the State should have been by two doors, one guarded by the State and one controlled by a different if not rival institution. To ensure a uniform education and standards for the elementary teachers of the nation it was now necessary to improve the normal schools where they were trained. So there were founded at Saint-Cloud and at Fontenay-les-Roses two primary higher normal schools, from which went out men and women to the departmental normal schools which, in their turn, produced the elementary school-teachers.

The greatest innovation was the creation of a new type of woman school-teacher. Her appearance was a far greater novelty than any mere alteration in the type of male teacher who, after all, had normally been a layman, not necessarily very devout, whereas the creation of an educational system for women not deeply marked by Church control was really revolutionary. Even Dupanloup, who took a far higher view of the possibilities of female education than did most Catholic leaders, had been most vigorously opposed to the attempts of Victor Duruy, in the last years of the Empire, to bring the secondary education of girls within the orbit of the State system. Not until 1880 were the first girls' *lycées* opened; and it was as significant that the legislative promoter of these *lycées* was a Jew (Camille Sée) as that the director of the Higher Normal School for Girls, Felix Pécaut, had been a Protestant minister. Men of Catholic background, even if otherwise completely alienated from the Church, still tended to think that a religious education was a good thing for their wives and daughters, a belief which helps to explain the scandalous success of one of the first literary results of the new system, *Claudine à l'École*. It was a long time before the bourgeoisie, which was neither Jewish, Protestant, nor bound by official position to display lay sentiments, began to send its daughters to the *lycées*.

The prohibition of all religious instruction by teachers in the State schools might have led to a great exodus from them, had it not been accompanied by compulsory education, which forced the children to go somewhere, and free elementary education, which penalized the zealous father who refused to send his children to the Godless school which cost nothing. Both reforms were opposed by the leaders of the Church, and Jules Ferry stressed the difference between the optimism of modern society and the pessimism of a Church which feared that more evil than good might come from general literacy, while the Republic did not care if the beneficiaries of her education only used it to read books of devotion. Conservative lamentations over the cost of the new schools, over the salaries of the schoolmasters (whose minimum was between £36 and £48 a year),[1] and over the interference of the State with the rights of parents, all only irritated still more the egalitarian feelings of the average voter and increased his conviction that the Church was the bulwark behind which the old privileged classes still resisted the work of the Revolution.

In those early days, the difficulties that later arose between the schoolmasters and the State were far off. It was easy to replace the old duty of teaching the child his duty towards God by a vague religion of patriotism and, a little later, by a heart-warming if not a very clear doctrine of 'solidarity'. It is true that the schoolmaster was completely at the mercy of the administration, as he had always been, but he was not now likely to suffer for unorthodox opinions. Indeed, his heterodoxy had become the new orthodoxy. The schoolmaster was usually the secretary of the mayor in the village, the official representative of Republican orthodoxy. The French State still supported an established Church but, in reality, it was not the priest but the schoolmaster who represented the real *ecclesia docens*—'the University'. The priest was merely a leader of the opposition paid—and so muzzled—by the Government. The schoolmaster had nothing to fear from him, whatever he might have to fear from a prefect who was in complete control of the educational machine and who might be the instrument of the vigilance or spite of local politicians. In other ways, politics was the serpent in this Eden, for there were still exceptions to the rule that all teachers must have passed through the normal schools. Men and women were admitted to fill unforeseen gaps in the personnel and these back-door entrants were usually, it was asserted, possessed of political backers, just as, it was believed, promotion went too largely by political favour.

The comparative ease with which Ferry carried through these reforms was due to his care not to alienate the bourgeoisie. Fervent Catholics were, of course, profoundly angered by his policy, but fervent Catholics were not the majority in the middle-classes, however much

[1] $180 and $246.

decorum might impose formal respect for religion on that majority. The class structure of French education was still intact.   State secondary education was neither free nor compulsory, although it was now lay.   A smattering of Latin still marked the male members of the bourgeoisie from the workers and from men who had risen from the working-classes.   Latin verse had been abolished in 1872 by Jules Simon, Latin composition went in 1880 and Greek was nearly a lost cause, but French middle-class education remained predominantly literary, with French largely replacing Latin, and English and German beginning to take the place hitherto given to Greek.

If in a legal sense the whole teaching body, from the Sorbonne down to the village schoolmaster, was 'the University', in reality only the upper branches counted.   The inspectors who controlled elementary education in the departments, like the prefects and the bureaucrats in Paris, like the minister himself, were products of the secondary-school system.   The elementary teachers, isolated in special (and presumably inferior) training schools, trained by professors who had themselves been produced by special (and presumably inferior) training colleges, were a proletariat, or at least were merely privates and non-commissioned officers in the great educational army. The officers were the professors, professors of *lycées*, of colleges, of faculties.[1]

The professors became, indeed, a new political class in France; what the men of letters had been under the Restoration and the July monarchy, the professors were now.   The higher strata of the older bourgeoisie were excluded from power in this generation, as far as it was Catholic or Royalist, and in mass it was both.   The gap they left was filled in part by Protestants, to a less degree by Jews, by aspiring lawyers—and by professors.   'Since 1870, Burdeau, Duvaux, Lenient, Compayré, Charles Dupuy, Jaurès, Jules Legrand, Étienne Dejean, Lintilhac, Mirman and how many others have been Deputies, Senators, Secretaries of State, Ministers, Presidents or Vice-Presidents of the Chamber.'   So wrote an eminent professor[2] in defence of the political rights of members of the University, although he was candid enough to admit that not all of the political activities of these scholars in politics did France or the University much credit.   In this generation only Conservative members of the University suffered for political activity. They could hardly be too careful in an age in which so good a Republican as Yves Goblot could be denounced by the zealous vigilance of the Republicans of Angers because he played duets with a countess!

There grew up what an acute critic of the régime has called the 'Republic of Professors',[3] and many, perhaps most of the great orators

[1] Colleges are local high schools mainly maintained by communes; *lycées* are high schools mainly maintained by the State.
[2] Gustave Lanson.   [3] Albert Thibaudet.

and debaters of the régime, had begun as teachers. They preserved a great deal of the ethos of their corporation and in the war with the Church brought a professional bias to bear that was not always admirable. A former professor like Lintilhac, advocating at a Radical Congress the establishment of a State monopoly of education, revealed, indeed, a curious family resemblance to Louis Veuillot, minus Veuillot's brilliant literary gifts. More important, as economic questions insisted in forcing their way into politics, was a curious defect in the system of higher education which has not yet been effectively remedied. Economics was taught and studied not in the faculties of letters or science, but of law. The new governing class was recruited mainly from professors of literature, of rhetoric, occasionally from professors of the physical sciences. Such economic teaching and investigation as was done in France, was done in a legal and formal atmosphere which accounts for the limited contribution of the French genius to this field of study in the last two generations: and it was done in a faculty which recruited its pupils mainly from the Conservative upper classes. The bright boy who rose by scholarships was far more likely to make his way to the École Polytechnique or to the École Normale, than to a faculty of law; and that bright boy, when he became a minister, had to fight a temptation to believe that the laws of economics, even of arithmetic, were inventions of reaction, to be safely ignored by the mandatories of universal suffrage, or to be refuted by eloquence.

III

Between them, the Revolution and Napoleon had given the system of higher education in France a character unknown in any other country. No institutions of the old régime in France were in more deserved disrepute than the universities. They had failed to adjust themselves to the new learning in the sixteenth century; and the general education of the French upper classes was thenceforward deeply marked by the literary bias of the Jesuits. The old faculties of arts became mere schools where some Latin and very little Greek was taught to boys who, if they pursued any further studies, did so in purely professional schools of law, medicine or theology. Even so characteristic a production of the French genius as Cartesianism was very slow in forcing an entrance into the universities. France continued to be a teacher of Europe, but it was not her universities which could claim the glories of a Mabillon or a D'Alembert; great monasteries or the academies were the centres of learning and research. Outside Paris, the universities were poor and sometimes venal. In the eighteenth century, apart from Strasbourg, only Montpellier preserved some of its ancient renown and revenues, and Strasbourg was half a German university. It is true that Oxford and Cambridge were at their lowest depths, but they were not poor. In the golden age of Glasgow and Edinburgh and of the German universities, the French universities were, even more than in the age of Rabelais, condemned by public opinion as the homes of 'Sorbonnards and Sorbonnicoles'. Strasbourg, despite a justified plea that it was more like Halle or Göttingen than like the decadent Sorbonne, was condemned by the National Assembly with the rest. France turned from the débris of the Middle Ages to a brand-new system of special schools.

Until the end of the nineteenth century, higher studies in France were centred in a number of specialized institutions, differentiated as much by the future careers of their pupils as by the studies pursued in them. The most famous of all was the École Polytechnique, which trained gunners, military engineers and civil engineers entering the State service. There was the Museum which dealt with natural history (biology), the École Normale Supérieure, which trained teachers for secondary schools, the École des Chartes, which trained archivists, the Conservatoire des Arts et Métiers, which evoked the admiration of the young Charles Eliot, the École Centrale des Arts et Manufactures, which trained technicians for private business. Each new need was met by the creation of a new special school; there was thus a multiplication of overlapping institutions: and these great schools were all in Paris, so that there was a further intensification of that intellectual grip of Paris on the provinces which was so widely deplored. Entrance to and exit from these schools was by competitive examination, the examination for entrance to the École Polytechnique being the most revered of these tests. The French schoolboy, from an early age, was brought up not to be educated but to be examined. Each great school had its famous 'promotions', the good years when all the stars competed together and the schools—and the public—had an insufficient appreciation of the difference between an Edmond About and a Taine.

To these special schools, Napoleon I had added the faculties. As far as these were organizations of teachers of law or medicine, no serious criticism could be made of them, but the faculties of letters and sciences were very maimed versions of true university faculties. Outside Paris and one or two of the greater provincial towns, these faculties remained what they had been, examining bodies which, in addition, gave public lectures of a popular type to the local seekers after culture. A great man, even under this system, could do great things, and when Strasbourg had Pasteur in its Faculty of Sciences and Fustel de Coulanges in its Faculty of Letters, it could not be contemptible. But even in cities which had four or five faculties, there was no university; neither morally nor legally were they united.

The chief critics of this system were the Germanophile scholars who were so powerful a force in French intellectual life all through the century. From the time of Madame de Staël and Charles de Villiers, the merits of German learning were fervently preached in France and the fruits of the German renaissance eagerly culled. Among the admirers of German learning and its organizational methods was Napoleon III, who had been educated in Germany and one of whose academic collaborators, Louis Renier, was a convinced admirer of German scholarship although he had no first-hand knowledge of it. The Emperor was anxious to see in France some equivalent of the German Catholic faculties of theology, but his efforts to create in Paris a new Tübingen or Munich failed, mainly because of the opposition of Pius IX. More success attended the efforts of the greatest French Education Minister of the nineteenth century, Victor Duruy. He created, it is true, just another special school, the 'École des Hautes Études' (School for Higher Studies), but unlike the existing schools, this did not train for a specified career or prepare for a State examination; it was a graduate school of advanced research.

The war of 1870, so shattering to French conceit, was followed by a national stocktaking, and the defects of the French educational system were blamed for the disasters. It is true that the criticism varied with the critic. To many pious Catholics the fault was in the moral looseness that came from un-Christian education.[1] To the pious Pasteur, it was due to the neglect of advanced science; to Renan, to French frivolity and Jesuit education. All were agreed that something should be done and the restoration of the universities, the grouping together of the separate faculties in local bodies each autonomous, with its own revenues and common government and subject only to general supervision, was the dream of the reformers, especially of those who had studied in Germany. These questions did not excite much interest outside professional circles and, inside them, there were plenty of defenders of the old order, especially defenders of the strongest parts of the old order, the examination-ridden 'great schools' of Paris. The fight over secondary and primary education was politically more interesting and profitable, and as 'pure politics' became the main business of the Ministry of Public Instruction, 'the main thought was the expulsion of the Jesuits and the friars', as Gaston Paris put it.

A further difficulty in the way of a serious university reform was the ambitious character of French secondary teaching. It was the common practice to consider the teachers in the *lycées* and the teachers in the faculties as parts of the same body, 'the University'. The degree of bachelor, won by examination at the end of the secondary-school stage, was a passport to all special studies. 'In France,' said Ernest Bersot, 'you make your first communion to be done with religion, you pass the bachelor's examination to be done with learning, you marry to be

---

[1] Napoleon III attributed it to the effect of such poisonous books as *Mademoiselle de Maupin*.

done with love.' Success at the competitive examinations for entrance to the great schools was the main object of secondary education in the eyes of the average parent, and it was the success in these competitions of some of the schools belonging to the religious orders that most irritated the old-fashioned champions of the University. Even at a later stage, the higher examinations were still competitive and it paid far better to do well in the 'agrégation', the annual examination for a limited number of privileged places in the secondary-school system, than to have written a brilliant doctoral dissertation or have received a first-class training in research at the École des Hautes Études. But, however slowly, the movement for the creation of regional universities made headway. The faculties themselves were given some autonomy and then in 1896 were linked in sixteen local universities,[1] usually in cities which had had universities in the past, like Caen, Besançon, Poitiers.

The new universities could receive gifts, receive subsidies from communes and departments and, if still under central control to a degree unknown in Britain, the United States, or Germany, they were far freer than the faculties had been. They were not richly endowed, either by the State, the communes or by individuals. Salaries were low: even in Paris a full professor only received £380 a year [2] and unless he could hold several jobs at the same time, he had to live on the level of a minor bureaucrat, a disability of less consequence than it would have been in other countries, but not negligible. As M. Ferdinand Lot pointed out, it was rare for rich men in France to give large gifts to any public object that was not religious, and, indeed, some of the independent Catholic universities, like that at Lille, received more gifts than did their State rivals.

Understaffed, ill-equipped as far as libraries and laboratories went, the French universities, like so many other French institutions, did wonders on meagre resources. Nancy, which had, in French minds, replaced lost Strasbourg as the University of the East, was housed, as M. Lot put it, in a stable, while the Germans had housed Strasbourg in a palace. Thirty years later, a Marseilles journalist compared the University of Glasgow to a castle and the faculties of Aix-Marseille to rabbit-hutches. In Paris, the re-built Sorbonne was cramped for space since piety had made it impossible even for the Republic to move the University from the sacred 'montagne Sainte Geneviève' to a more commodious site. But for all its weaknesses, the new university system was a vast improvement on the old. Associated with it in Paris were the École des Chartes and the Institut Pasteur, to name two widely different institutions, each deservedly a centre of world-wide admiration. The resources for advanced learning might be used more by foreigners than by Frenchmen, but it fell to the Third Republic to

---

[1] Including the University of Algiers.   [2] $1,900.

restore the glories of the French university and to make the name of the Sorbonne as splendid as it had been in the thirteenth century.

IV

The violence of the reaction against the Ferry decrees was no surprise to the astute old man in the Élysée and was a cause of great discomfort to the Prime Minister. He, like his predecessor, was a Protestant and it was significant of the extent to which the upper classes in France were hostile to the régime, that the first Grévy cabinet had five Protestant Members out of eleven—and Protestants were less than 1 per cent. of the population. Freycinet did not desire to appear as the instrument of a persecuting policy. It was all very well for his combative minister to receive addresses from the Freemasons of Toulouse congratulating him on his fight against 'the enemies of society', but society had more and, from a bourgeois point of view, more dangerous enemies than the Jesuits. The more violent anti-clericals were delighted that the Government had been led to such drastic measures as the decrees, but Grévy did not share their pleasure and he told his Ministers so. The same objects might have been attained, he thought, by less dramatic means.

Both Grévy and Freycinet wished to avoid further conflict and they knew that at Rome, whatever sympathy was felt for the Jesuits, the new Pope, Leo XIII, was much less disposed than his predecessor to let the best be the enemy of the good. The other orders, it was hoped, might be induced to apply for authorization, and thus along with the secular clergy, be separated from the Jesuits. A tactfully ambiguous letter from the orders was drafted and the Prime Minister gave broad hints that a compromise was under way. On the Right, the Royalists, whose one hope of survival was the continuance of the war between the Republic and the Church, sabotaged the negotiations by calculated indiscretions; while on the Left, Gambetta's representatives in the Ministry resigned in protest against this pusillanimity. Freycinet gave in and Grévy took up the presidential trowel; plastering was tried again, and the new Prime Minister was Ferry. Other orders followed the Jesuits into exile. Laicity was safe.

Neither Grévy nor Ferry could prevent Gambetta from being the first man in France. At a great fleet review at Cherbourg, the President of the Republic was eclipsed by the President of the Chamber; on a visit to his native town of Cahors, Gambetta was received much as the Prince President had been on those tours which had been the preface to the Empire. Not only did Gambetta give arms to those who talked of cæsarism; at Cherbourg he had spoken of 'an immanent justice' which would undo the wrongs of 1871. The German papers protested; and it was easy for Gambetta's enemies, from the President downwards, to represent him as a warmonger. Gambetta had his own political projects, the abandonment of the single-member constituency, the *scrutin d'arrondissement* which already was a powerful vested interest, and a limited revision of the Constitution. The first project was an offence to the deputies who saw in small constituencies their source of independence in face of the executive and, while any reform of the Constitution alarmed prudent Republicans, a limited reform was beneath the contempt of the Left. Gambetta was howled down at an election meeting in Belleville, and provoked into denouncing his tormentors as 'drunken slaves whom I shall pursue into their dens'. How different was this language from the political bargain struck with his electors of Montmartre by the leader of the new Radical party, Clemenceau! No limited revision for him; the Senate (of which he was so long to be a member) and the Presidency (for which he was to be an unsuccessful candidate) were both to be abolished. Universal lay education, the gradual replacement of the Army by a militia, separation of Church and State, income tax, abolition of the death penalty; this was the old Belleville programme of 1869 brought up to date. Gambetta's first love was still plaguing him!

The Republicans could afford, however, to indulge in violent disputes and in competition for the votes of the extremists, for the Right was demoralized and disorganized. The evil effects of the feud between the Orleanists and the Legitimists did not grow less. The Comte de Chambord and his organization in France were far from repenting past errors; they regretted, as far as they regretted anything, that they had ever made any concessions to the liberal ideas of the junior branch. Under the leadership of Dreux-Brézé, committees were established which, if without any influence outside the narrow circles of Legitimists, effectively discouraged Royalist zeal among the ex-Bonapartists and the Republican Catholics angered by the militant anti-clericalism of the Republic. Until the death of the Comte de Chambord in 1884, the official claimant to the throne showed that he had forgotten nothing and had unlearned what little he had learned. Characteristically, he bequeathed his property away from his Orleans heirs to the family of Bourbon-Parma and his death was followed by the dissolution of the Legitimist organization. The Comte de Paris only inherited the barren title of Pretender; the Orleanist leaders were left without troops.

It was natural that, in such circumstances, Bonapartism should have revived. It was far more popular than either Legitimism or Orleanism; it had far more adherents among the people; and the Army, like the administration, was still largely manned by Bonapartists. But the chances of a concentration of Catholic and Conservative sentiment on the Imperial cause were destroyed by news from Africa. In 1879, the Prince Imperial, heir of Napoleon III, fighting as a volunteer with the British troops, was killed by the Zulus in South Africa. The young Prince had been the most promising of the Pretenders, if only because he was young, contrasting with the elderly Comte de Chambord and the middle-aged Comte de Paris. He was, too, a familiar figure; he had grown up in France and he had been regarded by millions as the heir to the throne. He had been too young when the Empire fell to have incurred personal odium and he had been too young, when the question of the régime was decided, to have failed as a Pretender like the Comte de Chambord, or to have refused to become a Pretender like the Comte de Paris.

It was not only the loss of the most marketable of the contending princes that disorganized the Bonapartists. The legal heir of the dead prince was Prince Napoleon. But he had been a nuisance to Napoleon III, and his ideas were so opposed to those of his cousin that the young Prince's will had vainly attempted to leave the political inheritance of the dynasty to Prince Victor Napoleon, the son of Prince Napoleon. Yet the new head of the Imperial house illustrated in his own person the vagueness of Bonapartist doctrine. The Prince Imperial had been a pious Catholic, determined to be a protector of the Church. The new chief of the party was notoriously an unbeliever. He lived in open adultery, separated from his wife, the daughter of the usurping King of Italy, and he had made public both his anti-clerical and his Republican views. The latter were taken no more seriously in 1879 than they had been by the Prince's uncle, King William of Würtemberg, thirty years before. His anti-clerical views were more important, for most of the leading Bonapartists were convinced that an alliance with the Church was a necessity for the party.

The flirtations of Napoleon III with the anti-clerical elements in France, his Italian and his educational policy in the last decade of his reign were, to this section, the main causes of his downfall. They hoped that the new Pretender would resign his claims in favour of his son or that he would make a bargain with the leader of the Bonapartist party among the higher clergy, Cardinal de Bonnechose of Rouen, or that he would at least remain silent on the clerical question. Only so could the party be held together and such vigorous polemists as Paul de Cassagnac be saved from the temptations of Legitimism. Prince Napoleon went his own way; he continued his scandalous (and public) private life, and to the horror of many of his formal supporters, he announced his support of the expulsion of the congregations. To the Bonapartist leaders, who had hoped that the anger of the Catholics at this persecution would drive them into the arms of the only rival to the atheist Republic which offered any hope of deliverance, this policy was personally offensive and politically disastrous. But they were compelled to admit that the rank and file of the party in the provinces were less scandalized than were the upper-class leaders; that there were many adherents of the fallen Empire who had no love for the Church, that, as Napoleon III had discovered, in the alliance of Empire and Church it was far from certain that the Church brought as much as it took away.   Popular Bonapartism (and its strength lay in its popularity among the lower classes) was very different from the respectable Bonapartism of the salons—where the line between Legitimist and Imperialist was sometimes hard to draw.   Without some great popular movement, the sulky opposition of the best people in Paris and the provincial capitals would exhaust itself in social snubs to the agents of the detested Republic.

The despair of the Conservatives was revealed by the feeble efforts they made in the general election of 1881.   The leaders of the Bonapartists fought on the same side as the two Royalist factions, but the rank-and-file were indifferent.   The total anti-Republican vote was only half what it had been in 1877.   The Republic seemed to have triumphed definitively over all its external enemies.

CHAPTER III

THE PARLIAMENTARY REPUBLIC

I

THE new Chamber was controlled either by Gambetta or by Ferry; neither was safe without the other, but Gambetta was still the dominating figure, especially as the sudden difficulties of the Tunisian expedition[1] made Ferry's position impossible. Turning over the Presidency of the Chamber to Brisson, Gambetta was ready for the succession. Entangled in a mass of parliamentary formulas, the Ferry Government could not get the Chamber to support or disavow the Treaty of the Bardo. Gambetta saved not the Ministry but the treaty, and even Grévy realized that he must be given his chance.

For many months, public opinion had been dazzled by the thought of the return of Gambetta to power. If it was his enemies who launched the phrase 'the great Ministry' to describe the future Government, France and the world, which made such a difference between Gambetta and all other French politicians, *did* expect a great Ministry, no mere fourth plastering over of parliamentary cracks. It was to be a ministry of All the Talents. Ferry, Freycinet, Léon Say, were to be the supporters of the great man. Ferry was not asked, as he would have refused; Léon Say made impossible conditions, 'no loan, no conversion of the debt, no nationalization of the Orleans railway line'— and the prudent Freycinet abandoned the ship before it was launched instead of after it began to sink. The Ministry could only be great by the merits of its chief, not as a coalition of the great Republican leaders. What was to have been a Cabinet of All the Talents seemed, when its composition became known, to be a one-man show. It is true that the Minister of the Interior was Waldeck-Rousseau, who was to be a great figure in the Third Republic, but in 1881 he was simply a rising lawyer. Paul Bert went to the Ministry of Public Instruction and Public Worship where his combative anti-clericalism-cum-gallicanism was in place in the circumstances, but the composition of the Cabinet seemed to the suspicious to be evidence of the dictatorial tendencies of the Prime Minister. He wanted, it was asserted, only partisans and satellites round him.

[1] See p. 225.

From the first the Ministry was in difficulties. The question of amending the Constitution gave the Radicals their chance. How, demanded Clemenceau, could Gambetta limit in advance the sovereign authority of the National Assembly? How could he prevent it from abolishing the Senate whose mere existence was an affront to orthodox Republican doctrine? Practically, Gambetta's reason for limiting the action of the Assembly to a programme agreed on in advance between the two Houses was conclusive. Unless the Senate agreed, there could be no meeting of the National Assembly at all. It is true that once the Assembly met, deputies and senators lost their separate characters, but even a firmly Republican Senate which the Upper House now was, would not risk its own abolition. Clemenceau's point was only a debating point, but it was none the less effective with the many deputies who were looking for good doctrinal reasons for deserting the man who had been the great Republican leader.

Waldeck-Rousseau had infuriated practical politicians as much as Gambetta had annoyed theorists by a bold circular in which he announced his refusal to pay any attention to complaints or requests from deputies that were not sent through the prefects. To Waldeck-Rousseau this circular was merely asserting the obvious rules of administrative discipline; to the deputies it meant a substantial loss of effective power and, on a higher plane, meant that decisions affecting electors might be made by non-Republican officials, instead of by the men whom universal suffrage had chosen to see that no ill befell the Republic or Republicans. Gambetta, too, showed an indifference to this truth by giving important posts to a general and a journalist who had been more or less involved in the Sixteenth of May.

The real battle was fought over the electoral system. It was, or had been, standard Republican doctrine that the single-member constituency was a danger to effective popular sovereignty, as it had been a belief of the Right that their only chance of success was in the use of local influence. Experience had now taught the Republicans that they could do very well in single-member districts, and, while there was a platonic sentiment in favour of electing all the deputies of a department on one list (*scrutin de liste*), it was hard for deputies to be deeply hostile to a system that had worked so well for them. So when Gambetta tried to force the hands of the Chamber, by making electoral reform part of the proposed constitutional reform, the partisans of the *scrutin d'arrondissement* were angered. The view that in the *scrutin d'arrondissement* lay the safety of the Republic was not yet dogma, but the Republican cause was now a great vested interest in most districts. If these districts were merged, the local machines might find difficulty in functioning. It was all very well for the partisans of Gambetta to assert that France saw herself in a 'broken mirror'. If Gambetta had his way, it was feared, France would have no chance to see anything but Gambetta and his teams of carpet-baggers sent down from Paris with a specious programme drawn up by the great demagogue and competing successfully with local men whose appeal was not very potent outside their own small circle. The committee appointed to consider Gambetta's proposal had only one partisan of the Prime Minister on it. It reported against his measure and the Chamber backed it up. Gambetta resigned: the great Ministry had lasted seventy-seven days.

Gambetta had written to his mistress, Léonie Léon, a fortnight before he fell, that he was playing 'double or quits. They will pass under the Caudine Forks or I shall leave them to their irremediable impotence'. The Chamber did not want any person or institution to be potent save itself; to the degree that a large assembly can govern a country, the Chamber would govern it. What the Chamber could not do would not be done—and, in the Radical Republican tradition, there was a strong element of anarchical suspicion of all government. Above all, that tradition was suspicious of the government of one man.

The vested interests of the deputies were now safe and so were other vested interests, for Gambetta had dreamed dreams of drastic reforms of the taxing system and in Allain-Targé he had found a Minister of Finance who was not to be intimidated by the rulers of the Bourse or by the great companies. He was a predecessor of the numerous left-wing financiers who have assailed the Jericho of high finance with noisy attacks which the capitalist Jericho has successfully resisted—of course, it has never had to fear much more than noise.

In the grand penitence that followed the war, the National Assembly had projected a rigorous reduction of public expenses, by the abolition of such useless officials as sub-prefects, by the reduction of the large incomes of the departmental-treasurers whose rôle as Government bankers had very little obvious justification in a country now unified by railways and telegraphs, by the abolition of the many minor posts in the bureaucracy which had few duties if low pay. It proved harder to abolish the sub-prefectures than the Empire, and, by the time the Republicans were well in the saddle, their horror of jobbery had lost its old fanatical character. The general prosperity which helped to anchor the new régime in popular esteem, also deprived its leaders of any temptation to pursue an ascetic financial policy. It was possible to reduce unpopular taxes and yet produce impressive budgets. It was also possible to resume the policy that had accounted for so much of the splendour of the Second Empire, the policy of great public works. It was not merely a matter of finishing the new Opera or building the Trocadero. It was by building railways and roads that Napoleon III's Government had made its beneficence visible in many remote regions of France. The Third Republic was soon to surpass the Second Empire.

The programme of 'great public works' was launched very appropriately in 1878, after the submission of the Marshal, in the year of
the great Exhibition that advertised the triumph of the Republic.
It was backed by the advertising genius of Gambetta, the technical
competence of Charles de Freycinet, and the financial competence of
Léon Say. It was Say who found the means of borrowing the
cost at 3 per cent. without swamping the market, and Freycinet who
was in charge of the investigations of what was needed and how it was
to be done. The desire of Gambetta to make the Republic splendid,
as well as to win to it the allegiance of the great masses which still
hankered after the flesh-pots of the Empire, made him a warm sup-
porter of the great enterprise. If the scheme did not do all that its
authors hoped for, it was not altogether their fault. The good years
of the late 'seventies were followed by the bad years of the early
'eighties, and the financing of the schemes became less easy as the
question of what to do with the budget surplus ceased to have any
urgency.

More serious were the extravagances and follies that resulted from
the weakening of executive authority. A strong Ministry, sure of a
long life, might have been in a position to defy the demands of deputies
and senators where those demands had only electoral justification.
One main object of the scheme, for instance, was to do for Le Havre
and Marseilles what Germany had done for Hamburg, to create great
modern ports fit for all the demands of trade. But there were many
little ports which were not willing to see a few great rivals get all the
money, and, in order to get the programme through, it was necessary
to burden it with port-works of no real utility, except to the contractors—and, of course, to the local politicians. The main object of
the great project was the completion of the railway system, the resumption of one of the greatest enterprises of the Second Empire. Here,
too, the comparatively modest plans of the engineers were overloaded
with more optimistic projects for lines without any economic justification, lines whose only freight would be votes or which, if baptized
by the magic name 'strategic', had no relation to any strategy but
that of electoral campaigns.

The amount of pure waste must not be exaggerated. Even the
numerous light railways laid down in rural districts, if impossible to
justify from an accountant's viewpoint, did break down the isolation
of rural life and, in that way, spread Republican principles among a
Conservative population which was immediately gratified by the
money spent in its behalf and, in the long run, was shaken out of its
traditional way of life. The political lesson was easy to learn; no
prudence in the plan, no caution in its early execution could secure
any policy involving great public expenditure from the necessity of
having to pay a very heavy toll to politics. No Ministry could save

the general interests except at great political risk. In vain, critics from the old defeated parties, Buffet or Rouher, attacked Republican Finance Ministers like Magnin. The public was not moved if financiers were. This policy had an immediate consequence that made what the public thought of only intermittent importance. Republican finance soon came to involve constant borrowing, and politicians found, with an indignation in rough proportion to their naïveté, that it was not enough to want to borrow, one must find someone willing to lend or one must impose a system of really rigorous taxes which would be politically disastrous. Léon Say noted that many politicians thought it was as easy to pass a law raising a loan as a law on game licences: when they discovered that it was not, their righteous indignation at the tyranny of the bankers knew no verbal bounds.

For some years after the accession to power of the Republicans, the bankers got no chance to exercise their tyranny. In face of budget surpluses and a constant rise in both Government securities and in such private favourites of the investor as the obligations of the great railways, it was difficult to make the economical but timid French investor frightened by the very name of Republic and the first years of Republican control were boom years on the Bourse. There was a real-estate boom, too, above all in Paris, where the golden days of Haussmann seemed to have returned. It was easy for the Government to borrow, and to borrow cheaply, while the great rise in revenue that accompanied the boom made it practicable both to reduce the severity of the more unpopular taxes and yet to present budget surpluses. In the summer of 1880, the Minister, Magnin, could still justify a bold policy of reduction of taxes by admitting its boldness yet declaring that 'face to face with this great democracy, so prudent, so industrious, so thrifty, I have no fears'.

By the time Gambetta came into power these golden days were over. The 1880 budget was the last for a long time which had even an apparent surplus to show. A slump was under way, and it revealed itself in the limited success of the loan of 1881 which was adequate but no longer brilliant. The Government could no longer do without loans if it proposed to keep its extraordinary budget going; revenue just met the regular costs, all the extras would have to be paid for out of loans.

There was an effective deficit of nearly £30,000,000 in 1881 and no very obvious means of reducing it—except by reducing expenditure. That was politically impossible, for the Republic had already acquired a reputation for generosity that put the Empire to shame. Generosity in minor things like the 8,000,000 francs [1] that was voted to provide pensions for the victims of the *coup d'état* of 1851 and generosity in big things, for the educational reforms were costly and the Chamber, which

---

[1] £320,000 a year ($1,600,000).

had no desire to make them unpopular by putting some of the burden on the local authorities or, indeed, to encourage the view that educational expenditure, any more than policy, was subject to local control, put the whole burden on the National Treasury. From 1877 to 1882, the costs of education more than doubled, and if the total figure was still modest, a little over £4,000,000 on one calculation, a little over £5,000,000 on another,[1] it was not negligible in an era of deficits, when it would be necessary to borrow from classes in little sympathy with the objects of this particular expenditure. The Army, the Navy, the colonies, the Tunisian expedition, salaries, pensions, all cost more.

The Republican fiscal administration was more 'popular' than that of the Conservatives had been. The rigid and, in many ways, deservedly upopular tax system that had remained fundamentally unchanged from the time of Napoleon I, was among the first departments of Government to feel the effects of the emollient character of Republican administration. There were far fewer prosecutions for evasion of taxes, delays were more easily secured, and if these benefits were in some degree justified by the onerous nature of the cumbrous system whose working these adjustments oiled, the methods whereby they were secured had a less defensible side. For it was soon realized that to get a tax collector to see light it was advisable to call in the influence of the local Republican deputy or senator, who would very often successfully go to the tax-collector's chief, the Minister, or when the system had got really working, avoid bothering that busy man with details and go straight to the bureau chief. It was widely suspected that in making these representations to authority, deputies and senators went on the principle that the Republic owed justice to all, but favours only to its friends, a belief that increased the number of friends but did not make for general confidence in the impartiality of the fiscal system. In the long fight over income tax in France, many silly things were said and many disingenuous arguments used against the system, but some of their emotional force came from the general belief that taxes were collected with more rigour from the enemies of the régime than from its friends—and among the potential income-tax payers, there were more enemies than friends.

In mass and in detail, the deputies, by 1881, had made it plain that the rules of financial orthodoxy had little appeal for them. Lip service might be paid to it when it was necessary to submit to the admonitions of a purist like Léon Say, but as soon as it was possible to do without such symbolic figures, the politicians fell back on their old unexpressed principles; never raise by taxes what you can borrow, never, in any case, raise taxes before an election, spend your surpluses, if any, and leave your deficits to be liquidated by your successors. The Right might sneer and scold, but who cared what they said?

[1] $20,000,000 or $25,000,000.

The average elector was content with a fiscal policy whose immediate results were gratifying and whose dangers were stressed only by the enemies of the Republic and the friends of the Jesuits. Such a system put a great deal of power into the hands of the large body of Republican deputies, powers which, in less enlightened ages, might have been used for discreditable ends, but in a republic what was to be feared? 'Probity,' said Charles Floquet, 'that old, vulgar probity . . . ought to remain the distinctive mark and the stainless flag of all the true Republicans.' No one could say fairer than that.

However great the supply of probity (it was less than Floquet's electors believed) it was no substitute for credit, as Allain-Targé discovered. It was all very well for Gambetta's Minister of Finance to announce, in those confident terms to which the French public has had so much opportunity to get accustomed, that the budget had been planned with the intention of 'securing an unshakable financial foundation to the democratic policy' that was, of course, to be followed. The pessimistic prognostications of Léon Say that had made him refuse the Finance Ministry—except on his own terms—and had found expression in his subsequent writings, were all too well founded. There was a very large and increasing floating debt; there was a real deficit in the neighbourhood of £24,000,000.[1] If the floating debt increased there would be a general expectation of a loan, and in the depressed state of the market, borrowing would be expensive, conversion impossible, while the buying up of even one railway would be but another extension of the range of Government financing, already stretched too far by the Freycinet plan.

A strong Government might have been able to put the railway companies in their place. Were they not, as Gambetta's organ, *La République Française*, had declared, 'a State within the State . . . a power left in the hands of directors whose chief claim is that they are the most open enemies of our political institutions'? But the collapse of the Gambetta Ministry saved the companies from attack and the Orleans company from nationalization. If Republican institutions could not produce a strong Government, they could not hope successfully to combat great economic combinations whose rulers were not harassed by their shareholders as Ministers were by the Chamber.

Allain-Targé was replaced by Léon Say, who thought that a Government which could not pay its way had to humour the people from whom it proposed to borrow the money to carry on. He proposed to consolidate the floating debt, to cut down the 'extraordinary expenses', that is, the deficit, by two-thirds, though that meant diminishing the supply of manna and quails that was so helpful politically; and, far from attacking the railway companies, he proposed to get them to find the money to meet the new net deficit of £10,000,000 by

[1] $120,000,000.

a loan which would be set off against their obligations to the Treasury. Gambetta was only too right; the era of perils was over and the era of difficulties had come—and the Republican political system was much better fitted to deal with perils than with difficulties.

The immediate cause of the financial troubles that befell France and its Government was the 'krach' of the *Union Générale*. From small beginnings in Lyons, this bank had grown very rapidly. It was to free (so its chief, Bontoux, declared) the Catholics of France from their dependence on the two great groups that dominated high finance, the Jewish and Protestant bankers. Its operations were followed with blind faith by all classes of Catholics; its stock soared to fantastic heights and its activities had a great deal to do with the boom of 1880 and 1881. By November, 1881, ordinary shares of the *Union Générale*, whose nominal value was 500 francs, were selling round 3,000. Within a year the decline had set in and it turned into a collapse, whose consequences spread to every part of the French financial system. Although the *Union Générale* foundered, the other interests involved were salvaged, and by the end of February, 1882, the worst was known. The assault on the Jewish-Protestant hegemony had failed, failed as thousands of ruined Catholics believed, because those allied powers had seen, with pleasure, the ruin of a powerful rival.

This belief was naïve. It is unlikely that religious fanaticism induced bankers to run the risk of demoralizing the whole capital market, but if the older banks did not kill, it is possible that 'they did not strive officiously to keep alive' an institution with such special facilities for tapping savings as a great Catholic bank would have had in France. If the failure weakened enemies of the Republic, it weakened the Government too, for although the panic was kept from spreading, it effectually killed the boom, ended the seven fat years, and helped to breed the anger and scepticism which was to endanger the very régime that had seemed so secure when universal suffrage had given its blessing to the dominant party in 1881.

The toll taken by the phylloxera,[1] the deficits in international trade balances caused by bad harvests, the general depression of world economy that affected politics in all countries, all combined to make the unreality of some sides of French politics apparent. It was all very well for the eminent political chemist, Paul Bert, to drink at Auxerre to the destruction of the phylloxera, 'both kinds of phylloxera', that is both the disease that was ruining so many wine-growers, and the Jesuits. If the Burgundian peasants were satisfied with these pleasantries, the town workers were not. They wanted more than priest to eat.

If Gambetta's fate proved that it was easy to fail by attempting too much, Freycinet's second administration proved that it was possible to fall, less gloriously, by attempting nothing at all. While Léon Say

---

[1] Phylloxera, the deadly disease that almost killed European wine-growing.

was retreating in good order from the advanced financial positions occupied by Allain-Targé, his chief was faced with a problem affecting the position and prestige of France which divided the Chamber into two strongly opposed groups. Should France do nothing in Egypt? Should she do a great deal, thereby risking a good deal? The Radicals were for doing nothing, taking no risks, of loss of life, or of money, and, of course, of moral strength, in repressing the revolt of a people rightly struggling to be free. Gambetta was indignant at the abandonment of a great French diplomatic asset. Freycinet did a little, enough to anger Clemenceau, not enough to please Gambetta. What did this policy of sending troops to the Suez Canal mean? 'Is it peace?' asked Clemenceau. 'No, for troops are to be sent. Is it war? No, for they won't fight.' The Chamber refused to support this policy by an overwhelming majority.

Freycinet was out and, after refusals by himself and Ferry to attempt to form Governments, the 'seaside' Ministry of Duclerc was formed. The Chamber was anxious to go on holiday and this elderly contemporary of Grévy, with a Ministry largely composed of Gambettists, would do to manage the current business till the Chamber came back. The office of Prime Minister had changed hands six times since Grévy had taken office. It was no wonder that authority was contemned, that there were riots, Socialist demonstrations, Legitimist demonstrations, Imperialist demonstrations, or that the Chamber, when it returned, should have demonstrated its irritation by attacks on the families of the Pretenders who represented a principle of executive authority very unlike that which the Republic was revealing as her own. The Duclerc Government fell.

A few days before, on December 31st, there occurred a greater blow to the principle of a strong executive than the fall of the Duclerc Ministry. Gambetta had died. He had long been in poor health; he was more and more preoccupied with his mistress,[1] and an accident that would not have mattered to a more robust man was fatal to him. There was, of course, a national funeral and formal sorrow. Victor Hugo took his grandchildren to look at the coffin and said, 'There lies a great citizen'. The active politicians did not want great citizens in their trade; the safe great man of the régime was to be a symbolic figure like Victor Hugo or like Anatole France or, once he had been dead for some years, Jean Jaurès. A living great man in politics was just a nuisance: for, except in dire emergency, the Third Republic had no more use for them than the First had for chemists. M. Clemenceau was to learn that.

The holiday Ministry of Duclerc, absurd as it was, was more impressive than the Fallières Ministry that followed. Not merely was

[1] Léonie Léon, who was to him what Kitty O'Shea was to Parnell, a serious distraction from politics.

this a further plastering, but it was a poor job at that; it lasted less than a month and it was Ferry's turn. He was now in a strong position; the Chamber was, if not ashamed of its frivolity, at least conscious of the need for some stability, and the death of Gambetta cleared the way for the dour Lorrainer. His followers and those of Gambetta had an overwhelming majority over any combination of Right and extreme Left. If they supported him, Clemenceau and Cassagnac could speak and combine in vain. The coalition thus formed was provided with an admirably descriptive name that was adopted by all parties. The 'Opportunists' were the sagacious Republican members whose hearts were with the Left, of course, but who realized that fundamental reforms should not be put through until the time was opportune, which, again of course, it seldom was. The elections of 1882 gave this party an equally complete control of the Senate. It was ready to make concessions to the sentiments of the uncompromising Left by enacting a law of divorce, a law which still further angered the Catholics. By giving trade unions full legal status and rights it attempted to win the tolerance of the elements that shouted Gambetta down, while professing, perhaps sincerely, to believe that the organizations of the workers, thus recognized by law, would stabilize the 'militants' and make of them sound, careful, trade-union leaders of the English type.

Two reforms of great political importance were closely connected. By removing the limitations on the rights of large communes to elect their own mayors, a real measure of decentralization was achieved, but one whose importance was as much political as administrative. The mayor, now chosen by the councillors, was still an officer of the Central Government, obliged to do a great deal of work for it and liable both to close control and to removal by the Minister of the Interior and his agents, the prefects. But, partly because of the political importance of local government elections from the point of view of recruiting the Senate, and partly because of the general passion for politics that marked the country, local elections were seldom fought on purely local issues. The personnel of local government bodies was composed of active politicians of all ranks, and the mayor of the big town and the chairman of the departmental council was almost always a deputy or senator and often a very important deputy or senator. Whatever the legal fiction might be, a prefect, or even a minister, would think twice before exercising his legal authority against a mayor who might be a maker or unmaker of ministries, especially if he were head of a great local dynasty like the Chautemps family in Touraine. In the next generation, Poincaré in the Meuse, Augagneur and then Herriot in Lyons, Clementel in the Puy-de-Dôme, were only examples of the intermingling of local and national politics which made it impossible to say offhand how much independent power a French municipality had. It depended on who was at the head of it, at least as much as on the formal law.[1]

With the freedom of election of all the communes, the question of reform of the Senate was inevitably connected in consequences if not in origin. The Radicals had not yet repented their dogmatic opposition to any second chamber, and the tactical reasons that had led Gambetta to try to make a deal with the Senate before asking it to agree to the meeting of the National Assembly were as powerful as ever. The Senate would not risk a revision unless the Chamber tied its hands in advance. No Radical Medea was going to get a chance to reform the Senate out of existence by putting the whole Constitution into the melting-pot. The Senate could afford to give satisfaction to the Left by abolishing public prayers and by accepting a declaration that no member of a former ruling family could be elected President, and that the method of constitutional revision could not be used to abolish the republican form of government, gestures which were superfluous or meaningless.

More important were the amendments which affected the Senate itself. The system of life senators was abolished, the existing life senators would remain, but, as they died out, their seats would be given to the more populous departments, although the representation of the departments remained far from equal, for the least populous department had three senators, while the most populous, even the Seine with Paris and its suburbs, had only ten. The Senate was still weighted against the industrial areas and it was still weighted against the big towns. It is true that the arrangement of 1875, whereby the tiniest village and the largest city in a department had each one vote in the college that chose the senators was done away with. The number of senatorial electors from a commune now ranged from one to twenty-four, according to the size of their municipal councils and so, rather remotely, according to their population. But the great cities, which were far more than twenty-four times as populous as the villages, were still greatly under-represented; the real beneficiaries of the reform were the middling county towns, the homes of the lawyers, doctors, *lycée* professors who were becoming the new governing class. The Senate was no longer predominantly rural; it was now mainly a body representing the fears, the prudence, the sentiments of the petty bourgeoisie of the scores of little local capitals of around ten and twenty thousand inhabitants.

The reform of the Senate was all to the political advantage of that body. Whatever chance the idea of life senators of great personal eminence had had was gone from the moment the Legitimists sold out to the Left. The replacement of the beneficiaries of parliamentary jobbery by elected representatives of the local political organizations

[1] Paris has remained divided into arrondissements, each with its own mayor.

could only strengthen the Senate. For the new members were bound to be either really important people in their own districts, or the representatives of really important people. Elected for nine years by ·a body composed of all the effective politicians, great and small, of his department, a senator was now the recipient of a mandate which if less mystically impressive than that conferred on deputies by universal suffrage, was yet a good deal more concrete.

As long as both houses remained of the same general political complexion, both Opportunist and only differing a little in the keenness of sight that enabled them to see how inopportune real change was, the strength of the Senate was not apparent. It was useful in that it allowed the Lower House, especially when an election was in the offing, to pass bold measures, directed against the Church or in favour of the workers, confident that the Senate would smother them. The tactics of the Senate in these matters was masterly and simple. It simply ignored the inconveniently radical measure and left it to moulder until the formal political demand became, over a period of years, a real demand which it was convenient to meet half-way. By that time, the demand had usually become more radical, so that the Senate when, at last, it got around to acting on the proposal, had to choose between a mild bill received some years before and a more violent one which the Chamber had passed in real or simulated indignation. Of course, it chose the mild bill which was resurrected from the grave where the Senate had laid it. No more effective device for avoiding the dangers of democratic rashness has been discovered. Of course, acting in this way, the Senate had to choose its ground with care, not to show the obstinate folly of an English House of Lords or the occasional pig-headedness of the Senate of the United States. It is a tribute to the sagacity of the French Senate that it has almost always managed to fight its battles with the Chamber from safe defensive positions. The shrewd politicians in the Upper House were— and are—excellent judges of the way the cat is jumping and can translate fiery words and lavish promises or threats into intelligible political language. Consequently, it has been mainly on finance that the two houses have differed, for the Senate knows full well that, as M. André Siegfried has put it, if the Frenchman's heart is on the Left his purse is on the Right.

It was not until 1896 that a Radical Ministry, and so one differing in character from the majority of the Senate, first came into office and proposed the desperate remedy of an income tax. The Senate took the offensive and passed votes of no confidence in the Ministry, thus claiming that the Cabinet was responsible to both houses, not merely together but separately.[1]

---

[1] As usual the Constitution cast no light on the problem. It merely said that the Ministers were 'responsible before the Chambers'.

Such a claim was outrageous, so the Radicals thought, but the Senate did not care what they thought. It went on strike, even going as far as to refuse the necessary vote of credit for the Madagascar expedition. The Radicals were angry; they were pathetic; they appealed to the sacred rights of universal suffrage and threatened with its wrath the mere representatives of restricted suffrage. Léon Bourgeois, the Prime Minister, was an eminent academic politician, but even he knew when he was beaten. He resigned and, from his time to the time of M. Léon Blum, Prime Ministers have learned that in a battle over finance with the Senate, the odds are on the Senate. It never fights the battle unless it is sure to win, that is unless it has strong reason to suspect that the Frenchmen-in-the-street and, still more, the politician in the local committee-room, is more worried about the financial situation than about the mystical dogmas that are so useful at elections but wear so badly when they have to be paid for.

The power of the Senate was not purely negative, for it became a reservoir of ministers. Its membership included many veterans past their best, but it also came to include more and more of the real leaders of the Republic. To sit for nine years instead of four, to be elected not by emotion-ridden electors but by sage and practised politicians and to suffer no real political disabilities in consequence, made the delights of being a senator appeal to more and more notables. As ministers, they could speak in either house and senators were just as likely to be ministers as were deputies. They were even more likely to be effective ministers, for, from the turn of the last century on, the Prime Ministers who have not been transient and embarrassed phantoms, the Prime Ministers who have carried programmes and carried Parliament with them, have all been senators. Waldeck-Rousseau, Combes, Clemenceau, Poincaré. That such careers were possible was, in great part, due to the reform of the Senate carried out by Jules Ferry, a reform which so greatly strengthened the body he was soon to adorn.

For the moment, however, Ferry was in command of the Lower House, at least as much in command as anybody could be. For it was now evident that French parliamentary practice and the ideas on which it was based gave little hope of providing a strong executive. The failure of Gambetta's attempt to build up a united and disciplined Republican party made the Prime Minister dependent on the allegiance of several groups. The misuse of the right of dissolution in 1877 had made it impossible for recourse to be had to that method of appealing from the delegates of universal suffrage to their theoretical master, the electors. The abolition of *scrutin de liste* had meant that the electors were tempted to choose local men on local issues, contenting themselves with formal adherence to vague doctrines of no immediate moment. No effective charge of disloyalty could be made against deputies who voted against their nominal leaders—if they were given an excuse to do so by an astute wrecker of ministries.

Procedure made it easy to provide the excuse: in the 'interpellation', the deputy was provided with a weapon against the Ministry that made the life of the latter a long or short series of hairbreadth escapes. Every deputy or senator was entitled to demand, in writing, an explanation of a specific act or a declaration of policy from the Government. The ministers were thus forced to make a declaration that might alienate some of their unstable supporters. The advantage was with the attack which could choose its ground ingeniously and frame questions of the classical 'have you stopped beating your wife?' type and, even if repulsed in that assault, could keep on coming back until the Government was put in a position in which it must offend one section or another of its indispensable nucleus of support. Then it was doomed; a new Government was formed, composed, as a rule, of some members of the old and of some of the more ingenious assailants.

Few systems could be more calculated to weaken the sense of common responsibility in the Cabinet or of honesty in opposition in the Chamber. It was true that the absence of an effective formal opposition, the belief that, whatever happened, the Conservatives were too weak to replace the Republicans, made the game possible without endangering the régime—for the moment. All that suffered was the independence of the executive, the strength of the administrative system and the long-term interests of France. Apart from any other drawbacks, the system imposed an intolerable burden on the ministers who were forced to be continually in the breach and whose time, when Parliament was sitting (as it was for more than half the year), was necessarily devoted to securing a respite until the rising of Parliament freed them for administration.[1]

The Chamber, and to a less degree, the Senate, from the first years of the constitutional system of 1875, made it plain that effective sovereignty was in their hands, that the Cabinet only held its power by a temporary delegation that might be, and very often was, quickly withdrawn. For the effective exercise of this power, however, the Chamber was not well organized, and the Senate was even less so. Whether from a repulsion from the precedent of the governing committees of the Convention which bred a resolution not to create a new Committee of Public Safety, or from mere reluctance to delegate any part of its power, the Chamber was very slow to organize an effective committee system. Before 1902 the only permanent committee was on finance. All other

---

[1] When it is remembered that it is possible to have a vote on each phrase of a resolution of confidence or no-confidence, following on an interpellation, it is easy to see what opportunities for ingenious drafting fall to an opposition leader. If he can pick up enough support on any part of the resolution, the Government is fatally weakened. Even if the Government carries a vote of confidence, it is in order to try to add an amendment which in effect reopens the whole question.

committees were set up to deal with one particular proposal or problem and were recruited, not straight from the Chamber in proportion to the size of each group, but from the *bureaux*. The *bureaux* were simply groups of deputies to which members were assigned by lot and for one month at a time. A *bureau*, then, did not need to be possessed of any homogeneity and could not, owing to its short life, develop any corporate spirit or tradition. As the committees were chosen on the basis of so many members from each *bureau*, the accidental character of the composition of the *bureaux* might result in committees being very unrepresentative of the temper of the house. Thus the committee which dealt with and reported against Gambetta's constitutional proposals in January 1882 was far more hostile to his Government than the Chamber as a whole was. If the majorities in the Chamber had been more stable and party discipline could have been relied on, this would have mattered less, but a committee reporting adversely on a Government project or giving a hostile turn to an investigation was not faced with a loyal Chamber rallying to its leaders, the ministers, but with an amorphous body, often more anxious to spot the winners of the next cabinet crisis than to support the winners of the last one.

It was a tribute to Ferry's courage and tenacity that he was able, with such institutions, to carry out his ambitious colonial programme, to secure the limited revision of the constitution and to enact such important financial measures as a conversion of a large part of the debt. He was strong enough, too, to make a settlement with the great railway companies on terms favourable to the latter and very offensive to the proclaimed principles of the Radicals. He had, by suspending for a short time the law that made it impossible to remove judges, 'purified' the Bench, that is removed judges whose loyalty to the new order was suspect. This was a very great blow to the Catholic bourgeoisie who saw one of the most prized of their preserves taken from them, and though there had been vague talk of using the occasion to cut down the number of judges which was certainly too great, the vacant jobs were of course not abolished but given to the deserving members or friends of the new governing class. It was not this measure, any more than the war on the Jesuits, or the secularization of education that brought down Ferry and introduced a new period of indiscipline, but the course of the war in Tonkin.

The dying Chamber had realized how detested the colonial policy had become and the continued depression had diminished the popularity, if not of the Republic, at least of the Republicans. It did not appreciate these facts at their true importance or it would not have run the risk of restoring the *scrutin de liste*. That system was excellently designed to let great waves of public opinion sweep away local issues and local men. Had the Republicans been united, had Gambetta lived or Ferry not been overthrown, the damage might have been slight. But in 1885 the Conservative vote more than doubled; on the first ballot, there were only 127 Republicans elected—and 176 Conservatives.[1] Panic drew the Republican factions together. 'Republican discipline' was invoked, that is the Republican candidates who had got the highest vote in the first ballot were given a clear run against the Conservatives. The final result gave a handsome majority in seats to the Republicans, but the popular vote showed a recovery of the Conservatives or a loss of faith in the Republicans that was, on the surface, as ominous as the opposition gains in 1869 had been for the Empire. The régime, then, was not as stable as it looked and the new Chamber had no such central dominant block as the alliance of the followers of Ferry and Gambetta had provided in the old. There were things that united the new majority; such as the unseating of twenty-two Conservative Deputies for electoral offences, in accordance with the traditional French principle that only members of the minority are ever elected illegally, but there was no person and no group in command. The Brisson Government had only held office to carry through the elections. Its refusal to provide for the immediate evacuation of Tonkin was the ostensible cause of its fall, though the continuance of French rule in Tonkin to this day makes this cause seem rather inadequate; but a new Ministry had to be found. So the 'white mouse', the pliable Freycinet, obliged and, as a sop to the Radicals, took as his War Minister, Boulanger.

[1] French law and custom, like American, distinguish between a majority and a plurality. In an election, if no candidate gets a clear majority over all the other candidates, a second ballot is held at which a mere plurality, i.e. the receipt of more votes than any other candidate, suffices. Between the first and second ballot, the real party adjustments are made, the winner in the first becoming the candidate of all the allied parties and groups. The first ballot is thus like an American primary, a means of discovering which section or which leader of an electoral alliance appeals most to the voters and so is the destined standard-bearer.

BOOK IV

THE REPUBLIC IN DANGER

And every one that was in distress, and every one that was in debt, and every one that was discontented, gathered themselves unto him; and he became a captain over them.

I *Samuel* xxii. 1.

CHAPTER I

BOULANGER

On July 2nd, 1886, the British Ambassador in Paris, Lord Lyons, wrote to his chief that 'the Republic here has lasted sixteen years and that is about the time which it takes to make the French tired of a form of government'. No régime since the Revolution had lasted twenty years. The Republic, in 1886, was giving signs to the world and to France, that she, like her predecessors, might well prove mortal when attacked by the diseases that had killed them, the diseases of habit, of boredom, of being something that the new generations now coming to maturity had not made for themselves, but had inherited from their fathers. Since 1789, no form of government in France had survived the ordeal of the younger generations knocking at the door. 'How lovely the Republic was under the Empire,' the lapidary phrase of the comic artist, Forain, summed up all the disillusionment with which the political zealot, young or old, looked on a Government without brilliance and without stability, but above all, without glory. The hopes of a speedy revenge on the victors of 1870 were now dead in the breasts of most of the rulers of France. Grévy had been right, it seemed.

This policy of renunciation (which could not be openly avowed) had no popular appeal, and in the overthrow of Ferry, two forces had been at work, a sceptical pacificism that doubted the value of the colonial triumphs and strongly objected to their cost, and an indignant nationalist feeling that saw in Ferry a traitor, playing Bismarck's game, turning the eyes of Frenchmen from the Vosges and wasting, on the banks of tropical rivers, blood and treasure that should be husbanded till the day came when France would fight for her share of the Rhine. Which of these two sentiments was the stronger in the country remained to be seen. There was no doubt which was stronger in Paris. The continued isolation of France, the lack of glamour in the Government, the reluctant appreciation of how solid the work of Bismarck was, and all the personal and general passions these facts provoked or covered, would have found some outlet had Georges Boulanger never been born, but luck and a curious combination of assets made the general who, in January 1886, became Minister of War in the Third Freycinet Cabinet,

183

appear to be the predestined instrument of all the enemies of the Republic of Ferry—and of Bismarck.

Young as modern generals go, Boulanger was under fifty.[1] In Africa, in Italy, in Cochin-China, the young officer redeemed by great bravery and several wounds a far from distinguished career at Saint-Cyr. He later returned to the military school as instructor, a chance that enabled him to gain the admiration of many future officers, to escape the disasters that led most of his comrades to early captivity in Germany, and to win very rapid promotion in the defence of Paris. Luck did not desert Colonel Boulanger, for he was wounded again at the beginning of the fighting in Paris, thus earning further promotion and also escaping that responsibility for the massacres of the *communards*, which was to weigh so heavily on the reputations and careers of soldiers like Gallifet. Boulanger continued to climb. His war-time promotions were finally confirmed and, so long as it paid, Boulanger was a model of Catholic and Conservative sentiment and practice. He was sent to America to represent France at the centenary of Yorktown and then made chief inspector of infantry. By 1881, however, Boulanger was a devoted Republican and on good terms with the Radical leader, Clemenceau, like him an old boy of the *lycée* of Nantes. Sent to Tunis to command the Army of Occupation, he showed that, Republican as he might be, he would defend the rights—or privileges— of the Army against mere civilians like the Resident, Paul Cambon. Boulanger's methods recalled a little too much the soldiers of the First Empire, and the 'pékins' [2] finally manœuvred him out of his position. He was thus available for the political combinations of Clemenceau, whose will it was that made of the youngest general in the Army, the new Minister of War.

Boulanger had owed his rise to luck, bravery, and ardent ambition, combined with the talents of a courtier. Now that he was a public figure, he had other assets to put on the market. Blue-eyed, reddish-haired, giving an impression of youth and energy, the new Minister made one of his most important decisions when he let his blond beard grow. France had before her, surrounded by drab civilians, this attractive figure, and in contrast with the grey whiskers of the President, the blond beard of the Minister of War.

Boulanger had shown that he could cultivate the right friends in the right places at the right time. He was now to show that he could flatter mobs and regiments as well as individuals. As Minister of War he was energetic and, what was more important, he was noisy. His predecessors had only slowly realized that the change from a professional Army of the old type to one based on universal service, involved new

---

[1] He was born in 1837 of a Breton father and a Welsh mother.
[2] Contemptuous slang term for 'civilian'.

standards of cleanliness and comfort, more intelligent and flexible discipline. Some minor adjustments had been made; others were planned. Boulanger quickly put into effect most of those which had been planned and accepted credit for those carried out before him. The food, the lodging, the clothing of the troops was improved and special efforts were made to win the gratitude of the non-commissioned officers. The morale of the Army was looked after. Regimental spirit was encouraged; recruits were welcomed with military music; sentry-boxes painted in the national colours; all trifles, but important trifles. It was the veteran Orleanist general, Changarnier, who said that Boulanger had again taught the French Army to 'wear its cap on the side of its head'.

Boulanger was the Radical Minister as well as the protector of the rank-and-file. The Radicals had put him in the War Office, what would he do for them? What he did was symbolic but none the less important. The success of the Conservatives at the elections of 1885 had alarmed and irritated the Left. The votes cast for the Conservatives had not been much less than those given to the Republican parties —and the Pretenders were living in France! The Comte de Paris was very rich; he lived in the capital and in his châteaux like a sovereign. In Parisian society, he was the chief, and no social climber like Swann would for a moment have thought of preferring an invitation from any Republican dignitary, from the President downwards, to one from the Comte de Paris. A Royal marriage, celebrated in Paris with a social splendour far beyond the resources of the Élysée, was the excuse for a Republican counter-attack.[1]

A law was speedily passed exiling from France the heads of former reigning families; and members of these families could not enter either the Army or Navy. The restriction, on the face of it, applied only to those princes who might wish to become soldiers or sailors; it preserved the rights of the princes who were already serving. But Boulanger, passing beyond the text of the law, deprived of their commands all the princes, chief of the victims being the brilliant Duc d'Aumale, under whom the Minister had served. This decision was an outrage to the Royalists, a token of good faith to the Radicals who now felt like some old Jacobins after the execution of the Duc d'Enghien, that this implacable enemy of the Bourbons was indeed their man. An indignant letter of protest by the Duke led to his exile and to a duel between Boulanger and a Royalist partisan in which the pistol of the Minister of War failed to go off. More important, if not quite as ominous, was a controversy in which Boulanger, who had been taxed with ingratitude, denied owing anything to the Duc d'Aumale. When a letter of his was

---

[1] According to one story, Clemenceau was held up for a long time by the traffic jam caused by the reception given in honour of the marriage, and this was one of the causes of his anger.

printed in which he thanked the Duke, in very warm words, for his kindness, he denied the authenticity of the letter. When it was published in facsimile, the Minister replied with vague threats and protestations of Republican loyalty. The hero of the Radicals was revealed as an energetic but incompetent liar, but those Frenchmen who wanted a hero were not shocked; after all, Bonaparte himself had had no blind devotion to veracity.

Boulanger gave new proof of his intention to republicanize the Army. He removed from their usual garrisons regiments whose officers were suspected of too overt devotion to former dynasties; he imposed public rebukes or dismissal on officers far senior to himself who seemed to question his authority: and he gave indisputable rhetorical proof of his love for the people during the great strike at Decazeville. The violence of the strikers had been answered by a military occupation, a normal enough reply, but one dangerous to the reputation of a political soldier like Boulanger. He escaped from his dilemma by the most famous of his speeches, in which he defended the Army against Socialist charges. It was not attacking the miners, he declared. 'At this moment, perhaps every soldier is sharing his rations with a miner.' This kindly thought enabled Boulanger to escape both horns of the dilemma. He was a friend of order—and of the workers. Who else was both?

It was the great review at Longchamps on July 14th, 1886, which revealed to the astounded and irritated politicians that, for the first time since Gambetta, perhaps for the first time since the rise of Napoleon III, one man had captured the hearts of millions of Frenchmen. Nothing like it had been seen since that day, used by old Parisians as the standard of popular frenzy, the return of the Army of Italy in 1859. Mounted on a black horse which became at once almost as famous and popular as its rider,[1] Boulanger, in full uniform, surrounded by his staff, completely eclipsed the President. Boulanger rode back to Paris as part of Grévy's escort: the ride was a new triumph and the night was another. He had ceased to be a general on the make, or an Army reformer; he had become an idol and the incarnation of a great national movement.

He received his consecration from the popular songs. Fletcher of Saltoun's wise friend might have regarded the music-hall singer, Paulus, as the real author of Boulangism. *En revenant de la revue* became the first and most famous of the innumerable songs written in honour of the national hero.[2] Millions repeated the lines:

---

[1] Critics said that 'Tunis' was a poor specimen of its kind and Boulanger an indifferent rider, but from the point of view of the man in the street Boulanger and his horse were just what they should be.

[2] Some assert that Paulus had thought of celebrating other military heroes and merely chose Boulanger because he was in the public eye at the moment.

Gais et contents
Nous marchions triomphants,
En allant à Longchamp,
Le cœur à l'aise,
Sans hésiter,
Car nous allions fêter
Voir et complimenter
L'Armée française.

With the success of the song sung at the Alcazar, a new Boulanger appeared. It was not as the friend of miners or the enemy of princes that he had been acclaimed by the crowds which had poured out of Paris to 'pay its respects to the French Army'. It was as the emblem of French military pride and hope, the man who would make the Army of Sedan, the Army of Austerlitz. Soon he was to be 'General Victory'.

Regardez-le là-bas! Il nous sourit et passe:
Il vient de délivrer la Lorraine et l'Alsace.

A year later Jules Ferry was to refer contemptuously to Boulanger as a 'music-hall Saint-Arnaud' [1] but, as Jacques Bainville said, it is not given to everybody to become a music-hall hero. The sneers of Ferry, or of any other French politician, mattered little to the fanatics who now rallied round the general, for Boulanger was, by German testimony, above all by the testimony of Bismarck in his speech in the Reichstag on January 11th, 1887, the greatest danger to good relations between France and Germany. Whatever doubts the man in the street had had were swept away. Bismarck had named his enemy. There could be only one reply, a rally to the hero by all true Frenchmen. They could now see him in his true light:

D'un éclair de ton sabre, éveille l'aube blanche,
À nos jeunes drapeaux, viens montrer le chemin
Pour marcher vers le Rhin, pour marcher vers le Rhin:
Parais, nous t'attendons, ô général Revanche.

[1] Marshal de Saint-Arnaud was the Minister of War who carried out the *coup d'état* of December 2nd, 1851.

CHAPTER II

DÉROULÈDE

THE idea of revenge for 1870, of a war to recover the lost provinces, had in France its regular and open organization and its chief in the League of Patriots and Paul Déroulède. Few Frenchmen in their hearts had abandoned all hope of undoing the Treaty of Frankfort and fewer would have dared to admit their final acceptance of the treaty in public, but there were so many other internal and external questions. The odds against a French triumph, single-handed, over Germany lengthened. The nation was not willing to devote all national resources and all national thought to this one question. Paul Déroulède was. He had served in the war. He had been a prisoner in Germany but had escaped; and had fought against the Commune. The disasters of 1870 had made him the man of one idea and he grouped round him the most active members of the minority of Frenchmen for whom there was only one question. Déroulède was a great orator; he had written immensely popular patriotic poems, but he had never managed to create a great mass movement. With the death of Gambetta, whom Déroulède had trusted, it became obvious that there was nothing to be got from the politicians. The League of Patriots, which Déroulède had attempted to keep non-partisan as long as all parties were united in their resolve to undo the crime of 1871, became more and more an organization for revising and reforming the Constitution as a means to the war of revenge. Only a strong executive could plan and carry out a policy so bold, calling for such foresight and tenacity. And the inevitable fate of constitutional reform under the present régime had been made manifest by the way in which Jules Ferry had been able to make the revision of 1884 farcical.

Déroulède had been in touch with Boulanger since the general had come to the War Office as Inspector of Infantry and he had sounded him when he became Minister. As was his habit, Boulanger listened, uttered polite formulas of agreement and committed himself to nothing. Nor for the moment did Déroulède want more. His great scheme was to win over Russia to a French alliance by affecting public opinion in that country and the opinion of the Tsar himself through the influence of Katkov, the famous Panslav editor. With Russia detached from Germany and a strong Government in Paris, the good work could begin. Déroulède did not realize that the Boulangist agitation, far from impressing the Tsar, made him more suspicious than ever of a State in which such disorder could be permitted and in which a man like Boulanger could be so powerful.

The time for testing the strength of the Russian cobwebs spun by Déroulède and Katkov was not yet come. First of all, Déroulède had to convince the general that it was his duty and interest to put himself at the head of a great national movement. He promised Boulanger the support of his '300,000 leaguers', a vast exaggeration of their numbers, but they were not negligible all the same. As long as Boulanger was a Minister, he was bound to some loyalty to his colleagues—and Boulanger liked being Minister. Boulanger, too, had reason to suspect that the politicians who had welcomed him into the Government would now gladly usher him out of it. His Army reforms, his demands for money for the new magazine rifles he was determined to issue to the troops, even his love of the limelight, could be tolerated or approved, but though Boulanger remained at the War Office when Freycinet was replaced by Goblet, his fundamental frivolity alarmed the more prudent politicians. When Bismarck named him as a danger to peace, he seemed prepared to do everything to justify the Chancellor's fears. Only the timely confession of a subordinate revealed and prevented his despatching a personal letter to the Tsar and, when the Foreign Minister taxed him with this extraordinary usurpation, Boulanger fell back on his standard defence, announced that the accusation was a lie and left the Cabinet meeting.

German military preparations were now on a scale that was, for those simple days, unprecedented in peace-time, and Boulanger was active in counter-measures. It was, and is, hard to decide whether Bismarck or Boulanger was really the aggressor, but Bismarck knew what he was doing and Boulanger did not. The War Minister was all for drastic measures: he was alarmed, he said, as to the results of letting Germany begin war when she was ready and France was not. Grévy, who was convinced that if there was a war France would be beaten, coolly told Boulanger that the only difference was that he would have to fight his battle on the Marne and not on the Saar. Grévy and the civilian Ministers, as Bismarck realized, were all for peace; the danger was a seizure of power by Boulanger—or an incident. The incident came, the arrest of the French frontier agent, Schnaebele, by the German police. The French asserted that he had been seized on French soil; the Germans denied this and declared that he was an organizer of espionage in Alsace, which was true. There was all the raw material of a war of honour, but the fortunate discovery that Schnaebele had been invited in writing to meet his German colleagues and so was covered by what was equivalent to a safe-conduct, enabled Bismarck to release the prisoner. Boulanger, who was the main organizer of the spy system of which Schnaebele was part, had displayed all his usual frivolity. The public did not know this. They knew only that Bismarck had appeared to retreat. His climb-down must have been due to his fear of Boulanger. Déroulède, who had resigned the Presidency of the League of Patriots just before the Schnaebele affair, in despair at the timidity of the Government had lost heart too soon.

The Goblet Government fell in its turn and it was not easy to find it a successor, for the Chamber was divided between the Radicals, who still looked on Boulanger as one of their own, and the more cautious elements who regarded him as an enemy of peace and perhaps of the Republic. A campaign of Rochefort, the most violent of Paris editors and darling of the left-wing mobs, got 39,000 votes for the general at a by-election in Paris, although he was not a candidate. Such a success frightened more moderates into the belief that no Government was big enough to hold Boulanger. The Senate, too, let it be known that it would vote against any Ministry of which he was a part and, at last, with Catholic support, a Rouvier Ministry was formed—without Boulanger. For a moment, there had been fear of a *coup d'état* by the over-mighty Minister, but with outward good grace, he surrendered office. To return to the War Office was now his main ambition, and as the orthodox Republicans made it plain that he could never return with their permission, Boulanger began to listen to the bold men who now surrounded him and who saw in his popularity a way to power. Boulangism as a sentimental mass movement was stronger than ever. Boulangism as a party was being born.

The problem of the Government was what to do with Boulanger, for he must be got out of Paris before the 14th of July. An Elba was found, the command of the 13th Army Corps at Clermont-Ferrand. Buried in Auvergne, it was thought he would be able to do no harm and might soon be forgotten, but he was not yet in Auvergne. He was due to leave the Gare de Lyon on July 8th, but Paris was as upset at this news as at the flight of Louis XVI. An immense mob filled the station and the surrounding streets; there were shouts of 'To the Élysée'; there were fights with the police. If Boulanger had wished to put himself at the head of an *émeute*, there were all the materials present, but he was not ready for such drastic action. The hysterical mob singing the *Marseillaise*, the men who lay down on the rails to keep the train from moving, the feverish atmosphere of one of the 'days' of which Paris had the secret, all this intimidated rather than stimulated Boulanger. He allowed himself to be put on another engine and smuggled out of the station. He may have let an opportunity pass, but his party was not yet firmly constituted and he was not the bearer of a great name like Louis Napoleon, who could afford to risk failure.

The demonstration at the Gare de Lyon was only one sign, among many, of the mounting popularity of the general. Business had seen its opportunity and every kind of article was put under the invocation of his name and picture, as is done with royalty in coronation years. There were short and cheap lives of the general on sale; floods of verse; scores of songs. There were children's toys, the most interesting being a model which always bounced back on its feet 'with energy . . . a popular emblem of a France respected and the Republic saved'.

Once Boulanger was settled in Auvergne, the hopes of the Government seemed likely to be fulfilled. The general quarrelled with Jules Ferry and tried to force a duel on him. He inspected his troops; he tried on the phlegmatic Auvergnats the arts that had won the Parisians; but he seemed now a seven days' wonder whose power was gone, and the politicians, who had begun to fear him, recovered their equanimity.

CHAPTER III

THE CRISIS

I

'THE association of purity of morals with the Republican form of government, for which history furnishes no justification, is one of the most striking results of the pseudo-classical basis of the French Revolution.' Such was the comment of the most acute foreign observer of French affairs [1] on the Wilson scandal which interrupted and forwarded the development of the Boulangist crisis.

It was a private quarrel between two women that opened the sluices of scandal. One lady of indifferent morals had borrowed a dress from a kindred spirit and had refused to return it. The lover of the infuriated and defrauded woman denounced the borrower to the police as an agent in the sale of decorations; and 'la Limouzin', this odd fish from the Parisian underworld, was thrown up on the beach to public view, accused of espionage as well as of traffic in decorations. La Limouzin was trapped, and then came the turn of General Caffarel, who broke down, confessed and was dismissed from the Army. Caffarel was no shady nonentity; he was the soldier whom Boulanger had chosen as deputy-chief of the General Staff. He had a brilliant military record and, like so many more of his class, he had been ruined by the collapse of the *Union Générale*. After Caffarel came Senator and General Count d'Andlau who prudently disappeared, as well as a long train of minor agents in graft. Even M. d'Andlau was a small fish compared with the great political whale into whose hide the Captain Ahabs of the Paris press were now ready to hurl their harpoons. For the chief agent of corruption, it was asserted, was no less a person than that veteran Republican politician, Daniel Wilson, who, long important in his own right, was still more important since his marriage in 1881 to a daughter of President Grévy. The trail of scandal led straight from the dingy offices and hotels of the Paris of confidence tricksters and ladies of the town, to the Élysée, where M. Wilson resided as the permanent guest of his father-in-law and from which it was soon discovered (as the insiders had long known) that he had plied his trade.

At first sight, this state of affairs, however deplorable, did not

[1] J. E. C. Bodley.

directly involve the President. Had Grévy quickly disowned Wilson, he, and the presidency, might have escaped fatal discredit, but the family feeling of the Grévys was excessive even by the high French standard. One brother had been made a General, one a Senator and Governor-General of Algeria, and it was a current jest that it was a pity that no Grévy was a priest, for he would have been a cardinal. Grévy was ready as a good family man to protect his son-in-law and, in any case, he had a high regard for Wilson himself. His foreign name made it easy to attribute Wilson's character to his ancestry. He was said to be English or, as Lépine put it, a 'Yankee', but in fact, though of partially Scottish origin, he was descended on his mother's side from a member of the Convention.

It was perhaps this ancestry that suddenly turned one of the most lively men-about-town of the Second Empire into a Republican deputy and opponent of the régime and induced him to spend on politics the fortune which had hitherto earned him the grateful admiration of so many ladies. Even before his marriage, Wilson was a powerful political figure. His private political machine was well oiled with money, with private favours, with financial combinations, which if not strictly dishonest were far from exemplifying public purity. In a less brilliant way, Wilson was a Republican Morny. He used his position to bring pressure to bear on the Administration to make things easy for commercial friends of his and, in one of these acts of good fellowship, he was thwarted by the heir of a greater name than Grévy,—Carnot, the Minister of Finance. The main political expense for which Wilson needed irregular revenues to augment his own was the building up of a chain of newspapers. It became known that it was wise to patronize the Wilson press. It was also believed that it was easier to have your merits recognized by the grant of the Legion of Honour if M. Wilson had reason to think kindly of you, and it had long been known that Wilson conducted his private and political business from the Élysée, thus avoiding the expense of office rent and postage.[1]

The popular song that immediately made its appearance, 'What bad luck to have a son-in-law', did not convince the mob that all that Grévy suffered from was bad luck. For the President had developed one French quality to excess; he was reputed to be very mean and to be as ready as Wilson to save his own pocket at the public expense, and, unlike Wilson, he had no past of lavish generosity to earn pardon for present parsimony. Yet the President of the Republic was handsomely paid and lavishly provided for in other ways. He received £48,000 a year,[2] of which a very large proportion was saved.

It is true that economy in the Élysée was no novelty. Madame

---

[1] It was this abuse of franking that alone seems to have angered Wilson's loyal constituency in Touraine.

[2] $240,000. Grévy left £280,000 ($1,200,000), mostly saved from his presidential salary.

Thiers carried thrift to pathological extremes, but not only was there something grandly Balzacian in her behaviour, Thiers was not Grévy. France got her money's worth from Thiers, even if the presidential fruit was rotten, but Grévy's chief rôle was to incarnate the formal, not the real authority of the State, to imitate MacMahon not Thiers, and the Marshal Duke, as befitted a *grand seigneur*, had left office poorer than he entered it. In the reaction against Grévy this contempt for his meanness was mixed with the general dislike of his excessive self-satisfaction.

Grévy, who had been famous as the opponent of any presidency at all, once in office took up his rôle with a profound conviction that all was for the best in the best of all possible republics, with a Ciceronian belief that France was indeed lucky to have such a President and with an assumption, which his re-election fortified, that his right to be chief of the State was, if not divine, at least indefeasible. It was this illusion that made Grévy turn a deplorable but minor scandal into a great political storm in which the Republic nearly foundered. For the 'sale' of decorations to provide funds for political journalism was not, in itself, enough to discredit the régime, and the application to English politics of the severe standards defended by some of Wilson's critics would, in modern times, have kept the House of Lords a good deal smaller than it is.

Public opinion in Paris was in no mood to listen to the apologists, and a series of new scandals inflamed it even further. Indiscreet letters involved an ex-Minister of War. General Thibaudin was one of the few sound 'Republican' generals, and he was military governor of Paris. It was this bulwark of the régime who had written to La Limouzin, on the night he had given up the War Ministry,—'a word of farewell', begging her permission to put into that word 'all the thoughts which dominate my heart, and can inspire a great spirit which loves you'. Worse still, the rash General had denied anything but the most formal relations with the lady. Why had he risked so dangerous a denial of what he was soon to have to admit? Thibaudin followed Caffarel and Andlau, but the real prey of the assailants was still at large.

From the beginning of the trial of the traffickers, the public waited for the introduction of the name of Wilson. At the third sitting of the court the explosion came. Two letters of Wilson's had been seized among the other papers of La Limouzin. They were harmless enough; one merely noting an application for the Legion of Honour, the other expressing the interest of Wilson and of Grévy in the career of General Thibaudin. Both dated from 1884. Marcel Habert, the defender of La Limouzin, asked that the letters should be shown to an expert witness, representative of the firm that made the note-paper for the Chamber. The expert testified that the water-mark showed that the paper had been manufactured over a year after the dates of the letters.

The originals had been stolen and replaced by new and, it was assumed, much less damaging letters.

Now far more than Wilson was involved; the régime itself was suspect and in Parliament the indignant (and exultant) Right demanded light on the mystery. The Republican politicians, like any other hierarchy anxious to avoid scandalizing the laity, tried to resist. The Minister of Justice made the farcical excuse for doing nothing, that the course of justice must not be interfered with, that course of justice which was being assisted by a forger lodged somewhere in the administrative machine. Already the politicians had evaded the issue by appointing a parliamentary committee to inquire not into the 'dustbin',[1] as the Wilson affair was called, but into any kind of abuse that they thought fit, a successful method of boring the public. But such tactics could not be repeated. It mattered little now who had directed the tampering with the dossier [2] or whether the changes were important. The Republic had been caught out defending its own and it could only be saved by sacrificing somebody. Wilson would no longer be a big enough sacrifice: Grévy must go.

Nothing was further from the mind of the aged if no longer venerable President. The attack on his dear Daniel was mere political spite. 'I shall be like a rock,' he said, and the man who had been elected to be the obedient servant of Parliament now convinced himself that it was his duty to save France from the disaster of his removal from office. The rock was soon attacked by formidable miners. Clemenceau displayed all his genius for invective, and Rochefort found in the Wilson affair a chance to display his talent for scandal, for irony and all his hatred and contempt for the politicians who had let him rot in New Caledonia.

The Rouvier Government once overthrown, the obstacle that Grévy could not overcome was a parliamentary strike. No politician of any weight would form a Ministry without the promise of Grévy's resignation. The old man, more and more a comic character, alternated between indignant resistance and embittered acceptance of his fate. Rochefort asserted that innocent citizens could not sleep at night for fear of being awakened by orderlies from the Élysée asking them to form Ministries. He went on to suggest that the only remedy was to put up a notice: 'Commit no nuisance. Ministerial portfolios not to be deposited here.' The motives attributed to Grévy were not flattering: 'Every day I hang on, I get 3,333 francs.'

Even Grévy could not hold on indefinitely, and when he went, who would replace him? There were three candidates and three only,

---

[1] 'boîte à ordures'. The same tactics were used at the same time to extend the inquiry into the authenticity of the letters attributed to Parnell by *The* (London) *Times*.

[2] M. Dansette argues plausibly that Grévy had the letters destroyed, and Wilson, realizing that they were not likely to do him any real harm, wrote new versions. But for the neglect of the water-mark, all would have been well.

Freycinet, Floquet and Ferry, and the strength of Ferry suddenly converted some of the bitterest enemies of Grévy into defenders if not friends. To the Radicals and to the men of the extreme Left, Grévy was at worst merely a pompous knave, Ferry was a traitor, or so they had always asserted, and whether they really believed it or not, the men who had brought down the 'Tonkinois' had obvious prudential reasons for keeping him out of the Élysée. The ex-*communards* like Rochefort, Eudes and the rest, thought of Ferry as the accomplice of Thiers, of Gallifet and the other murderers of the workers. Lastly, the Catholics had never forgiven the author of Article Seven. They had taken their revenge in 1885; they were not satisfied with that. Their votes, added to those of the supporters of Ferry in the Chamber and the overwhelming 'Opportunist' majority in the Senate, would elect Ferry, but he was not merely the patron of the 'Godless school', he had affronted public hypocrisy by a purely civil marriage. He must repent, go to Canossa and give definite assurances of friendliness to the Church to get Catholic support. Ferry had too much pride to accept such terms and, if his supporters stood firm, he could win anyway.

The enemies of Ferry had two courses open to them: they could try to find a candidate to beat Ferry or they could avoid an election altogether, swallow their words and try to save Grévy. The Radical newspapers now began to throw mud at Ferry, recalling the financial triumphs of his brother, Senator Charles Ferry, of which they gave unpleasant explanations. 'There are brothers who are worth just as much as sons-in-law.' One last effort was made to save Grévy. At the headquarters of the Grand Orient,[1] Clemenceau, Laguerre (the future Boulangist leader), Rochefort, Camille Dreyfus, Eugène Mayer, the flower of Radical and anti-clerical talent assembled, but Clemenceau hesitated. How was the agitation against the unpopular Grévy to be calmed? It could only be done by using a popularity great enough to cover the President. Boulanger must return to the War Office. Meantime, Floquet and Freycinet must be induced to give up their claims—but the emissaries returned to report that Floquet and Freycinet was each convinced that he was President-elect in all but name and, under this illusion, naturally refused to give up not a hope, but a certainty.

Déroulède and his League of Patriots were willing to swallow all their words to save Grévy, or at any rate to keep him in office long enough to block the way to Ferry. The longer the agitation against Ferry lasted, the more frightened the more timid of his supporters would become—and all the world had had proof of how easily they could be frightened. On November 29th, 1887, the 'Equals' of Montmartre placarded their manifesto: 'People of Paris! The Republic is in danger! The Congress of Versailles is about to name Grévy's suc-

---

[1] Headquarters of the strongest section of French Freemasons.

cessor. And it is Ferry-Famine,[1] it is Ferry-Tonkin, Ferry the valet of Bismarck, to whom a monstrous coalition wishes to deliver up the Republic. . . .'

The rumour that Ferry might get Catholic support increased the anger of the Left; and the danger of mob action, whether real or not, stirred the politicians to further efforts. That night, Georges Laguerre gave a dinner-party in his house in the Rue Saint-Honoré, across the street from the Church of Saint-Roch, famous as the scene of young General Bonaparte's whiff of grapeshot. Clemenceau was there, and a more important figure than Clemenceau, Boulanger, the only man who could keep Grévy in office long enough to build up a coalition against Ferry. The new Cabinet, it was suggested, would prorogue the hostile Chamber and perhaps get the Senate to dissolve it. 'I see Augereau clearly enough, but afterwards,' said Clemenceau,[2] 'what will the garrison of Paris do?'—'It will stay in its barracks,' replied Boulanger—and Clemenceau saw that his Augereau was really Bonaparte.

If the chief of the Radicals at last saw where his protégé was going and withdrew, others were less cautious. The ex-Prefect of Police, Andrieux, was to be Prime Minister, so the story runs, Rochefort, Minister of Fine Arts,—and Boulanger, Governor of Paris. The 'historic night' of November 29th passed without any final decision and without any results—except one carefully kept from the left-wing allies of the General, for Boulanger had taken time out during the meeting at Laguerre's to go to see the Royalist leader, the Baron de Mackau.

Grévy was still wavering between patriotic submission to the outrageous demands of the Chamber and refusal to let France suffer the disaster of losing his services. The Prime Minister, Rouvier, who had only continued to serve on a promise of the immediate resignation of the President, duly announced to the Chamber that since Grévy had not resigned, the Government would.

Paris was in an uproar; a quasi-revolutionary committee was sitting at the Hôtel de Ville, threatening a renewal of the Commune; Déroulède's 'League of Patriots' was ready for action; the only trouble was to unite the rioters who chiefly wanted to get rid of Grévy, with those who mainly wanted to keep out Ferry. The Minister of War ordered Boulanger back to Clermont-Ferrand and was obeyed. Buoyed up by his conceit and his trust in the letter of the law, Grévy still struggled, but at last he succumbed and Rouvier was able to read to the Chamber on the Second of December (ominous date)[3] Grévy's letter of resignation. Coming from a monarch of ancient line, abandoning the throne

---

[1] An allusion to Ferry's rôle as Mayor of Paris during the siege.
[2] Augereau was sent by Bonaparte, in 1797, at the request of the Directory, to purge the legislature.
[3] On December 2nd, 1851, Louis Napoleon had overthrown the Second Republic.

after an active reign, the manifesto might have been touching. Coming from the astute but unamiable lawyer who had been made President to ensure that the office would be as innocuous as was possible, the phrases of the abdication were richly comic. 'I appeal to France! She will say that, for nine years, my government has assured peace, order and liberty; that it has made her respected throughout the world.' The Chamber was too surprised to laugh.

Now came the real crisis, the election of a successor. The danger of Ferry's election was greater than ever, and there seemed only one way to prevent it, to frighten the electors with the scarecrow of an *émeute* in Paris. All the parties which preached or tolerated violence were in the streets against Ferry—and Versailles, where the election was to take place, was not far enough away for the deputies and senators to recover their equanimity. The Socialist deputy, Basly, who had defended the lynching of the engineer Antrin by the strikers at Decazeville, went off to consult the revolutionary committee at the Hôtel de Ville. His political colleagues had no desire to be victims of that 'popular justice' which Basly had defended! It did not matter very much that the excitement in the streets was largely confined to professional rioters, or that indignation over Wilson, Grévy and Ferry was not very profound. There was enough to frighten timid men, and the politicians who had deserted Ferry in the past had not become much braver with the lapse of years.

Preliminary soundings showed that already Ferry's supporters were deserting him, but it was not easy to find a substitute who would win all the deserters without losing his own supporters. It was Clemenceau who finally found the man. 'Vote for the stupidest', was the formula put into his mouth to justify the choice of Sadi Carnot. Yet Carnot was not in the ordinary sense stupid; he was a brilliant engineer, but his political career was due not to his merits but to those of his ancestors, to his grandfather, the great organizer of victory of the Revolution, and to his father, Senator Hippolyte Carnot, one of the surviving patriarchs of the Republican cause, still living and overshadowing his worthy but dull son.

The election of Carnot marked another stage in the decline of the presidency. The third President, like his predecessors, had been forced out of office, but unlike them, not over any question of principle. He had been succeeded by a nonentity. Thiers had been chosen as the greatest living French statesman; MacMahon as the most honourable French soldier; Grévy had been elected in 1879 because of what he had said in 1848; Carnot was elected in 1887 because of what his grandfather had done in 1793. Carnot's election had meant, too, that no Frenchman of real eminence could be President if mob violence or parliamentary jealousy could be roused against him. It was not hard to rouse a Paris mob; it was still easier to rouse the egoism of the politicians. The real victor of the crisis was Boulanger, happily for him, in exile in Auvergne.[1]

II

As the Royalists were the strongest section of the Conservatives in the Chamber and as they had great Press and financial resources, it was natural enough for Boulanger, when he began to look for allies on the Right, to turn to them. But apart from personal barriers between Boulanger and the Royal house, there were other reasons why his feelers to the Right were not limited to contacts with the Royalists. Boulanger, after all, had been an officer of the Imperial Army; his ambitions were almost entirely military and the name of Napoleon had for him a prestige that no Bourbon could rival. Then, for all his faults and follies, Boulanger had an understanding of the masses and he knew how much more lively and how much more widespread potential Bonapartism was than the hereditary loyalty of a diminishing number of families to the Bourbons.

Even if these thoughts did not spontaneously occur to Boulanger, they were implanted in his mind by an energetic young journalist who had experienced, in his own career, the narrowness and futility of Orleanism, and who was convinced that only one dynasty could be of any real help to the enemies of parliamentary domination in France. It was Georges Thiébaud who now persuaded the commander of the 13th Army Corps to take the great risk for an officer on active service of leaving his command and visiting a Pretender.

Prince Napoleon, nephew of Napoleon I, and head, in his own estimation, of the House of Bonaparte, was at the time of the Grévy crisis living at Prangins on the Lake of Geneva, and although Thiébaud had kept in touch with him, the Pretender's first thought on seeing before him a man claiming to be Boulanger was that he had to deal with an impostor, an *agent-provocateur*. The General had managed to throw the detectives who were shadowing him off the trail and, face to face with the nephew of the Emperor, he displayed a proper awe in the presence of the custodian of so great a tradition. There was, indeed, a good deal of common ground between Prince Napoleon and Boulanger. The Prince's programme, officially, was not the restoration of the Empire, but the creation through a plebiscite of a strong executive. Boulanger and he could work together for the plebiscite, each confident

---

[1] After various vicissitudes in the courts, Wilson's lawyers were able to get him acquitted on all charges, usually on technical points. Other less prominent members of the firm were not so lucky. 'All saved but honour,' Wilson took his seat in the Chamber ignored by all; in disgust at his impudence in taking his seat, the deputies voted to suspend the sitting. Wilson did not leave, and when, after an hour, business was resumed, Andrieux walked up and shook hands, saying 'I don't like baseness.' Georges Thiébaud, who had no high opinion of parliamentary honesty, said of the outraged virtue of the deputies, 'It's the whores keeping clear of the woman taken in adultery.'

that the choice of France would fall on him. The Prince put his finger on the immediate weakness of the General's position, the want of money, but apart from a vague offer to harbour him if his enterprise failed, he did nothing to help Boulanger to put money in his purse. That tangible proof of confidence had to be sought elsewhere.

The expulsion of the Comte de Paris had restored him to the profession of Pretender. He had now nothing further to lose, and at Twickenham, unlike Paris or Eu, he had nothing else to do. The great Conservative assault of 1885 had been successful enough to anger, even to frighten the Republicans, but it was not a purely Royalist triumph—and in any case it was not much of a real triumph at all. The Republicans might not be an overwhelming majority of the country, but they had a firm grip of the Government. There was no legal way of restoring the monarchy, and the assets of a party whose aims are illegal and whose methods are both legal and futile are bound to be wasting. The Comte de Paris would not be called back by a great popular movement expressing itself through the normal political channels. Boulanger was a far greater threat to the régime than were the heirs of Henri IV and Napoleon. He might be Cromwell—or, as Lord Lyons had early foreseen, he might be Monk.

There were very great difficulties in the way. Boulanger was not merely a Republican General; he was an ostentatiously Republican General. He had far more to expiate than had Monk—on the other hand, he had far less to expiate than had Fouché, who had yet been so serviceable to Louis XVIII. A more serious objection to using Boulanger was that the tradition of the House of Orleans was parliamentary and liberal. The appeal of Boulanger was not merely military, it was Bonapartist in method. It was an appeal to the masses, to plebiscites, appeals fully in the tradition of the heir of Napoleon, but in complete contradiction to all that either branch of the House of France had stood for hitherto. The younger Royalists, discontented with the drab and fruitless counsel of the 'Burgraves', were not impressed by this objection. Popular discontent was less with the Republic than with parliamentary government, and France would hardly turn out a parliamentary President to replace him with a parliamentary King. In the Royalist party itself there were many old Imperialists, like its parliamentary leader, the Baron de Mackau, who had gone over to the Bourbons when the death of the Prince Imperial had ended the chances of 'Napoleon IV'.

To the plebiscitary view, the middle-aged Pretender in September 1887 announced his conversion. The return of the King would be ratified either by a Constituent Assembly or by a plebiscite. There was to be only one plebiscite; it was not to be a regular instrument of government like the Imperial plebiscites, and the contingency that the plebiscite might turn against the King was not contemplated. It would be a new contract between France and its hereditary ruler. There was to be a strong government and the parliamentary responsibility of Ministers was abandoned. A Bonapartist paper was not unjust when it declared that 'the Orleanist monarchy . . . incapable of understanding the doctrines of the Empire is trying to find a way of exploiting them'.

These doctrinal recantations would normally have mattered little; they would only have hastened the decomposition of the Royalist party had there been no movement of opinion against the established order. There was such a movement: and it was incarnate in one man. If the Comte de Paris was to see any results for his efforts, in some way or other Boulanger must be made an ally or a tool. As long as Boulanger was still on the active list of the Army and as long as he could hope to return to the War Office by some deal with the politicians who had got him out of it, he was unlikely to do anything so rash as really to commit himself to revolutionary negotiations with the Royalist party. But the appearance of Boulanger as a candidate in several elections (against his will, he asserted, untruthfully and implausibly) and the launching of a new paper, *La Cocarde*, made the politicians resolved to finish with him. They first suspended him for his military offence of coming to Paris without leave, and when the martyr was triumphant in the first ballot in a by-election in the Aisne,[1] they dismissed him from the Army. He was both indignant and demoralized by this ending of his military career, the only public activity for which he thought himself fitted and for whose honours and powers he really cared. It was too late to repine; he could only recover his lost rank by force; force in Parliament or out of it.

Other elections followed. In the Aisne, Boulanger withdrew; in the Dordogne he was again elected and, finally, in the most industrial department in France, the Nord, Boulanger for the first time openly stood as a candidate. He stood on a platform of patriotism, of constitutional revision and for the necessary preliminary—dissolution of the Chamber. The result was an overwhelming triumph for Boulanger. The Opportunist majority of 20,000 became a Boulangist majority of 100,000. Nothing like it had been known since the triumphs of Louis Napoleon.

Boulanger had already been in touch with the Royalist leader, Mackau, during the Grévy crisis and, but for the delay in receiving instructions from the Pretender, the Boulangists and the Royalists might have combined during the presidential election. Always ready with promises, Boulanger had allowed Mackau to understand that he was ready to play the Monk, but his failure to get back to the War Office forced on him the rôle of a Bonaparte, a Bonaparte who, after

---

[1] At the bottom of the poll was the young Radical candidate, Paul Doumer, later murdered while Conservative President of the Republic.

making his *coup d'état*, would gracefully call in his rightful sovereign as the Comte de Provence had hoped to induce the First Consul to do. The adoption of the plebiscitary policy by the Pretender had won the hearty approval of the chief ex-Bonapartist journalist, Paul de Cassagnac, and Eugène Veuillot, who had succeeded his brother as editor of the *Univers*, after abusing the General, was converted by the results of the election in the Nord. 'Boulangism is ceasing to be a farce and becoming a force.' The editor of the most uncompromising Catholic newspaper forgave the Radical minister who had, to the delight of the Left, promised to make the future priests serve in the Army. 'The parson with the knapsack on his back' had been a boast of the General's that rendered him even more odious to the Right than had his conduct towards the Princes. As the worldly-wise Arthur Meyer, editor of the fashionable *Gaulois* put it, 'the General is the best weapon forged against the Government; let us take hold of it without inspecting the hilt'. And it was the converted Jew, Meyer, who found the way to get a hold on the Boulangist sword. The General needed money, or rather his campaign manager did.

The manager called himself Comte Dillon, but the Franco-Irish noble family of that name refused to recognize this company promoter who had learned his trade in the United States and had now set about selling Boulanger to France, as he had sold stock to America. Dillon saw that for the great campaign he had planned, a campaign whose methods were either praised or blamed as American, great sums of money were needed. Meyer found the money, that is to say, it was through him that the very rich Duchesse d'Uzès, a passionate Royalist, was induced to subsidize the war against the Republic. The Duchess was not the only backer of the General, for the great Austrian Jewish banker, Baron Hirsch, subscribed handsomely to a cause dear to the leaders of Paris society. Who knew? It might open doors hitherto closed to him, even though he was a friend of the Prince of Wales!

Dillon's position was difficult; he was a Royalist himself, but the original Boulangists had been Radicals and the most prominent members of the party were such enemies of the bourgeoisie and the clergy as Rochefort of the *Intransigeant*, Eugène Mayer of the *Lanterne*, most scurrilous of priest-eaters, Naquet, the author of the divorce law, and Paul Déroulède who, though a Catholic and a defender of the social order, professed the most rigid Republican orthodoxy. To combine extreme Right and extreme Left in order to promote the cause of a man whose word was worthless and who did not always even bother to give his word, required great tact.

The Comte de Paris was slowly giving way to the pressure that the Boulangists brought to bear on him, despite the scornful contempt of his uncle, the Duc d'Aumale, for his old enemy. Too open an identification of the Royal cause with that of the General was dangerous to the latter; and it was in the dark that the diverse elements of the attacking army advanced.   Only one thing held them together, the belief that in Boulanger was the only weapon able to break through the defences of the régime.   Naquet, who had long preached revision of the Constitution; Déroulède, who saw in the system a barrier to the war of revenge; the Catholics, maddened by the renewed anti-clerical threats of the Government; the Royalists and Bonapartists despairing of legal victory; all pretended not to notice who their allies were, or, if that was impossible, to forget and forgive until the 'slut' was strangled.[1]

The first step was to demand the revision of the Constitution, and, if that was refused, the dissolution of the Chamber.   On June 4th, the Deputy for the Nord, president of the 'National Republican Party', read to the Chamber a vague programme of reforms from which it was not clear whether he wanted a Senate or not, whether there was to be a President or not.   What was clear was that he wanted a change.   By what right, asked the Prime Minister, Floquet, did Boulanger attack French institutions and demand changes?   Where were the victories that could cover such impudence?   'At your age, General Boulanger, Napoleon was dead.'

There was, of course, no chance that the majority would oblige their enemy and, until a revolutionary situation had been created, the obvious method was to make Boulanger stand for every vacant seat, resigning after each victory and thus prove his claim to represent France against the machine politicians of the Chamber.   But the Radical Boulangists did not like to commit themselves to one man and one man alone.   The memory of Napoleon III was too much for them, so in the next election in the strongly Bonapartist Charente, they ran not Boulanger but Déroulède.   The Imperialists were ready to sacrifice their own candidate to the General, but not to a Republican carpet-bagger, and Déroulède ran a bad third.   The Boulangist leaders ordered their supporters to transfer their votes on the second ballot to the Opportunist candidate!   That is, in deference to 'Republican discipline', they went over to their enemies and attacked their allies. This manœuvre was not only absurd, it failed.   The Bonapartist won, because more than half Déroulède's supporters continued to vote for him and most of his remaining supporters went over to the victor. The prudent Eugène Mayer saw the light and resigned in a great show of indignation.   On the Left, only the really revolutionary leaders remained, men whose hate of the existing order or hopes of the results of a general upheaval blinded them to the way the General was going.

The new Royalist affiliations of the General were the harder to hide since Boulanger had discovered the delights of Society.   He had always been a climber and he was now dizzy with the flattery and adulation

[1] 'La gueuse' was the Bonapartists' term of abuse for the Republic.

with which he was surrounded. The pink, which was his emblem, was all the wear; great ladies were delighted to be his hostesses; and it was rumoured that he was received with semi-royal honours. The General was delighted. His erotic activities had long been notorious and there were now stories that suggested that he seemed to think that a *droit du général* had replaced the *droit du seigneur*, but the great world was ready to overlook many things in the predestined deliverer. The aristocracy, despite warning voices from the elders, was convinced that the Republic was doomed and their optimism spread to the diplomatic corps. Only one ambassador, it is said, refused to believe the good news, and his reason was simply that the members of his very smart club were all convinced that nothing could save the régime— and from many years' experience, he had discovered that his fellow-clubmen were never right. The Pope, it was said, at first shared the scepticism of the ambassador, and the Comte de Paris showed that his own faith was weak by refusing the pleas of Dillon for money. The Duchesse d'Uzès, however, had no doubts, and she gave £120,000 ($600,000) to the Comte de Paris, all 'to be staked on Boulanger'. The bargain was concluded at Coblence, place of ill omen for the Royalist cause.[1] If the conspiracy succeeded, the King of France would repay the gift of his loyal subject.

The campaign had its sinews of war and it was vigorously pursued. Again Boulanger addressed the Chamber and demanded a dissolution, a formal act of propaganda only important because the violent encounter between Boulanger and the Prime Minister led to a duel, a duel which, by every ordinary political rule, ought to have ruined Boulanger. For the elderly lawyer easily defeated the soldier, and for two days Boulanger lay at death's door. It was not the only shock to the party. Boulanger was badly beaten in the Ardèche and the politicians were sure that their enemy was down and out. They spoke too soon. Boulanger was a candidate in three departments, and Dillon poured out the money of the Duchess with a generosity and skill worthy of Mark Hanna. He won all three elections and the figures showed the ominous fact that his increasingly open alliance with the Right as yet cost him little on the Left. It was a complete revenge for the duel and Boulanger enjoyed it, not with the chiefs of his party, but with the mistress with whom he had been madly in love for over a year. While the Republic apparently bled to death, Boulanger was in Africa on his irregular honeymoon. That it had to be irregular was due to the obstinacy of Madame Boulanger, who refused to facilitate a divorce, and to the Court of Rome, which refused to aid the hero of Catholic France by granting an annulment. Irritated as the Boulangist leaders were by the amorous distractions of their chief, it did not seem to matter much in the autumn of 1888. The Republic seemed doomed.

[1] At Coblence the émigrés of 1792 had assembled to invade France and restore the King.

The tactics of the Republicans were not wholly defensive. A 'League of the Rights of Man' had just been founded to resist Boulangism and it was ready with a programme of reforms. There were old political stand-bys like income tax and the election of judges; there was the separation of Church and State, that panacea which had never failed in the past to rally the townspeople in defence of the Republic and Republicans—and there was the revision of the Constitution. After all, that had been the Radical slogan before the General had stolen the idea. The Opportunists were quick to criticize the proposals of the Radicals. Floquet, at a time when the Republican majority of the Senate might be the only barrier to a Boulangist Chamber, wished to make a legal revolution easy. At a time when the strength of Boulangism was being daily increased from the Right, an anti-clerical campaign was to be undertaken in order to drive those Catholics whose prudence had kept them aloof from Boulanger into his arms.

The disunion in the Republican camp was equalled by that on the other side. The 'National Republican Committee' was alarmed by the patronage of a Royalist candidate whom Boulanger could not disown. The Royalists of the 'Committee of National Consultation' were alarmed by the zeal of all sections of the Imperialists for the plebiscite which was to ratify the power of Boulanger—or another. Boulanger could only fall back on his standard tactics—lies. He distributed assurances of complete fidelity to all his nervous supporters, but the most warm assurances were given to the Royalists, for on them he was now completely dependent for money. Neither the Republicans nor the followers of Prince Napoleon could compete with the Duchesse d'Uzès, and the attempt to get the Empress Eugénie to contribute failed. Her Majesty had no faith in Boulanger and even less in Prince Napoleon, and, in any case, before the final collapse of the negotiations with the Empress the great crisis was over.

The complacency that Floquet had displayed in his ill-timed projects of revision did not desert him now. There was a parliamentary vacancy in Paris. Boulanger's previous victories had been in Bonapartist or clerical strongholds, or so it was asserted with uncritical confidence. In Paris, anti-Clerical and anti-Imperialist and anti-Monarchist, the true heart of France beat. An inoffensive candidate, the President of the Conseil-Général of the Seine,[1] was chosen to carry the banner of the united Republicans. M. Jacques would be the new Barodet. The Government quickly fixed the date of the election: January 27th. It was to be a short and decisive campaign. The Boulangists were as confident as the Government, and all the enemies of the régime in Paris rallied to the support of the General. Rochefort and Eugène Veuillot; Albert de Mun and Granger; Catholics and

---

[1] Roughly equivalent to the Chairman of the London County Council.

communards; the League of Patriots of Déroulède, the nascent anti-Semitism of Drumont and his allies; the ex-Radicals, Naquet and Laguerre; all combined in the decisive campaign.

Against the resources of the Government and the municipal political machine, the money of the Duchess was poured out. In the seventh arrondissement the Boulangists put up 1,500,000 posters, enough to have covered all the vacant spaces in the district several times over, but the game was to hide the placards of the enemy. The rival armies of bill-stickers not merely plastered over each others' posters as fast as they went up—thus delighting the printing trade—they fought in the streets until the campaign became more like an American newspaper circulation war than a mere parliamentary election.

Not all the political leaders of Paris followed Boulanger or the certified Republican candidate. The Guesdists, in their gloomy orthodoxy, ran their own candidate, Boule, but the action of the Guesdists was reproved by most other Socialist leaders as much as was the desertion to Boulangists of some of the Blanquists. Neither set of traitors to Republican unity, it was felt, would be able to take many supporters with them. Had not Paulus gone over to the Government and provided a song to rival the Boulangist anthem, a song that appealed to anti-militarist feelings, asserting as it did that 'the people had never had friends in barracks'?

What if Boulanger did succeed despite Floquet and Paulus? That was not merely what the Government wanted to know, but what the Boulangist leaders wanted to know. If he won, would he take the obvious course, cash in on the plebiscite by making a *coup d'état* or, to use the Boulangist euphemism, that 'sweeping-out' of the deputies and the Government which the country expected? The General would not commit himself. He had been brought up to detest the *coup d'état* of December 2nd. What would history say of him if he laid a sacrilegious hand on the Republic? Had he not read in the *Châtiments*:

> France! à l'heure où tu te prosternes,
> Le pied d'un tyran sur ton front,
> La voix sortira des cavernes,
> Les enchaînés tressailleront?

Revealing his inmost preoccupation, Boulanger asked how could one be sure of success? To risk infamy and yet to fail!

On the night of January 27th, the Ministers met in the Élysée, and, a mile away, the Boulangists met with their chief at Durand's Restaurant, beside the Madeleine.[1] Floquet was still confident, but despite military and police precautions, there were signs that the régime was ill defended. It was by no means certain that the Army would act vigorously or at all against its former chief, and the Police was full of Boulangists. As the results began to come in, the only question was

[1] Now the chief Paris office of Thomas Cook.

how great would be the Boulangist majority. The streets round the Madeleine and in front of the Boulangist newspaper offices were packed with enthusiasts. They sang the *Marseillaise*; they sang the Boulangist songs. Round the Élysée there was darkness and within it gloom.

> C'est Boulange, lange, lange,
> C'est Boulanger qu'il nous faut,
> Oh! Oh! Oh!

The extent of the electoral victory justified all Boulangist hopes.[1] A march on the Élysée was, indeed, an amateurish way of beginning a revolution for which no preparations had been made, but on that intoxicating night, the hopes of the victors, the fears of the defeated, showed that the ordinary rules were suspended. It would have been a new Fourth of September, not a new Second of December.

Boulanger was not convinced; legality had paid him well so far. He was not the only Boulangist leader to oppose the night march. Déroulède had another plan. Boulanger was to go to the Chamber, next day, he would be followed by 20,000 regular supporters and 200,000 others would follow them. He was to ask for revision and dissolution. It would be refused, then 'Come out and we will go in.'

The General had other thoughts in his mind. He left his triumphant supporters for a time; left them to join, so they thought, his mistress. No one knows to-day what she said,—indeed, no one can prove that she was at hand, but when Boulanger returned, Rochefort reminded him that it was a quarter past eleven. Outside the mob was roaring, and among the demonstrators stood the detective ordered by Floquet to arrest Boulanger if he made any illegal move! Boulanger's mind was made up and Rochefort had to make the best of it. Finally, Georges Thiébaud looked at his watch, 'Five past twelve, I'm a bear of Boulangism.'[2] The General made his way out of Durand's and was driven off amid frantic acclamations. With him went Déroulède, trying to shake his chief's determination. 'The Empire died of its origins.'—'It lived on them for eighteen years,' retorted Déroulède.

At the Élysée the Ministers were bewildered and then frightened; elsewhere the leaders of the coalition so ignominiously defeated met to discuss their humiliation, Clemenceau asking the ex-prisoners of the Commune what life in New Caledonia was like, while they all awaited news. A message from the irrepressible Floquet assured them all was well. All was not well but the Republic was saved. President Carnot slept in the Élysée; Boulanger, it is thought, in the arms of Madame de Bonnemains.

---

[1] Boulanger got 245,000, Jacques 162,000, Boule 17,000 votes. As the normal strength of the Right was about 90,000, Boulanger must have polled nearly as many normally Left votes as Jacques; and since Jacques presumably got most of the Opportunist votes, Boulanger must have been supported by the majority of normally Radical and Socialist voters.

[2] 'Le Boulangisme est en baisse.'

CHAPTER IV

THE COLLAPSE OF BOULANGISM

I

ON the next day Boulanger not only avoided all revolutionary demonstrations, he did not even go to the Chamber to take his seat. If the chief of the revolutionary movement was idle, his enemies were not. It was through an ingenious use of the rules of the game that Boulanger had put the Republic in danger. The rulers of the Republic could and did change the rules. *Scrutin de liste* was abolished; it still had enough loyal adherents on the Left to make the majority small, but it was done. Paris would never again be allowed to consecrate a dictator by her united voice. By prohibiting multiple candidacies, the law now made it impossible for Boulanger to run in every department at the approaching general elections and, thanks to *scrutin de liste*, to carry his partisans in with him. The General was far stronger than any of his supporters; that strength would have to be spent in one constituency only. The abolition of *scrutin de liste* was the abandonment of a reform preached by great Republican leaders, and the prohibition of multiple candidacies was a direct attack on the free choice of universal suffrage, but the Republicans were, for the moment, cured of their mystical deference to that political God. 'It is a question of eating or being eaten,' wrote Jules Ferry, 'and the Republican party will deserve all the scorn of history if it can oppose the revolution that is being organized with nothing but a fatalistic reliance on principles.' What was wanted was a realist policy devoid of encumbering scruples and Floquet had not merely mismanaged the election, but he still clung to the dangerous project of constitutional revision.

To resist Boulanger a sort of inverted Morny was required, one who could make a *coup d'état* against the plotters of a *coup d'état*. The new Prime Minister was Tirard, but the real head of the Government was the Minister of the Interior, Constans. No one had ever accused Ernest Constans of pedantic and untimely adherence to awkward principles, for he was a political *condottiere* on whose commercial past his enemies rather than his friends liked to dwell.

Constans had a sense of humour and was indifferent to the most scandalous charges, whether of collusion in corruption in Indo-China, or of tampering with the official rate of exchange in China. His political speciality was elections, and it was as an expert manipulator of universal suffrage that he was now called in. The frightened deputies trusted this technician; he was their 'fetish', said Ferry a little scornfully, but then Ferry had so little reason to admire his colleagues. On the night of January 27th, Constans had observed the revolutionary opportunity and, like Georges Thiébaud, he had concluded that it would probably not return. Boulangism was weakening, but it had seemed to be weakening before. There were those who said that before Constans decided to destroy Boulangism he was ready to consider an alliance with it, but the Boulangist leaders would have no compromise.

The first move was against the League of Patriots; taking advantage of .any text of the code which gave colour to the Government's action, the League was prosecuted. How were the Boulangist leaders to be convicted? It was certain that a jury trial would result in triumphant acquittal. Fortunately the constitutional laws of 1875 had provided for the trial of offences against the State by the Senate, transformed into a High Court. There was no doubt that the Senate would find enough law and enough facts to convict the Boulangists. It was, as Clemenceau was later to boast, a truly Jacobin tribunal. Just as the Revolutionary Tribunal had found it convenient to prevent such appeals to the people as had marked the trial of Danton, it was desirable that a great political trial should not unite on the same defendant's bench, a popular idol like Boulanger and such orators as Laguerre and Déroulède. They must not be given the chance to repeat the success of Gambetta under the Empire with a living Baudin at their side. The way out was to frighten Boulanger into flight. He was already nervous, and he got Naquet and Laisant to write him letters advising him to leave France; thus covered, he took the train for Brussels. The Boulangists managed to keep this first flight secret and the volatile General returned next day. With his usual frivolity he now agreed to let Laguerre launch a fresh attack on Constans and that attack ended any hope of a bargain with the Minister.

Circumstances were forcing both Government and Boulanger to appeal to the Right. The new Prime Minister, Tirard, had appealed not merely to Republicans but 'to all Frenchmen' to rally to the Government. So it was time, the Right thought, that Boulanger gave them some public evidence of his loyalty. With such old pillars of 'laïcité' as Ferry and Challemel-Lacour courting the Catholics with kind words, Boulanger might safely do the same. The manifestation of the conversion of the anti-clerical General to religious peace was at first planned for the Ardennes. Boulanger was to speak at the unveiling of a memorial to a priest who had given himself up as a hostage to the Prussians to save the lives of some married men of his parish. This was Thiébaud's idea; Boulanger would be covered by the patriotic memories evoked by the ceremony, and the Ardennes was a Conservative part of the country where applause could be guaranteed. The General finally decided to speak at Tours, in a region where the clergy were not excessively popular. It was, in fact, the constituency of Daniel Wilson. The Republicans were prepared, when March 17th came, to prevent the General's success being a success. The school-teachers, at this moment perhaps the only completely faithful body of functionaries in the country, had distributed whistles to the school-children, and the procession through the city got a mixed reception. Boulanger only gave the Catholics the standard kind words; he promised tolerance and an end of 'the Jacobin heritage of the present Republic', but those kind words irritated and alienated the Left masses who had elected Boulanger in Paris. Their faith was shaken; it could all the more easily be destroyed.

In the next few weeks, the rôle of the ex-anarchist Naquet was more important than ever before. He, the author of the divorce law, went further than Boulanger in his courting of the Catholics, and, what was more important, he encouraged or did not resist the determination of the General to flee if his arrest was imminent. Naquet tried to persuade his colleagues that the flight would please the General's sup-porters. The working-men, he asserted, would be glad to see him too smart for the police, but it was rightly retorted that Frenchmen would prefer the General to be less smart and more brave.

Boulanger was getting less brave every day; preparations for calling the High Court were well advanced; a new *procureur-général*, Quesnay de Beaurepaire, known for his vigour and lack of crippling pedantry, was appointed to play Fouquier-Tinville before the High Court. The ingenious Constans indeed allowed a friend of the General to see the warrant of arrest—accidentally. The constant pressure told; Boulanger took the train for Belgium—and the Government with an amply-rewarded self-restraint, let him go.

II

The General had fled very appropriately on April 1st, and on April 2nd the Boulangist newspapers tried in vain to treat the rumours flying round Paris as an All Fools' Day hoax. The last hope of the leaders was to induce Boulanger to return to Paris quietly and confront the sceptical newspaper men. Laguerre promised that the meeting would take place at midnight at the office of *La Presse*. Midnight came, but no General; instead there was a substitute, a letter to Arthur Meyer of the *Gaulois*, announcing Boulanger's refusal 'to submit myself to the jurisdiction of a Senate composed of men blinded by their personal passions, their foolish rancour and the consciousness of their unpopularity'. No letter had wrought such a change in French politics since the days of the Comte de Chambord.

The resemblance with the Pretender did not end there; the agony of Boulangism, like the agony of the Restoration, was prolonged by futile deputations to Boulanger in Brussels, in London, in Jersey, beseeching him to return, to lead his followers, at first to victory then to a defeat which would at least be honourable. Boulanger had now no ambition that could compete with his resolution not to be separated from Marguerite de Bonnemains. He had, moreover, developed a view of himself as an incarnation of the popular will that was as disastrous as the divine-right obsessions of 'Henri V'. He believed that the electors would rescue him from his exile and restore him to his rights. When the elections of 1889 resulted in a crushing defeat for his leaderless army, the exile ceased to be Chambord at Frohsdorf and became Napoleon at Saint-Helena. He turned again to the Left, he declared himself a revolutionary Socialist and sponsored a little weekly paper, *The Voice of the People*, which preached this new doctrine, much as Napoleon had devoted his exile to the creation of the legend of the revolutionary pacifier of Europe. Boulanger's mistress was now dying of consumption, and they left Jersey for Brussels, where she died on July 16th, 1891. The few faithful adherents of the General thought he might still play a part in politics, but his last link with reality was gone. On September 30th he shot himself on her grave. In a note written the day before he killed himself, Boulanger asserted that 'history would not be severe' towards him, and his dramatic end evoked some easy sympathy. The romantic Séverine said that he had 'begun as Cæsar, continued as Catiline, and ended as Romeo'. A juster verdict than the lady's was the brutal epitaph of Boulanger's quondam protector, Clemenceau: 'Here lies General Boulanger who died as he had lived, like a subaltern.'

Long before Boulanger killed himself he had killed his party. The High Court, as was planned, condemned Boulanger, Dillon and Rochefort to imprisonment in a fortress, but all three were safe in exile. The trial made it easy to vilify the absent General, to reveal his sexual activities, which shocked the elderly senators, and to imply that Boulanger had used, for private and immoral purposes, the funds given him for his campaign. It was difficult to prove an actual conspiracy, for there had been no organized plot; that the Senate was still there to try the Boulangists was due, in all probability, to the refusal of their chief to conspire seriously. The trial did not begin until August, and it was too much to expect that Paris could remain at the white heat of January till then. There were too many distractions; the new Eiffel Tower, the most striking and attacked feature of the Great Exhibition which was commemorating the centenary of the Revolution; there was Buffalo Bill; there were endless celebrations of the great events of 1789.

When the elections came in September, the Boulangists were defeated in advance by the alterations of the electoral laws, by the vigour of Governmental pressure and by the absence of the General. The Ministry had no illusions about the risks of allowing elections free from all pressure. Constans took the matter in hand with his usual skill. The Minister of Public Instruction warned the schoolmasters that they were not to take shelter behind 'a kind of false professional impartiality'. On the other hand, the clergy were threatened with the rigours of the law if they forgot that a rigorous impartiality was their duty.

The Boulangist campaign was based in the country on an alliance with the Conservatives, and in Paris on an attempt to repeat the winning of the Left that had produced the victory of January 27th. Boulanger met the Comte de Paris in London and the electoral bargain was struck. Already defections had begun. Georges Thiébaud, disillusioned by the cowardice of his chief, opposed him in his Paris constituency. Worse still was the anarchy of the organization; there were rival Boulangist candidates and the necessity of accepting Royalists among the faithful was bitter to the surviving Boulangists of the Left.

It is true that the fault was not wholly Boulanger's. He was only an 'agent of the discontented' and the discontents were so many and so varied that only a most skilful driver could have kept from upsetting a coach drawn in so many directions by such fiery horses.

Popular favour had chosen Boulanger: so what could Déroulède or Naquet or Mackau do in face of that consecration? As Jules Ferry said, Boulanger was 'a Messiah, a Mahdi'. Once he had become the incarnation of popular hopes, it was inevitable that all the enemies of the régime should try to use him. For a revolution, Boulanger was not ready. Although an ill-disciplined soldier, he was a soldier, and needed orders, and no one of his associates acquired enough ascendancy over him to counteract his own timidity and the influence of Madame de Bonnemains. When invited to meet the General, the boulevard wit, Aurélien Scholl, had replied that he would be with Boulanger right 'to the 17th Brumaire'.[1] Boulanger himself .was of Scholl's mind and in that scruple or fear was the final cause of ruin for Boulanger and his party.

That ruin affected far more than the narrow circle of original Boulangists. It did not merely reduce the ambitious and courageous Georges Laguerre to a life of provincial obscurity and poverty, send Rochefort again into exile and end the careers of many minor partisans. It ruined the political strength of the Conservatives. The Duc

[1] On the 18th Brumaire, Bonaparte had overthrown the First Republic.

d'Aumale, Cazenove de Pradines and the other old Legitimist and Orleanist leaders had proved right in their forebodings, and the Comte de Paris accepted the responsibility of his choice. In the General Election, less than twenty candidates dared to run as Monarchists. From this disaster it was impossible to save hope or honour.

For the Republicans, the narrowness of their escape was a salutary lesson. Another important political lesson had been learned. The rural classes had, in the main, escaped the Boulangist fever. As they supported the established Government in 1870 when it was the Empire, they supported it in 1889 when it was the Republic. The division between Paris and the provinces was marked, for the revolutionary Boulangism of the capital was very different from the Conservative Boulangism of the country. Only by violence could Paris have asserted its old predominance. No tempting policy of revenge could shake the resolution of the peasant not to be led off on adventures. An apologist for Boulanger's hesitations on January 27th, attributed to him as a reason for them the fear that Bismarck would make war on a Boulangist France. It is doubtful if any such motive influenced Boulanger, but rural France certainly preferred a pacific Republic with all its faults to a policy that might mean war. To war, Boulanger might well have been driven by forces more potent than those that led Napoleon III to Sedan; and a war conducted by Boulanger would have ruined France, to translate into proper language the vigorously expressed opinion of General de Gallifet. The men who defeated Boulanger were not all of them admirable servants of the State and, in defending the Republic, they were defending themselves. But the purity of their motives matters little; in saving France from the dictatorship of this shoddy hero, they deserved well of their country. And for the defeated party, even honour was not saved, for a Boulangist Deputy, Terrail, who called himself 'Mermeix', began the publication of *The Inside Story of Boulangism*.[1] With a treacherous candour, he revealed all the General's duplicity, his contradictory promises to Republicans and Monarchists, the secret of his finances, the quarrels of the leaders. 'Mermeix' had provided the Republicans with more mud to throw than Wilson had supplied to the enemies of the régime. Consistent to the last, Boulanger lied with his usual effrontery and incompetence and the great movement of national regeneration ended in ignominy.

[1] *Les Coulisses du Boulangisme.*

BOOK V

FRANCE OVERSEAS

Et plus en heur ne peult le conquerant regner, soit roy, soit prince ou philosophe, que faisant iustice a vertu succeder. Sa vertu est apparue en la victoire et conqueste. Sa iustice apparoistra en ce que, par la volunté et bonne affection du peuple, donnera loix, publiera edictz, establira religions, fera droict a ung chascun, comme de Octauian Auguste dict le noble poete Maro:

> Il, qui estoit victeur, par le vouloir
> Des gens vaincus, faisoyt ses loix valoir.

Pantagruel.

CHAPTER I

THE OLD EMPIRE

I

IN 1815, the British Government returned to France those parts of the French Colonial Empire which were not needed for British strategical security. That did not leave France much. Her most valuable colony, in 1789 the most valuable colony in the world, San Domingo, was now independent. A few West Indian islands like Martinique, Réunion in the Indian Ocean, Saint-Pierre and Miquelon in the St. Lawrence, Cayenne in South America, a few decaying trading posts in India, a few more on the African coast—these were the scattered fragments of what had once been a great colonial system. In the generation that followed, Algeria, Tahiti and a few Pacific archipelagoes were added. A beginning of African expansion on the Senegal and Asiatic expansion on the banks of the Mekong had been made, but there was little reason to anticipate the outburst of energy that, in the next generation, was to create the second greatest colonial empire in the world.

There was a natural connection between the defeat of 1870 and the renewal of colonial activity. As the hopes of immediate revenge grew less, the more energetic Army and Navy officers became bored with a life of preparation for an ordeal and an achievement that never came. It was this boredom, frankly admitted, that drove one of the two greatest of French empire builders to seek service in Tonkin, and less brilliant and less vocal officers than Lyautey must have felt the same urge. In the colonies a young soldier like Marchand could rise from the ranks and enter world history. Africa and Asia were, to the men of the generation that followed 1870, what Algeria was to the men of the generation that followed 1815. It is true that this search for glory and for promotion on non-European battlefields was looked at askance by many soldiers. 'If you were to bring me all the empires of Asia and Africa . . . they wouldn't in my eyes be worth an acre of the earth where I fought in 1870 and where the cuirassiers of Reichshoffen and the Zouaves of Froeschwiller lie.' So, it is reported,[1] General Garnier des Garets told the young Mangin. It was public property that Bismarck

[1] By M. Lucien Corpechot.

encouraged the expansion of French energies overseas and that in French colonial controversies with Britain the normal German attitude was cordially pro-French, so the numerous party that thought good patriotism and good sense meant doing what Bismarck did not want, was strongly opposed to a policy which meant the spending of French troops and resources abroad and the distraction of public attention from the blue line of the Vosges. Moreover, colonial wars were very unpopular, once the principle of universal military service was accepted. It was not to die of wounds or of fever in a colonial war that the conscript and his family accepted the blood tax. As far as possible, professional troops, the Marines, the Foreign Legion, or native troops like the Senegalese were employed, but in emergencies these were not enough and each death of an ordinary soldier or sailor made enemies of colonial expansion.

It was not as a substitute for battles in Lorraine that colonial expansion was preached by the politicians. In the reaction against the free trade policies of the Second Empire, the traditional mercantilism of the French people was given free play. France, a late starter in the industrialization of her economic life, was reasonably apprehensive as to her chances of competing in world markets, and to win for nascent French industry a closed market was a natural ambition. Even so hard-headed a statesman as Jules Ferry saw through very rosy spectacles when the economic possibilities of the new empire were in question. Thanks to an empire in which French goods would have a preferential right of entry, the industries of the nation and the welfare of the working classes would both be benefited, or so it was believed.

There was much less reality behind another ambition of the colonial school. France had no surplus population to export and, in any case, few parts of the old or new empire had any room for white settlers. The possible 'colonies of settlement' were two only. New Caledonia, though small, remote, and hampered in its economic life by a tariff system that cut it off from its natural Australian market, did offer some good land, in a tolerable climate. But New Caledonia was used, like early Australia, as a dumping-ground for convicts, and though many of these were, like early Australian convicts, victims of unjust law or political mischance rather than of their sins, their presence did not encourage free settlement. As for the attempt to build up a colonial population out of liberated convicts in Guiana, it never had even a plausible case for presentation. In that tropical region, a liberated forger or burglar settled on the land was, if anything, worse off than when he was in prison.

More serious were the possibilities of settlement in Algeria. Although the weakening of French authority that followed the war of 1870 produced the great rebellion of 1871, in fact the natives were not only materially, but spiritually, helpless. The French conquest had lasted for over twenty years; it had been terribly expensive in men and wealth for both parties, but it was final. In that long war, the native aristocracy and bourgeoisie of the coast, so far as there was any, had been swept away. On the one hand there were the conquerors, on the other a cowed and demoralized population, cut off from the conquerors not only by recent bloody memories, but by the far more important barrier of Islam. On the one hand were the millions of the Faithful, on the other the scores of thousands of invading Infidels.

Napoleon III, in one of his generous dreams, had thought to find a solution of this problem in juxtaposition. Except where the European settlement was already in progress, the Arabs were to be maintained on their lands; Algeria was to be an 'Arab Kingdom'. He was too late: settlement had begun. Behind the armies fighting in the marshes of the Tell, had come the sutlers and the women. From these enterprising groups had come the first settlers, for they had discovered that if fever and the natives spared them, men and women who grew vegetables and were at hand to deal with the Army could make handsome profits.[1] The Roman precedent was ever before the minds of the conquerors. Had this region not been (it was believed) the granary of the empire? Where the Arab had made a desert there had been great cities, Hippo and Constantine, Timgad and Lambessa. The symbolic story of the conquest was that of the General who having fought his way through a difficult pass, sent pioneers ahead to clear the face of a cliff on which the achievement was to be commemorated. On the face of the cliff was to be seen the name of the Third Legion! With the Roman precedent before them, could the French forget Gracchus and Cæsar and leave the vast neglected country to the Arabs? In any case, by using Algeria as a dumping-ground for its political enemies, a milder version of Siberia, the Empire both increased the immigrant population and concentrated energetic and hostile elements on the edge of the Arab kingdom. Official military colonists of the type associated with the reign of Louis Philippe; political exiles of the Second Empire; energetic men (and women) who had seen a chance to gain economic independence in the new territories (many of the last being not French but Italians, Spaniards, Maltese); these were the classes whose opportunity came with the fall of the Empire. For not only did Sedan destroy the authority of the chief patron of the natives, but it weakened the prestige of the soldiers who, if not converted to the Imperial ideal, were yet hostile to the political and economic claims of the immigrants. Marshal MacMahon as Governor-General of Algeria had a prestige which, a few years later, the prisoner of Sedan could

---

[1] The early settlers had to be tough to survive the ordeal of life in a region as dangerous as Kentucky's dark and bloody ground. In the village of Boufarik, now one of the most prosperous settlements in the neighbourhood of Algiers, between 1835 and 1841 out of 400 to 500 inhabitants, 58 were killed and 38 carried off by the Arabs.

not claim. What the settlers wanted above all was the access to the great areas of potentially fertile land in Arab hands.

Eugène Étienne, himself born in Algeria and, for a long life, spokesman of the settlers, put their view-point with admirable clarity and a fair degree of candour. 'Algeria . . . has an area equal to France's—more than sixty million hectares— . . . this land is reputed to be the most fertile in the world.' Unfortunately nearly all this treasure house was in native hands. As long as they were allowed to keep their lands, as they were under the bad old system of Napoleon III, they were insulated from European culture and incapable of rising in civilization. How was this deplorable state of affairs to be ended? [1] By making of the mere tribesman an individual with his own legal name and legal property. Property rights of course would be respected, that is in the case of those 'who really occupied land with proper title to it'. As happened to the English peasant when his betters enclosed the common lands, many Arabs who thought they owned land found that they did not. It was made very easy for individuals to demand the sharing out of land held in common. Such a demand presented a simple native group with economic problems which it was ill-trained to face. An ingenious dealer could usually find some shiftless native who, for a few francs, would insist on a partition of the family holdings; once the partition was made it was usually easy to buy up many of the allotted pieces cheaply; in a few years all but the most prudent and tenacious natives in the group were being introduced to European civilization as landless wage-labourers on soil that, a few years before, they had owned.

Buying land in this fashion became a flourishing business which gave openings to the commercial talents of the Jews of Algeria. The Algerian Jew had many qualifications for the work; he spoke Arabic, he knew the country and, by the Crémieux decree of 1870, he was a full French citizen whereas the Arabs were only subjects, with many legal handicaps. The project of naturalizing all the Algerian Jews had been favourably considered under the Empire, but it was actually put into effect by the venerable Minister of Justice in the Government of National Defence. He was himself a Jew and he was rightly confident that his co-religionists would rapidly assimilate French culture. For the moment, however, the naturalized Jew, not otherwise unlike the unnaturalized Arab, was an unpopular if necessary instrument of the modernization of Algeria.

The economic results were striking. Where there had been brush and swamp were now great estates. Once the illusion that Algeria was destined exclusively for wheat was got over, the prudent settlers who had acquired land cheap made money, for the phylloxera killed so many of the French vineyards that the new Algerian capitalist

[1] The confiscations following the rebellion of 1871 had helped a little.

wine-growers had little difficulty in ruining many sections of their French competitors. The French population of Algeria grew, though not nearly as fast as the Spanish and Italian population. The old pirate capital of Algiers has become a great modern port; on the rocky site of Constantine, glass and steel buildings of the utmost modernity crown cliffs at whose foot primitive people still live in caves.

Like other backward peoples, the natives of the coastal areas of Algeria bought civilization unwillingly and at a high price. They provided labour for a new ruling class of great capitalist farmers in the country and a ruling race of European artisans, clerks, business men and officials in the towns. In North as in South Africa, a European society was transported into a populous native society. The edifice built in Algeria in the first generation of the Republic was splendid, but it was a house divided. A European society had been superimposed on the native society; it owned all the capital resources of the country; and if a native bourgeoisie began to grow up, it was in the frame-work of the European system that these lawyers, doctors, officials lived. Only in the South did the native aristocracy hold its own, partly because the conquerors, by the time they reached the edge of the desert, were less ruthless than the men of 1830, partly because it proved impossible to do without the native shepherds in a region whose wealth is purely pastoral, and it proved equally impossible to break the links that bound the shepherds to their hereditary chiefs. Europeans might be sleeping partners with the Kaids in their enterprises, but the kinsmen of Abraham—or of Masinissa—saved themselves from the ruin that befell the rulers of the Tell; where the plough could not go, the French heirs of Rome could not go either.

The settler population in Algeria had more reasons to dislike authoritarian rule in the colony than those furnished by the Arab policy of Napoleon III. The authority given to the military under the Empire was necessary in the frontier districts on the edge of the Sahara, but unnecessary, so it was asserted, in the settled regions which were simply three departments of France.[1] This claim was denied by the existence of military Governors-General like MacMahon before 1870 and Chanzy after it, and, from the settler's point of view, normality did not begin until Albert Grévy, brother of the President, became Governor-General and proceeded to carry out the policy of 'attachment'. This meant the breaking up of the separate centralized administration of Algeria and the 'attachment' of the various departments to the relevant Ministries in Paris, general administration to the Interior, fiscal matters to the Ministry of Finance and so on. Such a policy meant the reduction of the Governor-General to the rôle of a filing-clerk or a post-box. The departments of Algeria were to be governed from Paris, as far as possible, like any other departments. Algeria's

[1] Algiers, Oran, Constantine.

needs and special problems were to be represented by her elected representatives who would make their views heard in Paris, not in Algiers.

In Algeria was displayed in all its oddities the system of colonial representative government at the centre which is the French solution for the fundamental Imperial problem. From the beginning of the great Revolution, this solution had been applied to the old Empire, and each revival of Republican ideas had restored it. So, under the Third Republic, Algiers was given representation in both Houses of Parliament as were, with one minor exception, all the colonies in existence in 1870. This system had more justification in Algeria than it had in decadent sugar islands, or than in the absurd French enclaves in the mass of British India. In the islands, representation merely meant the selling by the coloured electorate of their votes to the highest bidder in a good-humoured and frank fashion. In the Indian settlements, things were done in a more decorous way, recalling less a Pennsylvania primary election of the good old days, than the auctioning of safe seats to opulent candidates by Conservative Associations in the south of England. There was no Boss in the West Indies as masterful and competent as the all-powerful Madou-Chanemouganelayoudaméliar who delivered the vote of Chandernagore, Pondichéry and the other Indian towns. In Algeria, elections were no more violent or corrupt than they were in Marseilles, and there was all the difference in the world between the representative character of a Thomson or an Étienne and that of the successful bidders for the votes of the Negroes of Martinique or the Brahmins of Pondichéry. But the Algerian deputies and senators (like the deputies sent by Cochin-China), if they represented a real political community, represented only one interest in the Algerian community, the settlers. The only indigenous community which could vote was the Jews, and that did not conciliate the Arabs. It is true that the Arabs could acquire, by naturalization, all the rights of French citizens; all they had to do was to abandon their status in Moslem law, adopt monogamy, accept the full principles of the civil code: in short, by their standards, cease to be Moslems. Few were willing to pay this price, so that the vast majority of the inhabitants of Algeria were reduced to an inferior caste with no political and only limited civil rights.

The attempt to treat Algeria as a part of France soon broke down. The deputies and senators from the three departments had, in fact, many economic interests in common with the rest of the inhabitants of Algeria, and they could not ignore the fact that the financial relation of the colony to the metropolis was not that of a department in France to the central government. Indeed, as they were anxious to explain to sceptics like M. Doumer that the fiscal burdens imposed on Algeria were intolerable, they were not tempted to deny this obvious fact. The absurdity of the attachment system, with its false premise of an almost complete identity of Algeria and France, became common knowledge, thanks largely to reports on the situation by such eminent Republican authorities as Jules Ferry and Burdeau.

In 1896, the system of 'attachment' was reversed, the authority of the Governor-General restored, and two years later a more significant step was taken, the establishment of the 'financial delegations', consultative bodies entitled to express local opinion on fiscal matters. With a Governor-General in effective command of the local administration and with an increasingly effective organ of local opinion (that is, in the beginning, settler opinion) set up, the fiction that Algeria was merely an 'extension of France' was slain. Yet the results of colonization and attempted assimilation remained. In Algeria a fifth of the population was now of European origin. Government, education, economic life was organized on French lines; there were many exceptions to the rule, but the rule was that they order these matters better in France. The worst iniquities of the new land law were done away with; the era of wholesale expropriation was over and the most indurated Moslem conservatism could not escape the effects of railways, roads, schools, military service (which did not become formally compulsory for the native until the eve of the last war). The economic transformation of Algeria, the coming of a wage economy, of capitalist farming, of modern mining, the rapid increase in native population, all ate into the carapace of Moslem society. Yet, as the new century dawned, Algeria was still a country of two nations, one on top and one below. Members of the presidential suite who accompanied Loubet on his official visit to the great colony could still be horrified at the insolence of the rulers to the ruled, but that was only one sign of the barrier between the two races. The native Algerian had been conquered, but he had not yet been won.

CHAPTER II

TUNIS

THE fate of Tunis was really settled when the French had secured military control of Algeria. The Regency itself was defenceless, its natives unwarlike, its sea and inland frontiers open. Its conquest would be a very different thing from the long and bloody war against the warlike mountaineers of Kabylia. The French disasters of the war of 1870 made it, for a moment, seem likely that the Italians would take advantage of the military prowess of the Germans not merely to take Rome but to take Tunis, for by 1870 the question of the future of Tunis had been simplified. She would be ruled by France or by Italy. On the one hand France was far richer, stronger, and was an immediate neighbour. On the other hand, the connection between Sicily and Tunis was old and the conquest and development of the Regency were probably within the powers of the new Italian State, now that the French had made the western frontier safe. As for the Tunisians themselves, few knew or cared what they thought.

Like Algiers, like Egypt, Tunis was vaguely connected with the Turkish Empire. Now that the great days of piracy were over, the Bey was a territorial prince ruling over the old domain of Carthage.

Under pressure from Europe, one Bey had granted a constitution which meant special privileges for Christians and Jews; he had contracted a large national debt; in short, as far as his means allowed, he had imitated Ismail Pasha in Egypt. His splendour, however, had no such monument as the Suez Canal. Palaces, one of which housed a harem more numerous if not more splendid than Solomon's, more or less modern and decidedly expensive weapons of war, new taxes that Western ingenuity had thought up—these were the chief fruits of the modernization of Tunis. Another Bey came who had no use for his predecessor's harem, but could be influenced through a handsome young man.

In the capital, British, French, Italian bankers, lawyers, adventurers exploited the decadent Government; the Tunisian peasant paid more and more in taxes and the Bey made vain efforts to play one European power off against another and even attempted to make of his nominal suzerain, the Sultan, an effective protection against his fate. At the Congress of Berlin, both Britain and Germany allowed France to know that they had no objection to a French liquidation of the bankrupt concern. The Italians might protest but they could not resist. There was a lively war of concessions, law-suits and intrigues between the French consul, Roustan and the Italian, Maccio. Native discontent against France was fanned by Arabic journals printed in Sardinia, and under cover of commercial competition both Governments subsidized political rivalry. It was an uneven contest; and as soon as France could find an excuse for intervention, Italy would have to submit. She might —and did—show her anger by joining the German-Austrian alliance, but that would not get the French out of Tunis, once they were in. A temporary Italian success in the diplomatic war in Tunis made it advisable to act quickly. A Tunisian tribe was making a nuisance of itself on the Algerian frontier, and the patience of the French authorities suddenly snapped. An army crossed the border and the threat of recognition of a Pretender made the Bey see reason. Three weeks after the troops had entered Tunisia, the Treaty of the Bardo was signed. Under polite disguises, it gave complete external and preponderant internal control to France and, in return, ensured the dynasty its survival.

The speed of the first campaign was essential for the political survival of its author, Jules Ferry. The Prime Minister, in obtaining credits for the expedition, had assured the Chamber that 'the Government of the Republic does not seek conquests', but he had refused to give the assurances demanded by suspicious deputies of the Opposition parties that nothing more was intended than a punishment of the marauding Kroumirs. Thanks to the speed of the Army and the feebleness of Tunisian resistance, Ferry was able to present the Chamber with a treaty which, however much critics on the Left like Clemenceau and critics on the Right like Cunéo d'Ornano might object, was certain to be gratefully received. But Tunisia was not yet conquered; a revolt broke out, mainly in the south, whose suppression meant more effort than the first military promenade. The Holy City of Kairouan, the Mecca of North Africa, was occupied; Sfax was attacked from the sea; Gabès occupied. By the end of 1881, the authority of the Bey, that is of France, was restored all over the Regency. The 'rebellion', the heavy losses from sickness among the troops and the widespread belief in Paris that the conquest of Tunis was proving highly profitable to financial interests of which Roustan was the mouthpiece, all made the position of the Ferry Government difficult. It was, indeed, overthrown, but Gambetta secured a vote accepting the Treaty of the Bardo. Clemenceau might see in the triumph only a Stock Exchange affair; Rochefort, prince of all the journalists who 'private dirt in public spirit throw', might accuse Roustan of corruption and be acquitted of libel by a jury; Tunis was securely French.

The new acquisition was valuable. In general it was fertile and both more easily conquered and more easily held than Algeria, but its political problems were more complex. Those very elements which had been shipped off to Constantinople in 1830, when Algiers was taken, were preserved in their rank and perquisites, if not in their power, by the treaty. Not only persons but institutions like the great religious estates were preserved from simple expropriation on the Algerian model. Tunis, too, was more populous in proportion to its area than was Algeria and offered less chance for settlement. Lastly, what European settlement there was in the years immediately before and after the conquest, was not mainly French. Italy might be excluded politically but not the Italians, and as France was only a protecting power she had to make far more concessions to the other European Governments than she had done in Algeria, which she had annexed outright. The Italians were very numerous in the eastern department of Algeria (Constantine), as Spaniards were in the western (Oran). But the children of these settlers were French citizens. They had to serve in the French Army and they normally went to French schools. Thus the son of an Italian settler was, in the next generation, to be famous in French politics, but in Tunis a René Viviani might easily have remained legally and spiritually an Italian. Italy at first refused to recognize French action in Tunis and when she did, she did so on her own terms. There were not two legal classes in Tunis, natives and Europeans; there were three, Tunisians, French and Italians. The French language had not only to fight against Arabic, but against Italian, and French enterprise had to compete with Italian. There was, it is true, a natural division of labour among the Europeans. From Sicily came peasant settlers, hardy, industrious, sober, able to live as cheaply as the natives and work harder. They provided a necessary labour force for the development of modern Tunis, while France provided the skill and the capital for great works like the canal that turned Tunis into a port or created European towns like Enfidaville or the great olive groves of Sfax. France, too, provided the spiritual direction, for the Archbishop of Algiers, Cardinal Lavigerie, moved to Tunisia, built a cathedral on the site of the citadel of Carthage, and made it the headquarters of his famous missionary order of the White Fathers, who warred against barbarism and the slave trade in Central Africa and for the spread of Christianity and French influence. The main sufferers were the Italian bourgeoisie, who saw the administration in French hands, with its direct power over the jobs and its indirect power over the contracts.

Under cover of the beylical authority, order, health, finance, roads were improved. The Bey was deprived of the power to pledge State property and his subjects given a chance to accept the blessings of Western civilization. In Tunisia, Arabic civilization was more deeply rooted than it was in Algeria. The sedentary, trading Tunisians were more sophisticated and better able to look after themselves than the Algerians had been. For the moment, the drawbacks of the protectorate system from the French point of view were ignored. The ease with which French authority had been established and maintained was in gratifying contrast to the troubled history of Algeria, and the merits of indirect rule, of using, not abolishing, the native authority were preached with conviction by leaders of the colonial party. In other parts of the growing Empire, the Tunisian precedent was to be rather uncritically followed.

CHAPTER III

EGYPT

IF some French sentiment about Egypt was awakened by the memory of the crusade of Saint Louis and the Egyptian captivity of the holy king, far more was evoked by the memory of Bonaparte's expedition. The France of the Revolution had awakened Egypt from her slumbers; the Rosetta stone which made possible the study of ancient Egypt and the creation of a modern Egyptian State by the Albanian adventurer, Mehemet Ali, were both fruits of the French invasion. All through the early nineteenth century, French interest in Egypt was lively. In defence of Mehemet Ali she almost went to war with Britain; the disciples of Saint-Simon saw in Egypt a field for the application of the technocratic ideas of their founder: and, in 1869, one great work inspired by them was completed, the Suez Canal. In face of British scepticism and hostility, the dream of Alexander the Great and Napoleon I had been made a reality: and it was the wife of Napoleon III, cousin of the builder of the Canal, who officially opened it. In the next year, the Second Empire fell and an exhausted and humiliated France could not defend the special position she had acquired. Worse, the success of the canal attracted British attention to the country and it was inevitable that the British Government should try to undo the harm done to her position by Palmerston's mistake. The Khedive Ismail was one of the Oriental rulers who were anxious to modernize their countries, but the European financiers who advanced money to the Khedive for railways and opera-houses, telegraph lines and palaces, exacted an extortionate price for their services and the reforming ruler made Egypt responsible for a debt charge of nearly £20 per head of population. In the course of his rake's progress Ismail had been forced to realize his shares in the Suez Canal, and by buying them under the nose of the Broglie Government, Disraeli got Britain that footing in Egypt which she now needed. The British Government did not acquire a majority vote on the Canal Board, but she was by far the biggest individual shareholder—and 80 per cent. of the shipping passing through the Canal was British. Nothing could make Ismail solvent; and his European creditors, whose claims on Egypt's wealth were of course paramount, insisted on getting protection from their Governments. In France, their complaints were most heartily supported, and to save the interests of the debt-holders became the main object of the French policy. The British Government, less frankly and less uncritically, backed France.

Egypt was taken under the joint financial tutelage of France and Britain, her finances and administration were reformed, that is, were reorganized so that four-fifths of the revenue of the country could go to the debt-holders. It was a kind of condominium, but it was a limited condominium. The interests of the French and British creditors, though parallel, were not identical, and Britain had a direct political interest in the future of the country through whose territory ran the route to India. No British Government would tie its hands by making a hard-and-fast bargain with France. Gambetta discovered this when, in his short Ministry, he induced the British Government to consent to the sending of a joint note to the Egyptian Government promising the Khedive vigorous support against the growing Egyptian Nationalist party. This party, with its anti-foreign bias, had aims which were incompatible with the prompt paying of interest, but while Gambetta was ready for deeds to back up words, Lord Granville had no more in mind than the delivery of a sermon.

Despite notes and pressure, the Egyptian Nationalist movement grew. It was directed against foreigners of all types, against the great foreign commercial colonies of Alexandria whose immunity from Egyptian law and whose vigorous commercial methods evoked resentment, against the Turkish and Circassian officers and officials who had most of the good jobs that were not in European hands, against the powers whose solicitude for the legal rights of their citizens was seen in an unkindly light by Army officers whose pay was in arrears and whose peasant soldiers resented the crushing taxation necessary to keep Egypt solvent.

Parallel with the growth of Egyptian resentment, there had been a marked disposition on the part of the Eastern powers to keep the Western powers from acting entirely off their own bat. Bismarck was not now disposed to be cut out altogether and, although German interests in Egypt were trifling, a too close collaboration of France and England was not desirable in the eyes of the great diplomatic juggler. The solution favoured by the British Government was the use of the authority of the Sultan and, if necessary, of Turkish troops to restore order, that is, support the Khedive in what had now become an open quarrel with the Nationalists. France was strongly opposed to calling in Turkish aid. It was no long time since Tunis had tried to shelter behind the nominal authority of the Sultan and, unwilling since the fall of Gambetta to take strong measures itself, the French Government was now disposed to make the Egyptian affair the business of the concert of Europe and anxious not to be involved in any enterprise except as the mandatory of all the powers. Freycinet, the new Prime Minister, had never liked the complete identification of French policy with the demands of the bondholders, and in Paris the wrongs of the Egyptians and the greed of the bondholders, like the corresponding themes in the Tunis affair, were meat and drink to the Left. When the Army and popular feeling put the native leader of the officers, Arabi Pasha, in power for the second time, and when the authority of the Khedive and the security of the bondholders were both in danger, a French squadron joined a British off Alexandria. When native indignation was expressed in a pogrom directed against the foreigners in the city and the question of action became urgent, the mere hint that France might be seriously involved in military operations in Egypt was enough to provoke an outburst in the Chamber which moved the ardent Gambetta to patriotic rage. The 'gang of lackeys' had revealed the moral feebleness of France. 'Finis Galliæ,' he wrote to his mistress Léonie Léon, 'we are ripe for slavery.' However Gambetta might rage, no one was less likely to take a bold decision, to run counter to the feeling of the Chamber than the former Dictator's right-hand man. Freycinet defended his policy by stressing the danger that France would find herself isolated with only British support, which would be no great help if the great continental military powers combined against her. This, too, was Clemenceau's argument; and on the other side, the prudent Grévy thought it was more important that the restless Moslem world should be taught that it could not successfully defy any European power than that France herself should teach that lesson. If the British Army and Navy demonstrated this important truth in Egypt, France would benefit by it in other regions.

There was no support for intervention in Egypt and the Chamber even refused the timid Minister a small credit to enable France to share in guarding the Suez Canal. Both the enemies and friends of a vigorous Egyptian policy agreed that this was a worthless half-measure. Freycinet resigned and, although it was long before France reconciled herself to the fact, she was effectually excluded from the country in whose modern history she had played so great a part. The British Government repeatedly announced that it had no intention of staying in Egypt. After the destruction of the Egyptian forts at Alexandria and the defeat of the Army at Tel El Kebir, there was no danger of resistance to the Khedive and the British civil and military advisers who ruled in his name, but the great revolt in the Sudan meant a permanent danger to the Lower Nile and, in any case, deprived the Egyptian State of a great part of its territory. To end the Dervish menace and restore 'Egyptian' rule in the Sudan now became the object of British policy. Such a policy required money which, if it was to be furnished by Egypt, could come only from revenues which would otherwise go to the bondholders. Such a diversion of budget surpluses was impossible without the consent of the international commission which administered the

Egyptian debt, and it was by opposition to British policy on this body that France could best express discontent at the British occupation of Egypt. This opposition in turn forced Britain to look to Germany for support in her Egyptian policy, so that the Egyptian question divided the two Western powers and drove one of them to seek in German and the other in Russian aid, weapons in their war. France could do no more than hinder Britain; she could not permanently impede her policy by mere legal sabotage on the Debt Commission. If she was to recover any part of the lost Egyptian assets it would have to be by more active measures. There was another lesson to be drawn from the Egyptian failure. The new Chamber had overthrown Gambetta *and* Ferry *and* Freycinet; it was obvious that vigorous action abroad was impossible if the Chamber had to be kept fully informed of what was planned. Ferry, at least, learned this lesson and in his next colonial enterprise was careful not to come into the open; careful to represent each step in his scheme as the last and, by such methods, to secure for France a great empire far further from Europe, far more of a diversion of resources, far less connected with French interests and sentiments than Egypt was. By such methods the Chamber which had refused to run not very serious risks in a country where, as the event showed, war was a military promenade, was persuaded to vote the men and money needed for the long and exhausting war in Tonkin.

CHAPTER IV

INDO-CHINA

I

A T about the time that the Romans were conquering and romanizing the Celts of Gaul, the Chinese were extending both their authority and their civilization southwards into the most easterly of the great peninsulas of South Asia. Although the political authority of the Chinese Empire was overthrown at about the time of the establishment of the Carolingian Monarchy in what was becoming France, the cultural mark made by the Chinese conquest on the people of the eastern half of the Indo-Chinese peninsula was as deep as that made by the Romans on Gaul. It was, in some ways, deeper, for there was no nostalgic memory of a pre-Chinese State, no antiquarian cult of an Annamite Vercingetorix; and whereas the Roman Empire disappeared, the Chinese Empire remained, superficially not very different from what it had been in the first centuries of the Christian era.

Despite a brief resumption of direct Chinese authority, destroyed after a few years by native resistance, the real hold of China on the kingdoms to the south was cultural. Chinese literature was copied and political authority was in the hands of a class of classically-educated mandarins through whom alone the local divine monarch could exercise his authority. Chinese ideograms made the *literati* citizens of the cultural empire which stretched from the borders of the tropic Malayan seas to the frontier of Siberia. Chinese ways of life and thought, Chinese philosophy and Chinese superstition deeply marked the way of life of all classes of Annamites and Tonkinese.

French interest in this region was not new. The religious possibilities of the whole region did not escape the vigilance of the greatest missionary nation in the world. Siam and all the lands to the east were kept in view from the reign of Louis XIV on and the flag followed the cross since, on the eve of the revolution, the court of King Louis XVI was receiving ambassadors from Annam and French adventurers were· improving the military methods of a backward people. The Revolution put an end to this connection, but the missionary interest never died and it was stimulated in the early nineteenth century by a violent persecution of the missionaries and of their converts, a persecution that made the region as famous and dear to zealous Catholics as England had been in the sixteenth or Canada in the seventeenth century. As a Catholic and expansionist power, the Second Empire was naturally attracted to Indo-China and by 1870 a series of easy campaigns and increasingly ambitious treaties had secured for France control of the rich and sparsely inhabited delta of the Mekong, in which was created the colony of Cochin-China. The Spaniards, who from their Philippine base had aided the campaign, had been got rid of, and the existing feeble mandarin government had fled. France had acquired a valuable territory and the chance to extend it. It was a minor Mexican expedition differing from the other in scale and in being successful.

The Republic thus found herself in possession of a territory difficult to defend in its present form and tempting the man on the spot to adventure. To the west lay the decaying Indic civilization of Cambodia and Laos; a far feebler copy of Indian culture than Annam was of Chinese. To the north lay the Kingdom (or Empire) of Annam, a feudatory of the Chinese Empire like Korea, but separated from the suzerain power's capital by vast distances and encouraged to assert herself by the weakening of Imperial prestige and authority that had followed the unsuccessful resistance to white aggression and by the weakness revealed in the long course of the Taiping rebellion. On the west of the new colony was an aggressive Siam—and behind her, a potentially aggressive Britain. Within Annam, was the great territory of Tonkin, easy of access from the sea, not well provided with means of communication with the capital of the kingdom, discontented with the rule of the Annamite mandarins and influenced to some degree by loyalty to a deposed dynasty. And the great mother empire of China lay like a stranded whale unable to defend her capital, much less her extremities, from the outrages of the Western barbarians. She seemed to be a great prize, religious and economic, for whoever should seize her: and if she was too big to be swallowed by one power, each could slice-off a convenient morsel. She would die the death of a thousand cuts. It was inevitable, then, that the occupation of Cochin-China should be only a beginning. In the Red River lay an open waterway to the edge of southern China, and the country of the Red River tempted missionaries, merchants and adventurous officials like that young Protestant naval officer, Francis Garnier, who explored the region under Napoleon III and, in 1873, began the Tonkinese wars by seizing, with a handful of sailors, Hanoi, capital of the vice-royalty of Tonkin, only to fall into an ambush and be slain. At another time Garnier might have been avenged by the annexation of Annam, but the France of the Duc de Broglie was not ready for distant adventures and the Annamite authorities escaped with no more than a vague acknowledgment of the special interests of France in Annam and Tonkin and what the French took to be an acknowledgment of their right to control Annamite foreign relations. The mandarins of Annam were wise enough to see their danger. They, too, took steps to prepare for renewed French aggression. They punished, most rigorously, the native Christians who had helped Garnier and they renewed their relations with their nominal suzerain. Old feudal rites were now hurriedly performed, old tributes paid; the menace from the south—and from the sea—drove the rulers of Annam to rely on Pekin.

It was inevitable that this policy should lead to a violent dénouement. A France which was everywhere recovering from the numbness of the years that followed the war and which was especially active in colonial enterprise, was unlikely to rest content with the meagre gains of the Treaty of Saigon. China, still self-complacent but imitating barbarian arts in military matters, had refused to recognize the treaty and was adept in polite evasion. The second Tonkinese war was certain to come, but it came in a dramatic form, for the French naval officer sent out to Tonkinese waters was a romantic man of letters, Rivière, anxious to be both a hero and a member of the Academy. Like Garnier before him, he insisted on reparations for alleged or real injuries to French interests and regardless of the odds attacked and captured the citadel of Hanoi. Although Western arms and Western discipline could work miracles, they were not omnipotent. Rivière, like Garnier, was defeated and killed. This time no easy compromise was possible, for the honour of France was engaged—and behind the feeble Annamites was the power of China. There followed a diplomatic comedy of a type less familiar then than now. France and China remained at peace. Their ministers in Pekin and Paris negotiated and concluded agreements, evaded or amended by one side or the other. No war was declared, but French troops fought well-armed Chinese regular troops whose presence was officially denied. The 'Black Flags' were to the French dangerous bandits; to the Chinese they were Annamite troops or citizens. In fact they were agents of Chinese arms and policy. The war was laborious. The French behaved with the reckless daring of *conquistadores* in sixteenth-century America. With the entry of Chinese troops on the scene, the French were no better equipped than their foes, but they had a discipline and a confidence in victory that their opponents lacked, so attacks that should have been disastrously defeated were successful. Moreover, the French had command of the sea—and of the rivers. They could move along the coast and send parties up the labyrinth of water-ways, bombard old-fashioned Annamite fortresses (designed a century before by French engineers) from their gunboats and seize the nodal points of Tonkin's transport and commerce. They could not keep the Chinese authorities from sending men and arms into the disputed territory and, as long as that was done, no number of brilliant French feats of arms were of any lasting value. On the other hand, it was difficult to bring pressure to bear on China without declaring war. The other European powers were in the main anxious not to interfere with France. They had all a great deal to lose if she lost face in Eastern eyes, but Britain, at any rate, objected to the French attempt to have the best of both worlds, to exercise the rights of a belligerent and still remain formally at peace.

The war degenerated into two campaigns. . On land, there were brilliant successes followed by reverses when the French tempted fortune too much. Under the vigorous command on sea and land of Admiral Courbet fortune had favoured the bold, but when soldiers replaced the sailor, fortune was less kind. At sea, Courbet was only too anxious to get at the Chinese fleet, but on the one occasion when a Chinese squadron came in sight, the pugnacious admiral was thwarted in his plans for what would doubtless have been a complete naval victory, since the cruisers of Admiral Ting were a good deal faster than the battleships of Admiral Courbet. The Chinese saved their modern vessels by flight, although a brilliant and completely successful cutting-out expedition, which destroyed some old Chinese vessels at Foochow, was some consolation. To coerce the Imperial court, Courbet landed parties on Formosa, but he was far too weak from a military point of view to exploit local successes or to redeem the local failures of his subordinates. An occupation of the Pescadores islands was both more practicable and more likely to frighten Pekin, but the real threat to Pekin, the interruption of its rice supply by the Gulf of Pechili, was long postponed for fear of international complications.

While the war continued, the French naturally took the opportunity of regularizing their position in Annam. They imposed new treaties on the Government, leaving no loopholes for evasion; and once they had successfully defended the capital, Hanoi, deposed one Emperor and enforced recognition of their authority by their new nominee, the conquest of Annam and its dependencies was formally complete, limited by the outbreak of a general rebellion and the continuance of the war with China. Not content with this extension of authority, France forced comparable conditions on the King of Cambodia. A new empire had been founded.

The success in the field and in the palaces of the new client princes did not put an end to the war in the peninsula or to the opposition to it in France. As the campaigns continued, as it became necessary to call on the Chamber for repeated credits and on France for more and more men, the opposition to the war grew. Ferry, now Prime Minister for the second time, was unshakable in his resolution to impose a victorious peace on China and the Opportunists still supported him, but on the Left and Right, the enemies of the Prime Minister were vigilant and bitter. It is possible, of course, that had Ferry foreseen and had he announced the true cost in men and money of the conquest of the new empire, Tonkin would never have been conquered. By presenting the Chamber with a series of demands whose refusal would have meant French humiliation in the East, he had his way, but at the cost of increasing parliamentary irritation and of a growing conviction that the resolute Minister was aiming at more than he admitted. He was able to repel the assaults of critics like Clemenceau by pleading that too candid a reply to questions would leave him at the mercy of Chinese diplomacy, but as a treaty made in 1884 was, so the French Government averred, evaded by the Chinese, the war continued. The alleged duplicity of the enemy was to be punished; the Treaty of Tientsin was to be enforced; but French patience was wearing out. It was not evident to everyone that a satisfactory settlement with China was not possible and Ferry was in fact negotiating such a settlement when the blow fell.

The besieged French garrison of Tuyen-Quan was relieved in March 1885, and the Ferry Government had reason to hope that it could silence its critics with the double news of a settlement with China and a brilliant military finish to the war. That was not to be. The campaign which was now being fought on the Chinese frontier took an ugly turn. There was confusing and disheartening news and, with an election in the offing, the deputies of the majority were easily frightened by Clemenceau and were ready, if excuse were given, to abandon a policy and a chief whose unpopularity might cost them their seats. They were given their excuse. On the 29th of March the blow fell. A panic-stricken despatch from General Brière de l'Isle announced the defeat and wounding of General de Négrier at Lang-Son. Like the Empire at the news of Sedan, the Ferry system was doomed by the news of military defeat.

Unlike Napoleon III, the chief of the system went down fighting. He faced the Chamber knowing that his overthrow was certain, a Chamber full of bitter enemies applauding Clemenceau when he refused to have any relations with the Ministers who were no longer Ministers, but men 'accused of high treason'. By a great majority of Radicals, Monarchists and renegades, the vote of fresh credits for the war was rejected.[1] The Government was overthrown and the crowds in the streets were full of mischief; Paris seemed to be on the eve of one of its 'days'.

Ferry's spirit was unbroken. He had confronted the howling Chamber knowing that the preliminaries of peace with China were settled but that, if he announced the news, the Chinese might evade their engagements and the Chamber might, in its violence and panic, throw away the results of war and policy. He left the parliament building accompanied by a young official[2] who was appalled at the

---

[1] Freppel, the fiery Royalist Bishop of Angers, refused to vote against the *bête noire* of the Catholics who were defending France and Catholicism in the East.

[2] Gabriel Hanotaux.

sight of the furious mob barring the way, but Ferry kept his head. He sent Hanotaux off to the Ministry of Foreign Affairs to secure it against any explosion of violence and walked, unattended, towards the Élysée to tender his resignation to the President. The last that Hanotaux saw of him that day was his tall hat moving steadily westwards along the *quai* above the heads of the mob that howled 'Into the water with him'.

Although Ferry was overthrown, his work was done. Had he not been too sharp a bargainer he might have made a peace with China sooner, for the terms on which he finally settled with the Imperial Government were those which he could have had earlier. By securing the acceptance by China of French suzerainty over all the territories of the Emperor of Annam, he had made it certain that if France did not lose heart, her authority could be established without outside intervention—and left to themselves, the natives could not hope for successful resistance. Of this Ferry was well aware and in his retirement he saw in the conquest of Tonkin his greatest achievement. It was not merely a revenge for the loss of Egypt (although it was that); it was, he thought, the creation of a great market for French industry, a remedy for trade depression, a new and French means of entry through Yunnan into the immeasurably rich Chinese market. The reality fell a good deal short of the dream, but the reality was striking enough and the chief credit for the acquisition by France of her most populous and richest colony is Ferry's. But for him merchants like Dupuis, sailors and soldiers like Courbet, Garnier, Négrier might have laboured as fruitlessly as Dupleix or Montcalm.

II

In forcing their way into Indo-China, the French undertook the administration of a civilization, or rather of civilizations, more sophisticated and more unintelligible to Europeans than those of any other French colony. If they had had little success in breaking through the barrier of Islam in North Africa, that had not prevented the creation of a European society parallel with the native society. Indo-China offered no opportunity of repeating the methods which had created the French society of North Africa. It was too remote, too vast, too populous and the dominant race was too ingenious, adaptable and self-satisfied to be made French or safely left in its ancestral stagnation. The Asiatic world of which Indo-China was a part was not stagnant; it was beginning its great revolutionary transformation. The French were hardly settled there when the Chino-Japanese war of 1894 further weakened the traditional order in what was the spiritual mother country of the Annamites—weakened it to the profit of another Oriental people. The revolutionary movement that had long been smouldering in South China was rapidly spreading, and revolutionary ideas and victories in Canton were bound to have repercussions in Hanoi. The expulsion of the Manchus, following on the defeat of the Russians by the Japanese, inevitably encouraged hopes in the breasts of the Annamite Nationalists; and French policy for long did little to discourage the growth of Nationalism.

In the oldest colony, Cochin-China, the withdrawal of the Annamite officials with their tax registers and other apparatus of government had forced the conquerors to set up a rough-and-ready system which, since it was established by the naval officers who had conquered the territory, was known as the 'admirals' system'. Cochin-China was rich; it had a docile and sparse population; and the admirals made not a bad job of replacing the old system. They established a school for training European officials in the language and customs of the country and, however offensive their rule was to the separation of powers and other constitutional principles, it was suitable to the situation. The Republic could not and did not tolerate such anomalies. Civil governors replaced the sailors; the school of apprentice administrators was abolished and the new and ignorant officials sent out from Europe made no attempt to learn the difficult local language and were forced to rely on venal interpreters and on missionaries for communication with their subjects. French law was imposed, with disastrous effects in a country in which the moral unit was the family and in which the idea of the individual as the sole bearer of rights and duties was a blasphemous novelty. Cochin-China was added to the list of full colonies, given a system of local government which, in effect, gave power to the tiny minority of colonists; and, in 1881, the formal honour of electing a deputy was conferred on the colony, that is to say, on the same tiny minority. If the rulers of the colony had all obviously belonged to the conquering race, the inert if proud natives might have borne it, but a principle of race equality which was not observed to the advantage of the indigenous inhabitants of the colony, worked to the advantage of Negroes and Indians. The patronage of the colony was largely in the hands of the deputies for Réunion and Martinique, with some allowance made for the claims of the little French settlements in India. In consequence a foreign law was administered to a conquered people, not merely by the conquerors themselves but largely by members of other subject races. Even more irritating was the rôle of the Indian moneylenders, all being or claiming to be French citizens, while the natives were only subjects. It is a common drawback to the imposition of European order and respect for formal contracts on native societies that it makes things easier for usurers. Here the grievance was peculiarly irritating, for the moneylenders were transients, taking their profits out of the country, not linked by any real ties either to their rulers or the ruled and able, by their privileged political position, to make the best of both worlds.

It would be unjust, however, to suggest that all the faults of French administration were due to coloured officials. The French employed far more white officials than was customary in either British or Dutch practice. This excluded natives from jobs which they could have perfectly well filled, increased the discontent of the native intelligentsia as it grew in numbers—and did not make for efficiency. The French clerk who was willing to exile himself to further Asia for a salary of less than £200 [1] a year was seldom, either by character or attainments, an impressive representative of the ruling race.

For all its faults, however, French rule in Cochin-China meant peace and progress in the Western sense of the word. The problems of society were simplified by the clean sweep made of native institutions during the conquest which had its advantages, while the natural fertility of the soil was given an opportunity to yield its fruits and was even increased by bold and successful engineering works.

Far more complicated were the problems of the semi-independent kingdoms which had come under French rule during the Tonkinese war. In Cambodia and Laos, the native civilizations were in an advanced stage of decay. If Annamite society and institutions were rather crude copies of Chinese models, Cambodian and Laotian society and institutions were parodies of Indian models. A faint survival of a caste system, a sacred monarch, a docile population, neither anxious nor willing to advance or resist advance, ensured that French rule should have no very formidable opposition to face. Indeed, encroached on to the west by the Siamese, to the east and north by the Tonkinese, the inhabitants of the Indian states of the peninsula had some reason to be grateful for the protection thrust on them by the French. It delayed, if it did not postpone for ever, their economic and political eclipse at the hands of their more energetic neighbours. The inhabitants of Laos had even more reason than the Cambodians to welcome the strong rule of the invaders; and, for the moment, French authority saved this decaying society as French science revealed the forgotten glories of Angkor-Vat.

Where French diplomacy was skilful, where French agents were tactful, the reverence of the natives of Cambodia and Laos for their hereditary sovereigns was used to win acquiescence in the rule of the foreigners. It was difficult, indeed, for officials bred in the official irreverent French masculine education to take seriously the sacred rites of the comic court of King Norodom. When Governor Thomson of Cochin-China forced his way into the royal bedchamber in 1884 to force the King of Cambodia to accept effective French control, he behaved naturally but foolishly and the price of his brusqueness was a rebellion led by the King's brother, Prince Sivotha, a rebellion which though not so serious from a military point of view as the activities of

[1] $1,000.

the Black Flags in Tonkin, was an expensive nuisance all the same. It was not sufficiently appreciated that it was impossible to display public contempt for the King and to expect, at the same time, that his subjects should preserve to the full their traditional reverence. Under superficial docility, the Khmers went their own way and the native officials were able to disregard the well-meant reforms imposed on them from above, the more that a system which gave the kingdom fourteen Residents in eighteen years, was incapable of rigorous control.

In Laos, the idle, cheerful, incapable people went their own way protected from their dangerous neighbours the Siamese and the Annamites, on good terms with the Chinese who provided the necessary minimum of economic energy, and isolated from the rest of Indo-China by a happy difficulty of communication. What their white rulers did or thought they were doing was no concern of the subjects of the petty kings of Luang Prabang and was even less the concern of the mountain people over whom French and Laotian authority was for long hardly even nominal.

In Annam and its dependencies, the problems were far more complex. In his deliberately isolated capital of Hué, the Emperor lived his semi-divine life, performed the sacred rituals and embodied the spirit of *tinh*, the same spirit that animates tigers and elephants. An elaborate civil service on the Chinese model administered justice and collected taxes from the thousands of village communities of the Empire. As conceited as their Chinese prototypes, the Annamite mandarins were angered rather than impressed by the military prowess of the Western barbarians. In the Emperor they had a sacred symbol whose value they refused to see depreciated. It was in this spirit that they forced an Emperor, who had received French envoys in person, to commit suicide, and the lack of tact with which successive French agents treated the incarnation of the dragon race who sat on the throne of Hué was bitterly resented. So far as Annam was concerned, the French had some appreciation of the situation, but they regarded Tonkin as a conquered appendage of Annam, still loyal to the deposed Le dynasty and ready to be delivered from the Annamite yoke, which meant, in fact, the rule of the *literati*, the ruling caste of scholars whose prestige depended on their knowledge of the Chinese classics.

Whereas the formal authority of the Emperor was acknowledged in Annam, in Tonkin a system much more like the direct rule of Cochin-China was instituted. The French overestimated the degree to which the Tonkinese disliked Annamite rule or overestimated the capacity of the Tonkinese to see the difference between one alien rule and another, and they certainly underestimated the solidifying force of the age-old system of government. In the long run, the natives came to share the contempt of their white rulers for the old learning, and the examinations for the mandarinate were abolished in 1915 with no great opposition.

But an unnecessary strain had long been put on the patience of the subjects of the Emperor, both in Annam and in Tonkin. Emperor after Emperor had been deposed, until there was some resemblance between modern Annam and the Japan of the age of Genji; and there were other vacillations in policy which were inevitable with rapid changes in personnel. (Tonkin had thirty-one and Annam thirty-two Residents in the forty years between 1886 and 1926.)

These were long-term problems; the immediate problem facing the French authorities on the conclusion of peace with China was how that formal peace should be made real. Whatever may have been the character of the original armed bands who resisted the French, by the formal end of the war banditry had become endemic. One of the young French officers engaged in the pacification of the frontier, Captain Lyautey, was convinced that banditry was deliberately encouraged by the Chinese mandarins of the frontiers who profited by it, as eighteenth-century British governors in North America sometimes profited by piracy. After years of wearying campaigns, the methods of Colonel Galliéni told, mainly because they were not merely military. By his system of the 'splash of oil' an area once pacified became a spreading centre of attraction for the great majority which wished to live peacefully. Peace helped markets; loyal villages were armed to defend themselves; and, by the time that Galliéni went off to pacify Madagascar, the back of the military problem was broken.

There remained a problem which is not yet solved. In the reaction against the forward policy of Ferry, the Paris Government showed its bias by a rigorous economy. The newly-conquered Empire had to try to pay its way. As little as possible of the cash and credit of the metropolis was to be at the disposal of Indo-China. Starved of funds, the French administration was able to do little more than preserve formal order: Indo-China, for the first fifteen years after the conquest, was very stagnant indeed. From this state it was rescued by an energetic Governor-General, Paul Doumer. That determined politician came out to the peninsula resolved to make his title of Governor-General a reality. The separate colonies and protectorates were to be forced to work together; their economic resources were to be pooled and a great programme of public works to be launched. He created a budget for the federation separate from the local budgets: he insisted that Cochin-China should pay out of her abundance a due share of the total cost of running the federal system: and he was authorized to contract a great loan on the credit of the federation itself. He made effective the three great monopolies of opium, alcohol and salt, all very lucrative, all very unpopular, all in varying degrees harmful. With the proceeds of the loans and the rising revenue, a great public works programme was put in hand. Roads and railways were built; the whole federation was united economically and, in France, the contempt for the possibilities of Indo-China that had long prevailed gave place to a modified version of Ferry's golden dreams.

Modern Indo-China owes a great deal to Doumer, but in one department he was quite incompetent. He increased the dislike felt by the natives for their European rulers, which was natural since the immediate cost of his great developmental schemes fell heavily on the peasants. The natives had other than financial grievances. They were excluded from effectual authority in their own country, and subject to the rule of a race whose egalitarian principles seemed to suffer a sea-change between Marseilles and Saigon. It was noted that even priests in their churches sometimes drew the colour-line and that even members of the League of the Rights of Man wore their principles with a difference in Indo-China. As in British India, the European women were declared to be an obstacle to the free intercourse between the races that had marked the earlier days. The very absence of colour prejudice in France, made the student who came home to an inferior position in his own country, after some agreeable years in Paris, all the more bitter and dangerous.

Yet there were improvements. The law, if it still in practice differentiated between colonist and native, did so in less striking degree. The worse abuses of the monopolies were attacked and modified in response to criticism in the press and Parliament. A few natives were added to the advisory 'Government Council', but discontent was rife among the intelligentsia and, perhaps more ominous, there was a recrudescence of banditry in Tonkin. To Albert Sarraut fell the task of supplementing the material development of Doumer's régime with political development. He came out in 1911 resolved to go back to the more sympathetic policy associated with the names of Paul Bert and Lanessan. He greatly improved the tone of the Civil Service, getting rid of the white official proletariat, throwing more jobs open to natives, insisting on a real knowledge of the native languages. He resisted the French passion for uniformity and the conviction that what is right in Paris must be right everywhere. More place was given to native law and to native administration of the law. What Doumer had done in the material, Sarraut did in the political sphere, and, on the eve of the Great War of 1914, France's greatest colony was far more prosperous and far less discontented than even an optimist could have anticipated in 1900.

CHAPTER V

MADAGASCAR

As in the origins of the conquest of Indo-China, tradition played a part in determining French action in Madagascar. In the reign of Louis XIV there had been designs on the island and the proximity of the great French colony of Mauritius kept the interest alive, but Mauritius was conquered by Britain during the Napoleonic wars. It was British, not French influence, that was active at the court of King Radamá I, who set about creating a modern kingdom in Madagascar at about the same time that another monarch of the same race was attempting the same task in Hawaii. Kamehameha had a simpler task than had Radamá, for Madagascar is the third largest island in the world, larger than France and not much smaller than Texas. Its population, though containing a considerable Arab and Negro mixture, is predominantly Polynesian and Melanesian, and the arms and policy of King Radamá established the predominance of the inhabitants of the central plateau, Imèrina, a people usually known as Hovàs. To the outside world the ruler of Imèrina was ruler of Madagascar. English arms were not the only allies of the Hovàs. English missionary activity benefited by and reinforced the authority of the Queens, for with brief intervals, the rulers of Imèrina all through the century were women.

Had Hovà authority been really coextensive with the island, France might never have got a foothold there, but many of the outlying tribes were as little contented with Hovà rule as the outlying tribes of the Ethiopian Empire were with Amharic rule. It was possible for the French to find client tribesmen like the Sàkalàvas, and from this client relationship came those opportunities of intervention and those quarrels over minor matters which led to the usual sequels—naval bombardment, landing-parties, a treaty giving France control of foreign relations and outright sovereignty over the magnificent harbour of Diégo-Suarez. By the treaty of 1885, France in Madagascar reached the position she had attained by the treaty of 1873 in Annam, but thanks to missionary effort, the main commercial and cultural ties of the island were with Britain, and the Hovàs were almost as much clients of the London Missionary Society as unwilling protégés of France. France had recognized that Queen Ranavalona III was ruler of the whole island, which was not true, and in return France expected to rule the island through her—which was optimistic. Even so, as experienced an administrator as Le Myre de Vilers, one of the founders of Indo-China, could make nothing of the division of authority. No reforms were introduced; there was no security for European property and so no development. It was realized that a real protectorate on Tunisian lines must replace the barren 'right of protection', and had the Queen been more sensible or less spirited, she might have settled down to the rôle of a protected sovereign with nominal powers.

The Queen and her noble kinsmen, the aristocratic masters of Imèrina, continued to resist French authority. The man who was to conquer the island, Galliéni, attributed the recalcitrance of the Hovà ruling class to a reasonable calculation. Their wealth came from plundering the lower castes and from the profits of alluvial gold-mining. 'It was evident that in the long run, with the coming of an honest administrative system and an incorrupt system of justice, it would be more difficult to squeeze without mercy the lower classes.' Galliéni added, with perhaps unconscious cynicism, 'The coming of numerous prospectors in search of gold would very soon dry up the other source of income.' However natural these fears were, the Hovà aristocracy was ill-advised to provoke French hostility, so ill-advised that Galliéni attributed their folly to the bad advice of the English missionaries who had assured their clients that the French were a vacillating people who could easily be diverted from their aims. This was an error. A French force under General Duchesne easily occupied the capital, for the Hovàs were not formidable military antagonists like the Maori, and, although the first conquest cost the French over 5,000 lives, only 20 of these were lost in battle. The rest were lost by disease, and the mismanagement of this expedition was soon a stock argument of the anti-militarist party in France. The Queen submitted; her anti-French Prime Minister was exiled and a more pliable one supplied. As it was the custom for the Prime Minister to marry the Queen, Her Majesty rebelled at this substitution. General Duchesne was not a very great soldier, but he was a Frenchman and he saw Her Majesty's point of view. His own candidate, he admitted, was 'already old, fat and with no physical attractions. So Her Majesty screwed up her face and several times put the question whether she was bound to have personal relations with him. I had to give her the assurance that she need not'.

This question settled, the Hovàs and the French might have settled down, the more that French action in recognizing Hovà rule as extending by right all over the island, actually favoured the rulers of Imèrina. Madagascar was just Tunis or Annam all over again. But not only was Madagascar not Annam or Tunis, in that there was no central generally recognized authority worth conciliating and working through, a protectorate of this type could not avoid leaving great power, economic and social, in the hands of the men-tors of the Hovàs, the English missionaries. France would establish law and order in the great island for the benefit of two hostile groups, the Hovàs and the missionaries. Because of defective com-munications, Duchesne had not received the order to *impose* conditions on the Queen in time and he had made a treaty with her. It is just conceivable that the treaty might have worked, even after the formal annexation of 1896, but the Malagasys, Hovàs and non-Hovàs alike, thought that their protectors were weak and undecided. There was a general uprising. The real conquest of Madagascar was still to be achieved and for that a new man was needed—Galliéni.

The new commander was the most famous of French colonial soldiers, trained in the hard school of the Sudan and Tonkin. He benefited from having no previous commitments in Madagascar and he saw his task as fundamentally simple; the influence of the Hovàs and their English friends must be destroyed. The non-Hovà tribes must be encouraged and, instead of vague professions of Hovà sove-reignty over the whole island, each natural unit must be won over to the French side, by tact and firmness. French authority would spread like a 'stain of oil'.

This policy involved a breach with powerful interests. To attack English influences meant attacking the missionaries, and that not merely meant alienating English opinion, but meant that Galliéni was suspect of clericalism. To that charge Galliéni replied that he ostentatiously kept himself apart from any Catholic religious observances, both because that was his personal habit—and good policy. He disliked the Jesuits, who were the chief Catholic missionaries on the island. He wanted the Jesuit Bishop replaced by a secular Bishop and other orders encouraged to come in. He wanted the French Protestants to take over the mission field of their English brethren, but he could not conceal from himself the fact, however distressing it might be to zealous Republican politicians in Paris, that the Jesuits were a source of French influence, cultural and political, while the London Missionary Society was a centre of English influence, and, in the colonial sphere at that time, 'England, there is the enemy' was as much a dogma of French colonialists as 'clericalism, there is the enemy' was of Radical politi-cians. The properties accumulated by the English missionaries through royal benevolence were taken over. Financial compensation was paid but the roots of English influence were cut.

Another aspect of Galliéni's policy which was soon under attack was his assertion that Madagascar was not and could not be a white man's country, that it could not be turned into a colony for settlement. Whatever was to be done, would have to be done through the native and his varied institutions. Through these institutions the Army was to work. It was, of course, to defeat and disarm the rebels, but its main task was to win them to acceptance of French guidance. The Hovà agents were to be got rid of (except in their own territories), and after a decent interval, the Queen was deposed.[1] The island was resolved into its natural tribal units and each unit dealt with on the lines suggested by its own character and possibilities. By 1902, the whole island was peaceful, although peace had been secured by methods distressingly lacking in uniformity. Lawyers, anxious to introduce modern conceptions of justice (and, Galliéni believed, not unmindful of the possibilities of a complete legal system set up in the midst of a litigious people); Treasury officials distressed by the irregular character of the tax system; all the political and administrative Haussmanns of Paris and Madagascar were highly critical of Galliéni's policy.

Galliéni was unshakable in his own convictions and he was able to resist political pressure. He treated the sickness of Malagasy society, a despair of the future revealed in a rapidly declining population, by using native society to work out its own salvation, by a system of taxation to force the idle to work—and by the use of this taxation for *obvious* benefits to the natives. The tax, in many regions, took the form of forced labour as education was made utilitarian, and the Malagasy was taught to cultivate his garden before he was taught to read *Candide*.

The success of this policy had its limits. The natives were not to be turned into industrious French peasants merely by the creation of legal peasant proprietorship and by compulsory labour. The population of the island was quite inadequate for rapid development. If the main lines of Galliéni's policy were never altered, there were occasional failures to imitate his Gallio-like indifference to the volatile religious life of the island. Governor-General Augagneur, who had been Mayor of Lyons, was an enemy of missionary activity, and in his own way as sectarian and ill-advised as any Methodist or Jesuit. The hopes based on the potentialities of the island as a large-scale producer of tropical crops, like the hopes based on an increased population brought about by assisted immigration, were groundless. Madagascar, if it was to be developed, would have to be developed by the Malagasy peoples despite their serious defects as members of a modern economic system. Ex-slaves, unemployed warriors, Hovàs put down from their seat of power—these were the raw materials of the new society growing up under French guidance. Some tribes failed to adjust themselves and continued to decline. Others took advantage of the peace imposed by France and of the new roads and new markets to move into the empty plains of the west, as the Tonkinese had moved, in the same circumstances, to the south. There a great cattle-raising industry grew up, and away from the depressing jungles of the east coast a new people slowly found its feet. As midwife and as nurse, France had succeeded.

---

[1] At the same time, the United States was ending the kindred monarchy of Hawaii.

CHAPTER VI

THE NEW EMPIRE

THE French commercial interest in Senegal dated from the early seventeenth century, if not earlier, and Saint-Louis and Goree had been prizes of war in the eighteenth, but there was and could be no effective conquest of the interior until the river steamer helped to solve the transport problem. Even that invention was of limited utility to the masters of the lower Senegal, since the river was safely navigable for only four months in the year and the good river highway of the region, the Gambia, was in British hands. It was the energetic Faidherbe who, under the Second Empire, set about turning the chain of trading posts into a colony, and the interest of the metropolis in the colony was mainly due to the importance of its geographical position on the way to South America. These advantages could not be exploited by the existing trading stations ; and the first step to the development of this asset was the creation of the new port of Dakar, which, at first, was merely a port of call for steamers bound for Brazil. As the limitations of the Senegal were realized, the remedy for the transport problem was seen to be the railroad, and in the first decade of the Third Republic, plans for joining the Senegal and the Niger were drafted, but their execution was long postponed.

In the scramble for Africa, Senegal was an obvious jumping-off ground. Its hinterland, of desert and scrub, was not at first sight attractive. A great French colonial official [1] compared it to a 'lunar landscape', but once its plague was remedied, the soil was less sterile than it seemed. The plague was human: slave-trading and tribal war. For nearly twenty years the history of the colony and of its expansion was the history of war with the Moslem chiefs of the military tribes. Chief of these was Samori, whose defeats and recoveries, flights and returns, made of him the local Abd el Kader. Pushing up the Senegal and across to the Niger, the French encountered the agents of other powers, chiefly of Britain. These agents, in their turn, were moving inland to the domination of the great emirates of what is now Nigeria. There were claims and counter-claims, and not till 1898 was the frontier question settled. By that time Samori was a prisoner; Dahomey had been conquered; and, after an initial disaster, a capable

[1] Van Vollenhoven.

engineer officer called Joffre had occupied Timbuctu. Existing French trading posts on the Ivory Coast and in Guinea had been linked up with the hinterland and a vast area had been added to French territory. It is true, as Lord Salisbury observed, that a great deal of that territory was light soil. There were dreams of compensating for superior German man-power with the aid of black troops, but not all officers shared the young Mangin's high opinion of African troops. Even though the Senegalese had proved admirable instruments of empire, there were not many of them, and the physically and morally inferior Negroes of the more tropical colonies were poor material for soldiers. In any case, poor or not, there were not many of them, for West Africa, wasted by war, the slave trade, and disease, was under-populated.

In all this region France was running a race with Islam whose progress, whatever effect it had in raising the cultural level of the natives, threatened to impose a barrier to their spiritual conquest by France whose impenetrability was fully appreciated by those who knew Algeria and Tunis. In other ways, West African society presented problems not easily solved by mere legislation. The abolition of slavery in 1901 was more or less nullified by the survival of domestic slavery in a society based on it. Only the prohibition of the slave trade was effective. The lesson of Algeria was learned in that there was no attempt to apply the disruptive principles of French land law and, as far as French rule impinged on native economic life, it was in the bias given to certain types of production rather than in direct alterations of the social structure. In Senegal, to produce ground-nuts; in the more southerly colonies, timber, palm oil, cocoa; and, in the hinterland, cotton; these were the general aims of French policy and in all except the last, the aims were achieved. The whole vast region could only be effectually developed by being free from its reliance on undependable rivers, and that meant great railway construction. The handsome profits of railway construction in Senegal encouraged a timid Chamber to authorize loans, and by 1923 the main railway system was completed. Not only was the hinterland provided with an outlet, but the isolation of the natives was broken down. With the growth of the railways went the growth of the ports. Dakar, from being a mere port of call, was given a magnificent artificial harbour and, growing like the prophet's gourd, became the capital of the whole of French West Africa.[1] In an area ten times the size of France, but with only a third of the population, a new civilization was being created.

In the basin of the Congo, French expansion was the work mainly of a remarkable explorer and man of action, Savorgnan de Brazza, an Italian by origin, an indefatigable traveller and a man of great nobility of character. It was largely thanks to Brazza that France secured a

[1] In post-war years the establishment of a permanent air service to South America has made it one of the key positions of French international commerce and communication.

foothold in the Congo basin between the Germans in the Cameroons and the agents of King Leopold of Belgium and Stanley, who were launching that ill-fated experiment in international administration, the Congo Free State. Officially an explorer under the direction of the Ministry of Public Instruction, Brazza was in effect an agent of French expansion. In the years immediately before the peaceful delimitation of tropical African colonies by the Berlin Act of 1885, possession was highly important, and treaties with venal native chiefs like Makoko, who had little idea of what they were doing, had yet a real diplomatic value. The little band of explorers, helped by and helping the French missionaries who were active in the region, secured for France what was thought to be a very valuable share of the spoil of Central Africa.

Before the spoil could be enjoyed it had to be prepared for use, and that took capital. A tropical jungle, with communication only easy by river, inhabited by the most disease- and superstition-ridden of Negroes, the debris of an African society plagued by the vices of the climate and demoralized by the slave-trade, was not immediately valuable, however great its potentialities. It was natural, then, that politicians should listen to the siren voices of company promoters who promised a rapid development if they were given great concessions of land and authority. Was not the same system working well in the Congo Free State? Was there not a growing demand for rubber from bicycle manufacturers and even from the new motor-car industry? After hesitations and amendments, concessions were given and economic control (which involved a practical exclusion of direct governmental control over great areas) was put into the hands of companies anxious to make rapid profits in a rising market. The profits were to come mainly from collecting wild rubber, for although there were conditions in the leases intended to encourage the growth of plantation rubber, no one took them seriously.

The example of the Congo Free State was followed. Natives were encouraged by payment in kind to collect rubber. If this did not stimulate them to industry, flogging, rape and murder were used. All the scandals of the Congo Free State were repeated on a lesser scale and the country which Brazza had sincerely hoped to civilize was devastated. The tormented natives rose in revolt and were easily and cruelly suppressed. News of what was going on reached the metropolis and evoked angry protest, especially from idealists like Péguy, who had seen in French expansion 'the introduction of justice, intelligence, humanity'. As the real source of evil was the exorbitant power of the companies, only the grossest abuses could be remedied unless the concessions to the companies were to be revoked. It was a fundamental maxim of French law that the State had to behave 'like an honest man'; and the concessions had many years to run. They could not be cancelled without compensation, and the Council of State was certain to rule that compensation would have to be very substantial.

In such circumstances the liquidation of the companies took time. In return for their vast temporary concessions they were induced to accept much smaller areas in absolute proprietorship. The attempt to develop the colony rapidly was over. In any case, the wild rubber industry was declining and continued to decline in face of competition from plantation rubber in the far-eastern colonies of Britain, Holland and France. The cession of a great part of the colony to Germany as part of the post-Agadir settlement, showed how little was now thought of the treasure-house won for France by Brazza and, although the Peace of Versailles restored the territorial integrity of the colony, it remained a poor relation.

Its depressed condition was in humiliating contrast to the rapid development of the Belgian Congo, now directly ruled by Belgium which, both economically and socially, was rapidly repairing the worst damage done by the Free State. Most striking proof of the stagnation of the French colony was the rapid fall in population: the spread of a deadly form of sleeping sickness reinforced the results of the growth of abortion. Without a native population, the colony could not be developed at all, but all schemes for introducing East Indian coolies or Senegalese failed. Only in recent years have improved hygiene and a more sympathetic handling of the natives begun to stop the rot. A 'back-to-Brazza' doctrine has been preached and, to some extent, practised, and although under-financed, public works at last are doing something to rescue this Cinderella.

If in North Africa and in Indo-China, in face of old, elaborate and self-satisfied civilizations, the assumption that French subjects could be fairly quickly and easily turned into Frenchmen was absurd, it was not so in tropical Africa. There, primitive institutions, illiteracy, a low level of sophistication and a mass of varying traditions and languages, none of them strong enough to play the rôle of Islam in North Africa or of Chinese culture in Annam, seemed destined to give way before the superior civilization of the conquerors.

The simple-minded rulers of the early revolutionary period of 1848 exemplified this belief by making the inhabitants of the old colony of Senegal, French citizens, not mere subjects, and giving them representation in the national parliament. The Second Empire, here as elsewhere, abolished parliamentary representation, but the Third Republic restored it.[1] The result was to create a privileged class in the 'four communes', the native citizens of which had the rank of French citizens without having to abandon their private family law. Their deputy might be an important figure in colonial politics and their municipal organizations were theoretically entitled to all the rights of a

[1] In the Chamber only; Senegal has no Senatorial representation.

metropolitan commune. As the colony of Senegal grew, this enclave was more and more anomolous and, without openly withdrawing its privileges, claims to share them were more rigorously scrutinized, and if communal autonomy was left intact, most of the important departments of local government were in practice removed from communal control.

Outside this area, the early government was 'assimilationist' but not egalitarian. Local native authority was ignored and, although natives were widely employed, it was outside the existing hierarchy of native society. 'Chiefs' were made and set over groups with whom they might have little or nothing in common and the power of native institutions was neglected and weakened by that neglect. The waste involved in such a policy was seen by such great administrators as Van Vollenhoven. 'Nine times out of ten,' he wrote of the necessary intermediaries between the white officials and the native mass, 'the intermediary is there: he is the chief with traditional authority.' Although the native authorities (where they really existed and had not been, as in the Congo, almost annihilated) were used, they were used to French ends, not to preserve native society but to hasten its elevation to French standards. All the time the objective was to supplant native ideas, as much as native techniques, with better ones. Native arts and crafts were, indeed, encouraged, but native ways of life were only temporarily tolerated if they stood in the way of the conquest of this barbarian society by French ideas.

The chief instrument of this progress was, and is, the French language. Of course, in addition to local native languages, there exist widely-spread native lingua francas like Mangingo, but as far as possible all literacy is literacy in French. Even in the schools for Moslem notabilities which have been established in those regions where Islam has a hold, the main language of instruction is French, with only the necessary minimum of Arabic for Koranic studies. The whole school system is designed to produce a French-speaking class useful to the Administration and a vehicle for the transmission of French ideas. 'To instruct the masses and discover and bring out an élite' is the basis of French educational policy according to a leading official.[1] The complete absence of a colour line in education, which means that children of the same class are educated together, without regard to race, makes this a practicable policy as it would not be in a British colony. Yet there are serious limitations on the degree to which a policy of assimilation has as yet succeeded. As native authorities are far more the agents of central governments than initiators of policy, and as all high posts are in French hands, the millions of Africans are in fact governed by a handful of officials. Nor is the representation of Senegal in Parliament any real remedy. Not only are the four communes a tiny oligarchical

---

[1] Governor-General Carde.

community, but comparatively little colonial legislation passes through Parliament anyway, as the President of the Republic is, for most purposes except finance, a law-maker for the colonies. It is, theoretically, not very difficult for a native of education or official rank to become a French citizen, but in fact only 2,000 or so have done so, and the great enterprise of Europeanizing so many millions of Africans is still directed from the top. The school and the Army, these are the main instruments of this policy, and in both of them the African himself is at best seldom more than under-master or a non-commissioned officer. But true to the Roman precedent that has haunted French colonial policy, France is trying to make of barbarians, men of the modern world if not complete Frenchmen.

The expansion from Senegal had, by the end of the nineteenth century, extended French authority over all the West African hinterland and to various sections of the coast. It was natural that this great French domain should be given a common government, as it was natural that Indo-China should be given one. A Governor-General was set up at the head of eight (now seven) colonies in what was styled a 'federation'. It was not a true federation, much less of a federation than Indo-China was. There were no authorities like the white colonists in Cochin-China or the Emperor in Annam to limit the authority of the Governor-General, and it is more realistic to think of the Governor-General delegating authority to the governors of the colonies and permitting them some local financial autonomy, than to think of the federal units delegating any authority to the Centre. A corresponding system was set up for equatorial Africa, but that poor and neglected region was in no position to work a federal system, and its local units were shifted about as changes of policy or financial stringency dictated.

It was not until 1894 that the growth of the empire forced the creation of a permanent Ministry of the Colonies, and that department, it should be remembered, has no authority, even to-day, over North Africa. Needless to say, the Colonial Ministry, like every other, suffered from the musical chairs of French politics. It was difficult for a Minister with only a few months in office to think out and impossible for him to apply a policy, especially as he might be Minister merely as part of some elaborate political combination. He was under the constant inspection of colonial deputies and senators and harassed by many different interests. It was notorious that colonial posts were often filled, from the highest to the lowest ranks, with men whose claims were political in the narrow sense of the word. Even the office of Governor was used in this fashion. As late as 1911, an energetic Minister [1] found the cadres of this rank full of 'elderly gentlemen who had been planted there in the early days of the creation of our empire in return for electoral services that they had rendered at Béziers or

[1] Messimy.

Chateauroux'. They were long absent from their posts and, as in the eighteenth-century British Empire, it was customary to have the work done on the spot by a deputy, while the nominal governor drew his salary at home.

It was fortunate that neither Ministers nor Governors were the only or the main makers and executants of policy. A 'superior colonial council',[1] representing not merely official, but unofficial opinion in the colonies (normally, of course, *white* unofficial opinion), was and is a check on mere ignorance and on bad faith. A more interesting, indeed a unique institution, is that of the inspectorate. These *missi dominici* have no parallel in other colonial systems, although individual officials sometimes fill that rôle by special commission.[2] These officials have the largest powers of inspection and can command any services needed for the purpose of their investigations from the local civil and military authorities, but they can give no orders and cannot occupy any administrative post. Every French colonial administration knows that every three years or so it will undergo a rigorous investigation by experts, with no local axe to grind, but with very great and varied experience of all parts of the Empire. In Paris, a Minister or a great official in the Ministry has always at hand a mass of critically sifted information which enables him to contrast like things with like and makes possible that minimum of efficiency in services which the same system produces in English local government.

In Africa, as elsewhere in the Empire, France has been far more willing to devolve financial power than political power. Where identifiable bodies can be found or created whose opinion on economic and financial questions would be of value, chambers of commerce, notables, or the like, they are usually given a chance to make their views heard. If these bodies have no real powers except that of publicity and pressure, these powers in a system whose central government is democratic are not negligible.

In its sixty-odd years of existence, the new French Empire has undergone many changes, nearly all for the better. After the first heroic years, there was a let-down both in personnel and policy; politics weakened the administration and too hasty measures to exploit the economic resources of the colonies led to great waste and, in some cases, to great scandals. There has been in the last thirty years a very marked improvement in the governing personnel and a corresponding improvement in the intelligence of the policy carried out. The passion for mere uniformity that provided Saigon with the handsome and absurdly ill-designed barracks that young Lyautey saw, that rode roughshod over native custom and governed ancient peoples in the

---

[1] Now known as the 'Superior Council of Overseas France'.
[2] In recent times the work of Sir Alan Pim in various British colonies has been like that of a French inspector.

spirit of M. Homais, is gone. Indeed, in sympathetic understanding of the cultural achievement of their subjects, the French have set a good example to other peoples. It may be true that French officials learn in Paris more of the philology of the ancient Khmer tongue than any command of current speech that will be of use to them in Cambodia, but they are less likely to have a philistine contempt for their *administrés*. The comparative immunity of the French from vulgar colour prejudice is a great psychological asset, combined as it is with a firm belief that any people, with time and trouble, can be trained to appreciate the highest of civilizations, i.e. French civilization.

The rigorous protectionist policy imposed on all parts of the Empire which are not covered by international treaties, on the whole works to the disadvantage of the colonies, although, of course, special colonial interests gain by their protected market in France. Yet, as France has become more and more industrialized, her colonies have suffered less than they did from their compulsory confinement to the resources of French manufacturers. The trend of the world has been towards those closed economic systems of which Ferry and the early colonial school dreamed. The long period of investment is now beginning to show results in Indo-Chinese rubber and in Sudanese cotton. Great capital investments, like the Tonkinese and African railways, have been indeed too systematically planned, with too much of an eye on imperial communication and too little on immediate economic needs. But they have been effective in breaking the cake of custom and, like military service, forcibly introducing backward peoples to modern civilization, in its best and worst aspects, to schools and hospitals, to alcoholism and tuberculosis. They have helped to create a common culture on the Senegal and to make easy the migration of hardy Tonkinese from their over-populated home to empty Cochin-China or the rich lands of the lotus-eating peoples of Laos. The hope of Frenchifying the sixty million Negroes, Arabs, Annamites and the rest is a dream, but when the French Empire goes the way of all empires, it may leave a spiritual and cultural mark on its former subjects more like that left by Rome and less like that left by Carthage than could be safely predicted of some rival colonizing powers.

BOOK VI

THE REPUBLIC SAVED

J'ai été nourri sous l'Empire, dans l'amour de la République. 'Elle est la justice', me disait mon père, professeur de rhétorique au lycée de Saint-Omer. Il ne la connaissait pas. Elle n'est pas la justice. Mais elle est la facilité.

ANATOLE FRANCE, *L'Orme du Mail.*

CHAPTER I

THE 'RALLIEMENT'

I

IT is a tribute to the power of Boulangism that, for a moment, it shook the confidence of Pope Leo XIII in the permanence of the Third Republic and halted, though not for long, his design of freeing the living body of the Church of France from the corpse of monarchy. Ever since he succeeded to the throne and the meagre assets of the policy of Pius IX, Leo XIII had contemplated, like a new Ezekiel, the valley of dry bones of French Royalist politics and had decided that (barring a political miracle) the cause of the Most Christian King was as dead as that of the Most Serene Republic of Venice. , The ignominious collapse of the conspiracy cleared the way for the long-matured papal plans and, if that was possible, increased the papal contempt for the tactics and judgment of the French Conservative politicians.

As Pope Leo saw the problem, France was a country which had determined, however regrettably, to abandon its ancient and modern dynasties. The Houses of Bonaparte and Bourbon were equally things of the past, and the Papacy, which had existed long before either of the rival families, should imitate, in the nineteenth century, the policy of the eighth. As Pope Zacharias had sanctioned the transfer of the crown of the Franks from the House of Clovis to the House of Pepin, a later Pope could ratify the definitive exclusion from power of the two families that had succeeded the House of Pepin. But although there was still a good deal of popular Bonapartism, and although the higher ranks of the Army and Navy had a large number of commanders who had served Napoleon III and would gladly have served 'Napoleon IV', 'Napoleon IV' had died before reigning. It was, not with the Bonapartes that the Pope was concerned, and they had, in fact, lost most of their leaders, like Mackau, Paul de Cassagnac and Baron Tristan Lambert, to the Royalist cause. The claims of the Bourbons were more serious. Most of the Conservative leaders in France were aiming at the restoration of the Comte de Paris. In this aim they had the sympathy of most active Catholics, priests and laymen alike. The Republic had become identified in the minds of its friends . and enemies with hostility to the Church.

In consequence, the Church was on the wrong side of the fence in France, constantly harassed in minor ways and unable to halt the constant drift of governmental policy towards a position of definite hostility. Pope Leo, who had to reconcile himself to the permanent state of war between his own Government and the usurping Government of the King of Italy in Rome, was not so enamoured of the situation as to reconcile himself to being equally alienated from the Government of France.

Pope Leo, if given less to illusions than his predecessor, was, like him, unwilling to recognize that the papal temporal power was lost for ever. The Italian State was poor, threatened by revolution, a *parvenu* treated with condescending patronage by its allies, Germany and Austria. If there was a general European war, or even a prolonged crisis, the papal diplomats thought that the whole rickety structure would collapse and, from the ruins, the Pope might recover, if not the old Papal State from sea to sea that had been partitioned in 1860, at least the territory lost in 1870. Such dreams necessarily involved taking a kindly view of the policy of the French Republic which was on exceedingly bad terms with Italy and undoubtedly ready, if the worst came to the worst, to use the Pope against the Italian State. Such an alliance would be more natural and much easier if Pope and Republic were on better terms. So, apart from his realistic contempt for the political folly of the Royalists, the Pope had his own reasons for wishing to make a deal with the infidel Republic. A successful ending of the feud between Church and State, the penetration of the Republican governing class by French Catholics, would be good for the Church of France and for the territorial policy of the Papacy.

The most important reason, from the point of view of the French Church, for a change of policy, was the need for an ending of the repeated sacrifices of Catholic interests to the lost cause of the Most Christian King. This was certainly the view of the most prominent member of the French episcopate, Cardinal Lavigerie, Archbishop of Algiers and of Carthage, the only French bishop of international renown. His foundation of the White Fathers had spread his fame all over the Catholic world and, as a leader in the war on the African slave-trade, he was known far outside the circles of the faithful. In Algeria it was impossible for the State and the Church to remain on the coldly formal terms of the mother country. The activities of the Cardinal-Archbishop were necessarily of importance in an overwhelmingly Moslem country, where the differences between one kind of infidel and another were not clearly understood and, as far as they were understood, not always appreciated as they were in enlightened circles in France. In Africa, Lavigerie was a power, especially after the occupation of Tunis, for the ardent cardinal set himself at once to restore the glories of the see of Carthage and to revive the memories of Saint-Louis who had died on Tunisian soil on a crusade. These activities were not unimportant to the French Government, faced not only with the problem of Moslem hostility but with the more immediate problem of the Italian colony in Tunis. Inevitably Lavigerie had become a powerful figure; very different from the docile administrators or political nonconformists who filled the sees of France.

Lavigerie had been first a Bonapartist and then a zealous Legitimist, but he was always a man of government; and he was as much an admirer of Gambetta as he had been of Napoleon III or the Comte de Chambord. It was natural, then, for him to regret the Royalist affiliations of the majority of the bishops and clergy. Before the elections of 1885, Lavigerie had been forced to accept close collaboration with the Royalists, but his politics were already suspect. The result of the elections strengthened the Cardinal in his judgment, for, however great the moral victory, the Conservatives were, in fact, beaten. The rally of the Republicans between the first and second ballots which undid the effect of the early Right victories was by many attributed to rash Royalist boasting. The Right had not won but had lost, on this view, because it was tainted with Royalism. France, the first ballot seemed to show, was ready to change her governors but not the form of government. A year before, Monseigneur Mourey, French auditor of the Rota, had prophesied as much. 'France', he wrote in his memorandum designed for the Pope's eye, 'is steadily moving towards the Republic. . . . What is to be done? Two things: first of all publish a doctrinal declaration on the adaptability of the Church to different kinds of political institutions and apply the traditional principles to the present condition of France; then tell our bishops to prefer a Republican candidate, if he gives adequate guarantees on religious matters.'

Thus was set out, before it was acted on, the policy of the '*Ralliement*', the acceptance by French Catholics of the fact that the Republic existed and was going to continue to exist, and the drawing of the conclusion that the Catholic elector should prefer a frank Republican (if otherwise acceptable) to the most pious and acceptable Royalist whose usefulness to the Church would be gravely limited by his rôle as a member of what was doomed to be a permanent opposition. The Government of France was left in the hands of professed enemies of the Church who were enabled to stay in office because the elector was offered as an alternative, not merely a Government more friendly to religion, which he might be expected to want, but a royal restoration which he most decidedly did not want. The most effective reply to this line of argument was provided by Monseigneur d'Hulst, the able and aggressive Rector of the Catholic Institute in Paris.[1] D'Hulst was

[1] The chief centre of higher studies for the French clergy and for some of the laity.

not merely a noble, Royalist by birth and breeding, he was a close personal friend of the Comte de Paris. He despised the Republic and the Republicans, extending his contempt to some, at least, of the bishops nominated by Republican Ministers. The policy suggested by the Mourey memorandum, he argued, was based on a false premise. It was a mistake to think that there existed a majority of French electors devoted to the Church or at least friendly to it and only forced to vote for anti-clericals by the monarchist tendencies of the official Conservatives. 'In forty or fifty departments of the Centre, the country people have little faith. They are attached to the outward observance of religion; they want to have a church, a parish priest, funeral services; but hardly anybody but the women make their Easter duties. . . . The town workers have higher feelings. When you can get hold of them individually, it is easier to reawaken Christian feeling in them; but taken in the mass they belong to the socialist sects.' It was useless to waste time lamenting a situation which could not be changed. The Republic was bound to get worse instead of better, but that had its advantages: 'there is a double current which pulls all the Conservative interests (including the Catholic interests) towards the monarchy [and] all the elements of disorder, including the hatred of religion, towards the other camp'. All good Catholics might be Conservatives, but not all good Conservatives were Catholics; in face of the danger to property and order presented by the radicalization of the Republic, all those classes, faced with moral and material ruin, were forced to unite and unite on the common ground of the monarchy, the sole remedy for the dire disease. Far from the Church suffering from her association with the Royalist party, she gained, thereby, the support of important sections of the population which had no real objection to the lay policy of the Republic.

The Pope had little reason to be tender of the feelings of the defeated party. Their chief, the Comte de Paris, had not only committed the folly of supporting Boulanger, but had allowed his daughter to marry a Protestant, Prince Waldemar of Denmark, without insisting on the customary religious guarantees. Many French Catholics had lamented too openly the good old days of Pius IX. There were some who even deplored the recognition by Pope Leo of the legal government of Spain under Alfonso XII. They had found a chief in Cardinal Pitra, whose conduct brought on him a rebuke of a severity not to be equalled for another generation but then to be excelled. Of course the drift in papal policy had not escaped notice, and finally Pope Leo got support from such purely orthodox journals as the *Univers* (though Eugène Veuillot had long fought such an abandonment of the policy of Pius IX) and from the *Croix*. The latter paper went so far in its attacks on Royalism and on the Pretender that the Comte de Paris thought of appealing to the Pope to silence the polemics. An enterprise that failed helped to break the ground for a new political edifice to shelter the interests of the Church of France. Albert de Mun, the most eloquent Catholic orator, had attempted to found a Catholic party, avoiding any doctrinal views on forms of government, but offering the workers a programme of legislation, 'inspired by the Church's spirit', which was to give the working-class 'the protection it needs against the abuses of power [and], in moral customs governed by its doctrine, the example and patronage which the upper classes of the nation owe it'. The success of the German Centre Party was noted in France, but the political frivolity of so many Catholic leaders was manifested in this programme, appropriately enough approved of by the 'League of the Counter-Revolution'. The Monarchists disliked it as much as did those few Catholics who understood anything of the spirit of modern France. Dazzled by their comparative success in the elections of 1885, the Royalists would have nothing to do with the new party. There *was* a Catholic party in existence, the Monarchist party; let it pick up a few hundred thousand votes more and the game was won. Assailed on all sides, the new party died still-born.

Some of the illusions that had gone to its begetting survived. As the centenary of 1789 approached, the Republic prepared to celebrate the beginning of the Great Revolution with an exhibition in Paris. Albert de Mun and his friends, inspired by a group of country gentlemen in Dauphiné, tried to counter these celebrations by a kind of parody of the original States-General, an assembly in which 'cahiers' [1] were to be presented purporting to show that the Revolution had been a complete failure and must be undone. When the time of the exhibition and the centenary came round, the Republic had just escaped from the Boulangist danger. The Revolution might be a failure but the Counter-Revolution was an even greater one. Yet there were plenty of stern and unbending Catholics to refuse to have anything to do with the accursed thing, ready to find Albert de Mun too ready to make terms with the Mammon of Unrighteousness, insisting, as Paul Vrignault wrote to Maurice Magnien, that the Revolution which was being celebrated 'is fundamentally impious'. But, alas! there was abroad in the land 'a spirit of conciliation and compromise at any price which is ruining the strongest characters'.

Paul Vrignault was soon to be given conclusive proof that this detestable spirit was strong in very high places, for the Pope had finally got tired of waiting for the natural leaders of the French Catholics to read the signs of the times. Although less than twenty candidates at the elections of 1889 had dared openly to call themselves Monarchists, the greater part of the Conservative and Catholic candidates were badly-disguised Royalists, making the worst of both words, losing the respect due to frankness and the chance of success offered by acceptance

[1] In 1789 the members of the States-General brought up lists of grievances, the 'cahiers'.

of the fact that France was a Republic and gave every sign of remaining one. Laymen like Raoul Duval had tried to get their co-religionists away from the barren ground of dynastic politics. Churchmen like Cardinal Thomas of Rouen had tried to free the Catholic cause from the imputation of ineradicable hostility to democracy. M. Jacques Piou, enlightened by the collapse of the Boulangist coalition, had attempted to found a 'Constitutional Right', which was to be a 'great Tory Party' disputing, within the framework of Republican institutions, with the 'Whigs' of the Left.

None of these efforts had shaken the loyalty of the majority of active Catholics to Royalism or, at least, their inert acceptance of the old links binding throne and altar together in a common impotent dislike for the institutions of modern France. There must be a dramatic assault on this inertia, and the Pope decided that Lavigerie was the man to give that publicity and force to the initiation of the new policy which it required. Lavigerie was more than ever convinced of the necessity of such a move, but he had some reasons for hesitation. His missionary efforts, his schools and his armed caravans, his hospitals and his new cathedral in Tunis, all took vast sums of money. He was the chief beggar of the French Church. He had no illusions as to the effect on many of his supporters of becoming the leader of a movement for reconciliation with the Republic. Many a man and woman who had contributed generously to his good works would cut off supplies if he publicly advocated acceptance of the Republic. Lavigerie foresaw such blows to causes he held dear as the resignation of Keller, a leading Catholic politician, from the Anti-Slavery committee in Paris which was one of the chief sources of money and power for the Cardinal's campaigns. But he was too much the good centurion to refuse: he was to be the mouthpiece of the Pope as soon as he could find a suitable opportunity.

He found it in the presence of the French Mediterranean fleet in the harbour of Algiers and in the absence of the senior officials who might have entertained the officers. The Cardinal stepped into the breach. To his astonished guests, Lavigerie gave a 'toast'[1] which included the assertion that 'when the will of a people had clearly declared itself, when the form of government has nothing in itself (as Leo XIII has recently declared) contrary to the sole principles by which Christian and civilized nations can live', it was the duty of good citizens to accept the form of government at whatever cost to personal feelings. The officers listened in icy silence. The Admiral, Duperré, who was notoriously a Bonapartist, simply proposed the health of the Archbishop and clergy. The first battle was a defeat for the Cardinal— and the Pope.

From October 27th, 1891, the leaders of the French clergy and

[1] This 'toast' was not what the word means in English, but a longish speech.

laity displayed a marvellous tenacity in trying to persuade themselves and the world that the flamboyant Archbishop of Algiers and Carthage had spoken only for himself. Lavigerie, who had hoped for speedy results, was bitterly disappointed with his episcopal brethren and with the chief who had sent him into battle but who showed no signs of openly supporting his champion. It is true that the Pope later declared that he had only given Lavigerie permission 'with my encouragement' to launch his appeal for the frank acceptance of the Republic by the Catholics of France. He had been impressed by the vigour with which the Cardinal had stressed the weakness of the Royalists.[1] Lavigerie, exposed to all the rebukes and reproaches of the angered Royalists and unsupported by his episcopal brethen, was of a temperament to which discretion did not come naturally. 'Hares in mitres', was his description of the French bishops. He had a good deal to put up with. The more dignified Royalist organs were merely pained and reproachful, but the ebullient ex-Bonapartist, Paul de Cassagnac, let loose on the Archbishop of Algiers a flood of abuse of the type usually reserved for Ministers and officials of the 'slut'. [2] 'There was in the past at Carthage a faith that has remained famous: it was called Punic faith. It would be regrettable if Cardinal Lavigerie were solely inspired by this bogus theological virtue.' The clergy could not be as frank as M. de Cassagnac, but there were priests whose opinions did not differ very much from his. The Bishop of Réunion and the Bishop of Annecy were the only open adherents of the new policy. The reasons given by the Bishop of Annecy in a letter to Monseigneur d'Hulst showed an acute sense of realities not common in the clergy. Isoard had no admiration for the Republic, but he knew that 'for the great majority of Frenchmen, the priest loves the old régime and wants the old régime, and this old régime frightens people. Now it died with Louis XVI. . . . The monarchy is gone for ever. It suited a state of mind which *only survives in the memory of educated people [but] of which the great mass of electors has no conception*'.[3] The conviction that the monarchy was dead was far more widely spread than the conduct of the bishops would lead one to believe. Cardinal Richard, the Archbishop of Paris, had been a spectator of the abortive Royalist rising in La Vendée in 1832 and had been convinced that, even then and in the most devotedly Royalist part of France, there was no real monarchical sentiment. Yet Richard dared not act on his convictions. Spurred on by d'Hulst and tied by his old relations with the Royalist leaders, he could only organize another neutral Catholic organization which tried to unite Catholics by ostentatiously avoiding discussion of what divided them. At the head of this organization, 'The Union of Christian France', he put Chesnelong, and the rest of its leaders were as symbolical of the

---

[1] Lavigerie, said the Pope, had called the Orleanists 'capons'. [2] The Republic.
[3] Italics mine.

old alliance of throne and altar.[1] But the appearance of the old gang at the head of the never-victorious Army irritated the younger generation. It was a veteran politician, Dugué de la Fauconnerie, who expressed (as far as he was concerned with unconscious prophetic force) their feelings. 'None of the men of the old parties! Not X! Not Y! Not Dugué de la Fauconnerie.'

The siege of Rome was undertaken by the fiery Bishop of Angers, Freppel, deputy for Brest. Freppel argued that Lavigerie's policy (it was still possible to feign to believe it was not the Pope's) was based on the erroneous belief that 'the Republic, in France, is simply a form of government as in Switzerland or in the United States for instance, and not a doctrine, a doctrine fundamentally and radically contrary to Christian doctrine'. It is true that the American example had greatly weighed with the younger generation of French Catholics. The names of Cardinal Gibbons of Baltimore and of Archbishop Ireland of St. Paul represented, for them, a policy of liberalism, of a readiness to accept the facts of the modern world that had not prevented the rapid growth of the Church in America while the policy of Royalist intransigence had not produced any very attractive political or religious fruits in France. Archbishop Ireland, indeed, did not shrink from carrying the war into France and with preaching the religious advantages of republicanism in face of shocked Catholics in Paris.

The reported readiness of the Pope to dismiss, as obsolete, the claims of the House of France, claims based on so many centuries of history, provoked bitter reflections. Freppel did not fear to hint that the same principle of acceptance of the accomplished fact might force the Pope to recognize the loss of his temporal power in Rome. For the Kingdom of Italy seemed just as secure as the French Republic.[2] But the time was past when, in Paris, the Nuncio, di Rende, had been a willing listener to the hopeful Royalists, as, in Rome, his house was a centre of credulous zealots who not only believed in the restoration of the Pope's temporal power, but in the restoration of the King of Naples and the Duke of Parma! The Pope's mind was made up; it would be vain for Royalist journals like the old *Gazette de France* to remind him of the Royalists who had died for the Pope at Castelfidardo and Mentana. Leo XIII at last came into the open and in an interview with the *Petit Parisien*, followed by an encyclical, he made the Lavigerie policy publicly his own.

The encyclical [3] distinguished between *constitution* and *legislation*. The Catholics were to accept the Constitution and alter the legislation, by all constitutional means. It was a fatal blow to the 'Union of Christian France'. As Chesnelong put it, the new policy

[1] The Vice-Presidents were MM. de Mun, de Mackau, d'Herbelot and Keller.
[2] Monseigneur d'Hulst harboured a peculiarly irritating suspicion that one object of papal policy was to win the support of French Ministers for diplomatic action against Italy.
[3] *Inter multiplices sollicitudines.*

needed new men. Even if he had thought the Pope right that would have been true, but he thought the Pope wrong and the Pope insisted on a formal acceptance of the policy of the *Ralliement*. Chesnelong submitted and, after reading without comment the papal message to the Catholic Congress that had met while still hoping to evade the issue, he left the hall, saying tearfully, 'Twice disowned; by the King and by the Pope'. Not everybody was as docile as Chesnelong. The Comte de Paris objected to the assumption that the political control of Frenchmen who were Catholics was in the hands of the Pope and remarked, ironically, on the triumph of the principles of Gregory VII involved in the papal confirmation of the Republic. His chief representative, the Comte d'Haussonville, who had, as a child, refused to wear a tricolour badge in 1830, was no more willing to obey the Pope blindly now than he had been to obey his mother then. Monseigneur d'Hulst was elected to succeed Freppel in the Chamber and managed to avoid committing himself (practising what the anti-clericals called the policy of the 'flag in the pocket'), but he found, to his distress, that the Breton priests to whom he owed his election were completely convinced of the rightness of the papal policy. They were 'Catholic-Republicans' to a man. For, despite the bitterness of the Royalists, bitterness made manifest in the attacks of his old friends on Albert de Mun when his acceptance of the papal policy became known, the action of Leo XIII had finished off a moribund 'party.

How was the papal policy to be received by the Republicans? By the Radicals it was of course received as another clerical trick, a new Trojan horse from whose belly would issue forth the enemies of the Republic if the Republicans were foolish enough to allow it entrance into the city. But the Radicals were not in power and their attacks did not do anything to make the prospects of a union of Conservative forces less attractive to many Republicans. Boulangism had frightened many of the governing classes, who had reason to wonder whether the violence of their anti-clericalism had not been in part responsible for the coalition of Left and Right that had nearly destroyed the régime. Old Gambettists like Challemel-Lacour expressed more kindly views of the possibility of domestic peace between Church and State than would have seemed decent a few years before. It was not only the memory of Boulangism that won some Republican support for the new policy. Behind the Radicals were the Socialists. On May 1st, 1890, had taken place the first of the annual labour demonstrations, borrowed from America, but which in France were given a far more definitely revolutionary character. May Day in Paris in the 'nineties of last century was not, in the eyes of the alarmed bourgeoisie, a mere proletarian version of July 14th; it was an annual rehearsal of a revolution. The Radicals had now rivals on their Left to force them into even more revolutionary ways. Can we wonder that Jules Ferry was ready to accept genuine converts to the Republic? 'The Conservatives who have rallied to the Republic will bring over others. This is natural and not at all disturbing.' The country had need, he declared, of religious peace, there was no question of going to Canossa. But there were real issues at stake; real interests which could be united on a common Republican ground. There were Catholics who for slight concessions, even for a mere cessation of further anti-clerical activities, would be willing to join in the defence of private property even with such former hammers of the Church as Ferry.

It was not only the Socialists who frightened the bourgeoisie. There were the Anarchists, whose bombs were, some Catholics asserted, the natural fruit of the tree of Godless education. Such views were not confined to Catholics. It was Séverine, the famous left-wing journalist, who said in her usual dramatic style that the lay State had 'shut up Heaven but had not opened the bakers'-shops'.[1] But while not all the world agreed that the wave of outrage was the result of the Godless schools and the collapse of traditional morality, the attitude of the Anarchists helped to force the timid on to common ground. On his way to the guillotine, Ravachol had sung the new Père Duchesne.

> Pour être heureux, nom de Dieu!
> Faut pendre les propriétaires!
> Pour être heureux, nom de Dieu!
> Faut couper les curés en deux.

A good many proprietors and priests thought that, if they resisted in common, they were less likely to be hanged or cut to pieces separately.

The welcome given to the *Ralliement* was not all based on fear or cupidity or political calculation. A generation had grown up since the establishment of the lay Republic and it could not be expected to share the bitter animosities of its elders. The psychological equivalents of the compulsory religious observances of the École Normale under the Second Empire that had embittered the young Aulard, or of the stupid snobbery of the richer pupils of the Catholic Collège Stanislas that had wounded Anatole France, were now as likely to be found in the lay educational system. The reaction of the younger generation against Republican orthodoxy in the schools was soon to find brilliant expression in the first of the great political novels of Maurice Barrès.[2] Now that Laicism and Republicanism were orthodox, youth, naturally rebellious, was ready to react against them. So there was noted in the generation coming of age around 1890, not merely a more lively

---

[1] This attempt to link up anti-clericalism with anarchism did not escape the vigilance of veteran guardians of the Republic. René Goblet wrote to Arthur Ranc to tell of an adventure of his in the provinces, his encounter 'with a gentleman, very agreeable by the by, [who] took trouble to meet me: he then tried, determinedly, to indoctrinate me with anarchism. Now, I have since learned, beyond all doubt, that he is an agent of the Jesuits, what is called a short-coated Jesuit, which does not prevent his publicly preaching radicalism, even socialism; anarchism he keeps for private discourse'.

[2] *Les Déracinés.*

and intellectual faith among those who had remained Catholics, but a certain sympathy with Christian ideas among those who had lost their faith or never had any.

The 'Neo-Christianism' of Henry Berenger and his school was not very long-lived, but it was part of the climate that made the *Ralliement* possible. The prestige of German and English thought had its part in weakening the older French Voltairian tradition of scepticism towards all that was not crystal clear. One of the leaders of the Catholic youth of this generation, Frederic Boudin, even invented a Germanic Ultra-montanism, and looked to America, to the disciples of Father Hecker, to free real France, that is Germanic France, from Latin formality and lack of spirituality. The times seemed ripe for what Spuller, the veteran ally of Gambetta, was to call 'the new spirit'. In the background, silenced if they were clergy, hampered if they were laymen, were many thousands of French Catholics only forced by papal authority into formal compliance. On the other were unconverted Republicans for whom the Republic was anti-clerical or nothing, who would far rather have had, in some cases, an anti-clerical king than a clerical republic. Both the uncompromising Catholics and their perpetual enemies would have agreed with Renan in the condemnation he had passed long before on 'clerical liberalism'. 'An old man is not ridiculous if he wears the clothes of his age; he is ridiculous if he puts on a red cap and assumes airs of youth which contrast with his baldness.' The Catholics who objected to assuming the red cap were confirmed in their aversion by the bursting of the great Republican abscess, the Panama scandal. Hopes revived; the Catholics who had rallied seemed ludicrous to the faithful remnant, since they seemed to have entered the Republican house just as it, at last, was doomed to collapse on their foolish heads.

CHAPTER II

PANAMA

I

IN 1888, when the Republic was in danger, the Socialist Deputy of Nîmes had declared in what, it was hoped, was a moment of southern extravagance, that the fuss made over the Wilson affair had been hypocritical. 'Among the thirty-three members of the Budget Committee there are at least twenty Wilsons.' It was no time for such charges, even when made in after-dinner speeches, and the rash Numa Gilly was sentenced to a year in prison, but the great corpse of Panama was beginning to stink.

The idea of a Panama Canal was as old as the day when white men first gazed on the Pacific, but the wild surmise did not become more than that until the success of the Suez Canal attracted attention to the possibility of repeating the success in Central America. Both Britain and the United States had a real interest in the region and in the problem, but neither public nor private enterprise in those countries was ready to take the risks. It was inevitable, too, that men's minds should turn to the maker of the Suez Canal and inevitable that the energetic and vain old man, whose dreams had once come true, should see, in Panama, a fitting crown to his romantic career.

Ferdinand de Lesseps had been born in 1805, the year of Austerlitz. He was sixty-four when the Suez Canal was finished and when he married his second wife, aged twenty-one.[1] To undertake a new enterprise on the scale of Panama when he was seventy-four was a heroic folly, as his family pointed out. Chairman of a 'Congress of the Interoceanic Canal' in Paris, he swept away the doubts of most of the experts, took over from Napoleon Bonaparte Wyse his Colombian concession and prepared to repeat in America his success in Egypt. That success had been due, more than anything else, to his incurable optimism. In the discourse of the Protonotary Apostolic at the opening of the Suez Canal, the prelate praised 'that superhuman faith in the accomplishment of this gigantic work'. Naturally, Ernest Renan, receiving Lesseps into the French Academy, was rather more ecclesiastical in his manner and

---

[1] He had twelve children by her, the last born when he was eighty.

quoted (in 'a positivist sense') the words of Holy Writ, 'If you have faith as a grain of mustard seed, ye shall say unto this mountain, Remove hence to yonder place; and it shall remove'. It was a bad prophecy, but an accurate diagnosis of Lesseps' mind. By faith, he had made the Suez Canal. By faith, he had kept the Company from liquidation in the early difficult years of its operation.

Lesseps, it should be remembered, was not a professional engineer, but, in the original sense of the word, an *entrepreneur*. One of his chief technical assistants at Panama, M. Bunau-Varilla, has described how politely and incredulously Lesseps listened to technical objections. 'He saw in them obviously only another of those engineer's ideas that had hampered him so much at Suez, and which he had got over by letting Nature and common sense have their way.' It was this bold empiricist who won over the Canal Congress to his pet idea, that the Panama, like the Suez Canal, was to be a sea-level canal, 'a new Bosphorus'. This inspiring idea was so magnificent that technical arguments for a canal with locks to get round the great difficulty that the canal had to be pushed through rain-soaked hills, not through a flat desert, were swept aside for what were largely æsthetic reasons. Faith would move mountains. Fundamentally, the Panama enterprise failed because faith was not enough; the back of the energy of the Company was broken in the unfinished Culebra Cut.

Lesseps was, like so many of his generation, influenced by the social ideas of the Saint-Simonites. Indeed, the Suez Canal was one of the main works which were to exemplify the faith of the sect. He delighted to think that the Suez Canal Company was not just another vast financial enterprise in the hands of a few financiers. Its constitution was (and is) designed to limit the power of the great shareholders [1] and Lesseps rejoiced to think that so many small shopkeepers, cab-drivers, peasants had had faith in him, had taken shares in the Suez Canal and that their faith had been rewarded. So, when the Panama Canal Company was finally launched, provision was made for holding the general meeting of shareholders in the *Cirque d'Hiver*.

Lesseps appealed to the small investor partly because he wanted to, partly because only from the small investor could he get the necessary funds without putting himself into the hands of the great banks. But to appeal to the small investor meant appealing to a credulous and timid class. They were incapable of reading a balance sheet, but they could be won over to trust the man whom Gambetta had christened 'the great Frenchman', the man who, with Victor Hugo as his only rival, incarnated what pride 1870 had left in French hearts. But they were timid; this was their all, their first adventure in high finance, or possibly their second, after they had tasted the sweets of Suez. Because

[1] For this reason, the British Government is not able to control the Company as effectually as its large shareholding would suggest.

they were timid, because the first attempt to raise capital was a failure, and because he was incurably optimistic, Lesseps repeated his Suez mistake. He underestimated the cost of the canal and asked only for 300 million francs.[1] He was offered twice as much, but even twice as much would not have been enough. From the start Panama was hampered by shortage of funds; crippled by the constant threat that money would run.out before the canal was finished. The original shareholders saw their share in the total future assets getting smaller and smaller; the way to get good terms out of Panama was *not* to have come in on the ground floor. To continue to raise funds, it was necessary to use, more and more shamelessly, the main asset of the Company, 'the Great Frenchman'; and that asset began to waste. To keep it from wasting, it was necessary to buy off critics: and so an increasingly great proportion of the money raised was spent on all classes of blackmailers, from very great figures of the journalistic world like Émile de Girardin and Arthur Meyer, down to the owners of the most obscure sheets, like the *Bee-keepers' Journal* and *The Line Fisherman*. Finally it became necessary to pay, not for favourable publicity, but for mere silence. The offices of the Panama Company became a kind of out-door relief organization for Paris journalists. These methods of exploitation were not unknown before Panama and are not unknown now, but there had never been such a prey. Gulliver lay there helpless, bound by the gossamer bonds of confidence which he dared not break— until the canal was finished.

The canal seemed ever further from being finished. After the collapse the whole story of Panama was told by its enemies, who had usually their own reasons for showing that it died of its own sins in Central America and was not bled to death in Paris. There was, of course, mismanagement, in the allotment of contracts, in the design of machinery, in the organization of work. The difficulties were prodigious. Until the science of tropical medicine had made Panama habitable, yellow fever killed Europeans as fast, at times, as they could be sent out. The chief engineer, Dingler, who boasted that Panama was really healthy, was refuted by the loss of his own family. Ships lost all their passengers and the records of the great school of civil engineering, the 'Centrale', had soon a roll of honour that recalled the Polytechnique in war-time. In such an atmosphere, moral relaxation was as inevitable as in war. Cargoes of newly-landed prostitutes were announced by the slang-code, 'lobsters arrived'. The isthmus became one vast gambling hell and the three most flourishing industries were brothels, gaming houses and coffin manufacturing. As the news of the daily plundering at home spread, it was difficult to keep a spirit of extravagance from affecting the men who were risking their lives to build the canal. So there came into being examples of conspicuous

[1] £12,000,000 or $60,000,000.

waste, like the chief engineer's villa, 'Dingler's Folly', and, back in Paris, the blackmailers had another weapon to use.

The real weakness of the canal was due to the fundamental miscalculation of Lesseps, his refusal to recognize the necessity for locks; as long as the dream of the sea-level canal continued, the main work of the engineers was wasted. The rumours of a breakdown grew as the appeals for fresh funds became more extravagant, and the Government at last took action and sent out to Panama, M. Rousseau, a distinguished engineer who, though cautious and non-committal in his public report, was pessimistic in private.

Distress was converting even the obstinate Lesseps, now over eighty. It is true that he would not give up his idea of the 'new Bosphorus' and the plans provided for the alteration of the locks into a sea-level system when revenue should justify it, but at least the canal was on the way to completion. The engineers had learned a great deal and the great initial error was being remedied. All that was wanted was money, but that was harder and harder to get. Despite the secrecy with which the report of M. Rousseau had been surrounded, there had been a leak, although how there could be a leak when the Minister of Public Works, the distinguished engineer, M. Baïhaut, was in office, was hard to see. For Baïhaut was not only a Republican Minister and not a Morny, he was a professional moralist, an officer of 'the Society for the Promotion of Good' and an orator who never let a month pass without a public testimonial to the advantages and attractions of virtue. He was his own Madame Husson and, like the hero of Maupassant's story, he fell. He fell twice; once by seducing the wife of an old friend who was not of a forgiving temper and again by allowing himself to be tempted by the opportunities open to a Minister of Public Works to get his share of the spoils of Panama. By the time Baïhaut saw his chance, all the ordinary means of raising funds had been exhausted. There only remained the issue of fresh securities sweetened by a lottery. A corresponding lottery had helped to provide the funds to complete Suez, but that had been authorized under the Second Empire. It would be harder to get the Republic to consent, even for a good object, to such methods, harder or, at any rate, more expensive. In 1886, the price for Baïhaut's support or silence was a million francs, but, as the bill did not pass, he only got 375,000.[1]

The raising of funds for Panama was so closely bound up with publicity (or blackmail) and politics (or corruption) that it needed expert attention. The first financier of the company was a banker called Lévy-Crémieux, but he was soon replaced by a more brilliant figure, the Baron Jacques de Reinach. Reinach was a German Jew, an Italian Baron and a naturalized Frenchman. His background made him one of the representative figures of the new world of cosmopolitan

[1] £40,000 ($200,000) and £15,000 ($60,000).

and mobile finance and, through his nephew and son-in-law, Joseph Reinach, he had close connections with the dominant French party, the Opportunists. Joseph Reinach had been a close associate of Gambetta's, was one of the editors of *La République Française* and a rising Opportunist deputy of Seine et Oise. Although the Baron refrained from open political activity, or, as he put it, 'from the list of candidates but not from the combat', he was active in many affairs closely associated with politics, financial combinations like the conversion of the *rentes*,[1] various railway schemes and other activities that had done himself, if not the State, some service. He had friends like Albert Grévy and Camille Dreyfus and he was on at least friendly terms with such eminently respectable figures as Léon Say. His large income was lavishly spent in splendid hospitality, in fostering the arts, especially those arts which, like the opera and the ballet, brought him into contact with young women. He was, as his relations with his son-in-law showed, a man of strong family feeling but there was nothing narrow about his affections.

It was Reinach, with the aid of another German Jew called Arton, who looked after those aspects of the financing of Panama that would look oddest on a balance sheet. Although the Opportunists were the party in power, that, in the French system, did not mean that the parties not in power could be neglected, for Ministries might come and go, but the Chamber and Senate remained to be cajoled and coerced. So the Radicals had to be won over too, and that side of the job (it is believed) was left to Dr. Cornélius Herz. Herz, unlike Reinach and Arton, was a native of France; he had been born in Besançon of Bavarian Jewish parents who had carried him off to America where he was naturalized. He had returned to France, where on the strength of jobs in a pharmacy, an insane asylum and a short period as an *interne* in a hospital, he was commissioned as an Army doctor in 1870 and given the Legion of Honour (as a foreigner). The new-made knight next tried to make a fortune in America, picking up a doctor's diploma in Chicago (then not hard to do), a wife and, somehow or other, a connection with the nascent electric-light industry. He managed to get accepted in Paris as one of the great pioneers of electricity, to make a good deal of money and some valuable friends. Most important of all, he made a friend or ally of Georges Clemenceau.

Clemenceau had his own medical and American experiences behind him, but was moved by different ambitions from the adventurer whom he allowed to buy a big share in his paper, *Justice*. He needed money for his paper and he had less than none of his own. He had extravagant tastes; he had run through all the money of his American wife and he had taken a mistress whose previous lover had been the Duc d'Aumale, who was not merely a prince of the blood, but a multi-millionaire.

---

[1] National debt.

Cornélius Herz had undoubtedly a talent for risky financial operations, but he owed a great deal to the general belief that behind him stood Clemenceau, who was not only the most formidable debater in France, but one of the most formidable duellists.

In a few years, 'the Doctor' was a great Parisian figure, if not in quite the same circles as those adorned by the Baron de Reinach. He was even given testimonies of esteem from General Boulanger and from the Grévys, Madame Grévy accepting from him two valuable bracelets for her granddaughters with an alacrity that astonished Charles de Lesseps. Herz, like Reinach, began his relations with Panama as a political and financial agent, but this simple sharing of the work became complicated by the transformation of Herz from a highly remunerated lobbyist for Panama into a blackmailer, on a colossal scale, of Reinach. What was the hold of Herz on Reinach is not known; some common crime, some unknown folly of the Baron's past; perhaps, as suspicious Frenchmen have suggested, knowledge of some treason of Reinach's that even his friends could not excuse or hide. Reinach was now, as was said,[1] a parasite who, when full of blood, was sucked dry by Herz and had to begin over again, and the final victim was the vast body of the Panama Company.[2] As the victim grew more and more anæmic, Herz grew more and more exigent and, as the directors of Panama grew more and more desperate, it was necessary to bring pressure to bear on them not to resist, for resistance meant that Cornélius Herz might blow everything up. Everything meant the parliamentary Republic, for it was 1888 and the final crisis of Boulangism was approaching. So Freycinet, Clemenceau, Ranc all combined to induce Panama to pacify the angry Doctor. But in this critical year, the Government did more than defend itself; it allowed the company to make a last effort, to float a lottery-loan for seven hundred and twenty million francs.[3] Both Houses accepted the bill; the Minister of Finance professing to be completely neutral. The loan was a disastrous failure; only two hundred and fifty-four millions were raised.[4] It was the end. Despite some convulsive struggles the Panama Company had to go into liquidation; work was stopped on the canal and it began to be realized that all the vast investment was lost.

II

The shareholders of Panama refused to believe their evil fortune and then, when the truth was known, appealed to the Government to aid them, by providing funds whereby work could be resumed before the concession fell in. In a smaller number of cases, they asked for

[1] By Barrès.
[2] A list found in Reinach's archives bore the simple legend 'Herz Blackmail'. The sum noted on the list was nearly ten million francs (£400,000 or $2,000,000).
[3] £28,800,000 ($144,000,000). [4] £10,400,000 ($52,000,000).

investigation of the affairs of the company. It is possible that with a comparatively small investment, the French Government could have finished the canal on the new plan. This would not have done much good to the shareholders, at any rate for a very long time, but it would have salvaged something for French national wealth and prestige, but the rulers of France had had enough of Panama.

Reluctantly, the Chamber asked the Government in 1891 to open an inquiry. In January 1892, Fallières, the Minister of Justice,[1] announced that no time had been lost, although his private attitude displayed no earnest hope that all speed would be made. The collapse of Panama was on so great a scale that, even had there not been special reasons, a Government might have hesitated to increase, by investigation or prosecution, the misery and anger of the unfortunate investors. They had lost nearly £60,000,000 ($300,000,000); it was the greatest disaster since the collapse of the Empire, the greatest purely financial disaster since the Mississippi scheme of nearly 200 years before. The governing class suspected that if the story of how the Panama bill had passed became known, it would be difficult to keep it from appearing to reflect on the system, as the Teste affair had reflected on the Monarchy of July, as Jecker's bonds had on the Second Empire. It must be remembered, in defence of the various Ministers who did their best to stifle the scandal even at the cost of an economy of truth, that they had the fright of Boulangism just behind them, and that they really believed that régimes died of scandals, especially Republican régimes, bound to be virtuous by their very nature. They had managed to hush up Panama long enough to kill Boulangism, perhaps they might hush it up altogether.

These hopes of silence were destroyed by the appearance of a series of articles entitled 'The Inside Story of Panama'.[2] The new 'Mermeix' called himself 'Micros'. His real name was Ferdinand Martin and he was an ex-employee of the company with his own grievances to put an edge on his zeal. 'Micros' had not really been in the secrets of the great company, but he kept the public interested and the Government frightened, and he distracted attention from Baron Jaques de Reinach, which was natural enough, as the Baron had supplied 'Micros' with some of the information for that very purpose. What was not quite so natural was that the Baron's chosen instrument of protection and aggression should be a new journal founded expressly to combat that international Jewish finance of which M. de Reinach was so striking a specimen. With Panama, the Libre Parole and its editor suddenly became important political figures.

La Libre Parole had been founded a few months before by the chief mouthpiece of anti-Semitism in France, Edouard Drumont. Its sub-

---

[1] President of the Republic, 1906–13.
[2] 'Les Dessous du Panama', which might also be translated 'The Dirty Linen of Panama'.

title was 'France for the French', a cry that has not yet lost all its force. For Drumont the enemy from whom France was to be delivered was the Jew. He did, from time to time, assail Italian immigrants, English monopolists of the sardine fisheries, as well as American women, frivolous and ill-behaved, who got foolish French noblemen to marry them by a pretence of wealth and, once the title was safely acquired, admitted that they were poor and that their husbands would have to keep them! He had, too, a poor opinion of French Protestants and one of his collaborators was the author of a book denouncing the political dominance of careerists from the south of France, but the real enemy was the Jew. In 1886, Drumont had published the book that made him famous, *La France Juive*. This twelve-hundred page tract at first fell flat, but a duel with Arthur Meyer, the Jewish editor of the smart society paper, *Le Gaulois*, a duel in which Meyer committed the grave sin of seizing his opponent's sword in his left hand while running Drumont through with his right, gave the necessary publicity.

La France Juive sold by the tens of thousands and its author became known and hated or admired, as the mouthpiece of the rising anti-Semitism of many Frenchmen. The book was not wholly undeserving of its fame. Drumont at his best was a resourceful pamphleteer, a combination of an inferior Veuillot with an inferior Proudhon. He had not taken part in the brutal press-war of French politics for nothing and he might have adopted *caritas non conturbat me* as a motto. The theme of his book was the conquest of France by the Jews. Beginning with some of the standard race mysticism about Aryans and Semites and complaints that official anthropology was in the hands of Jews so that their permanent physical and psychological marks were not sufficiently dwelt on, Drumont passed on to his real theme. A series of Jewish immigrants, headed by the Rothschilds, had come into France since the Revolution, penniless, and look at them now! They shot down honest peasants who did a little bit of poaching on the ill-gotten preserves of MM. Rothschild and Ephrussi, and under a pretence of Liberalism, they were active in the most violent attacks on Christianity and specially on Catholicism. These specific charges were eked out by a general résumé of Jewish crimes in the past and present, including a declaration of belief in the ritual murder charges and a translation of Chaucer's 'Prioress's Tale'. But for all his talents and for all the French appetite for verbal savagery, Drumont would not have become either a hero or a villain if there had not been plenty of fuel for his fire.

La France Juive appeared during a period of acute economic depression and Drumont provided an explanation of the workings of the trade-cycle that appealed to harassed shopkeepers or to small tradesmen feeling the first impact of large-scale industry. On Marxian principles, these victims of finance capitalism ought to have become aware of the

275

general class-war. Drumont showed them the source of their evils in the wealth of the Rothschilds. It was inevitable that an attack on 'high finance' would involve anti-Semitism for, while in France as in most other countries, high finance had its share of eminent Christian representatives, those bankers who were not Jews were often Protestants. Under the old régime and since the Revolution, banking, in Paris at least, had largely been Swiss, when it was not Jewish.

This state of affairs had been made more general and more deeply felt as a result of the failure of the *Union Générale*. This attempt, either to get a share of the loot or to free banking from its heretical servitude, had failed, not only with a great loss of money and prestige, but in circumstances that gave some plausibility to Drumont's charges that it had been ruined by the Rothschilds and by such political representatives of the existing banks as Léon Say—and Léon Say was a Protestant. The Protestants, it was asserted, like the Jews thought more of their spiritual kin outside France than of the rights of the country they helped to plunder. Like Monod they backed English missionaries against French interests in Madagascar, just as the Jews worked up agitations against such natural allies of France as Russia. Backed by English hypocrisy they aroused superfluous sympathy for the victims of Russian self-defence, while ignoring the far more serious wrongs suffered by the poor Irish peasants of Falcarragh 'the most gloomy and desolate part of Ireland' at the hands of British police egged on by London Jewry.

The grievances of the French Catholics against what were to be called, a little later, the 'métèques', were not confined to finance. The practically complete breach between the Church and the Republic had meant that, in certain departments of the administration, it was rare to find a practising Catholic in a position of power. A Jewish prefect could, with impunity, observe Passover, but a prefect who was as openly zealous in the observation of Easter might find himself under violent attack from a paper like the *Lanterne*, whose main stock in trade was anti-clerical scurrility and whose editor was a Jew, the great 'priest-eater', Eugène Mayer. The Republican purging of the administration of justice had resulted in the prominence in the courts of Jews and Protestants, and the anti-clerical policy of the Ferry Government had meant that the decrees had often had to be enforced on Catholics by Jewish and Protestant officials. Needless to say, many Jewish and Protestant officials were conscious of the delicacy of their position, but not all were, and even those who were most amiable in social relations with the Church were sometimes guilty of the faults of taste that Anatole France was to illustrate in the person of the Jewish prefect, Worms-Clavelin.

The Conservative party in France was still numerous, rich and even hopeful. Unwilling to think too deeply about the cause of their defeats, unable openly to blame either Pope or King, the Conservatives were grateful to the writer who expressed, with great polemical talent, their bitterness. Since the death of Louis Veuillot, there had been no authentic voice of the dogmatic and sometimes unfairly harassed country-priest; there had been no authentic voice of the little squire who, in his heart, hated having to accept an Orléans as King; there had been no authentic voice for the small tradesman or workman in those regions of the South where religion and politics had always been mingled and where to the old target of the rich Protestant, was now added the even more attractive target of the rich Jew.

Drumont was fitted by temperament if not by genius to replace Veuillot. The victims of his pen who were most harshly treated were not the Rothschilds, but the great nobles who courted them. Drumont did not spare the Royal Family, the Duc d'Aumale or the Duc de Chartres, or the bishops or, for that matter, the Pope. For him the *Ralliement* was the rescuing of a decayed régime by cunning Italians. The refusal of the Church to admit that, once a Jew always a Jew, was another cause of pain for an ostentatious Catholic like Drumont. One of his chief lieutenants, Jean Guérin, has recounted the disgust he felt when the famous Jesuit, Père du Lac, remonstrated with him for attacking some converted Jews named Dreyfus. Another early ally of Drumont, Jacques de Biéz, went about asking priests if it were true that 'Jesus Christ was a Jew? Drumont doesn't seem to mind, but I can't swallow it.' A few years before, a leading Catholic, Anatole Leroy-Beaulieu, had complained that the clergy, above all in its lowest ranks, was hostile to liberalism, thanks in part to a defective education, in part to 'sheets which, far from enlightening them about a society of which they know nothing, persist in deceiving them with dangerous memories and elusive hopes'. This naïveté had been well illustrated by the welcome given to the famous anti-clerical pornographer, Léo Taxil, when he had 'returned to the faith' and had invented in 'Diana Vaughan' a Catholic rival to Maria Monk. Drumont had not been taken in by Taxil, but by the time that he founded the *Libre Parole*, he had won the support of many priests, 'sons of the soil who have not the timidity of many shamedfaced conservatives. They like strength and willingly pardon even excesses due to a kind of generous indignation.'

Generous indignation was not enough to make *La Libre Parole* a great success. Duels and libel actions were the chief handicaps of Drumont's campaign, and while the duels usually paid one way or the other, libel actions were unprofitable. Within a few weeks Drumont was condemned to £4,000 ($20,000) damages and three months in prison for attacking the probity of a Republican politician whose character ought to have been above suspicion, since he had begun life as a preacher and teacher of the new Kantian ethics that was to replace in the schools of the Republic the older Christian moral theories. M. Burdeau, like M. Baihaut, was vindicated by the Republican courts. But for the Baron de Reinach, Drumont might have been silenced by the mere shortage of material. He had, it is true, the advantage of having been cool to Panama in its great days. He had attacked the first financier of Panama, Lévy-Crémieux, and, by accident or design, he had assailed, while they were still powerful, many of the leading figures of the financial and political world, Clemenceau, Freycinet, Burdeau, Baïhaut, Antonin Proust, Cornélius Herz, Arène.

Drumont was in prison for his libel on Burdeau when he began to receive from Reinach, through Andrieux, the ex-Prefect of Police who had gone over to the Boulangists, the materials for a fresh campaign, materials provided by the demoralized Baron on the condition that he should be kept out of the columns of the *Libre Parole*. In supplying Drumont with materials, Reinach had been too clever by half. *La Cocarde*, the chief Boulangist journal, had joined in the campaign, seeing in the scandal its way to revenge on the victors of 1889. Within the Government, Loubet, the Prime Minister, and, after some hesitation, the Procureur-Général, Quesnay de Beaurepaire, saviour of the Republic in 1889, had decided against prosecuting any of the directors of Panama; the politician because he feared the political consequences; the lawyer because he was doubtful if any legal fraud had been committed. Ricard, the Minister of Justice, was less content, and the Boulangists in the Chamber were already demanding replies to awkward questions and, if Ricard did not get his way, his resignation would be an even greater disaster than the prosecutions, for he could appear as a martyr of probity, prevented from doing his duty by presumably corrupt colleagues. No one wished to give the pompous lawyer who was known as 'La Belle Fatma' a chance to become a hero.

On November 19th, the parliamentary campaign began with a broadside from Floquet, the President of the Chamber. The conqueror of Boulanger had been charged with receiving 300,000 francs [1] for electoral purposes in 1888. His reply was brief, complete, and should have been conclusive. 'Not only did I demand nothing, but I asked for nothing, I got nothing, and I distributed nothing.' Except for a few cynics, the simple affirmation of the President was received with roars of applause which had just ended when members began to look at that day's copy of the *Jour* [2] which had spread on its front page an inspired statement in which a 'close friend' of Floquet's admitted that he had received the money but, fighting to save the Republic at death grips with an enemy provided with ample funds from unknown sources, he had asked some great companies, including the Panama Company, for 'their financial aid in the battle just begun'. Floquet had prepared two lines of defence, one true, one false. He had himself used the false one at the very moment that a friendly paper used the true one! It was a bad beginning for the notabilities of the Republic.

It was not the only breakdown in staff-work that day. In a

1 £12,000 or $60,000. 2 Not the *Jour-Echo de Paris* now published.

desperate attempt to save Reinach, Loubet and Burdeau had tricked Quesnay de Beaurepaire into postponing the arrests, but the Procureur had seen through their game and insisted on obeying the orders of his chief Ricard who had, in his turn, tried with little success to quiet the parliamentary storm by informing the Chamber that the machinery of justice was in motion and all was well.

While the parliamentary war was raging with doubtful fortune, the Baron de Reinach was engaged in his last desperate campaign. He had seen the *Cocarde*, he knew that the silence of the *Libre Parole* was no longer enough. One man could save him, Cornélius Herz, and he implored Rouvier and Clemenceau to go with him to make this appeal. The Minister of Finance, the most formidable politician in France, and the great financier set out together to act as ambassadors to the master blackmailer. Herz was inflexible, and Reinach tried a last card. Accompanied by Clemenceau, he visited Constans whose fine hand was seen by connoisseurs in part of the press campaign. Constans, like Herz could, or would, do nothing. There was a last unpleasant interview for Reinach with his nephew and son-in-law, Joseph Reinach, whose career would be compromised, perhaps fatally, by the conduct of his uncle. The Baron's allies had failed him; his family was embittered. He spent an hour or two with two young sisters whom he kept and, at one o'clock in the morning, got home. At a quarter to seven he was found dead in bed. One of the chief witnesses would never tell his side of the story.

If anything was needed to make of Panama a first-rate scandal, the death of the Baron supplied the want. It was impossible to avoid suspicion of foul play. The official cause of death, 'cerebral congestion', was believed by few; there was much talk of suicide and some of murder. It was against this dramatic background that Jacques Delahaye, the formidable and deeply unpopular Boulangist deputy, demanded of the Government and the Chamber, the appointment of a committee to inquire into the charges that the Panama Company had corrupted members of Parliament.

It was to be the day of light, not like the day of darkness when Reinach had died, like Polonius, a 'rat killed behind the arras'. The Shakesperian comparison is that of a young Boulangist deputy of the left-wing of the party, Maurice Barrès. Delahaye hated the system which he had failed to overthrow. Barrès did not altogether dislike a system that provided such admirable literary subjects as did French parliamentarism, but he despised the victors, the more that among them was his old philosophy teacher, Burdeau, who was to suffer the disaster of immortality at the hands of a pupil who had revolted against the man and the doctrine.

Delahaye was in a difficult position; he knew, through agents of the incriminated directors, that there had been corruption, but he had no proofs. His tactics were to make general charges, but to refuse to be drawn into giving particular instances which might be impossible to prove and thus to force the reluctant Chamber and the still more reluctant Government to set up the machinery for investigation. That done, somebody would talk! To every cry of 'names' he answered, 'Vote the inquiry'. It was a contest of nerves. 'The names! The names!' 'If I had to give the names of all involved there would have to be an all-night sitting.'

Floquet was still President, still with some rags of reputation and, abandoning his pretence of presidential impartiality, he, too, demanded names. As the accusation went on, over the protests of hereditary custodians of the Republic like Boissy d'Anglas, the Deputies banged their desks to add to the roar of their shouting, a noise, says Barrès, that 'recalled the sound of scorching followed by a scream made by the branding iron on the shoulder of a convict'. For all their shouts, the majority knew that Delahaye had won—that round. The inquiry was voted.

The Committee was presided over by Henri Brisson, whose reputation for probity was well enough founded to survive even this dangerous job. There were more immediately exciting investigations at hand. There was the trial of the directors of Panama for fraud and there was the trial of the politicians for corruption. The task of saving what could be saved of parliamentary dignity was too much for the clumsily cunning Loubet. The rumours of murder or suicide which had spread rapidly after the convenient death of the Baron had forced the Commission to demand an autopsy, and Loubet and Ricard had foolishly tried to evade the demand. The Government fell and the Baron was dug up, too late to confirm or refute the rumours that insisted that he had died by poison in the way, Herz had insisted, Reinach had earlier tried to kill *him*. Ribot succeeded Loubet and his tactics were subtler, to give in when he had to, but to treat the whole scandal as an attempt by enemies of Republican institutions to weaken the régime. 'French democracy would know how to take these calumnies.'

In the meantime, French democracy was treated to a series of new revelations, by the liquidator of Reinach's bank and by Gaston Calmette of the *Figaro*, who was to learn how dangerous a trade political revelations could be. Ribot did not deny that there had been corruption, but he concentrated his moral indignation on the directors who were charged with this grave offence—and with them, one politician, who no longer sat in the Chamber. What was to be called the 'Republic of Pals' was still in command.[1] The incriminated directors refused to play the game; they were determined not to stand their trial alone and the fatal cheques were released, or rather the stubs of the cheques with which parliamentary support for the last great loan had been bought.

[1] 'La République des Camarades.'

How many cheque stubs would turn up? What other evidence had Reinach left behind? What did Herz or Arton hold? What politicians, other than the Boulangists, were behind the attack? Was Constans playing the game of the opposition? It fell to Floquet, the now terrified Floquet, to announce to the Chamber the Government's request for the waiving of the parliamentary immunity of five deputies, Emmanuel Arène, Dugué de la Fauconnerie, Antonin Proust, Jules Roche—and Rouvier. It was a small number, but all, except Dugué de la Fauconnerie, represented the Republican parties; all were prominent and Rouvier was one of the most important politicians of the régime, *the* great financial expert of the system. It was Rouvier's defence that remained in men's minds. He admitted taking money from Panama, but it had been for the defence of the Republic. What was wrong with that? His personal honour was intact, conscious as he was 'of having been involved in the most important business of this country *without my fortune having increased abnormally*'.[1] It was a disastrous slip and cost Rouvier exile from office for the relatively long period of ten years. Five senators were also charged, one of them the inevitable Albert Grévy.

It was a Republican débâcle, even though Rouvier and others were masters of the tactics that have become classical, of reproaching their critics with past Royal or Imperial scandals. But there was bigger game even than Rouvier, and it was the emotional, unstable, but fearless Déroulède who dared to attack the most formidable figure involved in Panama. To whom was it due that Herz had been rapidly promoted to the high rank of Grand Officer of the Legion of Honour? 'You all know; his name is on all your lips; but none of you dare say it, for there are three things which you fear: his sword, his pistol, his tongue. Well, I defy all three and I name him: it is M. Clemenceau.' Herz, Déroulède went on, was a foreign agent and Clemenceau was under his influence. It was this charge that nearly ruined Clemenceau. His friendship for England and Englishmen, his command of the language, his rational dislike of any policy hostile to England which could only help Germany, all were remembered against him. His enemies, numerous in all camps including his own, were delighted to see him go down. Clemenceau's reply was a brilliant improvisation, but few were the faithful friends who stood by him. He was stamped as an agent of the British Foreign Office, not merely as the complaisant partner of a financial gangster. A duel was inevitable and, a sign of how his luck turned, the infallible marksman missed Déroulède three times. Déroulède missed him, too but that did not matter, for, as he said, 'I have not killed M. Clemenceau, but I have killed his pistol.'

The policy of making the directors of Panama, anybody except the politicians, the scapegoats, was aided by the fact that since Ferdinand

[1] Italics mine.

de Lesseps was a Grand Officer of the Legion of Honour, he could only be tried in an appeal court, that is to say without a jury, and his rank forced the other accused to stand trial before that court too. From the Government's point of view, that was an advantage, for who could tell what sophistical arguments might affect juries? The accused were Lesseps, his son Charles, Baron Cottu and Marius Fontane, all directors of the company—and M. Eiffel, the contractor whose tower had made him famous in 1889 and who had been called in, in the last desperate struggle, to lend his name and talents to the company.

The prosecution was vigorous and resolute. Republican justice would show its mettle. The lawyers for the defence were eloquent, but its real heart was the shrewd and courageous Charles de Lesseps. His father was now eighty-eight [1] and hardly conscious of what was going on. Charles de Lesseps painted a picture of filial loyalty, of doing everything for the salvation of the great enterprise and of being harassed and bled by the blackmailing gangs which were conspicuously not being tried. When he, Lesseps, told the story of how Baïhaut had extorted nearly 400,000 francs from the company, the President, with traditional judicial naïveté, asked solemnly, 'But in those circumstances, you go for the police.' There was abundant laughter in court and a wit put into the accused's mouth the retort, 'And when it is the police who are the thieves?' Pleas of piety, of pressure, of good faith in the most optimistic announcements of the company, did not shake the judges. The two Lesseps were given five years each; the other three two years each. The directors of the greatest companies could note; there were still laws and judges in France. [2]

A month later began the trials of the accused politicians, or rather of a few of them, for the examining magistrates had declared that there was not a sufficient case to go before the jury where Rouvier, Roche, Arène, Renault, Grévy, Devès, were concerned. These were, it is true, the most important politicians, the ex-Ministers, the leaders of parties and the well-connected; but the Republic, if it had shown in dealing with the Lesseps that it could be just, showed in dealing with Rouvier and Company that it could be understanding.

The remaining accused were Charles de Lesseps and Fontane, Baïhaut and his go-between Blondin and five members of Parliament, Sans-Leroy, Béral, Dugué de la Fauconnerie, Gobron and Antonin Proust. Charles de Lesseps having been sentenced for one crime and being now before a jury, made no attempt to get off by keeping his mouth shut. He did his best to shake the faith of the French people in their rulers, but all the political defendants except Baïhaut took the line of stout denial. Sans-Leroy, whose changed opinion had turned the parliamentary committee from an unfavourable to a favourable

---

[1] Charles de Lesseps died in 1923 at the age of 83, full of vigour.
[2] These sentences were duly quashed on a point of law by the Supreme Court.

vote, got the biggest laugh of the trial when he declared that his attitude 'had been that of a member of a committee who wished to be enlightened'. The jury accepted this story. They accepted all the stories that the politicians chose to tell. After all, they were no less plausible than the stories the examining magistrates had chosen to believe when told by Albert Grévy and the rest. Even the Royalist and Catholic leader, Dugué de la Fauconnerie, was believed. Only Baïhaut was convicted, but then he insisted on confessing, with a wealth of detail and a display of emotional repentance that recalls twentieth-century Russia more than nineteenth-century France. Baïhaut got five years; Charles de Lesseps and Blondin one year each.[1]

These trials, however satisfactory to the new privileged class whose Battle of Pavia had ended with all saved but honour, were not so edifying for the country, especially for those who had noted the evidence of Madame Cottu, who had testified that the head of Police, Soinoury, had promised to look after her husband if she would enable the prosecution to incriminate a member of the Right. It was not clear that Soinoury had acted off his own bat, but the Minister of Justice, the stern and unbending Radical, Léon Bourgeois, denied any knowledge of the proposed bargain. In all probability he was telling the truth, but so many Ministers, on their word of honour or oath, had had to deny such scandalous things.

During all the trials and acquittals and sessions of the Brisson Committee, two men who could have told all or a good deal more than could otherwise be known, had prudently left the country. Cornélius Herz had taken refuge in Bournemouth and Arton, who had his own private difficulties with criminal justice over the Dynamite Company, was travelling over the Continent, pursued, not very vigorously or successfully, by M. Soinoury's detectives.

The Doctor was as great a humorist in exile as he had been in Paris. He was, he asserted (and eminent doctors backed him up), very ill. He could not leave Bournemouth and could not be extradited. However, he was willing to give evidence if the Committee would come to see him. The comedy went on, with visits of doctors and members of the Committee to the Doctor who promised or threatened to tell all, but was able at every new demand to evade questioning on any vital point. An Arton comedy went on too, for that minor swindler was willing to sell information, or silence, in exchange for immunity. The hunt for Arton was a godsend to the music-halls, but in 1895 he was given away and arrested in London. In Paris he was only tried for his frauds at the expense of the Dynamite Company (the grounds of his extradition) and got eight years. Meanwhile the

---

[1] Arton was later convicted (in his absence) of bribing Sans-Leroy, who had been acquitted of the charge of being bribed. It may be remarked that in America, in similar circumstances, it was the politician, Fall, who went to jail and the businessman, Doheny, who was acquitted.

Panama Committee had laboured; it produced a great deal of distressing evidence, but except for the unfortunate Baïhaut, no politician went to jail for his sins; and it was noted, with interest, that while the heirs of various dead political beneficiaries of Panama were successfully forced to reimburse the ill-gotten gains by the administrators of the defunct company, the living successfully defended their spoil.

The pool into which Drumont, Gilly and the rest had thrown their stones at last returned to its old calm. The enemies and friends of the Republic alike believed, for a moment, that the régime was again in danger. Even the dim Prince Victor, head if not hope of the Bonapartists, found a lively phrase. 'The Empire built Suez, the Republic Panama.' But the Conservatives had more than ever to regret the waste of their assets in the Boulangist adventure. If the men who had defeated Boulanger had been shown up as knaves, their enemies had been earlier shown up as fools: and a peasant elector prefers a knave to a fool. As if to show how incorrigible they were, the Boulangists allowed one of the most feather-headed of their members, Millevoye, to charge Clemenceau in the Chamber with being a paid agent of England on the strength of some highly incompetent forgeries sold to him by a negro employee of the British Embassy. A party which could be taken in by Norton was not fit to govern.

There was more to come, for in the trial rising out of the Norton affair, the honour of the Marquis de Morès was impugned. Morès was a Spanish-Italian-French nobleman who had married a rich American and had lost a lot of money in America, lost it, he asserted, in fighting from his ranch in the Dakotas, the Jewish controlled beef-trust. Back in France, he had become the chief lieutenant of Drumont and had organized a gang among the butchers of the abattoirs of La Villette which he called 'the Friends of Morès'. He saw himself as the link oining the old nobility to the workers, a plan recalling the romantic dreams of young Mr. Disraeli. A real swashbuckler, Morès was a noted duellist and his killing of an inoffensive Jewish Army officer had won him even more admirers. Alas! it was now revealed, by the reckless marquis himself, that having incurred in a smart gambling club a debt of honour which he could not pay, he had applied to Andrieux for advice. Andrieux, who had a finger in every pie, told him to apply to Cornélius Herz. The Doctor had a sense of humour of a cruel kind and he insisted that he would only lend the money if Drumont would come and ask for it. Drumont did! Shakespearian comparisons were fashionable at the time. Renan had compared democracy to Caliban; Barrès, as has been seen, could quote Hamlet to advantage and Cornélius Herz insisted in parodying the 'Merchant of Venice', which play Drumont had publicly admired.[1]

[1] Critics had already noted that the first business-manager of *La Libre Parole* was a (converted) Jew.

In the elections of 1893, the French people showed far less moral indignation than had been hoped or feared. Several honest leaders of the *Railliement*, including Albert de Mun and Jacques Piou, were defeated, partly because of Royalist defection. The Conservatives lost badly; no moral reaction stayed their decline, while few of the incriminated politicians lost their seats. The most notable exception was Clemenceau and he was defeated in the Var, not because he was too close a friend of Cornélius Herz, but because he was, it was asserted and believed, an English agent, indeed a personal protégé of Queen Victoria. His speeches were interrupted by shouts of 'Aoh yes' and he retorted, unavailingly, with ferocious and indecorous humour. Some politicians had managed, like Cavaignac, to acquire a reputation for moral integrity and rigour that stood them in good stead later, but the great lesson of political morality (which Ribot had professed to hope for) was not given.

If there was any lesson at all to be learned, the town worker thought it was that all politics must be corrupt in a capitalist régime—and the Socialists rose from twelve to fifty. France was still predominantly a peasant country and the lesson the peasants drew, if they drew any, was based on the fate of Baïhaut. It reminded them of the celebrated anecdote of the condemned man who asked and was given permission to speak a few last words of advice to the crowd around the scaffold. He said only this: 'Never confess.' [1]

---

[1] A general line of Republican defence that was very successful was the assertion that the whole scandal was the work of the clericals! A more ingenious version of this is that of M. Debidour, who, distressed by the lack of moral indignation shown by the Republican electors, attributes it to the demoralizing influence of Catholic doctrine on these (anticlerical) electors, especially the devotion to Saint Antony of Padua.

CHAPTER III

THE REVIVAL OF SOCIALISM

I

IN his famous speech to the National Assembly on March 21st, 1871, Jules Favre had promised that Paris would be 'brought to heel and punished'. She had been, but there remained in the minds of the ruling classes a conviction that the last had not been heard of the dread society that, they thought, was the main author of the crimes of Paris, the International. Favre was hardly back in the Foreign Office before he was approaching the powers of Europe, trying to induce them to take common measures against the International. His approaches were received politely but nothing was done. Thile, one of Bismarck's assistants, listened to the plea of the French chargé d'affaires, the Marquis de Gabriac, and solemnly told him of the million members that the International had in England! And Gabriac foresaw a great and dangerous future for the International in America, where Marx had sent the headquarters in his desperate and unavailing fight with Bakunin to save the dying society, a flattering estimate that would have surprised even the optimistic Engels. In the first few months after the victory of order, Favre could be pardoned for asserting that 'All the filth of Europe was invited to Paris. Paris became the rendezvous of the perverted people of the whole world'. It is a little more surprising to find an editor [1] of an important paper like the *Journal des Débats*, asserting that the Commune had simply been a congress of the International. 'It opened on March 18th, taking this time the name of the Paris Commune.' It was natural, then, that the Assembly, sharing these illusions, should have legislated against this formidable organization, that believing that the workers of the world, or a good many of them, *had* united to raise rebellion in Paris, it should have struck with all the force of law against the society which claimed to be the unifying force of these enemies of society, that it should have shouted down Louis Blanc and Tolain and replied to the former's analogy of the English Trade Unions with cries of 'They haven't burned Paris'. That the workers and their leaders had been, as one

---

[1] Villetard.

of them[1] put it, caught in a trap sprung by the war and its consequences, was too simple an explanation; and the law of March 1872 made it a penal office even to belong to the dreaded association. The severe repression did not altogether stamp out the local sections of the International, especially in the south, but they were henceforward impotent to do more than act as scarecrows for the bourgeoisie.

For the moment it was only among the exiles that the work of reconstructing a worker's party and a worker's doctrine was possible. The two chief centres of the dispersed survivors of the Commune were London and Switzerland; London meant, in effect, encountering the influence of Karl Marx, and Switzerland that of the strong anarchist movement of the watch-makers of the Jura. Except for the comparatively small group of members of the International, Marx was hardly known in France, or, if he was known, it was as the assailant of Proudhon. Louis Blanc, according to Benoît Malon, was one of the few French leaders in 1848 who appreciated the importance of Marx and that, it may be suspected, was due in part to their common hostility to Proudhon. But twenty years later when Sainte-Beuve was writing his sympathetic life of Proudhon, the Dr. Marx who had attacked Proudhon was still that and nothing more. But the Commune changed that. The importance erroneously attached to the International by the French bourgeoisie was an advertisement for Marx, whose rôle, if misunderstood, was not underestimated. For the moment, indeed, Marx was taken more seriously in conservative circles in France than among the *communards*. For the acrid tone in which Marx criticized the way the Commune had been run was not pleasing to men who had just escaped the firing post, or exile to New Caledonia or death on the barricades. The intellectual power of the academic revolutionary in London was not fairly appreciated by men who had really taken the field against capital, with rifle if not with pen. And the feud within the International played into the hands of the enemies of Marx, for two of the most important future leaders of French socialism, Jules Guesde and Benoît Malon, were at the moment deeply influenced by anarchist views, although not formally anarchists. When it was discovered that the police spy who had betrayed the members of the International in the south of France had been chosen by the infallible theorist of revolution, the anger of Guesde overflowed in a bitter letter. Van Heddeghem had been authorized by the International to suspend the organization or a member of his district, until the General Council's decision was known. This was control of local French revolutionary action from the outside—and Van Heddeghem had turned out to be a weak fool who was the dupe of another agent of Marx, Dentraygues, who was a police spy. 'Under the pretence of affiliating the workers of our south to the International and

[1] Albert Richard.

thanks to the full powers given by Marx, he acted as a beater driving the Socialist game for the police.'

Paul Brousse, who was later to play an important part in French Socialist politics, was strongly in favour of an alliance with the Spanish anarchists, then active in the troubled politics of the first Spanish Republic. Even in London, where Marx welcomed the exiles and where Charles Longuet and Paul Lafargue were on the way to becoming his sons-in-law, the Blanquists disapproved of Marx's activities in the International which they denounced as 'timid, divided, parliamentary'. Divided among themselves and without any effective means of propaganda in France as long as the 'moral order' ruled, with military courts still seeking out and punishing *communards* and with the International completely disorganized and Marx largely discredited by the Dentraygues betrayal, French Socialism seemed dead. As Engels said in 1874, 'The absence of a theoretical foundation and of practical common sense is very evident.'

Within France, however, the workers were slowly emerging from the coma to which the failure of the Commune had reduced them. Many thousands of the most militant among them were dead, in prison, or in exile, and the Government was vigilant to repress any organization that seemed to be another head of the hydra that had not, it appeared, been killed in 1871. But the serious and sensible workers, on whose existence the ruling classes congratulated themselves, were not content to remain quite passive. There were slight reforms even in those dark days; the first effective Factory Act, for instance, dates from 1874; and the workers who went as delegates to the Vienna exhibition noted that they represented a working class which was better off than its Austrian peer, as the workers sent to the London exhibition of 1862 had been stimulated to agitation by the discovery that the English worker was better off than they. There was room for a reformist movement and it was supplied by Barberet with his groups of craft unions. Barberet was a very unrevolutionary leader, but the Parisian working-man, for the moment, was in a very unrevolutionary mood. Barberet was against even legal strikes, they were treason to democracy. Can we wonder that an optimistic bourgeois economist believed that 'the earnest workers have learned to their cost that strikes are a detestable way of gaining an increase of wages'? Barberet believed in co-operation, co-operation for production that is and also in 'social bazaars' where workers would exchange their products. Tolain, the expelled Internationalist, who was a deputy, encouraged this modest programme, although the nervous Government was frightened even by this faint stirring.

It was the collapse of the reactionary Government which gave the workers courage again. Their votes were valuable to the Left; prosecution of *communards* was soon to be stopped as was the maintenance of martial law and the other repressive means whereby the National Assembly had controlled the country. Not all of these shackles were cast off at once, but their end was obviously not far away. In 1876, a Workers' Congress was held in Paris. Workers' delegates had been sent to the Philadelphia Exposition of that year and, unlike those sent to Vienna, had had little reason to congratulate the French worker on his comparative good fortune. Some militants had refused the subsidy offered by Parliament to pay their expenses and there were signs that the days of meek submission were over. Yet the Congress was mild enough to reassure *Le Figaro* and to win an angry rebuke from the Blanquist exiles in London. But not all exiles were so censorious. Brousse was pleased that there should be any kind of Workers' Congress at all. And Jules Guesde noted that the members showed a clear class-sense. They had excluded from membership anyone who was not a worker, or a delegate of a group of workers. To free the proletarian from his dependence on and trust in bourgeois leaders and policies had been the aim of Proudhon. The Blanquists in 1872 had declared that the proletariat had 'finally become conscious of itself. It knows that it bears within it the elements of the new society.' The workers were giving signs that they had learned this truth. All they needed was a doctrine and leaders.

The leaders were numerous enough. As the Republicans got a secure grip on the State, more and more *communards* were pardoned and enabled to carry on their propaganda from within France. True to their traditions, the London Blanquists had founded a secret society, 'The Revolutionary Commune', and as long as Blanqui was alive, especially as long as he was in prison, his immense prestige made him a rallying-centre for many ardent if confused aspirations towards social justice and against the effects of the contagion of the world's slow stain on the purity of the Republican party. These militants were able to run Blanqui successfully against Gambetta's nominee, Lavertujon, at Bordeaux in 1879, and force the release of the 'imprisoned one', although he had been ineligible when elected. But with Blanqui's death next year, the party lost its leader and without him its doctrine was too thin to serve for a modern Socialist party. The 'Central Revolutionary Committee' which replaced the 'Revolutionary Commune' as the controlling body of the sect was originally a 'closed' body, that is to say its membership was limited to a small and select body of real and competent revolutionaries in the true Blanquist tradition. But Édouard Vaillant, who had been a very new member when the Commune was set up, and whose German education made him open to Marxian influences, was successful in his move to accept members from other Socialist parties and societies. Thus diluted, the Committee lost what unity it had had. 'General' Eudes was still a name to frighten the bourgeoisie with, and his supporters were still believers in the sudden stroke by the small, determined and disciplined band, but in the squabbles between the new and old school Blanquism decayed. Although it provided Socialism with some striking figures like Vaillant, it could not provide a doctrine.

That duty fell to Marxism which found, in Jules Guesde, the representative it needed. Guesde seems to have adopted many Marxian ideas before he had ever read any Marx. He was a Republican in that he believed that the Republic was indispensable for the workers, but otherwise he wanted the workers to form their own party and take over the State. Only thus could they put an end to the robbery inherent in the wage system, the source of all their evils. Guesde, a bourgeois himself, could not accept the view that only workers could represent their class. That doctrine meant, he later asserted, giving up Delescluze and accepting traitors like Tolain. *Le Radical* and *Les Droits de l'Homme* were vehicles for Guesde's propaganda and he found in a young German in Paris, Karl Hirsch, the necessary link with the new school of scientific Socialism. In the Latin quarter the Café Soufflet became the chapel where the new gospel was preached. Marx no longer depended on the denunciations of the righteous for his fame. To an increasing number of French workers, his doctrine became their living faith, not always very well understood, but none the less firmly believed in. The field was not yet clear of competitors, it is true. There were still Proudhonians; there were still Comtists; there were the Colinists who believed in the nationalization of the land as a solution of the social problem. But all these stars were paling before Marx's. A translation of the first volume of *Capital* was issued in ten-centime parts and in 1880 appeared the first *Revue Socialiste* in which Kautsky wrote and in which part of Engel's *Anti-Dühring* appeared, while in the revived *Égalité*, Lafargue published a translation of Engel's *Socialism, Utopian and Scientific*. 'The effect in France was enormous,' wrote Engels. The literary campaign for Marxism was well under way. It was still an undisciplined campaign. Benoît Malon, in his broad-minded eclectic way, wrote in 1881 that it was foolish to talk of the madness of doctrines that 'have for propagators people like Marx, Engels, De Paëpe, and for theoretical adherents, people like J. S. Mill, Spencer, Schaeffle, Letourneau and a score more of universally respected men of learning'. Marx would not have liked the company Malon and his sponsor, Jules Vallès, made him keep, but his name at least was known. And not only his name, for Gabriel Deville produced an epitome of *Capital* which, as the naïve M. Boilley wrote in 1895, 'is fairly lucid and well enough suited to our literary taste. Hardly anyone in France,' he goes on, 'reads more than this.' So eminent an academic as Émile de Laveleye thought Marx worth respectful refutation and so adroit a journalist as 'Mermeix' printed the Communist Manifesto in full. And if we are to believe the story told by Paul Adam,[1] copies of *Capital* in tatters, stained with coffee and cigarette ash, were passed from hand to hand in the cafés of the Latin quarter, while the students debated the theory.

Guesde knew that revolutions are not made by mere literary conversions. They are made by revolutionaries, above all by revolutionary parties. In 1878, in his weekly *Égalité*, Guesde had preached that the electoral struggle was the only possible one for the moment, although 'the source of evil does not lie . . . in a political organization which, however defective it may be, is only the effect, the resultant of the social organization'. The last number of *Égalité* appeared on July 14th, killed by fines, but Guesde was soon to find a more effective sounding-board, for he took advantage of the Exhibition of 1878 to organize an international Workers' Congress in Paris. It was prohibited. But its organizers went on, and they were arrested, on September 4th, a significant reminder of how little Republican anniversaries meant to the workers. His defence made Guesde far better known than he had yet been. 'We believe in the inevitability of a workers' 1789,' he declared, and when he was imprisoned he issued a manifesto from Sainte-Pélagie,[2] appealing not only to the wage-earners, but to the petty bourgeoisie of shop-keepers and peasants, trying to persuade them that they had nothing to lose by a revolution as the existing order of things was making them mere wage-earners anyway.

In 1879, the Workers' Congress, held in the Folies Bergère of Marseilles, was open to delegates of clubs as well as of workers and marked the defeat of the older and more cautious leaders like Finance, the Comtist who thought the workers were not yet prepared for the overthrow of the existing order. But the tide was moving away from such timidity. The exiles of the Commune sent a message defending the Commune that is very reminiscent of Marx's defence of it in 1871. There was a violent attack on that monument of revolutionary respectability, Louis Blanc, deputy of Marseilles, who was accused of having betrayed the Commune in 1871. He was soon to declare that 'if ever an insurrection was of a kind to justify and to demand a full amnesty, it is certainly the insurrection of March 18th', but the real militants were not satisfied with such belated conversion. There had been a marked growth in collectivist belief even since the Congress of the previous year at Lyons and an increased readiness to run the risks of workers' candidacies, despite the gloomy fears of Ballivet that the workers' representatives would be forced into dangerous alliances with bourgeois parties. The bright example of the good work done in the Reichstag by the German Social Democrats was held up to the French workers, who were also treated to a lesson from the German party

---

[1] To M. Lucien Corpechot. According to a more reliable witness, M. Alexandre Zévaès, the students read Proudhon, Blanqui, Bakunin and Stirner as well as Marx and the pamphlets of Guesde.
[2] He called the prison 'Pélagic', omitting the 'Sainte'.

whose fraternal message insisted on the need for a disciplined proletarian party. Ernest Roche, who was the organizer of Blanqui's successful election at Bordeaux, was there to show what political action could achieve. The resolutions finally passed contained chilly commendation of the co-operatives whose sickly life had been suddenly prolonged by the legacy of Benjamin Raspail, who left £60,000 ($300,000) to provide capital at low rates of interest, but the real heart of the Congress was in the acceptance of public ownership of the means of production and the organization of wage-earners in a class party with working-class candidates. The proletariat must 'cut itself off completely from the bourgeoisie and separate itself from them in every field, intellectual, judicial, political and economic'.

The new 'Workers' party' was organized on a regional basis. Its main centres of strength were Paris, Bordeaux, Lyons, Saint-Etienne, Lille and Roubaix. In the south, anarchism was still too strong for the party to have more than nominal existence and, even so, the local groups professed anarchist views quite out of keeping with the spirit of the new movement. That spirit was summed up for the moment in a minimum programme whose origin was of great significance, for in order to launch this new organ of French revolutionary activity, Guesde went over to London to consult Marx and Engels. The result was a list of immediate reforms like legal regulation of hours of work, a legal minimum wage and other desirable improvements which, if they did not alter the fundamental character of capitalist society, made fine talking-points in electoral campaigns. Marx was not altogether pleased at having to make these concessions to French illusions, but the desirability of getting a real Marxian party organized was too great for him to stick to rigid orthodoxy, if that would alienate the ignorant French. The tact displayed in drafting the platform did not save it from attack from two different sides. Felix Pyat, as unbending an ass as he had been in the days of the Commune, attacked it as pusillanimous. He wanted nothing to do with minimum programmes; only maximum programmes were good enough for him; meantime he had his own proposals, such as that for the erection of a statue to Danton on the site of the chapel erected to expiate the execution of Louis XVI. More serious was anarchist opposition, for fear of State tyranny was still strong, and the leader of the Marxists was not temperamentally fitted to dispel such fears. Jules Guesde, the Marxist leader in France, like his master in London, had many weaknesses as a party leader. He was suspicious, dogmatic, convinced both of his rightness and of his righteousness. Jean Grave, the anarchist, is a hostile witness, but it is not hard to believe him when he asserts that Guesde's intolerance of opposition, or even of questioning, made him far less effective as a leader than otherwise he would have been. 'Mermeix', while not unwilling to recognize the merits of Guesde, had to admit that 'he didn't inspire sympathy'. But the tall, meagre, bearded figure had the strength of firm belief and courage. 'Blanqui, young, minus his romantic side, more scientific and truly modern', so Paul Alexis described him to the inquiring Zola. In the rich Creole, Paul Lafargue, Guesde had a useful ally, bitter, unscrupulous, redeeming the suspicions his wealth and luxurious habits might have aroused by his marriage to one of Marx's daughters. In Jean Dormoy was a more typical representative of the French converts to the new faith.

That the intolerance of Guesde had a good deal to do with the speedy disruption of the party is certain, but there were other and more general causes. A Socialist party that descended from the high ground of abstention from all bourgeois politics, that, as Jean Grave put it, wasted money on elections that ought to have gone to buy explosives, was tempted, from the first, to play the game according to the political rules. Either it ran hopeless candidacies like that of Accollas in 1876 as mere demonstrations, a method of propaganda of limited value, or it really tried to make its weight felt, and that meant bargains with other parties; open bargains or tacit bargains. The organizer of resistance to Gambetta in his fief of Belleville was Reties, a member of the party, but opposition to Gambetta was far from being confined to the new party; there were the left-wing Radicals to profit by the campaign of the militant Socialists.

It was difficult to have a common enemy and common victories without being drawn into entangling alliances. The real Marxians were weak in Paris where the Blanquist tradition was strong and where the true factory proletariat was just beginning to appear. In the great textile towns of the north, there were the economic conditions for breeding a real class-conscious proletariat. Elsewhere, it was necessary to predict that the small craftsmen, shopkeepers, peasants and the like were going soon to be reduced to the condition of the loom-tenders of Lille or Roubaix, but prophecy was not, electorally, very appealing. After the victory of Blanqui at Bordeaux, the Radical Sigismond Lacroix had warned the old politicians that the 'days of idle chatter and of intrigues are over'. But Lacroix and Guesde were both unduly optimistic. It was possible to unite all sections and factions in campaigns like that for Blanqui, for the complete amnesty, for the election to the Paris Municipal Council of Trinquet, the exiled *communard* who was dear to the proletariat because, on trial, he had, unlike some others, refused to disavow his adherence to the revolution of March 18th. Beyond that, unity was hard to achieve. Men would willingly unite on what became, from 1880, the annual pilgrimage to the 'Wall of the Federals' in Père La Chaise, but it was harder to get them to unite on the programme Guesde had brought over from London. Even watered down to suit French tastes it was rather Germanic. The assumption that there was only one true Socialist doctrine was irritating to people who agreed with the policy of *Le Prolétaire* : 'Truth in social economy is not the property of any one school.' The admirably disciplined German Socialists had hurriedly snubbed *L'Égalité* when it offered its physical aid when the time came 'to answer force by force'. The haste with which *Vorwärts* rejected the offer had not been lost on the sceptics who thought that the French workers had no need of verbal lessons in revolutionary tactics from Germans, whether in Berlin or London. Soon Joffrin was objecting to a programme 'born in Thames fogs'. It might be all right for the north, but it was far too inflexible for the whole country; there must be local adjustments. Joffrin, Brousse and Benoît Malon were for a programme of immediate and practicable reforms, for getting what was possible. They were immediately nicknamed 'Possibilists' and, with an obvious reference to the corresponding split in the Republican party, Guesde said there was no room for Opportunists in the Workers' Party. 'What did you want to be?' asked Joffrin, 'impossibilists?' Was the party to confine itself to 'declining at every moment the word Revolution only as a piece of play-acting?' If that was so 'our activity is as worthless as the walk to the victim in the workhouse treadmill; we hate results'. The split came at the Havre Congress in 1883; two separate meetings were held and the new Workers' Party was cut in two. Brousse, who had old grievances against Marx, compared the policy of split to the separation of Church and State. The French workers were the state to be delivered from the tyranny of the new Ultramontanes, the Marxists. 'The Ultramontanes cannot obey the law of their country because their chief is in Rome. The Marxists cannot obey the decisions of the *Party* because their chief is in London.'

The anti-Marxian section took the name of The Workers' Revolutionary Socialist Party, but were generally known by their sub-title, the 'Federation of Labour Socialists of France', and more commonly still, as the 'Possibilists' or 'Broussists'. For the Marxian programme, Brousse and his party substituted the doctrine of 'public services', the taking-over of the great monopolies by the State as soon as they were ripe for nationalization. Municipalities were to run bakeries and butchers' shops. The days of violent revolution were over. Guesde attacked this gas-and-water socialism. Not only did it evade the fundamental question, the ending of the appropriating of surplus value by the capitalist, but its immediate reforms would make things worse. Rationalizing the bakeries and butchers' shops would greatly increase the number of unemployed, besides creating a discord within the working class between the consumers and the employees of the public services. But in Paris and the rural areas, the warnings of the 'Torquemada in glasses', as Clovis Hugues, the Socialist poet-deputy of Marseilles, called Guesde, were neglected. Blanquism, Broussism, Anarchism (the last reinforced intellectually by the prestige of Prince

Kropotkin) all divided with Guesdism the allegiance of the French workers. It was a story that was to be repeated; the hostility of the rank-and-file to an exotic doctrine that did not appeal enough to their own revolutionary tradition; the jealousy of leaders when one of them was the known representative of a foreign personality or doctrine; the sliding into mere politics of so many members, once safely elected to Parliament or to local bodies; the substitution (as soon occurred with the Possibilists) of mere political objectives like the abolition of the Senate for basic economic changes. The numbers involved in this party war were small; the vast majority of workers were as indifferent to Brousse as to Guesde, to Jean Grave as to Joffrin. But on a far greater scale, later leaders were to have to face the difficulties that were too much for Jules Guesde.

The split soon produced the usual bitterness. Electorally, the Possibilists naturally did better than the less practical Guesdists; indeed, the vote controlled by Brousse soon became a respectable asset in the Paris political market. Guesde was a candidate who inspired hostility in electors, but he was only defeated at Marseilles in 1885 by the intervention of Protot, the ex-Delegate for Justice of the Commune, who denounced Guesde as an agent of Germany, an ally of those German Socialists who were merely scouts for the armies of the Triple Alliance. The Conservatives, who had their own reasons for seeing clearly the menace to the complacency of their Republican fellow-bourgeois, noted that Socialism grew if the parties claiming to represent it did not. But the early hopes, shared by Guesde and Malon, of making the French worker exclusively class-conscious had died by the time the Boulangist crisis called all good Republicans to the aid of the party.

II

The Boulangist crisis had further embittered the relations between the Socialist sections, for some militants were seduced by the revolutionary promises of the General, while others, like the Possibilist leader Brousse, seemed more pleased that they had helped to save the Republic than anxious to transform it. It was the increasing absorption of Brousse and the other bourgeois leaders of the party in merely political aims, personal or general, that produced the next schism.

The ex-*communard* compositor, Jean Allemane, had watched with distaste and distrust the degeneration of the party into an electoral machine. He attributed this decline to the bourgeois character of the leaders, to the excessive importance they attached to being elected and to the excessively broad view they took of their duties to the party which had nominated them. Once elected they were more anxious, so Allemane thought, to get re-elected, to please the general body of voters and the leaders of other groups than to serve the interests of the proletariat whose delegates they were. The discontent within the party came to a head at the Congress of Châtellerault in 1890. The militants, who were soon to be known as Allemanists, were defeated, —defeated, they asserted, by sharp practice. They claimed to be the true heirs of the original party, although they left to Brousse the name of the 'Federation of Socialist Workers of France', taking the sub-title for themselves and becoming 'The Workers' Socialist Revolutionary Party'.

The new party, the Allemanists, was based on a strict class doctrine. Only the workers could liberate the workers. Its leaders must be men who knew the workers' lot at first hand, not bourgeois on the make, or even bourgeois sentimentally affected by woes they had not experienced. Any member of the party elected to a public body was to be closely watched by a committee of vigilance, the deputy or municipal councillor was to give a resignation in blank to the committee that nominated him; he had to turn over a proportion of his official salary to the party and to recognize that his duty was to it and not to the unorganized electors whom the Broussists were accused of 'basely flattering'.

The suspicion of bourgeois leaders, the insistence on the strict dependence of the political representatives of the party on its ruling committee, the belief in the general strike and in direct trade-union action, the attempt to make municipal Socialism the means of immediate benefit to the workers, marked off the Allemanists from the bourgeois-ridden Possibilists and from the doctrinaire Guesdists and Blanquists who diverted the workers from immediate gains to remote possibilities of complete revolution. Fear of being compromised with the bourgeois led to prohibitions of the electoral bargains with other parties which had been the bane of the old Possibilist policy, although, as candid members of the new party pointed out, it was in fact impossible to carry out the programme of municipal Socialism without alliances with other groups. Anti-militarism was another of the dogmas of the new group; with none of the reservations of the customary type, the Allemanists were opposed to any war, even a war for Alsace-Lorraine, and denounced the Army as a school of vice and idleness. In many of its doctrines, the party was marked by the influence of Proudhon, in its federalism, its suspicion of the bourgeoisie, its contempt for the patriotic gullibility of the masses. In other ways, in its belief in strike action, in the rôle of the trade unions, in its aversion from systematic dogma, it was an ancestor of the later syndicalist movement.

The Allemanists had their strongholds, and their activity led to the increase of Socialist activity in new regions, but ten years after the foundation of a united French Socialist party, it had split into four sections, each as anxious to fight the other groups as to combat the common enemy. It was a sign of the times that, despite this faction fighting and the discredit cast on all the leaders of all the Socialist parties by the charges of tyranny, corruption, incompetence and political thimble-rigging that were thrown about, it was Socialism, if not the organized Socialist parties, that profited in the elections of 1893 by the disgust aroused by Panama.

One result of these elections was underlined by a rising young lawyer who had moved from Radicalism to an undoctrinaire Socialism. 'The Panama case,' wrote Alexandre Millerand, 'has shown all the social forces of this country at the service and under the orders of high finance. . . . The nation must take from the barons of this new feudal system the fortresses which they have torn from her in order to dominate her: the Bank of France, the railways, the mines.' But, he went on, 'It is not by the waving of a wand, by a miracle or by violence, that social transformation will be brought about'. The electors had shown their disgust with the existing political personnel, not only by electing some of the leading members of the organized Socialist parties, but by electing nearly thirty independent Socialists.

The doctrinal feuds between Guesde, Brousse and Allemane had not prevented the growth of a general, if vague, Socialist sentiment. The poet deputy, Clovis Hugues, and the old *communard* Camélinat had represented this vague Socialism in the Chamber, and to it various deputies of other parties had drifted, men like Millerand and the brilliant young professor, Jean Jaurès, who had returned to the Chamber at a by-election just before the general elections of 1893, this time free from all his previous connections with the bourgeois parties.

The main bond of unity between these unorganized Socialists was furnished by the Socialist press, by Benoît Malon's *Revue Socialiste*, hospitable to all schools, and by *La Bataille*, founded by the *communard*, Lissagaray, a more polemical than expository journal, fighting its founder's battles over again rather than expounding the economic and social creeds of the younger generation. The *Cri du Peuple* of Jules Vallès also served as a common battleground to all the Socialist schools, although its founder was too independent in temperament to take kindly to any dogmatic system. After his death, the romantic Séverine edited the *Cri du Peuple* and her generosity and sentimentality made her a nuisance to rigid teachers and leaders like Guesde.

The contributors to these journals, like the independent Socialist deputies, were far from any general agreement on their programme. To some, Socialism meant little more than a generous hatred of bourgeois complacency and a vague dislike of the wage system; they owed much more to Victor Hugo than to Marx. The successes of 1893 made some clarification necessary, and the establishment of the 'Republican Socialist Federation of the Seine' and the taking over by Millerand of the newspaper, *La Petite République*, gave the Independents the rudiments of an organization and an organ, as the electoral success of Millerand, Viviani and Jaurès gave them leaders.

Millerand was the hardest-headed and politically the shrewdest of the leaders of the new party. His self-control marked him off from his colleagues as was noted by a Belgian Socialist,[1] who was rather scandalized by the violence of the feuds between Socialist factions in France. In Viviani, the group had one of the very greatest of French parliamentary orators, who, even when he had little to say, was a master of the art of saying it. More important than either of the young lawyers, was the young professor, Jean Jaurès. A brilliant schoolboy in a family more productive of sailors than of scholars,[2] he had been 'fort en thème' to a prodigious degree, the glory of the École Normale Supérieure, endowed with a prodigious memory and learned beyond the run of professors. To the new generation of members of the University, Jaurès was a hero. It was to him that the critical and enthusiastic youth of the *lycées* and faculties looked to redeem the credit of a corporation not highly honoured by the career of men like Burdeau or by the narrow conformist Republican orthodoxy of so many others.

The conversion of Jaurès to Socialism was not sudden. His Latin thesis for the doctorate had, indeed, been on the *Origins of German Socialism*, but in it Socialism was interpreted very widely indeed and, in its emphasis on the autonomy of moral factors in social evolution, in the importance attached to the liberation of the spirit achieved by Luther at the Reformation, in the comparative neglect of the economic side of the question, it was a profoundly un-Marxian work. As far as Jaurès ever became a Marxian (and there were idealist elements in his doctrine to the end), he owed it to the Alsatian librarian of the École Normale, Lucien Herr, who was to indoctrinate a generation of members of the University with Marxism or, at any rate, to infuse a generous dose of Marxism into the general Socialism that was becoming part of the mental atmosphere of the Rue d'Ulm. In Jaurès, Herr made his greatest convert. In a far higher sense than Viviani's, he was a great orator; there was a force of argument and a generosity of temper in all his speeches that were beyond a mere virtuoso. Not a first-rate judge of men as individuals or as small groups, Jaurès had an unequalled power of winning the trust of great masses and of inspiring reverence and affection in brilliant young men not wont to lavish either on their seniors. Two such different types as the sophisticated and wealthy young Parisian Jew, Léon Blum, and the robust, independent child of the workers of Orleans, Charles Péguy, testified to the power of the new leader's personality, and a subtle observer like Barrès spent years pondering the problem of the power and charm of this man who was the inspirer of so much that Barrès hated and feared. In Jaurès, French Socialism had at last found its predestined leader, and it was natural, given the temper of the two men, that the growing ascendancy of

---

[1] Émile Vandervelde.
[2] His brother, like his father's cousin, rose to be an admiral.

Jean Jaurès should be suspect to Jules Guesde, who had been the preacher of the word while Jaurès was still at school and who was forced to see in this eleventh-hour labourer in the vineyard, the born charmer of that multitude which Guesde sometimes impressed but so seldom won.

It was not Jaurès, however, but Millerand who, with his sense of the practical, laid the foundations of a closer unity between the old Socialist parties and the new loose Socialist group. Acting with them in the Chamber, it was natural that even Guesde and Vaillant should come to see some use in the newcomers who made the Chamber the sounding-board for a propaganda much more successful than anything hitherto achieved by the veteran zealots. It was Millerand who, in 1896, managed to induce all sections of the Socialist deputies, except the Allemanists on one side and a few vague semi-Socialists on the other, to accept a minimum programme called, from the name of the banquet given to celebrate the recent victories at the municipal elections, the 'Programme of Saint-Mandé'.[1] The guests included Guesde, Vaillant, Jaurès, Viviani, Clovis Hugues, nearly every shade of Socialism in the Chamber and the victorious mayors like Jean Dormoy of Montluçon. Guesde characteristically preached union, but union on conditions; there must be agreement on objects and it was in a sense a reply to this demand that was given by Millerand. 'No one,' he said, 'is a Socialist who does not accept the necessary and progressive substitution of social for capitalist property.' But, he went on, this progress was to be achieved by the use of the vote, not by violent revolution. The Socialists only asked 'the right to persuade the voters'. The speech was the affirmation of a minimum economic content in a joint Socialist programme, combined with the exclusion on one hand of the vague preachers of mere social reforms that left the property structure un-touched and, on the other hand, the criticism, if not the exclusion, of the believers in a sudden violent overthrow of the bourgeois state. The great change would come peacefully and gradually and by political means. Caution, the repression of Utopian dreams, the defence of the political system that opened to the workers the prospect of a peaceful conquest of power—these were the notes of the programme of Saint-Mandé, and they came fittingly to close a period when the old tradition of revolutionary action seemed to have been killed in the repression of the last desperate campaign of the Anarchists.

In the French Socialist tradition there had long been a strong anarchist element; it was not only that the influence of Proudhon was strong, but that there were so many minor Proudhons among the French militants. It was as natural for Frenchmen to be 'anti-

---

[1] The banquet took place, not in the suburb of Saint-Mandé, but in the remote eastern section of Paris on the edge of the Bois de Vincennes, then much more remote even than to-day.

authoritarian' as for Germans to see in party discipline and in the liberating authority of the State, the way to the new world. To Proudhonians, the way to make sure that the bourgeois state did wither away and did not merely change its title was to abolish it at the first opportunity. Against Lenin, Proudhon would have said that the time to accustom the people to 'observing the elementary rules of social life . . . without force, without compulsion, without subordination' was from the beginning of the revolution. Unless the State apparatus were rooted up at the start, it would not wither away.

Theoretical anarchism of this type was too abstract to compete with Marxism, and from the assumption of the Socialist leadership by Guesde, Lafargue and the other Marxians, it seemed doomed to extinction. Anarchism, however, had one real asset: it was actively revolutionary. It did not postpone the great day to some remote time when, by political organization, the capitalist citadel would be taken over by the leaders of the workers. The declaration by Caffiero and Malatesta in 1876 that 'the insurrectionary deed, designed to assert Socialist principles by acts, is the most effective method of propaganda', was welcomed. Malatesta was as good as his word and tried to raise a rebellion in Southern Italy—a hopeless effort which was severely condemned by the orthodox Marxists in France and Germany. There were still men in France, such as Jean Grave, who dared to defy the orthodox. 'Our propaganda among the people ought to show them that in a revolution, instead of going stupidly to the Hôtel de Ville to proclaim a government, we ought to go there to shoot whoever tries to set one up.'

Such language appealed to the romantic. The Anarchists, who if still few in number were sure of widespread sympathy, were prone to give arms to their enemies, the police. Spies were common in their ranks, and the verbal violence of Grave, Gautier and the others enabled the police to frighten the bourgeoisie with the threat of a new Commune, and facilitated the work of *agents provocateurs*. The preaching of violence was not without results; there were anti-religious riots in the Haute Loire and a bomb explosion at Lyons. The trial of the alleged authors or instigators of this outrage attracted much public attention, the more so that one of the defendants was the romantic Russian, Prince Peter Kropotkin. The accused asserted that 'all governments are like each other and one is as good as the other'. The court of Republican France showed that there was some truth in this by condemning Kropotkin and his associates to long terms in prison, and the man who had escaped from the fortress of Peter and Paul in St. Petersburg, found French prisons more efficient than Russian.

From the Lyons trial of 1882, for a period of twelve years, the doctrines and the deeds of the Anarchists became increasingly terrifying to the sober citizens of France and the subject of mutual reproach between Radicals and Conservatives. The bad times of the 'eighties gave Anarchist propaganda a chance, and an unemployed demonstration that ended in pillaging shops was credited to the movement. More serious was the case of burglary whose author, Duval, boldly proclaimed himself an Anarchist attacking directly the fortress of private property, and, in defending himself from arrest, had legitimately killed a policeman, agent of an iniquitous society. Whether to condemn or applaud Duval became a case of conscience with the leaders of the Left and, if most condemned, he found a warm defender in Séverine who condemned 'Socialist Pharisees'; which in turn led to the withdrawal of Guesde and the rest from the chief Left paper, the *Cri du Peuple*, which she edited. The celebration of May 1st of 1890 led to riots in the strongly Left city of Vienne and to the condemnation of Anarchist leaders; next year it was in Paris that the Anarchists and the police had their annual fight, and again there was a trial and condemnation of the leaders, some of whom had suffered more at the hands of the enraged police before trial than they did after their conviction.

It was obvious to the most zealous that these demonstrations did little or no harm to the capitalist state and were followed by severe repression of the militants. It was necessary, then, to take more drastic steps, and in 1892 the campaign began with bomb explosions at the houses of legal officials who had taken part in the trial of the Paris Anarchists in 1891. The author of these 'acts of propaganda' was Ravachol, who had murdered an old man and robbed graves for the good of the cause before attempting to avenge anarchy on MM. Benoît and Bulot. Some Anarchists refused to acknowledge Ravachol as one of theirs. Against the condemnation of Jean Grave was to be set the admiration of the most eminent and respected of French philosophical anarchists, Elisée Reclus, who, refusing to discuss the actual crimes of Ravachol, expressed admiration for his motives and his courage. More outrages followed, and the parliamentary Socialists had none of the hesitations of Reclus: they denied any sympathy with such compromising associates.

It was as well they did so, for parliamentary tolerance of extreme preaching and practice was tested very high when, in December 1893, an Anarchist called Vaillant [1] threw a bomb from the gallery of the Chamber of Deputies, wounding the priest-politician, the Abbé Lemire, and giving the presiding officer, Charles Dupuy, the chance to achieve a brief fame as the author of the remark, 'the sitting will go on'. No one died as the result of Vaillant's bomb, but the attack on the representatives of universal suffrage was punished with death, despite the plea of Lemire. It was to revenge Vaillant that Henri threw his bombs. To Henri, all bourgeois were criminals and the death of any one of them a just revenge for the death of Vaillant. On his trial he was

[1] Not to be confused with the Blanquist leader.

defiant. 'Hung in Chicago, beheaded in Germany, garrotted in Jerez, shot in Barcelona, guillotined at Montbrison and Paris, our dead are many; but you have not been able to destroy anarchy.' He was right; other outrages followed, in one of which the literary Anarchist, Laurent Tailhade, was badly wounded; the æsthetic admirer of earlier anarchist achievements did not repent of his defence of the beauty of propaganda by the deed.

The Anarchist campaign had its most important victim still to come. At Lyons, the President of the Republic was assassinated by an Italian called Caserio, who professed to be avenging Vaillant whom Carnot had refused to reprieve. After Vaillant's bomb-throwing, the Chamber had passed a law against Anarchist activities, and it now resolved to make an end of the menace. Despite the opposition of the Socialists and Radicals it was made an offence to advocate anarchy; and trials were not to be before a jury. By the standards of contemporary Chicago, the laws were mild enough and they were not very vigorously enforced. The 'scoundrelly laws' [1] provided the Socialists and Radicals with plenty of material for denouncing the Opportunists. It made a new line of demarcation and, as long as they were in opposition, the Radicals had no words harsh enough for the laws which they omitted to repeal when they were at last responsible for the government of the country.

An imitation of the *Carmagnole* called the *Ravachole* had denounced the 'magistrats vendus' and the 'financiers ventrus' along with the 'sénateurs gâteux' and the 'députés véreux'. Corrupt judges, pot-bellied financiers, senile senators and grafting deputies, it was against these types that the Anarchists protested.

> Mais pour tous ces coquins
> Il y a de la dynamite.

The same moral was drawn by Millerand. Under cover of protecting order, the corrupt politicians and their allies were gagging the press which had exposed their thieving.[2]

Parliament showed its anger and alarm by more than the new repressive laws, notably in the choice of a successor to Carnot, for they chose the President of the Chamber, Casimir-Périer. It was a superfluous gesture. The Anarchist campaign was over; rigorous repression did its work, and although Anarchist sentiment remained, and was especially strong in the trade-union movement where its defenders waged war on politically ambitious leaders, the movement lost its power even to frighten.

The election of Casimir-Périer to the presidency was a gesture of

---

[1] 'Les lois scélerates.'
[2] By what modern Left historians would think an unfortunate choice, Millerand gave as an example of the ruthless exposure of grafters, the *Vieux Cordelier* of Camille Desmoulins.

defiance. To make a millionaire, the nephew of a duke,[1] the grandson of the Prime Minister of Louis Philippe who had so rigorously maintained order, President of the Republic was to abandon the tradition of Grévy and even of Carnot, for the hereditary claims of Carnot were in the line of the Republican tradition, while those of the new President were Orleanist. It was natural that the election should arouse expectations that the presidential office would not be merely ceremonially filled. A cartoon by Forain showed a Radical deputy telling a worker that 'the Tree of Liberty had grown a bludgeon'.

That Casimir-Périer had any serious intention of using his bludgeon is very doubtful. He was proud, sensitive, and the limitations on any effective use of the nominal powers of his office irritated him. The social prestige and financial rewards of the Presidency meant nothing to the heir of so great a name and so great a fortune. It was through his fortune that he was most successfully attacked, for the rising Socialist party saw in the President of the Republic one of the chief magnates of the unpopular Anzin Company, the great mining and metallurgical trust. The President was infuriated by the attacks of a bold adventurer, Gérault-Richard, and he felt that his Ministers neither listened to him in private nor defended him in public. The foresight of Dugué de la Fauconnerie was vindicated. 'In six months a dissolution or a resignation', he had predicted when the election was announced. It was resignation.

On January 5th, 1895, the President resigned. 'The presidency of the Republic,' he wrote, 'deprived of means of action and of inspection, can only draw the moral force without which it is nothing from the confidence of the nation.' A system that allowed the chief magistrate to be slandered with impunity could not provide the necessary moral atmosphere in which a President could do useful work.

The Republic had had five presidents; two had been forced out of office, one had been murdered, two had resigned. Casimir-Périer's case merely showed, what was to be shown again and again, that the election to the presidency of a man of ambition, or of first-rate abilities, was a mistake. Either he had to resign himself to an unnatural discretion and to the achievement by influence of what he could not achieve by power—or he had to go.

The deputies and senators who had elected Casimir-Périer six months before were not impressed by his rebuke. They regarded him as a deserter, too sensitive for political life, a *dilettante*, not a professional inured to the rigours and broken in to the necessary loyalties of the game. They determined to make no such mistake again, and chose Félix Faure, a politician whose background of Havre business and family origins were not likely to make him indifferent to the social opportunities of the Élysée and who, in fact, developed a passion for the

[1] See Audiffret-Pasquier.

303

ceremonial side of his office that delighted satirists. The election marked another stage in the decline of the presidency, for the new President had neither personal nor ancestral claims on popular reverence; he owed all his prestige to his office, and the intrinsic prestige of the office was now not great. On the other hand, Félix Faure was an astute politician under his comic vanity, and what he wanted he was ready to try to get, within the limits imposed by the rules of the game. In the great storm that was blowing up, the fact that he and not Casimir-Périer was at the Élysée was important—and unfortunate.

CHAPTER IV

CAPTAIN DREYFUS

ON October 29th, 1894, the suspicious public of *La Libre Parole* read this note: 'Is it true that, recently, the military authorities have made a very important arrest? The charge brought against the arrested man is said to be espionage.' Drumont was well informed, for he had received a letter the day before from Commandant Henry of the French Military Intelligence informing him that the arrested man was Captain Dreyfus. Henry had written: 'the story is that he is travelling, but that is a lie spread about because they want to hush the business up. All Israel is on the job.' Drumont was delighted to reply to these alleged Jewish manœuvres and, on November 1st, he published the name of the officer. The day before, Havas had issued an official statement that an arrest had been made. France suddenly learned two things: that there had been treachery in high military quarters and that the suspected man was a Jew.

The counter-espionage department of the French General Staff, disguised as 'the statistical section of the Second Bureau', had known, for some time, that the German military attaché in Paris, Colonel von Schwartzkoppen, was in touch with various French traitors. In reply, the Statistical Section had got its own agents in the German Embassy; had managed to put microphones in a room used by Schwartzkoppen and had a careful watch kept on the movements of the German's attaché and on his Italian colleague and friend, Colonel Panizzardi. Official assertions by Count von Münster, the German Ambassador, that no member of the Embassy had anything to do with espionage did not shake the convictions of Colonel Sandherr, the head of the Statistical Service, and rightly so, for although Münster did not know it, Schwartzkoppen was, in fact, in touch with spies.

From the start, the French soldiers and French Ministers very naturally received with ironical politeness all German official and un-official statements. On September 24th, Commandant Henry had shown to his colleagues a piece of paper which had been torn up and which he had pieced together again. Here was conclusive proof that the Marquis de Val Carlos, Spanish military attaché and French military spy, had been right when he said, 'there is a wolf in your sheepfold'. The document shown by Henry was the *bordereau*; it was, that is to say, a list enumerating various pieces of military information which the unknown writer proposed to sell to Schwartzkoppen, who was obviously an old customer.

It was decided, rather hastily, that the author of the *bordereau* could only be an officer of the General Staff in the War Office at the moment. The field of research was thus limited; the document was photographed and circulated to the heads of the various bureaux but no one recognized the handwriting. Major d'Aboville decided that the mystery was being tackled in the wrong way. What must be done was to deduce what kind of officer *could* have written it. He must be a gunner; he must have been recently in touch with several sections of the General Staff, and only the staff officers in training moved from one section to another. So the traitor must be a 'stagiaire'. D'Aboville and his chief, Fabre, then examined the list of possibles. One name suited all the conditions, except for the remark at the end of the *bordereau*: 'I am going off on manœuvres'. The suspect had not gone off on manœuvres, but, they reflected, he had gone on a 'staff ride' in the East. Alfred Dreyfus was their man. Then they compared the writing of the *bordereau* with the writing of Captain Dreyfus and were 'stupefied' at the resemblance. They consulted their chiefs, who instructed them to go ahead, and the agreement of all, including Sandherr, was notified to the Chief of the General Staff, General de Boisdeffre. A talented officer, M. du Paty de Clam, who, among other artistic and semi-artistic hobbies, was an amateur graphologist, agreed with his colleagues. The Minister of War, General Mercier, was told, and he immediately told the President of the Republic, Casimir-Périer. A Cabinet Meeting was called and the course to be taken discussed. The Minister of Foreign Affairs, Gabriel Hanotaux, was in favour of hushing the matter up, which was also the advice of the Military Governor of Paris, General Saussier, but Mercier objected that the fact that there was a traitor was too widely known to be kept secret; the investigation must go on. Handwriting experts were called in; one, the expert of the Bank of France, gave a hesitant reply; the other, Alphonse Bertillon, the famous inventor of criminal anthropometry who had recently set up as a graphologist, was much more positive. The arrest of Dreyfus was decided on.

Alfred Dreyfus was a native of Mulhouse in Alsace, where his family were rich business men. He had chosen to serve in the French Army and had had a distinguished career (he was the first Jew to enter the General Staff of the Army). He was able, conscious of the fact, and not popular. He was well off; indeed, by the standards of French army officers, he was rich. He was married and had two children. He had, in short, a great deal to lose and very little to gain by treason. He had, of course, connections with Germany, as he was an Alsatian, but that was common enough; Sandherr was an Alsatian, for instance, and it was difficult, at first sight, to see why a man who had chosen to go with France and had chosen to serve in the French Army should suddenly turn traitor. There were many readers of *La Libre Parole* who knew that Jews would do anything for money, but Dreyfus, by entering the Army, had given up the chance of making money in business as his brother did, and was it likely that he would run all the risks of espionage for the sums likely to be paid to a comparatively junior officer by the Germans?[1] Nevertheless, there was a *prima facie* case, and du Paty de Clam was ordered to lay a trap for Dreyfus. Fragments of the *bordereau* were dictated to him and his writing was found to resemble the original closely enough to reassure his superiors. He was immediately arrested and kept in the closest confinement in the military prison of the Cherche-Midi.

The arrest took place on October 15th and the secret was well kept. Madame Dreyfus was told it would be in the interests of her husband to keep the fact that he had been arrested secret, so that Dreyfus, protesting his innocence, was completely cut off from the world, while Mercier and his subordinates prepared the case which would justify their neglect of the prudential advice of MM. Hanotaux and Saussier. Dreyfus was subject to constant interrogations from du Paty de Clam and, according to the latter, once cried out, 'My race will take vengeance on yours'. It was just what a Jew would say, according to the doctrines of *La Libre Parole*, and Sandherr and others had already asserted that there were other proofs of his guilt. Nevertheless, the inquiry was not proving very fruitful. Three more experts had examined the photographs of the *bordereau*; one said it was by Dreyfus; another that it was by Dreyfus 'or a handwriting twin'; the third refused to say that it was by Dreyfus. It was difficult to go on with the case, and as the arrest had not yet been made public it was possible to drop it without too much loss of face.

It was at this point that Commandant Henry warned the vigilant Drumont. To give up the case now was far more serious, especially for a War Minister fond of politics, but not sure of his footing in that treacherous field. Mercier was ambitious; and although the evidence comes from a later time, when Mercier was becoming an active politician, it is worth noting that one of Drumont's collaborators, Raphaël Viau, described him as the 'most politically-minded and publicity-hunting officer' he had ever known. Even a less politically-minded War Minister might have been frightened to drop the case once Drumont and his allies got hold of it, for there had been repeated rumours of treachery, and Drumont had already declared that Dreyfus would escape, though he had 'admitted everything a fortnight ago', because he was a Jew. His very name was damaging; as bad as Lévy

---

[1] We now know that Schwartzkoppen thought that £40 was a very big sum to pay. Dreyfus had about £1,000 ($5,000) a year of his own.

or Mayer. Had not Drumont in *La France Juive* denounced Ferdinand Dreyfus 'one of the tribe who crawl over France'? It is true that Alfred was not a relation, but what did that matter? In the same way, in an endeavour to find out what motives could have led Dreyfus to treason, inquiries were made into his private life. He was found to have had a few affairs with women before marriage and one after, but none likely to provide a motive; but a police spy, confusing him with another, declared that he was a regular frequenter of gambling houses. The Prefect of Police, Lépine, sent in a report that Alfred Dreyfus was unknown in the gambling world and had been mistaken for his namesakes. Commandant Henry did not allow this information to confuse the minds of the judges.

On December 19th the trial began before a court-martial, none of whose members was an artillery man, a weakness in a court which would be called on to decide various questions of probability which involved familiarity with the professional vocabulary of gunners. The counsel for the defence was Maître Demange, an eminent Catholic lawyer, who only accepted the case on the condition that, should he find from examination of the records that Dreyfus was guilty, he would throw up his brief—with all the disastrous consequences for his client that such an action would involve.[1] Mathieu Dreyfus and Alfred accepted this condition.

Despite the protests of Demange, the trial was heard *in camera*. There was testimony that only an officer could have got hold of some of the information mentioned in the *bordereau*; there was contrary testimony that it could have been known to clerks and non-commissioned officers. There was evidence advanced that Dreyfus had talked a lot about espionage and counter-espionage, that he had displayed an unhealthy curiosity. There was counter-evidence of character. Du Paty de Clam testified that Dreyfus had trembled when he wrote [2] 'hydraulic brake'. When asked to show where the trembling had affected the writing, he replied that an innocent man would have trembled, and that if Dreyfus had not, it showed what a good actor he was.

The case for the prosecution was not going well when Henry asked to be heard and testified that an 'honourable person' had told the Intelligence Department of the existence of a traitor and, later, that he was an officer of the Second Bureau. Turning to Dreyfus Henry added, 'There he is'. He refused to name the 'honourable person'. 'There are secrets in an officer's head which his cap ought not to know.' It was the first of those appeals for complete trust in his own reliability that Henry was to make. The burly ranker officer was, in some ways,

---

[1] Demange had successfully defended Morès in the trial arising out of the duel in which he had killed a Jewish officer.
[2] The trick dictation had been given on a very cold day.

an odd personage to find in the Intelligence Service. Physically he was of a type that would have seemed eminently at home in the uniformed police, and although the main business of his office was concerned with Germany, he knew no German.[1]

Despite Henry's affirmation, the judges were still reluctant to convict on the evidence produced, and Demange had reason to expect the acquittal of his client. Henry's solemn affirmation impressed nearly all who heard it. It even impressed Lépine, but it left cold Colonel Picquart, who knew that the honourable person was the Marquis de Val Carlos whose claim to honour was open to suspicion since he accepted pay for spying on his brother attachés. The time had come to play the trumps which the prosecution had up their sleeves, the sealed packet of documents which Mercier had authorized du Paty to give to the judges in private.

These documents, if du Paty was right, were final. There were four documents, all involving Dreyfus more directly than did the *bordereau*. One, above all, was decisive, if du Paty was right, for it was a letter signed 'Alexandrine' which had passed between Panizzardi and Schwartzkoppen, referring to 'that dirty dog D' who had sold plans of Nice.[2] At the time that this document had been intercepted,[3] no one had thought 'D' could be an officer, or his plans of any real value. Nevertheless, du Paty now declared that 'D' was Dreyfus and he was believed by the judges. The document was concealed from the defence; none of the judges of the court-martial seeming to know or care that they were breaking the regulations for the conduct of courts-martial.

The Minister of War, however, did, and his motive (on his own authority) was the safety of the nation. The traitor could only be convicted on evidence which, unlike the *bordereau*, directly involved the attachés of Germany and Italy. The *bordereau*, after all, had only been sent to Schwartzkoppen; he had not in fact received it. But the letter of 'Alexandrine' was from Schwartzkoppen (or Panizzardi); it directly involved the military attachés of the two powers of the Triple Alliance who had frontiers bordering on France. Even though the trial was *in camera*, Mercier could not rely on the discretion of the defence and a leak might mean war. And, the most vehement defenders of Mercier assert,[4] war in disadvantageous conditions. 'Germany was ahead of us in the re-equipment of the artillery, we were in the midst of changing our mobilization plan, we were in the dark as to the intentions of the new Russian Emperor [Alexander III had just died]; finally, the very

---

[1] According to a story that circulated in the Army, Henry owed his promotion to his excellent management of General de Miribel's eating and sleeping arrangements on manœuvres. The only job open at the time when he was to be rewarded was in the Intelligence.

[2] 'ce canaille de D.'

[3] The letter was not dated and no record had been kept of the date of its arrival in the War Office!

[4] 'Henri Dutrait-Crozon.'

motive of the war would have put us in a bad light in Europe.' The judges were convinced; they voted unanimously for conviction and sentenced Dreyfus to imprisonment for life in a fortified place, to be deprived of his rank and to military degradation. Dreyfus was overwhelmed and Demange said, 'Your condemnation is the greatest crime of the century'.

Mercier had won; whether he had saved his country or not, he had saved his own reputation. The secret documents were brought to him; he destroyed the 'life' of Dreyfus written by du Paty de Clam and ordered that the other documents should be scattered in the files. Sandherr and Henry disobeyed; the documents were kept in one envelope, initialled by Henry and put in the safe kept for secret records. All that was wanting, now, was a confession from Dreyfus, but although later it was asserted that he had confessed, no record of this interesting confirmation of the judgment was noted at the time. Dreyfus continued to protest his innocence to the governor of the military prison, Forzinetti, who believed him. He talked of suicide, but Forzinetti persuaded him that it was his duty to live to clear his name for the sake of his wife and children. The sentence was confirmed; the solemn degradation took place in public but there was still no confession, only a stoical submission and a cry of 'Vive la France! I am innocent'.

Except for the Dreyfus family, his lawyer and some persons with their own private reasons for knowing the authorship of the *bordereau*, there was a general rejoicing that a traitor had been exposed and that the fears early expressed that the wealth of the accused would secure his escape were groundless. Legal procedure seemed to so many Frenchmen designed mainly to secure the escape of the obviously guilty. The rules of the Bar and Bench, the limitations they imposed on the members of the profession, seemed, as a popular comic song suggested, to affect only details. A lawyer 'couldn't ride a bicycle', so the refrain ran, but he could do anything else. Courts-martial seemed to be free from the weaknesses of the ordinary courts. It is true that the rising Socialist deputy, Jean Jaurès, complained that while privates were shot for disobedience, the court had let an officer off with his life, but in fact, the court had imposed the heaviest sentence in its power. A law was passed making Devil's Island, off the coast of Cayenne, the place wherein Dreyfus was to expiate his great crime. In a nation distrustful, with good reason, of its rulers, the conviction of Dreyfus was consoling. When Bazaine was tried for treason in 1873 he had excused his conduct by reminding the court that, after September 4th, there was no regular government to pay allegiance to. But the President of the Court, the Duc d'Aumale, destroyed this sophism in a phrase. 'There was France.' In an age of corruption and weakness, one institution had shown its vigilance. There might be no government that the man in the street could trust, but there was the Army.

CHAPTER V

THE RUSSIAN ALLIANCE AND FASHODA

I

SINCE 1870, the idea of calling in the power of Russia to redress the balance in the west had haunted the minds of Frenchmen. It was to Russian intervention that, as Decazes allowed the public to believe, was due the deliverance of France from a new German invasion in 1875. There were French politicians who dallied with the thought of using Austria as a check on Germany, if not with the idea of avenging Sadowa and Sedan in one joint effort; but it was evident to all but the most blind that Austria had, by 1880, definitely resigned herself to the position of brilliant second to Bismarck's Germany. Association with England appealed to many more, but from a military point of view British help (even could France have counted on it) would have been of slight importance, and, at sea, British naval support was unnecessary, as the French fleet was vastly superior to Germany's. There was, in fact, only one ally who could do what France wanted, could reassure the timid Frenchmen (and there were millions of them) who were less concerned with avenging 1870 than with preventing the recurrence of another invasion and could inspire the more ardent souls who dreamed of recovering Alsace-Lorraine by a fortunate war fought with the active support of the countless soldiers of the Tsar.

There were, it is true, some very cautious Frenchmen who did not believe in a Russian alliance for any purpose, because they thought the only safety of France lay in her reconciling herself to her dependent position. That was Grévy's view. There were others who did not think that the Russian alliance was as valuable as public opinion imagined. Such soldiers as Appert and Boisdeffre, who knew Russia at first-hand, knew how much would have to be done before the Russian Army would be in a position to attack quickly and effectively, and knew that there was a risk of France's being over-run before the lumbering giant had got ready to strike. Economists, like Paul Leroy-Beaulieu, knew how much was rotten in the state of Russia, economically, politically, socially; the giant had not merely feet but legs of clay. But the isolation of France was such a humiliation to some and such a nightmare to others that scepticism was deemed unpatriotic. An alliance with Russia was the ideal solution of the problem of French foreign policy, whether it was considered as insurance that there would not be another Peace of Frankfort or as giving high hopes that the crime of 1871 would be expiated.

With these hopes in the air, it was natural that French public opinion should be on the alert to notice and magnify all signs of strain between Russia and Germany; that the importance of the anti-German sentiments attributed to the new Tsar, Alexander III, should be exaggerated; that Russian resentment at the rôle of Bismarck in the Congress of Berlin in 1878 should have been dwelt on and that such leaders of the anti-German party in Russia as General Skobelev and the Panslav journalist, Katkov, should have been credited with more influence over imperial policy than they had. Indeed, Conservative writers on the origins of the alliance, like Ernest Daudet, or diplomatic commentators, like M. Toutain, have given the impression that the alliance might have come sooner had France not been a Republic, or had she been one less ostentatiously. It is probable that France did suffer a little in monarchical Europe from her political character. She could not oblige the Tsarist police, at that time, by turning over Nihilist conspirators like Hartmann, or refuse to imprisoned anarchists like Prince Kropotkin, the benefits of a general amnesty. It is not unlikely, too, that Republican suspicion of professional diplomats did some harm at St. Petersburg. Gambetta's choice, in 1881, of his chief diplomatic agent of 1870, the Comte de Chaudordy, as ambassador, a nomination which fell through with the collapse of the Great Ministry, was a better selection than the sending of the politically sound but very ill-equipped Admiral Jaurès.[1] Nor did the chronic instability of French Cabinets impress a ruler like the obstinate Alexander III who, as he said, did not like 'new faces'.

French opinion exaggerated the importance of these obstacles to an agreement with Russia. It was unfortunate that so prominent a politician as Floquet was reputed to have insulted Alexander II on his visit to Paris in 1867 by shouting 'Long Live Poland!',[2] but Alexander III was not so blindly pious a son as to allow such memories to influence his politics twenty years later.

The real obstacle to an alliance was Bismarck and the real maker of it was William II. Germany, in Bismarck's time, was still a saturated power; in the Chancellor's opinion no change in the territorial *status quo* was worth the risks of a war. It was his basic policy to preserve Austria as a great power; so if he were forced to choose between Russia and Austria, he would have to choose Austria, but he hoped to avoid having to choose. He kept the line open to St. Petersburg by the 'Rein-

[1] Benjamin-Constant Jaurès was the cousin of the father of Jean Jaurès.
[2] When the reputation for this display of Republican sentiment had become rather a handicap, Floquet declared that it was not he, but Gambetta, who had shouted at the Tsar. Unfortunately a declaration by Floquet cannot be taken as ending the matter.

surance' treaty, so that he was allied to two rival powers at the same time. He used Italy's British connections to make Britain a silent partner of the Triple Alliance in the Mediterranean, thus checkmating any French plans of coercion of Italy by the use of her superior navy. Perhaps only Bismarck could have kept so many balls in the air at the same time, for Britain was as hostile to Russian designs on Constantinople and the Straits as Austria was to Russian designs on Bulgaria; and Bismarck had to keep on good terms with all three. He managed to do it, and even, by backing up French colonial policy, to achieve something more than formal good relations with France, although the fall of Ferry and the rise of Boulanger showed how transient such a *détente* was bound to be.

As long as the balls were kept in the air, Bismarck could afford to take lightly the efforts of people like Déroulède and Katkov to unite France and Russia on a common basis of Germanophobia. Even the Tsar's dislike of the German elements in the Russian Empire, his measures against the German language and against German subjects in the frontier provinces, however irritating, were no proof of anything but a policy of internal Slavification quite like Bismarck's own policy of Germanization in Prussian Poland. As long as the old Emperor William I was alive, with his memories of the aid and protection afforded by the Tsar Alexander I to his father in the War of Liberation from Napoleon I, the traditional connection of Hohenzollern and Romanov would stand a good many strains. It would certainly stand the strain of resisting naïve propaganda from a State whose system of government seemed to be at the mercy of an adventurer like Boulanger.

It was the refusal of the young German Emperor, William II, to permit Bismarck to carry on with his policy of juggling, of which the Reinsurance treaty was the main feat of legerdemain, that at last gave reality to the dream of a Franco-Russian rapprochement. If Germany was going to move decidedly into the Austrian camp, Russia's position was highly dangerous, for there were powerful groups both in Berlin and in Vienna in favour of liquidating the old Austro-Russian feud by a preventive war. In Italy, Crispi, exhausting the credit and resources of the country in an armaments race and a tariff war with France, was almost eager for a conflict; at any rate, he was earnestly asserting his belief in the imminence of a French attack on Italy. Russia and Britain had many causes of conflict. Europe was more of a powder-magazine than ever and it was no time for Russia to be left alone without any secure friendship to rely on. France was no longer merely a suitor: she had a good deal to give in exchange and, by financial pressure, could make Russian political worries even more disturbing.

In clearing the way for a Franco-Russian agreement, Bismarck's financial policy greatly helped. The attacks by the Russian Government on the German interests in the Baltic provinces had been, of course, resented in Prussian circles, and the Chancellor may have had genuine doubts as to Russian financial stability and may have thought, in addition, that he could force Russia's hand by denying her the resources of the Berlin money-market. For whatever reasons, he refused, in 1887, to permit the perennially hard-up Russian Government to borrow in Germany and thus forced it to apply to Paris. This was an astonishing blunder, since for the use of financial power for political ends, Paris was much better equipped than Berlin. Under the Second Empire, Paris had rivalled London as a money-market and although, for the first few years of the Republic, French savings were almost exclusively devoted to paying for the war, there was then a rapid revival in foreign investment which even the depression of the 'eighties, following on the great losses in Austrian securities, associated with the rise and fall of the *Union Générale,* could not seriously check. France was the most attractive country in the world for the foreign borrower. The interest rate in Paris, right up to 1914, was almost always lower than in any other great capital; the French people went on saving faster than a stationary population and a slowly-growing industry could absorb the surplus, and local and general government borrowing was much less important in France than in most countries. No country had as much ready money as cheaply available.

The French money-market was, even more than others, subject to government control. It was not impossible, but it was difficult, to borrow money if the French Treasury objected. This power had already been used, along with tariff weapons, to make Italy repent her adherence to the Triple Alliance. Russia was a borrower on a greater scale than Italy and seemed likely to be more solvent in the long run. Despite slight improvements in Franco-Italian relations, the ban on Italian borrowing lasted until the end of the tariff war in 1897. Germany had had, indeed, to support the credit of her ally, and it may be said that in this financial war, Germany and France changed partners. Russia was very soon given proof of the degree to which her new friend was prepared to use financial power for political ends, for in 1891 when Russian finances were even more desperate than usual, the Paris Rothschilds refused to back a new Russian loan, ostensibly on account of the anti-Semitic policy of the Russian Government, really, it was believed, because the French Foreign Office was determined to tie Russia down to something more definite than vague expressions of goodwill.

The renewal of the Triple Alliance, by making it clear that despite the temporary exclusion of Crispi from power in Italy, that country could not be coerced by France into abandoning her allies; the disastrous repercussions on Franco-German relations of the failure of the visit of the German Emperor's mother to Paris; the brief flirtation of William II with Britain; all these moves left Russia and France isolated. The two losers in this game of musical chairs were naturally thrown together.[1]

France could and did press Russia for some definite understanding and, while the negotiations were going on, the French fleet visited Kronstadt. The visit was a diplomatic gesture of the most open type; it was not misunderstood anywhere, and when the Tsar stood bareheaded as a Russian band played the *Marseillaise* (regarded in every European country save France as the revolutionary hymn *par excellence*), it was known that the Republic was at last out of the dog-house.

The visit to Kronstadt was, it is true, followed by a French naval visit to Portsmouth, and it was not yet possible to tie Russia down. Nevertheless, the coming event cast its shadow over all Europe. The Russian Ambassador, Mohrenheim, was a strong partisan of an alliance,[2] and he talked. A desperate famine left Russia, in the winter of 1891–92, weak from a military point of view and on the edge of bankruptcy. Hitherto all that France had to show for her political and financial support was a letter from the Russian Foreign Minister, Giers, to Mohrenheim, affirming a desire for the maintenance of a peace threatened, it was implied, by the Triple Alliance and Britain. The Russian and French Governments undertook to 'consult together on every question that endangers general peace. . . . In the event of this peace being seriously endangered, and especially if one of the two parties should be threatened with aggression, the two parties undertake to come to an agreement on the measures of which the realization of this eventuality would necessitate the simultaneous and immediate adoption'. This jargon was vague enough to satisfy the cautious Giers, but it was too vague from the French viewpoint. Nor did personal negotiations between Giers and Freycinet in Paris improve matters. Russia, Freycinet learned, had no designs on Turkey and would give only moral support to France in Egypt. A Russian loan had failed on the Paris market; the new friends had reason to regard each other in a chilly enough fashion.

It was for France to force Russia's hand and to demand something concrete, specifically a military convention. This appealed to Alexander, who was, for the moment, very anti-German, dreaming of dismembering the parvenu empire. With the arrival of the Deputy-Chief of the French General Staff, Boisdeffre, real work began. From a military point of view, simultaneous mobilization was the crux. Could Russia assemble her armies quickly enough to save France from

[1] Much to the disgust of professional patriots, the Empress Frederick had visited Paris, officially *incognita* but, in reality, with plenty of publicity. Her visit was to have been the herald of better relations, but she visited the ruins of the Château of Saint-Cloud, destroyed in the war of 1870, and this exhibition of Anglo-Prussian tact enabled the patriots to gain a great deal of support from less fiery sections of French public opinion. As a political move the visit was worse than useless.

[2] There was suspicion in Russia that the Ambassador's views were coloured by financial advantages he drew from his advocacy of an alliance.

being overrun?   Should France be allowed to evade the obligations of
the Alliance unless Germany were involved, that is, be allowed to
ignore the Austrian threat to Russia's security?   It was finally decided
that each power was to aid the other if its enemy (Italy or Austria)
was being aided by Germany or if either was attacked by Germany
alone.   Each country was to put in the field against Germany an agreed
number of troops, 1,300,000 in the case of France, seven hundred to
eight hundred thousand in the case of Russia.   Technical measures
would be studied and neither party would make a separate peace.
This was the gist of the Boisdeffre-Obruchev agreement, designed, so
its preamble asserted, to aid in the preservation of peace and having
'no other object than that of providing for the necessities of a defensive
war, provoked by the forces of the Triple Alliance against one or the
other (party)'.[1]   This convention made plain how limited were the
objectives of the Alliance, how far from justifying the dreams of
Déroulède.   The Panama scandals came almost at once to make the
Tsar very suspicious of the new ally; Austro-Russian relations improved
and, more important still, there seemed reason to believe that
William II was going back to the old Bismarckian policy of being on
good terms with Russia.   Russia, too, refused to support France in
Egypt where British control was being strengthened, and the arrival in
power of Gladstone meant that Germany could no longer rely on
Britain as a sleeping partner in the Triple Alliance.   The political
situation that had forced Russia towards France had greatly changed
for the better, but a tariff war between Russia and Germany and the
survival of the régime in France limited the possibilities of manœuvre.
In Germany, the Government felt itself bound to dwell on the danger
of a war on two fronts to justify its military programme and, by the
summer of 1893, the Franco-Russian Alliance had stood its worst
initial strains.   It was merely a *mariage de convenance* at the moment,
but it was at least that.

As often happens in a marriage of that kind, the benefits were
decidedly limited from the point of view of one party.   France had
escaped the dangerous isolation of the past, but she had been in less
danger of German attack than she thought, while by tying herself to
Russia, she actually incurred new risks.   Should a conflict break out
over Russian aims, Germany, whether involved directly, or through
her Austrian ally, would be forced to face a war on two fronts, and
that fact, given the views of the German Staff on the military potentialities of France and Russia, meant that France would have to bear the
burden of the first German attack.   Whether the disasters of August
1914 should be put down to the debit side of the Alliance is open to
question.   The Germans were sure to think that a speedy victory over
France was easier than a speedy victory over Russia; it was not the

[1] 18th August, 1892.

treaty that made them think that, and it is arguable that, from a military point of view, it was not the German attack on France but the attempted French attack on Germany that led to the great disasters. A more serious criticism, borne out by the event, is that war, when it did come, came from the east; that it was in support of a Russian client state that France underwent the ordeal of 1914–18; that, both in peace and war, France gained far less from the Alliance than had been fondly hoped for in the optimistic early years.

The first power to suffer in the esteem of the world as a result of the Franco-Russian rapprochement was not Germany but Britain. France, in Egypt, in Africa, and in Asia, had many grounds of difference with Britain. The dispute between France and Siam over the control of the Mekong involved a clash with Britain, which wished to preserve Siam as a buffer state; but however far Rosebery might be willing to go, Gladstone was not willing to risk a war for the rights of the Siamese. The French were able to send warships to anchor off Bangkok and impose a treaty that seriously damaged the prestige of Siam's presumed backer. Worse still, it was for a moment believed that the French commander had ordered British ships away from Bangkok, a step Rosebery wished to treat as a *casus belli*. A war with France, at that time, would have been no joke, as the Russian fleet might have been thrown into the scale and the great reorganization of the British Navy was not complete. Rosebery appealed to the Kaiser, who was then in England, for help, but before any decision could be made, the news came that the crisis was a false alarm. The crisis left the German diplomats convinced that Britain had given way, that she needed German help—and would have to pay for it; while the French were given a chance to develop illusions as to the ease with which Britain could be forced to climb down.

Paradoxically, the Alliance that in the minds of the professional patriots of Paris was to deliver Alsace and Lorraine, seemed to have its use, if it had any, in the game of bluff and claim-jumping that was going on in Africa and Asia. Britain was isolated, and Italy, the common link between the Triple Alliance and Britain, was exhausted by the tariff war with France and by economic misery that brought about a rebellion of the wretched Sicilian peasants. It was a change from the days when the Triple Alliance powers with their British associate, had had it all their own way. But it was a change that helped to defend the *status quo* in Europe; its other result was to increase tension between Britain and France, a popular enough result at the moment, when, as Clemenceau discovered, any English attachment was fatal, but not quite what Déroulède had planned. Europe was settling down into two camps; it was as yet uncertain which camp Britain would join, but war for European causes was less, not more, likely than it had been a few years before. As the critics of the Alliance put it, the new system preserved all the existing arrangements in Europe including the Treaty of Frankfort.

The Alliance did more than that. It tied France so closely to Russia that when the policy of the latter power involved good relations with Germany, it involved France in those relations. France was thus made a not very willing member of the triumvirate of European powers that forced Japan to relinquish most of her gains after her victory in the war with China in 1894. She was debarred from too ostentatious sympathy with the Armenians during the period of revolution and massacre in 1896, for Russia as well as Turkey had her Armenian problem. Far from making a vigorous anti-German policy possible, the Alliance led to a renewal of the policy of more friendly relations with Germany, accompanied by an intensification of the colonial rivalry with Britain. France even sent a squadron to the celebration of the opening of the Kiel Canal, a gesture which one of the most formidable critics of Republican diplomacy was to make a symbol of the vacillations and reversals which, he asserted, were inherent in the system.[1]

As the offensive weapon of the revenge policy of Déroulède, the Alliance was a complete failure. Whatever the French negotiators may have thought, it was in Russian eyes purely defensive, in Europe at least. Moreover, as critics pointed out, since the Alliance was a reply to the Triple Alliance and would die with it, it would cease to be effective just at the moment when the European diplomatic game would offer possibilities for a forward policy: for example, if the death of the Emperor Francis-Joseph broke up the Austrian Empire. Of course these limitations were hidden from the crowds which mobbed the Russian sailors of Admiral Avellan on their visit to Paris in 1893. That visit was the occasion of the greatest exhibition of Parisian enthusiasm since the Boulanger review of 1886. The visit of the young Nicholas II and his wife in 1896 was not such a popular success. No coloured posters showing the dull and timid young autocrat caracoling on a fiery charger in a semi-Cossack uniform, no lush poetic prose from the hysterical pen of François Coppée, could make Nicholas II a great popular idol, and no courtly blindness could conceal the lack of warmth which the young Empress showed to her hosts. The return visit of President Faure was more formally significant, for at a naval review off Kronstadt, Nicholas II spoke of the 'two friendly and allied nations', the first official statement of the existence of the Alliance.[2] Even after that public proclamation of the bond between the Republic and the Autocracy, the Alliance was not an effective anti-German instrument, and if it had any effect on France's position, it was to bring her face to face with the danger which had been the nightmare of the early years of the Republic, the danger of war, but this time not war with Germany, but war with Britain.

[1] Charles Maurras in *Kiel et Tanger*.　　[2] 26th August, 1897.

II

The success of Brazza's explorations and political activities in the Congo, at the time they were made, bred more hopes than the intrinsic value of the region seemed to justify. If, from bases on the Niger and the Congo, French power could be extended eastwards, it might be possible to undo what was (from the point of view of the Colonial party) the greatest error of the Third Republic, the help unwittingly given to the British occupation of Egypt. If France could extend her power right across Africa from the Congo basin to the frontier of Abyssinia, she would be in a position to bring pressure to bear on Britain. She would be in control of the waters of the Nile by which Egypt lived; modern engineering technique could make this control more than a metaphor and then France would undo the mischief that the feebleness of Freycinet had wrought. This plan, or these vague ideas out of which a plan might come, were not merely incompatible with the security of the British position in Egypt, but they would make impossible the realization of the dream that then delighted the less realistic British imperialists, the vision of an All-Red route from the Cape to Cairo.

This contradiction in aim between the two great expansionist powers in Africa was itself bound up with the whole complex European situation. The degree of freedom allowed to the agents of the two rival Governments in Africa was largely determined by the balance of power in Europe. How far Britain would go depended on the degree of security she felt in face of France's ally Russia, which, in turn, depended on such contingencies as the possible acquisition by Russia of the right to send her Black Sea fleet into the Mediterranean or the completion of the Trans-Siberian railway. Not only so, British policy could count on a more or less free hand according to the state of Anglo-German relations which, in turn, might depend on conflict over rival claims in Samoa. So we see the British Government at one time trying to induce the German Government to advance its own Cameroon frontier to Lake Chad and, when this fails, agreeing to let King Leopold's Congo Free State acquire residuary rights in the Bahr el Ghazal, nominally part of the Egyptian Sudan, and, at the same time, getting from the King a right of way for the All-Red route. This move served to bring together both France and Germany, who were easily able to intimidate King Leopold, if not Lord Rosebery. That particular method of keeping the French out of the Upper Nile failed, having had no more beneficial results than that of throwing Germany and France together.

In this game of African musical chairs even Russia was involved, for both France and her ally took a great if selfish interest in the independence of Abyssinia. After the death of the Emperor John at the hands of the Khalifa's army, the Italians who, like the French and British, had established themselves on the seaboard of the Abyssinian plateau, soon quarrelled with their quondam protégé, Menelik. He, in turn, was supported morally and materially by France and Russia, the French having a *locus standi* as owners of the port of Jibouti, the Russians as patrons of all Eastern Christian peoples. The British, on the other hand, supported the Italian designs on Abyssinian independence. It was convenient to have another and innocuous European power on the flank of the Khalifa and still more convenient to avoid having the head-waters of the Blue Nile under the control of a client state of France.

It is against this background that the French designs for seizing a post on the White Nile, not for its intrinsic value but for its possibilities as a bargaining weapon in negotiations with Britain over Egypt, must be seen. British and French policy in turn would succeed or fail, less in terms of its intrinsic soundness than in terms of the general European situation. Britain was in the stronger position since she was firmly settled on the Lower Nile, while France was only moving towards the Upper Nile, but she had not made it quite clear that her claims (on her own behalf and on Egypt's) were geographically continuous, that is to say that, from Uganda to the mouth of the Nile, all the river valley was to be under British or 'Egyptian' control. Between the northernmost limit of British claims and the southernmost limit of Egyptian claims there was a possible gap into which France might insert herself, a gap whose chief town was Fashoda and whose chief importance was that it might be used to secure control of the Nile waters. As long as Britain seemed open to argument, both about the evacuation of Egypt and the settlement of African claims, France might hold her hand, but there were rumours, and justified rumours, that France and King Leopold were both preparing expeditions to stake-out claims in the vast region which was controlled, as far as it was controlled at all, by the Khalifa in Khartoum, and which the British Government, as the trustee for Egyptian claims, looked on as its own.

Not all agents of British policy in Egypt wanted to extend control over the Sudan much south of Khartoum. When Egypt could afford it, Cromer thought, the death of Gordon would be avenged and a more secure frontier acquired, but it was not necessary to extend Egyptian rule into the vast tropical swamps wherein it had died once before. There had been a famous warning, given in 1895 by Sir Edward Grey,[1] that 'the advance of a French expedition under secret instructions right from the other side of Africa right into a territory over which our claims have been known for so long, would be not merely an incon-

---

[1] Then Parliamentary Under-Secretary for Foreign Affairs and mouthpiece of the department in the House of Commons.

sistent and unexpected act, but it must be perfectly well known to the French Government that it would be an unfriendly act, and would be so viewed by England'. This was, on the surface, plain enough, and it was approved and denounced by Englishmen according to their sympathies with a forward and exclusive policy in the Sudan. But the French Government naturally refused to be frightened off merely by strong and vague words, for it was not wholly clear what the British claims were, and the British assertion of a right to have an option on a vast territory, while reserving to herself the choice of a time to take it up, was bold. Britain laid down the law and seemed to bar all compromise, a diplomatic method whose drawbacks she herself fully appreciated when, a few months later, President Cleveland, in an even more blunt fashion, issued what was almost an ultimatum over British claims in Venezuela.

Nor was the British position merely made uncomfortable by the Venezuela dispute; in South Africa, the Jameson raid was made and failed, with a consequent loss of prestige by a power some of whose leading figures found themselves associated with an absurd episode which, since it failed ignominiously, was certainly criminal. This blow was followed by the telegram of the German Emperor to President Kruger congratulating him on his successful defeat of the filibusters, a gesture which infuriated a proud people conscious of not looking its best in the eyes of a critical world. Lastly (and of even greater moment in Central Africa), at the Battle of Adowa, the Italian invasion of Abyssinia was not merely repelled; a European army was annihilated and the friend of Britain was humiliated by the client of France and Russia. From Adowa sprang the necessity or excuse for British action to relieve pressure on the Italians. The first move towards the re-occupation of the Sudan began; and from 1896 on, there was a race between the British and French agents. Which would first reach the Upper Nile and in what force?

III

From the moment that the British Government decided to push forward with the reconquest of the Sudan, the French Government had little excuse for believing that a mere formal occupation of a post in the disputed territory would serve any good purpose. At the moment, France, backed by Russia, was successfully preventing the International Debt Commission from advancing money to the Egyptian Government for the cost of the war, thus forcing Britain directly to underwrite the financing of the campaign. There was no longer any real hope of the settlement that a year or so before had been discussed between the French Minister of Foreign Affairs [1] and the British Chargé in Paris.

[1] Gabriel Hanotaux.

The bluster of the short-lived Radical ministry of Léon Bourgeois had added to British resentment of French action and, if we may believe a good witness,[1] Hanotaux, who had returned to replace the luckless Marcellin Berthelot at the Foreign Office, knew this perfectly well, since he told the soldier who had been chosen to lead the expedition, 'You are going to fire a pistol shot on the Nile; we accept all its consequences.' The young man to whom this was said was equally ready to accept his share of the risks.

Jean-Baptiste Marchand was just over thirty when he was chosen to march to the Nile.[2]   He was a soldier by choice, enlisting as a private in the Marines, the famous 'Marsouins', to whose valour the modern French Empire owes so much. His ability was noted and he was admitted to the military school at Saint-Maixent and commissioned. In Africa, his courage and powers of leadership soon won him fame; he was twice wounded in the wars against Toucouleurs and Tuaregs; he learned to command native troops and to win the trust of his fellows. Ambitious and bold, he had not waited for destiny to strike him, but had put himself in the way of it, haunting, when on leave in Paris, the Foreign Office and the new Colonial Office,[3] trying to persuade Ministers like Chautemps and his successor, Guieysse, to turn the tables on the English.

The design was not new; a few years before, the same mission had been entrusted to Monteil, who was then diverted from his first destination. Marchand was passionately partisan, Anglophobe like most of the French colonial officers of that age, convinced that Britain had armed Samori against the French, and very willing to enter into amicable relations with her enemies, the Dervishes of Khartoum. Nor did the plan of the Minister and the soldier stop there, for missions were to be sent to Abyssinia from whence they were to descend towards the valley of the Nile and join hands, cutting off the British in the south who were rushing the Uganda railway to completion, from the great expeditionary force in the north that was being assembled for the reconquest of the Sudan. It was a design worthy of the bold French adventurers of the eighteenth century and, like their designs, it called for resources far greater than a government bound to keep its main strength ready in Europe could possibly supply.

Formally, the Marchand mission was pacific. The soldier was to be subject to Victor Liotard, the energetic civilian governor of the Upper Oubangui, one of the most zealous partisans of the forward policy. All the attempts to give this 'mission' a pacific character were so much ingenuity wasted. It was intended to upset British policy— if necessary in amicable agreement with the Dervish power with which Britain was preparing to wage a considerable war. Whatever verbal

---

[1] Baratier.   [2] He was born in 1863.
[3] This Ministry was given a permanent organization in 1894.

distinctions M. Hanotaux might reassure himself with were not likely to be appreciated in Cairo or London.

The story of Marchand's march across darkest Africa is one of the glories of modern French history. At the beginning, there were difficulties with Brazza who did not like to have soldiers traversing his territories and upsetting his natives. There were the customary difficulties over porters—indeed more than the customary difficulties—for the Mission was bigger and its itinerary far more ambitious than was usual. Marchand was not a Frenchman for nothing; he knew how to wangle, and he was resolved to get to the Nile, to get there by river and, when he had got there, to have means of transport; so he commandeered the steamer *Faidherbe*, which he took to pieces, even managing to bring the boiler with him by rolling it on logs for hundreds of kilometres through the tropical forest. The hull, lightened by the removal of the machinery, was towed on the rivers when there was water and mounted on wheels when there was not. It was a fantastic, impossible scheme, adding greatly to the difficulty of finding porters, but it succeeded.

Marchand was not the only exceptional leader on the expedition. The ingenious engineer, Souyri, whose time of service was up, but whom Marchand persuaded to join him to reassemble the *Faidherbe*, Baratier, Doctor Emily and a young soldier who had already fought at Marchand's side and who was destined to even greater fame, Mangin, —these, almost as much as Marchand, were heroes. Spare parts were fetched from Brazzaville, and month after month, the Mission moved on, negotiating with Dinkas and harassed by orders from Paris for speed. When the Bahr el Ghazal was reached, the main obstacle was the vast masses of vegetation which choked the rivers and in which it was possible for a ship to be blocked as effectually as in the midst of an ice-pack. A year after Marchand had left Liotard, he was safely settled in the Bahr el Ghazal, though racked by fever and by impatience to measure himself with the English, an honour delayed until the River Soueh rose enough to float the *Faidherbe*. On July 5th, the little steamer at last reached the waters of the White Nile and, going on ahead, on July 16th Marchand was at Fashoda.

Fashoda had been an important centre of trade and of Egyptian power, but the revolt of the Dervishes had reduced it to a ruined village. At once work was begun to make the ruined fort safe from a *coup de main* and, by a hasty sowing of vegetables, to have some resource against famine, while every effort was made to win the friendship of the natives while awaiting the arrival of the *Faidherbe* and of the messengers of the Abyssinian Mission. But the *Faidherbe* was slow in coming and the messengers from the east did not come at all; the little garrison was cut off from its base and from all news, even the news that, to the north, the Dervish power was in its last agony. When ships at last appeared, it was not the *Faidherbe* but armed Dervish steamers which made brave but futile attacks on the fort and were driven off with great loss. Four days later, the *Faidherbe* appeared, with food, supplies, and instructions, the last ordering Marchand to get into touch with the Abyssinians who were reported to be moving west. There were no Abyssinians, and the success of a treaty with the local chief, putting his territory under French rule, was clouded, a fortnight later, by the arrival of two messengers from Kitchener. They announced the destruction of the Dervishes at Omdurman—and the intention of the victorious Sirdar to come himself to Fashoda. Marchand could only congratulate the victor, announce his own occupation of the Bahr el Ghazal—and await events.

He had not long to wait. Five hours after the letter, five gunboats and a whole flotilla of other vessels brought to the fort three battalions of infantry, a strong force of artillery—and Kitchener. The captain faced the general, the leader of the little band of Senegalese riflemen, the leader of the army which had just annihilated the long-victorious troops of the Khalifa. Which would give way? For the moment neither did and, by a compromise that did credit to the self-control of each, the Egyptian flag was hoisted but the French flag was not pulled down. Kitchener admired the flower garden that had been created, talked in his good, stiff French with the officers—and sent the garrison some newspapers. From them they learned that their native land was torn in two by the Dreyfus case, yet unless they were supported to the uttermost by the home government, their great journey would be simply a fruitless raid, and what chance had they of support now?

They had none; the rest of the story of Fashoda is simply the story of the constant pressure under which the French Government, faced with the certainty that Britain would make the retention of Fashoda a *casus belli*, tried to find the easiest way of retreat. As the general European situation had favoured France two years before, it now favoured Britain. Germany was no longer ready to back up France against Britain, and Russia was unwilling to support, diplomatically or in arms, the claims of her ally. The new Minister of Foreign Affairs, Delcassé, had been a prominent member of the Colonial party, but he was clear-sighted and resolute and he could see that France would be reduced to fighting a solitary war against a country with all the trumps in her hands. At Fashoda itself, Marchand would of course be overwhelmed—and elsewhere? Elsewhere could only mean at sea, and there the French Navy, if in a better position than Marchand, was in no condition to fight even a moderately successful war against Britain. France, it is true, was still the second naval power in the world, but that was not to say that she was in any position to fight the first naval power.

It was natural that, after the war, the Navy should have been starved. France's complete naval supremacy in 1870 had not helped the French much or seriously hindered the Germans. It was necessary that all the resources of the country should be spent in re-building the Army; and after the first strenuous years were over and it was possible to do something for the fleet, bad habits of false economy were deeply rooted. For example, in order to use up the vast stocks of seasoned timber France continued to build ships with wooden frames, long after advances in naval technology had made iron frames indispensable. The weakening of administrative authority had prevented very necessary reforms. France had five naval dockyards, which was too many, and instead of closing down the smaller ones, like Rochefort, or at least making each yard do a special kind of work, naval construction was carefully portioned out to preserve the vested interests of the dockyard towns, and in consequence, building became fantastically slow and costly. Nor was naval policy consistent. Under Admiral Aube, the school which believed in small, fast, light craft, torpedo-boats, cruisers and in a war of commerce destruction, was popular, but neither Aube nor his opponents had their way, so that the French fleet was not designed to carry out any general theory of naval war. The battle fleet was not homogeneous. The cruisers were insufficient in number and, more serious, too badly provided with overseas bases to make a commerce war as formidable to Britain as was necessary if British threats against France were to be effectually countered by French threats against Britain. No plans, no preparations for a war against Britain had been made, and the Government got no very comforting counsel from its naval advisers.

Very different was the spirit in London. The more irresponsible papers were full of ill-mannered abuse; the more serious made it plain that even if it meant war, France would be excluded from the Nile Valley. Men like Rosebery thought that a war with France now would not be altogether a bad thing, and Joseph Chamberlain was busy with the ill-judged diplomatic schemes in which he delighted. Salisbury, though quite immovable on the subject of the Nile, had no desire for a war, although that war could hardly fail to be successful even if, as was unlikely, the Russian Navy reinforced the French. Delcassé had to give way; Marchand was forced to evacuate Fashoda. Too late to be of any help, the Abyssinians at last appeared on the horizon, but the adventure was over. It only remained to liquidate it, and Britain seemed in no hurry to do that, but in March 1899, having secured her position in the Sudan by her agreement with Egypt, she was ready to deal with France. The latter was to be totally excluded from the Nile Valley, but to be left with all her recent acquisitions west of the watershed. The dream of a French barrier across Africa from Atlantic to Red Sea was over. Jibouti and French Somaliland remained as pathetic relics of those dreams. On the other side of the ledger, France had at last secured the whole hinterland of West Africa.

From the Mediterranean to the Congo, all the continent was hers, save for enclaves, some tiny, like the British colony of the Gambia, some large, like the British colony of Nigeria and the German Cameroons; only one was not yet under European control—Morocco.

Fashoda was a bitter humiliation for France, coming as it did at the very height of the Dreyfus crisis. The inglorious denouement provided plenty of ammunition for the embittered Nationalists, and in many French circles hatred of England seemed destined to replace hatred of Germany. There was a growth, too, of scepticism about the value of the Russian Alliance, but resentment of English manners and methods was too deep to allow room for much anti-Russian sentiment; it even fostered a shallow growth of feeling in favour of real co-operation with Germany. Étienne, one of the leaders of the Colonial party, expressed the contemporary sentiment. He was tired, he declared, of sacrificing French to English interests. 'There are other people in the world, with whom France can make a good bargain. All right, France will remember all the good turns of the past and all the bad turns of the present.' This was not the lesson learned by the new Foreign Minister. For Delcassé, the lesson was the need not to let the reach exceed the grasp, to reach an agreement with the odious nation which had just won so brilliant a triumph over France. For Delcassé was too good a Gambettist to forget for a moment the wound of Strasbourg under the influence of the irritation of the scratch of Fashoda.

BOOK VII

THE AFFAIR[1]

Gesta Dei per Francos

---

[1] The French word 'affaire' is usually translated 'case', but 'l'Affaire Dreyfus' was no mere case and it has been called simply 'the Affair'.

CHAPTER I

A GHOST WALKS

I

FROM the point of view of the French Army and the French nation, the Dreyfus case was better forgotten. A traitor had been unmasked, but it was humiliating that an officer in a confidential position had betrayed, although less humiliating when it was remembered that the traitor was not a real Frenchman but a Jew.[1]

The desire to let the matter rest was not uncommon among French Jews, especially among the richer French Jews; the very best that could be hoped for was that the business would be forgotten. Mathieu Dreyfus was not ready to follow this prudent line. He was convinced that his brother was innocent, both because of his knowledge of his brother and because of the meagreness of the evidence against him. Like Maître Demange, he could not understand how the court-martial could have convicted Alfred on the very inconclusive testimony known to the defence. Since Alfred was innocent, someone else must be guilty; since the evidence was weak, there must be some mystery behind the conviction. So the Dreyfus family set themselves to find out who had really written the *bordereau* and what had really happened at the trial. They were at first more successful in the second part of their task, for the trail which they had followed to lead them to the real traitor, petered out. The judges of the court-martial had not been discreet and it soon became known that secret documents had been shown to the judges which had been kept from the defence. Among those who learned this was Demange, and this breach of the rules of procedure gave the Dreyfus family its first hope of getting a re-trial on legal grounds. Such a re-trial could not be had without the consent of the Government and the military authorities, and they were not willing to risk the political storm that a re-trial of a rich Jew would have brought, as long as they believed that justice had been done in however irregular a fashion. The sacred 'chose jugée'[2] could not be upset on a mere point of law.

[1] The world of the Affair is so remote, that it is hard to remember the sense of shame and alarm felt at the news of the treason of a mere temporary staff captain. The high standard in treachery, at the very top of an Army, set by Soviet Russia was then unthinkable, as was the comforting reasoning that shows how much an army gains from the revelation of such colossal conspiracies.

[2] Legally over and done with.

Destiny, which had been unkind to Alfred Dreyfus, at last relented. That disease of Colonel Sandherr which perhaps accounted for the initial mistake now made it necessary for him to retire and soon killed him. His successor was not the semi-illiterate Henry, but a highly cultivated officer, Colonel Picquart, who was like Sandherr, Dreyfus, and so many others in the case, an Alsatian. However disappointing to Henry the nomination of Picquart may have been, it was from the point of view of the General Staff not only suitable but safe. For Picquart was a Catholic and an anti-Semite[1]; if there was any move for the Dreyfus case being reopened, it would not come from him.

Picquart was that rare type, a man who really cares for justice, no matter where his care for it may take him. He really did believe *fiat justitia ruat cœlum*, or it might be better to say he believed that righteousness exalteth a nation. There were to appear in the course of the Affair many men who boldly asserted that they, too, put justice before all questions of party and doctrine, but their claims were not, in fact, severely tested, for their party interest and their doctrinal interest ran in harness with their sense of justice. Picquart's did not; justice for him involved a breach with the loyalties and beliefs of his whole life.[2]

Picquart did not doubt that Dreyfus was a traitor; what puzzled him was the problem of why Dreyfus should have betrayed. While that problem was still unsolved, a new one was perplexing Sandherr's successor; the sale of secrets to the German attaché was still going on. There were many signs of this, but the decisive proof came with the arrival at the Bureau (during a temporary absence of Henry) of an intercepted letter from the German attaché to a French officer who was obviously in treasonable relations with Schwartzkoppen. The officer was a Commandant Esterhazy. Picquart's first thoughts, on the receipt of the 'petit bleu', were that there was another traitor at work, not that Dreyfus had been innocently condemned, and when he began to investigate Esterhazy, he had no notion of where the trail would lead.

Esterhazy was a descendant of a great Hungarian family and well but not creditably known about town for his lively private life. He was in debt, distrusted in his own regiment, the 74th Infantry, abnormally interested, for an infantryman, in artillery matters—and an old acquaintance of Henry's. It was unfortunate, then, that Picquart thought it necessary or natural to entrust further investigation to Henry, since that tenacious officer was very unsuccessful in his attempts to discover much about Esterhazy. It was necessary to learn a good ·deal about the Franco-Hungarian: for he was trying, by the use of his

---

[1] Picquart is usually said to have been a Protestant.
[2] It is to be hoped that it is unnecessary to-day to emphasize the fact that left-wing doctrinaires can swallow just as preposterous defences of the indefensible, and produce *ex post facto* explanations of events whose possibility they had denied as hotly as any blind believer in Drumont or Rochefort.

political friends, to get appointed to the General Staff. This was a bad move, for the letters written by Esterhazy in his campaign were seen by Picquart and he had seen that handwriting before. It was the writing of the author of the *bordereau*. The resemblance was striking, so striking that du Paty de Clam, when he saw it, attributed the letter to Mathieu Dreyfus, and Bertillon to a man who had been trained by the Jews to imitate the hand of Alfred Dreyfus. Picquart thought that a simpler explanation was adequate. The writing of the *bordereau* was identical with that of Esterhazy, because Esterhazy had been a traitor in 1894 as he was in 1896. What remained to be done was to see the evidence that had resulted in the condemnation of Dreyfus. Had Sandherr and Henry obeyed orders, the evidence would have been destroyed, but it was still in the files, and Sandherr had called Picquart's attention to it when turning over the post to him.

When Picquart had read the famous dossier, his mind was made up; there was nothing in that collection of ambiguous papers to fix guilt on anybody. With some simplicity, Picquart now told Boisdeffre of his discovery; and the Chief of Staff, apart from annoyance at the discovery of Sandherr's disobedience, seemed to take the matter calmly. Picquart waited and continued to investigate Esterhazy, but not only did waiting mean that Dreyfus was still on Devil's Island but, hearing rumours of the activities of the Dreyfus family, Picquart pointed out to his chiefs how much better it would be to take the initiative while there was yet time. Further delay, he wrote to Gonse, would mean a crisis, 'a harmful, useless crisis, which could be avoided by doing justice in time'. It was the first of many chances given to the rulers of the French Army to retreat in good order.

The Dreyfus family had entrusted the task of writing up their case for a new trial to a brilliant young Jew, Bernard Lazare, who was a most courageous opponent of anti-Semitism, but they did not know how to call attention to the pamphlet. When at last they were ready to publish it, Mathieu Dreyfus had the ingenious idea of getting a British journalist to publish in a Welsh paper a false story of the escape of Alfred. The only result, at first, was to frighten the Minister of the Colonies, André Lebon, into ordering Dreyfus to be put into double irons and confined to his hut. Physical torture was now added to the mental tortures of the prisoner, but a second result of the story was to revive interest in the case and *L'Eclair* published an article asserting that there were many proofs of the treason of Dreyfus, including a reference to 'him' in a letter from the German to the Italian attaché. The opponents of a new trial were making the first false move; they were not content to stay within the fortress of the *chose jugée*; they thought to drive off the besiegers by sorties.

Picquart was still so much in the dark as to believe that the article was the work of the Dreyfus family, trying to keep the question alive, but an interview with Gonse began to shake his faith in his superiors. For Gonse informed him that, guilty or innocent, the Jew would have to stay where he was. Picquart, shocked out of official respect by this candour, retorted that he would not let this secret go to the grave with him. He was becoming a nuisance and at an awkward time, for Madame Dreyfus was demanding the re-opening of the case on the ground that the rules of procedure had been violated, and the press was beginning to take a new interest in the Affair if only to print further 'proofs' of the guilt of Dreyfus, proofs which complicated the position of the General Staff. So Picquart was sent off to inspect fortifications and then to the frontier of Tunis, a move which had the advantage of putting Henry in charge of the Bureau, but had the disadvantage of destroying Picquart's faith in his superiors.

It was not only the press and the Dreyfus family that were active. Nationalist deputies were beginning to use the case as a means of demonstrating their vigilance; interpellations were threatened, for, as was later said, the enemies of Dreyfus were not content to assert that he was guilty, they could not bear that anyone should assert that he was innocent. By the vehemence of their assertions these enemies got momentary applause and, no doubt, a warm sense of having deserved well of their country, but they were aiding the Dreyfus family to keep the question before the public mind. It was in a reply to a Nationalist interpellation that General Billot, the Minister of War, was in his turn provoked into leaving the security of the *chose jugée*, for he asserted that Dreyfus had been *regularly* convicted. This was untrue and was now known to be untrue to a large number of people, among them to Demange and Mathieu Dreyfus. Alfred Dreyfus, guilty or not, had not been regularly tried.

It was now very doubtful if even in the part of his trial that had been regular, he had been rightly convicted, for the *Matin* had published a facsimile of the *bordereau* and there were plenty of people in Paris who saw that the handwriting closely resembled that of Esterhazy.[1]

Henry, now in charge of the Bureau, was resolved that the activities of Picquart should not be allowed to create doubts in the mind of any other investigator. He began to tamper with the documents that had aroused Picquart's suspicion (not knowing that Picquart had taken the precaution of having the *petit bleu* photographed before placing it in the files), and other 'proofs' of the guilt of Dreyfus were manufactured and added to the dossier. The campaign for the defence of the *chose jugée* was well under way. Picquart, who was determined not to let his secret die with him, wrote a narrative which was to be

---

[1] Long after it was claimed that the *Matin*, in publishing the *bordereau*, had deliberately tried to help Dreyfus ; the *Matin's* comment on the case at the time shows that the newspaper, if that was its purpose, had very carefully concealed its aim from its readers.

sent, should he die, to the President of the Republic. He went further; as the hostility of Henry and, behind him, of Gonse and Boisdeffre became more and more obvious, he consulted Louis Leblois, an eminent Paris lawyer, like himself an Alsatian, and a schoolfellow at the Lycée of Strasbourg. He told Leblois of his conviction of the innocence of Dreyfus, bound him to secrecy and entrusted him with a watching brief over his interests. Leblois thought himself entitled to investigate the case, if he kept secret the rôle of Picquart in it and, talking of his doubts with a friend, Charles Risler, was astonished to learn that Risler's uncle was himself in doubt both about Dreyfus's guilt and what was best to be done.

The uncle in question was a notability of the régime, Scheurer-Kestner, member of one of the greatest Republican clans,[1] Vice-President of the Senate, most eminent of exiled Alsatians. He had been approached by the Dreyfus family as fellow-Alsatians, and his doubts of the guilt of Alfred Dreyfus had led him to make representations to his old friend General Billot, who had put him off by affirmations of the certainty of Dreyfus's guilt. Leblois had given him something concrete to go on, the opinion of Picquart and the attitude of Gonse. Leblois himself felt bound to remain in the background. He did not trust Billot or the military officials. 'A whole world will collapse when this business is cleared up. . . . Those fellows will defend themselves, and we know how unscrupulous they are.' So Scheurer-Kestner was not to open fire until he had approached the President of the Republic and the Ministers. Félix Faure was not responsive and the Senator tackled Billot. It was in vain, Billot was deaf to all warnings and encouraged the press to attack his old friend. The Prime Minister (Méline) was also approached, but, as Scheurer-Kestner had already discovered, Méline was not a Gambetta or a Ferry. At last he came into the open and by a letter in the *Temps*, addressed to another great figure of the Republic, Arthur Ranc, he declared for the reopening of the case, for 'revision'.

It was obvious even to the military mind that the attack was becoming serious. It was necessary to make sure that Esterhazy, who was no very reputable character, would not run away, or sell out to the Jews who were, in the opinion of the General Staff, capable of anything. So a comic-opera secret interview with Esterhazy was arranged in which du Paty de Clam wore a false beard.[2] For reasons which even now are not quite clear, the General Staff had resolved to protect Esterhazy, although they must have known how unreliable he was and

---

[1] He was Madame Jules Ferrie's uncle.

[2] Those Frenchmen who, like M. Jean Héritier, still assert the guilt of Dreyfus have to represent Henry and du Paty de Clam as being the innocent victims of Hebraic guile. They can only defend the two men by implicitly asserting that some of the most delicate and important work in the French Army was entrusted to men who would have bought a gold brick or Brooklyn Bridge at the bidding of the first plausible confidence trickster.

how dangerous an ally or protégé he might turn out to be.[1] The honour and security of the French Army were, from now on, in the hands of an incompetent forger, Henry, and a most disreputable adventurer, Esterhazy. Boisdeffre was ready to repress smiles when Esterhazy wrote that he had 'a heritage of glory to defend'.

In this laudable enterprise Esterhazy needed liaison officers to keep him in touch with the General Staff and two women were thus employed, the Marquise du Paty de Clam and a less reputable female, Esterhazy's mistress, commonly known as 'Tart Pays'. The plan of campaign was that Esterhazy should appeal to Félix Faure, who thus found himself approached on the one side by Scheurer-Kestner and on the other by Esterhazy who, when other letters had been left unanswered, uttered a threat of a kind soon to be familiar. He possessed, he asserted, the facsimile of a document that not only proved the guilt of Dreyfus but which, if published, would force France to go to war or to humiliate herself. It was a form of blackmail that was to be employed to excess.

Up to this moment the Revisionists [2] had been working in the dark. Picquart knew nothing of the activities of the Dreyfus family or of Scheurer-Kestner who knew nothing of the *petit bleu*, and Mathieu Dreyfus, so far, knew nothing of Esterhazy. But the *Matin* facsimile was reprinted by Bernard Lazare; the hand of Esterhazy was recognized and the news passed on to Mathieu Dreyfus, while Henry, through the *Libre Parole*, attacked Picquart without naming him and revealed yet more secret documents, another of those rash sorties of the defence. At last the Dreyfus family had found what they wanted, the author of the *bordereau*. It was no longer on a point of law that they asked for revision, but on the general question of guilt or innocence. In a letter to Félix Faure, Mathieu Dreyfus denounced Esterhazy by name. Esterhazy, confident in his protectors, demanded an inquiry and casting himself as a victim of the 'Jewish syndicate' whose misdeeds Rochefort was making much of, he was on the way to becoming a hero. Both the Italian and German ambassadors were increasingly irritated by the violence of the French press and both insisted with Hanotaux that Dreyfus was innocent. Outside France all well-informed people knew that Dreyfus was not the author of the *bordereau*, which proved them in the eyes of stout patriots, allies or dupes of the Syndicate.[3]

The demand of Esterhazy for an inquiry was granted, and the task

---

[1] One theory is that Esterhazy wrote the *bordereau* at the orders of Sandherr as part of a campaign of counter-espionage.

[2] I shall use this word to cover all those who wished the case to be reopened.

[3] It was one of the complications of the case that the Empress Eugénie and some of the Orleans princes knew, through their relations with Queen Victoria, that the Kaiser had told his grandmother that Dreyfus was innocent. But the old dynastic parties were not to be shaken by such weaknesses. It should be noted that the Bonapartist firebrand, Paul de Cassagnac, and the Orleanist newspaper, the *Soleil*, were for revision. But the *Soleil* had to climb down and replace its editor in face of the blast from its infuriated readers.

was entrusted to General de Pellieux, who was given a civilian legal official, Bertulus, to aid him. Henry had prepared for this emergency by accumulating documents that would have been conclusive against Dreyfus if they had referred to him or had been genuine. He was able to persuade Pellieux that Picquart was engaged in a conspiracy, with Leblois, to throw the guilt of Dreyfus on Esterhazy's shoulders. When at last Pellieux saw Picquart, who had been brought back from Tunis, his mind was made up. It was just as well, for the *Figaro* had secured from a cast-off mistress of Esterhazy some very revealing letters in which this French soldier abused the French Army and its generals, and wrote of 'a red battle sun, in Paris taken by assault and given over to be plundered by a hundred thousand drunk soldiers . . . That's the treat I dream of.' Esterhazy was henceforward known to the Revisionists as the 'Uhlan', but by denying the authenticity of some of the letters and representing the others as provoked by honest indignation, their author managed to keep his reputation as a patriot. Pellieux declared that the charges against Esterhazy were baseless, but that the conduct of Picquart should be investigated, and when, on Esterhazy's demand for a court-martial, another investigator backed up by three experts declared that the *bordereau* was not by Esterhazy, the General Staff breathed freely again.

The court-martial when it came was more a trial of Picquart than of Esterhazy. It took the judges three minutes to acquit him: he was cheered by the Nationalist mob and lauded by the Nationalist press as if he had been a new Napoleon or at least a new Boulanger. Picquart was arrested and the campaign seemed to have been won, but every move that attracted attention to the Affair threatened the security of the official thesis and the Esterhazy trial was no exception.

Among the newspapers which had taken up the revisionist cause was the new journal founded by Vaughan for Clemenceau, *L'Aurore*. The political career of Clemenceau seemed to have ended with his defeat after Panama, but with heroic tenacity he had decided to make a new career with his pen. It was he who, in a flash of genius, chose as the title to put at the head of the open letter to Félix Faure written by Émile Zola, *J'accuse*. Zola was no longer as popular as he had been, and if the violence of the attack on *La Terre* had done its authors more harm than it had done Zola, none of the bright young men of letters took very seriously the literary or sociological theories of the novelist. But outside France and among the common readers of France, Zola's reputation was still immense. He had been converted to revisionism by Leblois and had begun a campaign in the *Figaro* which that paper had had to drop. In *L'Aurore* he had found a more sympathetic and more formidable audience than in the fashionable readers of the *Figaro*. He accused the Army leaders, Mercier, Billot, Boisdeffre, of deliberately concealing the evidence that showed Dreyfus to be innocent, and 'the judges of the Esterhazy court-martial of knowingly acquitting the guilty. He added in a prophetic phrase, 'What I do is only a revolutionary method of hastening on the explosion of truth and justice'.

It was, indeed, a revolution that was now threatened, not, as the stupid political soldiers thought, a mere revolt. For with Zola the *intelligentzia*, or as they were called at that time, the intellectuals, entered the campaign. Anatole France, Claude Monet, Carrière, Charles Richet, Louis Havet, young Marcel Proust were among them. The war of doctrines was beginning.

To deal with Zola it was ingeniously decided to try him only for one part of his letter, that in which he had declared that the court-martial had acquitted Esterhazy *by order*. Picquart was tried for communicating documents to Leblois and ordered to be discharged from the Army, but the sentence was not carried out until after the Zola trial and, for the moment, Picquart was kept in Mont-Valérien. The trial was another Pyrrhic victory for the General Staff. Zola was convicted, but the Revisionists had managed to bring before the court the communication of the secret documents in the Dreyfus court-martial; and the Army witnesses, while they had not admitted this, had not dared to deny it. Henry was bolder; he alluded to a mysterious document that could not be produced. His impressive discretion was not imitated by Millevoye, who had already shown his credulity by his attack on Clemenceau over the Norton forgeries.

Millevoye told a meeting at Suresnes that there was in existence a *bordereau* proving the guilt of Dreyfus since it was annotated in that sense by the hand of the Kaiser! It was not the dramatic nonsense of Millevoye that influenced the jury, but the testimony of Pellieux, who asked what would become of the Army if it had to fight under discredited leaders? In another of those dangerous sorties, he hinted that there was in existence a document proving that Dreyfus was guilty. Boisdeffre and Gonse were not ready to let this document (which Henry had providentially discovered in 1896) be produced. Zola was convicted, but the conviction was quashed on a point of law and a new trial ordered. Professors and officers who had professed revisionist sympathies were suspended; Picquart was compulsorily retired from the Army; Zola deprived of the Legion of Honour; Leblois of his rank as assistant mayor of the seventh arrondissement. The Government, true to the principle of its chief, was determined to prove that there was no Dreyfus case, merely a handful of troublesome clerks.

The Prime Minister, Jules Méline, was unfortunate in the time he had come to power. In a quieter age he might have been a real success. He based his politics, almost as candidly as had Guizot under Louis Philippe, on economic interests. A high protectionist, he had saved the French peasantry from the worst effects of the great fall in world prices. In policy he was all for conciliation on a basis of interest; he would not repeal the lay laws and he did not enforce them with any zeal. He was sympathetic to the policy of the *Ralliement*, to a union of all forces of social conservation, with no doctrinal questions raised or answered. Unfortunately, he fell into the midst of a violent doctrinal quarrel. His political subordinates, like the too zealous Louis Barthou (who was all for rigorous measures against the Revisionists) and the noisy generals, were nuisances. Generals and politicians *would* insist on improving their position by new discoveries, new theories; a whole mythology had grown up round the case in which the astute Méline could not believe, but which hid the beauties of his sound budgets and his high tariffs from a people that, no more than fifty years before, was content with a naked policy of interests. The elections of 1898 were morally a defeat for the Ministry, and within a few days the new Chamber had overthrown Méline.

It was the continued refusal of the Army, or of the politicians who thought they were serving the Army, to remain within the stronghold of the legal decision that finally gave the Revisionists their chance. The instrument of destiny was the Minister of War in the Cabinet which Brisson had formed after the fall of Méline. Godefroy Cavaignac was by birth, by education, by career, the model Republican. He was the heir of his family tradition, of the general who had saved the Second Republic from anarchy but who had not saved it from the Empire. He had been, as a schoolboy under the Empire, a conspicuous Republican; and under the Republic he was a kind of Cato. It was an anti-Dreyfusard interpellation that gave him the opportunity to declare his conviction of the guilt of Dreyfus—and to give reasons. The reasons were various documents which might refer to Dreyfus and, if they did, proved him guilty, a confession which it was belatedly found that Dreyfus had made—and a document that did undoubtedly refer to Dreyfus. The speech was brilliantly successful. Only a small minority of Socialists refused to vote it the honour of publication on every official notice-board in France, but with the abstaining Socialists was the astute Méline, who had been told by the Italian Ambassador that the document referring to Dreyfus and supposed to have been written by the Italian attaché was not genuine. Méline knew, moreover, that Dreyfus had not confessed.

The Dreyfusards were pleased, for Cavaignac had moved away from discussing the *bordereau*, the only legal basis of conviction, and the lawyers were given a chance to attack the procedure of the court-martial which had had no other evidence before it in the eyes of the law but the *bordereau*. It was Picquart who was chosen to launch the attack; he declared that the minor documents cited did not apply to Dreyfus and that the document which did was a forgery. Cavaignac determined to crush Picquart by charging him with a breach of the law on official secrets. Esterhazy was also arrested and Zola, appealing on a point of law and finding that his new trial would still go on, refused to appear in court. He was condemned and fled to England. The climax was approaching.

The arrest of Esterhazy was bound to alarm Henry, who was deeply involved with the 'Uhlan', and, while Esterhazy was being investigated by one judicial official, Picquart was being investigated by another. The results were more damaging for Esterhazy, that is for Henry and for du Paty de Clam, than for Picquart. Cavaignac was becoming worried and was foolish enough to propose to arrest and send for trial before the Senate a long list of Dreyfusards, including Jaurès, Clemenceau, Scheurer-Kestner and Mathieu Dreyfus. This was too much for his colleagues, but for a Government convinced of the strength of its cause the Brisson Cabinet was strangely jumpy. They had reason, for the expert ordered by Cavaignac to verify the letter in which Panizzardi was supposed to have talked of Dreyfus, found that it was composed of fragments of two letters.[1] It was or rather should have been a crushing blow for Cavaignac, the more that Esterhazy had been retired from the Army by a court-martial which found him guilty of habitual bad conduct.

Henry was not immediately taxed with the forgery and when he was he tried at first to lie. But the evidence was too strong and he confessed. The first person to appreciate that the turn of the tide had come was Boisdeffre. 'Recognizing that his confidence in Henry . . . was misplaced,' he resigned. Nor could all the arguments of the Minister induce him to return. Henry was arrested and sent off to the fortress of Mont-Valérien, and the press was informed that Henry had admitted forging the document which, had it been genuine, would have set all doubts at rest. General de Pellieux took the line of Boisdeffre. 'Dupe of dishonourable men', having lost confidence in superiors who had given him forgeries to work on, he too resigned. The Governor of Paris, Zurlinden, persuaded him to withdraw his resignation and the Prime Minister had no official knowledge of a letter so devastating in its implications for the *chose jugée*. Boisdeffre, Pellieux, all but the most blindly partisan could see the implications of Henry's forgery. As the document had not been before the court-martial of 1894, it could not have affected its judgment one way or the other, but what had affected its judgment was the testimony of Henry and the introduction of documents not known to the defence. As far as the original conviction had depended on the account of his own actions given by Henry, it was now morally as well as legally undermined. For the good of the French State as well as of the French

---

[1] The weave of the fragments was different; it was the same error of the forger that helped to damn Wilson.

Army, it was a pity that the rulers of both did not know when they were beaten. The news of Henry's confession was followed by the news of his suicide. He had written a letter to his wife, asserting that the letter was a true copy. 'You know in whose interest I have acted.'[1]

For the moment almost all the enemies of revision were silenced and the reopening of the case seemed inevitable. But Cavaignac refused to admit that anything had happened to affect his opinion, and, by resigning, he forced Brisson to find a War Minister who would undertake to reopen the case. His first choice was Zurlinden, who was soon convinced by his subordinates that Dreyfus was guilty and was more anxious to bring Picquart before a court-martial than to reopen the original case. Picquart announced that he was not going to commit suicide and if he were found dead like Henry, the public would know what to think. Zurlinden had resigned and Brisson had been weak enough under the pressure of his successor, General Chanoine, to restore him to his old post of Governor of Paris. Picquart's fears may have been needless, but they added to the melodramatic atmosphere in which the Affair was now bathed.

After their first moments of stupefaction, the enemies of Dreyfus, of the Jews, and of 'the Syndicate' had found a theory to allow them to defend Henry. His forgery had been, said Ernest Judet, like a banknote; it was of no value in itself but it represented a great deposit of wealth. There were real but unpublishable proofs of the guilt of Dreyfus; it was on this hidden store of gold that Henry had drawn his note. It fell to another, and until that moment obscure, writer to make of Henry not merely a witness of worth but a great national hero. In the little read and venerable Legitimist newspaper, the *Gazette de France*, Charles Maurras became famous overnight. Henry, he said, until he manufactured the Panizzardi letter, had been a gallant soldier, and as his forgery had injured only the enemies of France, his action must be interpreted favourably. From that general principle it was easy to deduce that the dead man was a hero and a martyr. Maurras admitted that this deduction would not be accepted by everyone. 'Our bad half-Protestant education' had kept us 'from estimating justly so much moral and intellectual nobility . . . But your unlucky forgery will be reckoned among your finest feats of war.' To educate the French public to this view of political morality was the task set himself by the critic and journalist who had now provided the anti-Dreyfusards with a doctrine fit to resist all criticism.

The prosecution of Zola was ominous for the critics of the General Staff, or even for the cautious politicians who were not willing to give

---

[1] This cryptic phrase has puzzled many commentators. M. Armand Charpentier has furnished an ingenious explanation which suggests that the whole Affair began as the result of a mistake by Sandherr, and it was as the heir of Sandherr, the trustee for his policy, that Henry had acted and had killed himself rather than betray his dead chief.

blind credit to any assertion made by one or more generals. It was during the Zola trial (February 1898) that one of the political chiefs of Dreyfusism, Trarieux, launched the idea of founding a society for the protection of the principles of '89 now threatened by the soldiers. The new society took the name of 'The League of the Rights of Man'. It was to rally 'all those who, without distinction of religious belief, wish for a sincere union between all Frenchmen and are convinced that every kind of arbitrary action or intolerance threatens civil disturbance and is a menace to civilization and progress'. The new League was to serve as a kind of general staff to the Revisionists. By its formal neutrality and the publicity of its activities it distinguished itself from Masonry and among its founders was one of the most eminent Catholic defenders of Dreyfus, Paul Viollet of the École des Chartes. Viollet soon discovered that the new League was incapable of preserving the delicate distinction between opposing the activities to which the vocal majority of French Catholics had given adherence and opposing the activities of French Catholics in general.

For the moment the League did bring together those who felt that in the Affair there was involved more than the innocence of one man; that there were endangered by the arbitrary action of the generals, the Government lawyers, the complaisant politicians, the major conquests of the Revolution. The memory of the traditional miscarriages of justice of the past, of Calas, of Sirven, was awakened. It was this powerful tradition running back to Voltaire that brought so many *dilettanti* over to the new League. It was this tradition that turned the Epicurean ex-Boulangist, Anatole France, into the defender of Zola and the symbolic figure at great demonstrations of the Paris workers. The Catholic polemics of Ferdinand Brunetière had already awakened anger in the disciple of Voltaire and of Diderot, but what was now threatened was something more serious than dogmatism from the Sorbonne, or from the *Revue des Deux Mondes*. The sceptic found that he cared about scepticism, and, having refused, with his father, to believe in the infallibility of the Pope or the divine right of kings, Anatole France was hardly likely to accept the infallibility of courts-martial or the divine right of Ministers of War or of Justice, with Rochefort or Drumont.

II

It is difficult to-day, perhaps impossible, for most persons to understand the passions provoked by the Dreyfus case. It is hard to see why the Army and the partisans of the Army ran such risks, took such extreme courses, forced themselves to steer narrowly between equally dangerous positions and, in the name of the security and dignity of France, compromised themselves with fools or knaves. It is even more difficult to realize that the partisans of Dreyfus could assert, in all sincerity, that they sought only justice, that a wrong done by the State to one man must be undone, at no matter what risk. There were, of course, old Boulangists seeking only revenge; there were old Panamists seeking rehabilitation; but there were thousands of zealots on both sides who believed that what they were fighting for was the greatest thing in the world. M. Léon Blum has given a convincing picture of his disillusionment when his literary idol, Barrès, whose support for reopening the case he had confidently promised to secure, first evaded and then refused. Barrès had been for so many of that generation 'not only the master but the guide'.[1] In a short time, Blum was telling Jules Renard that he was afraid to re-read Barrès, that he could not be as good a writer as they had thought him!

Among the educated classes in France, the case became a dividing sword. It separated Lavisse from Rambaud, the Duc de Guermantes from the Prince de Guermantes, it bred quarrels and feuds which it took a generation to heal. It was not, or it soon ceased to be, the question of the guilt or innocence of Dreyfus, a victim who was not much hated by his enemies and not much loved by his friends. The question at issue was much deeper; should the Army, which, for so many, was France, be endangered, its prestige and self-confidence weakened merely to remedy a hypothetical injustice? In addition to Dreyfus, there was, so the opponents of revision asserted, a neglected victim, France. The hostility of foreign opinion to the official French thesis irritated rather than shook the conviction of the enemies of 'the Syndicate'. They doubted, with some reason, the complete *bona fides* of English, German, and American critics who implied that such things could happen only in France. As far as it was true, it was deplorably true. Only in France would fundamental questions of the safety of the State and the established order of things be debated at all. On the other side, the friends of revision saw, in the claims of the military authorities to impose their view of the facts, a claim to set up a new ruling class, to exempt, from due process of law and from the working of the critical spirit, a body of men whose claims to public respect were never overwhelmingly impressive and, since the confession and suicide of Henry, open to serious question.

It is possible that if the Army leaders, the 'great chiefs' of the Nationalist press had accepted the necessity of revision after the suicide of Henry, the Affair would not have developed its revolutionary character. The honour, that is the pride, the record for consistency, the not unjustifiable resentment, the hopes of long-delayed triumph, all combined to betray the classes and sections most closely allied with the

---

[1] A modern parallel to this shock is furnished by the refusal of M. Romain Rolland to pay attention to the testimony of Mr. Eugene Lyons. The writer who had once been 'above the battle' had taken sides and did not, any more than Barrès, propose to discuss evidence against his faith.

Army chiefs, into indefensible follies. It was not merely that after the suicide of Henry their case was bad, but that they were in no position to defend it successfully even had it been good.

The incorrigible folly of the old Conservatives had been abundantly displayed at the elections of 1898. The Legitimists, reduced to a sulky silence by the papal policy, had bitterly resented the choice of an old Republican, Étienne Lamy, as the head of the Catholic organization. At the elections they sabotaged the efforts of the Catholic leaders and were in a great degree the authors of the check administered to Méline. Well might Albert de Mun quote the Cardinal de Retz, 'it is easier to fight one's enemies than to get on with one's friends'. In the approaching crisis it was of importance that so many of the Conservative voters in France had managed to persuade themselves that the experiment of the *Ralliement* had failed; that no orthodox Republican Government, no matter how lukewarm on the question of laicity, that no Republican leader, not a Spuller or a Méline, would ever make those concessions which the zealous Catholics demanded as a minimum, the abandonment of the policy of laicity in the schools and the compulsory military service of the clergy.

The elections of 1898 exalted the spirits of the extremists, while they depressed the timid moderates, and there were few Conservative leaders who were not in either class. So comparatively sagacious and so generous a man as Albert de Mun saw in the agitation for reopening the Dreyfus case merely a conspiracy to make the French soldier distrust his officers, to 'cast doubts and suspicions on his leaders'. Even the moderate Jacques Piou, writing long after the event, had only the mildest words of condemnation for the follies of the zealots and the excesses of zeal that led Henry to forgery and Christiani to a mean and childish brutality.[1]

The development of the case into a crisis brought the veteran leader of lost causes into the field. Déroulède turned from writing historical dramas on Duguesclin and Hoche, to politics. He was elected in the old Bonapartist region of the Charente and he began to plan another military *coup d'état*. His *Duguesclin* and his *Hoche* were improved Boulangers, but it was time to turn from the pen to the sword. So the League of Patriots was revived, ready to be the ally of whatever general could be induced to save France and the Republic from the politicians. 'The Army will be our ally. It must have, when the moment comes, all the decent people on its side. And if it turns out not to be enough to follow it, we will go ahead of it.'

Déroulède was not the only Boulangist to see in the case an attempt by the corrupt profiteers of the Republic to recover the ground some of them had lost after the Panama explosion and, in the increasing bitterness of the agitation on both sides, a chance to renew the assault on the

[1] See p. 349.

parliamentary Republic and avenge the humiliations of 1889. Rochefort, Barrès, the old Monarchist leaders were all tempted to follow the popular course; and their contempt, not unmerited in many cases, for the sudden moral fervour of their enemies, blinded them to the folly and meanness of their own allies.

The Boulangist element in the anti-revisionist ranks was the source of many illusions. The failure of Boulanger as a dictator had made people forget how effective he had been as a mascot. It was in vain that 'the great chiefs', Boisdeffre, Gonse, Mercier and the rest, were presented to the public as deserving a reverence that would have been excessive if given to marshals of the First Empire. The prestige of these soldiers was purely official; they owed it to their rank, not to personal popularity or to personal achievement. Nor did the habit of talking of 'the Army' show much more judgment, for the Army was not the officer corps but the vast majority of conscript soldiers, many of whom must have felt that a judicial error by a court-martial was not at all beyond credence.[1] The group of aristocratic generals, falling back on blunt assertions of authority, were very far, from a political point of view, from equalling Boulanger; and the hatred of the Jews was too artificial and limited an emotion to replace the passion for the *Revanche* that had carried Boulanger and his black horse to the very threshold of dictatorship. In putting all their money on the generals, the defeated notables were backing the last hierarchy that had survived the liquidation by the Republic of the old order of society, the last group of men whose authority and prestige were independent of the only two authorities recognized by the Republic, the politicians and the rich. And as had happened in the case of the other hierarchies, the generals put too great a strain on the real authority that they still had. The Affair, once it became a question of the right of the generals to implicit trust, was a new Sixteenth of May. It was fitting that the Duc de Broglie lived long enough to support, with what prestige he had left, this disastrous imitation of his own folly.

III

While the politicians were manœuvring and the academicians signing manifestoes, the most vehement of the Nationalist orators and leaders was again ready to try his old recipe for the evils that were eating away the foundations of the French State. Déroulède was preparing to renew Boulangism without Boulanger. It was a serious handicap, for the cause in 1889 had had a leader under whom Déroulède and Naquet and Mackau could have fought, if the leader had ever dared to

---

[1] One of the leading anti-Dreyfusard intellectuals, M. Louis Dimier, was many years later to learn from the experience of his son that military discipline and military justice were not exempt from very serious faults.

fight. Now there was only Déroulède. Age had not increased his prestige or his stock of political wisdom. He was ostentatiously Republican and suspicious of the Royalist connections of some possible allies. Anti-Semitism, whether plebeian like that of Drumont, or aristocratic like that of Barrès, was uneasily worn by Déroulède for, in the past, his anxiety to accumulate any kind of assets for his foreign policy had led him to praise Cornélius Herz. Drumont, indeed, had only with difficulty concealed his scorn for Déroulède, who was foolish enough to think that the German was the main or only enemy, whereas Drumont had maintained that, in 1870, both 'Aryan' peoples had been victims of Jewish high finance, which needed a war to allow Bleichröder to combine with Rothschild to plunder France. Worse still, Drumont had warned France against a new war prepared by a fake quarrel between 'Mayer and Mayer' and only needing an imbecile to start it: and he had added, the imbecile was there, Déroulède.

Faced with the problem of freeing the Republicans from the charge of war-mongering and from the difficulties of preaching a formal policy of revenge without any active measures to that end, Gambetta had found the magic formula, 'clericalism, there is the enemy'. It was the weakness of the Right that they could not find so powerful a lever with which to turn popular feeling against their enemies. They could not even agree which of the two or three weak tools they possessed, they were to use. They suffered, too, from a weakness that was inevitable in a party which had never known power; the leaders were nearly all newspaper editors, appealing to a limited public that might, in its unsteady enthusiasm, switch its support from *L'Intransigeant* to *La Libre Parole* and, a little later, from the *Libre Parole* to *Action Française*. The Republican parties had their own newspaper wars, but Jaurès and Briand, if not M. Gérault-Richard, had in Parliament and the platform more effective sounding-boards than any newspaper afforded. The fate of *La Petite République*, *L'Humanité* and later of *Messidor* mattered little compared with the survival of the party.

It was a tribute to the respect shown by or expected of the French people towards the established intellectual Church, the 'University', that the manifesto of the 'Intellectuals' in favour of revision should have so profoundly irritated the other side. The signatories might be denounced as useless mandarins attacking the indispensable institutions of a State which protected and paid them; the manifesto, nevertheless, had to be answered. If the question at issue was one of mere guilt or innocence, one of the mere exercise of critical judgment, then the opinion of men whom the nation had agreed to treat as intelligent, professors, academicians and the like, was highly relevant. That an eminent mathematician, chemist, historian or man of letters could be just as credulous and prejudiced as any peasant was not generally realized. That the motives that made one academician come out for

Dreyfus and another against him were not in most cases purely intellectual was a heretical view, not widely held on either side, except as far as each doubted the good faith of its opponents.[1]

It seemed, then, to some young professors of the 'Université' that it would be worth while to organize a counter-manifesto and from this there sprang a permanent organization. Composed of citizens indignant at 'seeing the most disastrous of agitations being prolonged', it was given the name of the *Ligue de la Patrie Française.*

The *Ligue de la Patrie Française* was welcomed by many thousands of sincere and honest people whose critical judgment was not very acute, by people who had been taken in by Léo Taxil, old readers of Drumont, old readers of Rochefort, used to believing any absurdity of their enemies, but not necessarily either fools or knaves for being only moderately impressed by the moral beauties of the Dreyfusard crusade. The transference of the case from the mystical to the political plane which Charles Péguy deplored, though he realized that it was inevitable, was now well under way. The sudden moral fervour of so many survivors of Panama (although it was often genuine) naturally aroused the anger and disbelief of men devoted to another tradition than that of 1793, as it evoked the ironical scepticism of a man like Georges Sorel, who was to welcome Lenin, but who was not reverential enough to be swept off his feet by merely verbal and historical revolutionary 'action'.

It is unlikely that any resistance to revision could in the long run have succeeded, but the form which it took was peculiarly futile. Begun as a reply to the manifesto of the 'intellectuals', the League might, in a country used to reverencing constituted authority, have carried some weight. But the news that a majority of the French Academy was against revision was less important than the academicians thought; it was a repetition of the mistake of the 'moral order', the belief that the 'notables' were still intrinsically powerful. Under this illusion, the fight against the united Republican *bloc* was begun under the leadership of a distinguished if not profound literary critic, Jules Lemaître. His reputation was perhaps enough to offset that of Anatole France on the other side, but as Maurice Barrès noted after a speech of Lemaître's, 'a doctrine was missing'. The League, avoiding every theme which could divide the mass of Nationalist and Conservative voters and subscribers that it wanted to enrol, would not have known what to do with a doctrine, even if Jules Lemaître had been the man to invent one. The time was to come when he would have a doctrine, but it would be a doctrine evolved in a stronger head: and Charles Maurras was still a

---

[1] It was of course a great delight to enemies of the *intelligentzia* to show it up. Anti-Dreyfusards were never tired of telling how Salomon Reinach, brother of Joseph and a great State archæologist, bought a bogus 'tiara of Sataphernes' for the Louvre. Fortunately, although Salomon Reinach, as an old man, was again a victim at Glozel, he had enough fellow-victims to escape a solitary pillory. The very sections which made fun of Salomon Reinach, or attacked the logic of Henri Poincaré, were proud of their own scientific partisans.

minor figure beside the elegant academician. Lemaître had, of course, one thing to bring to the League, large financial resources, for his mistress, Madame de Loynes, played the rôle of the Duchesse d'Uzès in the Boulangist campaign.[1] If the campaign was to be an affair of matching academicians, the choice of Lemaître was defensible. But the other side was not led by Anatole France or Jules Claretie. They were like the princes in the old German Army, ornaments given a prominent place in the foreground, but the Ludendorffs of the Dreyfusards were highly trained professional politicians like Clemenceau.

The new League inevitably invaded the field already occupied by Déroulède's *Ligue des Patriotes*. Déroulède having failed to find a saviour for France in Boulanger, or in General X, or in any politician, had cast himself for the rôle. He was very sceptical of the value of mere electoral campaigns like that waged by the new League, but he loyally collaborated, although some of his supporters, like George Bonnamour, were resentful of the way in which local triumphs, which they thought due to the militant tactics of the old League, were credited to the oratory of the new.

The question whether Déroulède was to lead France to salvation was soon settled. The Brisson Government had decided to take the first legal measures for making a revision possible, but ten days after the Court of Cassation had begun its work on the case, the new Minister of War, General Chanoine, stabbed Brisson in the back by declaring to an astounded Chamber that he shared the opinion of his predecessors and resigned on the spot.

The Brisson Government fell and Dupuy was called on by Faure to take over the inheritance. The two critical posts of Justice and War were given to the mediocre Lebret and the evasive Freycinet. Quesnay de Beaurepaire, with his usual vehemence, attacked the judges of the criminal section of the Court of Cassation,[2] and although the Government denied any intention of reflecting on the judges, they introduced and passed a bill transferring the case to the whole court, a victory for the anti-Dreyfusards. At the same time, the charges against Picquart were pressed, and not only the Generals but the incorrigible Cavaignac affirmed their faith in the rightness of the early decisions. Any hopes which might have been formed that the Court of Cassation would be allowed to do its work in peace proved baseless. The agitation on both sides was more heated than ever, but fortune favoured Dreyfus, for France was startled, if not shocked, to learn that the President had died suddenly on February 16th.

The death of Félix Faure was a blow for the opponents of revision, for the President was determined to do all he could to postpone or

---

[1] There were some anti-Dreyfusards who attributed a lack of combativeness in Lemaître to his reluctance to expose Madame de Loynes to the full blasts of French controversy.
[2] The President of this section was unfortunately named Loew.

defeat the project, and, although a President could do little if faced with a united and determined majority, there was as yet no such majority; and a skilful President might prevent its being formed. The death, so awkward for one side, so fortunate for the other, naturally further inflamed a public opinion which was, in any case, far from calm. There were rumours that the official cause of death, a stroke, was not the real one and that there were strange circumstances surrounding the last day of Félix Faure. In the *Libre Parole*, the charge of murder was openly made, although in terms that were not incompatible with the other less startling rumours that ran round Paris.[1]

Whatever the cause of death, the politicians felt the need of having a safe man in the Élysée. The anti-Dreyfusard party, so far as it had one candidate, was for Méline, but that cautious man refused to run, and the Radicals, combining with the prudent, elected Loubet, famous for his efforts to diminish the scope of the Panama scandal. This election was taken as an affront by the extreme Nationalist groups, who were distressed by the loss of Félix Faure and, so far as they were old Boulangists, were also infuriated by the election of the friend of the 'chequards'. When the presidential cortège entered Paris from Versailles, it was assailed by shouts of 'Panama' and other party cries which showed that central Paris, at least, was in the mood of January 1889. Some ardent spirits wanted Déroulède to lead his leaguers and the mob to attack; but, with a characteristic romantic gesture, he replied 'There is a corpse in that house'.

Whatever chance there was of a *coup d'état* on February 18th, was lost, but Déroulède had his plan. He proposed to take advantage of the funeral of Félix Faure on February 23rd to make a *coup d'état* with the aid of the troops under arms for the funeral procession. Whether he ever had any real hopes of aid from a general or generals is uncertain. His enemies, anxious to show him up as a frivolous play-actor, declared that he had not, that his only hope was to induce a general, on the spur of the moment, to lead his men to the Élysée. But whether with or without military connivance, Déroulède made his own plans. He prepared a proclamation declaring the Constitution of 1875 abolished and calling for a new constituent assembly. Although he represented his attempt as a new and bloodless September 4th, his proclamation had a decided ring of December 2nd, 1851, when with the aid of the Army, President Louis Napoleon Bonaparte had destroyed the Second Republic. Déroulède was not President and he was not a Bonaparte, and his forces were disunited by their different views as to what was to follow the ending of the parliamentary republic. Déroulède was very sensitive about any suggestion of crypto-Royalism and afraid that the Pretender, the young Duke of Orleans, was in

---

[1] These rumours suggested that the President had simply died from over-exertions of a type dangerous to one of his age and physique.

347

hiding in Paris and would suddenly appear to reap the fruits of Déroulède's success. The chief of the League of Patriots was determined not to play the Monk, so he regarded with suspicion the collaboration of Jean Guérin and his 'Grand Occident', for Guérin was already suspect of taking money from the Royalists on behalf of the 'Predestined One'.[1]

Armed with his proclamation, his pockets full of notes and gold, and with straps ready to secure his trousers when he led his army on horseback to the Élysée, Déroulède waited for the arrival of the troops in a porter's lodge off the Place de la Nation in the company of Maurice Barrès. At last the troops appeared, led by General Roget. Whatever hopes Déroulède may have founded on any general were not founded on Roget. Déroulède later asserted that the Government had altered the plans for dispersing the troops after the funeral, so that it was Roget and not another who appeared in the place where Déroulède had assembled his 500 Leaguers. There was no time to change the plan, so Déroulède rushed forward, caught the bridle of the General's horse and implored him to lead his men to the Élysée. Roget, who may not have heard what was being said, shook off Déroulède; and the troops marched on, pursued by Leaguers singing the *Marseillaise*, in which many spectators joined, and by Déroulède and Marcel Habert hoping that Roget would yet change his mind. Where were the troops going? Déroulède suddenly realized that they were approaching Reuilly barracks; the troops were going home. He shouted to his Leaguers to bar the way, while Habert, thinking the soldiers were on their way to the Place de la Bastille, let them advance unopposed. They entered the barrack gates carrying the two conspirators with them. Roget was only anxious to get rid of Déroulède and Habert, who were equally anxious, now that the coup had failed, not to be taken lightly. While the General tried to get them to leave, Déroulède burned his papers in a stove and tried to win over the young officers; until, at last, the police arrived and arrested him. Whether Déroulède had planned a December 2nd or a September 4th he had, in fact, managed to do what had been thought impossible, to parody the attempts of young Louis Napoleon at Strasbourg and Boulogne.

---

[1] Guérin afterwards retorted by saying that he saw many notorious Bonapartists among the patriots assembled under Déroulède's orders.

CHAPTER II

REVISION

I

BY submitting the question of whether the case was to be re-opened to the Cour de Cassation,[1] the Government helped to educate the public in the substance of the case. The special law that transferred the decision from the Criminal Section to the whole Court, made no real difference. Indeed, from the Dreyfusard point of view, it was all to the good that the judge who finally announced that the *bordereau* was the work of Esterhazy, was not M. Loew of the Criminal section, but the 'Aryan', M. Ballot Beaupré. The new trial was ordered and, before it could take place, the bold Commandant Esterhazy had at last lost his courage or his trust in his old protectors. He confessed that he had written the *bordereau*; he could afford to admit it, for he was safe in London. Du Paty was less fortunate; he was in his turn sent to the Cherche-Midi, and there was a movement to send Mercier before the High Court.

On the other side, Picquart was released from prison, Zola returned to Paris and Alfred Dreyfus was ordered to be sent back from Devil's Island to stand trial for a second time before a new court-martial at Rennes. That, a day or two later, a jury had acquitted Déroulède for the Reuilly affair, mattered little. If the Government stuck to its guns, it had little to fear from a *coup d'état* or from regular political opposition. But would it stick to its guns? It was made to seem doubtful when, at Auteuil Races on June 4th, Loubet, the new President of the Republic, was assaulted by the Baron de Christiani, who smashed the presidential tall-hat with his stick. The assault was mean and childish; the day for such *muscadin* tactics had passed or had not yet come.[2]

Like the assault on Senator Sumner, the assault on Loubet revealed, or seemed to reveal, to many hitherto lukewarm defenders of the Republic a serious threat to the dignity, if not to the safety of the

---

[1] The highest French court; it is not in the English or American sense a Court of Appeal. It does not decide finally on the merits of a case but, if it 'breaks' the decision of a lower court, the case is sent to be re-tried by another court, in this case a new court-martial.

[2] The *muscadins* were smart young men-about-town who beat up Jacobin sympathizers after the fall of Robespierre.

régime. Generals and colonels were still talking mutinously. The Dupuy Ministry would not promise to send Mercier before the High Court and was bitterly attacked for its failure to guard Loubet. When it was the President's duty to attend another race-meeting, this time at Longchamps, he was accompanied and guarded by an immense outpouring of the Paris workers. The crowds which had lent strength to the cause of Boulanger were now on the other side. This demonstration reassured many frightened Revisionists, who had despaired of rousing the people, and opened the eyes of many prudent politicians to the justice of a cause whose support was no longer dangerous and was soon to be highly advantageous. It no longer paid to steer skilfully between the Scylla of 'yes' and the Charybdis of 'no'. Dupuy was overthrown: the task of ending the threat to the régime and to internal peace, the task of dealing with the problems which were sure to become acute after the new court-martial, were too much for a mere standard parliamentarian.

Loubet had tried a young and able lawyer, Raymond Poincaré; but partly because Poincaré wished to include his friend Louis Barthou, who as a former member of the Méline Cabinet was suspect, and partly because he wished to include Casimir-Périer, who was known to be a Dreyfusard and whose prestige might have helped the new Government, time was lost and the attempt had to be abandoned. It was then that Waldeck-Rousseau consented to take up the task of crushing the enemies of the régime. The new Prime Minister was a Breton of Catholic family; he had been one of Gambetta's bright young men, but seemed to have long abandoned politics for the bar, where he was one of the most respected lawyers, counsel for great interests. Waldeck-Rousseau had been and still was an Opportunist. It was necessary for him to express vague social sympathies, to wish mildly for the progressive replacement of the wage system by some kind of profit-sharing, but this grave, severe lawyer was very far from the Left. But to carry out the Government programme he had to seek support on all sides; and only a man of great political courage would have found the solution. As Minister of War, he chose General the Marquis de Gallifet and for Minister of Commerce, the Citizen Alexandre Millerand. Gallifet was a very distinguished soldier, but to the Left he was, above all, the ruthless represser of the Commune, the smiling butcher of the *fédérés*! 'His sword,' said one orator, 'is red to the hilt with Republican blood.' That a Republican Ministry should contain this elegant courtier was extraordinary enough, but that the same Cabinet should contain a Socialist leader of the calibre of Millerand was incredible. It was like an alliance between Cromwell and O'Connell, between Jefferson Davis and Sherman. It was no wonder that Deputies like Boutard and Zévaès protested furiously when the Cabinet met the Chamber or that the sitting opened to cries of 'Vive la Commune!'

Waldeck-Rousseau was not to be intimidated by the rage of the Left or the irony of the Right. He had undertaken to save his client, the Republic, from the dangers of expropriation at the hands of reaction and to secure his client against future annoyance. In his choice of tactics, as in his choice of men, he showed his mastery. He denounced the religious order that had made itself most conspicuous and most noisy during the Affair; and the attack on the monks who were business-men, on the monks who were politicians, struck home. 'Les moines ligueurs' recalled the bad days of the wars of religion when the Catholic League had allied Paris with Spain against Henri IV, when the monkish demagogues had betrayed the national cause.

Waldeck-Rousseau might regard himself as the heir of the great lawyers, the *politiques*, who had helped the good king to bring peace to France. Then his reference to the 'milliard' at which he estimated the wealth of the unauthorized religious orders was a master-stroke. Not only was a milliard a nice round sum,[1] but it recalled the 'milliard des émigrés', the sum given to the ancestors of the noble enemies of Dreyfus under the Restoration as compensation for their losses during the Revolution. It was not necessary to do more to hint that the seizure of the 'milliard des congrégations' was simple justice, compensation for the sums handed over to the nobles by Villèle. In any event, the prospect of getting hold of the milliard was in itself highly attractive. From that spoil so many (lay) good works could be subsidized!

Before the attack on the religious orders could be launched, or indeed, before the new Ministry could be secure in its authority, it was necessary to convert or silence vociferous critics on the Left. These critics detested Gallifet, but more serious, they saw in the entry of Millerand into the Ministry, a betrayal of the self-denying ordinance that the Socialist leaders had imposed on themselves, a breach of the bases of the unity of the Socialist sections which had been accepted and a return to a new 'possibilism' with far greater prizes and far greater temptations offered to the leaders than Paul Brousse had ever had to resist or succumb to.

It was the first great triumph of Jaurès as a party manager that he managed to convince so many Socialists that the Republic *was* in danger; that it *was* a matter of moment to the workers whether it was saved or not; that the entry of Millerand into the Government *was* a necessary move in its saving and that, in addition, a Socialist Minister could *help* Socialism in his ministerial capacity, not merely profit by Socialist professions to reach the highest offices in the bourgeois state. For years to come, it was Jaurès, not Millerand or his imitators and successors, who held a large section of the French workers to an alliance with the bourgeoisie which produced no very striking benefits for the proletariat and seemed to deny the premises of the class-war. Only a

[1] £40,000,000 or $200,000,000.

man of the personal probity of Jaurès could have done it, and even Jaurès could not shake the dogmatic adherents of Guesde who saw in Jaurès a sophist and in Millerand a traitor and a begetter of traitors.

The refusal of Guesde to collaborate with bourgeois, any bourgeois, parties in the defence of justice was not unnatural. It fitted in with his rigorously doctrinaire temperament. What was Dreyfus, a rich bourgeois, to the workers? What were these quarrels between one section of the oppressors and another to the workers' leaders? Nor was the sectarian side of the struggle likely to escape his critical eye. He was inevitably as a good Marxian, an anti-clerical, more deeply anti-clerical, perhaps, than the romantic and sentimental Jaurès, but he had regarded the standard French anti-clericalism of the bourgeoisie as a dodge 'to turn the anger and the efforts of the proletariat from the grabbers of the earth to the exploiters of an imaginary heaven; to substitute for the necessary and fruitful war against the employer, the useless and harmless war against the priest'.

In any case, the fact that his party was strongest in the north was bound to affect Guesde's policy; in Lille, in Roubaix, the Church had a far stronger hold on the workers than it had in the Midi. No excess of anti-clerical zeal on Jaurès's part could harm him in Carmaux. All his supporters wanted that kind of thing, and those who did not like it would not have voted for Jaurès anyway. In French Flanders, however, there were plenty of workers who might be induced to vote the Socialist ticket, but who were yet sufficiently attached to the Church to resent too obvious a mixture of anti-Catholic with Socialist propaganda. To concentrate all the efforts of the party in an attack on the Church would mean for Guesde, in his own stronghold, a long, bitter, difficult and not very profitable battle. Guesde had other reasons for steering clear of the dangerous connections which his Republican and humanitarian zeal was commending to Jaurès. These recruits to Socialism from the University, from the ranks of the lawyers, these Millerands, Vivianis, Jaurès, all were suspect in the eyes of the grim zealot. Their popularity, their ability to rouse great audiences to enthusiasm and faith were not very agreeable to the unpopular pontiff of absolute Socialist truth. The policy of Saint-Mandé was not the policy of uncompromising believers in the class war. It was necessary that the primary and genuine workers' party should avoid contamination,[1] that it should not be a

---

[1] M. Alexandre Zévaès tells us that Guesde was careful not to repel the millionaire recruit to Socialism, Alfred Edwards, but that he steered him away from Guesde's own party, the French Workers' party, towards the Blanquists. Edwards, through his wealth and his control of several important or at least widely-read papers, was useful to the cause, but the sincerity of his conversion was open to question. He was, at the moment, Waldeck-Rousseau's brother-in-law, and there were cynical souls who thought that the Socialism of M. Edwards was put on to annoy Waldeck-Rousseau. It is worth noting, too, that this Levantine adventurer, notorious or ridiculous since his controversy with Barrès over the nature of French nationality, was just the type of the 'métèque' suspected by the Anti-Dreyfusards of being conspirators leagued against the honour and security of France in the interests of international Jewry.

ladder for ambitious exploiters of the resentments and the hopes of the victims of the system of capitalist exploitation, victims as deserving of aid as Captain Dreyfus but a great deal less likely to get it.

II

When the first public session of the court-martial opened at Rennes on August 7th, 1899, it was true, so far as it is ever true, that the eyes of the civilized world were on the *lycée* of Rennes. One mistake of 1894 was not repeated. There were several distinguished artillery specialists among the seven officers who made up the court and, with the removal from high commands of most of the more ebullient Generals of the earlier trials and the rigorous discipline enforced by Gallifet, there was less danger of a repetition of the scandalous scenes of the Zola case.

The streets of the dull Breton city were filled by journalists from all over the world, including in their ranks the brilliant star reporter of Mr. Alfred Harmsworth's *Daily Mail*, G. W. Steevens, who, with Anglo-Saxon firmness and robust brilliance, was to pass severe moral judgments on the conduct of the French. A more subtle observer was Maurice Barrès, combining the rôle of dogmatic and intolerant Nationalist pamphleteer with that of the student of the individual and the society of which he was a more or less integrated part. For Barrès professed to believe that Dreyfus was not a fellow-countryman, scarcely a fellow-human being, since he was a member of a race with different standards, different views of the good life. Less sophisticated versions of the same doctrines were set out in anti-Semitic tracts hawked in the streets. Jaurès was there, too, to see in the demeanour of the witnesses the confirmation of his theories.

The trial itself produced little that was new. The two actors who could have cast most light on the early acts of the play were absent: Henry was dead and Esterhazy was in London, from which city of refuge he refused to return. The prosecutor was an elderly and incompetent officer called Carrière; the chief defending counsel were Labori and Demange. The first great sensation of the trial was the shooting of Labori by an unknown young man; the fact that the wound turned out to be slight did not ease the tension much, since it gave the Anti-Revisionists a chance to say the attack was a fake. Labori was soon well enough to take part in the trial, but his vehement manner, his refusal to profess belief in the good faith of an obviously evasive, or deliberately misleading witness, were thought dangerous, and it was Demange, therefore, the respectful Catholic and brilliant advocate, who made the final speech for the defence.

The main novelties of the trial were the testimony of Casimir-Périer for the defence and of Mercier for the prosecution, and the intervention of an Austrian adventurer called Cernuski, whose story of an Austrian official's story of a German officer's admission of German relations with Dreyfus was a poor substitute for the Henry forgeries. The Anti-Revisionists pinned their faith to Mercier. His evidence was going to be final, for it was boldly asserted he would produce a photograph of the decisive document, the annotated *bordereau*. According to the classical version of this story, the original *bordereau* had been written by Dreyfus on thick paper and traced by Esterhazy on thin paper. The damning original could not be used, because it bore annotations in the hand of the Emperor William II commenting bitterly on the greed of Dreyfus.

It was to prevent the publication of this proof of imperial participation in the work of subornation of treason, it was asserted, that the German Ambassador had delivered an ultimatum to the French Government in 1894. It was under the threat of war that Mercier had discussed the situation on a 'historic night' with Casimir-Périer. If the truth were now told, war was again a danger; it was to such perils that the agitation, subsidized by the 'syndicate' with vast sums from abroad, had brought France! Such was the dramatic story that stirred the readers of the most popular organs of the Catholic and Nationalist press. The editors of these journals stressed the danger of war. The poet, François Coppée, was willing to pay that price to know all, so he wrote in the *Gaulois*, but he counted on the prayers of Joan of Arc. Others were willing to run the risk without the aid of the saints.

There was no risk. Mercier was too astute a man to assert his belief in this nonsensical story in court. He had to face, in any case, the awkward testimony of Casimir-Périer who denied the story of the 'historic night', and to explain away the fact that the démarche of the Ambassador had taken place after the condemnation of Dreyfus, so that it could not in itself have prevented the prosecution from using the annotated *bordereau* if it existed. Mercier had to evade this point. The War Office, he said, did not know anything of this rumoured document *at that time*. Mercier was adroit and he was prodigal of hints, playing the game of sealed lips like an old House of Commons master, but all but the most zealous were a little tired of hints and secrets too terrible to be revealed. Even a letter from Esterhazy, repeating the story of the danger of war if the whole truth were told, did not add much to the value of Mercier's testimony.

The Anti-Revisionists were anxious; they were especially anxious because of what they surmised of the attitude of Commandant de Bréon. At first sight no member of the court should have been safer. An aristocrat, a most pious Catholic, an Anti-Semite, he had sent money to that subscription for the widow of Henry which had seemed so like a posthumous testimonial to her husband. Commandant de Bréon's religion was very deep and very personal. His brother was one of the small group of Dreyfusard priests and it was known that his confessor had advised him to follow his conscience. Attempts were made to counter the effects of this deplorable clerical influence. His cousin, Colonel de Villebois-Mareuil, reasoned with him in vain.[1] The trial dragged on for weeks, but when the time came to decide it took the seven judges only an hour to make up their minds. By five to two they found Dreyfus guilty, but with extenuating circumstances, and they reduced the penalty from life to ten years. It was an absurd decision: for, if Dreyfus were guilty, there were no extenuating circumstances, an argument that two of the majority were consistent enough to accept. In the eyes of many the minority of two was as important as the majority of five. Colonel Jouast had joined Commandant de Bréon; the President of the Court, and the member of it whose character for probity was highest, had refused to accept the official thesis.[2]

The verdict for the moment prostrated Dreyfus, whose health was extremely bad, and it infuriated Waldeck-Rousseau. The Prime Minister was ready to have yet another trial, but Gallifet pointed out that a new court-martial might do the same as the others. It was resolved to pardon Dreyfus, but here the obstacle was the Dreyfusards. They had been startled and infuriated by the verdict to a degree which the reaction of many Americans to the Lowell Committee report in the Sacco-Vanzetti case furnishes a pale parallel. To accept a pardon, to abandon the right to appeal for a new trial, was to accept a new iniquity. Clemenceau, Picquart, and many others were bitterly opposed to this surrender, but the Dreyfus family had no stomach for vicarious heroism. They accepted the pardon, even though it involved, in effect, an amnesty for Mercier, du Paty de Clam, and the rest. Gallifet justified the pardon on the grounds that Dreyfus was in very bad health and had already served half of the sentence of the Rennes court, but these formal reasons deceived nobody. In a proclamation to the army on September 21st, Gallifet declared that 'the incident is closed. The military judges, surrounded by the respect of all, have decided in entire freedom. We have accepted their decision without any mental reservations. We shall do the same before the decision which a feeling of profound pity has inspired the President of the Republic to make. . . . I ask you and if it was necessary, I should order you, to forget this past in order to think only of the future.'

Tacitus had long ago remarked that it was easier to be silent under orders than to forget, but the Flavian emperors had had resources to induce silence in their subjects that were not available to the rulers of the Third Republic. What had been possible, as late as the few weeks that followed the suicide of Henry, was no longer possible. In what

---

[1] Villebois-Mareuil was soon famous in another rôle. He went off to fight for the Boers in South Africa and was killed in defence of a cause which the whole civilized world (outside Britain) thought just. The indignant Mr. Steevens died in the same war on the other side.
[2] A distinguished French officer, at that time in the Far East, who had never doubted of the justice of the verdict of 1894, was converted on the spot when he learned the names of the dissenting judges.

had become a kind of civil war, one side had been victorious; it was a good deal that it consented not to exercise the full rigours of vengeance against Mercier and the other military leaders of the defeated party, that it accepted an act of amnesty.   It could not and did not accept an act of oblivion and, even if it had, the other side would not let it.   The guilt of Dreyfus, the existence of the annotated *bordereau*, the existence of a conspiracy of the Jews and other foreign powers to ruin France, these were still articles of political faith for hundreds of thousands.   On the other side the agitation for a complete legal rehabilitation of Dreyfus, for a recompense for Picquart, never died down.   As the victorious party got firmer in the saddle, it found time to undo the crimes of 1894. At last, in 1906, in a decision which the extreme Nationalists of the *Action Française* said was as gross a violation of the letter of the law as anything charged against the court-martial of 1894, the conviction of Dreyfus was quashed by the Cour de Cassation.   The victim was restored to the Army with pomp and ceremony.   He was given the Legion of Honour and Picquart was made a general and was soon Minister of War, but save for a few zealots on both sides, the person of Dreyfus had long been lost sight of in the great debate between the parties.   He had been a symbol more than a man, and men still battled round his name but no longer round his person.

CHAPTER III

THE DREYFUS REVOLUTION

I

IF there was to be no personal vengeance carried out in the form of
law, the Prime Minister was resolved that there should be an end to
a state of things in which insubordinate soldiers, in league with troublesome clerks, upset the peace of the nation and weakened the authority
of the State. He had told his brother of the horror which he experienced when he came into office and discovered the disorder and indiscipline which infected the public service. That the Republic was
in any real danger in 1899 is doubtful, but certainly public order and
Governmental efficiency were.

The Reuilly plot had failed miserably, but it was not forgotten.
Nor could it be, for the incorrigible Déroulède was still hoping for a
great revulsion of public opinion that would sweep away the agents of
the 'syndicate'. The signal that Roget had refused to give would be
given, he thought, by the shattering testimony of Mercier. But without
waiting for Mercier to testify, the Government arrested the conspirators
or those of them who, like Déroulède, had not got away in time. One
of these laggards was Guérin. He saw his opportunity to await delivery until popular wrath against the syndicate had risen high enough,
so his friends said, or to gain notoriety as his enemies suggested, and he
took refuge, with forty or fifty members of his 'Grand Occident', in
their headquarters, which from the name of the street was soon known
as 'Fort Chabrol'. There they were 'besieged' by the Paris police.

If the Reuilly affair was comedy, 'the siege of Fort Chabrol' was
farce. Indeed, as the siege continued into its fifth week, Parisians and
tourists who had been accustomed to visit it as one of the sights of the
town, grew bored. The makers of the mineral water and other supplies used by the garrison advertised the fact; there were bickerings as
to the terms on which the Fort would surrender; but finally, when the
Government had reaped all the advantages of ridicule, surrender it
did. The good fortune of the Republic continued, for if Guérin
parodied Déroulède, Max Régis, the anti-Semitic Mayor of Algiers,
parodied Guérin. He had his own Fort Chabrol in Algeria, but it
only held out a little over a week. Even Boulanger at his weakest

had been a more impressive figure than these various comic-opera conspirators.

Déroulède had been tried and acquitted by a sympathetic jury, but however farcical his activities, they were more than a joke. So, as in Boulanger's case, the Senate was called in and it duly convicted Déroulède, Buffet, Guérin. The conspirators, after varying but brief periods in prison, were exiled and the days of active conspiracy were over. If there was to be a revolution it would not come from romantic patriots or the dwindling band of the partisans of exiled pretenders.

It was not Déroulède and his kind, however, who were worth powder and shot. It was their most potent allies, the religious orders through whose preachers and press the anti-Dreyfus agitation had been kept at white heat, the noisy clerical auxiliaries of the Army whose numbers and wealth had been tolerated as long as the *Ralliement* and the 'new spirit' had ruled the attitude of the chiefs of Church and State. But Méline was for ever fallen from power, while the voice of the Church had seemed to be indistinguishable from the voice of Drumont, Judet, and the defenders of Henry. That corporations of such doubtful legality or certain illegality should not merely defy the law by existing, but should throw themselves into the thick of a bitter political battle, was foolish on their part and infuriating to the victorious side. This was what came of letting the policy of Ferry slip into innocuous desuetude! It was time to think of that 'milliard' of which the Prime Minister had spoken, time to deal with these organized enemies of the spirit of the age, the authority of the State and the anti-clerical tradition of French polity.

The chief sinners, politically and morally, were the noisy and foolish priests of the order of the Assumptionists. A new order, lacking the prestige and the traditions, as well as the wisdom of the Jesuits or Dominicans, the Assumptionists had been among the most verbally loyal servants of the policy of the *Ralliement*. Through their newspaper, *La Croix*, they had a vast audience all over France; and among the country clergy their paper rivalled Drumont's *Libre Parole* in popularity and influence. As the struggle over the Affair grew more bitter, the Assumptionists grew more violent. They no doubt believed what they said, in the press and in the pulpit; but it is probable that the delights, dear to so many clerics, of adventitious popularity, were not without their heady effects. To be on the same side as a great popular movement directed against the enemies of the Church who were also enemies of that more popular institution, the Army, was delightful. Who knew? Men who began by hating the Jews might end by loving God!

If French Catholics had been accustomed to take thought for the morrow, they might have reflected how hostile French tradition was to political priests, they might have doubted whether it was wise to involve the cause of religion in such an ambiguous crusade as that defended in deed by Henry, in writing by M. Maurras. But the intoxication of the moment was too much. The bishops were discreetly silent, as was their wont, for they had not changed much since Lavigerie had expressed his candid opinion of them. Laymen and clerics alike committed themselves to the doubtful cause of the honour of Henry, the honesty of Esterhazy, the most rabid illusions of Drumont, the most preposterous fictions of Rochefort. There were Catholics who, for higher reasons than mere prudence (although their action was the highest prudence), did not see what the honour of the Army had to do with lying and forgery, who thought that even Jews deserved justice, who had no use for the bogus science of Drumont or the more sophisticated version of it preached by the gloomy atheist, Jules Soury, to the elegant agnostic, Maurice Barrès. These men, priests and scholars, formed a 'Catholic Committee for the Defence of Justice', words which, if some zealous defenders of the faith were to be believed, had no place in true, French, Catholic mouths.

In resisting the aggression of the religious orders in the political field, Waldeck-Rousseau was, of course, very much in the tradition of the French lawyer statesmen. The dependence of the orders on Rome and their immunity from the authority of the bishops were an old grievance. Many a statesman of the old régime could, with a few verbal changes, have made his own Waldeck-Rousseau's distinction between the ordinary clergy whose position was regulated by the Concordat and which had its hierarchical chiefs 'between whom and the State there exist defined and agreed-upon relations' and 'certain militant organizations, constantly growing, constantly getting more aggressive'.

The most obvious example of these aggressive bodies was the Assumptionists who were promptly dissolved; but it was necessary, if the campaign against the orders was not again to end in practical toleration of unauthorized property-holding, trading, and teaching bodies, to go much further, to regulate the whole matter of the right of association. It was no longer enough to fall back on the richly-stored arsenal of all French Governments, Royal, Imperial and Republican, for decrees against Jesuits and the like, for that arsenal was full of weapons which could equally be used against trade unions, Freemasons and almost all kinds of collective activity. To 'draw on the boots of the Empire', as a critic put it, was convenient but not dignified for a Republican Minister.

If the immediate grievance against the orders was their activity in the Affair, an older and more permanently resented one was the success of their schools. It was infuriating to the good Republican that, a century after the Revolution, more than half of the pupils in secondary schools should be the pupils of priests and brothers. In all departments of the Government, the contrast between the anti-clerical if not anti-Catholic personnel of the elected bodies and the attitude of so many officials was striking. To some it was a danger to the safety of the State (and the Affair did not make this view less plausible); to others it was intolerable that the right to serve the Republic for pay and prestige should be open to men whose education was based on hostility to the Republic as the embodiment of a philosophy of life, if not as a form of government. To put an end to this state of affairs, or to pretend to put an end to it, the Government introduced a bill which would, in effect, have made it impossible for anyone, no matter how well qualified otherwise, to enter the State service who had not first passed through the State schools. Waldeck-Rousseau defended the project with ingenuity. It was, he said, an elementary test of loyalty to demand of those who wished to serve the State that they should not 'repudiate its [the State's] teaching, or turn their backs on its schools'. But the applause this view evoked was more noisy than warm. It was not only that it was, or seemed, unjust to bar for life from the civil service men who had had the ill-fortune to have zealous Catholic parents—the Chamber was full of good Republicans who had had that misfortune, as indeed the Prime Minister himself had had. It was still more serious to alienate so large a portion of the bourgeoisie in face of the Socialist menace and, as was constantly found when the partisans of an educational monopoly seemed near the attainment of their goal, there were not enough Republicans with blind confidence in the University to establish a new educational church. The bill was buried in committee.

It had been the profession and the desire of Waldeck-Rousseau to impose on the congregations an effective control by dealing, once for all, with the right of forming associations; the orders would not be named as such but would be covered in the general law; the most noxious would have their existence made impossible, the less dangerous would be given a new legal status that would make them fiscally and politically subject to the State. This statesmanlike proposal was altered by the action of the militants, who controlled the committees in both Houses, into a general law on the right of association with special provisions to deal with the religious orders, which were now named and whose rights were to be severely limited. No order could now be legalized except by a definite law. The prohibition of any teaching by any member of a religious order that had not been authorized created a new class of Frenchmen with fewer rights than any other, a departure from the common law that was justified on the ground that it forbade teaching by orders which were propagandists for the 'Counter-Revolution'. Even this justification presented difficulties. To condemn to silence the organized enemies of the Revolution of 1789 was one thing, but was the condemnation to extend to organized preachers of a new revolution? The Socialists secured an amendment that saved them from any such danger and they, like the Masons, had to be careful that legislation directed against bodies with international affiliations did not affect them.[1]

The law established complete freedom of association in France as it was already established in America and Britain. There was only this difference, that those Frenchmen or Frenchwomen who wished to exercise this privilege to live in common for religious motives were only to be allowed to do so if a special law were passed. Waldeck-Rousseau's decree, implying that a congregation was not to be dissolved until both Houses had refused the request for authorization, saved the orders from immediate dissolution. It would suffice for the Senate not to act at all to preserve the *status quo*. Some of the orders like the Jesuits did not ask for an authorization that they knew was sure to be refused, but most determined to get out of the law all that they could.

The parties of the Right hoped at the elections of 1902 to recover the ground lost in the course of the Affair. The veteran leader of the *Ralliement*, Jacques Piou, led the union of groups which called itself the *Action Libérale* which absorbed most of the old Conservatives. The *Ligue de la Patrie Française* also hoped to lead the rescue of the nation from the agents of the 'syndicate'. Both sections were bitterly disappointed. The difference in the number of votes cast on each side was not great, but the Left had an overwhelming majority in the Chamber and the miserable showing of the League was its death-blow. The Revisionists were now in power without the need of moderate support. They marked their triumph by replacing Deschanel in the presidency of the Chamber by Léon Bourgeois and electing Jaurès to the vice-presidency. More significant for the moment was the resignation of Waldeck-Rousseau before the new Chamber met, and the resignation was made more important than it might otherwise have been by the choice of a successor suggested to President Loubet by the outgoing Prime Minister. His choice was Émile Combes.

II

The new Prime Minister was very unlike his predecessor; he was no Parisian lawyer but a provincial doctor of medicine of a common enough type. M. Combes shared all the ideas, prejudices, hates, principles of the small-town anti-clerical, but before he had become a doctor of medicine he had been a doctor of divinity. Destined for the priesthood, he had not been ordained, but he preserved something of his clerical training, not in the form of the unction that Renan cultivated, but in a dogmatic combativeness. Had he stayed in the Churc' it is very unlikely that he would have been one of the modernist cler' who dreamed of reconciling the modern world with the ancient f?

[1] The modern Communist party might have had to be condemned on the strict tion of the law of 1901.

He might well have been a somewhat credulous reader of Veuillot or Drumont. It was his sturdy resistance to the opinion of Paris, his indifference to the social pressure which the provincial Radicals saw as the chief source of the seduction exercised on so many of their leaders by 'Reaction' that endeared 'the little Father' to the rank-and-file and that, even to-day, makes some of the older generation see in this narrow, obstinate and self-satisfied little man, the ideal Republican statesman. No dreams of social success, of a seat in the Academy, of a place at a directors' meeting shook the resolve of the new Prime Minister. He would finish, once for all, with the enemies of the Republic, in every department of the State. The old maxim that the Republic owed justice to all, but favours only to its friends, would be practised with all the rigour of the game, even if it involved treating as favours what many persons thought of as justice.

It was this firmness in face of the temptations of society and the criticism of persons whose sound Republicanism had been weakened by sophistries about justice and liberty, that endeared Combes to the scores of thousands of men who prided themselves on being abreast of the spirit of the age in hundreds of little towns. It was his acceptance of power as a delegation from a resolute majority, not as a general commission from the whole Chamber, that won Combes the real as apart from the formal confidence of the victors of the elections of 1902. He was their man and they could forgive him minor faults and even major ones like that untimely profession to a startled Chamber of 'spiritualist' beliefs which shocked for a moment the heresy hunters of the Left.[1]

Combes was ready to use the law when it was a convenient weapon and to evade it when it was a handicap. As Minister of Cults in the Bourgeois Cabinet, he had contested the right of the Pope to veto the nominations of bishops made by the Government. According to the Roman theory, the Republic merely presented names to the Pope and he decided, for whatever reasons seemed good to him, whether the candidates were suitable or not. It had consequently become the custom to sound the Pope in advance, and episcopal nominations were the result of previous negotiation between Paris and Rome. Combes had objected, both on the ground of the absolute right of nomination reserved to the State by the Concordat and on the ground that the papal veto kept sound Republican clerics from the episcopal bench. Now that he was Prime Minister he was more insistent than ever on the rights of the State and, in Pius X, he had a Pope far less ready than Leo XIII had been to meet the State half-way.

The quarrel was not a new one. Under the Second Empire there had been something like a strike and lock-out; the Minister, Baroche, refusing to fill vacancies until the Pope accepted previous

---

[1] Spiritualism in its French sense, as opposed to materialism, not as involving a belief in the possibility of communication with the dead.

nominations and the Pope preferring to leave sees vacant rather than give in. Combes was soon in the position of Baroche, and one of the main advantages of the Concordat from the point of view of the State was lost. If the State could not control the filling of the higher ranks of its religious civil service, for what reason did it maintain it? This administrative point of view was further offended by the action of the Pope in summoning to Rome two bishops of whose conduct serious complaint had been made. To Combes, these bishops were not only victims of their Republican principles, but important officials whose obedience to the State that paid them came first. They were forbidden to go to Rome, but short of taking part in a schism they could not long resist papal pressure; they gave in and resigned. From the Pope's point of view, two unworthy pastors had been removed; from Combes's point of view, two important State officials had been dismissed by a foreign authority.

In such conditions was the Concordat worth maintaining? But before the question of church establishment was ripe for solution, the orders had to be dealt with. To Waldeck-Rousseau, the question of the orders was one of political prudence. They were numerous; their accumulation of property presented those problems that become acute in the most pious nations every three or four generations; some of the orders were, in addition, a political nuisance; and all of the orders, as far as they competed with the official educational system, were a danger to the moral unity of the nation. Waldeck-Rousseau saw the question from the point of view of a lawyer and an administrator; hostile to all fanaticism, he did not like either the political monks or the political anti-monks. Like Ferry before him, Waldeck-Rousseau was willing to distinguish varying degrees of incompatibility with the modern State and modern society. He asserted, and probably believed, that the Church could flourish without any orders, as, he asserted, the acceptance of the Concordat had shown was the view of Pius VII. But once the State was made secure, he was willing to allow for the fact that a great many Frenchmen and Frenchwomen did not agree with him. He had no desire to alienate more honest and sincere people than he could help and he did not estimate the soundness of his policy by the extent and bitterness of the opposition it provoked among the 'enemies of the Republic'.

Combes took a simple view of his duties; he was a delegate of the majority for a special purpose, the extirpation of the clerical menace. In internal policy, a unity was given to the policy of the Government not merely by the personality, simple and obstinate, of the Prime Minister, but by the new organization of the Chamber. The rules were at last re-cast to provide a general system of permanent committees parallel with all the main departments of the Government. The *bureaux* had been only constituted for a month at a time by lot; they had assembled members with nothing in common and reshuffled them before they had time to acquire any common knowledge or attitudes. The Chamber of 1902 finally broke away from this system. The *bureaux* still survived and it was from them that the new standing committees were recruited, a system that led to committees being, at times, quite unrepresentative of the real sentiments of the Chamber: accident might have assembled all the leaders of the majority in a few *bureaux*.[1]

The new system had then, and has still, bitter critics. Poincaré denounced the committee system as one of the chief causes of ministerial weakness and instability, but the instability had far more deeply-rooted causes than the committee system and the weakness of the Ministries flowed from their instability. It could, indeed, be argued that the permanent committee, assembling in one long-lived group the deputies interested in a special branch of government, provided a very necessary substitute for the missing ministerial stability and authority. In the committee on one branch of government, there were normally to be found the specialists in that field or the deputies who were preparing to become specialists. There were the ex-Ministers and the future Ministers. No doubt both types of member were often excessively anxious to return to or to enter the Cabinet, but that was an inevitable part of the system. At any rate, the ambitious deputy got an opportunity, as 'reporter' of a bill or of a section of the budget, to master the details of government that the English system does not offer. Believing, as the French deputies did, in the necessity of an effective and continuous inspection of the activities of the administration, the system of specialized and permanent committees was a necessary reform.

The Combes Cabinet was supported by a coalition of Radical and Socialist groups with a few Left Centre adherents. To hold this majority together there was set up a steering committee called the 'Délégation des Gauches', representing all the sections of the majority. It was to this committee that Combes felt himself responsible. He was constantly in touch with it and when he had got its assurance of support, he was able to count on a majority of the Chamber and so was freed from the nightmare of sudden reversals of parliamentary fortune that threaten most French Cabinets. The moving spirit of the 'Délégation' was Jean Jaurès, now wholly committed to the policy of collaboration with bourgeois parties in order to save the Republic and to secure reforms.

Saving the Republic meant, at the moment, crushing the orders. Whatever Waldeck-Rousseau may have thought was the intent of his law, Combes had no desire to give any legal status to any orders if he could avoid it. He declared that he would apply the law 'in form and spirit, without bothering too much with certain juridical interpretations

---

[1] The Chamber of 1910 allotted members to committees in proportion to the strength of their groups, ignoring the *bureaux*. This system was adopted by the Senate after the last war.

of it'. Schools were shut on a great scale; there were riots in Brittany; there were furious debates in the Chamber; but Combes held firm. The Council of State ruled that the refusal of one House to authorize an order involved its immediate dissolution, and Combes proposed to authorize only five orders; for the others, the simple system was adopted of refusing authorizations *en bloc*. It was, the Catholics believed, a kind of revocation of the Edict of Nantes—at their expense this time. The orders of women followed, and even the authorized orders were assailed, but the few remaining teaching orders among them were allowed ten years' further life as it was impossible to replace them at such short notice.

There were special difficulties in enforcing such laws which arose from the liberal character of the French state. In a modern state it is very easy to suppress orders or ban whole sections of the community like the Jews, because there is no general code of public liberty to hamper the executive. But in a country that allowed free choice of domicile, free disposal of property, the right to teach, the right to religious freedom, it was hard to enforce the laws against the orders without infringing these rights. It was necessary to attribute to the member of an order a permanent status that the law had pointedly refused to notice when the orders were still tolerated. Monks and friars who did not wear robes, who did not directly hold property in common, who merely lived in small groups in private houses might constitute disguised religious communities. How, except by inquisitorial means, could the truth be discovered? Soon the Catholic press was full of stories of administrative action that could be made to seem, and often was, petty tyranny. What was to be done with sisters, members of the same convent, who came home and lived in their father's house? If members of societies, dispersed by law, were allowed to preach or teach near their old haunts the dispersal of the order might be more nominal than real; but if they were to be given a special and inferior status, what became of the liberty of the citizen?

The profound irritation caused by the criminal folly of many of the orders made these questions seem mere forensic tricks even to that part of the majority which was not, under cover of defending the Republic, carrying out its own sectarian purposes. Moreover, the Catholics who relied on the general respect for the nuns were handicapped by the revelation of serious scandals affecting two convents. The stories of dirt and cruelty that were revealed in the courts were not edifying. Worse still, one of the chief grievances of the old-fashioned French politician against the orders was their direct connection with Rome, their refusal to accept the authority of the relevant State officer, the bishop. And in one of the cases, the efforts of the local bishop to reform the convent had been rendered nugatory by the slowness of the Roman tribunals to which the accused nuns had appealed.

The bitterness bred by the Affair was increased by the policy of the Combes Ministry. A form of religious activity that all Catholics thought necessary to the well-being of the Church, if not to its mere existence, was made practically impossible in France; and exile was imposed on many thousands of men and women revered by millions. Nor were the financial results as gratifying as had been hoped. The 'milliard' that was to have been secured for social reforms turned out to be much less. The liquidators appointed by the courts were slow —and sometimes worse than slow. Litigation was long and costly though profitable to lawyers like Millerand. The Radical answer, that these difficulties only arose because the liquidation had been turned over to the courts and not to the administration, in order to please the moderates, was a terrifying defence to many timid souls for whom the project of a direct confiscation of property and the settlement of all questions arising out of it by administrative action was a nightmare precedent. But the majority of Frenchmen remained either indifferent or approving spectators of what the Catholics and Conservatives thought of as spoliation. It was no wonder that many of the most ardent members of the defeated party despaired of the Republic.

III

On trial before the Senate, Paul Déroulède had defended himself warmly against the charge of Royalism, declaring that Parliamentary Royalism was the most unpopular cause in France. He was not far wrong; the old Orleanist tradition had always been the doctrine of an élite and that élite was not recruiting itself. Fatally injured by the collapse of Boulangism, it lingered on with ebbing life. The Dreyfus case was the last blow. No anti-Semitism on the part of the Pretender, no ill-timed adulation of Esterhazy by a prince of the blood, could give any appearance of life to the cause. There were still many thousands of Royalists, old Legitimists, old Bonapartists, enemies of the Republic by family tradition or convinced of its incorrigible vice by the way in which it responded to the manœuvres of 'the Syndicate', but they had no leaders, no doctrines, only impotent hates.

These elements in French society were now to be given a lead by a man of genius whose power of argument, of sophistry, of tenacity, served to give an appearance of life to the dead monarchy and who provided a framework of political doctrine within which nearly all the critics of the Republic on the Right were to work and which was not without its influence on some critics of the Left.

Even if Charles Maurras had not been among the first to rally the demoralized troops of the Right after Henry's suicide, even had he not been the Desaix of a Marengo that was lost after all, he could hardly have failed to win support from the angered, defeated and bewildered Right. For Maurras knew what was wrong and, since he was uncompromising and since the people to whom he appealed wanted some explanation of their defeat that was not too humiliating, his simple, consistent, clearly-stated thesis won the assent of thousands. The basic doctrine of the new school of politics was that politics came before anything else. *Politique d'abord.* The economic, the social, the intellectual life of France could not be healthy and could not be cured until the common cause of their ills was removed. The Republic was the source of most evil, and what little could not be explained as flowing from that fountain of poison was inherent in human nature. For Maurras was no optimist; human life at best was hard; the wise man accepted this fact and adjusted himself to the world as it was and ever would be, a world in which the race was to the swift and the battle to the strong, in which mere sentimental pity was a weakness and an intellectual crime. Like Nietzsche, Maurras despised Christianity and thought its politically dangerous sentiments of 'he hath put down the mighty from their seat and hath exalted the humble' order highly noxious. In his early writings he gave free expression to this hostility, but as a realist, a positivist, he had to admit that France had been profoundly marked by the teaching of the Church; and as a practical politician, he had to face the fact that many of his potential supporters were likely to be alienated by the frank expression of his distaste for Christianity. So whatever regrets he had for the old gods, he had to recognize that they were conquered, that the day of the 'laurel, the palms and the pæan' was over.[1] He accepted the fact that the French tradition was Christian, but, fortunately, Christian with a Roman and Hellenic superstructure. The dangerous, revolutionary Hebraic doctrine had been humanized by the Church, which was one of the most perfect instruments of order, of organization, of the classic virtues endangered by the vague, romantic barbarism of the North. At the Reformation the barbarians had broken away from the healthy discipline of the Church and it was the Reformation, letting loose in Europe the poison of Hebraic doctrine, that had ended the union of Europe. Since that day it was futile to aim at a restoration of unity; the national state was the highest good, the necessary framework within which the individual could develop. It was the great crime of the Dreyfusards that they exalted a vague and unrealistic ideal of 'Justice' above the concrete conditions within which the human race alone could attain to as much justice as was possible. It was folly to put justice before the state; there had been states without justice but there was no justice without the state. For a Frenchman the good life was possible only within a strong France. That was the condition of justice for French-

---

[1] According to a former disciple, M. Louis Dimier, M. Maurras in conversation did not despise the other pagan assets listed by Swinburne and banned by Christianity.

men. Was that France to be weakened fatally because of some artificially raised doubts about the guilt of one man?

That the question could be debated was a sign that France was in a parlous way, for it showed that she was open to the intrusion of the ideas and the interests of the 'four confederated states', the Protestants, the Jews, the Masons, the *métèques*. These four groups had in common their alienation from the true French tradition; two of the groups were Frenchmen who had gone wrong, the Protestants by their adherence to the anarchical doctrines of the Reformation, the Masons by their adherence to the internationalist doctrines of the eighteenth century, doctrines which were Protestant at one remove. The Jews and the *métèques* were not French at all. The true country of the Jews was world-wide Israel. They thought as Jews not as Frenchmen; their kinsmen, in England or Germany, were closer to them than were the Gentile citizens of the State that had foolishly admitted them to full political rights. The whole agitation over Dreyfus showed that. The *métèques* were the recently-naturalized foreigners, too quickly and too easily admitted to high places, formally French, but connected with other nations by family, by religion, by education. The Protestant Franco-Swiss-Danish family of Monods were examples of the *métèques*.[1]

Thanks to the exploitation of anti-clerical sentiments, the four groups had managed to get hold of the French State and, once in possession, did everything to dig themselves in, attacking such strongholds of the national tradition as the Church and the Army. It was futile to attempt to defeat the conspirators by constitutional means, they had the machinery in their hands and, as they had shown in Boulanger's case, they did not mean to let the machinery of the Republic be used against them. Nor was it any use appealing to a vague patriotic sentiment as Déroulède had done. It was necessary to strike at the fundamental cause of the ills of France, the Republic, and to do it by the only means possible, the 'coup de force', by some form of violence. A Royalist revolution was the necessary condition of the deliverance of France.

The King was a real thing not a vague ideal like the Republic. Governments were always governments by men and not by abstractions, and not only governments by men, but by families. That was the strength of Rome, of Carthage, of England, of the great oligarchies. They could be far-sighted; they could take thought for the morrow because the good of the State would be the good of their children and grandchildren. Better still was the identification of the State with one

---

[1] Maurras had used the term before the Affair in the Nationalist paper, *La Cocarde*, which Barrès had run. The metics in ancient Athens were the resident foreigners who had to serve the Athenian State and who were given some privileges, but who were carefully excluded from the full rights of citizenship. In France, alas, the *métèques* were not kept in their proper place, but given the full rights of the city. The term was quickly taken up by all parties and used to describe any type of foreigner in France which the critic did not like.

family, with the House of France. No one had such good reason for taking a long view as the King; no one had less temptation to reap quick profits than a man whose office had come to him from his fathers and would descend to his children. The truth was illustrated even in the Republic, for France *was* governed by families, by groups, but these families and groups were those of the four confederated states who had elsewhere their abiding city, in Jerusalem or Geneva.

This doctrine was stated in a series of political tracts of great ability. The possibility of a monarchical restoration was demonstrated in *The Inquiry into the Monarchy*;[1] the contradictions of the foreign policy in *Kiel and Tangier*; the dangers of Protestantism and of crypto-Protestantism among Catholics in *The Religious Revolution*. The doctrine was just what was needed by the demoralized parties of the Right, or rather by their most ardent members.

The collapse of the *Ligue de la Patrie Française* had left many homeless militants and they had already become discontented by the vagueness and respectability of the League. Henri Vaugeois, a courageous member of the University, had founded a more combative organization, which was to be militant for French ideals and French interests, not for a vague general humanitarianism. This *Action Française* went over to the monarchical ideas preached by Maurras, and the Republic as an organization was now subjected to a constant criticism from some of the most talented polemical writers in modern French history. Maurras himself was an indefatigable writer whose style, if monotonous, was in daily doses very effective. With him were associated one or two brilliant young members of the University, the art critic Louis Dimier and the writer on foreign policy, Jacques Bainville. There were others, notably those indefatigable enemies of Dreyfus and the Dreyfusards, Delebecque and Larpent, who wrote together under the name of 'Henri Dutrait-Crozon'.

But the most formidable of Maurras's allies was Léon Daudet. As his father's son, he had had the *entrée* to the new ruling class; he had grown up with the sons of Marcellin Berthelot and had married a granddaughter of Victor Hugo. Daudet had qualities Maurras lacked; he had a sense of humour, a much less doctrinaire attitude to letters and the arts and an astonishing gift for scandalous controversy. He was a more coherent Rochefort, a less solemn Drumont; his nose for scandal was superb and his taste for it could hardly be restrained even when an ally was in question. The Republicans were now the ruling class with the advantages of being the ruling class, but with the disadvantages too, the high proportion of humbugs in the higher ranks, the fatty degeneration of the controversial muscles that accompanies success.

To be an orthodox Radical, in the early years of this century, was as discreditable for a young man, in the eyes of his contemporaries, as to

---

[1] *L'enquête sur la monarchie.*

be an Imperialist was in the last decade of the Empire. The student population, profoundly aroused by the Affair, was now ready for rioting; and for more serious reasons than the right of the Four Arts ball to have semi-naked models on show.[1] There were constant street affrays, and the young men who had joined the new league were organized in bands of newspaper-sellers and their guards; these 'Camelots du roi'[2] were tough, combative, athletic young men spoiling for a row. Whatever danger there may have been that the brawlers of the Sebastian Faure, Charbonnel and other Left gangs would have it all their own way, was past. It was not long before bourgeois and noble families were familiar with the results of police methods applied to their own sons; and the unfortunate guardians of order in Paris were in danger of attack from Right as well as Left. The Camelots, like the *Action Française* itself,[3] were small bodies, but they were noisy, talented and brave, and they had far more sympathizers than members. The revolutionary doctrine of a Conservative party backed by fighting squads of ardent young men was a French invention, destined to do great things outside the country of its birth.

The rise of the *Action Française* did more harm to the parliamentary Conservatives than to the Republic. Its violence, its dogmatism appealed to the sections of the Conservative forces which had never accepted the *Ralliement*; to the Legitimists, to the contemners of compromise. The attitude of the new Pope, Pius X, had something to do with this revulsion, for his attitude was more like that of Pius IX than that of Leo XIII. Louis Dimier, on a mission to Rome, was able to appeal to the new Pope's dislike of liberalism and perhaps to encourage him in dangerous optimism by talk of a Government of order, whose character, Royalist, Imperialist, Republican, was a matter of indifference to the Holy See. The days when, as the zealous Abbé Barbier put it, 'the conscience of the Catholics of France has been kept lethargic by the calculations of a too human prudence', were over.

This was the lesson learned by Marc Sangnier, the ardent ex-officer who had founded *Le Sillon*[4] which was to organize the Catholic democrats, to impress Catholic social doctrines on society, to resume the work of the *Ralliement*, not on the narrow grounds of political forms, but in every aspect of public life. *Le Sillon* appealed to many young priests as well as to laymen; it turned its weekly into a daily; but it had many enemies, especially among the Catholics of the *Action*

[1] A serious riot had broken out over this question; the ladies were clad in costumes that would, to-day, cause censorious remarks at a conservative seaside resort, but the authority of the Republic was thrown on the side of the prudish Senator Berenger. The brutality of the police on this occasion helped to alienate a good many young men from Republican orthodoxy.

[2] 'The King's Hawkers.'

[3] The name 'Action Française' is applied both to the movement and to the journal of the movement which became a daily newspaper in 1908.

[4] 'The Furrow.'

Française; its Leader was, perhaps, unduly ambitious; he welcomed non-Catholics to his ranks; he was rash in statements of doctrine and his enemies succeeded in inducing the Pope to condemn the movement. Perhaps to the disappointment of his enemies, Marc Sangnier submitted; but the lesson was learned; the days of the *Ralliement* were over as long as Pius X and his Secretary of State, Merry del Val, were in authority. The *Action Française* was open to as great objections from the doctrinal point of view as *Le Sillon*, but although the theologians condemned it, the Pope, who loved it for the enemies it had made, suspended sentence. The most vociferous section of French Catholics were now violent dogmatic enemies of democracy, of liberty in the ordinary sense of the term, of 'Social Catholicism'. They were not the authorized representatives of the Pope, but they were men whom he delighted to honour and to whom much was forgiven.[1]

IV

On the Left, the Affair and its aftermath bred new hopes of a reconstruction of French society. Socialism became more than ever the fashionable doctrine among the young intellectuals. There seemed a danger that the clever young men from whom, by custom, French politicians were recruited, would all be won over by Jaurès or by Maurras. The Radicals were, in the circumstances, delighted to welcome to their ranks an occasional brilliant intellectual like Édouard Herriot. Prudent and realistically-minded young men like Anatole de Monzie might wonder how the rigours of Marxian doctrine were going to be applied to the French countryside, with its millions of tenacious peasant proprietors, but the alliance of the workers and the more intelligent and honest of the bourgeoisie which had defeated 'Reaction' in the Affair was still solid, or so it was hoped. Certainly it was zealously cultivated, and not merely in the field of politics.

The young intellectuals and some of the older generation had been awakened to the danger in which their way of life and their ideals had been placed by the Nationalist campaign. They realized that the defeat of the Nationalists was more due to the combative strength of the Paris workers than to the testimony of the Professors of the École des Chartes on points of textual criticism or than to the testimony of eminent mathematicians on the application of the theory of probability to the arguments of Bertillon. Their gratitude took the form of establishing 'People's Universities', that is the organization in the working-class districts of Paris and of some provincial cities of courses of lectures

[1] It is worth noting as illustrative of the tenacity of Conservative memories that according to M. Dimier, when the *Action Française* was believed to be on bad terms with the Pretender, the Duke of Orleans, subscriptions began to come in from old Legitimist families which had never become reconciled to the fact that the heir to the throne was a descendant of the hated usurpers.

which would, it was hoped, raise the intellectual level of the workers and make them fit to take over the capitalist state.

The practicability of such teaching, the possibility of building a common culture for the workers and the left-wing intellectuals were exaggerated. The very name of 'Universities' showed a grandiloquent refusal to face realities. It was easy for intellectuals to over-estimate the desire of tired workers to sacrifice their meagre leisure, their interest in their gardens or in cycle-racing, to listen to lectures on art, philosophy, science and the rest. To the intellectuals it was a great novelty; as to the Russian revolutionaries of a generation before, this 'going out to the people' was a source of genuine spiritual refreshment if it was, as in Russia, often a source of bewilderment to the workers. It was all very well as long as the 'Universities' were just enthusiastic public meetings where the great ornaments of the Left, like Anatole France, could indulge in generous generalities. Such visits from the great were flattering to the workers' self-esteem. 'The working class,' wrote Guieysse, 'honours them and asks them to appear at its festivities to put before it strongly the few simple ideas of which it feels the need to be soaked in in order to finish its job thoroughly.' That is, the 'Universities' were to be sources of Socialist propaganda of a simple kind, without any irritating displays of that scepticism which was disliked by militant workers as much as by embattled officers. In this activity, as in all others of the same kind, the workers had to develop their own organizations: and the only body, not itself under workers' control, that was able to build up any organizations among the workers, or to be with them in their daily lives, was still the Church. The attempt of the intellectuals to be a priesthood for a body of working-class believers broke down before that ironical distrust of his social superiors that marks the French working-man.

The despair of the Right, doomed as it seemed to be to perpetual defeat on constitutional battle-grounds, was in contrast to the hopes of the Left or to that part of it which followed Jean Jaurès; he had managed to win to his side the majority of French Socialists. They believed that constitutional action could do a great deal for them. By preserving the Republic it saved them from the danger of that 'government with a punch' of which the Right was always dreaming and, by winning if not the gratitude, at least the prudential collaboration of the frightened Left *bourgeoisie*, it made possible the extortion of useful immediate reforms. The time would come when the *bourgeoisie* would have given all that it dared, but that time was not yet. Against this policy, Vaillant for the Blanquists and Guesde for the orthodox Marxists preached and manœuvred. To them, Jaurès was a dangerous seducer of the workers. Jaurès was too kindly and too tactful to retort in the same bitter fashion, but he had no high opinion of the political sense of the doctrinaires. Yet, despite these quarrels, bitterly waged on one side at least, the movement towards the union of the Socialists factions went on.

The authority of the central body set up to harmonize the actions of the various sections was weak and, although Millerand improved the conditions of work in Government establishments and in the factories and workshops of Government contractors, made factory inspection more efficient and carried a factory act limiting the hours of work to eleven which was later to be reduced to ten, these reformist gains were nothing in the eyes of the militants compared with the scandal of a Socialist being a member of a Government that had, at Châlon-sur-Saône, shot down strikers. Worse still, to keep the Government in office, some of the Socialist Deputies voted for an order of the day condemning collectivism. A new split was inevitable; the Blanquists and Guesdists combined to form the 'Socialist Party of France'; the rest forming the 'French Socialist Party'. On the one hand were Guesde and Vaillant; on the other the younger men, the lawyers, the brilliant *Normaliens*, united under their most brilliant comrade, Jaurès, in close alliance with the Radicals and in unshakable support of the Ministry that had saved the Republic and was about to crush the Church.

The policy of Jaurès might have remained compatible with Socialist orthodoxy in France had only French Socialists been concerned. But ever since the re-establishment of the International in 1889, the schisms in the French Socialist ranks had been a scandal to the better-disciplined parties of other countries, especially to the German Social-Democrats, then at the height of their fame. There was, indeed, a great contrast between the well-disciplined regiments led by Bebel, with their powerful trade-union allies, their elaborate and wealthy party organization, their rich press and the feud-ridden, poverty-stricken French Socialists. The Second International resolved not to tolerate such a scandal any longer and, by preaching union to the French, it played into the hands of Guesde. He took over a resolution voted by the German Socialists at Dresden which had condemned a policy of concessions to the established order, a policy which would make of a party that ought to be a party of class war, 'a party content to reform bourgeois society'. It was easy for the German Socialists to condemn Jaurès; they were not tempted to collaborate with the Government, since no German Government wanted their aid. But at Amsterdam, the dogmatists had their way; the policy of collaboration with bourgeois parties was condemned and the French Socialists were ordered to unite. In 1905, the schism was officially closed. The new united party took the name of the 'French Section of the Workers' International', commonly known as the S.F.I.O. It declared that it was 'not a reforming party but a class and revolutionary party'. Guesde had triumphed and not only formally, for Jaurès, once defeated, accepted most loyally the policy of the victors; the experiment of the Republican *bloc* was over.

But before that had happened, the *bloc* had achieved its greatest triumph, it had made inevitable and imminent the separation of Church and State, that deliverance which had been promised by the Radicals since Gambetta's Belleville programme of 1869. After the suppression of the orders, the relations between the Republic and the Pope could hardly remain more than formally correct. Some bishops and some priests may have thought that the disappearance of the orders was not without its bright side for the secular clergy, but they were too loyal to the general interests of the Church to rejoice in a freedom from rivalry that had such a dubious source:

In any case, such credulous members of the ordinary clergy as rejoiced in the disappearance of their regular rivals and took literally the professions of esteem for the paid and disciplined clergy of the Republic which had been lavished on them when the fight against the congregations was beginning, were soon to be disillusioned. For, once the orders had been dealt with, the turn of the Established Church was at hand. The old Radical promised land of the separation of Church and State was about to be entered, with Combes as Joshua, happily delivered by death from the presence of a protesting Moses in the person of Waldeck-Rousseau.

V

The announcement of the projected official visit of the President of the Republic to the King of Italy in Rome was the occasion, not the cause, of the final conflict, but it was an occasion which put most of the blame for the breach on the side of Rome. It was the claim of the Vatican that the head of a formally Catholic state should not visit the usurping King in what was by rights the Pope's capital. The Secretary of State, Cardinal Merry del Val, confronted with the approaching visit of Loubet, sent a protest to all Catholic states as well as to the French Government. The note was not published, even by France, but Jaurès, who now had in the newly-founded *Humanité* his own newspaper,[1] had his first 'scoop'. He published the text with an addition not present in the version sent to France, that the Nuncio was only waiting at Paris for 'very serious reasons'. This was taken to be a hint that the fall of Combes was expected. Nothing could have better suited the enemies of the Concordat. Here was the Vatican both attempting to dictate the foreign policy of the Republic and discounting the fall of a Ministry which was supported by a strong parliamentary majority! And the occasion of quarrel was the old question of the temporal power to which so much French Catholic strength had been sacrificed. If the Pope and his Secretary of State

[1] His earlier organ, *La Petite République*, had suffered in repute from the sales-methods of its proprietor, Gérault-Richard.

thought that the unity of Italy was going to be undone, the more fools they; if they thought that so important an element in French foreign policy as the coaxing of Italy away from the Triple Alliance was going to be sacrificed to mere clerical *amour propre*, more fools still. Even the old defenders of the Concordat like Ribot could not swallow this: and many a French Catholic must, in silence, have wondered at the papal sense of proportion.

The time for an ending of the connéction of Church with State had clearly come. There was no political or moral justification for it any longer. Under previous Governments, if the Concordat had been looked on as a useful bridle to keep the Church in order, it had at least been administered by men who, like Baroche under the Second Empire, or Jules Simon or Dufaure under the Third Republic, wished the Church well as long as it did not intrude on the domain of the State. Such politicians could not now attain office, and the Minister of Cults was far more likely to be a Paul Bert or a Combes, awaiting with varying degrees of patience the death of superstition and using the Concordat to keep the dying Church quiet and harmless. On the other hand, the old Gallican illusions were dead in all but the most obstinate breasts. It was not possible to dream of reviving Bossuet. The Church as well as the French State had had its night of the Fourth of August; the old immunities, the old traditions, like the old local rituals, had been swept away by the Napoleonic centralization of the reign of Pius IX. The French State was unwilling any longer effectually to aid the Church in its attempts to make or keep France Christian; the French Church was unwilling any longer to aid the State to keep the bishops and clergy tame.

Separation was inevitable, but what kind of a separation? There were simple souls who thought that all that was needed was a simple denunciation of the Concordat. But the Concordat only bound the Pope and the Republic; were it to be abolished overnight there would still remain many and important questions to be settled between the French clergy and the Government. How were the vested interests of the clergy who had entered a State service in good faith to be preserved? Were they to be preserved? Who was to own the buildings from Notre-Dame and the Seminary of Saint-Sulpice to the humblest village church and village presbytery? To zealots all was simple. The clergy had no rights or hardly any; the example of rough Republican justice meted out to the orders was worth following in the spirit if not in the letter. But a Government which had had enough trouble with the orders, did not intend to run the risk of expelling thousands of country priests from their homes or of turning the churches into secular establishments. There would be no repetition of the errors of the First Republic, no persecuted clergy saying Mass in private houses and barns, while the new Republican cults of the Masons or the Socialists were observed in the secularized churches. If only to be baptized, married, and buried in, a church was a necessity of French life, as all but the blindest of fanatics knew.

The liquidation of the State Church, if it was to be carried through with any regard for internal peace, could not be the work of men like Allard. It was, in fact, the work of a man whose record, if superficially examined, seemed to make him totally unfit for the job. It was Aristide Briand, the preacher of the general strike, the mouthpiece of the syndicalist militants, the defender in the capitalist courts of the leaders of the class war, who, as 'reporter' of the committee which drafted the Bill, undid the work of the First Consul.

Briand was not a doctrinaire. He was ironically humble in the presence of the distinguished academic Socialists of *Humanité*, and he had none of the caste feeling of the University. He was a born negotiator; he had clerical friends and he did not rejoice in making personal or doctrinal enemies. If it had been possible to negotiate a concordat of separation, to arrange an amicable divorce with Rome, that would have been the best solution, but neither Combes nor Pius X were the men to make such an arrangement. The new settlement would have to be one-sided, but before it could be undertaken the Ministry had fallen. It had long been in danger. The alliance between the Socialists and the Radicals had become less close, and Jaurès had not been re-elected Vice-President of the Chamber, while his preoccupation with the anti-clerical policy of the Ministry made him the butt of attacks, not only from Guesde and the other orthodox Socialists, but from Millerand. On the other side, the discontent of the more conservative supporters of Waldeck-Rousseau had been growing. The Ministry had been on the point of dissolution when the final breach with the Vatican gave it a new lease of life. When its time came it was to die with less dignity than would have graced its fall if it had come earlier.

A Combes ministry would not, perhaps, have attempted or allowed an attempt to make the separation as easy as it was the wish of Briand to make it. The fundamental question was that of the property rights of the Establishment. On the extreme anti-clerical side there was a desire to make the Church as poor as possible. If the clergy continued to live in the same houses and control the same buildings, what good was the separation? But Briand and the majority of the Chamber, from motives of prudence as well as of justice, were anxious to avoid any appearance of persecution. They wished to leave the clergy in effectual control of the churches and other ecclesiastical property. But what was meant by the clergy? Was every parish to be treated as a unit? What was to happen if two persons claimed to be the priest of a parish? If the bishop was to decide, he was in effective control of the clergy and the assets—and the Pope, henceforward, would name all bishops without any voice being left to the State. To avoid this, 'religious associations' were to be set up which would be given the effective property rights in the churches, presbyteries and the rest. Priests would receive salaries for four years to come, but on a descending scale, and existing pension rights were secured. From the point of view of the majority it was a generous settlement and, from the point of view of many Catholics, it was less rigorous than they had feared.

The hopes of an amicable arrangement were upset by one internal and one external event. The law provided for inventories of Church property, and it was not made clear enough that the most sacred emblems of the Faith would be respectfully treated. There were riots in which the new militant Royalist party won its spurs in street fighting, and the Prime Minister, by this time Clemenceau, suspended the inventories. A candelabrum was not worth a human life, he thought.

On the other side, Pius X condemned the Law of Separation on the ground that the law 'attributes the public celebration of religion not to the hierarchical organization divinely set up by Our Saviour, but to a lay organization'. The defenders of the law pointed out that control of the property and finances of the parishes was in lay hands in Germany. The papal objection, however, was not groundless. The German Governments recognized and enforced the authority of the bishops; they were, in any case, not hostile to the Church as such, which the French State was. Moreover a difficulty arose from the fact that, in a great many French villages and in most French towns, the real Catholics were a minority. It was possible to foresee cases where the control of the Church would be in the hands of very lukewarm Catholics indeed, a danger that did not often arise in the Rhineland or Bavaria.[1] Yet the papal condemnation, though loyally observed, was not gladly accepted by all French laymen or even by all French bishops. The stern, unbending attitude of the Roman authorities imposed burdens not on them but on the French clergy, and the new Minister of Cults, Briand, was able to taunt the defenders of the Pope's policy in the Chamber with the notorious disagreement of the French bishops on the question of the religious associations.

What was to be done? There was no danger that the celebration of Mass would suddenly cease. Church services were treated as public meetings, but that meant asking for authorization, which the Pope forbade the clergy to do, and the simple remedy was found of abolishing the last restrictions on the right of public meeting for everybody. The use of the churches was permitted to the clergy, but they had no strict legal rights and, worse still, while the Communes could receive gifts for the upkeep of the churches of which they were now the owners, they

---

[1] Exactly the same difficulty arose when it was attempted, after the last war, to give autonomy to the Church of England. How was one to distinguish between the nominal Anglican and the real Anglican? The fight over lay control of Church property was, of course, familiar to such American Catholics as knew their own history.

did not need to accept them and, if they chose, could let the churches fall into ruins. The action of Pius X thus deprived the Church in France of a great deal of property and imposed great burdens on the laity. Not until after the last world war was a settlement reached which, it is perhaps fair to add, would not in all probability have been acceptable to either side in the bitter atmosphere of 1905–7. At long last, the dream of a 'free Church in a free State' was achieved. It was not freedom as Archbishop Ireland of St. Paul, whose teaching was held up to admiration by some French Catholics, would have understood it. Monastic life was prohibited; in cities and towns as far apart as Clermont-Ferrand and Bayeux, religious processions, many centuries old, were now stopped by local authorities; and the clergy lost all official status in a country where that was not unimportant.

The hopes of the Viviani school and the fears of the old Gallicans were both proved baseless. The Church suffered far less from the separation than had been anticipated. In many districts it was difficult to recruit the clergy, but that was already an old story; some parishes had to be abandoned altogether, but this was merely the public recognition of a state of affairs barely hidden by the legal establishment. On the other hand, the effects of freedom were often bracing; a new missionary spirit was awakened among the clergy and the old bureaucratic attitude grew less common. In varied ways, the Church tackled the problem of keeping a hold on the people. It organized women's clubs in the country; it organized boy scouts; the Christian trade unions gradually freed themselves of the crippling association with the employers; and, in every department of life, the one great organization that could compete with the French State showed its renewed life. There were no schisms and few scandals. The Catholic Church was now the Church of a minority of faithful and zealous people, not the nominal and official religious organization of nearly all Frenchmen. It did not lose by the change.

The dissolution of the orders, the separation of Church and State, some social reforms, a more generous legal interpretation of the rights of associations (if they were sufficiently lay) were the main, but not the sole, achievements of the Waldeck-Rousseau and Combes ministries. The classical character of French secondary education was further assailed in a fashion which shocked the devotees of tradition and the numerous recipients of a sound classical education who defended a system that had made them what they were. It was no accident that the defenders of the new system included such academic ornaments of *Humanité* as Gustave Lanson, and the assailants of the intellectual treason of the new Sorbonne found their most vehement spokesmen in the *Action Française*. All traditions seemed to be assailed and defended together. The censorship of plays was abolished as well as the Concordat; theatrical licence of spectacle or the liberty of theatrical art was a victory of the spirit that freed Dreyfus.

More serious and more offensive to the embittered Nationalists was one of the most popular acts of the government of the *Bloc*—the reduction of the term of military service to two years.

This reform was really egalitarian, for the three years' nominal service had, in fact, been exacted from only a part of the conscript population. Reduction in the term of service for various reasons and the privileges given to possessors of certain educational qualifications had made the average period of service less than two years, to the great and natural discontent of those who had to serve three. The new law insisted on a full period of two years with the colours for everybody, and it was held, by some optimists, that one result was to reduce anti-militarism among the educated classes. As long as they could cut short their stay with the colours, the time spent in the regiment was regarded as an unpleasant interlude in their careers. Under the new system the possessors of educational qualifications could gain advantage from their diplomas, not by a reduction in the term of service but by qualifying as reserve officers, and that involved taking the profession of arms seriously, and the acceptance of a reserve commission, while not incompatible with pacifist or anti-militarist views, usually tempered the zeal with which they were held and propagated.

Since the Affair began with a purely military question, it was fitting that it should end, morally if not legally, with another purely military question or scandal, a scandal which was educational in that it again showed that the French people, if not its professional leaders, had a lively sense of justice and public decency that even the strongest political vested interests defied at their peril.

VI

When Gallifet retired from the War Office in the summer of 1900, the choice of his successor was of the greatest importance for the Republican character of the Ministry. If it was the religious orders which aroused the most politically profitable resentment in the breasts of the voter, it was the generals who had been the leaders in the campaign against Dreyfus which had provoked the scare of 'the Republic in danger'. In the alliance of 'the Sabre and the Holy-Water Sprinkler', the Sabre was the senior partner. The folly and the arrogance of the leaders of the Army was not merely, it was thought, a result of the demoralizing effects of a military life, although that view was increasingly popular; it was, above all, the result of the clerical education and affiliations of the higher officers. Although Mercier had been, when appointed, regarded as slightly anti-clerical, most of the officers involved in the conspiracy against Dreyfus, whether as conspirators or as dupes, had been both aristocratic and Catholic. The very names of MM. de Boisdeffre, de Pellieux, du Paty de Clam stank, in Republican nostrils, of the *ancien régime*, of the rule of the Jesuits, of barely concealed disloyalty to the Republic.

How had it come about that so many high places in the Army were filled by Catholic aristocrats? Because, it was asserted, the whole machinery of promotion was in the hands of a Catholic and anti-Republican clique. This clique filled all the promotion boards with its nominees; all reports on candidates for promotion were made by members of the clique. A good Republican, above all a good Republican who was also a Jew or a Protestant, had little chance of rising in the Army. As the nation grew more Republican, the Army grew less so, and the change was made dramatic for the man in the street by the picture of the Jesuit, Père du Lac, who kept, it was said, the Army List on his table and who made and unmade military careers. That promotion in many cases went by favour was certain. The French Army was a human institution. That well-connected young men in the Army, like well-connected young men in other services, did rather better than their obscure if talented contemporaries, was probable. The main difference was that the kind of connection that helped in the administrative services was not as powerful in the Army as in the Foreign Office or the Ministry of the Interior. Catholic and Conservative origins, which were a crippling handicap in the case of a would-be prefect, were, at worst, no handicap, and often a decided asset in the career of a would-be general.

The difference in temper and origin between the Army and the Civil Service was not due merely to favour. It represented an important change in the position of the Army itself. The practical exclusion of the Conservative and Catholic classes from most branches of public life made the Army more than ever the natural career of the sons of these classes, and the Liberal and non-Catholic bourgeoisie had not merely many more opportunities for distinguishing themselves than were afforded by an Army where only colonial wars offered even meagre glory, they were now rather disposed to despise that kind of glory. Anti-militarism was increasingly popular among the educated classes which had freed themselves from many of the traditional values of French life—or thought they had. Although it was still not at all uncommon for a good Republican family to send a son into the Army, especially into the learned arms, it was becoming less common. The future Admiral Jaurès kept up the naval traditions of his family, but his brother's teaching was hardly likely to encourage a hesitating boy to choose the career of arms. For an able young man of Royalist origin like Lyautey, the Army was often the only career open. It was inevitable, therefore, that the higher ranks of the Army and Navy should represent, to a disproportionate degree, the Catholic and

Conservative bourgeoisie, and that the cavalry, above all, should represent to an even more disproportionate degree that declining class, the Aristocracy.

Nor did promotion from the ranks remedy this state of affairs. As France remained at peace, there was far less chance of winning a commission by brilliant service in the field. In the colonies, it is true, as the career of Marchand showed, there were still opportunities, but the tradition that every French soldier carried a marshal's baton in his knapsack was very implausible by 1900. It is true that the facilities for such promotions were much more lavish than in most armies, but it was a handicap to have been educated at the ranker's school, Saint-Maixent, instead of at Saint-Cyr, and, of course, still worse to have become a gunner by passing through Versailles instead of receiving the most highly esteemed education in France at the École Polytechnique.

The new War Minister was himself a distinguished artilleryman, and although the fact that he had begun his career as an officer in the Imperial Guard raised some doubts as to his right to be regarded as an original Republican, there was no doubt that, by 1900, General André was as sound an anti-clerical as could be found in the French Army, and, as far as opinions went, admirably qualified to carry on the work of republicanizing it, begun by General Boulanger. André took very seriously his task of 'protecting Republican officers and men against the arbitrariness of a reactionary staff', to borrow a description of his activities from an eminent academic Republican.[1] His duty, as he saw it, was double: to make sure that good Republicans did not suffer for their opinions and that reactionary officers did not benefit from theirs. He had drawn up for his own use a double list of sheep and goats, the list of sheep being headed 'Corinth' and the list of goats 'Carthage'. It was his duty as War Minister, so he thought, to extend these lists, to make certain that not everybody would be allowed to attain 'Corinth' and that the names listed under 'Carthage' would, if not deleted, be put back on the promotion lists. Justice would at last be done—but how? The official system of promotion-boards was useless for this purpose; it had given France the higher command that had been defeated and disgraced in the Dreyfus campaign. The boards could be abolished, promotions taken directly into the hands of the Minister, but on what information was he to act? Reports on candidates from their superiors were worthless, since it was the superiors who were suspected. Moreover, these reports would bear only on the real or alleged military merits of the candidates, not on their political soundness. André was forced,[2] he thought, to apply for information

---

[1] Charles Andler.

[2] It is asserted that André had his own domestic reasons for disliking the intolerance and snobbery of the Catholic wives who set the tone in most garrison towns.

outside the regular channels, to take account of parliamentary opinion, to call on the prefects and other officials of soundly Republican branches of the Administration. Official reports were not enough; other sources of information were needed, and André turned to that soundly Republican and worldly-wise body, the Freemasons, or rather to the dominantly political and anti-Catholic section of the Masons whose headquarters were the Grand Orient of the Rue Cadet.

André had as his personal staff officer a zealous Mason, Captain Mollin, and it was Mollin who was instructed to get in touch with his brethren. He set about this task with genuine zeal. He shared all his chief's suspicions of the clerical conspiracy; indeed, he exaggerated them, for although he was, at the moment, a son-in-law of Anatole France, Mollin resembled M. Homais a good deal more than he did M. Bergeret. He had no scruples and no fears. No wrong was done to the non-Republican officer who was not promoted, since apart from the operation of seniority, promotion went by favour and there were so many capable Republican officers that the Army would not suffer from the exclusion from the higher ranks of all politically suspect officers.[1] In any case, 'the brain which is able to adapt itself well to the republican idea should, by that very fact, generally speaking, be superior, not only in the domain of abstract thought, but also in those of concrete realities, to the brain which evolves towards the monarchical idea, which is an idea of stagnation and tradition and consequently of reaction'. With these convictions, Mollin went ahead, convinced not only that he was saving the Republic but improving the Army.

Mollin's usefulness came from his Masonic associations. The Grand Orient was turned into a research centre, field workers sent in reports on officers of every rank, reports sent first to the Secretary of the Grand Orient, M. Vadecard, and made available by him to Mollin. The 'fiches', that is the forms on which the reports were made, were kept secret, as is always desirable in espionage. But it was not possible to keep the system wholly a secret, and General Percin, shocked (or scared) told Waldeck-Rousseau in 1902 that non-official sources were being consulted. Waldeck-Rousseau took the matter up with Combes, pointing out that such a system was wrong—and dangerous, but the 'Little Father' paid no more attention to his predecessor in this than he did in other matters. In any case he was accustomed to let his colleagues run their departments as they liked. André, like Delcassé, was given a free hand.

The information collected was sometimes favourable to the officer

---

[1] It is worth noting that of the five French Generals who won the Marshal's baton in the last great war, four were bad Republicans by Mollin's standards (Foch, Pétain, Lyautey, Fayolle). The fifth, Joffre, was, if not a clerical, a friend of clericals. Two of the high officers most closely associated with Mollin had unfortunate military careers in the field. It may be, of course, that in addition to being unlucky, they were the victims of their past.

reported on. A lucky colonel was described as 'perfect in all respects; excellent opinions.' Less lucky was the commandant who, although he was a 'good officer, well reported on, takes no part in politics', let his wife have her own way and send her six children to religious schools and, sharing his wife's opinions, 'goes to Mass with his family'. Worse still was the officer who, though a bachelor, went to Mass, and worst of all, the officer who both went to Mass and manifested reactionary opinions as well as philosophical errors. While it was easy for the local Masons to see what officers went to Mass, sent their children to religious schools, or otherwise gave exterior signs of unfitness for military command, it was harder to catch the dangerous type whose internal treason only manifested itself at the mess among comrades. For information on this class, the only good source was a brother officer. It was not always possible to find officers whose sense of Republican duty was so strong that they could overcome reactionary scruples about reporting the after-dinner conversations of their brethren, but many regiments did produce at least one good Republican willing to denounce his equals and superiors for the good of the nation and, occasionally, for the immediate good of the Service: for if two officers were candidates for promotion at the same time, and one successfully denounced the other, the Army not only benefited by the elimination of a reactionary from high command, but gained by the promotion of a Republican whose loyalty had stood this severe test.

If it had been noted before 1900 that it paid to have reactionary and religious opinions, it was now noted that it paid to be a staunch Republican; even a little anti-militarism did no harm. As Mollin complacently wrote, 'It happened often enough that one saw an officer who in 1901 had his sons at a Jesuit school and openly displayed sentiments hostile to the Government, in 1902 sending his sons to the *lycée*, and in 1903 displaying his respect for our institutions'. As a Corps Commander put it in a letter to Vadecard, with the help of the Masons one had good hopes of uncassocking the Army of the officers infiefed to Sarto'.[1] With luck and ordinary fidelity, the Masons might have given France an Army as wholesomely Republican as espionage, delation and hypocrisy could make it.

There was a weak link in the chain that joined up the local grocer denouncing or approving his military customer, the ambitious major denouncing a rectionary colonel, to the zealous captain who had the ear of the Minister of War. Vadecard's assistant at the Grand Orient was a certain Jean Bidegain who, from his own account, had always been a lukewarm Mason as well as an anti-Semite.[2] His conscience pricked him, so he later affirmed, as he saw the work of secret reporting

---

[1] Sarto was the family name of Pope Pius X.
[2] He had, he asserted, started a Masonic lodge, along with Deslinières, from which Jews were excluded.

going on; only the thought that he made his living by carrying out the orders of Vadecard kept him from resignation, and when he finally offered a large and varied collection of the 'fiches' to the secretary of the *Ligue de la Patrie Française*, he did so on the promise that he would get 40,000 francs in compensation. The secretary, Gabriel Syveton, rightly thought that the secret of the 'fiches' was cheap at the price. There had been for months rumours of the working of some such system, and various newspapers had talked indignantly, but with insufficient proofs, of the iniquities of the War Office.

Bidegain's 'fiches' were admirable ammunition, for he had carefully covered his tracks and there was hope that the mine could be sprung under the Government without any preliminary counter-mining being possible. The firing of the mine was entrusted not to Syveton, but to a retired officer, Guyot de Villeneuve, who read out to a startled Chamber specimens of the 'fiches', choosing naturally those in which the zeal of the Masonic informers had run away with their manners, 'fiches' of the type which denounced a general as 'a Jesuit, a dirty Jesuit, a threefold Jesuit who soils the Army'. He named, too, some of the officers who had helped to reveal the un-Republican character of their colleagues. The mine exploded with all the force its authors had hoped for. André, frightened by the press campaign, had told Mollin to take the 'fiches' away so that it might be said truthfully that there were none in the War Office, but this precaution had been taken too late. The War Minister was in an extraordinarily difficult position. He might allege that Mollin had gone much further than he had been authorized to go, but that would seem like an attempt to put the blame on other shoulders and would be no credit to the efficiency of the Minister himself. He might, as his Republican predecessor Boulanger had done in like circumstances, deny the authenticity of the 'fiches', but from the moment that Guyot de Villeneuve began reading, André had the dreadful certainty that the Reactionaries had got hold of the genuine article. Even had André had the moral standards of Boulanger, stout denial would have been too risky. So the astounded Chamber, waiting—on the Left at least—for an indignant refutation of the slanderous charges of the Right, had to put up with a feeble promise to look into the matter from André and a vigorous 'You're another!' from Combes, which, however adequate for the devoted supporters of the Prime Minister, was not quite enough for the deputies who had been telling the world and France, for six years past, how unlike clerical methods was the true Republican art of government.

There was a grave danger that the Ministry might fall. It was saved by the only man who could have saved it, by the only man whose reputation could have covered André and Combes, by Jean Jaurès, glory of the intellectuals, the philosopher in politics, incarnation of the public conscience awakened by the Dreyfus case. Jaurès [1] brushed aside the minor moral question and, with all the resources of his intoxicating rhetoric, implored the good Republicans of the Chamber not to do the work of the reactionaries and bring about the fall of the Ministry. The days of 'let justice be done though the heavens fall' had passed. Even Jaurès could only induce the Chamber to pass, by a majority of four, an evasive order of the day. Outside the Chamber, public opinion was less easily placated. Despite the formal anti-militarism of the electoral majority, the Army was still semi-sacred, and it was hard to persuade even left-wing voters who, after all, were mostly ex-soldiers, that its discipline and efficiency were improved by Mollin's methods. Those who were not affected by this argument were, too often for the security of the Ministry, affected by moral scruples. Within the ranks of the League of the Rights of Man war raged. Charles Gide, Rist, Hauser, Bouglé, Eisenmann, asked for a condemnation of espionage and secret delation, but Francis de Pressensé, who was the most prominent representative of the Protestant conscience in the ranks of the Socialists as well as President of the League, was not to be moved. He pointed out that a condemnation of André's methods might and would help the reaction; he treated the whole question as one of tactics, talked of the bad effects of obstruction in the Chamber, reminded the troubled Dreyfusards what Parnell had done to the discipline of the House of Commons, and suggested that the time for expressing an opinion on the moral question had not yet come. In this M. de Pressensé, like M. Jaurès, acted as a practical politician. He was backed by one of the most eminent young academics with political ambitions, the mathematician, Paul Painlevé, [2] and when Joseph Reinach, taking care of his reputation both as a patriotic Gambettist and as a Dreyfusard, resigned from the committee of the League, his place was taken by Anatole France.

. The position of the Masons was more difficult. They were forced to realize that for reasons they did not wholly understand, the public was not grateful for the services they had rendered the Republic. Laferre, President of the Grand Orient, was a deputy, but he had preferred not to defend the action of the great organ of lay morality when the storm first burst in the Chamber. His courage soon returned and he and his colleagues issued a manifesto reproaching the Republican majority of the Chamber with its cowardice, a majority which contained so many Masons! The manifesto lamented that the chance of declaring that Masonry 'had deserved well of the Republic' had been

---

[1] Jaurès showed his courage in defending a system that made the religious practices of a wife proof of the bad Republicanism of a husband, for he had more than once been delated to his own party for allowing his wife to bring up his daughter as a Catholic, to let her make her first Communion and, as some asserted, to send her to a Church school.

[2] Painlevé was later to claim credit for promoting the Catholic generals, Foch and Pétain, during the last war.

lost, but the weaklings were warned that the eyes of their brethren were on them. M. Laferre's apologia was not well received, for the public found it hard to understand why the Masons were both so proud of what they had done and so angry with Brother Bidegain for revealing it. They had done good by stealth and blushed to find it fame. As M. de Pressensé pointed out, it was a mistake to have left the contents of a powder magazine in the keeping of a traitor and a badly paid one at that.

Denials, defiance, evasion and honest anger with the disloyal M. Bidegain all left the public cold. The 'fiches de délation' killed the Combes Ministry as the Henry forgery killed the anti-Dreyfusard cause. The death agony was shorter. The vigorous and brutal Nationalist deputy, Syveton, had allowed Guyot de Villeneuve to reap the glory of the first day, but after a debate in which Jaurés, Combes, and André had each shown his particular talent for evasion of the issue and which resulted in a majority of two for the Government, Syveton, before the counting of the vote was finished, walked over to André and slapped him repeatedly on the face. This assault by a young man on an old one saved the Government for the moment and a vote of confidence was passed by a large majority. The attack, as Syveton in an apologia declared, was an act of civil war, and many on Syveton's side deplored his brutality, but for many more he was a hero. Although the immediate result of the assault was the passing, by a large majority, of a vote of confidence in the Combes Government, the situation remained dangerous. André was bitterly humiliated and Syveton, if he were put on trial, would have every chance of exposing the whole system of delation, of demonstrating that André and Combes had been evasive in their explanations to the Chamber, perhaps of showing, through the evidence of the indignant Captain Mollin who had been made the scapegoat, that they had been more than evasive. The day before Syveton was to face the jury and to make himself the accuser and André and his system the accused, the hero of the Nationalists committed suicide, faced as he was with a sudden double charge of sexual offences with his daughter-in-law and of embezzling the funds of the *Ligue de la Patrie Française*.[1]

The death of Syveton did not save Combes for long. André resigned, but Combes was now his own Jonah. His candidate for the Presidency of the Chamber, Brisson, was beaten by Paul Doumer, and although the faithful Socialists and the more obscure Radicals gave the Ministry a majority of six on a vote of confidence, Combes resigned.

---

[1] Needless to say, many of Syveton's friends said he had been murdered. The real mystery is why his daughter-in-law should suddenly have become indignant over the fairly remote loss of her virtue and should suddenly have confessed all to her mother. Because the sudden production of these charges was so convenient to the Government it would be as rash, as in the similar case of the sudden moral indignation of Captain O'Shea against Parnell, to lay too much stress on *cui bono*.

The great ideological conflict that had renewed in France the passions of the Wars of Religion and of the Revolution, that had affected every aspect of French public and intellectual life, ended in a stink of shabby spying and lying and in the obscurity of a vulgar sexual scandal. It ended, as it had begun, in darkness. Had France had an Andrew Marvell, he too might have thought that the cause was too good to have been fought for ; but it was fought for, and bloodless civil war took its toll, on both sides, of honour and truth. Yet as Monsieur Daniel Halévy found it necessary to remind his countrymen a few years after, an innocent man *had* been saved, bad men *had* been punished. Such triumphs of justice over passion and interest are not common in any land, even when justice is aided, as it was in France, by passion and interest.

BOOK VIII

THE SHADOW OF WAR

Les ténèbres s'évanouissent
Quand le soleil se lève.

HÉGÉSIPPE SIMON.

Ancestral voices prophesying war.

COLERIDGE.

CHAPTER I

THE ENTENTE CORDIALE AND THE MOROCCAN CRISIS

I

IT had fallen to Delcassé, to a determined opponent of any fundamental agreement with Germany, to make, as gracefully as he could,
the surrender of Fashoda. The Minister who began his career at the
Quai d'Orsay under such a humiliating necessity, was to stay there for
six years and, almost ignoring his successive colleagues as the necessities
of politics changed them, he was to carry out a bold and dangerous
reorientation of French policy. To forget Fashoda and come to terms
with the triumphant English would take time, and for the moment there
were other more urgent things to be done: to make the Dual Alliance
stronger and the Triple Alliance weaker.

In the first place, Delcassé was worried, as he wrote to President
Loubet, by the possible dissolution of the Austro-Hungarian Empire
which might follow on the death of Francis-Joseph and which would,
formally at least, make the military arrangements of the Dual Alliance
void. It was to remedy this defect that, in the summer of 1899, Delcassé made his secret visit to Russia, secret in that its precise object
was unknown. From Russia he brought back a substantial modification of the existing arrangements. The understanding between France
and Russia was extended to cover not the mere *status quo*, but the
'balance of power'; and the military convention was no longer to
lapse on the dissolution of the Triple Alliance. Superficially, Delcassé
had succeeded in his design. The policy of Russia, her diversion of
interest in the Far East, the absorption of her resources in the building
of the Trans-Siberian railway, the Tsar's action in calling the first
Hague Peace Conference (whether it revealed economic strain or genuine
pacifism) had all made it highly doubtful whether France could get
much help, in any independent designs, from her ally. But by adding
the 'balance of power' to the objects of the Alliance, France was making
it likely that, when and if the question of the Austrian Succession
became urgent, the Alliance would bind her to follow Russia in her
policy, for the balance of power *would* certainly be in question if Austria
dissolved. It was in vain to boast, as Delcassé did, of 'the far-reaching

plans' now made possible, unless he could be sure that these plans would be at least half-French. He was to learn, in a few years' time, how little regard for the interests and even for the dignity of her ally Russia could display.

More successful, if looked at from a realistic point of view, was the lessening of the tension between France and Italy. The ending of the tariff war in 1898 was mainly the work of Delcassé's predecessor, but it was Delcassé who reassured a nervous Italian Government that France had no designs on Tripoli. It took time for the economic peace to be followed by political consequences but, by 1902, the time was ripe for written assurances to Italy that her claims in Tripoli would be safeguarded and that Italy would remain neutral should France be attacked by one or more powers. Even if France, as a result of 'a direct provocation', should be forced to declare war, Italy would still be neutral. What was a 'direct provocation'? The Italian Foreign Minister, Prinetti, reassured Delcassé by examples which could hardly be comforting to Germany: the Ems telegram, the Schnabele affair, and 'certain developments' of the Fashoda crisis. It was all very well for the German Government to minimize the secession of Italy, to talk of wives waltzing with men other than their husbands and yet remaining faithful. No one knew better than Chancellor von Bülow that Italian flirtations were liable to have quite serious consequences.[1]

Delcassé had, in his own mind, cleared the way for a more difficult achievement—a settlement with England.

At the beginning of the twentieth century, the existence of the independent Moroccan Empire, bordering on Algeria by land and only separated from Spain by the Straits of Gibraltar, was an anomaly. A vast area, reputed to be rich, occupying a most important strategic position on the Mediterranean and the Atlantic, was ruled, as far as it was ruled at all, by a curious bureaucracy, the *Makhzen*, which had some points of resemblance with the mandarinate of Annam and, like it, formally obeyed but usually controlled the monarch whose authority and prestige were increased by an alleged descent from the Prophet. The Sultans and the *Makhzen* had been fully conscious, ever since the conquest of Algiers, that their independence and authority were threatened by the infidel. Taking advantage of the anarchy produced by the French conquest of Algeria, the Moroccans had advanced eastwards, but after their great defeat at the hands of Marshal Bugeaud, in the Battle of Isly in 1844, they acquired a healthy respect for their new neighbours.

France was not the only threat, for Spain, clinging to her garrison

---

[1] The Chancellor's wife was an Italian lady of very high rank who had eloped with Bülow when she was still the wife of the German Ambassador in Rome and Bülow was on her husband's staff.

towns like Ceuta, waged war on the Sultan, and under the vigorous leadership of O'Donnel and Prim, forced concessions from him. Other powers followed suit, and it was in vain that the *Makhzen* tried to maintain a policy of economic and political isolation, rather like that imposed on Japan by the Tokugawa Shoguns. A more practicable policy was to assert the authority of the Sultan in the eastern frontier regions where the French colonists of Oran were covetously eyeing the rich lands of the neighbouring tribes. While the *Makhzen* was thus trying to make its authority effective, it was also trying to play off one power against another, especially Britain against France.

The vigorous Sultan Moulay el-Hassan was helped, of course, by the eclipse of French prestige after 1870; but when he died in 1894, a bold Minister, son of a negro slave, made a child the Sultan, and the decline of the imperial authority set in. The child, Abd el-Aziz, might have delayed the fatal event by playing off British authority, as represented by the famous Kaid MacLean and the more important Walter Harris, Tangier correspondent of *The Times*, against French, but dying at the age of nineteen, he left a serious debt and a threatened succession. From 1900 onwards, Morocco was plagued by wars started by pretenders to the throne, by bankruptcy, by tribal revolt, by rival concession hunters, by all the symptoms of the political and economic maladies which, in Tunis and Egypt, had made possible the imposition of European tutelage. The Moroccans were warlike; they detested the foreigner; they would resent the imposition, even under cover of imperial authority, of foreign rule; but if the European powers could agree, the independence of the Sheriffian empire was over.

M. Delcassé saw, or thought he saw, a way of making sure that the liquidation of that independence would be the task and the opportunity of France. She would step into the breach, restore and extend the authority of the Sultan and, in his name, open Morocco to development. This policy was a natural one; it made possible the rounding-off of France's North African empire, and it was certain that twentieth-century Europe would not indefinitely tolerate anarchy, barbarism, and the denial of opportunity for economic development in a large area at her very door. To the Colonial party, especially to the Algerian representatives of that party, the Moroccan apple was ripe. Étienne, the powerful representative of the settlers in Western Algeria in Parliament, advocated the forward movement among the politicians. No more than Stephen Douglas, faced with the problem of opening Kansas and Nebraska to settlement, was he worried by the moral side. It was time to extend the benefits of modern civilization westwards to the Atlantic and southwards to the desert.

When, in 1903, anarchy in Morocco and incidents on the Algerian frontier made it evident that some method of pacification and modernization of the Moroccan territory had become necessary, Jaurès attacked any policy of military action. But it was not, as yet, with a full realization of the dangers of the 'Moroccan wasp-nest'. If the thought of a war in Morocco appalled Jaurès, what he feared was a great colonial war comparable in difficulty and expense to the South African War. Jaurès attacked, that is to say, a policy of supporting and extending the authority of the Sultan under the belief that the Sultan could be controlled by France. Let France deal directly with the independent tribes and, by peaceful penetration and aid, win them to her side. To do any more than this meant uniting all Morocco against the invader and would lead to a long, bloody, and expensive war. A fraction of the money spent on that war would enable France to modernize Morocco on generous terms that would win Moroccan hearts.

There was some force in Jaurès' argument. The Moroccans were warlike and their country geographically was as difficult to conquer as Algeria had been. If that precedent was conclusive, a long and bloody war *was* in preparation. It was true, also, that the Sultan's rights over the whole vast area were a fiction. Yet there was force in Étienne's argument. It was impossible to negotiate 'with nothing', and apart from the imperial authority, there was no organized authority in Morocco at all. At any rate, the policy of controlling the Sultan, ruling in his name and extending French control over the whole Empire, was adopted. All that remained was to clear up the diplomatic situation.

That was the task of Delcassé. He had learned the lesson of Fashoda and was prepared to make a deal on a great scale with the main obstacle to French control of Morocco—Britain. Franco-British relations, embittered by Fashoda, had not been improved by the events of the Great Boer War. Within a few months of France's humiliation, British pride was being humbled in its turn by a series of ignominious defeats at the hands of well-armed farmers in tall hats. The press of the world took a cruel pleasure in rubbing it in, and the Paris press was, of course, more competently cruel than that of any other country. The sacred person of Queen Victoria was insulted and the anti-foreign passions bred by the Dreyfus case made matters worse. Nor did the attempt of the Right to use the hero of Fashoda as a stick to beat the Republican traitors with, conduce to good relations. Nothing could have seemed more remote, in 1900, than an 'Entente Cordiale' between France and Britain.

There were other aspects of the situation. The Boer War had not merely irritated British pride, it had revealed her isolation, for German public opinion and the press had been as hostile as the French, and the clumsy overtures of Joseph Chamberlain to Berlin had been brutally rebuffed. The coming of Lord Lansdowne to the Foreign Office in succession to Lord Salisbury meant that British policy was now in the hands of a man who believed that the days of 'splendid isolation' were over. Britain had had to draw close to the Triple Alliance ten years before; she now had to make friends somewhere. The official visit of the new King, Edward VII, to Paris was a bold stroke which turned out to be completely successful. The new British sovereign knew Paris well, and he was far better qualified to charm the Parisian population than was his nephew, the Tsar. It would be absurd, of course, to attribute too much or, indeed, very much, to the personal influence of the King, but a fondness for France and a dislike of his nephew, William II, made Edward VII a good symbol, if no more, of the willingness of both Governments to forget Fashoda—and Bangkok. A visit of President Loubet to London sealed the social side of the Entente. It only remained to complete the business deal. It was not easy, for as that eminent Francophile poet, Kipling, said, French and British adventurers and empire builders had been on each other's tracks for a long time in the past. But Britain was willing to pay a pretty high price to escape from the awkward position of having enemies on every side, ready to take advantage of her difficulties; and German rudeness, as well as the open German determination to build a navy big enough to threaten British naval supremacy, made it impossible to believe that much could be done in Berlin. As for France, the withdrawal of Britain from the German orbit was a great general diplomatic gain, and the settlement of all outstanding controversies would make the task of getting control of Morocco easy.

In 1904, the negotiations were completed by the signing of a general agreement. Most of the articles of the Franco-British agreements of 1904 were not important in their actual content. Long and tedious negotiations over the right of French fishermen to use Newfoundland beaches during the season, over the frontiers of Gambia or of Nigeria, over the *condominium* in the New Hebrides, or over the disputes between France and Siam, had little relevance to the main agreements except that they illustrated the willingness of both Governments to remove, as far as possible, *all* causes of dispute, even minor causes. Far more serious were the really important surrenders and exchanges, the abandonment by France of her long opposition to the British occupation of Egypt, her surrender of her powers of delay and wrecking, and the British recognition, in return, of a special French interest in Morocco, an interest which, if it was represented to the public as a bulwark of the *status quo*, was, in the minds of the negotiators and in the secret articles of the agreement, equivalent to the acceptance, in advance, by Britain of whatever action in Morocco should be determined on by France. If the condition of the rickety 'empire' of Morocco called for active intervention by France (as it would), British rights were saved by the agreement of France not to fortify the coast opposite Gibraltar; and Spanish claims, by the reservation to Spain of a special zone of influence.

If Delcassé's calculations proved correct, if he had really bought off all opposition, he had made a good bargain, for he had exchanged the barren right of being a nuisance to Britain in Egypt for exclusive rights of political interference in the rich and weak Moroccan state. The rest of Europe would be presented with an agreement which it might not like, but would have to swallow. The Dual Alliance had won the long struggle for the hand of Britain, a conquest not only intrinsically important but making it more certain than ever that Italy's loyalty to the Triple Alliance would be very lukewarm. But at the very moment of triumph, Delcassé's plans were endangered by the threat of war between Japan and Russia, a threat that became a reality two months before the formal signing of the agreement with Britain.[1]

The most prominent and most acute critic of the Franco-Russian Alliance had been Jean Jaurès. He had not been hostile to it in the beginning and he continued to oppose those uncompromising Socialists who expressed a doctrinaire intolerance of an alliance with the Tsardom. But Jaurès was rightly convinced that the hopes of Russian aid for a policy of revenge on Germany were illusions natural to romantic and unpractical agitators like Déroulède, but quite beyond credence by any responsible statesman. Like many, probably like most Frenchmen, Jaurès saw in the Alliance an insurance policy against sudden German invasion. But unlike most Frenchmen, Jaurès did not believe that such an invasion was seriously to be feared. He contrasted the prudence and restraint that had marked Bismarck's policy after 1871 with the megalomania of Louis XIV and of Napoleon I. While most Frenchmen, who thought of the matter at all, saw in the Triple Alliance only a menace to French safety, Jaurès saw in it, so he said, a stabilizing force. The Dual Alliance and the Triple Alliance were forces of equilibrium. He asserted that Europe had never known such peace as between 1871 and 1900, and he indulged in some polemics, not very candid on either side, as to the claims of the period that followed the Congress of Vienna and the period that followed the Peace of Frankfort for the pre-eminence in peace.

According to Jaurès, the question of Alsace-Lorraine would be solved when the workers of France and of Germany had freed themselves from their bourgeois and aristocratic masters, but war to free Alsace-Lorraine would be a crime. Who knew what would come of that war? The true Jacobin tradition was one of peace, and, with historical accuracy, he contrasted the pacific policy of Robespierre in 1792 with the combative follies of the Gironde which brought on the war in which the Revolution exhausted herself. By tying herself to Russia which had no interest in restoring the lost provinces to France and a serious political interest in not aiding the anti-authoritarian forces in Germany,

[1] Without declaring war, the Japanese attacked and sank the Russian squadron in Port Arthur harbour on February 8th, 1904. The agreement was signed on April 8th, 1904.

France had, in fact, renounced all hopes of a restoration of Alsace-Lorraine by force. Why should she not admit this fact and orient her policy accordingly, instead of alarming Europe by verbal provocations which she had no intention of turning into deeds? Were France to renounce the idea of military revenge, Europe, even capitalist Europe, might look forward to peace. For with an optimism that ignorance alone could justify, Jaurès asserted that the great questions of nationality that had convulsed Europe in the first half of the nineteenth century were now settled. There were irritating problems still to be solved but they were minor. In spite of them 'there is no longer a single people in Europe which cannot know the pride and joy of national development, and the great upheavals, either the passionate efforts of nationalities which wished to establish themselves, or the attempts at repression which crushed them, have ended. . . . No nation has now a vital interest in altering the map of Europe.'

Holding this belief, Jaurès was naturally opposed to any excessive deference, in internal or external policy, to the presumed wishes of Russia. Jaurès wished to be on good terms with the Tsar, with the King of Italy, with the Kaiser. He rebuked the Italian Socialists for their opposition to a visit of the Tsar to Rome and hinted that he looked forward to the day when there could be a mutual exchange of visits between Paris and Berlin. But he felt free to criticize Russian policy in the Far and Near East and to denounce such atrocities as the Kishinev pogroms. Whatever could be said for the Alliance as long as it was confined to Europe, there was nothing to be said for extending it to Asia, where it could only result in renewing the old enmity with England and producing a totally unnecessary alienation of Japan. Jaurès incurred the enmity of most of the Right and of a good many Radicals by the energy with which he denounced the dangers of a servile following of Russia. Only the clergy, anxious to save the monks and nuns, could support such a policy, he declared, and whether he believed this or not, it was a good debating-point. The attacks on the Republican Ministers of War and Marine,[1] whom Jaurès himself had recently denounced for jingoism, were represented as being part of the reactionary-clerical conspiracy.

The anxieties felt by Jaurès were not felt by him alone, and by no one were they more deeply felt or resented than by Delcassé, whose bold and hitherto successful foreign policy was suddenly endangered by the folly of the rulers of Russia. As an ally, Russia had never been satisfactory, always exercising a pressure approaching blackmail on her partner. In the conduct of her quarrel with Japan she displayed no regard for her own or French interests. For not only did the diversion of Russian strength to the Pacific mean that she was not an effective counter-weight to German military predominance in Europe, but her

---

[1] General André and Camille Pelletan.

rival in the Pacific was the ally of Britain. France was now in the ridiculous and dangerous position of close association with the ally of the enemy of *her* ally. When war finally came; when for, reasons that scandalized the French diplomats by their venal frivolity, the rulers of Russia refused all compromise, the situation grew worse. There were a few optimists who trusted in the Russian Army, but as defeat followed defeat, their numbers dwindled. The Paris bankers, whose clients had swallowed so many of the Russian loans in the past ten years, were alarmed at the need for financing the war. The press might be induced, by means involving considerable expense, to keep from the investing public the depressing truth that the Tsar's Government was faced with certain defeat and probably with revolution; but that truth would out. To persuade Russia to make peace while there was yet time was a tempting policy. Russia could not fulfil her part of the bargain while the flower of her army was in Manchuria, and France's financial support of her ally was coming to look like throwing good money after bad. But to advocate peace was to endanger the tepid loyalty of the Tsar to the Alliance. Nicholas was obstinate and was egged on by his cousin, the Kaiser, who had hopes of detaching the Tsar from his republican ally. The Tsar, it was decided, must be left to find out for himself that he could not win.

The same calculations lay behind a very risky policy that Delcassé felt himself bound to follow. The last Russian hope was the use of the Baltic fleet to take command of the sea. That involved a voyage half round the world for a squadron without any bases *en route* and whose port of destination, Vladivostok, could only be reached after defeating or evading the enemy fleet. It would have been a very serious undertaking for an efficient squadron; and the Russian squadron was very far from efficient. Unless French naval officers would help, the Baltic fleet would never reach Japanese waters. But how could help be given without discovery which would infuriate the Japanese and their English allies? As far as Russian incompetence allowed, French aid was given to the Baltic fleet whose commander had refused the not disinterested advice that he should approach Japan from South America, a route which would make it impossible for the French to help.

There seemed for a moment to be no way to save both the Alliance and the Entente, for in crossing the North Sea, the nervous (and possibly drunken) Russians fired and sank some British fishing vessels which they took for lurking Japanese torpedo boats. There was panic in Paris. War between Britain and Russia would be the last straw, but Russia climbed down and an international investigation was agreed on. Meanwhile the doomed fleet moved on; to Dakar, to Diégo-Suarez, to Indo-China, everywhere producing a bad impression on the French officers who had been chosen to help it to evade the rigours of neutrality.

The Japanese were not deceived by the elaborate comedy and the ingenious French evasions of their obligations as neutrals. There was some ground to fear that the Japanese might attack the fleet as it lay in Indo-Chinese waters, but that danger passed and the Russians sailed on to be annihilated at Tsushima.

The game was now up, and the best that could be hoped for was a speedy peace which would enable the Tsardom to defeat the revolution that was obviously on the way. Although the Peace of Portsmouth came in time to do that, Russia was, as an ally, almost useless. If there was to be a showdown with Germany, France, from a military point of view, would have to depend almost entirely on herself.

II

The possibilities of the situation were not missed in Berlin. The Franco-British agreement showed up, as baseless, the great illusion of German policy, the belief that Britain would *have* to accept German terms for collaboration, as she could not successfully settle her disputes with France. The war in the East offered two possibilities of action. As the Russian defeats continued, the authority of the Tsardom was increasingly weakened; Russia was entering on a time of troubles and the Kaiser might hope to play on the fears of his cousin, the Tsar. Britain, after all, was the ally of Japan; Germany could make attractive offers of support to Russia, and the Tsar in turn, to save himself, could (it was hoped) force France to choose between the new Entente with Britain and the Alliance with Russia. On the other hand, if it was possible to show France in some conspicuous way that British support would be feeble, the French, in their disillusionment, might abandon the Delcassé policy and leave Britain once more in unsplendid isolation.

Which of these policies would be tried depended on the general situation. The French, by sending the Tallandier mission to Fez to impose 'reforms' on the Sultan, and by making a bargain with Spain, obviously intended to dig themselves in in Morocco before any opposition could be organized. Bülow, against the wishes of the Kaiser, determined to strike a dramatic attitude. On March 31st, 1905, the Kaiser and the Chancellor landed at Tangier and in a speech that was heard round the world, William II insisted both on the interest of Germany in Morocco and on the full independence of the Sultan whom the French were obviously trying to reduce to the position of a client prince. It was an Ems telegram over again.

It was Delcassé's obstinate refusal to face the fact that France was running exactly the risk which had been the nightmare of the statesmen of the early years of the Republic, that alarmed his colleagues. However confident he might be that Germany was bluffing, he could not be certain. However plausible might be his formal replies to the German

399

complaints that they had been kept in the dark over the Moroccan settlement, they did not affect the realities of the situation. He *had* stolen a march on Germany; he *had* greatly extended French power in one of the few important areas still open to colonial expansion. The greatest military power on the Continent saw no reason for submitting to such an exclusion. The British Navy and the tiny British Army could not save France—and the French Army under André, like the Navy under Pelletan, was not in the highest state of efficiency, while the state of the public mind was made plain by the political necessity of the reduction of the term of military service from three years to two.

The shrewd financier who had succeeded Combes as Prime Minister was fully aware of all these considerations. Rouvier, unlike the 'Little Father', did not allow his Cabinet to disintegrate into a collection of departmental Ministers each doing what was right in his own eyes. The anarchy within the executive, which had arisen from the concentration of all the energies of Combes on the war with the Church and had allowed Delcassé to carry on, without any supervision, his own foreign policy, was now over.

The professional diplomats, who admired Delcassé's energy and firmness of purpose, yet saw clearly enough that he had kept his colleagues and his countrymen, as well as the Germans, too much in the dark. The France of 1905 and 1906 was not prepared to fight an almost hopeless war to exclude Germany from any share in the Moroccan settlement. If Germany was willing to go to the edge of war, France would withdraw. It was possible that Germany was bluffing, but it was certain that France was not in a position even to bluff.

Delcassé in vain tried to blind his colleagues to the realities of the situation by lavish promises of British help, promises that do little credit to his candour or, alternatively, to his judgment The daring pilot was dropped, and Rouvier had to steer the ship away from the rocks and, after wriggling a little, accept the German demand for an international conference. It was a spectacular triumph for Germany which, at the same time, had managed to induce the panic-struck and isolated Tsar at Bjorkö to sign an alliance treaty with Germany, a treaty that Nicholas II had to renounce, but whose mere existence showed how broken a reed the Russian Alliance was.

As long as Germany had any hopes that the Tsar would keep his word and bring France over to the German side, she was willing to make handsome concessions to France in Morocco. But when the pressure of Russian and French Ministers had forced Nicholas II to withdraw his signature, when American intervention under the energetic direction of Theodore Roosevelt was securing the end of the Japanese War, Germany, if she was to reap any benefit from her

activity, must do so in Morocco itself.   In this last policy she was only
in a minor degree successful.   Only Austria gave her any real support
at the Algeciras conference.   Britain defended the French thesis with
great tenacity; the Entente had stood the first strain put on it—and a
secret but decisive event, the threat of war, had been followed by staff
negotiations between Britain and France; begun by a Conservative
Prime Minister they were continued by a Liberal.   If any country was
isolated it was Germany.   In return, the actual situation in Morocco
was left more ambiguous than Delcassé had hoped for.   The Sultan
was not yet reduced to the situation of a Bey of Tunis, and the French
and Spanish rights of intervention were not only limited, they were
regulated by an international agreement which meant that the development of the Moroccan situation which was sure to produce further
opportunities for French action would, at the same time, make that
action of the greatest diplomatic interest to the signatories of the treaty,
especially to the country which had played for such high stakes and
had gained so little.

III

France had been lucky.   The Japanese War, followed by the first
Russian revolution of 1905, the forcing on the Tsar of a parliament
and the struggles between the Duma and the Autocracy, had made
France's ally useless in the European balance of power.   Germany
had, in fact, lost a chance of easy military victory over France, a chance
which grew less with every month that passed, for the Tsardom survived.
Russia began, very slowly at first, to recover from the war—and, excluded from the Far East, to turn her attention to the Balkans where,
of course, she ran across the interests of Austria.   The German
diplomatic difficulties which had plagued Bismarck plagued his
successors.   Vienna and St. Petersburg had to be kept, if possible,
from irreparable hostility, but if a choice had to be made, it would
have to be Vienna.   Worse still, the Anglo-Russian agreements of 1907
meant that the old wedge that might be driven between Britain and
France, the hostility of France's ally, Russia, to France's friend,
Britain, had lost its dividing power.   The Entente of 1907 might be
a good deal less cordial than the Entente of 1904, but it marked un-
mistakably the decision of Britain, if she *had* to take sides, to take the
anti-German side.   From the French point of view, the diplomatic
situation was rapidly improving.   She had a powerful and, as
Algeciras has shown, a dependable friend in Britain, and she had a
convalescent and, as the aftermath of Bjorkö had shown, a moderately
dependable ally in Russia.   Italy, at Algeciras, had not even pretended
to support her nominal ally, Germany, and France did not need to

401

worry seriously any longer about the Italian front, even if the soldiers were not as fully aware of this as were the diplomats.[1]

In Franco-Russian relations, the great power of a debtor was now fully revealed. France was committed to Russian financial stability; about a quarter of French foreign investments were in Russia, mainly in Government loans, and the number of French investors with Russian holdings was over a million and a half. In such circumstances, it was difficult to avoid throwing good money after bad. Despite the obvious shakiness of the Autocracy and the opposition of the Socialists—and of others—to the financial bolstering up of the tottering tyranny, Witte was able to finance his 1906 loans and thus defy the Duma. Not only did Russia blackmail her creditor, she was able to dictate or, at least, strongly to influence the course of French investment in other countries. It was due to a Russian protest that Hungarian loans were no longer admitted to the Paris market; and, in loans to the Balkan states, Russian views were allowed to influence the choice of clients, of Serbia over Bulgaria, for instance. Of course, the forces at work were not exclusively Russian. The fact that the armies of the Balkan League of 1912 were trained and armed by French officers and French firms was largely due to the conditions attached to loans to these countries. Lule Burgas and Kumanovo were victories for the French loan market as well as for the Creusot guns and the French military missions. In the same way, the better relations between France and Italy were reflected in increased French holdings of Italian loans, while, in any case, Italy, unlike Russia, was no longer at the mercy of foreign money markets where Government financing was concerned. By 1914, the fifty-two Russian securities listed on the Paris market and totalling over 12,000,000,000 francs [2] held France firmly to her imperial ally. She could make conditions, that loans should be spent on strategic railways for instance, but that was all.

In her relations with Germany, France might have used her financial power much more adroitly. The privilege of admission to the great source of cheap money, the Paris market, was worth a great deal to a rapidly expanding economy working on a rather narrow credit basis. To make Germany pay for financial privileges in return for concessions over Morocco was a plan attributed to M. Caillaux who, in any case, was not very enthusiastic about Russian loans, and Germany was, at times, ready to talk business. But sentiment and the widespread conviction that financing Germany was merely financing a future

[1] One consequence of the Entente was the withdrawal of British support from Siam. That kingdom had been pursuing, through most of the later part of the nineteenth century, an aggressive policy towards its feeble eastern neighbours in Cambodia and Laos. There was constant friction, but, in 1907, the main aim of French policy was achieved, the two Cambodian provinces occupied by Siam were retroceded and French control of the Mekong was secured, as well as a greater share for France in the development of Siam itself. It was a substantial if not conspicuous gain for the Colonial party.

[2] About £500,000,000 or $2,000,000,000.

enemy were too strong. German firms were, of course, in close connection with French industry, especially in the steel industry, but the savings of the French peasant and bourgeois went, not to foster German war preparations, but to the diminution of the complete unpreparedness for war of Russia.

CHAPTER II

THE PLEASANT LAND OF FRANCE

I

THE Germans have a simile 'as well-off as God in France' which, whatever its exact origin, reveals the awe and envy with which less fortunate lands regarded France before the revolutionary impact of modern industrialism. There were other countries as fertile as France, there was England for example, but no other country was as fertile and as large. The King of France and Navarre, in 1789, ruled as many subjects as the Empress of All the Russias or the Holy Roman Emperor, but how much better worth ruling were the increasingly rich subjects of Louis XVI than the inhabitants of the poverty-stricken lands of the Romanovs and Habsburgs! From the flax and cereals of the north, to the vines, the olives, the oranges of the south, the wealth and variety of French production was incomparable. Bad political and social organization, the backwardness of many regions, the inferiority in technical skill of the south (where the iron plough was still a rarity) to the north, could not weaken the economic strength of a people so industrious, so resourceful, so abundantly provided by nature with the sources of natural wealth. More truly than Virgil's Italy, France was 'magna parens frugum'.

That France did not preserve this superiority was due in some degree to the wars that followed the Revolution; those wars gave England a great start. But that was not the whole story, as the case of Germany showed. The fundamental change that slowed up French relative progress was technical. What France lacked was what suddenly became of overwhelming importance—coal and iron. Coal was not merely relatively scarce in France; it was poor in quality and deposited in small and scattered pockets, hard to work and hard to reach. Only in the north was there the basis for a great modern industrial area. France was not so badly off for iron, but her abundant deposits in Lorraine, because of their high sulphur content, were unusable for modern industrial purposes. Moving from an industrial economy based on wood and iron to one based on coal and steel, France suddenly found herself handicapped, not helped, by nature. Nor was this all, for the Revolution, by greatly accelerating the growth of a peasant proprietary, diminished the supply of helpless, poverty-stricken labourers so opportunely provided for the needs of the new manufacturing class in England and Germany.

French heavy industry was slow to develop and backward in almost every respect. It was thought necessary, not merely to protect it by high tariffs, but by absolute prohibitions of imports. It was not until the Cobden treaty of 1860 with England that competition was legally permitted, and that treaty, sacrificing heavy industrial production of the new type to the needs of the basic French forms of production, wine and silk, showed how strong was the bias in favour of the old forms of economic activity, for, if the treaty had to be imposed by the will of Napoleon III, it was welcomed by the more vocal elements of the class which the Emperor cherished above all others, the owners of the soil of France. Like a Chinese Emperor, the Emperor of the French was the protector of the plough, the hoe, the silkworm.

France was still very rich; war and defeat were to prove that, but she was not rich in the new ways. Her Manchesters, her Pittsburghs, her Essens and Elberfelds were small; progress was turning only a few regions of France into imitations of Lancashire, Westphalia or western Pennsylvania. The growth of French wealth was, as far as export trade was concerned, still based on the skill of highly-trained, highly-individualistic workers, workers on the land or on special raw materials. What two experts said of the price of Burgundies was true of far more than wine. 'Quality, that is the essential cause of the variations of the price of a product which is a monopoly, sought after by the customer because of its fineness and its flavour.' [1] French external commerce was mainly in luxuries and in unique luxuries at that. This, as much as the scarcity of coal and iron, accounted for the relative decline of the French merchant navy. The typical French export was valuable but not bulky, whether it was a case of Romanée Conti, a Worth or Paquin hat or dress, the novels of Zola or the person of Sarah Bernhardt. With a stable population which did not provide even the minimum crude labour force for such new industries as grew up, there was no French equivalent to the mass emigration of British and German and Italian subjects that enriched the United States and the shipping lines. Many emigrants took ship for America at Cherbourg, but few of them in French ships and still fewer of them were French. France was not of the first importance in the new world commerce that was growing so rapidly. She did not want the mass crude imports of wheat, wool and the like that were needed by Britain and Germany and she had no surplus of mass-produced exports, alive or dead.

Even as late as 1906, when high tariffs had encouraged the concentration of capital in the home market and when modern industry was at last taking hold of France, the second most valuable French export

[1] MM. Germain Martin and Paul Martenot.

was wine and the first was silk-goods; the latter largely, though to a decreasing degree, still made from silk grown in France. Other French industries working largely for external markets, cosmetics, early fruit, flowers, luxury sweetmeats, in the aggregate not contemptible items in the international balance of payments, were simple extensions of French agriculture. If the great oak forests of the Centre, planted by Colbert to provide, every hundred and sixty years, timber for the fleet, were now merely relics of the past, the great plain of the Beauce, out of which the Cathedral of Chartres rises, and many other regions of France were still producing wheat on a scale not contemptible even by the standards of Minnesota or Manitoba. Horses and cattle, the highly integrated beet-sugar industry of the north, the sacred names of the great wine regions, the Clos Vougeot, Hermitage, Haut Brion, Châteauneuf du Pape, Cognac and Epernay, seemed to show that the land of France was as fruitful as ever, as great a store of material and moral wealth as it had ever been.

The decline in the French birth-rate had many consequences, but one of the most striking was the effect on the countryside. From the middle of the century on, rural depopulation began to trouble observers, especially those who really believed, what nearly all Frenchmen professed to believe, that the peasantry was the backbone of the nation. The rural population that had been 75·6 per cent. of the total in 1846, had fallen to 64·1 per cent. in 1886 and was to fall to 57·9 per cent. in 1906. And these figures were worse than they looked. For many persons included in the rural population were not directly connected with the land; they were officials, policemen, schoolmasters, *rentiers*, little tradesmen. With the decay of the handy-man on the farm, there was room for more specialized workers, carpenters, wheelwrights and the like in the villages and little towns. If the true farm population was computed, it was shrinking faster than even the census figures showed.[1]

The class that diminished most rapidly was that of the day-labourer who owned a little land of his own. Sometimes, the decline of this class represented a social advance; the labourer had acquired enough land to keep him and no longer needed to go out to work. But more commonly he had sold his scrap of land and had migrated. In some regions economic disaster accounted in great part for the decline in population. In the mountainous parts of western Burgundy, bad prices for wool and timber made life too hard. The ravages of phyl-

---

[1] There were many difficulties in using the comparative figures; the standards of exactness in the early censuses left a good deal to be desired. Thus an apparent rise in the number of women engaged in agriculture merely reflected a more careful discrimination: farmers' wives were now counted as part of the farming population, but the number of unmarried women working on the land was falling. There were, too, minor causes of error in the formal figures. Thus in one region of Burgundy the figures of rural depopulation, bad as they were, would have been worse had it not been for the numerous boarded-out children from Paris sent there by the municipal social services. In some communes they were 10 per cent. of the population.

!oxera ruined many little wine-growers all over central and southern France. Improved communications weakened the economic position of the wine-grower who produced a good local wine that had had its own market, until the railway brought Burgundy and Bordeaux to compete with his speciality. As for the growers of coarse and cheap wines, the disease not only destroyed the vines, but as the purchase of the immune American stocks cost money, made recovery impossible. There was a proletarianization of a large class.[1] When it was discovered that wine could be profitably produced on the sandy shores of the Mediterranean, the new vineyards represented capitalist enterprise on a big scale and, when the competition of the great Algerian bonanza vineyards came in, the day of the small grower was almost over. He sometimes abandoned the fight altogether and grew potatoes or other ignoble crops where once the rows of vines had run; more often he abandoned the land where so little profit was to be made and moved into the towns.

Not all, not nearly all, the rural depopulation was due to economic disaster. Some of the richest and most fertile parts of France were the worst sufferers, and some of the most famous and virile stocks seemed to approach extinction without any very tangible material reason explaining their decline. In lower Normandy and in Gascony, the race seemed doomed to death. In Normandy, excessive drinking added a high death-rate to a low birth-rate to hasten the decline of that 'bold peasantry a country's pride' which 'once destroyed can never be supplied'. If there were not many deserted villages, there were plenty of deserted cottages. For want of workers the most fertile land lost value: a loss which, in turn, weakened the economic strength of the rural bourgeoisie and petty gentry.

There was a sharp, in some places a disastrous, fall in the price of land in the bad years of the early 'eighties, a fall which was just being recovered-from before the beginning of the war of 1914. The loss did not fall on all types of land equally. Where valuable cash crops like beet were possible, the values held up, but in general, arable land suffered much more than pasture. But land was no longer an asset that was sure to increase in value. The traditional French peasant, so land hungry that he was ready for the most desperate labour and the most rigorous thrift to buy an acre or two, was no longer to be found in some regions of France. He did not even care to own his house. That pride in becoming a 'proprietor' which had anchored previous generations to the soil was now not always a strong enough motive to conquer dislike of the dullness, the hardships, the poor monetary returns of work on the land.

In the old days, the poorer regions had exported their surplus popu-

---

[1] Not implausibly, M. Maurras attributes the decline of the Royalist party in Provence to the ruin of the bourgeois by the phylloxera.

lation, not for good but for a season, to the more fertile regions. Brittany, Auvergne, Flanders from their teeming populations had provided labour for other provinces. Sometimes the labour exported was not farm labour but special crafts. The Creuse was famous for its wandering masons. But now these regions were less ready to supply seasonal labour. It was not that they could or did hold their population. There was still a great Breton emigration, but it was not an annual movement to the farms for the harvest, but to the new industrial centres for life. A mountain region like the Aveyron had half its young men living outside the department, most of them little likely to return.

France still needed seasonal labourers, but more and more she got them from outside. If the nomadic workers of the Cambrésis still moved south to hoe the beet, then to reap the wheat in the great plains round Paris, the 'Camberlots' were followed by Belgian Flemings, organized in little squads with a French-speaking leader. In the east, before the war of 1914, the first Polish labourers were beginning to appear, while in the eastern half of the Midi, Italians and, in the western half, Spaniards were coming in to replace the vanished Frenchmen. There were even attempts to bring in Kabyle labourers from the mountains of Algeria. The immigrants, however indispensable, forced down the wages of the surviving French labourers and still further accelerated the flight from the land.

Yet the productivity of the land did not fall: it rose. The disappearance of a cheap and abundant labour force compelled landowners to turn to machinery. It was not surprising that between 1892 and 1908, the number of reapers and binders in a Gascon department (Haute Garonne) rose from 60 to 1,200. The bigger proprietors were forced to experiment with new fertilizers, new crops, new seeds. It was easier now to do away with the remnants of the strip system. The Revolution had held up the French enclosure movement and there were still many tiny properties scattered over a wide area and jealously watched by their owners. To avoid manuring a neighbour's land, strips were left to nature to fertilize. A high level of cultivation was impossible; even in a department as near Paris as the Oise, on the Montagne de Liancourt the strip system made the use of the plough impossible.

The tenant-farmers who, in the north, were the most enterprising exploiters of the soil were now in a good bargaining position. Leases became longer; eighteen years was not uncommon, and as it was customary to negotiate the renewal of the lease three years before it fell in, it was possible for the outgoing tenant to deal on equal terms, not only with his landlord but with the new tenant. In some regions a kind of tenant-right sprang up. The peasant proprietor usually worked much less land than the lease-holder did; he had less capital and less interest in improvements, but the big capitalist farmer, whether owner or tenant, was now an industrialist in temper. Gone were the days when an annotated edition of the *Georgics* was regarded as a suitable method of inserting a few notions of scientific farming into a purely classical and mathematical education. Each department had had, since the secure establishment of the Republic, a departmental professor of agriculture, and there were demonstration plots, model farms and travelling demonstrations. But the obstinacy of the small farmer made him less ready to learn than was desirable, as his shortage of capital debarred him from some improvements, while his ferocious independence made the organization of co-operatives very difficult. There were regions where co-operation succeeded brilliantly: among the dairy farmers of the west; the wine- and olive-growers of Provence and Languedoc; and among the cheese-makers of the Jura—where it was an old story. But compared with Denmark or Belgium, if not with England or America, co-operation was backward in rural France. Yet the worst years were over by 1914; there had been a rapid rise in the standard of living; the worst losses from the crash in land values had been recovered; the economically weakest members of the rural community had been swept off the land.

There were still black patches. The wine-growers of Languedoc and of parts of Champagne had serious price grievances which they brought to the public attention by strikes and riots. More ominous, for those who thought of the rural population as necessarily politically 'healthy' and 'stable', were the first inroads of trade-unionism of an extreme type among the farm labourers, especially in the Centre, and the rising tide of revolt among the share-croppers, the *métayers*, whose bargain with the owner of the land was likely to be one-sided.

The wood-cutters of the Centre, badly underpaid and exploited by middlemen, were often on strike in the last years of the nineteenth century. There were local trade unions and they were generally successful, but their success brought about an almost equally complete organization of the employers; and the fact that so great a part of the forests of France belong to the State complicated matters further. The class war had entered Arcady.

The growth of capitalist wine-growing in the south had as a corollary the growth of a rural labouring class without much hope of escaping from the wage system and consequently with plenty of reason for combative organization. There were strikes in such regions as that round Béziers and a marked shift to the extreme Left in local elections. Optimistic Socialists threatened and timid proprietors feared something like a new *Jacquerie*. But the unions were, as a rule, not long-lived, and the movement merged with that of the general protest against the low price of wine and other general economic grievances led by Marcellin Albert which culminated in the famous mutiny of the seventeenth infantry.[1]

[1] See p. 424.

The share-cropping system in France was very old and, despite the criticisms of many experts, showed no signs of disappearing in the pre-war years. It could work well, for both parties, where the bargain was concluded on really equal terms and where the proprietor was personally interested in the land he owned. But in some regions, especially in the Centre, between the working share-cropper and the owner there was a middleman, who bore the odious name of 'Farmer-General'.[1] The middleman dealt with the landowner on one hand and the would-be tenant on the other. He was a speculator: and in his hands the ownership of the land appeared in its ugliest aspect, as a naked property right without any social obligations and without any very obvious social utility. The *métayers*, bidding against each other, were forced to accept annual leases; they were forced to buy fertilizers and machinery from the same middleman; there was nothing to set-off against this tyranny, since the middlemen usually refused to make repairs. Some of the worst abuses of eighteenth- and nineteenth-century Ireland were repeated in twentieth-century France. Indeed, these abuses had been one of the great rural grievances of 1789. But the burden which was thought most intolerable was the 'settler's tax'. The whole principle of *métayage* seemed to be summed up in its etymology: it was a half-and-half system; the owner of the land provided the land; the tenant provided the labour; the results of this partnership were equally divided. That, in addition, a payment in cash should be enforced was considered a breach of natural justice and was far more resented than were the extra payments in kind enforced in the west. It was no wonder that the region where the cash payment was most common and most burdensome, the Bourbonnais, should have been for a century past notorious for its Left politics.

In the region round Paris, the social problems of agriculture were not those of the *métayers* but of the labourers. This fertile region, so near a great market, was in the hands of small proprietors working their own land and of great capitalist farmers holding on long lease, in some cases working the same farm for generations. The socially and politically disturbing body here was the farm labourer working for the capitalist farmer. He had many grievances; he was often so badly lodged that he openly admitted he was better off in the Army; his food, when it was supplied, was monotonous, and he wanted and did not always get what he thought his due, a ration of wine or cider with each meal. He also wanted a rise in wages or, still more, a regular wage, for more and more he was employed on piece-work, paid a good deal at the most busy times and little or nothing in the slack season. He was assimilated in many ways to the town worker and reacted in much the same way. The great strikes that broke out in 1906 and in subsequent years were,

---

[1] The Farmers-General of the old régime were the tax-farmers; their rapacity was part of the historical tradition of all Frenchmen.

in some regions, directed against piece-work which the rural labourer was coming to regard with the same dislike as the factory worker. The militant trade-unionists of the Paris region saw a chance to spread their syndicalist doctrines, and there were riots, attacks on farmhouses, mass intimidation of blacklegs, all the warlike apparatus of an industrial strike. Taken by surprise, the farmers yielded, and there followed on this success a sudden spread of trade-unionism among the farm workers. But all agricultural unions were shallowly rooted; they never enrolled more than a small minority of the farm workers and these chiefly among specialists, the forest workers of the Centre, the market-gardeners of the Paris district. By 1914, rural unionism was little more important than it had been before 1906.

In the year of her great ordeal, from an agricultural point of view, France was better off than her chief enemy or than her chief ally. She was normally capable of feeding herself; she ranked next to the United States and Russia, though at a distance, as a wheat producer, and against the decline in the production of flax, hemp, silk, wool, could be set great increases in cattle, cereals, wine and fruit production. If her rural population was declining, it was more important than was the case in either Germany or England. It was from the land that there came most of the infantrymen who lived, and fought, and died so hard. In Macedonia, where the English infantryman was so often at a loss, the tough French peasant from Auvergne or the Jura was soon as much at home as the Serbians or Greeks. Despite the loss of so much of her most fertile and best-farmed land, France, in 1914–18, was not at the mercy of blockade and counter-blockade. There were in 1914 many urban critics who thought that the peasant was pampered, by protection, by subsidy, by praise; that he was too conservative, too individualistic, too little affected by the great currents of the age. In peace-time, most of these charges could be justified, but in war-time the great fault of the French peasant was that he was now not numerous enough; there were not enough men to fill the ranks, not enough women to feed the nation in arms. Or rather, there were just enough, to hold out to the end.

II

The speciality of French industry for centuries had been luxuries, and French predominance in the agreeable arts of life was greater in the nineteenth than in any previous century. In all the western lands the growth of a great new middle class provided a market for all kinds of luxuries that, in previous centuries, could be sold only to great nobles, to financiers, to a few great merchants. In place of Lord Bristol making the grand tour and leaving his name to innumerable hotels, there were thousands of middle-class tourists, less lavish in the individual case, but far more important in the mass than a hundred English peers. Many countries benefited by the rise of the tourist traffic; the hitherto grim and despised Switzerland more than most, but France was the greatest gainer of all.

Paris had been a rendezvous of Europe since the thirteenth century, but now she surpassed herself. As a centre of intellectual as well as of other fashions, she was unrivalled. The modern Cagliostro, Candide, or Casanova found in Paris what his predecessors had found in Venice, diversion or victims. By the end of the Second Empire it was already true that 'good Americans when they die go to Paris' and more and more Americans were in a position to anticipate death. It was not only Paris that benefited. New watering-places, Trouville, Biarritz, brought visitors who would have been bored by Pau or Cannes. The unification and moralization of Germany, with its adverse effect on such gambling resorts as Baden-Baden, made a place for Monte Carlo in the providentially independent principality of Monaco. The little Italian town of Nizza became the greatest tourist city of the world and, as Nice, became and remained one of the largest French cities, more populous than Nantes or Bordeaux. Vichy, Aix-les-Bains, and the rest replaced Homburg and the other German spas as the greatest of inland watering-places; and to the world of feminine fashion, if not to the improvers of horse-breeding, Auteuil and Longchamps became more important than Ascot or Goodwood.

In addition to the temporary or permanent pleasure seekers, France, and above all Paris, became the Mecca of artists. Thousands of young men and women began to think of being artists as, in an earlier century, they might have thought of being monks and nuns. There were some genuine vocations among the many false ones, but real and bogus artists had this in common—they all regarded Paris as the one place to learn or practise their craft. Gone were the days when a visit to Rome or Florence or, odd as it may seem, to Düsseldorf, was essential to the English or American aspirant to the status of artist. In the visual arts, Paris was now as dominant as any Italian city had ever been. Not only were most of the greatest as well as the most popular artists French, but those who were not were profoundly influenced by France, and for shorter or longer periods dwellers within the sacred precincts. Van Gogh, Sisley, Picasso, Modigliani were almost as much the glory of France as Monet, Manet, Cézanne or Degas. The immediate economic result of the work of Sisley or Cézanne was not great; it was only the fact that he was heir to a sizable fortune that saved Cézanne from the depressing life and early death of Sisley. France had it both ways; she had the artists who, in the long run, were to be the best lock-up investments, for dealers like Vollard as well as for Moscow and Philadelphia millionaires. But she had also the immediately popular artists, Doré, Detaille, Carolus Duran and Van Dongen. More wealthy foreigners than Mr.

Thaddeus Sholto helped to enrich France by being 'partial to the modern French school', meaning by that, those later Corots and the Bouguereaus of all epochs which are so poorly esteemed to-day.

Another source of French wealth and influence was the invention, or the description of the life of the professional 'artist', in letters or life as well as in paint, by Murger. The new sea-coast of Bohemia was in Paris, and from George du Maurier to Rudyard Kipling, George Moore and Ernest Hemingway, literary men encouraged the migration to Paris of large numbers of persons, the expense of whose social and artistic education was an important invisible export for France.[1]

Even more profitable, economically, was the growth of the old Paris industry of female dressmaking. Paris had long been the leader in fashion, but fashion had been less versatile and the concern of fewer persons than it became in the nineteenth century. To dress his wife in the latest Paris fashions was even more the duty of an American millionaire than to fill his French château on Fifth Avenue or Nob Hill with bad French pictures. Not only the dressmakers, but the jewellers, the makers of cosmetics, the designers of furniture, made Paris the Mecca of rich women with money to spend, and the heroine of *Gentlemen Prefer Blondes* showed sound economic sense when she concentrated her attention on Coty, Cartier and the other historic names. Paquin and Worth were symbolic names in the total French economy, worthy of a place beside Clicquot, Panhard and Hennessy.

The immense importance of these luxury trades helped to maintain in France the tradition of the small workshop, of the semi-independent producer, of the man who could do something better than anybody else or something that nobody else could do. Even as late as 1870, Paris was still overwhelmingly a city of small workshops, and the lists of *communards* which give their occupations show how far from being a homogeneous, factory-organized, uniform proletariat was the working population that fought, unknowingly, for the Marxian tradition of the future revolution. Not only in Paris did the small shop survive; watchmakers in the Jura, knife-makers in the Forez, silk-weavers in the Lyonnais gave to French industry and French life its stability, its resistance to modernization, to trustification, to what most of the outer world thought progress.

Yet even France could not resist the spirit of the age. Modern capitalist industry on a great scale was beginning to affect French society profoundly under the Empire and it advanced with giant strides under the Republic. The application of power-driven machinery to many industries hitherto employing only human labour came later in France than in England or Germany. But the hand-looms that had

[1] In an age when Hiram Power's nude 'Greek Slave' could only be shown in parts of its sculptor's native land if wrapped in muslin, and when the schools of the Royal Academy in London did not allow persons under twenty-one to draw from the nude unless they were married, it was easy for Paris to attract custom.

eked out the incomes of the labourers in the northern departments were destroyed by the new power-looms. Even industries like lace-making, that were still monopolized by home workers, suffered badly from the competition of machine-made substitutes. The best lace of Bayeux or other centres could not be successfully copied in a factory, but cheap machine-made lace destroyed the market for the hand-made. All but the most expensive pottery suffered in the same way. Old potteries might continue to flourish, but machines largely replaced men. Yet these changes not only came later in France than elsewhere, they came less completely. Only in the heavy industries, in mining and metallurgy, did the great capitalist unit completely replace the old workshop. There was still room, if narrowing room, for the small master with a few workers or the individual worker employing only himself. This section of the petty bourgeoisie resisted, with more success than one would have thought possible, the rivalry of the factory system.

Another section of the lower middle-class that suffered from new methods was that of the shopkeepers. Paris was a pioneer in the development of the department store; the great shops, Samaritaine, Printemps and the rest were among the sights of the city, and the American tourists of the *Quaker City* type spent as much time in the Grands Magasins du Louvre as in the Museum. Every sizable provincial town had its imitation or branch of a great Paris shop, and there followed the growth of the chain grocer's shops, sometimes faintly disguised as co-operatives, chains with hundreds of branches whose managers increased the numbers of the salariat if not of the proletariat. The son or daughter of the lower middle-class family, forced to become an employee in any case, naturally preferred, if possible, to be an employee of the State. The great fortunes of the millionaire drapers and grocers were accumulated at the social cost of weakening the ambition and tenacity of the lower middle-class, while on the other hand, they not only in general reduced the costs of distribution, but by adopting fixed prices saved time and diminished interest in purchasing.

Forced by the quasi free-trade of the Cobden treaty to modernize their equipment, French manufacturers in the 'sixties held their own, though with difficulty. The return to protection assured them of a home market and, in some branches of industry, above all in those connected with shipping, the Government helped by actual subsidies. There was a circular process at work. High tariffs on raw materials, such as steel, made it impossible for French shipyards to compete with English, so they were subsidized. High prices for French ships made it impossible for French shipowners to compete, so they were subsidized. The subsidy for shipbuilding had one absurd effect, for since it was more easily earned by building sailing ships than by building steamers, France saw her sailing fleet doubled at a time when in all other countries the sailing ship was obsolete. And however well adapted for some forms of traffic, like the transport of aluminium ore from New Caledonia, the sailing ships were, they were in general a poor investment, as was finally recognized in 1903, when the subsidy law was amended. But the main cause of the decline of France from her place as the second maritime power has been given above; she did not export or import the bulky cargoes which were the basis of profitable shipowning and, consequently, French shipowners found it hard to compete in the open market of international transport. For her size and wealth France had a smaller overseas trade than her rivals and the proportion of that trade carried in French ships was only 30 per cent. on the eve of the last great war.

In certain industries France was hardly a competitor at all. She was not, for instance, in any way able to compete with the German dye industry; her old vegetable dyeing industry, the madder dyes which were used for the red trousers of the infantry, was killed by the competition of the German synthetic dyes. The woollen industry was not in such a bad way; its output grew considerably and thanks to high tariffs it was able to monopolize the home market, but it was organized largely on an export basis, as its carding and spinning sections were more important than its weaving, and even the weaving section was more important than the home market justified. But in the early years of the twentieth century, the foreign market for French woollen goods was being captured by English and German firms and, at best, the industry was stagnant except in the highest luxury branches.

The great French textile industry was silk and that was still flourishing, though it was beginning to be threatened by artificial substitutes. But a lowering of prices, a great increase in consumption and the invention of mixtures of wool and silk kept the trade prosperous as a whole, if the lot of the hand-loom weaver, who was still strong in the industry, was increasingly hard. In cotton, high tariffs secured a home and imperial market that might have been hard to find on a strictly competitive basis.

The location of industry was often determined not only by tradition, which had put the woollen mills in Flanders, or by political changes which had transferred so many Alsatian cotton mills across the new frontier, but by mere accident. It was the chance that a kinsman of the Mackintosh family settled in Auvergne that made Clermont-Ferrand the centre of a French rubber industry which replaced the declining macaroni factories of the region, and it was the return from America to Fougères of an emigrant to the United States, that resulted in the establishment there of modern shoe-manufacture with hired American machinery.

In the development of industry, modern machine-tools and other forms of machinery were of increasing importance, and France, in many sections of industry, was dependent on her competitors for machinery.

415

Her textile mills drew a great part of their equipment from Germany and England, her agricultural machinery was mainly American. But in one growing mechanical industry France was a pioneer. The motor-car industry was one in which all countries started at scratch; the general excellence of French roads (by the standards of those days) made the new invention more immediately useful than in some other countries, and France became one of the great automobile producers of the world. In 1913, 35,000 workers produced what was, for the time, the enormous number of 45,000 cars a year.

Not all the developments of technique were either to the disadvantage of France or not to her advantage. The growth of electrically-driven machinery provided for France a new source of power, the 'white coal' of her abundant water resources. In the Alps, the Jura, the Vosges, the Pyrenees, that is on all her frontiers but the north, France had valuable reserves of power and, in the mountains of the Massif Central, there was another. With the improvement of long-distance transmission systems, these sources of power were made available in some of the industrial areas, while new industries, like aluminium, went to the scattered sources of power. But the full exploitation of water power was postponed until after the war of 1914. Coal was still cheap enough and abundant enough to provide the main source of power, although the proportion of that coal which was of French origin was steadily falling.

More dramatic and important was the result of the application of the Gilchrist-Thomas process to the iron deposits of Lorraine. In drawing the frontier of 1871, the Germans had, as they thought, secured for themselves all the valuable mineral resources of the divided province. But bad geology misled them as to the location of the main deposits and, when the new process made it possible to use the Lorraine sulphurous ores, it was discovered that in Lorraine, and mainly in French Lorraine, was a source of iron ore second only to the Minnesota ranges. From 1886, France, hitherto so poor in the resources necessary for a modern industrial society, became one of the key countries. Above all, her position became decisive for the German steel industry. The marriage of Lorraine iron and Saar and Westphalian coal was a necessity for both parties, and close financial links were created between the French mining companies of the Briey basin and the great German steel cartel. The discovery transformed Lorraine. Iron mining on this scale implied capitalist industry in its most developed form and the Lorraine iron-masters were soon great powers in the land. But the development was not confined to mining; a great steel industry grew up on the spot, eclipsing the older centres as far as the production of metal was concerned, if its manufacture was still mainly an affair of places like Saint-Étienne and Le Creusot.

Financially, the steel manufacturers dominated the new iron-field;

they owned the ore and disposed of it as they thought fit, to their own steel works or to their competitors in Germany. Steel making was an old industry in Lorraine, the *Comité des Forges* that grouped together the steel producers of the region had been founded in 1864. But the scale was now quite different. Great vertical combines grew up covering every stage of the industry, and the old ironmaster family of Wendel became leaders of the new order. The name first appears in the industry in 1701, but it was now as much a symbol of the French iron industry as Carnegie had been of the American, and the special character of the Lorraine industry was underlined by the fact that the M. de Wendel in France had as partner Herr von Wendel in Germany. Across the frontier that angered patriots so much, modern industry stepped without much . difficulty. There was a good deal of easy indignation, but the relationship between the German and French industry was not only imposed by the inability of the French coal-fields to provide enough coke for the steel mills, but by the fact that the French steel industry could not use all the available ore. Alone among the great steel-producing nations before 1914, France was a great exporter of ore. Her reserves were estimated at nearly a fifth of the available world supply, so she could afford it.

In industry as in agriculture, a basic fact was the stabilization of the population. In 1870 Germany and France had had approximately the same population. In both, the birth-rate fell rapidly between 1870 and 1914, but in 1870 the French birth-rate was already lower than that of Germany in 1914. France had a long start in the limitation of births, which meant that her population was older than that of other nations as well as proportionately smaller. In 1914, the two nations which had been equal in 1870 were now far apart; Germany's population was approaching 65,000,000, France's was around 40,000,000. Great Britain and Austria-Hungary, as well as Germany and Russia, were now more populous than France, and Italy was rapidly overtaking her.

The reality was in fact worse than these figures suggested. There were fewer French men and women than forty years before. The balance of births and deaths was about equal; in some years there was a positive loss. The number of children per marriage was only a little over two. But for immigration, France would have been on the way to depopulation. The main sources of immigration were Belgium and Italy, and there were always around a million foreigners resident in France, the children counting as Frenchmen and new immigrants keeping the figure constant. The Lorraine iron-field, located in a province whose population was falling, had to recruit its labour force from Germany, Belgium, Luxembourg and Poland. It was a humiliating contrast with the neighbouring Saar where there was a native industrial population.

The reasons for the fall in population were social and psychological.

Those departments where the Church was strong were still populous; where it was weak, no amount of preaching of patriotic duty had any effect. The lay state had many good things to its credit, but it was unable to prevent, even if it did not actually promote, a great and distressing historical event—the rapid decline of the proportion of Frenchmen to other Europeans. In a rather timid way, attempts were made to encourage large families by fiscal privileges, but the French taxation system did not then easily lend itself to such measures. Indeed, as it so largely depended on indirect taxation, it could only aggravate the burdens of the father of a large family. Attempts to preach the virtues of a higher birth-rate were often assailed as clerical or militarist propaganda. Nor were the efforts of great industrialists to encourage fertility much better received. As a rule the employers who, by family bonuses and other subsidies, direct or indirect, or by housing schemes and nurseries, attempted to make parenthood less burdensome, were zealous Catholics, and their efforts were associated in the minds of the suspicious and stubbornly independent French workman with attacks on his freedom of action. Too many employers were crude practitioners of the doctrine of Le Play that made the employer a sort of feudal chief of his workmen. A man of great ability, sanctity and sincerity like Léon Harmel, might make this rôle tolerable, even welcome, to his dependents, but there were not many Harmels. The French worker wanted to be left alone, not to be coerced or bribed into having more children, or going to Mass, or anything else. Yet the idea of family allowances, destined to an important post-war rôle, was taking hold in some highly organized industries where it was possible to spread the cost over the whole industry in a way that did not penalize the individual employer or the father who, if his high wages had had to come from one pocket, would soon have been unemployable.

With a stable or diminishing population, with resources for the new machine industry inadequate except in the case of iron ore, with the very merits of the population, its tenacious individualism and its high degree of ingenious initiative handicaps in a world calling for more and more robots (to use a word not then known), France seemed to fill a less important place in the economic world than her past or than the brilliance of her contemporary contribution to civilization made seem natural. Her industries were, in general, organized on a smaller scale than those of her neighbours; with few exceptions, they were less modern in methods and equipment; and, momentous fact, they were nearly all on the frontier. Fertile, self-sufficient in most of the necessities of life, with greater resources than her population could fully use, France in 1914 seemed stagnant, an easy victim of more dynamic, more modern, more enterprising nations.

CHAPTER III

THUNDER ON THE LEFT

I

THE trade-union movement that grew slowly in France after the Commune and not very rapidly even after the full legalization of union activity in 1884, was originally, as a national movement, little more than a side-show of Guesdism. It was political in aim, and it asserted that the political conquest of the State was the necessary preliminary to any bettering of the lot of the workers. But Guesde was not able, in the unions any more than in the more purely political organizations, to impose his arid and pessimistic doctrine on all the militants; and the foundation, in 1895, of the *Confédération Générale du Travail*,[1] the 'C.G.T.', marked the triumph of the preachers of industrial action over the politically-minded Guesdists. The new body was weak in numbers and resources, but it was destined to command the loyalties of French working-class militants until 1914.

Parallel with and in rivalry to the national federations of trade unions were the *Bourses du Travail*. As their name suggests, they were supposed to be labour exchanges; on the analogy of the Stock Exchange they were to collect information about the day-to-day price of labour. But in addition, they were to be centres of workers' education, social life, trade-union organization, and, according to their historian, Pelloutier, to be the instrument of the workers' liberation. As labour exchanges, they were often subsidized by municipalities, which was a considerable advantage in a country where dues-paying was often regarded as servile. But this had disadvantages, for the municipality might and sometimes did try to confine the *Bourses* to the narrow duties of a labour exchange and, as far as the workers' movement in a town had become dependent on the *Bourse* and the *Bourse* on the subsidies, the movement was at the mercy of local politicians. They might display an unworthy suspicion of the book-keeping methods of the *Bourse* as was done at Dijon; the Municipal Council might change colour as happened in Paris; the Prefect might insist on the observation of legal rules that were hampering to a semi-revolutionary organization. Almost all the *Bourses*, sooner or later, suffered from their connection

[1] General Confederation of Labour.

with the local authorities, suffered by the reduction of grants or their abolition, or by the actual suppression of the *Bourse* as happened in Paris in 1906. But for all their difficulties, the *Bourses* performed a useful function. In many small towns the national federations of the trade unions had little authority or utility. In the *Bourse* all the leading militants of the crafts could meet and get to know each other. If the municipality was suspicious it was sometimes possible to run a parallel organization to the *Bourse*; the *Bourse* obeyed all the rules and got the money, but the real organization, run by the men who ran the *Bourses*, was free to do as it pleased.

Within the trade-union movement, two types of unions were in conflict. According to the law of 1884, trade unions, like any other organization, had to keep accounts, lists of members, names of officers and in other ways submit to Government inspection. The authors of the law looked forward, so they said, to the growth in France of stable, wealthy, highly organized unions on the English model. Some unions did develop on those lines; they accumulated funds and acquired a fairly effective control over the working of the industry. A sample of this type was the great printing union, the 'Fédération du Livre'. But such unions were not admired or desired by all militants. A union that had large funds had thereby given hostages to fortune; its funds could be impounded by the Government if it turned to revolutionary action; and a strong, rich, national union could be run only by a bureaucracy which was distasteful to the average highly individualist militant. There was thus a conflict between the rich, centralized and rather conservative unions and the small, poor and often short-lived militant unions. The militants were, or said they were, sceptical of the value of mechanical organization, large and regular subscriptions, and attempts to get all the workers to join. The really militant workers in any industry, it was said, were always a minority. If all the workers joined the unions, the militants would be outvoted and compromises would be forced on them. Strikes brought about by small active minorities, subsidized by special funds collected while the battle was on, were more likely to be successful than strikes fought, after hesitations and negotiations by amorphous bodies, led by union bureaucrats and subsidized by accumulated funds. Rich unions would avoid strikes to save their funds.

What could small unions of workers do against their employers or against organized capitalist society? They could use 'direct action'. Although this phrase came to mean in the common usage of politics and polemics, violent, extra-legal action, the theorists of trade-union tactics originally meant by it merely any kind of union activity. It was, according to Émile Pouget, 'simply trade-union activity . . . any spontaneous or considered manifestation of working-class decision'. It was easier to say what was *not* direct action; political action was indirect action, the use of political means to attain class ends was indirect action —and it was, if not always condemned, at least always highly suspect. This disapproval of political action did not mean that the workers had no concern with the State. If, by their militancy, they could intimidate the State into making concessions that was all to the good, since the concession was squeezed out of the State by direct action.

The phrase, however, came to be associated with a special type of union activity. It was associated with various forms of sabotage, from 'strikes on the job' (the careful and obstructive obedience of all regulations by railwaymen for instance) to deliberately bad work, of which one famous example was that recommended to barbers, the infliction of non-fatal cuts on the clients of the employers! But the final weapon was the 'general strike', the paralysis of bourgeois society by the concerted action of the indispensable workers of the basic industries.

In the campaign for the adoption of the general strike as a substitute for direct revolutionary action of the old Blanquist type, as well as for the dangerous and deceptive method of political and parliamentary action, the chief orator was a young Breton lawyer, Aristide Briand, who had been at school with Pelloutier and who was the mouthpiece of the theorist of the *Bourses*. His eloquence and his extraordinary powers of personal charm made him a danger to the regular politicians in the unions and in the Socialist parties. He was a Pied Piper whose piping seemed, at times, almost as seductive as that of Jaurès in the ears of the French workers. The existence of two rival groupings of the not very numerous body of organized workers was obviously absurd and, in 1902, the *Bourses* were nominally absorbed by the C.G.T. But not only was the new organization organized on a double system of local *Bourses* grouping all the unions of an area, as well as a national organization by industries, the united organization was deeply marked by the doctrines of Pelloutier. It was hostile to politicians and in favour of incessant warfare with the employers, especially through the method of the general strike.

The new spirit among the militant workers found its prophet (after the event) in Georges Sorel. Of sound bourgeois origin, a graduate of the École Polytechnique, a retired State engineer, Sorel was no more a proletarian than Marx. But like many members of the bourgeoisie, he was contemptuous of the ideals and practices of his own class. Although he was a Marxian after his own fashion, Sorel, like so many French revolutionary thinkers, was at least as much in the tradition of Proudhon as of Marx. He, like Proudhon, was an unashamed moralist, the pursuer of an ideal, the believer in the utility of myths. He was to call Marxism a kind of 'social poetry', and his own doctrine which reached its classical form in the *Reflections on Violence* [1] was marked by an epic character. He idealized the workers who, in their day-to-day

---

[1] Published in 1906.

struggle with the capitalist class, above all in the semi-warlike action of the strike, were revealing themselves as the new ruling class and training themselves to be it. The workers were better than the bourgeoisie; they were the makers of the new society; that was the basis of their right, not any sentimental democratic doctrine. For the doctrine of the sovereignty of the democratic state was just a new version of the divine right of kings.

It was round the doctrine of the general strike that Sorel's teaching centred. By the use of the general strike, the militant workers exercised their maximum power of pressure against the bourgeois state. It was not certain that the pressure would be enough, but the encouragement of the 'myth' of the strike among the workers fostered in them the proper fighting spirit and saved them from the seductions of parliamentary manœuvring. What would be the effect of the failure of a general strike, of the discovery that the myth was merely a myth, was a question that Sorel, who after all was a bourgeois seeking a heroic element in modern life, hardly concerned himself with.[1] It is, indeed, not for his influence on the active labour movement or as an interpreter of the labour movement to the public that Sorel is significant. But his cult of violence, of the heroic, his contempt for the timid rationalism of the dominant Radicalism marked him as a contemporary of Barrès (with his cult of energy), of Bergson (with his depreciation of the mere intellect), of Maurras (with his love of violence, his contempt for formal democracy). As with the *Action Française*, it was not in France that the new doctrine found its most zealous adherents, but in Italy, where it served as the philosophical basis of revolutionary socialist action before becoming the basis of one side of the doctrines of fascism.

In the same year as saw the publication of the *Reflections on Violence*, the C.G.T. adopted the programme known as 'the Charter of Amiens'. It was deeply marked by the hostility of the old *Bourses* to parliamentary action for immediate reforms, a policy which still had defenders from the strongly Guesdist regions of the North. The general strike was to be the weapon which would liberate the workers, not any parliamentary intrigues or alliances. The reckless launching of strikes, with their natural sequel of violence, made the activities of the C.G.T. a nuisance to the more sedate Socialist leaders, especially to the deputies among them, and made Socialist relations with the Radicals very difficult. This was especially the case after the Confederation made anti-militarism its main activity. Its *Manuel du Soldat* was highly subversive of discipline, at any rate in intention, for, seen from the point of view of the C.G.T., the Army was simply the main bulwark of the exploiting capitalist state.

The hostility of the programme of the *Confédération Générale du*

[1] There is a curious parallel between the doctrine of the offensive at all costs as taught by Grandmaison and the myth of the general strike. Cf. p. 469.

Travail to open collaboration with any political party was partly caused by fear of estranging non-political workers, but much more by a fear that active participation by the unions in politics meant the flooding of the *cadres* by ambitious politicians on the make and the use of the unions as part of the electoral machine which sent climbing bourgeois to the Chamber, but did nothing else that was very clearly beneficial to the workers. This scepticism might have been lessened had the result of political activity been more obvious. It had been the calculation of Jaurès that once the clerical menace had been successfully crushed, the Radicals, for want of an active programme of social reform, would be forced to give way to the Socialists or, if they did not, to accept the Socialist programme or a great part of it. But in gratitude for the saving of the Republic, or in irritated contempt for the purely negative attitude of the Right, the electors in 1906, in addition to increasing the strength of the unified Socialists, greatly increased the strength of the Radicals. Clemenceau was able to ignore the attack of Jaurès as long as his own party stuck by him. He was even able to rub in the fact that Radicals and Socialists differed on fundamental questions; they might unite to defend the Republic and laicity, but they were separated by the deep gulf of property rights.

Outside the Chamber, the militants did not make things easier for Jaurès. There were repeated strikes and riots in which the Government took a high line, enforcing the law, preventing attacks on non-strikers and forcing Jaurès to choose between frightening the Radical bourgeoisie and alienating the workers. The parliamentary Socialists could hardly defend the violence and they could certainly not appear to condone the vigorous enforcement of the law which resulted in such distressing episodes as the firing on the crowd at Draveil. Such an event enabled Clemenceau to attack Jaurès as an agitator leading ignorant men to violence and, at the same time, lent plausibility to the argument of the extremists who said that the bourgeois state was the enemy of the workers and could be nothing else: that it was a Republic mattered not at all. Despite the fine flourishes, the programme of social reform, income tax, old age pensions remained a mere programme; it did not become law. The legislative machine seemed to be impotent where the workers were concerned but highly efficient where the deputies were concerned, for the same Chamber that could do nothing for the people hastily and secretly raised the salaries of its members from 9,000 to 15,000 francs.[1] Such a salary seemed princely to the average peasant or worker, and his jealousy of the wealth of the deputies increased as his opinion of their probity went down. The Socialist party taxed the salaries of its deputies, but the tax was very small; the chance of being elected a deputy was still very attractive even if it led to no more than that. And it often led to much more.

---

[1] From £360 ($1,800) to £600 ($3,000).

There was Millerand, who had built up a great practice at the Bar, helped, it was universally believed, by his political prestige and power. There was Viviani prospering the same way. Briand was not so obviously profiting as a lawyer, but he was a Minister and part of a Government that repressed the workers who now acted as he had talked.

Nor was the alliance with the Radicals on political questions very secure. One of the promises made by the victors in the Affair had been the reform of courts-martial, and the Clemenceau Government introduced a bill to that effect. But the wine-growers of Languedoc, suffering from a crisis of local overproduction and from the competition of Algeria, had broken out in a series of riots. Troops sent to restore order were drawn from the local regiment, the 17th Infantry, and they had mutinied, refusing to fire on the mobs. The Government had not taken severe measures; it had merely sent the regiment off to Tunis; but the mutiny frightened many moderate Radicals and the bill for reforming courts-martial was abandoned. It seemed to be no time to be tampering with military discipline. The affair of the 17th revealed a spirit in the Army detestable to the Jacobin at the head of the Government; he was willing to make concessions to the indignant wine-growers, but the Army was as sacred to the old enemy of the Generals as it had been to the most zealous anti-Dreyfusards. Did not Clemenceau make a zealous Catholic, a man with a Jesuit brother, head of the Higher War School, putting Colonel Foch in charge of the training of the future chiefs of the Army in full knowledge that he was as clerical as any protégé of Père du Lac? Had not the Prime Minister gone back to his native province of La Vendée and there celebrated the warrior virtues both of his own party, the Blues, and of the misguided Chouans, the Royalists? After all they were the same race, 'the last square of the Celts, of the Gauls, facing both the armies of Rome and the hordes of Germany; often beaten, but never surrendering'. Even had Jaurès been less sincere in his detestation of military glory, less convinced that it was an enemy of the true Republic of the workers, he would have been forced to resist such appeals to the combative patriotism of which Frenchmen were only now being cured by the action of his party.

The clash between the Clemenceau Government and the militants on the Left was not confined to mere doctrinal questions. The C.G.T., with its doctrine laid down in the Charter of Amiens and provided with a very dogmatic leader in Victor Griffuelhes, was in a decidedly combative mood. It fell foul of the Government by its attempts to organize the lesser civil servants, who had very serious grievances to complain of. Wage scales, promotion, terms of service were all chaotic; political influence was rampant and it was difficult to enforce discipline in a body of public servants whose normal rules of service were altered whenever it was convenient for a Minister to oblige a powerful politician. These grievances were not confined to minor officials. Even so distinguished a body as the *chartistes*, the trained archivists who had passed through the École des Chartes, found the prizes of their profession given to the protégés of politicians. Each Minister, on taking office, formed a 'Cabinet', that is a staff peculiar to himself; these ministerial staffs grew in size and were usually recruited from aspiring young politicians. When their patron went out of office they should have gone too, but it was customary to plant out the most favoured protégés in the higher ranks of the service. What was done at the top was done at the bottom, and the arbitrary nature of official discipline was one of the chief causes of the demand for a 'statute', that is for a legal definition of the rights and duties of the civil service. The crisis came with a postman's strike. The strike was technically a great success; it tied up the mails and the telegraphic and telephone services, and although Clemenceau made the usual speeches about not submitting to coercion, negotiations were begun. The strike leaders demanded the dismissal of the unpopular Under-Secretary, Simyan. The Prime Minister refused to accept such dictation, but the strikers thought that this refusal was purely formal, that Simyan would be got rid of. The strike was called off and Simyan stayed on. A second strike was far less effective; the immediate grievances of the strikers had been met and there was no general tie-up. The power of the unity of the Government servants had been exaggerated.

The next great test of the power of the C.G.T. was met not by Clemenceau, but by Briand. As the election of 1910 drew nearer, the combative attitude of Clemenceau in face of the extreme Left distressed the sentimental and practical politician alike. But the vehement Minister dug his own grave. The French Navy suffered more than did the Army from the various political storms of the Affair. During the Combes Ministry the Navy had, under Camille Pelletan, been watched with a truly Republican vigilance. The workers of the dockyards found in the Minister a vigilant defender; and in addition, M. Pelletan had his own theories of naval construction. A series of disasters whose number seemed to exclude mere bad luck shook public confidence in the administration of the Navy, and when on March 12th, 1907, the battleship *Iéna* blew up in Toulon harbour, with the loss of over a hundred lives, the patience of Parliament was exhausted. A committee of inquiry was set up under the chairmanship of Delcassé, which had little difficulty in forcing the resignation of the Minister of Marine, Thomson. But the campaign was not over. A new committee with very wide powers was appointed and Delcassé was again made chairman. His report was devastating and he insisted that the Clemenceau Government was to blame. The Prime Minister lost his temper and his judgment and instead of replying to the criticisms attacked Delcassé personally. 'I have not humiliated France, but I say that Delcassé has humiliated her.' The Chamber, already restive, did not tolerate this reference to the Tangier crisis. The Cabinet was overthrown on the spot.

The idea of Briand as Prime Minister had its comic side; but the former preacher of the general strike was to prove the truth of the adage that reformed poachers make the best game-keepers. Briand was an excellent judge of men and he knew what was lath and what was iron in the militant organization of the C.G.T. An internal row had led the imperious Griffuelhes to resign, but after a brief interval of moderate triumph, a young militant disciple of Griffuelhes, Léon Jouhaux, was appointed to succeed his master. The militants were again in control; the men who, like Merrheim of the Metallurgical Unions, wanted no collaboration with the State, no subsidization of the *Bourses du Travail* by the municipalities, no trust in even the most eminent Socialist politicians, by the organized workers.

The trial of strength came on the railways. The wages of railway workers had not risen for ten years; only by working overtime could the railway men make ends meet; and confidence in their own power, combined with anger at the inflexible attitude of the companies, especially of the Nord Company, made the unions ready to try the effects of the strike weapon whose potency had been so lyrically preached by the Prime Minister. But when the strike broke out, Briand was ready for it. He arrested the strike leaders, even when they took refuge in the offices of *Humanité*. More deadly blow, he called up the strikers as Army reservists. He talked vaguely of a great sabotage plot, the companies made some financial concessions, but the strike was beaten. The defeat was, of course, followed by recriminations and by complaints by the rigorous Griffuelhes that the strike leaders were highly incompetent. But more obvious to the rank-and-file was the impotence of the Socialist deputies to do anything for the strikers in face of the power of the Government. The bourgeois parties had rallied to Briand, leaving Jaurès and Guesde to utter academic protests. Even honest and sincere Socialist politicians could do little or nothing for the workers, while dishonest or insincere ex-Socialist politicians could do them great harm.

That Briand should be the agent of crushing the general strike was peculiarly maddening. Had he not risen by preaching it in company with his old schoolfellow, Pelloutier? It was this man who had not merely stretched the law to defeat the strike, but had boasted of it. This was worse than Clemenceau's candid admission that he was now on the other side of the barricade. Leader after leader of the workers had risen to power by the violence of his language, by the verbal audacity of his revolutionary energy. As the old Radicals talked of the cause and of their militancy as if they were still treading the dangerous road that led to Nouméa and Lambessa, when they were in much greater danger of dying as Senators or as Governors of great colonies, so a series of brilliant young men got their foothold on the ladder by finding words to express the revolutionary passion of the workers—and, the ladder no longer needed, kicked it away.

The slanders of the Right failed to shake the justified faith of the workers in the probity of Jaurès, but he, too, was a politician, forced to make bargains with other politicians, forced to shut his eyes to betrayals and abuses. In a political system where a genial tolerance was the custom of the country, a savage virtue was out of place and, if displayed too boldly, did not evoke admiration but irritation among an unpriggish body of men like the deputies. The average voter was not very surprised, not very disillusioned, for he took with plenty of salt the professions of faith and the promises of works of the candidates. He no more thought of believing every word that they said than he thought of believing every word the seller said when praising a horse or a cow to a prospective purchaser. But the zealots, who are as characteristic of French politics as the ironically sceptical majority, were less tolerant: and it was they who were tempted away to 'direct action' by their indignant resentment of the rules of the parliamentary game. It was they who treated as a description of treason the dictum of Robert de Jouvenel, which its author had stated as a mere law of parliamentary psychology. 'There is more in common between two deputies, one of whom is a revolutionary, than between two revolutionaries one of whom is a deputy.'

II

It was evident by 1910 that collaboration between the Socialists and the Radicals and other Left groups was producing very limited results, from the point of view of the Socialists. Yet as long as the electoral system remained the same, single-member constituencies with the second ballot, at election times it was necessary to make a bargain with the Radicals. Without such a bargain there were many safe Socialist seats which would be endangered, including Jaurès's own. The Socialists, then, with all the other groups except the Radicals, became converts to proportional representation, which would free the party from Radical patronage as well as helping the little groups of independent ex-Socialists like Briand, Millerand, Viviani and the rest who were in danger of being crushed between the two masses of the S.F.I.O.[1] and the Radicals. Proportional Representation would also help the Right, so that the question of electoral reform cut across the normal division. The elections of 1910 did not give the Radicals an absolute majority, and the disorganization of parties that followed was marked by a series of short-lived Governments and the ending of the long Radical

---

[1] 'French Section of the Workers' International', the official title of Jaurès's party.

427

domination of the Chamber; the great party, indeed, was so deeply divided that it could seldom provide a Prime Minister.

But if the electoral question brought together Jaurès, Briand and Albert de Mun, the question of peace and war, of foreign policy and militarism linked Jaurès and an important section of the Radicals. They realized that Europe was entering on a dangerous epoch of imperial rivalry and they were anxious that France should run as little risk as possible of being involved in the struggle. This policy of prudential pacificism made Jaurès overlook many faults in the Radical party and in that section of it which followed M. Joseph Caillaux.

In the Socialist party, anti-militarism and something like dogmatic pacificism were almost universally accepted, and what was true of the S.F.I.O. was truer still of the C.G.T. There was, of course, a remnant of the old Blanquist tradition incarnate in men like Édouard Vaillant, but it was a dying creed. The doctrine that the 'worker has no country' was replacing the old Jacobin tradition of the 'country in danger'. The Paris working men who, twenty years before, had sung the jingo songs of the Boulangist music-hall artists, were now on the surface violently anti-militarist. The song that now went the rounds was not a new 'En revenant de la revue', but a naïve ballad that praised the brave lads of the 17th for not obeying the orders which, if obeyed, 'would have killed the Republic'.

The reaction against militarism and against political Nationalism went very far. Although the Radical Governments had been patriotic, anxious to explain that they wished the Army to have all due honour, they could not help giving aid and comfort to simple hostility to any army. They might and did commemorate such triumphs of Republican arms as the defeat, followed by mass executions, of the 1795 royalist expedition to Quiberon. Hoche had his statue where he had defended the Republic and the inscription read a not very obscure lesson to the heirs of the émigrés who had suffered the heavy hand of the Republic a century before. But such commemorations of civil war, though gratifying to a taste common to all French parties, were not enough for the zealots.

There was Yves Guyot, a most vigorous critic of the French Army and of all armies. There was a vigorous body of critics of the traditional patriotic history which they regarded as the source of strength of their enemies and the betrayal of the true interest of modern France. For it must be remembered that France was profoundly divided over her own history. Benedict Arnold is not a hero to any Americans; Guy Fawkes only a comic hero to Englishmen. But Frenchmen, on both sides, had heroes whom the other side regarded as traitors, victories which were, for other Frenchmen, defeats. La Rochelle was, for one section, the heroic city that had defended Protestantism, and Protestantism had many more partisans in France than the tiny body of formal Huguenots would suggest. For others, La Rochelle was the traitorous city that had called in the English to resist Richelieu. Even within the Left parties, there was soon to be a feud over Danton, for that one-time hero was soon to be condemned as a rogue and a traitor by eminent scholars who saw in him not only the enemy of the true Jacobin tradition, but the exemplar of so many modern corrupt and compromising Republican politicians. It was only ten years or so since Clemenceau had declared that the Revolution was a 'bloc'; it was a bloc that was splitting as the orthodox patriotic Republican tradition felt the impact of the new Marxian criticism of all wars but the class war.[1] The most noisy spokesman of the anti-patriotic school was a teacher in the Yonne, Gustave Hervé, who expiated a youth of Déroulèdism by an equally violent reaction against the common platitudes about the country, the flag and the rest of the symbols of national religion. His career was lively; as editor of the anti-militarist *Piou Piou de l' Yonne* [2] he scandalized the bourgeoisie in the traditional fashion, lost his job in the *lycée* and spent a good deal of time in court, defending himself against charges of inciting to mutiny by repetitions of his scandalous doctrine. The rising left-wing lawyers who made a reputation by their defence of political prisoners, men like Briand, usually managed to save Hervé from the punishment due to his violence, but Hervé was irrepressible and he did not always get off. A Parisian jury proved less touched by the eloquence of the defendants' counsel than a provincial jury had been. Guyot and Hervé were both convicted and sent to prison, to be released in a general amnesty a few weeks later. Hervé's conviction, like his trial, aroused a good deal of more or less genuine indignation. Was the Army to be protected against criticism as in the bad old days when Lucien Descaves had been prosecuted for publishing *Sous Offs?* More important was the effect of 'Hervéism' on the newly united French Socialist party. Anti-militarism and pacificism was one of the most popular parts of the party programme among the militants. They read Hervé's speech to the jury with approval. 'We shall not let ourselves be shot down like rabbits. We shall reply to the mobilization order by revolt. . . . Civil war is the only war that is not stupid. . . .' This was the stuff that the ardent party worker wanted to give the troops.

'Hervéism' was profoundly distasteful to Jaurès. He was more and more convinced that the immediate menace of the capitalist system was not the direct impoverishment of the worker, but his death and mutila-

[1] There was even a violent controversy over Joan of Arc. Many Republicans tried to resist the attempt of the Right to make her a Nationalist asset by reminding Catholics that she had been burned by the Church, and the Royalists that she had been abandoned by the King. Some went further and, like M. Thalamas, spoke of her in terms that provoked the just indignation, or the intolerant violence, of the Right, according to your opinion of M. Thalamas's taste.

[2] 'The Tommy Atkins of the Yonne.'

tion in a fratricidal war with his fellow-workers, brought on by the vulgar covetousness and stupidity of the bourgeoisie.

But the noisy anti-militarism of Hervé hampered the work of warning the public against the intrigues and follies of the warmongers. By his violent and ill-considered attacks on patriotism, Hervé exposed the Socialist party to the deadly charge of being ready to betray France to Germany. Jaurès allowed for the deep-rooted patriotism of the average Frenchman, and he understood that to affront it was not to make of the peasant or worker a nationless member of the international proletariat, but to drive him into the arms of the Nationalists, perhaps to renew that alliance of the workers and the Nationalists which had made Boulangism so much more formidable than the anti-Dreyfus campaign had been. On the other hand, he knew that to rebuke Hervé too severely would be to expose himself to attack, for a kind of resigned pacificism was spreading in the party, especially among the school-teachers and in the ranks of certain of the more militant trade unions. He had to avoid the dangers of appearing to be another of those patriotic Socialists of whom a young German Social-Democrat, Herr Noske, was soon to be abused as the representative. So he translated 'Hervéism' (much to the disgust of Hervé) into something much less offensive. The famous 'flag on the dung-heap' speech was made a defence of true as against false patriotism; and the right of national self-defence was recognized. The workers of the world had a good deal to lose besides their chains, as miners had a good deal to lose by the destruction of a mine, even though that mine was, for the moment, the property of a usurping bourgeois. Hervé's noisy sympathy with the Moroccans was turned against him, for if it was right for semi-barbarous Moroccans to resist invasion, why was it wrong for Frenchmen? [1]

It was not necessarily true, said Jaurès, 'that an idea which shocked the vast majority was thereby proved to be right'. But in French Left politics, as in French extreme Right politics, outrageousness was very often the test of truth. To imagine that war could be avoided in a capitalist society, even by working-class pressure, was an illusion, so the critics thought. Jaurès, undaunted, saw in working-class action the only serious hope of avoiding the blood-bath, and as the feebleness of that action, as the inability of the working-class to develop a really potent organization of resistance grew more evident, the great leader shut his eyes more and more determinedly to the detestable truth. If, on the one side, Jaurès was attacked as compromising with the nationalist and militarist danger, he was attacked on the other as an agent of German demoralization. There was, it is true, something childlike in the admiration Jaurès felt for the country of Luther and Marx. He

---

[1] Twenty years later, another vehement denouncer of all compromise, Citizen Doriot, vehement Communist leader, was zealous in the cause of Abd el Krim. Hervé lived to become a noisy Nationalist and Doriot a Fascist.

was very proud of his German scholarship and envied the German Socialists their unity, their discipline, their doctrinal thoroughness. He noted, but did not attach enough importance to, their somewhat mechanical spirit of discipline, and although he once rebelled against the patronizing attitude of Bebel, reminding him that the German Socialists owed their privileges to monarchs who might take away what had been given not won, criticism of the greatest of Socialist parties was not welcomed. It was, then, a blow in the house of a friend when one of the most eminent of French authorities on modern Germany, Charles Andler, attacked the genuineness of the anti-militarism of the German Socialists, called attention to a change of tone if not of doctrine in their references to war and militarism, and accused Jaurès of misleading French Socialists as to the true nature of their German comrades' views. Andler was a close friend of Lucien Herr, who was the chief intellectual inspiration of Jaurès; so the scandal was all the greater. It was naturally exploited by the parties of the Right, and the picture of Jaurès as the agent of German policy was imprinted in foolish minds. It was not the fault of Andler any more than it was the fault of Jaurès; the dilemma of all Socialist parties as the crisis drew nearer was simply more acute in France than in any other country. The party, there, had more influence on the Government, was more vociferous and uncompromising in its language and yet as powerless as the Socialist parties of other countries to escape from the chain of fatality.

CHAPTER IV

RUMOURS OF WAR

I

THE easing of the European situation that should have followed Algeciras lasted, if it ever appeared, for only a few months. There were in the European system conflicts which it was almost impossible to solve peacefully in a world of sovereign states in which national rights were replacing supernatural hopes as the popular religion. Convinced that wars had mainly economic origins, the leaders of the Left in France, above all the Socialist leader, Jaurès, talked and acted as if Morocco were all that mattered. But a far more serious problem than the liquidation of the Moroccan empire was that of the liquidation of the Austrian and Turkish empires, each threatened by forces as fanatical as and more formidable than the Moroccan tribesmen. The Slavs of the Balkans were profoundly interested in the fate of their brethren under Turkish and Austrian control. The murder of King Alexander of Serbia in 1903 was a triumph for the forward party in Serbia; the discontent of the Bulgarians with their nominal feudal dependence on Turkey was growing ; Greece was troubled by military conspiracy and by nationalist fervour, directed to the formal acquisition of Crete and the redemption of Hellenes from Turkish rule.

In Vienna, the dangers of the situation were understood. As long as Bosnia-Herzegovina, the only acquisition of the Hapsburg empire in a century of losses, was nominally Turkish territory merely 'administered' by Austria-Hungary, there was a danger of Serbian attempts to unite the inhabitants with their brethren in the kingdom and a danger that a renascent Turkey would try to upset the *status quo*. These Austrian preoccupations chimed with Russian designs. Driven back from the Pacific, the Russian Government needed, or thought it needed, diplomatic success somewhere and naturally tried to get it in the region in which the Russian peasant, if he had any interest in imperial designs at all, had his, in the Balkans. The new Russian Foreign Minister, Isvolski, had long been planning the acquisition by Russia of the right to send her fleet through the Straits to the Mediterranean. He had tried in vain to get British support for this scheme when negotiating the settlement of 1907. He now turned to Vienna, where he met a kindred spirit in the new Austrian Foreign Minister, Aerenthal. In return for Russian consent to the annexation of Bosnia, Austria would support Russian claims in the Straits question. Nothing however was to be done until all could be done together at a conference of the signatories of the Berlin treaty of 1878. Isvolski was happily on tour, sounding out Germany and Italy, when he read in a Paris newspaper that Aerenthal had jumped the claim, that Austria was to annex the occupied territory and her protégé, Ferdinand of Bulgaria, was to proclaim his independence and take the title of Tsar.

Aerenthal's policy had some excuse, for in Turkey a military conspiracy, run by a body calling itself the 'Committee of Union and Progress', composed of young Army officers who were usually Freemasons,[1] had forced the Sultan Abdul Hamid to accept a constitution and to call a Parliament as a first step towards the reorganization of the Ottoman Empire. There was a danger that Bosnian deputies would be summoned to that Parliament; there was a danger that, in face of the new situation, the Serbians would try to get their share of the spoil, so Aerenthal acted at once and presented Europe with a *fait accompli*. It was a complete defeat for Russian policy.

Whether Isvolski was deceived by Aerenthal or not, he had certainly, by the standards of power politics, got himself 'into a mess' (the metaphor was his own); and no one was very ready to get him out of it. There was no chance of undoing or modifying the Austrian *coup* at a conference, since Germany would back her ally and France was very unwilling to contemplate the risk of war for so remote and, from her point of view, unimportant an issue. Russia, herself, was in no condition to fight; there was nothing to do but give in and accept, as Turkey did, the annexation. But that was not enough for Austria. For her, the annexation was a precaution against Serbian designs. Belgrade must be forced to accept it, to renounce its expansionist policy and to promise to be in future a good neighbour. Germany made it plain that she supported Austria, so Russia could do nothing and her client state was, for the moment, abandoned. The great Slav power, forced back into Balkan politics by her eastern disasters, had suffered a diplomatic defeat as severe as her recent defeat in war. The Tsardom, many of its leading councillors thought, could not afford another defeat. Russian foreign policy was discredited and the relations of Russia with France and Britain were now very chilly. Only Vienna and Berlin had shown real solidarity—as Europe noted.

The triumph of the Austrian thesis in the Balkans was not merely a great blow to Russia, it was a cause of great uneasiness to Austria's nominal ally, Italy. So Italy was ready to deal with Russia and, at Racconigi, Italy and Russia agreed to support the Balkan *status quo*, a move which made Vienna ready, in turn, to placate Rome by promises

[1] Among them the future Atatürk.

that there would be no further Balkan annexations—unless Italy had been told in advance and had been 'compensated'. Flirtation did not end there, for Germany tried to separate Russia from Britain by promising not to support Austrian forward policy in the Balkans if Russia would cease to support Britain. In short, the fidelity of Russia and Italy was rightly suspected by their official partners, and Europe was still not certainly divided into two unbreakable *blocs*.

It was obvious that Europe was not settling down; and, at the elections of 1910, the Socialists had put among the articles of their election manifesto an attack on the forward policy in Morocco. But the average elector never had any definite opinion on foreign policy and, in any case, the elections were particularly confused. Briand, as Prime Minister, had attacked the single-member constituencies in a phrase recalling Gambetta's image of the 'broken mirror'. For Briand they were 'stagnant pools', but he proposed to let them stagnate for one more election, fearing, as he candidly admitted, that the immediate adoption of proportional representation would increase the strength of the extremists with whom he was in conflict. The Radicals had tried to improve their discipline by setting up a party committee in an office in the Rue Valois, and the name of the street came to have a Tammany Hall ring in the ears of the enemies of the dominant party, enemies who were numerous, especially in the highly literate classes.

The calculation of Jaurès was that, with the separation of Church and State, the Radicals would be deprived of their standard programme. But the veteran campaigners of the Rue Valois were not at a loss. The 'defence of the lay school' was the latest version of their war against the Church. It was not untimely. Briand, who had never been a zealot of the true blue stamp, had aroused Radical suspicion by talk of 'appeasement', which was to the Radicals what abandoning 'the bloody shirt' would have been to Republicans in America in the generation following the Civil War. The bishops had launched a campaign accusing the schoolmasters and the authors of school manuals of undermining the official doctrine of 'neutrality'. It was, of course, very difficult to be neutral. It was easy enough to expurgate the works of La Fontaine, to remove the un-Republican word 'God' before putting his poems in childish hands.[1] But it was hard to teach without suggesting some view of life to the children; and the view of life of the average elementary schoolmaster was likely to be, in the eyes of a bishop, very dangerous. The bishops denounced the teachers whom they thought to be breaking

[1] This prudery was carried to fantastic lengths. An official who had to speak to the great authority on the Tuaregs, Père de Foucauld, was torn between his good manners, which suggested that the hermit should be addressed as 'Mon Père', and his duty as a Republican official. Odder still, long after the ending of the war of 1914, a high official of the educational system lecturing on folklore made the heroine of one of his legends address herself in difficult circumstances, 'to the divinities', thus avoiding the use of the un-laic names of God or the Saints.

the law; and the Radicals discovered, with pain if they were naïve, that the separation of Church and State worked both ways. The bishops were no longer officials with salaries that could be stopped and duties to their employers. They were private citizens, expressing freely their private opinions. Schoolmasters could, singly or in groups, sue them for libel; and that was done, but that was all. However, the electoral advantages of so useful a battle-cry as 'the schools in danger' more than compensated for the practical drawbacks.

The results of the elections were not satisfactory to any party except the Socialists, who had gained a good deal. It was they who launched the attack against the Briand Government. But the Prime Minister defended himself with skill and with boldness. A reconstruction of his Cabinet strengthened his hand, and when Briand at last fell, it was not over his repression of the railway strike or any other social question, but over his real or alleged lack of energy in enforcing the lay laws. Briand protested that the accusation was baseless. 'If you want to kill your dog, you say that he is mad. . . . When you want to over-throw a Ministry, you accuse it of clericalism and of making a bargain with the religious orders.' The ingenious parliamentary tactics of an uncompromising young Radical, M. Malvy, were not completely successful, but Briand's majority was too small for any hopes of ministerial stability to be possible and he resigned. His formal successor was the inoffensive and ineffective M. Monis, but the real leader of the new Government was its Finance Minister, M. Joseph Caillaux.

II

Few candid persons had believed that the Algeciras settlement could in any case have lasted long. If Morocco was to be developed (or exploited), more was needed than a control of the police of the ports. The attempt to create a grand port and centre of European influence at Casablanca awakened native fanaticism, and a massacre was followed by punitive bombardment and landing. The Moroccans were quite intelligent enough to know that their independence was in danger, that the punitive raids from the Algerian frontier under Lyautey, like the landing-parties of Drude and d'Amade, were preliminary to a general occupation. A violent dispute over the harbouring by the German consul at Casablanca of deserters from the Foreign Legion was finally settled at The Hague Court and was followed by an agree-ment between such great French firms as Schneider-Creusot and such great German firms as Krupp to work together for the development of Morocco, but the French would not extend this economic *condominium* to the Congo; and the Germans were resentful of what they could not unreasonably call bad faith.

Worse still was the situation provoked by the civil war between the Sultan Abd el-Aziz and his brother, Moulay Hafid. The Sultan, as the protégé of the Christian powers, was very unpopular and he was easily dethroned by his brother. The new Sultan was recognized by the Powers but he could not, of course, be permitted to continue to exploit the anti-foreign sentiments to which he owed his throne. He was forced to recognize the existing debts, to pay compensation for the Casablanca outrages, which meant high taxes and provoked a new rebellion. He was besieged in Fez and appealed to France for help. To save the Sultan and the European colony, a French column relieved the city (May 21st, 1911), and, at the same time, Spain increased her area of occupation. The Algeciras settlement was dead. After the experience of 1905, it was evident that Germany would not permit a simple nullification, or evasion, of the settlement without exacting a price. There could be no repetition of Delcassé's mistake. This was decidedly the opinion of the most important member of the French Cabinet, the Finance Minister, Caillaux. The Germans gave no sign of what they wanted as compensation and, at Kissingen (a watering-place very like Ems), the French Ambassador, Jules Cambon, learned from the German Foreign Secretary, Kiderlin-Waechter, that Germany would indeed expect compensation, but what and when was left open. Germany had, in fact, decided to repeat the tactics of Tangier, but before the game was begun the Monis Government had fallen, its Minister of War having with undue candour announced that, in war-time, the final responsibility for the conduct of the war should be in the hands of the Government and not in those of a Commander-in-Chief. The new Cabinet had as its chief the Minister of Finance of the old, M. Caillaux.

In the new Prime Minister, the Radicals seemed to have found the new leader they needed. Joseph Caillaux was, by origin, very unlike the typical Radical. He was the son of a Minister of the 'Sixteenth of May', a member of a rich Catholic and Conservative family of the upper bourgeoisie and, apart from any bias due to such an ancestry and environment, he had served in the highest ranks of the bureaucracy, in the Ministry of Finance. It was Waldeck-Rousseau who had first made him head of the department which his father before him had ruled and whose inner mechanism he knew so well; and, by 1911, M. Caillaux was the hope of those stern and unbending Radicals who hoped to see a progressive income-tax established before they, like so many other Radical Simeons, died. The new Prime Minister was not merely sound on this reform (so many had been that!) but he had the reputation for knowing what he was talking about, for being a master of all the arts of the bankers and capitalists and bureaucrats who had, for over a generation, prevented the adoption by the democratic Republic in France of a measure of financial justice familiar in imperial

Germany and in aristocratic England. The very absence in the Radical leader of the social affability so popular among the political personnel of what a great pamphleteer was soon to call 'the Republic of Pals'[1] inspired respect, if it bred dislike. His haughty manner hurt him with the workers, as did his origin, which he neither concealed nor apologized for. His extreme confidence in his own judgment did not endear him to his touchy colleagues, who may have suspected that he could have stood very well the ordeal that was too much for the Satrap in *Zadig*.[2] That he ought to be well pleased with himself was no news to M. Caillaux. He was not very well known to the rank-and-file militants of his own party, who had little opportunity to see through the exterior graces of their leader to the zealot for peace and fiscal justice who was hidden behind the smart clothes and aloof manner. In all ranks of politicians, he was more admired than loved, more feared than trusted. A devoted admirer[3] has admitted that his hero was ill-fated to be understood 'in a *milieu* where an easy tolerance and a rather vulgar friendliness are common'. Like Shelburne in his mastery of finance and in his boldness of conception, he was, like him, permanently weakened by the failure to win the goodwill of the members of his chosen profession of politics.

His associations in the world of business and his lack of moral indignation, at the beginning had alienated Jaurès, but on one point the Radical and Socialist leaders were agreed, in their aversion to war and in their conviction that it was not inevitable. What Jaurès hoped to achieve by mobilizing working-class opinion in France and Germany, Caillaux hoped to achieve by a mixture of economic and political negotiation. He proposed to make opportunities for economic development in Morocco really open to German enterprise; he was sceptical about the policy of supporting Russian finances and he hoped to bring about a real lessening of Franco-German tension by the fulfilment under happier circumstances of the economic agreement of 1909. He was not left much time to work out his plans, for his Ministry was only three days old when, on July 1st, 1911, M. de Selves, the new Foreign Minister, was informed by the German Ambassador that his Government had decided to send the gunboat *Panther* to the Moroccan Atlantic port of Agadir to protect German interests there. Germany, that is to say, by giving this public proof of the seriousness of her intention to exact a price for her consent to a modification of

---

[1] Robert de Jouvenel in *La République des Camarades*.
[2] His ingenious Sovereign cured the Satrap of his conceit by having a choir frequently sing to him,

> 'Que son mérite est extrême,
> Que de grace, que de grandeur,
> Ah, combien monsiegneur
> Doit être content de lui-même.'

[3] M. Charles Paix-Séailles.

the Moroccan settlement, was ready to take the risks inherent in a policy that might easily be interpreted as one of intimidation; and the form of the proof, a German warship in an Atlantic port, was one peculiarly fitted to make the British Admiralty nervous. The new Prime Minister of France might preserve his *sang-froid*, but in France, in Germany, in Britain, the makers of public opinion had now plenty of material to work up.

On the other hand, the German Government and German political opinion saw no reason why they should surrender their power of hampering France in Morocco except for a substantial consideration. The French talk of evacuating Fez was unworthy of belief; the French would stay in Morocco as the English had stayed in Egypt. France would have to pay the price for the undisputed right to control Morocco, as England had had to pay France for the same opportunities in Egypt. It was complicated by the fact that the price England had paid *was* Morocco, but France had to buy it again from Germany. Germany had something to sell which the French public might easily be led to think France had already bought and paid for. The German price, it appeared, was a high one, the whole of the French Congo. This was not in French hands a very valuable asset, but in German hands it would link the Cameroons to the Congo, give a common frontier with the great Belgian colony: and, should that colony come on the market, Germany might secure it and thus possess a continuous belt of territory right across Africa from the Indian Ocean to the mouth of the Congo.

If the German demands were great, French offers or even hints of offers were vague. The Colonial party was strong and it had to be considered. The Minister of the Colonies [1] was involved, as much as the Minister of Foreign Affairs, and there were justified complaints from Ambassador Cambon in Berlin that negotiations were not conducted either swiftly enough or firmly enough.

There were complications in Paris. Russia was as cold to the idea of fighting for Morocco as France had been to the idea of fighting over the status of Bosnia, but a belligerent speech by Mr. Lloyd George warned Germany that Britain would stand by France. By August 1st, France had made her first offer; it had become a matter of haggling, a breakdown was not impossible but it was unlikely, since for all practical purposes M. Caillaux had taken the affair out of the hands of M. de Selves, and M. Caillaux was a realist. France wanted to end, once for all, any right of any power except herself to political authority in Morocco; if Germany accepted that, she could get, not the whole of the French Congo but what was for her the most important thing, access to the river and a promise by France not to exercise her right of pre-emption of the Belgian Congo—if it came on the market—without previous agreement with Germany. There had been nasty moments,

---

[1] M. Lebrun, now (1940) serving his second term as President of the Republic.

there had been a panic on the Berlin bourse which may have been provoked by the French Government as a hint to the Germans, but on November 4th, 1911, the agreement was signed. Europe had escaped her third war crisis in six years.

Caillaux, like Rouvier, was a financier, and like Rouvier in 1906 he was anxious to make of this settlement, not a mere truce, but a foundation for real Franco-German co-operation; but not only were there still important sentimental obstacles, exploited and increased by non-sentimental people and interests, but the Moroccan crisis had led to the invasion of Tripoli by Italy and this attack on the territorial integrity of the Turkish Empire was only the beginning of a new menace to general peace.

It was natural that Italy, once it was fairly certain that the Franco-German negotiations were going to end in a settlement, should try to take up the option on Tripoli that she had held since 1902. The invasion of Tripoli did not result in a walk-over; outside the coast oases, the Turks stimulated Arab resistance to good effect and a considerable part of the Italian Army was tied up in a rather inglorious campaign. It was a source of weakness for Italy, a drain on her finances and temper, and she attempted to shorten the resistance of the Turks by use of her fleet. This brought her into conflict with France over a couple of French ships, seized with doubtful legality, but more serious was the occupation of Rhodes and the Dodecanese, the carrying of the naval war into Turkish home waters, for that excited the appetites of the Balkan states.

These little Christian states had seen, with alarm, the attempt of the new rulers of Turkey to unify the state, to impose Ottoman nationality on all Turkish subjects in a way unknown under Abdul Hamid. If the Sick Man got well, his recovery would end the hopes of the Balkan states. The Italian war weakened Turkey and it was inevitable that the Balkan states should try to strike while the iron was hot. Thus, as far as the Moroccan dispute and settlement encouraged Italy to try to get something, it was a factor in creating the war danger in the Balkans.

Russian diplomacy had not forgotten or forgiven Aerenthal's coup and vain efforts were made in 1911 to reopen the Straits question. Russia could not hope to get the Straits opened for her fleet alone, unless the three Great Powers were willing to bring pressure to bear on Turkey to that end and none of them had any real reason to desire such a settlement and some had strong reasons for disliking it. Whatever dreams Isvolski and the Ambassador in Constantinople, Charykov, might have of a deal with Turkey, the Ministers in Belgrade and Sofia were busy with the traditional Russian policy, busy organizing a Balkan League which would take advantage of Turkey's embarrassments, even if that meant war with Turkey. Sazonov, Isvolski's successor at the Russian Foreign Office, when he took over at the beginning of 1912 found himself faced with the problem of maintaining Russia's position in the Balkans without running the risk of a local war which might well turn into a general war. There was, indeed, no solution of the problem except abandoning the forward policy, which Sazonov refused to do.

It was the news of this 'Balkan League', formed under Russian auspices, that startled Poincaré when he arrived in Russia in the summer of 1912. France's ally was committed to a policy that might well mean war with Austria as well as war with Turkey, and no more than in the less-important Japanese affair had France been told anything until it was too late. Sazonov's excuse, if it was an excuse, might have been that France had been decidedly chilly to hints of an active Balkan policy that had been dropped a few months earlier, and his palliation of his action was a belated effort to induce the Balkan states to stop short of war. But, as Poincaré said, this attempt to put on the brake came from the people who had started the engine. It failed; the Balkan powers went ahead and no concerted attempt to stop them was or could be made. For to stop them by the joint pressure of the Powers would be again to make Russia the instrument of betraying the hopes of the Balkan states, and by the time a formula of joint warning by Russia and Austria was found, it was too late. War had begun.

One general illusion was that the war would either be quickly concluded by a Turkish victory or by a long-drawn-out contest. But, like Napoleon III in 1866, the rulers of the Great Powers had been wrong. The war was brief and marked by a series of brilliant and easy victories for the Balkan states. By the end of the year, Turkey in Europe was reduced to Constantinople and a few isolated fortresses besieged by the victorious armies of Bulgaria, Serbia, and Greece. The solemn warnings that the Balkan states would not be allowed to profit by warlike action which had seemed impressive in October, seemed merely silly in December. It was too late to save Turkey in Europe; it was necessary to save Austria-Hungary and the position of the Triple Alliance.

The Balkan war suddenly tipped the balance of power against Berlin. Her protégé, Turkey, had been ignominiously defeated by nations politically influenced by Russia and by armies that had been armed and trained by French firms and French officers. Worse than this blow to German prestige, was the menace to Austria. Serbia was now much stronger in economic resources and in prestige; having settled her Balkan problem, she could now turn north and begin to support her fellow 'South Slavs' in Bosnia, in Croatia, in Slovenia. Serbian ambitions were, for the moment, concentrated on getting a port in the Adriatic and thus escaping from the landlocked position which had put her economically at the mercy of Austria. But this meant the occupation of Albania, and such a change in the *status quo* was a danger both to Austria and to Italy, which collaborated with unusual cordiality in creating an independent principality of Albania. It was this settlement that brought about the second Balkan war. For Serbia, baulked of her Albanian outlet, demanded a larger share of Macedonia, and when Bulgaria refused, formed a separate alliance with Greece. The Tsar was called on to arbitrate the differences between the quondam Allies as had been provided for in the original treaties, but Bulgaria, over-confident, launched a surprise attack on the Serbians and the Greeks and was defeated. This was another blow for Austria since Serbia was more formidable than ever, and if Bulgaria was now out of the Russian orbit, that mattered less since two powers closely associated with Germany and Austria, Rumania and Turkey, had joined in the attack on Bulgaria. By the time the wars were finally ended by the treaty of Bucarest (August 1913), Austria's position had been definitely endangered. Czechs, Slovaks, Rumanians, Italians as well as Croats, Bosnians and Slovenes began to wonder if the day of liberation were not at hand. What was loosely called 'the Great War', but what would more justly be called the 'Second War of the Austrian Succession', was imminent.

It was realized in Vienna and Budapest that a critical period had begun, and but for German restraint it is possible that Austria might have backed Bulgaria openly at the beginning of the Second Balkan war. But Germany was less alarmed than was Austria. She had military preparations on a great scale to complete and she was, on the other hand, on better terms with Britain than usual. A preventive war fought over Balkan disputes was not, in 1913, inevitable and so it was avoided. Europe had had her fourth escape from catastrophe in seven years.

To France, the events of 1912 and 1913 were both gratifying and sobering. The victories of the Balkan peoples were, like the rapid expansion of French air power, gratifying to French pride; like the Lebel rifle in Boulanger's time, they made defeat in war less feared, although war, for most Frenchmen, was still to be avoided, if not at all costs, at all costs except security and honour. The failure of the Haldane mission to Berlin in 1912 made it certain that the Germans would go on building that navy whose power of menacing British security was the best guarantee of British fidelity to the Entente. The transfer of most of the French Channel Fleet to the Mediterranean, so that the British Mediterranean Fleet could be despatched to the North Sea to restore the balance of naval power' there, involved, in fact, an implicit bargain that France should not suffer for this subordination of her naval needs to those of Britain. The crisis of 1911 had been followed by tighter military relations. Arrangements for the use of the British Army on the continent were completed, and although Britain refused any commitment on paper, the French Government naturally assumed that two countries which had dovetailed their defence arrangements so completely were, if not Allies, something more than mere friends.

Even the independent course of Russia had something to commend itself to those persons in authority in France who suspected that a show-down between the two groups of powers was inevitable. For Russia, in disputes arising from French interests, had never inspired full confidence. Who knew if the only way to avoid being left in the lurch by Russia was not to be sure that, when the crisis came, it was concerned with what Russia would consider a vital interest? In what turned out to be a minor matter, Russia and Austria had combined to prevent Kavala going to Greece, and France and Germany had found themselves together on the opposite side. The secretiveness of Sazonov on this question had shown the French how limited was their knowledge of the aims of Russian policy and had increased their nervousness as to Russian loyalty. Germany might have felt the same for, on a general promise of German support, the Austrian Foreign Minister, without further consultation, sent an ultimatum to the Serbians imposing on them the necessity of abandoning some Albanian lands which they were defiantly holding. The Serbs gave way; it was a minor victory for Austria, a minor defeat for Russia; but the main Balkan situation remained the same. Rumania was drifting away from the Triple Alliance; and although Italy had renewed the Triple Alliance and was making military arrangements to fight on the German side of the Rhine if war came, these arrangements did not inspire much hope in Berlin or much fear in Paris, as Italy's loyalty to her Allies was estimated at its true worth.[1]

Austria had little reason to be satisfied with the success of October 1913. The nationalities question, whose solution (if, indeed, there was one) had been made impossible by the intransigence of the Sudeten Germans in Bohemia and the Magyars in Croatia and Transylvania, was a cancer eating away the flesh of the monarchy. An operation was necessary; the buying-off of Rumania; the destruction of Serbia; the conclusive proof to the disloyal Slavs of the Empire that the great Slav state could do nothing for them; these were necessary steps if the Dual Monarchy was to hold together.

If the practical conclusion of a colonial settlement between Germany and Britain gave hopes that this particular cause of conflict was now unimportant, the tension in the Balkans grew. There was danger of a war between Greece and Turkey, and the relations of Germany and Turkey were shown to be as close as ever by the appointment of a German General, Liman von Sanders, to a high post in the Turkish

---

[1] The belligerent head of the Austrian Army, Conrad von Hötzendorff, wanted a preventive war against Italy as well as against Serbia.

Army. The imminence of a fifth crisis was expected by all competent observers. Austria and Turkey were both in danger of dissolution, which, however deplorable, had to be provided for. Germany had to shore up her ally and her client; Germany's rivals had to provide for the crisis.

The Agadir crisis had shown that the policy of diplomatic *laisser-aller* that had prevailed from the fall of Delcassé to the opening of the Moroccan crisis was no longer adequate. Radical intellectuals might dream their dreams, but, although for a Foreign Minister not to be like M. de Vergennes was easy, it was not enough.[1] France could abandon her interest in the balance of power and trust that Germany would not abuse the great increase in freedom of action that such a change involved. Or she could go further and get a good price for her benevolent neutrality. Or she could strengthen her links with the states with which she was associated. But all these policies, even the first, involved coherence and resolution in execution. For the first involved a frank admission that the question of Alsace-Lorraine was closed and that the Republic was not and could not be active in European politics, as the democratic organization of the state was incompatible with an effective military and diplomatic policy. The Republic would have to admit the truth of the charges brought against her by the Nationalists and rejoice in her disability. This was to be the thesis of a famous Socialist tract that had a *succès de scandale*.[2] But this policy of deliberate withdrawal of France from power politics was not one that could just be let happen; it had to be planned, or the retreat in good order would be a rout; and no one was ready, officially, to accept responsibility for that retreat, that is to give Germany the necessary assurance that France would let her be judge of her own interests east of the Vosges.

A policy of active collaboration with Germany could, perhaps, have been carried out by a man of great courage, energy and personal dignity. Jaurès, had he been in power, might have done it: at any rate if there had been any hope (as there was none) that somebody like Jaurès would be in power in Germany. M. Caillaux had all the qualifications for the operation except the necessary one of personal immunity. He was not immune, for he had numerous enemies and these enemies were well armed against him. So great a change in the formal French outlook on the world could only have been carried out if one ideal, peace, anti-militarism, the creation of the 'true Republic', could have fought against the other ideal of national greatness, national honour, national pride. A leader fit to lay such potent ghosts as Joan of Arc and Napoleon, to eradicate such deeply-rooted memories as Jena

[1] Vergennes was the great diplomat who organized the coalition against Britain to which the United States owed its independence. To the French professional diplomat he ranked with—or above—Talleyrand as a model.

[2] Marcel Sembat's 'Faites un roi sinon faites la paix' ('Let's have a King or have Peace').

and Sedan, had to be a French Gladstone. Caillaux the realist, Caillaux the businessman, Caillaux the zealous and not too scrupulous party manager, was, at best, a Blaine or a Joseph Chamberlain. It was distrust of the man as well as of his policy that had brought about Caillaux's downfall and made it certain that his successor would not be a mere imitator of the fallen Minister. The alarmed politicians of the old school of power diplomacy saw in Caillaux a dangerous diplomatic gambler, who was willing to throw away acquired French assets, like the Russian Alliance and the Entente with Britain, for problematic deals with Germany, deals which involved surrenders of present French rights to Germany as well as the abandonment of the old protest against the mutilation of France. There were, too, critics like Briand who denied that only Caillaux could deal with Germany and insisted that the idea of economic co-operation with Germany, in Morocco and elsewhere, went back to the Clemenceau and Briand Ministries and that Caillaux and his friends, by their defeat of the proposals to admit German enterprise to the French Congo, had irritated Germany into the policy that led to Agadir. The Congo treaty with Germany would, of course, have to be accepted and ratified, but it was idle to pretend that the complacent belief that Europe was on the eve of a long peace was still a tenable opinion.

III

To find a successor to Caillaux was not easy; that is, to find a successor whose prestige and character would make the new Government resistant to foreign and internal pressure. M. Caillaux was not a forgiving man and his hold on the Radicals was growing every day; and although he had not yet conquered Socialist distrust, he was on the way to doing so. Briand hoped that he might be given a chance to resist his enemy, but it was finally to Poincaré that Fallières turned. The new Prime Minister had striking points of resemblance to Waldeck-Rousseau. Like him he was a great lawyer, not a brilliant forensic orator like Briand, but a master of detail. He was endowed with an astonishing memory and a prodigious industry. He had entered politics young; he was a deputy at 27 [1] and a Minister at 33. Yet at 35 he abandoned active politics, devoting himself to his work at the Bar, and it was as an almost silent deputy that he saw France pass through the crisis of the Dreyfus case and the war with the Church. He was a Dreyfusard, but not too soon and not too vehemently; he was a *laic*, but more in the spirit of Waldeck-Rousseau than of Combes. He entered the Senate in 1903, which made it easier for him to keep apart from the feuds and alliances of the Chamber. A period in Sarrien's Cabinet as Minister of Finance did little more than show

[1] He was born in 1860.

that he was still in politics. That a man so withdrawn from the ordinary political life of Parliament, so unlike the dominant political figures of the Left, dry, reserved, eloquent from the head not the heart, legal representative of great corporations, should become Prime Minister was sufficient proof of the disorganization of the parties. But it was proof of more than that—the shock to the French nation that had been administered by the Agadir crisis.

The new Cabinet was something of a 'Ministry of all the Talents'. It contained two of the most eminent ex-Socialists, Briand and Millerand; it contained that emblem of Radical intellectualism, Léon Bourgeois; it contained Delcassé. By adopting and pressing a project for electoral reform, a kind of proportional representation, the new Government pleased all the parties except the Radicals, who regarded any alteration of the present system as a blow at the majesty of 'universal suffrage', as it certainly was a blow at their control of the electoral machine. Debated and altered in the Chamber, the reform was to be buried in the Senate. In any case, it was in foreign policy that the Poincaré Government was to be noteworthy, for it was in order to give France 'a feeling of security' that it had been formed, according to its own declaration of policy.

The diplomatic situation was indeed alarming. The bargain of the Racconigi agreement,[1] when it was revealed, was almost as disturbing to the ally of Russia (for France had been ignored) as to the ally of Italy (for Germany had been deceived). As the Balkan war followed the Italo-Turkish war, the situation of France, if she was not to abdicate her position as a great power, was in serious danger. This was very evident to Poincaré, who had learned, during his visit to Russia in the summer of 1912, of the dangerous game that was being played. It was the general sense of increasing risks and the resolution that France should have some policy that, as the term of President Fallières came to an end, made the question of the succession more important than usual. If the rules of the game were to be observed, a docile second- or third-rate Left politician would be chosen: but should the rules apply at such a moment? There was a genuine feeling that they should not, as well as a natural jumping at the chance of dishing the Radicals on the part of the dissenters of Left and Right. A safe, dignified, and non-Radical candidate might have been Ribot, but his chances vanished when, stimulated by Briand, Poincaré allowed his own name to be put forward. For a politician of such eminence and weight to be elected would be a minor revolution. He was of the calibre at least of Casimir-Périer or of Grévy, not of Loubet or Fallières. His candidacy was an affront to many Radicals, above all to Clemenceau, who may have had designs on the Élysée himself (after all, he was now over seventy and his active career, presumably, at an end). Clemenceau

[1] Cf. p. 433.

the President-maker had, failing himself, a safe candidate. He had refused to accept Antonin Dubost, so the orthodox Left vote was cast in the preliminary meetings for a M. Pams. But Poincaré refused to retire in favour of a minor member of his own Cabinet and, as the votes had been almost equally divided between him and Pams, he was sure to be elected if his supporters stuck by him, as the Right far preferred him to Pams. Such a decision infuriated Clemenceau—it was, he asserted, a breach of Republican discipline to run after being beaten in the preliminary vote, no matter how narrow the margin. The conventions apparently required that the candidate of a little more than a third of the National Assembly should defeat the candidate of a good deal more than half. But Poincaré was not going to be argued or intimidated into surrender, and he was elected.

It was an election that created a precedent, for the Left was never able again, no matter how great its formal majority in the two Houses, to elect the candidate it had agreed on in the preliminary meetings. At the final election, enough members of the majority always went over to the other side to elect a compromise candidate. The presidency ceased, that is to say, to represent a particular majority at the moment of election. It represented the fundamental political caution and conservatism that lie beneath the superficial extremism of the French politician. The election meant more than that, for Poincaré took it as support for his belief that the nation wanted a reinforcement of the presidency—which was to take it too seriously, for the new President was too legalistically minded to step outside the bounds of law and precedent and, inside them, his power of independent action was small. Lastly, the election was a defeat for Clemenceau; his authority had been successfully defied and the new President was now added to the long list of politicians with whom 'The Tiger' had a score to settle.

Briand succeeded Poincaré as Prime Minister, but the ingenious emasculation of the electoral reform bill by the Radical technicians of the Senate (led by Clemenceau) caused him to resign, and it fell to Louis Barthou, close friend and ally of Poincaré, to carry through the measure which revealed to people and politicians the seriousness of the diplomatic situation, for before Briand's fall the Ministry had announced its intention of raising the period of military service from two to three years.

No project could have been politically bolder. The reduction of the term of service had been in line with the development of the whole military policy of the Republic and it had been almost the only concrete result of the victory over the Army in the Dreyfus case. The crisis of 1911 had forced a reconsideration of military policy and a stocktaking of military resources on the Government. The Army had a new Commander-in-Chief designate in General Joffre, and he was insistent that there was a great deal to be done before the French

Army could take the field with confidence in its ability to defeat the Germans. What was to be done called for great financial effort, but it also called, so the General Staff asserted, for great personal effort.

The War Minister in the Poincaré Government was Millerand, who won the confidence and respect of the chiefs of the Army by his great abilities and his firm belief in all they told him. He had done a great deal to restore to the Army the prestige it had enjoyed before the Affair. The Army was no longer a dangerous wild animal on a chain, but a faithful watchdog that required encouragement. Like Boulanger before him, Millerand knew that the man in the street and the soldier liked, in peace-time at any rate, the exaltation of the 'pride, pomp and circumstance of glorious war', and as far as it was possible in an Army whose traditions laid no stress on 'smartness', Millerand advertised the rebirth of mutual confidence between the Army and the Nation.[1] The energetic Minister fell as the result of an astonishing lack of political sense in a former member of the 'Government of Republican Defence'[2]; but his policy was continued. Yet reforms in administration, projected reforms in the artillery, even the proposal to put the French Army into a less murderous uniform than the blue coat and red trousers of not very old tradition [3] did not solve the military problem.

The Turkish defeat in the Balkan War had made the military position of Germany and Austria less good, and Germany reacted by a great programme of rearmament and a great increase of her peace-time strength. France could find the money for technical improvements, but could she find the men? Her population was stationary, that of Germany still growing. Already France had had to lower her standard of physical fitness to keep her regiments full. What could she do now? There was only one remedy: to increase the term of service with the colours. As France had only two thirds of the population of Germany she must remedy that by keeping her sons under the colours for three years, as against the German two. Involved in this argument was a military conception that was violently and ably attacked by Jean Jaurès. Jaurès, who had never been much at home in the economic side of Socialist argument, had been more and more oppressed, since 1906, with the danger of war and with the problem of the Army in a democracy. Not living in idyllic simplicity on an island or on an isolated continent, not believing that it did not matter whether France was ruled by Frenchmen or Prussians, he could not fall back on either sentimental or revolutionary unilateral disarmament

---

[1] One of his devices was the encouragement of torchlight parades. This gave the critics who had not forgiven him for his desertion of Socialism a chance to make a pun on the double meaning of 'retraite' (parade and pension). He had 'promised the workers old age pensions, he gave them torchlight parades'.

[2] He reinstated du Paty de Clam in his rank as a reserve officer.

[3] They dated not from Napoleon but from Charles X. The proposal to dress the Army in a drabber costume and make officers less of a target was violently attacked in a Right paper as part of a conspiracy to lower the dignity and authority of the officers.

as a remedy. Solutions that were not fantastically irrelevant to the problem in London or New York, were irrelevant in Paris. It was with this in mind that Jaurès, ably briefed by some critically-minded soldiers, wrote his brilliant plea for 'the New Army'.

The fault of the existing French Army, so Jaurès argued, was that its leaders thought entirely in terms of soldiers with the colours. They wanted a long period of service with the colours, because they thought that the war would be decided in the first few weeks by the first-line troops. Reserves would only be useful to exploit a victory already won. More than that, they wanted long service because their tactical ideas were based on a mechanical psychology. They put their trust in soldiers drilled to automatic action; and it took time to produce such soldiers. To train a man in the use of arms and in the elements of the military arts took months; what took years was the 'making a soldier of him', that is, the production of the blind habit of obedience which the generals believed—and Jaurès did not believe—was necessary to producing an efficient soldier. Because this obedience was thought necessary, troops spent too much of their time on barrack squares in endless repetitive drill, too little in real preparation for war in country camps. It would be possible to give France a more efficient defensive force at a greatly less cost in time and money if the Generals could be cured of their beliefs that only the 'active Army' counted for much and that it must consist of men who had put away civilian habits of thought and action. If the two-year law had failed, Jaurès argued, it was because the heads of the Army had never tried to make it work. They had merely lamented the reduction of the term of service instead of recasting all their ideas of what an Army should be. They had clung to the ideal of a 'great army' but had not tried to realize the more practicable and efficient ideal of a nation in arms.

It was this thesis that was the basis of the most impressive criticism of the three-years law. It was idle to pretend, as was pretended then and has been asserted since, that the reorganization of the German Army could be a matter of indifference to France; it could only be a matter of indifference if France, first of all, completely recast her foreign policy and, indeed, her view of the nature of the national state. If she had done so, she would have been unique among the great powers of Europe, but there was no chance of her doing so. In all probability, Jaurès exaggerated the merits of the militia system he advocated, however just were his criticisms of the mentality of the rulers of the French Army. The constructive side of his doctrine suffered from his association, however involuntary, with the noisy enemies of patriotism and preachers of revolutionary methods of ending the danger of war. And some of the supporters of the new law, conscious that it was not likely to be popular at the coming elections, may have resented the fact that Jaurès was choosing the electorally better part. But the arguments for the new law were often of very doubtful validity. The threatened superiority of the German Army was not decisive. The vision of that Army throwing itself on France in the first days of war without waiting for its reservists was rather a naïve nightmare than an actual threat.[1] But there was a real disparity of forces between Germany and France, and it was idle to ignore it.[2]

It was significant that the law was passed under the leadership of Barthou and that a Chamber in which the Radicals were so strong followed non-Radical ministers in this unpopular course. Of course such prudence saved the face of the Radical leaders. The most unpopular result of the changed military policy was the retention with the colours of the men who would normally have been discharged; there were many demonstrations and some minor outbreaks against military authority. The Chamber found the solution; it provided that the age of calling up should be twenty, not twenty-one, and that two classes should be called to the colours at the same time. The implied bargain with the serving soldiers was thus kept and, in 1914 there was in existence an extra class of trained men.

So great a sacrifice as the increase of the blood tax imposed on the workers, demanded some compensation. The Barthou Government, therefore, promised that the extra cost of the rearmament programme would be met out of the proceeds of the income tax which was at last to be instituted. This promise was not a new one. As long ago as 1907 M. Caillaux, as Clemenceau's Finance Minister, had introduced a bill for income tax that was to be progressive in its incidence, that is, which would be flexible enough to make the rates heavier on high incomes than on low. It was to replace some of the old direct taxes dating from Napoleon I, taxes which were now not productive enough and which were very unjust in their incidence, not only as between individuals but as between areas. The burden was to be shifted from landowners to security owners, a move which was just and which was popular with the numerous class of landowners. But the proposal to levy a tax on the income from *rentes* was condemned by the Senate as a breach of public faith. Had the income from the national debt not been guaranteed by the law of *Vendémiaire* in the year 1797? The Third Republic must keep the promises of the First.

Even apart from this threat to the implied contractual rights of the public creditor, where the Senate betrayed a sensitiveness worthy of John Marshall, the spirit behind the Caillaux proposals was terrifying to the bourgeoisie. For, as Jaurès pointed out, the information got by

---

[1] It should be remembered, however, that in the first days of the war two important attacks were made by frontier corps, one, the German attack on Liége, was a partial success; the other, the French attack in Alsace, a complete failure.

[2] The argument, dear to some French critics of the law, that the increase in the German Army was still merely a Government project is of no importance. Whatever might be the case in France, no Reichstag ever successfully resisted a demand for more armaments coming from the Imperial Government.

an effective income tax would make it possible to estimate what the possessing classes could be made to surrender for 'works of solidarity'. Not only would the privacy of family finance be violated, but it would be violated to enable politicians to pay the money of the thrifty over to the idle! The Chamber adopted a bill more radical than Caillaux's which, possibly to the surprise of its authors, the Senate referred to a committee which took nearly five years to report. After the three-years law, with its increase of the cash and social cost of the Army, the time had come to take some steps to fulfil the promises made for so many years. That generous leader of the Right, Albert de Mun, wished his political bedfellows to show that they meant what they said when they talked of equal financial sacrifice, but he found that he had taken them too literally; they did not intend that the needs of national defence should be made the occasion for revolutionizing a tax system from whose deficiencies they did not suffer very much. The debate went on for over a year, with various projects being sent to the Senate and being trimmed there of their dangerous features. But the great deficits of these years educated even the Senate and, on July 15th, 1914, the principle of a progressive income tax was at last voted. Its rates were low; its exemptions generous, and it avoided all unnecessary prying into private affairs by providing that a taxpayer who volunteered a statement of income was to be believed unless the authorities could prove him wrong, while if he made no statement he was to be assessed and had to prove the assessment wrong. It was a very thin end of the wedge, but the wedge was at last ready for the Treasury to hammer in.

It was not the Barthou Government that carried this reform. It had proposed to raise a large loan to cover the deficit and the loan was to be tax free. This was to deny the Radical thesis in the matter of taxation, and the Chamber revolted. Elections were drawing near; it was absurd, if not dangerous, that the dominant party should not rule the country till the elections were over, so the Radicals came back to office. The nominal Prime Minister was Doumergue; the real power, Caillaux, who was back at the Ministry of Finance. It was Caillaux who had launched the Radical programme with his speech at Pau— income tax and the return to two years' service. On the other side, the ·leaders who had been cut off from power by the resurgence of the Radicals and who were responsible for the three-years law, formed, under Briand's leadership, the 'Fédération des Gauches'; and the approaching election seemed to reduce itself to a duel between Caillaux and Briand with the military law as the theme. Jaurès led the orthodox Socialists in a real though not formal alliance with the Radicals, and as the Senate refused to tamper with the *scrutin d'arrondissement*, 'Republican discipline' could be trusted to defeat both open and concealed reaction, the feeble remnants of the Right, the waverers of the Centre and the more dangerous 'Fédération des Gauches' which united so many of the ablest parliamentarians.

Before the electors were given a chance to decide, the political system received a new shock that seemed to the jaundiced critics on the Right to justify all their contempt for the Republic and may have persuaded foreign observers that France was in almost as bad a way as her neighbour Britain. If she had no great party encouraging rebellion and mutiny, she had a scandal of the traditional type that predicts the ruin of the State—if old-fashioned moralists are to be believed. When the news spread round Paris on the evening of March 16th, 1914, that the editor of one of the chief Conservative newspapers had been killed in his office by the wife of the leading member of the Government, even the most blasé were startled. The campaign run by Calmette's paper, the *Figaro*, against the leader of the Radicals had been bitter even by French standards. It had consisted largely in the publication and threatened publication of those letters which even wise politicians write to women but which, when published, are so hard to get taken in the proper spirit.[1] They affected seriously M. Caillaux's reputation for political candour and consistency, and it was believed that Calmette was determined to go through to the end, to pursue his campaign against the powerful Finance Minister, regardless of the latter's violent temper, pride, and power. Attempts to silence Calmette failed, until Madame Caillaux tried the remedy of killing her husband's accuser or slanderer.

It is characteristic of the odd atmosphere of the 'Republic of Pals' that the Prime Minister, M. Gaston Doumergue, although of sound Calvinist stock, should have attempted to keep M. Caillaux in the Government. M. Caillaux had more sense and realized that his position, for the moment at least, was impossible. His place was by his imprisoned wife, whom he hastened to visit in the company of the young Radical Minister, M. Malvy. The Cabinet was reorganized; Renoult succeeded Caillaux and, more important, Malvy succeeded Renoult at the Interior. The Empire had found it harder to adjust itself to the murder of Victor Noir by Prince Pierre Bonaparte than, at first, the Doumergue Cabinet did to the killing of Calmette.[2]

There were violent scenes in Paris, crowds expressed their disapproval by the usual methods of cat-calls and hissing, but the machine of police and politics worked, at first, smoothly. But the vacant chair

---

[1] The letters were written to the second Madame Caillaux and had been stolen by the first.

[2] M. Thalamas, whose objections as a professor to the Nationalist exploitation of Joan of Arc have been mentioned (cf. p. 429), contributed the oddest document to the odd dossier of the case. He sent Madame Caillaux an open letter congratulating her on her achievement. He knew from experience the sufferings of those who had dared to combat wealth and clericalism. 'Make what use you like of this letter. Find in it the voice of an honest man who is shocked and of a journalist-deputy who is made heart-sore by the goings-on of those who dishonour the Press and Parliament.' Madame Thalamas, the world was informed, was writing an approving article for the *Dépêche de Versailles*.

of M. Caillaux was hardly filled when, on March 17th, the Chamber was the scene of a St. Patrick's Day row worthy of a place beside the attack on André, perhaps even worthy of comparison with the attacks on the Panama 'chequards'. It began in the traditional way with a demand from Jacques Delahaye for information about a letter whose existence had been asserted by Calmette, a letter proving, it was said, that in 1911 MM. Monis and Caillaux had brought pressure to bear on the Procureur-Général, Fabre, to secure the postponement of the investigation into the business affairs of M. Rochette.

M. Rochette was a financier on the edge of respectability. He had fallen foul of Clemenceau, who, as Prime Minister, had taken legal steps against him, an act of distrust that earned for Rochette the patronage of Jaurès. The best friends of the great tribune were the first to admit that he was no very good judge of character, especially of the character of sharks like Rochette. But it was not unimportant that by 1914, when Rochette was not even a hero to those who thought him a financial genius or a martyr to those who thought him the victim of Clemenceau's tyranny, he should once have been a stick used by the extreme Left to beat the Government with. By 1911, Rochette had been convicted, but had appealed. It was the postponement of the hearing of his appeal that was the favour Rochette, according to rumours, had asked of Monis and Caillaux and which had been granted after improper pressure had been brought to bear on the judicial functionaries whose business it was to deal with the matter.

The rumours involved more people than M. Monis and M. Caillaux, for the arrest of Rochette was declared to have been due to a conspiracy to break the market, a conspiracy to which M. Clemenceau had lent his aid, innocently or less innocently. When the affair was first investigated by a parliamentary Commission, Fabre, the Procureur-Général, refused to discuss the question of whether the postponements of the trial which allowed Rochette to continue his operations were due to political pressure. He hinted that they were, but refused to expand his hint. The Chairman of the Commission, M. Jaurès, summoned M. Monis to tell his story, but M. Monis was averse, he asserted, to increasing the amount of scandal. 'I will be the victim if you like, of your injustice, but I will be the proud and silent victim.' M. Jaurès did not insist; the mystery was left unprobed and Rochette had his first conviction quashed.

Assassination is enough to make ghosts walk, and M. Monis thought that being a proud and silent victim would not now impress the Chamber as favourably as it had the Commission. M. Monis, like M. Floquet, fell back on stout denial. He had not been concerned in any attempt to postpone Rochette's trial. That slander, he implied, had been scotched by the Commission whereby he passed the ball to Jaurès, who demanded that, if the document that proved these charges existed, it should be produced. Doumergue followed. Delahaye had admitted that he had only seen a copy: where was the original? The Radicals were triumphant but not for long, for M. Barthou, rising in his turn, declared that the original existed, that he had seen it, that in fact he had it in his possession, there it was! The document was decisive; it told how, under pressure from Monis and Caillaux, Rochette had been given a respite; the motives of Caillaux may have been of the highest, he may have been in all sincerity desirous of not upsetting the market at a critical moment by a new scandal, but his enemies had triumphed.

Behind the campaign of scandal there was a bitter personal feud. Caillaux, by his arrogance, his pride, his energy, had made many enemies, and his contempt for many of his collaborators was so great that he did not remember that a politician who wishes to pose—or act —as the defender of the poor against the rich, of the Republic against its enemies, cannot afford some kinds of acquaintances. His friends, for example, were active in launching a new left-wing journal, the *Bonnet Rouge*, which was not dangerous; but among the respectable politicians and journalists who backed the new paper, were men whose characters were vulnerable, men like M. Almeyreda. Caillaux, the enemy of embattled high finance, had too many friends or acquaintances on the edge of low finance. Moreover, he had made dangerous political enemies, notably Aristide Briand, whose good nature was one of his chief assets, who managed to be on good terms with the most diverse men and women, but who never forgave Caillaux. It was to Briand, as Minister of Justice, that Fabre confided the damning document and Briand had handed it on to his successor, Barthou. It was the publication of this report by Calmette that was the sword hung over Caillaux's head. It was to silence Calmette that all resources of pressure had been adopted, and they had been so far successful that Calmette, pressed not to use the Fabre letter, had printed the private letter which had infuriated Caillaux and driven the second Madame Caillaux to murder.

Opposed to Caillaux were very astute persons indeed, among them Louis Barthou. When he received from Briand the sealed Fabre letter, Barthou decided, he told the Chamber, that it was not an official document and that he was not justified in handing it on to his successor, so he kept it.[1] It was the knowledge of the existence of this explosive document that accounted for the desperate efforts of Doumergue and Monis to hush it all up; but why, knowing that it did exist, they should have risked their reputations in such dangerous denials of the truth is more hard to explain. There was a third Com-

---

[1] Barthou was an enthusiastic collector of autographs and of rare books; his methods were later the subject of a violent attack by Maurras in the famous tract *Le Bibliophile Barthou*. This particular example of the collector's point of view was rebuked by Jaurès, whose sense of humour was never his strong point and who was in an awkward position.

mission, which reproved the activities of Caillaux and Monis, rebuked Briand and Barthou and, of course, dealt severely with M. Fabre, who was not a deputy. The laws of political responsibility were not mocked.[1]

If Briand, Barthou, and the other leaders of the 'Fédération des Gauches' were naïve enough to think that the revelations of bad memory and plastic morals in high quarters would help them in the elections of 1914, they were undeceived. The real victors in 1914, as in 1893 after Panama, were the Socialists; they returned 102 strong, while Caillaux's Radicals were over 160 strong. So far as the country had expressed an opinion, it was hostile to any policy of domestic appeasement and against the three-years law. The authors of that law might lament, as they did, that a great question of high policy had been debated in circumstances in which the easy way was sure to win votes; the new Chamber had a mandate to end three-years service.[2] Poincaré regarded himself as the trustee of national interests, interpreting those interests in a simple nationalist fashion. He was determined to guard the sacred three-years service law and was naïve enough to do it by trying to foist on the Chamber a Ministry publicly committed to its defence. But the ignominious collapse of the Ribot Government made it necessary to bow to the verdict of the electors and of the new Chamber; the task of forming a Ministry was entrusted to René Viviani, who took office on June 16th.

The choice of Viviani, as the least unpleasant way for the President to retreat, was very natural. No one could be more eloquent in defence of the immortal principles of the Left than the ex-Socialist leader. But he was of Italian origin and, like Gambetta, fond of a *combinazione*. Moreover, he was a leading member of the Bar, and the uncharitable hinted that his success there owed something to the kindness of that even more successful leader of the Bar, Poincaré. For a man of Viviani's talents it was not impossible to find a way out of the dilemma for himself and for Poincaré. It was necessary both to carry out electoral promises and to keep the bargain with the President, and the new Government was considering the problem of how to repeal the three-years service law while keeping the troops with the colours for thirty-six months, when events made this compromise impossible and

---

[1] There were, of course, many other elements in the Caillaux-Calmette feud. The relations of Caillaux with his first wife and with his second wife (while she was still married to someone else), the relations between Monsieur and Madame Calmette, the fight for the control of the *Figaro*, all were involved. It was not a triangle but a maze (with as many doors as the set of a Palais Royal farce) which was brought to the attention of the French public by Madame Caillaux's pistol shot. It may be worth while adding that Madame Caillaux was acquitted. She had been defended by Labori.

[2] Caillaux took his triumphant return by his faithful voters of Mamers as a rebuke to the slanderers who had tried to defame him because he was for peace and fiscal justice. That opposition to a settlement with Germany and to an income tax were among the motives of Caillaux's detractors is undoubted; it does not follow that M. Caillaux, by his conduct, had not diminished his utility as a public servant defending the public interest against private wealth. But electors did not expect too much.

superfluous.[1]   The news of the assassination of the heir to the Austro-Hungarian throne in the capital of the annexed provinces of Bosnia-Herzegovina on June 28th made less of a sensation in Paris than had the killing of Calmette.   Diplomats were more impressed, for the murder of the Archduke could not fail to make Austro-Serbian relations even worse—if possible.   At the moment of the murder, the Austrian Foreign Office was busy with plans for a diplomatic isolation of Serbia; and the murder gave it an opportunity to press forward with those plans. But the secret of the decision to end, once for all, the Serbian menace to the existence of the Dual Monarchy was well kept.   Poincaré and his new Prime Minister, Viviani, were due in St. Petersburg on a visit planned by the President to reaffirm the Alliance and to smooth over the difficulties between Britain and Russia that were making the working of the Entente difficult.   It was decided to carry out the programme.

The position of Austria was simple.   She suspected, although she could not prove, that the assassination was the work of agents of Serbian officials.   She was convinced that the tide was running against the Monarchy; that the Balkan situation had to be ended or mended. She could not be content with a mere diplomatic victory like that of 1909 or 1913.   An independent Serbia could not be on good terms with Austria, for she was bound to try to play the rôle of a Balkan Prussia or Piedmont, to attempt to unite the South Slavs under her leadership.   Austria wanted to create a situation in which a war against Serbia would be made possible.   After victory, Serbia would be partitioned among her neighbours, Rumania, Bulgaria, Albania, who would thus be bound to the Austrian side.   A rump state might survive under Austrian domination, but there would be no annexation of Serbians to the Monarchy, which was already in danger of death from too many Slav subjects.   Austria hoped that the war would be localized and, if she could get German support, hoped to frighten off Russia.

On July 6th, Germany, with great rashness, undertook to back up her ally, and, with this trump-card in his pocket, Berchtold, the Austrian Foreign Minister, drafted an ultimatum so constructed that Serbia could not accept it and remain independent.   Each year that passed strengthened Russia, from a military and economic point of view.   She was rapidly improving her army and, in the years since the peace with Japan, she had made great economic progress.   No delay could help Austria.   Then, too, the military measures taken by Germany, the war levy and the great increase in military force, could not be repeated very soon.   France, on the other hand, had not had much time to reap the benefits, such as they were, of the three-years law, and the reform of her artillery had only just begun.   Britain was preoccupied with the Irish

---

[1] Isvolski, who did not lack shrewdness, realized that the three-years law was safer in the hands of a Left Ministry than in those of an openly reactionary and therefore weak Ministry.   Only the Left was, in fact, capable of carrying out the policy of the Right.

crisis. If it was true that a show-down with Serbia was necessary, the calculation that 1914 was the year and the Serajevo murder the occasion was correct. That, in the long run, it ended in the collapse of the Austrian political structure does not show that this policy was ill-timed except in being too late. And if the Germans were right in thinking that the survival of Austria was indispensable to their security, they were right in backing Austria, although wrong or imprudent in letting Austria have a free hand in deciding the nature of the steps to be taken.

The gravity of the crisis was fully understood in Belgrade, as was natural, for several members of the Serbian Government had known of the assassination plot and had done nothing effective to prevent its execution, while important Serbian officers were actually behind the conspiracy. In 1914 it was much harder than it would be now, when Balkan habits have spread over so much of the world, to make Western nations realize that there were countries in which high officials used murder as a political weapon and who thought a world war a slight price to pay for national unity. Nor did Austria's own record help her, for she had unfortunately allowed her *bona fides* to become suspect in a famous trial in which a zealous Pan-German historian had been the victim of forgers anxious to damn some Croat patriots. Such mistakes are made in all countries, as *The Times* in London should have remembered, but the zeal of the Austro-Hungarian State to convict Croat nationalists, like the zeal of Lord Salisbury, Mr. Joseph Chamberlain and others to discredit Parnell, was more damaging to the repute of the dupes of the forgers than they realized. The Friedjung trial [1] made it harder for the sound part of the Austrian case to be accepted by Europe. The terms of the ultimatum when they were published made a bad impression, especially since Serbia was only given forty-eight hours to accept or refuse *in toto*.[2] The Serbians were quite astute enough to take advantage of this situation. Like Cavour in 1859, they put the Austrians in a bad light by accepting almost all the demands. To the world in 1914, as to the world before Ems in 1870, one power had gained a great diplomatic victory and was soon to appear as a warmonger by not being content with it. This was not merely the reaction of the Entente but of the German Emperor. Berchtold and his colleagues could not openly avow what was, nevertheless, their conviction, that no diplomatic victory over Serbia was any good. Serbia must be made impotent by war. It was the contention of both Germany and Austria at this stage that the war could and should be localized: but the decision on that point would be made in St. Petersburg.

During the visit of Poincaré and Viviani, Russia had been assured

---

[1] The too zealous defender of German culture who played the part of Cavaignac or Lord Salisbury was a Jew.
[2] This note was delivered in Belgrade on July 23rd, 1914.

by France that her ally would stand by her. As in 1912, Poincaré, although anxious to avoid war, was equally anxious not to give Russia an excuse to abandon the Alliance or to let it fall into desuetude. Clemenceau and Pichon had run that risk in 1909 in the Bosnian crisis. Poincaré and Viviani would not run it in 1914; they would not take any steps to bring pressure to bear on Russia which might suggest to the Tsar, or to Sazonov, that France was indifferent to Russia's Balkan interests.

Those interests were, in fact, involved; the Serbian question was not a matter of life and death for Russia, but the annihilation of Serbia would put an end to Russian influence in the Balkans, bring Rumania back to the Triple Alliance and end the use of Panslav patriotism as a cement for the Autocracy. The Russian Army and bourgeoisie, if not the peasantry or town workers, were convinced that the abandonment of Serbia was to be avoided at all costs, even at the cost of a war with Austria that could hardly avoid becoming a war with Germany. What Sazonov wanted was to convince Austria and Germany that Russia was serious this time. He wanted assurances from France that she would back up Russia. He got them; he wanted assurances from Britain that she would back up France; he did not get them. Poincaré and Viviani had sailed for home a few hours before the publication of the Austrian ultimatum, with its disclosure of an intention to reduce Serbia to a satellite power, if not to destroy her altogether, but the French Ambassador, Paléologue, who had been sent to Russia to replace a less vigorous diplomat, was a good disciple of his former chief, Delcassé. So far as Russian action was affected by the certainty of French help, then Paléologue was responsible for stiffening Sazonov, and Poincaré for making those assurances of support, *if* the worst came to the worst, seem reliable.

As a means of bringing pressure to bear on Austria, Sazonov wanted to mobilize in those Russian military districts which were opposite the Austrian frontiers. Here a point of military technique became of the greatest importance. Germany hoped to get the Entente to let Austria deal with Serbia alone, and Russia was anxious to avoid appearing to intimidate Germany. But it was impossible to mobilize effectively against Austria without mobilizing in the Warsaw district, and that was a menace to Germany. For it must be remembered that Germany's chances of success in a war on two fronts were thought, in the opinion of all experts, to depend on her ability to mobilize much faster than Russia. Every day of peace and mobilization was a serious loss for Germany. A Russian mobilization then must involve war or the loss, for every day that it went on without war, of an increasingly large part of the chief German military asset—time.

Sazonov was able to delay mobilization and even to force the withdrawal of such an order which the weak Tsar had been induced to give.

But Sazonov was determined, even at the cost of a war, to make it impossible for Austria to destroy Serbia; and, by declaring war on Serbia (July 27th), Austria had made it plain how far she was willing to go and how hard it would be for her to retreat. Her German partner, repenting belatedly of her rashness, tried to get Austria to halt her invasion of Serbia till some compromise could be worked out. The British Foreign Secretary, pulling France along with him, was working desperately for a settlement. But there remained the unescapable fact: Austria thought the destruction of Serbia, and Russia thought her rescue, worth a great war. Each hoped to get what she wanted without a general war, but even the certainty of a European war would not have deterred the rulers.

These rulers, by the end of July, were not the statesmen but the soldiers. And the soldiers in turn were the prisoners of their machines. From the moment Russia mobilized, war was certain; for if mobilization did not mean war in France or Russia, it did mean war in Germany. To mobilize without war was to the advantage of Russia; to allow that situation to continue was impossible from the German viewpoint. It was obvious, by July 30th, that in certain circumstances Russia would fight and that France would support her; it was known next day that Russia had mobilized, as it was rightly suspected that she had been taking military precautions which cut down the German margin of security for some days before that. The attitude of Britain was a cause of uncertainty and worry to both sides. Sir Edward Grey could not promise aid to France and he could not threaten Germany with British intervention, for although he thought British honour and interest were involved, if a war came, in backing France, he was not sure that the Cabinet would support him. It is possible that had Grey been able to give a firm answer to German questionings, Germany would have brought a stronger pressure to bear on Austria. It is also possible that the result would have been to stiffen further the Russian resolve to prevent Austria doing what the rulers of Austria had decided must be done at any price.

In Paris there was great anxiety but no panic. London refused to give the comforting assurances demanded of her, and it grew more and more likely that war was coming. In such circumstances it was desirable not to repeat the mistake of 1870; desirable, that is, not to declare war. Germany in 1914 was less adroitly led than Germany in 1870. The news of the Russian mobilization made a German mobilization inevitable; especially as the French Government (whose Ambassador in Russia had failed to inform it of the Russian mobilization for a day after it occurred) at last gave way to Joffre's insistence and ordered a general mobilization an hour or two before Germany did. The two decisions were not directly connected; but they showed that the military necessities were regarded in the same light in Berlin and Paris.

The German Ambassador was ordered to ask the intentions of the French Government, and if they, by some miracle, said that they would remain neutral, he was to ask for the surrender of the great fortresses of Toul and Verdun as a guarantee. But as Viviani answered with polite evasions, the Ambassador did not need to present his demand. On July 26th a sealed letter had been sent to the German Minister in Belgium containing an ultimatum to be presented on further instructions. It demanded a free passage through the country whose independence and neutrality Prussia had twice guaranteed, a demand backed up by the plea of military necessity and by some quite superfluous lies about French designs on Belgium. And the declaration of war on France did not confine itself to stating, what was true, that France was the pledged ally of Russia with whom Germany was at war, it based the declaration on alleged and false French violations of German territory, while as a gesture, which did not in fact involve much military loss, if any, the French covering troops had been drawn back on an average 10 kilometres from the frontier to avoid any awkward incidents and to make a good impression on the world.

Germany was by now careless of what impression she made. She attempted to get Britain to promise an unconditional neutrality, promising in return that France should not lose any territory in Europe, but without extending the guarantee to the colonies. In London, Paul Cambon was trying in vain to get a definite announcement of his intentions from Grey. All he got was a promise that the German Fleet would not be allowed to enter the Channel, which, of course, would be a serious breach of British neutrality. The invasion of Belgium ended all British hesitation and, by the night of August 4th, both the great European combinations were at war, although it was a week or two before Austria and the Western powers were formally at war, and Italy, taking advantage of the good legal point that she had not been consulted about the ultimatum to Serbia, was neutral, ready to put herself on the market when the time came.

In France the whole crisis, as far as the people knew, had only lasted a few days; there was no warlike feeling in the masses; there was a powerful force of organized opposition to a war incarnate in Jean Jaurès. On July 31st the tribune was murdered, the first and one of the greatest of French losses. In all countries the nations believed that their rulers were the victims of aggression or of plots. They were all victims of a system. It was, by the ideas of the age, legitimate for Serbia to try to unite the South Slavs and legitimate for Austria to resist. Both Governments overstepped conventional limits in their pursuit of their legitimate but wholly incompatible aims; that was all. At the last moment, the Tsar made a despairing reference to The Hague tribunal, but no statesman, in Russia or out of it, thought for a moment of submitting the dispute to any third party. How could the right of the Habsburgs to rule the lands they had held for centuries be weighed against the resolution of the Serbs to unite their 'race'? It is possible that the war would have come anyway; but it did come because of the failure of Europe to find any way of settling peacefully the Austrian question. If there was any one group that, more than another, bears the responsibility for the war, it is the Magyar nobles and the Austrian Germans, above all the Sudeten Germans, who made a racial settlement within the old empire impossible.

BOOK IX

THE WAR

Allons, enfants de la patrie,
Le jour de gloire est arrivé.

La Marseillaise.

C'est la lutte finale,
Groupons tous et demain,
L'Internationale sera le genre humain.

L'Internationale.

CHAPTER I

THE FRONT

I

THE strength and weakness of the French Army in 1914 had curious resemblances to its strength and weakness in 1870. There was the same reliance on one or two weapons, without a sufficient study of their tactical use, their possibilities and limitations; there was the same under-estimation of the potential numerical strength and efficiency of the enemy. In the years that immediately followed the disasters of 1870, the military policy of France had been deeply marked by a sense of inferiority. It was, consequently, defensive in spirit; some critics might have said timid. The Peace of Frankfort had imposed on France a frontier deprived of one of its great barriers, Metz, but a frontier that still offered serious possibilities of fortification. These opportunities were fully exploited by an elaborate system of fortresses and forts, named after its chief designer, the system of Séré de Rivière. From north to south, the four major fortresses of Verdun, Toul, Epinal, Belfort, supported by many minor works, blocked all the ways into France, either across the Vosges from Alsace or from the twin fortresses of Metz–Thionville which were now the advanced bases of German military power in Lorraine. Twenty years after Sedan, a German advance into France was only possible if these fortresses (and the gaps that they covered) could be taken, covered or outflanked. And the temptation to outflank them grew, as German military opinion settled down to the study of the problems of the war on both fronts made probable by the Franco-Russian Alliance. For the French had not continued their frontier defences behind the Belgian frontier, where Maubeuge and some lesser works were a poor substitute for the ad-mirably-planned system of the eastern zone.

If the frontier barrier imposed on the German General Staff the duty of finding a way through it or around it, it imposed for over twenty years on the French Staff the duty of making the most of it. Even when the pessimism bred by 1870 and the real weakness that followed it had both given way to a reasonable degree of confidence and strength, the various French plans of campaign proposed to leave to the Germans the task of opening the campaign, of committing themselves to some solution of the very difficult problems set them by Séré de Rivière and of taking advantage of the difficulties inherent in any solution. Let the Germans engage themselves in the desperate assault on the frontier barrier and, when they were deeply involved, take such aggressive measures as the situation demanded.

Such were the prudent councils followed by the French Staff. But as the years passed, the prudence or timidity of these plans became distasteful to the men who were coming to the top in the French Army. That Army had, by 1890, not only recovered confidence in itself, but had impressed its high opinion of itself on outside observers. It was in many ways a pioneer; it had adopted the first magazine rifle, the Lebel, in 1889 [1]: and, in 1897, produced the 75-millimetre quick-firing field-gun, a weapon that was not only the first effective quick-firer, but which in 1914 was still the best, superior both to the German 77-millimetre gun and to the British 18-pounder. Nor was the prestige of the French Army due solely to its armament; the theory of war, the study of military history, the whole intellectual training of the officers who were to exercise the higher commands were raised to a high level. In General Bonnal, in Colonel Foch, in Commandant Colin, it had produced military historians and theorists whose writings were studied with respect in all the great armies. And the doctrine of war taught in the French military schools, especially by Foch and then by his disciples, became hostile to the whole policy of letting the enemy make the first moves. The main lesson of 1870 was, it was asserted, the importance of taking the initiative, of not submitting to the will of the enemy, for if one did so, the chance of repairing one's own mistakes or of profiting from those of the enemy was lost. The object of war was to impose one's will on the enemy until he surrendered or was rendered incapable of effective resistance; the means of imposing this surrender on the enemy was battle, and no defensive battle could give the results of an offensive one. At best, it prevented the enemy from carrying out, at that time and by that means, his projects; it did not force him to submit to yours and it did not in itself prevent him from trying again. The object of the French plan of campaign and consequently of the peace-time preparation of the Army should be to take the offensive from the start, not to allow the Germans to dictate the nature of the campaign by leaving them a free initiative. It was no longer enough to await the German attack in the shelter of the fortresses; they were to be spring-boards, not shelters. From those springboards the French Army was to deliver the 'blow that cannot be parried' which it was the object of the general to make easy.

[1] The Lebel was not a real repeating rifle like the later Mauser (German) or Lee-Metford and Lee-Enfield (British). Its magazine held eight cartridges, but each was inserted separately so that, in combat, once the magazine was emptied the rifle was reduced to being a single-shot weapon. This weakness was not remedied until some time after the outbreak of the war of 1914.

The successive French plans of campaign thus began to change in character, but even in 1910, the sixteenth made since 1870 was marked by a semi-defensive character. It was still dependent for its development on the revelation of the character of the German attack that would come with the outbreak of war, it involved an abandonment of portions of French territory from the very beginning, and it was a plan that suffered, in addition, the defect of ignoring the possibility that the Germans would turn the line of fortresses by invading Belgium. Worse still, it was a plan based on military resources grossly inadequate for the tasks assigned them, for it opposed only forty-two French divisions to sixty-five German. No system of fortification could supply such deficiencies, especially since the fortifications could be turned.

Such were the views of the new chief of the General Staff, Joseph César Joffre, who would have to command in time of war and who entered on his functions in July 1911 when the storm-clouds on the horizon were more and more ominous. The new General-in-Chief was just under sixty.[1] He was from the south, a native of Rousillon, but in physique and temperament very unlike the typical *méridional* of fiction. Burly, blue-eyed, phlegmatic, he had risen fast, displaying great organizing ability in the colonies, and earning the commendations of his great chief, Galliéni, in Madagascar. An engineer, he had taken part in the fortification of the frontier, but as a colonial officer he had commanded mixed units, and in his march to Timbuctu had displayed a capacity for command and a readiness to take responsibility which earned and deserved high commendation. Grave differences of opinion between General Michel and his colleagues of the Committee of National Defence[2] led to the resignation of Michel, and after the refusal, first of Galliéni, then of Pau, the post was offered to Joffre, who had been for a year past a member of the committee.

Joffre at once set about recasting the plan of campaign as fast as his resources would permit him. He managed, by calling on reserve divisions which the old plan had neglected, to raise the forces put into the field immediately on mobilization to sixty-three divisions against the sixty-five which the French Intelligence Service attributed to the Germans. In this way the inferiority of French numbers was diminished and Joffre (who had, for a time, specialized in railway work) believed that it was possible by a better use of the railways to give to this mass a sufficient flexibility and mobility. The next problem was that presented by the Belgian gap in the French defensive system. This gap presented a political and a military aspect. It seemed increasingly probable from the disposition of German forces in peace-time that an invasion of Belgium was part of their war plan. The Government was asked whether it would be admissible, if there was danger of a German

---

[1] Born January 12th, 1852.
[2] I have thus translated the title 'Conseil supérieur de la guerre'.

attack on Belgium, to take the initiative and move into that country. London was discreetly sounded to the same effect and the decision was made that only in the event of a German attack on Belgium would the French Army cross the frontier.

This decision was politically extremely prudent, but it had one military defect: it made very difficult any preliminary agreement with the Belgian military authorities as to a common plan of campaign. In fact, the Belgian plan provided for a massing of the Belgian Army in three groups, one to defend the country against Germany, the other against France, the other against a possible British landing. This vagueness as to the character of the danger and help that might come from Belgium was one reason why no detailed plan of campaign was drawn up. Apart from massing all possible forces on the frontier and being resolved to take the offensive as soon as possible, the actual decisions to be taken were left to the outbreak of the war. According to the joint Franco-Russian military agreements of 1913, both countries would take the offensive at once, and this necessity for joint action and for reassuring the Russians was one reason why the policy of a defensive recoil and a waiting attitude was abandoned.

To carry this plan into effect it was necessary, so thought Joffre, to do more than utilize all the resources of the existing military system; it was necessary to augment them.

The growing international tension, the great increases in the numbers and resources of the German Army which were announced, the success of the campaign of national revival, resulted in the conversion of the Chamber and the voting of the law of three-years in August 1913. This law provided a peace-time army of 700,000 men, less by over a hundred and fifty thousand than that which the new German law provided for, but, it was thought, sufficient (with the promised Russian aid) to make an offensive feasible as soon as mobilization was completed.

Joffre had hitherto merely modified Plan XVI; he now replaced it by Plan XVII, under whose direction the campaign of 1914 was begun. After a year's work, the immense task of drafting detailed instructions was over and by May 1st, 1914, the office preparations for putting the plan into effect were completed. Two great masses of troops were constituted; one on the south between the Moselle and the Vosges, one on the north whose junction with the southern wing would be secured by an army facing Metz–Thionville, and an army of reserve which would either move to the left of the right wing or to the right of the left wing. The armies would be numbered from right to left (south-east to north-east); the 1st and 2nd joined to the 5th by the 3rd and the army of reserve; the 4th, inserting itself *either* between the 2nd and 3rd or between the 3rd and 5th. Which alternative would be adopted depended on the German plan. If Germany invaded Belgium, the

4th Army would move north-east and help the left wing; if Germany respected Belgian neutrality, the 4th French Army would add its weight to the offensive of the right wing of the French mass. Certain minor units were earmarked as the special reserve of the General-in-Chief, and the great fortresses were provided with garrisons of reserve troops. Twelve territorial divisions of middle-aged reservists, indifferently trained and equipped, would undertake the less-important garrison' duties. When the mobilization was completed, the French Commander-in-Chief would have under his hand nearly two million men.[1]

What was the military value of this great force? It was great, but it was less great than it might and should have been. Its main striking force was infantry and field-artillery. The equipment of the infantry, with its defective rifle, its insufficient equipment in machine-guns, its conspicuous uniform of blue coat and red trousers, had made no real progress at a time when the German Army had in its equipment and training made a great deal.

The field-gun, the seventy-five, was still the best weapon of its kind, but it was not the only kind. Although the attacking French Army would have to begin its attack in hilly and wooded country, its artillery, admirable for rapid and accurate fire in open country, had a flat trajectory. The new Commander-in-Chief was conscious of this weakness and he was anxious to equip his armies with a mobile heavy artillery. This the Germans had done, and the weaknesses of their seventy-seven were largely compensated for by an adequate supply of mobile heavy artillery capable of mastering the seventy-fives. But Joffre failed to secure in time the funds necessary for a new artillery (though the plans and models of such guns were in existence) and had to content himself with the adoption of a device enabling the existing field-guns to fire at a higher angle and so be of a little more use in hilly country than they had been.[2]

Even more serious than the defects of equipment were the defects of tactical training. French military thought had been preoccupied for forty years with the question of the lessons to be drawn from 1870, but it had not continued to draw the same kind of lessons. Immediately after the war, the tactical teaching of the French Army had laid great stress on the effect of fire; it had recognized, as the Germans had been forced to do, that the chassepot *had* worked wonders and that, supported by a better artillery, it, or its successors, could still work wonders. And the lessons taught by the chassepot at Gravelotte had been repeated by the Remingtons of the Turks at Plevna. The improvement of modern

---

[1] 1,865,000 men of whom the garrison of Paris and a spare reserve division in the environs were under the authority of the War Office, not of the Commander-in-Chief.

[2] The history of this artillery question is curiously like that of 1870. The device that improved the seventy-five was the equivalent of the alterations in the fuse that were the reply of Lebœuf to the new Krupp guns, except that the improvement of 1914 was real if slight.

weapons had strengthened the defence. But in the decade before 1914, this obvious truth was neglected. Arguing that the purely passive methods of 1870 made useless the temporary tactical successes won by rifle fire, the advocates of the offensive, in greater or less degree, added to their general doctrine of the strategical offensive, a doctrine of a tactical offensive. This led them, even the greatest and most cautious of them, Colonel Foch, to minimize the reinforcement brought to the defensive by the improvements in equipment, the magazine rifle, the effective machine-gun, the quickfiring field-gun and smokeless powder. The teachings of 1870 were repeated in South Africa, in Manchuria, but despite heretics like Colonel Pétain, for a time professor of infantry tactics at the Staff College,[1] the dominant military teaching in France either denied or minimized the truth that a man standing still, or more likely lying down, fires more rapidly and more accurately than a man advancing on his feet or even on his belly, and that this was true of the other weapons as well. To arguments like these, the reply was given that troops could be trained to stand any losses in their advance, and that once the enemy line was reached, the power of the offensive would more than compensate for the preliminary losses; the bayonet would redress the balance of the rifle, and the enemy, driven out of his position, would suffer more in his hasty retreat than the victors had done in their brisk advance.

This gratifying result was to be obtained almost entirely by infantry action. The rôle of cavalry was to explore and to pursue; a reasonable enough doctrine, but the rôle of artillery was almost as limited. Until the infantry attack had made the enemy disclose himself, the guns were, in general, to remain silent, then they were to *support* the attack but they were not to *prepare* it. It was a strange doctrine for the most famous artillery in Europe; and a military doctrine which laid so much stress on developing a theory in accord with national capacities and traditions might have reflected a little more on the tradition of Bureau and Bonaparte.[2]

The new doctrine's triumph was not complete when Joffre took command; and when the professor of infantry tactics at the Staff College was asked to prepare an infantry manual, he insisted on the importance of machine-gun fire. But the higher powers would have none of this timid, mechanical teaching, and in April 1914 the manual of the new orthodox doctrine was issued. It was a doctrine of the offensive at all costs, attributing a virtue to the physical movement of masses of men animated by the *furia francese* which might have been in order before the Battle of Pavia (1525) but was highly unrealistic in

---

[1] École Supérieure de Guerre.

[2] Though not yet issued, a heavy field-gun, the 'one hundred and five', was being manufactured, and each *army* had some heavy artillery allotted to it. It should also be remembered that the first British forces in France had no heavy artillery at all, and their field-guns had only shrapnel, no high-explosive shells.

1914. But the 'Young Turks', who were now in the ascendant, went far beyond Foch, for as their chief representative, Colonel de Grand-maison, asserted, their faith was that 'in the offensive, imprudence is the best safeguard. If we push the offensive spirit even to excess it won't perhaps be enough.'

And in 1913 and 1914 it was possible to neglect the lessons of the Russo-Japanese war in favour of the apparently more comforting lessons of the Balkan wars, where the armies trained and equipped by French officers and French armament makers had defeated the Turks trained by German officers and equipped by Krupps. It was possible to dwell on movement and on the moral qualities of an offensively-minded infantry and forget that the victorious Bulgarians, before the lines of Chatalja, had been as helpless as the most defensively-minded army could have been.

In the few days before the outbreak of war, the main effort of General Joffre was directed to limiting the damage done by the peaceful gestures of the civilian Ministers, to limiting the withdrawal of troops 10 kilometres within the French frontiers to as short a period as possible, to putting into effect the preliminary measures for mobilization and, finally, to wringing from a reluctant Government the order for general mobilization. On August 1st the placards announcing the mobilization of the 'Armies of Land and Sea' were on the walls of every town and village and, despite the statement of the President of the Republic that 'mobilization is not war', few can have doubted that war had come.

The problems of the first days of war had long perplexed the Government chiefs. The vociferous anti-militarism of so many French leaders had bred a fear that the national ordeal would begin with an attempted sabotage of mobilization. But in face of the danger from the east, French national unity reappeared under the surface of faction and hate. And this union was helped by the reassuring discovery that the mobilization was proceeding with an ease and smoothness very different from the improvizations of 1870; the French Army, in this department, had learnt its lesson, and it absorbed its reserves and sent them off to the front as fast and as easily as did the Germans. Given the accuracy of the statistical information at the disposal of the French General Staff, Joffre had every reason to suppose that he would be able to assemble a mass equal to that of the Germans as soon as the Germans.

Joffre was right as far as the speed of concentration of the two armies was concerned, woefully wrong as far as numbers went. For in 1914, as in 1870, the French leaders refused to believe that the Germans could make good soldiers out of all reservists. Reconciled to the addition of more than an equal number of reservists to their own peace-time strength, but recognizing that the French reserve divisions were not at all on the level of their active divisions, the French chiefs had learned without perturbation that their German opposite numbers had prepared to put into the field complete army corps composed of reserve troops, but, since they did not believe that such troops were of any value, they refused to take their existence seriously. But the Germans had gone further; they had created entirely new formations, the 'ersatz' (substitute) units composed of the troops left over in regimental depots when the ranks of the active and reserve units had been filled, and of these extra formations the French Intelligence Service had no news of any kind. This double mistake was to be dearly paid for. During the first three weeks of war the repeated reports of great German masses on the extreme right of the German line, some of the reports being remarkably detailed and accurate, were completely disregarded since they *could* not be true, all the active corps of the German Army being accounted for. The Belgians, from whom most of this information came and who had good reasons for believing in it, were not allowed to disturb the peace of General Headquarters with stories of the invasion of their country by the Germans in force. The French cavalry corps sent into Belgian Luxembourg failed almost completely to penetrate the German screen and failed to report to Joffre the few fragments of truth it discovered. And that truth was very disconcerting, for the main German effort was directed to turning the French left flank by sweeping right across Belgium, not merely (as the French believed) confined to seizing the Meuse bridges and extending their right a little beyond their own frontier. The French attack, that is to say, was to be delivered against an enemy strong enough to withstand it and, at the same time, with enough extra strength to develop its own plan of campaign almost undisturbed. It took a little over three weeks for this to be made evident to Joffre, and during those three weeks the French Army was led blindfold to a great disaster.

II

It will be remembered that the main variation of Plan XVII depended on whether the Germans kept to their own territory or not; on August 2nd, as soon as the invasion of Luxembourg was known, Joffre ordered the 4th Army to take its place between the 3rd and 5th. This was a recognition that a great part of the German Army would act north, not south of Metz, but it was a decision made before anyone could know how far north and west the German right would march. The French Army now presented a continuous front from the Swiss frontier to the eastern frontier of Belgium. The 4th Army was no longer available as a strategic reserve; and as it became evident that, somehow or other, the Germans *were* massing troops in central and western Belgium, the only reply possible was the extension westward of the 5th Army. This was earnestly demanded by its commander, Lanrezac, who was convinced that a more formidable German force was on his left than was believed at Headquarters, but who was allowed by Joffre to do as he wished.

The first French move was a raid by the covering troops into Alsace, a raid that easily occupied Mulhouse, as the German plan left Alsace unguarded for the moment, and so produced a mood of patriotic exultation in Paris, but a mere raid that ended in a hasty retreat. It was in fact rather like Saarbrücken over again. But it was not until the 14th of August that really serious operations began, with the advance of the two right-wing armies (1st and 2nd) against the inferior forces that the Germans had entrusted with the guard of their southern wing. A new army of Alsace under Pau was got together and resumed the attack on Mulhouse, while its neighbours advanced in Lorraine. By the time the critical moment had come (August 19th and 20th), the Army of Alsace, thanks to the prudence of its commander, had been saved from advancing in the air, but was still too far away to help its neighbours whose attacks had been extremely costly, whose advance had been slow, and who were now vigorously counter-attacked by the Germans and forced into retreat. The right wing of the French Army had run into superior forces and its rôle was reduced to keeping those forces busy, while Joffre sought for victory on his left. On the left, the advance was necessarily delayed a little by the necessity of waiting until the British Expeditionary Force took its place in the line on the extreme left, and this was impossible before August 21st.

Joffre could not remain wholly indifferent to the news of the German masses on his left; but, still under the erroneous belief that no reserve corps were available, he could only account for the strength of the German right by assuming that they had weakened their centre. He decided, therefore, to leave the task of dealing with the German flank to his 5th Army, to the British and to the Belgian Army, now that the Belgians had been successfully withdrawn from the doomed fortresses of the Meuse (Liége and Namur). His centre armies, the 3rd and 4th, would strike at the enemy's centre and, if successful, seize its means of communication. But this scheme was based on an illusion; the German centre was not weaker but stronger than the French centre, and the 3rd and 4th Armies advanced in hilly and wooded country to be bloodily repulsed by an enemy stronger in numbers, in excellent defensive positions, and much better equipped for the only kind of war possible in the Ardennes and on the Meuse. The second French blow had failed and failed more completely than the first. And the main German blow was just being delivered, for against the 5th Army and the British were marching not seven but fifteen corps! The battles of Charleroi and Mons, the retreat of the last units of the Allied forces in line, followed. By August 25th the truth was revealed; the Allied Armies were in rapid retreat from an enemy greatly superior in numbers, anxious to force them to a new battle which, once joined, could only be disastrous, a battle which could be evaded only by abandoning the north of France to the enemy. It was a shock that tested the resolution of the country, of the Army and of its leaders, for the war of 1914 had begun with every appearance of being 1870 over again, only worse. The Army had not only failed strategically, but its tactical shortcomings had been revealed at frightful cost; 300,000 killed and wounded had refuted Grandmaison.

It is not to be wondered at that the natural pessimism that now struck so many Frenchmen should have had its counterpart in an equally natural exaltation in the German ranks and especially among the generals. For things had gone even better than had been planned; the left wing of the German Armies had defeated the French with almost as much ease as had the centre and right, whose business it had been to do the main job. The original German plan had been merely to turn the French left, but now there was the possibility of turning *both* flanks, of rolling the broken fragments against their own fortified line, of creating the possibility of a far greater Sedan. The organization of the German Army fostered such illusions, for it was like a loose federation rather than like the tightly-centralized army over which Joffre ruled. Each army commander exercised and was supposed to exercise a great deal of initiative. The far-away Commander-in-Chief in Coblence and Luxembourg never saw his Army commanders and was sometimes reduced to picking up their wireless messages to each other to discover what they were doing. The German Commander-in-Chief was Moltke, the nephew of the victor of 1870; his uncle had commanded in this fashion and the recipe was to be tested again.

For a week the pursuit went on, with each German commander anxious to emulate the exploits of the others and not very willing to recognize that another army than his might be the best one to give the *coup de grâce* to the fleeing foe. And this failure to co-operate in perfect harmony was accentuated by the fact that, on various sections of the advancing German front, there was evidence that, despite the initial disasters and the speed of the French retreat, the enemy was not yet incapable of resistance. On the east, the attacks of the armies in Lorraine made but slow progress against the French, strongly posted on fortified heights and, in some places, able to call on the fortress artillery to aid them to repulse the repeated and expensive German attacks. Even at the opposite extreme, the British 2nd Corps at Le Cateau and the French 5th Army at Guise showed that they could still fight to some purpose; but as the headlong advance continued, as the magnet of Paris came nearer, it was harder to keep one's head in the various headquarters of the German armies.

It was even harder to do it in Joffre's headquarters, where so many illusions had been shattered in less than a week and where the dreadful responsibility of being the organizer of defeat was always before the

General's mind. But Joffre had always had a talent for shouldering responsibility and he was now called on to exercise it to the full. From the moment that the collapse of his plan of campaign had been made evident, he had cleared his mind of the old illusions and set about reconstructing his front. He projected and had to discard successive plans for standing on various lines as the full weight of the German advance was felt, but each new disappointment left Joffre calm. There were none of the nervous fits of indecision which were weakening the judgment of his opponent; the French Commander was a man who had always kept early hours, and while the Government at his imperious suggestion was getting ready to abandon Paris, while the Minister of War, Messimy, a retired officer and Radical politician, was alternating between despair and the more comforting memories of Carnot and '93, Joffre slept soundly every night (though necessarily in different beds as headquarters moved rapidly south).

The reflections of the French Commander had led him to one solution of his problem. The final blow had been the concentration of the Germans on the western wing; he, too, must concentrate on that wing and try to turn the German flank as they had turned his. So while the Armies were retreating, Joffre was stripping his eastern wing of corps after corps and sending them by rail to the west; the same high degree of technical skill shown in the plans for mobilization was now shown in shifting the centre of gravity of the retreating armies.

While this shift was going on, Joffre was menaced by a gap in his line which could only be filled by tact. Sir John French, the Commander of the British Expeditionary Force, was profoundly disillusioned by his experience of fighting beside the French. His little army had been exposed to an attack in overwhelming force, had been forced to retreat and was now exhausted and in danger of being involved in the complete collapse that seemed impending. Sir John believed that his instructions forbade him to risk such a disaster and he announced his intention of withdrawing south of the Marne to rest and refit, and he had already begun to move his bases from the Channel to the Bay of Biscay. In short, he proposed to do as other British generals had done before him, to secure his own army and save it from annihilation as Sir John Moore had saved his in 1808. The news struck Joffre not with panic, but with consternation; not only was a gap to be created in his lines, but the moral effect of a failure to induce the British to join in the decisive battle would be disastrous. The British Government was warned and Lord Kitchener, the Secretary for War, came in person to impose on French the duty of staying in line. But Joffre needed more than that; for he had begun to accumulate to the west of the British Army a new group, the 7th Army under Manoury, whose advance against the German flank was to be the signal for the general advance. And for that flank blow to be effective it must have the co-operation of the British. In an interview in which French began by sulking, Joffre, who knew when to be dramatic, thumped the table and told his colleague that the honour of the British Army was at stake; and the co-operation of the British was secured. In Paris, the Governor, Galliéni, Joffre's former chief, was assembling all the troops he could, and with the entrenched camp of the capital as the bastion on one side, and the great eastern fortresses on the other, the preparations for turning the flank of the German advance went forward. They were helped by the Germans, for the Commander of the 1st German Army, Von Kluck, was turning away from Paris, following the retreating French to give the *coup de grâce*. The Germans thus outflanked themselves, presenting their right to any force in Paris. The time had come at last. On the night of September 3rd-4th, Joffre and Galliéni learned from various sources, but most accurately from British aviators, of the movements of the Germans. The only remaining decision to be made was that of the time when the blow was to fall. Should it be the 6th or 7th of September? The new Commander of the 5th Army, Franchet d'Esperey,[1] persuaded his chief to attack on the 6th. At ten o'clock on the night of September 4th the orders went out for the attack and, on the 6th, Joffre issued his order of the day to the Army: 'At a moment when a battle is beginning on whose issue depends the fate of the country, everyone must remember that the time for looking back is over; every effort ought to be directed to attacking and driving back the enemy. A unit that cannot advance must, whatever it may cost, hold the ground it has won and be annihilated on the spot rather than retreat. In the present circumstances no failure can be tolerated.' The Battle of the Marne had begun.[2]

The change of fortunes that followed the beginning of the battle and the long-run importance of that change were so great that it was natural to talk of 'the miracle of the Marne'. But if there was a miracle, it was a moral miracle. First of all there was the miracle of the self-control of the French Commander-in-Chief and of his staff. With every excuse for panic they kept their heads. They managed to exploit the possibility of manœuvre offered them by that movement of all the German forces *east* of Paris which ensured that any field force based on the entrenched camp of the capital would be on the German flank. The German errors and the French exploitation of them were part of the solution of the problem as seen by Joffre. And it is not to his discredit

---

[1] Although Lanrezac had shown a far more acute sense of reality than had any other army commander, he had become very difficult to work with, whether through his fault or Joffre's it is impossible to say. Joffre removed him and gave the 5th Army to the Commander of the 1st Corps, the future Marshal Franchet d'Esperey.

[2] The question of the relative merits of Joffre and of Galliéni in the genesis of the Marne has been much debated; it is not a question of great importance as the outflanking manœuvre was simple enough in conception. The greatest of soldiers said the same of war in general, 'a simple art, all is in the execution of it'. In execution, Joffre and Galliéni collaborated; each doing his part well; the part of Joffre being that of the responsible Commander-in-Chief.

that he only took advantage of the errors of an over-confident enemy. For the errors of Kluck and his 1st Army in 1914 were no greater than those of Steinmetz and his 1st Army in 1870. The difference was the difference between Joffre and Bazaine. In the decision to precipitate action, Joffre was well advised. The Germans had begun to realize that the war was not over and that the bold methods of their right wing were dangerous. And there were several minor weaknesses in the German position that time would speedily remedy. The continued existence and activity of the Belgian Army based on Antwerp involved a diversion of strength. The fact that Maubeuge did not fall until the 7th of September kept a complete army corps out of the first stages of the battle. Maubeuge, it is now believed, might have held out longer if the defence had been better conducted, but unlike Metz in 1870, it did hold out long enough to be useful. And the Russian menace that induced Moltke to divert troops to the east was at this very moment being exposed as hollow in the great German victory of Tannenberg, but too late to affect the Marne.

Yet all these auxiliary causes of temporary German weakness would have availed Joffre little, if the second and greater miracle of the Marne had not taken place, if the rank-and-file of the French Army, after a series of great disasters and a rapid and exhausting retreat, had not responded to the appeal of a leader whom they had, as yet, no reason to trust. The strain of pursuit was no doubt physically as great in those broiling August and September days as that of retreat and the German victories had been fairly costly in men, but the advancing Germans had all the pride and confidence of victory. It was 1870 over again on a greater scale and with victories less dearly bought. The cavalry had already sighted the Eiffel Tower; they had seized the racing stables at Chantilly; after one last assault on the defeated enemy, Paris would again know a German Army of occupation. Many of the French rank-and-file must have begun the battle as the more intelligent French officers had begun the campaign of Waterloo, without fear and without hope.

The battle was quite unlike the later battles of the war; the struggling armies were often separated from each other by great gaps. The initiative of individual officers and men, their courage or their panic, might, in a few minutes, decide an important local struggle and, in the mass, the whole struggle. A French regiment, sorely tried, broke in panic and the artillery officer in support drove his guns through the retreating fugitives and opened fire on the triumphant Germans with such speed and efficiency that they, too, broke in turn. It was the first feat of arms of Colonel Nivelle. The commander of the 20th Corps was sent off by Joffre to take command of a scratch collection of units which was, a few days later, to be called the 9th Army. *En route* he picked up, at a railway station, a young cavalry officer with an attaché-case who was to be the chief of his hastily-scraped-together staff. Colonel Max Weygand and General Ferdinand Foch thus began their famous partnership. Out of Paris, in a fleet of taxis, came a few thousand soldiers to join Manoury in the flank attack that menaced all the German right and rendered barren their continued and increasingly successful attacks on the French centre.[1]

From the beginning of the battle the Germans were outmanœuvred; the only question was, could they by tactical superiority overcome their disability? If the French armies that they had pursued from the frontiers broke, the technical outflanking of their right would matter as little as the pressure of the Austro-Russians on Davoût had mattered at Austerlitz. But the French armies did not break and the German retreat began. In the east, the Kaiser, who had come to follow the victorious attack of his son's army by a triumphal entry into Nancy, had to postpone that pleasure indefinitely. Hausen's Saxons of the 3rd Army, called on by their neighbours on both sides (and not aided by their commander's inopportune dysentery), made no real progress, while on the western flank, Kluck and Bülow were fighting for their existence. Behind and beyond them was Manoury, and between them and their neighbours was a great gap into which the Allies were moving, but very cautiously. Too cautiously, for though from various sources, and especially from the British Air Force, came news of the great gap, the leaders of the left, Manoury and Franchet d'Esperey and French, refused to take the risk of a great turning movement and a great forward drive that would have had a chance of routing the enemy, not merely of repulsing him.

Yet it was a field of battle that might have inspired boldness in French soldiers, for the battle lines moved round Champaubert and Montmirail and Château-Thierry where, a hundred years before, the Emperor had given the most brilliant examples of his virtuosity. One French general was, indeed, full of this spirit and it was Foch who best responded in spirit to the plans of Joffre. But even he could not drive forward the weary troops who had borne and survived the desperate assaults of the Prussian Guard. The German right escaped; and it was only slowly that the Allied Armies followed. It was in reading the names of reoccupied towns, of La Fère and Senlis and Rheims and Lunéville, that the French people and the world realized that the tide of invasion had turned. The Government, now at Bordeaux, just escaped from disaster, could hardly realize its good fortune or the duty of telling the world that the invincible German Army had been defeated, if not routed. But whatever the rulers of Germany might tell their people and neutrals, they passed their own verdict on the campaign and on the battle. On September 14th, Moltke was

[1] The legend of the taxis grew so fast that it was soon believed that all Manoury's Army went to the front in cabs.

removed and replaced by the Minister of War, Falkenhayn, although to conceal the implications of this decision the change was kept secret. It was six weeks since the war had begun; in 1870 the same length of time had brought Moltke's uncle to Sedan.

III

As the Allies cautiously followed up the enemy, the confidence of the more enthusiastic spirits at Allied headquarters rose. The British officer, Henry Wilson, who represented the main link between French and Joffre, agreed with Berthelot that they would all be on the Rhine in three weeks' time. But the Germans were recovering their nerve and accumulating reserves. Their right was brought back into line with the rest of their Armies and, north of the Aisne, their infantry began rapidly to put into effect its excellent peace-time training in the making of field-works. The 7th French Army (Manoury) was still beyond the German right, but not much, and all attacks made on the new German position failed. A new German offensive on the French position was out of the question and both sides began to move troops west, looking for that open front where the war of manœuvre for which alone they had prepared could be resumed. So began the 'race to the sea'. Castelnau and French were sent off to the west and, everywhere, they found the Germans moving with them. Antwerp had fallen, but the Belgian Field Army had got away and was now standing at bay in the last corner of its country, on the strip between the Yser and the sea. The possibilities of action were limited on both sides by the practical disappearance of artillery ammunition, for both the French and German gunners had planned for a short war and had exhausted their reserves.[1]

It was Joffre's idea to turn the German flank in Artois and then in Flanders since he could not do it in Champagne. But the Germans had the same idea and greater resources. Their reconstituted divisions, their new battalions of volunteers, were thrown against the hastily-constructed Allied lines. Whatever mutual suspicions of their ally's fighting power had been entertained by French and British vanished in the great battle of Flanders. The British infantry before Ypres; the French marines on the Yser; the French cavalry reduced to using its lances on foot to repulse the German infantry; the Belgians who flooded the tiny fragment of their country as their Dutch kin had flooded theirs against the then invincible Spaniards; it was to these that was mainly due the credit of the defeat of the second great German onslaught. But if the campaign of Flanders was mainly a soldier's battle, it gave to one French officer the chance to learn the difficult art of inducing Allies to fight together in a desperate battle. Foch had been chosen by

---

[1] These were about equal; fifteen hundred shells for each field-gun.

477

Joffre to represent him in the north. And it was by his coaxing, ordering, rhetoric, bluff, that the Allied front was held together for six weeks of constant crisis. On November 15th, the last German attack was made and failed, and from the North Sea to the Swiss border there stretched an unbroken line of trenches, a front without a flank, presenting military problems that were new, or new to soldiers dazzled with the memories of the great captains of the past. Germany had made two great efforts to destroy the French Army. Both had failed, but she had succeeded in building a great fortress in France in which her armies were to resist all attacks successfully until, in the great sortie of 1918, she put all to the touch and lost.

IV

Technically the French Army was even less well prepared for the type of warfare now imposed on it than it had been for the campaign of 1914. A vigorous policy of recruitment of first-line formations and the slow growth of the British Army saved it, for the moment, from the danger of being overwhelmed by superior numbers, but it was hopelessly outdistanced both in training and equipment by the Germans. In training, although the more naïve illusions of 1914 had been lost, there was still a reluctance in high places to realize that a war of siege had begun and that the technique of that war had to be learned. Dreams of brilliant manœuvres like that of the Marne delayed, at Headquarters, the objective study of the tactical problem presented by the creation of a great German fortress in France and Flanders.

The Germans had, and knew that they had, their enemies at a disadvantage. Their own plan of war had not, indeed, foreseen the development of a continuous entrenched line from the Vosges to the sea, but their tactical methods had always given a large place to the defensive and they had studied the problems of the defensive backed by modern weapons with thoroughness and objectivity. Their appreciation of the rôle of heavy artillery stood them now in even better stead than during the war of movement and their troops had been trained in peacetime in the use of field-works. 'Sweat saves blood' was a maxim of the Prussian Army, and the spade was never put to better use than in the months when the German Army dug itself in. In addition to its better equipment and training, the invading Army in the nature of things had strategical advantages too. It could choose its line with far less fear of political or psychological repercussions than could the French Army, which was expected, and knew that it was expected, to drive the enemy out of France at all costs—and soon. The German Army, once it was free from the pursuit that followed the Marne, could utilize the tactical assets of the countryside it occupied.

In general it occupied all the ranges of hilly country that ran across northern France; from its heights it looked down on its enemies, observing their movements and imposing on them very great difficulties, both for the infantry attack and for the war of the guns which was now beginning to dominate the infantry attack. For three years to come, the Allies were to waste their strength in desperate assaults on the natural advantages of the German position, striving to drive the enemy from Vimy Ridge, from Nôtre Dame de Lorette, from the Argonne, from the Heights of the Meuse, from the crest of the Vosges, everywhere battering against the natural and artificial obstacles behind which lay the open plains, the way to Germany and victory. It was during these years that the price of the initial defeat and of the limited exploitation of the Marne was paid.

This grim future was hidden from Joffre as 1914 came to an end with the knowledge that both the great German attacks had been held. The time had surely come for an offensive action to end the war in 1915 and to rid France of the invader? Thus the diplomatic defeat of the Turkish intervention on the German side, with its crippling effects on Russia, would be redeemed; thus Italy and the other hesitant neutrals would be encouraged to rush to the aid of the victor.

For such an offensive the French Army was not, in fact, prepared at all. It was able at most to hold its own. The brilliant strategical objectives, the cutting of the east and west lines of communication of the invaders, were mirages; indeed, it proved impossible even to recover the Saint-Mihiel salient which cut across the main line from Nancy to Paris and thus hampered that manœuvre of reserves from wing to wing which had won the Marne.

The tactical inferiority was mainly an artillery inferiority. The importance of gunnery was now realized and the first crisis of munitions shortage that had almost brought the campaign to an end, on both sides, had been overcome. Gone, too, was the old dogma that 'you don't make cannon in war time'. Not only was the task of replacing ammunition taken seriously,[1] but strenuous efforts were made to increase the number of guns, if only to equip the numerous new divisions and corps created since August. The number of '75's' was very rapidly increased and, for their new task, they were provided with a far higher proportion of high-explosive shells. This change meant a serious problem of supply of fuses, and in the race for quantity, quality was neglected. So all through 1915, artillery calculations were complicated by the fact that many of the new guns and new shells had the bad habit of bursting in the French instead of in the German lines. But compared with the problem of heavy guns, that of the '75's' was simple. As soon as the importance of heavy field-artillery was appreciated, the existing stores

---

[1] In the peace-time plans, arrangements were made, though very inadequate ones, for the continued manufacture of shells though not of guns: 50,000 men were allotted to the task of providing for the needs of the Army. By the end of the war, 1,600,000 were so engaged.

were stripped of guns. Forts not in the firing line, the reserve stores of the navy, artillery depots that had been kept filled in a spirit of conservative antiquarianism were all forced to give up their cannon. The result was a rapid increase in the number of heavy guns, an increase that concealed the weakness in power. None of the artillery thus sent to the front was, with one exception, worthy of comparison with that on the German side of the line. The one exception was the '105', a weapon with a respectable range and a capacity for rapid fire. But the manufacture of the '105' had only been begun when the war broke out and a year later the whole Army had only eighty in service. Nor was the task of filling the deficiences taken in hand fast enough; the war might end any day; the manufacturing resources of the country were barely adequate to keep up the supply of the existing models. So it happened that the new guns, like the '155', designed to reply on even terms to the Germans, were only ordered slowly and in limited quantities, and when a more adequate programme was decided on, it could not be completed before the summer of 1918 and for some types was not designed·to be completed before the summer of 1919! In the meantime, the French infantry paid in blood for the imperfections of a heavy artillery, a considerable proportion of which dated from the artillery reforms of Bange that followed the war of 1870.

In the desperate and futile attacks that marked the winter and spring of 1914–15, the last straw was often the weather. An army commander pointed out to Joffre the absurdity of expecting swift and irresistible blows from infantry stationed in water-logged trenches from which it was very difficult to climb out. The men who managed to get over the parapet were too often killed and wounded at once, their bodies fell back into the arms of their comrades, and when the remnants did get out, they found their rifles clogged with mud; and that mud made any manœuvring by the attackers impossible. They could only move forward slowly in face of numerous and admirably-placed machine-guns, protected by a powerful artillery that could too often afford to neglect the French batteries and concentrate on annihilating the French infantry. Four months of futile assaults of this type cost the 4th Army 100,000 men, and the same story could be and was told all over the front. As early as December 1914, General de Maud'huy had insisted that only a commanding superiority in artillery gave any hopes of success for the infantry attack—and added the pessimistic estimate that, at most, such a superiority of numbers could be assured on only 1,500 metres of front!

Such a doctrine was quite incompatible with the optimistic stratical conceptions that Joffre entertained at headquarters. Maud'huy might be written down as a pessimist, but Foch, who was now Joffre's right-hand man, used for all difficult tasks and finally given command of one of the three groups of armies that were constituted in 1915, was optimistic to the point of fanaticism and had been the great theoretician of the power of manœuvre. But experience, if it did not shake the faith of Foch in the importance of strategy, gave him a healthy respect for tactical necessity. He recognized that mere infantry assaults, no matter how gallant, were hopeless, that the tactical problem came first and that, after the experiences of the winter and spring of 1914–15, the Allied Armies did not dispose of the necessary means of imposing their will on the enemy and breaking through his lines at one great stroke. But Joffre refused to listen to the advice of his right-hand man; and even after the experience of the summer, in the great September offensive of 1915, he and Castelnau still dreamed of a single brief battle, breaking through the sides of the great fortress that the Germans had built in France.

These hopes were, if not made more plausible, at least made more natural by the desperate position first of Russia, then of Serbia, against whom the main effort of the Central Powers was directed. France must sacrifice her troops to relieve Russia in 1915 as Russia had sacrificed hers to save France in 1914. The Germans must be made to pay for the boldness with which they had concentrated their strength in the east.. And in each successive operation, gallantry combined with luck produced local situations in which it seemed, for a moment, that the break-through was imminent. But the defence was always able to rally; the effort of storming the front lines exhausted the attackers, whose artillery and infantry reserves never arrived in time. In vain great masses of cavalry were assembled ready to emulate Murat. The German lines stood firm; for a moment, it is true, the attacks of September did alarm the local German commanders, but Falkenhayn had firmer nerves than they and vetoed any idea of withdrawal to rear positions. His courage was justified. The battle had to be broken off. It had cost the French 230,000 killed and wounded; the British, whose first great effort it was, lost 100,000. The Germans lost 141,000 killed and wounded and 25,000 prisoners. In a famous phrase, Joffre had talked of 'nibbling at the enemy', but this kind of attrition resembled trying to bite through a steel door with badly-fitting false teeth.

It is easy to be wise and censorious; Joffre did make serious efforts to study the reasons of the failure of each vain battle, even if he was too willing to see those reasons anywhere but at Chantilly where he now had his headquarters. It would have been difficult for any French Commander-in-Chief to remain passive in face of the taunt hurled at the Government by the new Cato, Georges Clemenceau, 'The Germans at Noyon'. Like the Spartan fortress in Attica, the German fortress in France distorted the strategy of the power to whose sacred soil the presence of the enemy was a disgrace as well as a menace. But the education of the higher command and of the country was expensive. Since the war began France had suffered two million casualties, of whom 600,000 were dead.   Whatever illusions the Germans may have had as to French fortitude before 1914, they could have none now.   If the French were to be defeated, it was not because they did not know how to die; the question was rather 'is knowing how to die enough'?[1]

The question was asked with the more anxiety that the year 1915 had been marked with disasters everywhere; the rosy illusions of the winter of 1914, of French and Russian Armies meeting together in central Germany, were gone.   The Russian Armies had been driven back with immense losses and the great diversion of the Dardanelles expedition had failed.   In that expedition, France had surrendered control, both on sea and on land, to Britain, although the Mediterranean was by agreement her special sphere.   At sea, the joint attack on the Straits failed with serious losses to both fleets and, despite the opposition of the French Admiral, Guépratte, the attack by water was given up.   On land, the campaign was conducted with no deference to the military plans of the French Commanders.   In the first month, the French corps, under British orders, lost more than half its effectives, a proportion much higher than that of the British forces, and by the end of the campaign the French losses were a third of all the troops engaged.

The intervention of Italy had far less effect on the strength of the Central Powers than had been anticipated, and the defeat of Russia was followed by the destruction of Serbia.   Mainly through French insistence, Allied troops were hurried to Salonika to aid the Serbs and to persuade the Greeks to accept the interpretation of their treaty obligations which was advocated by Venizelos and was most convenient to the Allies.   But it was too late, and the Balkan Army had to dig itself in; the result was a locking-up of forces in and around Salonika which the Germans came to describe as their greatest concentration camp of Allied prisoners.   The one slight comfort that the situation had for Joffre was, that among the Allied soldiers so locked-up, was General Sarrail.

It had been one not unsubstantial claim of Joffre to succeed Michel that he was a 'good Republican' and, at the same time, was not on bad terms with those numerous generals who were not 'good Republicans' in the Radical sense of the term, for although he was not a Catholic, he was closely associated with such eminently Catholic generals as Foch and Castelnau.   From the outbreak of the war, Joffre had shown himself to be a severe judge of men, and of the twenty-one corps commanders of 1914 he had removed seven, while of the five army commanders, two, Lanrezac and Ruffey, had been speedily replaced by Franchet

[1] By the end of 1915 France had lost in *dead* almost as many men as Great Britain was to lose in the whole course of the war and two-thirds of the total losses of the whole British Empire.   In a period a little less than that during which the United States was a belligerent, France lost seven times as many men as the United States, out of a population a little over a third as great; i.e. over an approximately equal period of belligerency, about twenty Frenchmen were killed for one American.

d'Esperey and by Sarrail. The successive Ministers of War, Messimy and Millerand, had supported these exercises of authority, but all the prestige of the victor of the Marne was needed when it came to removing Sarrail himself. That general had two claims to respect; he had stabilized the front of his army in September, refusing to take advantage of Joffre's permission to abandon Verdun to stand a siege, and he was the most favoured general of the Radical politicians.

At the very beginning of the War M. Caillaux (at the moment out of office) had pulled all possible wires to be sent to Sarrail as paymaster. As the left-wing anti-clerical deputies saw the rapid rise of Foch (who had a Jesuit brother) and of Castelnau, a nobleman and a perfect 'monk in uniform', they clung to the comforting thought that there was at least one general who would not desert the Republic. As long as Sarrail had a great command, Combes and André had not lived in vain. Unfortunately, luck had deserted Sarrail; while other armies merely failed to gain ground, his lost it. A series of local German successes bred discontent all through the 3rd Army and finally Joffre instructed Dubail to make an inquiry, as a result of which Sarrail was 'put at the disposition of the Minister'. It was a bold stroke for which many politicians never forgave the Commander-in-Chief; but Sarrail was not a man whose friends would let him be left in idleness and it was he who was sent to Salonika to prove that he was a victim of bad luck and of clerical malice. The Sarrail episode was only one of the signs that the politicians were settling down to the fact that the war was going to last for some time and that the early days of uncritical national union were over. In August 1914, the dogmatic Marxian, Jules Guesde, might justify his entry into the 'Government of Sacred Union' by the declaration that 'when the house is on fire it is no time for controversy. The only thing to do is to take a hand with the buckets.' A year later, it was obvious that, although the house was still on fire, it was not going to burn down at once, and political hands could be spared for politics.

It was not either unnatural or unwise that this should be so. In the early months of the war Joffre had been all-powerful: before the Marne because of the general fear, after it because of his achievement. The civilian Minister of War, Millerand, made it his simple rule of conduct to follow the lead given from general headquarters at Chantilly, and deputies learned, with increasing misgiving, that whatever the Constitution might say, the real authority over the armies of the Republic was in the hands of Joffre, not of the Minister who acted as his mouthpiece in Parliament.

The dislike of this situation was not based merely on constitutional grounds. The French soldier, less than any other, was likely to overlook faults of intelligence and good sense in his superiors. He might and did obey the most fantastic orders, but he was under no illusions about their absurdity. Like the soldiers of the Army of the Potomac in 1864, the French soldiers of 1915 wrote letters, talked when on leave and managed to spread the justifiable conviction that the methods of war of the High Command were often unrealistic, to put it at its lowest. And among these soldiers on leave were deputies who had chosen to serve at the front instead of in Parliament. Among them, for instance, was the ex-Minister of War, Messimy, who had been a regular captain and was now a divisional general, but there were many more, like Desiré Ferry, who had first-hand experience of the limitations of the tactical resources and methods of Joffre's headquarters and who soon began to voice complaints. In vain Joffre protested and demanded assurances against the infractions of discipline involved in the political action of soldier-deputies and of officers with political friends. The assurances demanded (and given) would have been capable of fulfilment only if the complaints had been purely political and factional, without serious foundation. But what the deputies and their informants were saying was only what Joffre's combatant subordinates were telling him. The group of staff officers at Chantilly acquired more and more the reputation of theoreticians, of *embusqués*,[1] spinning their fine theories in safety and comfort and leaving their impossible execution to the fighting troops. And the deputies who, leaving questions of tactics and strategy to soldiers or to civilians who liked that kind of thing, concentrated their attentions on the food, the clothing, the wine, the leave of the men in the trenches were, no doubt, often playing politics in the traditional fashion, but they were also fulfilling a very useful public function. For only if the man in the trenches could be convinced that his grievances, even if not remedied, were at any rate voiced, was his morale likely to stand the prodigious strain put on it.

Although the politicians might grumble and although some were doing more than grumble, the position of the Commander-in-Chief was too strong both in the country and with the Allies. As far as there was any united conduct of the war it was organized by Joffre through the inter-Allied conferences. The politicians most feared in Paris were seldom known in other countries and, when known, were not always admired or trusted. So Joffre was strong enough, when he organized a General Staff of the whole Army, apart from his own staff of the 'armies of the north and north-east', to give the chief post to Castelnau. And when Millerand had been replaced by the sick Galliéni, the politicians who thought that, by making Joffre's old chief and rival for the glory of the Marne, Minister of War, they would restore the authority of the Rue Saint-Dominique [2] over Chantilly were mistaken. Galliéni disliked many of Joffre's collaborators and expressed bitter criticisms of the professors of the Staff College who had neglected everything that had happened since 1870, but Joffre's position was unshaken. On December 2nd, 1915, Joffre was given the title of Commander-in-Chief

[1] Slackers. [2] The French War Office.

of all French Armies and made responsible in form, as in fact, for the conduct of operations in all theatres of war. Galliéni was dying and was soon replaced by the ineffective Roques at the War Office. Joffre had, in fact, full authority to plan the campaign of 1916.

His freedom of action was seriously limited by the removal of Sir John French from the command of the British troops. Whatever difficulties had originally arisen, Joffre had found how to manage French, the more that French was deeply under the influence of Henry Wilson, who was deeply under the influence of Foch. In place of the Anglo-Irishman, came the silent and self-confident Scot, Haig, who might be managed, but if so could only be managed by other means. And it was most important that he should be brought to collaborate. At long last, the British forces were on a scale commensurate with the resources of the country; their collaboration with the French was no longer mainly of psychological importance. The French Higher Command and the French people would decidedly not understand it if the British troops did not take a much bigger share of the western fighting than they had done so far. And it was not certain that they would. French was a thorough 'westerner'; as convinced as Joffre himself that the war could only be won in France. It was by no means certain that Haig shared this belief and, even if he did, his position as a new commander was weak. As far back as December 1914, Joffre and Foch had dissuaded Kitchener from replacing French by Ian Hamilton, and now that Kitchener had had his way, it was he who had to be persuaded that the main military effort of the British Empire should be made in France and, if made in France, should be made according with the general strategy of the French Armies.

There was in Britain a powerful party which regarded this war, like so many previous wars, as one in which the main British contribution should be naval and economic. Command of the sea plus the most lavish use of the 'cavalerie de Saint-Georges' [1] combined with a moderate and *independent* use of the army had been the downfall of Napoleon despite Austerlitz and Jena. They would be the downfall of William II despite the possible temporary triumphs of his arms in France or Poland. And it was argued, with force, that Britain could not be expected to provide the dominant navy and a first-class army as well. She had just, slowly and reluctantly, adopted conscription, a breach with national tradition far more revolutionary than any continental country could realize, and she was already finding the financing of herself and of her weaker allies a severe strain. But though neither side realized it, British and French fortunes were far more deeply intertwined than those of Britain and of any former ally had been. For the first time

---

[1] i.e. money, so called by the French from the figure of Saint George on the gold guineas and sovereigns, with which for two centuries British statesmen had paid their allies to fight the French.

since the Armada, mere command of the sea did not guarantee the island from all the serious dangers of war. 'England is an island,' Michelet had said, thus explaining all the peculiarities of British policy. But England (or Britain as the new British Commander-in-Chief would doubtless have put it) was no longer quite an island. She was like Holy Isle or the Mont Saint-Michel, joined in an incomplete fashion at certain times to the Continent; the *et penitus toto divisos orbe Britannos* of Virgil was, for the first time, only partly true.

Britain had now hostages to fortune on the Continent almost as important to her as Paris was to France. The channel ports, the Belgian ports, from them came or could come the aeroplanes, the submarines that might starve out the island or bring war home to its complacent inhabitants. Napoleon had talked of Antwerp as being a pistol pointed at the heart of England, but English nerves had borne the pointing very well, since the pistol was not loaded. Napoleon and the Grande Armée at Boulogne had been an empty threat, but the Germans at Boulogne or Calais, that was more serious, for the new German guns could make the use of the Straits of Dover very difficult and with submarines might make it impossible. The Narrow Seas were now too narrow for safety. This truth, if it percolated slowly into English minds, did percolate; it was no longer possible to write off a complete French defeat as the defeats of Austrians, Prussians and Dutch had been written off in the past. With the enemy in the Channel ports, able, in case of complete military victory, to make France open to German submarines, aeroplanes and destroyers, not merely Calais but Cherbourg, not merely Dunkirk but Saint-Nazaire and Toulon, the semi-island might have to make very poor terms.

If such thoughts guaranteed France from too cavalier treatment at the hands of her ally, they introduced a strategical complication, for they made it as much a British interest to get the Germans out of Flanders as it was a French interest to get them out of France. And while a complete victory would do both, short of a complete victory it was as natural that the thought that the Germans were in Ostend and Zeebrugge should distort British strategy as that the thought that they were in Noyon or outside Rheims should distort French. If the Germans were to be defeated in 1916, Joffre was convinced that it was indispensable that the main effort should be joint, that the British should not attempt an attack on the Flemish coast and that French offensives in Lorraine and Champagne were out of the question. The great assault must be made where the two armies joined, in Artois and on the Somme. And with diplomacy and tact, as well as with good military arguments, Joffre and Foch, who was to be the chief French executant of the offensive, talked with their British colleagues.

They were successful; the British Army in France was to be steadily reinforced and when it was ready, around July 1st at latest, the great drive would begin. To that drive Joffre would contribute his carefully accumulated reserves of men and, more important, of guns and ammunition. France would contribute the lion's share of resources, and the young and inexperienced British Army would (with all necessary tact) be induced to take its orders from the senior partner. But while Chantilly was planning, so was the German Headquarters, and on February 21st, after a bombardment of unprecedented violence, the troops of the Imperial Crown Prince moved forward to storm the outer defences of Verdun.

V

The design of Falkenhayn was not to deliver a great battle or, in the strict military sense, gain a decisive victory over the French. The total forces engaged at first were limited; the proposal of the Crown Prince to make a wide encircling attack was rejected. The calculation of German Headquarters was that it would be possible to force the French to give battle in a narrow area where the French reserves and French will to fight could be destroyed under a storm of artillery fire. The attack on Verdun was not a surprise. The French intelligence service had got wind of the German plans and preparations in time to make it possible to reinforce the normal complement of troops in what had been a fairly quiet area and to plan how the fortress was to be defended. But Joffre, thinking as a strategist, was unable to see what great gains the Germans could count on. Even if they took the fortress, there was no possibility of a great break through.

Verdun was, indeed, important psychologically. It was one of the three great barrier fortresses that had stood firm in August and September of 1914. Verdun, Toul and Belfort were sacred names.[1] Was it not at Verdun that the heroic Commander, Beaurepaire, in 1792 had committed suicide rather than surrender the fortress to the Prussians? As a fortress, Verdun had suffered the eclipse in public and professional esteem that followed the triumphs of the great Austrian siege-guns over the Belgian fortresses in 1914. Its forts had been dismantled and the elaborate trench-works created in their stead took little account of the possibilities of defence offered by the steel and concrete masterpieces of French military engineering. In the steps which were hastily taken to defend less the fortress than the position on the Meuse which the fortress covered, but which, it was thought, it had ceased to guard, reliance was placed mainly on heavy artillery, working according to carefully planned schemes of fire supporting the infantry divisions assembled to stop the German attacks. These preparations were not complete when the attack came and, even had they been, the German leaders were

---

[1] Falkenhayn had for a time thought of making his attack on Belfort.

confident that the weight of their artillery would render such defences useless. The weight and speed of German fire, it was thought, would annihilate French resistance and, covered by their artillery, the Germans would advance in comparative ease on the fortress. And, indeed, by ordinary standards, the Germans were right. All the legendary tales of great sieges were to be eclipsed in the narrow battle-ground, only a few miles square in all, on which more than half a million men were to be killed or wounded.

From the start, the plans of attack and defence went wrong. The German infantry, advancing over ground where all resistance had theoretically been blotted out, found that in the ruined trenches and in the great mud-holes made by the sixteen-inch shells there were little groups of French infantry who fought to the last. In those first hours took place the first of innumerable Thermopylæ under a sky darkened by more formidable missiles than the Persian arrows. In snow, and rain, and mud, the French, who were proud to think themselves the heirs of Athens, showed all the Spartan virtues. The startled Germans who were working the sixteen-inch guns were to see a Frenchman move tranquilly with his hands in his pockets from one shattered trench to another. Officers and men were to sacrifice themselves with as little concern and less self-conscious virtue than any heroes of the ancient world and, if the German attack failed, if crisis after crisis was survived in the five-months battle, it was first of all due to the simple resolution of the French soldier. If, in 1915, he had shown that the old *élan* in attack was not lost in the most hopeless circumstances, in the spring of 1916 he showed that he could die where he was put as well as any soldiers the world has seen.

It would have been in vain for him to die if his chiefs had not chosen well where he should die. At first, the efforts of the local command to be ready for the attack seemed futile; if the power of resistance of the isolated units which had survived the bombardment was a shock to the Germans, the breakdown of the elaborate plans of defence was a shock to the French. In the hurricane of fire that burst on Verdun, the ordinary organization of command collapsed in many sectors. The most disastrous result was the abandonment of the Fort of Douaumont by its surrounding troops and its capture (empty) by a Prussian company. Lieutenant Brandis had scored the most brilliant feat of war on the German side since Ludendorff had captured the citadel of Liége in 1914. The weight of the German blow, even before this disaster, had impressed Chantilly, where Castelnau had taken the grave responsibility of awakening Joffre to demand orders and to offer to go to Verdun himself to report. He was sent off at once; he reiterated the orders already given by Joffre that the right (east) bank of the Meuse must not be evacuated, even at the risk of the loss of the great mass of artillery accumulated there, and when the new defender of Verdun arrived at his command on the 25th of February, the decision to stand fast had been taken.

The first German blow—mighty as it had been and dramatic as was its success in taking Douaumont in German, in neutral and in French eyes—had been parried. The task of resisting the second, that all knew was imminent, had been entrusted to General Pétain, Commander of the 2nd Army, and the general who had best gained and earned the trust of the rank-and-file. That trust was, from the side of the French Command, the greatest asset of Pétain; because he had not, in the past, asked men to die in vain, he could now hope to be heard when he asked men to die in tens of thousands to save the bulwark of France.

From Pétain's taking over of the command of the front round Verdun, the battle on the French, as on the German, side was mainly a battle of guns. This was fully understood by Joffre, who poured out at Verdun the carefully husbanded reserves of guns and ammunition that were to have been used in the great offensive. It was not in quantity that the French Army suffered but in quality, for the heavy artillery was still largely composed of semi-obsolete types that fired more slowly than did the German guns. But with all their limitations the French guns were the indispensable background of the defence. It was the task of the infantry to stand or to advance under the cover of an artillery fire of an intensity of which there was no previous example in history. Both the French and German artillery experts showed admirable ingenuity in devising methods of destroying the opposing infantry, but it was discovered that the infantry (German and French alike) had an unprecedented capacity for enduring agony and death.

It was discovered, too, that not only flesh and blood had been underestimated. The forts stood the batterings of the great German guns with comparative ease; the shells plunged a foot deep in the concrete; the turrets vibrated like bells; men choked from poison gas or went mad from shock, but the forts were not destroyed and could be and were fought like battleships. To recover Douaumont, the French poured out their most valiant efforts in attack; to defend Fort Vaux they were equally lavish of their lives. Heroic legends, no more improbable than the facts warranted, sprang up and, within a few weeks of the beginning of the battle, the merely military side of the contest was less important than the political. To force the French to give up Verdun was, for the Germans, a symbol of their ability to force a separate peace on their chief land enemy. To hold Verdun, was to show the world and the Germans that the French will to victory was unshaken. Into the lists by the Meuse the flower of both Armies was drawn; division after division was destroyed in the ceaseless fighting. The system of battle adopted by Pétain involved, indeed, the use of many fresh units, for troops were brought into the battle-line and after a few days withdrawn, then, after a brief rest, sent back. Falkenhayn kept his divisions in line until they were past fighting. The French system was very expensive in reliefs; it involved great losses and there were tactical drawbacks to the constantly changing composition of the front line; but it kept ready for use many famous fighting units which the German system would have destroyed for months.

One problem was much simpler for the Germans than for the French. The fortunes of war had given the Germans command of the main railway line behind their front, while Verdun was only linked to its rear by a narrow-gauge railway and a road, the road now known as the 'Sacred Way', from Verdun to Bar-le-Duc. It was along this road that every night the careful organization of Pétain brought, in thousands of trucks, the greater part of the supplies of the battle. It was as indispensable a foundation of victory as the opening of a line into Chattanooga by Grant in the autumn of 1863, but it was a line under fire all day and night and menaced by an enemy far more dangerous than Bragg. March passed and April and June, and the drain on the French Army continued; the Germans extended the range of their attacks and, if the Crown Prince had lost faith in the battle, Falkenhayn still pressed it. The losses were about equal on either side, but the Germans could afford them better. Before the Allied offensive on the Somme could be launched, the fortress would fall and the definite superiority of the German arms be made manifest. The 'sword of England', the French Army, would be broken and, without that sword, the hastily improvised weapon that was the army of Haig was not to be feared. But though position after position was taken, the sword did not break.

The Germans, having falsely announced the capture of Fort Vaux, could not fully exploit their success when, after days of fighting in the cellars of the fort, it fell at last. The observation-point aptly called 'the Dead Man' was taken; the position of the French on the right bank of the Meuse was bad. But on July 1st, the long-awaited Somme offensive began. Pétain had become commander of a group of armies and left the immediate defence of Verdun to Nivelle who, Joffre thought, would be more ready to take the offensive when the German attacks ceased. But the Battle of Verdun was not over; in one last effort, on July 11th and 12th, a great assault was launched on the Fort of Souville whose fall would open the way to the inner defences of the city. But the garrison, manning the outer defences of the fort like sailors repelling boarders, repulsed the attack. Verdun was saved; its salvation had cost 300,000 casualties to the French, and failure had cost as many to the Germans.

VI

All through the assault on Verdun, the French command had been steeled in its resolution to hold out by the thought that it was thereby making the more easy the combined Allied assault that was planned for the summer of 1916. The Allies, whose plans were being thus forwarded, did not always show great tact in their acknowledgment of this service. At the beginning of the battle, Sir William Robertson, chief of the Imperial General Staff in London, had been rather pleased to think that the Germans were spending their resources in this wasteful fashion. He took, indeed, rather the line of the Irish landlord who wrote to his tenants (from London) that if they thought they could intimidate him by shooting his bailiff, they were very much mistaken. Haig quickly took both a more sympathetic and more realistic view of the situation: and no British reaction was as trying to Joffre's temper as the anxious demands of Cadorna [1] that the Russians should attack before they were ready in order to relieve Italy from the imminent Austrian offensive. As Cadorna was in a great numerical superiority, this demand seemed, at French Headquarters, to be an excessive example of that sacred selfishness which the Italians had candidly announced as their motto.

The great operation in France was to be a joint offensive on the Somme, an offensive from which Joffre hoped greater things than did most of his subordinates. The wastage of Verdun had made the French share in the battle less than had been planned, and if the German lines were to be broken, it would have to be largely by British efforts. The task of leading the French attack was given to Foch; and (whatever might be thought at Chantilly) at Foch's headquarters and still more in the headquarters of his army commanders, like Fayolle, it was realized that the offensive could succeed only so far as the artillery preparation succeeded. Indeed, Fayolle wrote as if the main use of the infantry was to occupy and to hold German positions made untenable by the guns. Foch was not quite so limited in his outlook, but even he seemed to optimists to write off too easily all chances of a break-through and of a speedy return to a war of manœuvre. But the wastage of Verdun forced Joffre to give way in great part to his subordinates, and the main object of the battle was now to wear down the enemy. If the infantry could not attack without an intense artillery preparation, and if the fact that most of the French heavy artillery was of the old slow-firing type involved an artillery preparation lasting days, surprise—and so manœuvre—was almost impossible.

It was something that Foch approved of an attack at all, for Pétain was firmly of the opinion that the French Army had done its share for

[1] Italian Commander-in-Chief.

that year and the heavy fighting ought to be left to the fresher troops of the British, Italians and Russians. But to take this line was to abandon the carefully nursed understanding with London, even if it had not been contrary to Joffre's own beliefs. So, on the first of July, the Allied attack began; with real though limited success on the French side, with some success but with frightful loss on the British. For the new British armies, whose first experience of battle this was, were sent forward in a dense and rigid parade order which was perhaps necessary, but which gave the Germans the best targets they had had since the mass attacks of the red-trousered French infantry of 1914–15. On July 1st, the British attackers lost 60,000 men, a loss unprecedented in British military history. And the ground gained was not enough to justify these losses; at any rate, in the eyes of the London Cabinet. The crisis of September 1914 was renewed. Haig, under pressure from home, talked of abandoning the offensive and Joffre, as in 1914, was forced to appeal to the honour of the British arms. A refusal of the British Government to stand a fraction of the losses endured by France might well have done what Verdun had failed to do, broken the will to fight of the French nation. 'England,' had run the German propagandist taunt, 'will fight to her last Frenchman.'

It was necessary to prove that this was not so. So the attacks were resumed, with no striking success, but at any rate with the effect of further exhausting the western German armies. When Ludendorff, who (with Hindenburg in nominal command) had replaced Falkenhayn at the head of the German war machine, came to France in September, he realized, for the first time, how much more serious war was on the western than on the eastern front; and the problem of resisting the constant battering began to perplex him. But all was not well within the French lines. There was constant friction between Foch and his subordinates and between Foch and Joffre. The methods of attack in this siege warfare were constantly changing and the Germans adapted themselves to the defence faster than the assailants did to the attack. The French public, which had expected a great deal from the Battle of the Somme, was discontented with the modest successes that seemed, to those who had won them, so remarkable. In this type of war, weather was of supreme importance. Fog or mist made artillery preparation based on air scouting impossible, and rain during the battle turned the battle-field, pitted with shell-holes, into marshes. By the middle of November, the battle had to come to an end and the enemy was still in France. He had lost some villages and a few square miles of territory, that was all. And this limited success had cost the French 200,000 men and the British over twice as many, while the Germans had held their ground at a cost of about half the total Allied losses. It was a poor balance sheet: and, as if to underline this fact, in two limited offensives, in October and in December, General Nivelle, in front of

Verdun, had recovered most of the ground lost in the great battle at comparatively little loss to himself and at a considerable loss in prisoners to the Germans.

It was natural that the French Government, and the French Commander-in-Chief, should regard this feat of arms with admiration, should wonder whether Nivelle and his chief executant, Mangin, had not discovered the secret that (on their own admission) was hidden from Foch and Pétain, the secret of how to break, quickly and cheaply, the fortified line against which for the third campaign the French Armies had been hurled in vain. And the general situation made some change politically necessary. The joy roused by the great Russian successes of June had been destroyed by the quick destruction of Rumania, on whose intervention such high hopes had been based. Sarrail's Balkan offensive had petered out after the capture of Monastir, the Italian offensive after the capture of Gorizia. On all fronts, the great Germanic fortress had resisted attack. It was not without a certain sympathy that Joffre listened to the proposals of the new Prime Minister, Briand, that he should give the immediate command of the armies in France to Nivelle and take over a general direction of the war.

Joffre set about creating a new central organization and it took him some days to realize that he was being politely removed from all command. His new office was purely nominal, all authority would be divided between Nivelle and the new War Minister, General Lyautey, who had been brought from Morocco where he had worked wonders and who was entirely new to the intrigues, as well as to the problems, of Paris and General Headquarters. After a few days Joffre resigned, and was made, in an oddly casual fashion, a Marshal of France, the first that had been made since 1870.

The fall of the Generalissimo was a great symbolic event. He had outlasted two German Commanders-in-Chief and no Allied chief had commanded as long. Abroad his reputation was still immense, and all the plans for 1917 had been made under the assumption that Joffre would be in power. Within France, his authority had long been contested and it was not only he but his collaborators who were *limogés*.[1] Foch, whose maintenance in active service after he had passed the age limit of his rank had annoyed the purists, was removed from the command of the northern group of armies and set to studying problematic German invasions of Switzerland. Castelnau was sent off on a mission to Russia and, symbolic act, the General Headquarters were removed from Chantilly at great cost and trouble to Beauvais and many of the members of the central organization sent to the front.

---

[1] Limoges was the town to which generals relieved of their commands were traditionally sent.

VII

The appointment of Nivelle has a curious resemblance to the super-session of McClellan by Lincoln in October 1862. As that was prob-ably the greatest mistake made by the Federal Government in the American Civil War, so was the appointment of Nivelle the greatest mistake made by the French Government in the World War. There was, it is true, a great difference between Nivelle and Burnside. Burnside's own opinion of himself was not much higher than the low one held by his subordinates, while Nivelle was a clever man and knew it. Of partly English origin, a Protestant, a new man who had been only a colonel when the war broke out, he had the gift of impressing civilians, for a time at least. The fall of Joffre in France had been paralleled by the fall of the Asquith Government in England, and the new Prime Minister, Mr. Lloyd George, was as disappointed by the results of the Somme as was the French Chamber.

Nivelle promised a victory in forty-eight hours; if, by that time, the German lines were not pierced and a campaign in open country made possible, the attack would be stopped. But Nivelle was sure that the lines would be pierced. By covering the German lines back to the rearmost position with a blanket of artillery fire, by sending the infantry forward in a great bound to the positions of the enemy's heavy artillery, the long and bloody combats of the Somme would be avoided. And to the sceptics, Nivelle pointed with no false modesty to what he had done outside Verdun. Reluctantly the elaborate plans of Joffre were scrapped. Sir Douglas Haig was induced to put himself under the orders of the new French Commander-in-Chief, who did not waste any time on the tactful diplomacy with which Joffre and Foch had nursed Franco-British collaboration to its comparatively healthy state. And the French Chamber and, soon, the French soldier, was given an assur-ance that the war was going to be won quickly and cheaply by a new method. The secret of their doom could not be kept from the Germans whose new chief was making his own arrangements.

Ludendorff had, in fact, decided to abandon a great part of the territory fought over the previous summer, to save troops by shortening his front and, by occupying a carefully planned and fortified position, to let the projected Allied offensive waste itself in the air. If the plans of Joffre had been carried out, the Allies would have been attacking about the time the Germans were retreating, but the change to Nivelle made certain that there would be time for the quiet execution of the retreat to the Hindenburg line. The German plans could not be kept secret and the rumours of a great retreat soon reached the Allied front lines, from which they were relayed to headquarters. There they received little credence, either from Haig or Nivelle, both of whom thought that such a retreat was an operation which no German general dared carry out; involving, as it did, the abandonment of dearly-won and dearly-held ground.

It is a little surprising that such ideas should have blinded the chief of an army that was familiar with the campaign of Austerlitz, and still more surprising that they should have affected the judgment of the chief of an army whose second greatest commander had been Wellington. But thanks to this blindness, the German retreat was begun in peace and all the Allied plans were delayed in their possibilities of execution. As the Germans withdrew, the Allies cautiously advanced, but the German retreat was admirably planned and executed; the region over which the withdrawal was carried out was laid waste with a completeness which owed a great deal to modern science and a great deal to national thoroughness. Wells were poisoned, traps were set which, when touched, exploded; all buildings that could help the advance or hinder the retreat were destroyed and, when there was any doubt, the answer was 'blow up'. Thus was the magnificent medieval castle of the lords of Coucy at last deprived of all military value.

To the advancing French, the aspect of German military thoroughness which struck home most deeply was the careful sawing down of the fruit trees. It was like the destruction of olive trees to the Greeks. The careful devastation of enemy territory was no novelty in war, but the English on the Scottish border under Henry VIII, in Munster under Elizabeth, the French in the Palatinate, Sheridan in the Shenandoah Valley, had never done so perfect a job. And it was unfortunate that the troops of the country across whose face this dreadful scar had been so efficiently drawn, were not, like the Scots or Irish or Confederates, doomed to defeat, but destined to victory. In less than two years' time, it was Germany's turn to be occupied by French troops whose tempers, in some cases, may well have been rather frayed by what they had seen in 1917.

The German retreat upset all the Allied plans for an offensive; or rather it would have upset them had the Allies been wiser, above all had the new French Commander-in-Chief been wiser. There could be no surprise now and as weeks passed in slow advance over the devastated area, the chances of German knowledge of the French plan increased. Not only did the Germans learn of the attack in general; the details became known through captures of officers with operations orders on their persons. The political scene, too, had changed. Briand, Nivelle's patron, had fallen because his War Minister, General Lyautey, had 'insulted the Chamber' by opposing the revelation of war secrets even in secret session. The new War Minister, Painlevé, was sceptical of the value of the promises of easy and quick victory that Nivelle was still prodigally issuing from headquarters, and the scepticism of the mathematician turned politician was shared by most of the leading officers of the French Army. General Micheler, destined to be the chief executant of Nivelle's plans, was rebuked for issuing orders that showed doubts of the ability of infantry to do much away from their artillery support. A corps commander who, when pressed by the Commander-in-Chief, avowed apprehensions was sent to another part of the front, as Nivelle asserted that faith was essential for the new system. To the sceptics he asserted that he would be victorious in two days or stop; the new offensive would be a different thing from the slow Somme advances. Had not the brilliant, speedy and economical triumphs of the 'Verdun team' been contrasted with the slow, costly and ineffective methods of the old gang? Painlevé was still unconvinced; the generals were consulted as to the prospects, a measure to which Nivelle took not unreasonable exception. A council of war was held on April 6th at Chantilly. The necessity of an offensive to support the Russians, who were being weakened by revolution, and to keep faith with the British was agreed on, but the atmosphere of doubt and the interference with his authority which the consultation of his subordinates involved irritated Nivelle to a degree that made him play his most formidable card, his resignation. In face of the enemy and still more of the Allies, a second change in the French command inside six months would have been disastrous. As Castelnau, back from Russia, put it, it was the duty of the Government to give Nivelle a free hand or to remove him. In the circumstances they could not remove him. His authority was confirmed.

Everything was against Nivelle; if faith was still possible in the lower ranks, it was difficult in the higher. Parliament was for the moment anxious to show its power; it had overthrown Joffre and Lyautey; deputies saw themselves as modern versions of the Jacobin 'representatives on mission'. Many of them were at or near the front, like the congressmen before Bull Run in 1861. Thus the political situation made anything less than a complete triumph no triumph at all. The weather was vile; snow made all the troops miserable and made the black troops on whom Mangin put such reliance almost useless. Postponement until better weather was urged on Nivelle, even by Mangin, whose offensive spirit was beyond doubt. But Nivelle was unshakable.

The offensive was to be begun on April 16th, a date too late to give any chance of surprise. Postponements had meant a prolongation of the artillery preparation with a consequent weakening in intensity. The necessity of firing on the rear German positions, imposed by the ambitious nature of Nivelle's plans, was a further cause of ineffectiveness. And lastly, the command of the air was in German hands. The attack, when it came, was vigorously delivered except by the unfortunate and frozen Senegalese. The weather was still vile; transport was fantastically difficult; in some places it took eighteen horses to move a single gun. Casualties in the next few days were heavy; some regiments lost half their effectives; the tanks did less than had been hoped for. But the advance, the prisoners, the losses inflicted were by the standards of the Somme not dearly bought for 120,000 casualties. But it was not merely a better Somme that the French Army and people had been promised; it was a new Austerlitz, a quick, complete, and final victory. That was as far away as ever; the Germans, as they had been apprehensive, were correspondingly exultant. Despite his promises, Nivelle had not broken through the German lines; despite his promises, he had not broken off the battle.

The great blow had been delivered, it had not produced the results expected, but Nivelle continued limited attacks, especially on the Chemin des Dames, that 'Ladies Road' built for the daughters of Louis XV, whose possession had been so valuable to the Germans and whose conquest by the French was a real gain. At another time, this success might have saved the General's reputation and place, but not now. Refusing to resign, Nivelle was removed after his most zealous collaborator, Mangin, had been vainly sacrificed. At last Painlevé had his way; the new Commander-in-Chief was Pétain and he was appointed barely in time, for what the German attack had failed to do in 1916, seemed on the point of being done by the French attack of 1917; the combatant spirit of the French Army seemed to be broken.

The mutinies of 1917 revealed a weariness not at all surprising when the ordeal of nearly three years' fighting is remembered. The French soldier was too intelligent not to know that many people had blundered and, if he had not been smart enough to find this out for himself, there were plenty of people to inform him. The unanimity of the national will to resistance in 1914 was, if not destroyed, weakened by 1917. The news of the Russian Revolution of March, with its promises of peace, came to reinforce political and social forces ready to think that a negotiated 'peace without victory' was not evident treason, if only because the chance of getting anything else seemed remote. But the root of the troubles of the Army lay elsewhere. The 'soldier had been too much tried' said a general—and he had.

It was not only the dreadful losses, suffered, as the infantryman had come to believe, in part at least because his commanders did not know their business. There were other grievances. The soldier had to suffer hardships for which there was no real excuse and that at a time when he believed that all civilians were making and spending money in a way unknown to a frugal country before 1914. His food, his drink, were monotonous, at best. The accommodation provided for him when he was resting behind the lines was often wretched. Leave was irregular and, owing to the delays of the offensive, it was hopelessly in arrears, as furloughs had been stopped since February. When the soldier did get leave, he had to make a long comfortless journey home, often to find that the family dependent on him was badly off, while the fortunate dependants of munition-workers were opulent. At home, the soldier was subjected to propaganda against which the Government took no steps. Moreover, the dislike of the French for extra-governmental activities in peace-time had its fruits in war-time. The voluntary organizations for looking after the troops, the Y.M.C.A. and the like, common to the British and American armies, were non-existent or far weaker and poorer in the French Army. The soldiers, thus sorely tried, had been promised a speedy end to their suffering if they made one great effort; they had made the effort and the promise could not be kept.

The mutinies were in most places peaceable enough. Troops refused to attack but were willing to go into the trenches,[1] other units talked of marching on Paris for the front was full of wild rumours of revolution, rumours without foundation, but not without plausibility in the spring of 1917, when every day brought new and strange news from Russia.[2]

Apart from refusing to obey orders, there was little positive violence. A general forced to descend from his car was about the most serious outrage to discipline. But for a month, the fighting power of the French Army was desperately weakened. And fortune which had favoured the Germans by giving them the plans of the great offensive now deserted them; they had no suspicion of the mutiny and Pétain, like Duncan during the great mutinies of the British Fleet in 1797, was able to bluff his enemy into leaving him alone while he set about restoring the morale of the Army.

For the work of healing, the new Commander-in-Chief was admirably qualified. Pétain was a man of great dignity of manner and nobility of person; no soldier was less of a demagogue, less afflicted by a false heartiness. But he was known as a man of his word; he had always been careful of the lives of his men, never calling on them for useless sacrifices [3] although, as Verdun had shown, capable of the utmost resolution. He made few promises, but those he made were kept. The food, lodging, leave, allowances of the troops were improved; a great gift of American money from private sources was spent on the most needy dependants; punishment was comparatively little used, although power was taken to execute without appeal to the civil authorities.[4] The Commander-in-Chief toured the whole line, talking to all ranks, appealing to honour and patriotism, promising redress of grievances and, by his example, restoring confidence between officers and

---

[1] The same causes produced the same weariness and passivity in the Army of the Potomac in 1864.

[2] There were some Russian troops in France; they were already in a state of disorganization comparable to that of their brethren at home. They had, however, voted to take part in the April offensive and had done so with courage if without skill.

[3] It was this claim of Longstreet on the loyalty of his men that made him more popular than either Lee or Jackson in the Army of Northern Virginia.

[4] Cf. p. 535.

men. In one group of officers assembled to meet him, Pétain noticed a young lieutenant who stood silent, and asked him what he thought was the main cause of trouble in the Army. 'The neglect of their men by the officers,' the subaltern blurted out. 'Well, gentlemen, you heard that?' Such neglect was now inexcusable, since it was a fault of which no one could accuse Pétain himself.

The Army rapidly convalesced, but it was not fit for violent activity. To restore its faith in itself, Pétain undertook a number of small operations, carefully planned and admirably successful, which were excellent for morale, if only for showing that an offensive need not be a bloody futility. The re-equipment of the Army went steadily on; heavy artillery was more abundant and more modern; the equipment and training of the infantry was improved and, by the end of 1917, the wounds of the spring had healed. It was time, for the healing of the French Army had had, as a natural if not necessary corollary, the bleeding of the British Army, if not to death, to a dangerous degree of anæmia. The autumn of 1917 was the blackest season of the war for the British. Deprived of French aid, anxious to divert German strength from Russia, the leaders of the British troops subjected them to an ordeal far worse than that endured by the French in April and, indeed, only surpassed by Verdun in duration and severity. In the mud of Passchendaele the fighting edge of the British Army was blunted. And to end the year came the complete collapse of Russia and Rumania and the rout of the Italians at Caporetto.

Both British and French generals and troops were sent to Italy; Foch, who had become Chief of Staff, went there too, and did not, it appears, think it necessary to waste any of his stock of tact, so useful in dealing with British Headquarters, on the Italian generals. The Italians stood on the Piave and, when the New Year dawned, if the eastern front had at last collapsed, the western fronts were intact. The lesson of the year had seemed to be that Allied campaigns must be more closely articulated, and experiments in Allied councils had produced committees for unified action which, it was hoped, would be able to secure as much unity as Joffre had achieved by prestige and personality. One soldier kept on insisting that this was not enough, but the complaints of Foch were not yet listened to, and the Allies awaited the expected German attack, relying on gentlemen's agreements for mutual aid. They were to learn that war was no place for mere gentility.

VIII

Both Haig and Pétain had been sceptical of the schemes of Foch for a central reserve and they relied on agreements for mutual assistance. It was evident that a great German attack was on the way. The army attacked was to call on its ally for help and, with their own offensive achievements as a guide to possibilities, the two Commanders-in-Chief can be pardoned for thinking that there would be time enough for divisions to be moved up in support.

On March 21st the attack fell on the British, as they had foreseen; not on the French, as Pétain had obstinately insisted was probable. The main German attack did not score any extraordinary success, but its right, directed against the British 5th Army, was successful in a fashion unprecedented since 1914; the British retreat was precipitate, and Ludendorff was presented with the opportunity (it was really a dangerous temptation) to neglect his main battle to exploit this great success, and instead of hammering the British Army to pieces, to try to separate it from the French and then destroy it. What Ludendorff saw as possible was also evident to Pétain and Haig; the German advance, if once it broke the union between the Allied armies, would force them to retreat in separate directions. The British could only fall back on the Channel ports and, if they were lucky, escape across the water like Moore's army at Corunna in 1808, or try to man a new defensive line based on the water, like Wellington at Torres Vedras in 1810. The French would have to fall back on Paris and fight for their lives without hope of aid from the British. There would be a new Ligny and then a new Waterloo, with no chance of a reunion of the Allies on the battle-field and therefore a complete victory for Ludendorff-Napoleon.

In this great crisis all mere agreements for mutual aid were useless. Pétain, always pessimistic, was ready to write the British Army off as a loss; help was sent, but slowly and in driblets. The French Commander-in-Chief shrank from the frightful risk of involving his own army in the disasters of the British. He had even better reasons for his attitude than Sir John French had had in 1914; his decision was even more pregnant with disaster. It was to meet this crisis that Haig appealed to London, that Lord Milner came over, and that Clemenceau, Milner, Poincaré, Haig and Pétain met at Doullens on March 26th. Pétain, according to one story, nodded at Haig, 'He'll have to surrender his army in the open field, then it will be our turn'. A local politician besieged Clemenceau with entreaties for information; if the battle were lost, would he make peace? All present showed stoicism or resignation, all except one. Foch had come with Clemenceau, and the never-shaken self-confidence that had marked him from his youth, was now welcome instead of being irritating. He was neither stoical nor resigned. He refused to think of defeat; 'They're no smarter than we are', he repeated, reinforcing his dogmatism with his boxing gestures. One thing, he asserted, was obvious. Amiens, the link between the two armies, must be held at all costs. These calculations of lines of retreat must stop. Haig, who had asserted that he could deal with a man but not with a committee, now suggested giving Foch the task of co-ordination. The hour had found the man, and when all criticisms are examined, they boil down to assertions that, had the hour been different, Foch would not have been the man.

Foch's immediate task was that of co-ordinating 'the action of the Allied armies on the western front'; he was to keep them together, and in that he was aided not only by his bold, not to say reckless spirit, that made him ready to take all risks, but by the exhaustion of the Germans. As French infantry moved up in their unimpressive and entirely adequate way, smoking, marching in apparent disorder, to the support of the British, as French aeroplanes attacked constantly, fatigue, heavy losses, the difficulties of supplies slowed up the German advance. By March 30th, the first great offensives were over; the blow had been parried.

On April 3rd the powers given to Foch were extended; he was now entrusted with the 'strategic direction of operations'. The three national Commanders-in-Chief were to be under his orders with a right of appeal to their own Governments. And on April 14th the last step was taken; Foch was given the title of Commander-in-Chief. Foch was optimistic and he had reasons for his optimism. Each month diminished German numerical superiority; their resources in men were bound to dwindle while, thanks to the Americans, those of the Allies were bound to increase. And if the new American troops were raw and tactically inferior, their spirit, their physique, their equipment more than compensated for their defects, defects that would in any case lessen as the battlefield educated the survivors. If the Allied line held through the summer, the German chance of a complete victory in the field was gone. But such a negative victory, a mere success in holding out, was not enough for Foch. He began at once to plan for the exploitation of the chances given him for counter-attack by the very German successes, each of which created new bulges, new salients which, when the time came, Foch intended to burst in.

The time was slow in coming; and there was a moment when it seemed that the chance, if it came, might fall to another general. In a series of battles the confidence of the Allies in their generals was strained to breaking point. The second great German blow took the form of an attack on Flanders in which the British Army, as its leader told his troops in a famous order, had its back to the wall. Haig added that French aid was on the way, but it was not coming in sufficient quantities, for Foch had no intention of engaging his main force as the enemy decided. He calculated that the British Army, with carefully doled out French aid, would hold its own, with heavy loss in men, territory and prestige no doubt, but with no fatal damage.

The third great German blow was directed at the French. Ludendorff had not abandoned his plan of finishing off the British Army, but the preparation of another great attack in the north took time. The area selected for attack was the position of which the Chemin des Dames was the most famous section. So completely had the fears of German attack in this region been forgotten, that exhausted British divisions were, by Foch's orders, sent there for a rest! The positions were not held in strength and the army commander, Duchêne, not only failed to notice or believe that an attack was being prepared but, when doubt was no longer possible, he deliberately held up his counter-battery fire until the attack was launched. His artillery, like his infantry, was blotted out by 4,000 guns. Surprise had been made easier by the frogs in the marshes which drowned the inevitable noise of preparation. It was March over again; indeed, the Germans advanced farther and faster; they took Soissons; they reached the Marne. By May 30th they were thirty-seven miles from Paris and the military results of their victory were less important than the potential political results.

Nerves in the capital were not good. Paris was now under steady bombardment from a great gun firing at an unprecedented range. Its effect was purely moral [1] but not the less important for that. The news of the German victory was a shock for the strongest nerves and many deputies had no claim to strong nerves. They demanded vengeance on the generals; and Clemenceau had to exercise all his authority to save them, but obviously Foch could not afford another disaster.

Ludendorff, as in March, could not resist the temptation to exploit his unexpected triumph. He still thought of the attack in the north as his major effort; he did not intend to change his bid, but he wanted to pick up some quick tricks. For, if Allied nerves were strained, German nerves were breaking; many of the people and many of the soldiers wanted peace; a victorious peace if possible, but peace.

Every day's delay was a serious loss, for every day meant increased strength for the British Army which was recovering from its terrible mauling; every day meant more Americans; every day meant the increased strain on the physical and moral strength of the Central Powers. Germany had to win quickly before her allies collapsed. Yet Ludendorff had now to give respite to the French as he had had to give it earlier to the British. And when the new attack was launched in June, it was no surprise, although there was an impressive early success which promised much. But any hopeful illusions were short-lived, for the French line did not merely bend without breaking; a counter-attack launched by Mangin on June 11th scored real if limited successes. Far more important was the fact that the attack had been broken and returned, although the Germans could reckon on a serious tactical gain, for the great lateral railway line from Paris to Nancy was cut: but that was not enough.

A month later Ludendorff tried again, but Foch was completely ready; he disregarded the protests of the British, before whom the

---

[1] The most famous achievement of the gun was the killing and wounding of a great part of the Good Friday congregation of the church of Saint-Gervais. On that day, at the request of the Archbishop of Cologne, the Allied air forces had refrained from their regular raids on the Rhineland.

reserves accumulated for the long-postponed battle in the north loomed as a menace. His gamble was based on very accurate information, for the time and place of the impending attack were exactly known, and two hours before the German barrage was ready, the French counter-barrage was loosed on them. It was the night of July 14th.

By the 17th it was obvious that the attack had failed; obvious to Ludendorff, who decided to cut his losses and move his offensive resources to the north. He had now no option but to play what trumps he had. He was not given even this chance for, on the 18th, the great counter-attack surprised the Germans. French, British, Americans, Italians were launched from the cover of the forests on the German flank. Only hasty retreat saved the mass of the troops, but they lost 30,000 prisoners and over 600 guns. It was not as great a disaster or as complete a victory as either side might have feared or anticipated, but it was enough. Although Ludendorff did not yet realize it, the initiative had passed from his hands to that of his opponent. He might still hope and plan, but all future battles would be fought where and when Foch decided. The Allied Generalissimo had, in his peace-time writings, compared the course of a battle to an inclined plane. The Germans were now sliding down the board, clinging desperately, but sliding. And the Allies, the whole world outside the beleaguered fortress, knew it.

On the 5th of August, Clemenceau visited Foch at his headquarters and drawing a paper from his pocket began to read it. 'At the moment when the enemy by a formidable offensive on a front of 100 kilometres [1] relied on being able to gain a decisive victory and to impose on us that German peace which would mean the enslavement of the world, General Foch and his admirable soldiers have beaten him. . . . The confidence placed by the Republic and by all the Allies in the victor of the Marshes of Saint Gond [2] and in the illustrious chief of the Yser and the Somme has been fully justified.' For a moment Clemenceau stopped, then went on reading the decree. 'Article One: the General of Division Foch (Ferdinand) is created a Marshal of France.'

It was not only in France that the tide had turned. The great British armies in Palestine and Mesopotamia were destroying what was left of the Turkish Army; the Austrian offensive in Italy had been broken in June, and Foch was now pressing the Italians to attack and showing increasing impatience at the refusal of General Diaz to take any risks. Foch had not done what he had done by refusing to bet on anything but a sure thing, and he was, perhaps unduly, intolerant of Italian prudence. But in his own immediate sphere he showed none of this temper. Known as a man of dominating manner and almost inordinate self-esteem, he now showed a tact and sympathy in his deal-

---

[1] 70 miles.   [2] 1914, at the Marne.

ings with his subordinates that were his greatest service to the Allied cause. He refused to order, to dictate; he suggested and received suggestions; he compared his position to that of the leader of an orchestra, but he insisted on far less unison than the metaphor implies.

From the 8th of August the main task of assailing the Germans fell to the British, now fully restored in strength and, although there had been sharp differences of opinion between Haig and Foch when the latter seemed to gamble with the safety of the British Army, the new Marshal of France showed the same diplomatic skill that he had displayed in 1914, with due alteration of tactics, since he knew well that Haig was not Sir John French. With Pershing the task was more difficult. Foch did not believe that the American staff organization was skilful enough to handle a great army; by the time it had learned its lessons the campaign of 1918 might be over. As a mere problem in mathematics the question was simple enough. To put American divisions under French or British commanders was the most economical way of using the fresh American troops. They had shown at Château-Thierry and elsewhere that their combative spirit was magnificent, but that was not enough. In any case, to aid the Allies in their desperate straits in the spring and summer of 1918, Pershing had willingly put his infantry at the disposal of Foch, saying 'we are here to be killed', and in the choice of troops to be sent over, preference had been given to the immediately useful infantry and machine-gunners.

The American troops in France were thus necessarily short of experience in the other arms. But Pershing, backed up by President Wilson and by the Secretary of War, Mr. Newton D. Baker, was unshakable in his determination to create and command an American Army in France, not to allow the American troops to be used as mere feeders for the veteran and weary French and British Armies. To this claim Foch was sympathetic; no doubt he would have liked to be able to draw on the American reservoir, but he had not insisted on the importance of moral questions in war for nothing. The Americans would fight better as an independent army under their own officers; tactical mistakes would be more than compensated for by better feeling. But Clemenceau (although he had had better chances of knowing the American spirit than had Foch) was indignant. Indignant with Pershing and still more indignant with Foch, who evaded hints and disobeyed orders to put the Americans in their place. Foch knew that, whatever his formal powers, he could not in fact order Pershing about as if he were a French subordinate; for that matter, he could not order Pétain about. So all through the autumn the Generalissimo had to persuade the political chief of his own country as well as the Allied generals; he had to choose continually the lesser of two evils; he was not in the position of his hero, Napoleon, or of his opponent, Ludendorff.

Thus the great British triumphs of August took the form they did as a result of Foch's accepting the modifications suggested by Haig, modifications fully justified by the result; and the decisions to let Pershing attack the Saint-Mihiel salient, at the risk of delaying the more important attack in the Argonne, was made under the pressure of American firmness and Pétain's plea for tact. Yet the clearing of the Saint-Mihiel salient was a brilliant success, even if hypothetical greater successes can still be won on paper, so much easier to manœuvre on than that deplorably unaccommodating soil.

The German resistance revealed that Ludendorff, in defence as in attack, was unable to bring himself to cut his losses soon enough. The day for offensives was over; but the German chief could not bring himself to abandon the territorial proofs of his former triumphs. He behaved like Napoleon in 1813, but perhaps with more reason, for it was desperately important to bolster up the feeble faith of the allies of Germany and of the German people. Despite the bluff reassurances of the political agents of the General Staff who were the nominal German Government, faith in victory was vanishing if not yet replaced by a despairing acceptance of defeat. Indeed, that despair was to strike at the head of the German Army before it began to paralyse its members.

At the northern end of the Allied line the British advance, supported by the French and soon to be joined in by the Belgians, showed that the orderly slow retreat of which Ludendorff had dreamed was impossible; there was to be no stopping on prepared fortified positions against which the Allies would batter in vain. At the eastern end the American Army, by a prodigious feat of energy, had been shifted from Saint-Mihiel to the region of the Meuse-Argonne. The Germans were completely surprised.[1] But the fears of the limitations of American staff-work were in part justified by the event. If there was, at the moment, a chance of ending the war by a great victory in the field, it was lost in the delays and breakdowns of the Argonne battles.

All along the line the desperate Germans fought with superb courage. There were weak and demoralized units; there were bad breakdowns; yet the western front, rapidly moving east as it was, was still a front. But the weaker sides of the great central fortress were now being opened. In the Balkans, Sarrail had been as trying and troublesome as in France, and his political friends could not save him. He was succeeded by Guillaumat and then by Franchet d'Esperey, but although the war-weariness of the Bulgarians was notorious, and although the deposition of King Constantine by the Allies had both secured the Allied rear in Greece and added the royal army to the

[1] There is a parallel here to one of the most famous feats of the American Civil War, the shifting of Jackson's army from the Shenandoah to Richmond in 1862. The parallel becomes closer when it is remembered how clumsily and slowly Jackson intervened. Here the comparison is to the advantage of the American generals of 1918.

Allied forces, the Balkan front was passive and the removal of the Commander-in-Chief was thought of.

Before that measure was taken, Franchet d'Esperey struck. Boldly he assailed the strongest part of the Bulgarian position with the French and Serbians; his boldness was rewarded; the British troops, weakened by malaria and poorly equipped, failed, but the Greeks succeeded. The whole Bulgarian front collapsed. A cavalry brigade, under a general who honoured the name of his uncle, Gambetta, seized the nodal point of railway communications, Uskub. The Germans hurried reinforcements south, but too late. Bulgaria surrendered and Clemenceau telephoned the news at once to Poincaré; a gesture that revealed his emotion. The British troops marched on Constantinople and the Franco-Serbians moved north. There was still caution in Paris, and Franchet d'Esperey was warned against the dangers of attempting to rush to the Danube, warnings that he acknowledged from the banks of the great river. The way into the centre of Germanic power was thus opened; and the army of the Balkans began to plan its advance on Prague and Dresden.[1]

Before this disaster was fully realized, the nerves of the man who had concentrated all power in his hands in Germany snapped. On the 29th of September, Ludendorff insisted that an immediate peace offer and demand for an armistice should be made to the Allies. The horrified civilians and even the nominal chief of the army, Hindenburg, protested.[2] But Ludendorff was not to be denied; he feared a rout in France; he feared, much more reasonably, the consequences of the Bulgarian collapse. He insisted that the announcement of the German request for an armistice should be made on the basis of the Fourteen Points of President Wilson which, since he had not read them, he did not realize involved not merely the abandonment of dreams of territorial gains, but the loss of most of the spoils of Bismarck and of Frederick the Great.

From army headquarters the panic spread to the rear, as was natural. But for six weeks the agony was prolonged. Ludendorff's nerves recovered, but the damage was done; all hopes of victory were gone; what remained was the hope of peace. Foch was preparing a great Franco-American attack on the eastern end of the line; the Belgians and British were advancing on the west; Lille and Bruges were recovered; the Italians were preparing at last to destroy an Austrian army whose political counterpart had already collapsed. Victory was in sight.

That victory was not solely the work of the armies. The overwhelming force that was now battering at the crumbling walls of the

---

[1] The proposal to remove Franchet d'Esperey on the eve of victory recalls the threat to Thomas on the eve of Nashville, as the battle recalls the battle of Chattanooga. There was a danger in 1918 that Haig would be replaced by Sir Henry Wilson.

[2] Hindenburg was still dreaming of annexations in France!

German fortress had been accumulated over a period of four years, during which one of the greatest of the original belligerents had been knocked out, to be replaced by a far more formidable power than decaying Imperial Russia. It was at the head of a great military coalition that Foch was triumphing: and the creation of that coalition was the work of Allied—and German—diplomacy.

Beginning the war with what they thought a preponderance of power which, barring a quick German victory, made ultimate triumph certain, the powers of the Triple Entente had the satisfaction of seeing the minor partners of the Triple Alliance find ingenious reasons for separating their fate from that of their allies. Rejoicing in the neutrality of Italy and Rumania, M. Doumergue, in the first weeks of August, instructed the French Ambassador to thank the Italian and Rumanian Governments and declare that France was not surprised at this action 'on the part of nations so civilized as Italy and Rumania faced with the odious aggression of Austria and Germany'. But the refusal of Italy and Rumania to march with their quondam friends was not based on moral scruples, but on an acute calculation of their own self-interest. It was the object of Germany to keep them neutral; it was the object of the Allies to win them over to active intervention by promising them a share of the spoil. As the fortunes of war favoured one side and then the other, the diplomacy of the Allies succeeded or failed. As far as France was concerned, that diplomacy was, with the formation of the Government of National Defence, in the hands of Delcassé, who brought all his old tenacity and energy to bear. On September 5th, the signature of a treaty in London binding Russia, Britain and France not to make a separate peace, at the very darkest moment of the war, on the morrow of Tannenberg and the eve of the Marne, created that formal coalition against Germany which was ultimately to embrace in its ranks the greater part of the nations of the globe. The first accession had already taken place: Japan had declared war on Germany and laid siege to Tsingtao, the German naval base on the Chinese coast. It became an obsession of French diplomacy, as soon as the early dreams of speedy victory were over, that the fortunes of war would be decisively inclined to the Allies by the active intervention of Japanese troops; as a corps of volunteers on the western front, or as a regular army on the eastern front. As the war dragged on, France was willing to go to great lengths to secure active Japanese support, pressing the irritated Tsar to cede the northern half of Sakhalin to secure Japanese aid. But the rulers of Japan had secured all that they wanted; they sent a few destroyers to the Mediterranean, but that was all.

The first effective fresh military force added to the fighting armies was added to the German side. Turkey, from the very beginning of the war, had made her decision, although that decision was concealed from the not very perspicacious Allies for some months. With the accession of Turkey to the German side, Balkan politics became of overwhelming importance. To Russia it gave an opportunity of seizing the most glittering of prizes—Constantinople. The design was not openly admitted at first; but when it was, the Western Powers could not oppose the designs of their indispensable ally. In war, as in peace, the Russian Government was apt in the use of blackmail. The Foreign Minister, Sazonov, was always ready with hints that *he* was the main partisan of war to the end, and he might resign. It was soon evident that, despite her treaty with France and Britain, Russia was by no means to be blindly relied on. If she did not get her way she sulked, and her sulkiness was a threat of worse things to come. In the Balkans, Allied policy tended inevitably to be Russian policy, and it suffered from the impetuous character of Sazonov, who was precipitate and irresolute.

The Allies dallied with the idea of uniting all the Balkan states against Turkey. But Bulgaria, smarting under her recent defeat, could only be won over by promises of territorial concessions from her despoilers, and Serbia, Greece, and Rumania were asked to give up territory they now held to Bulgaria, in return for future and uncertain shares in the spoils of Turkey and Austria-Hungary. Bulgaria was not won and the other Balkan states were alienated. Russian policy insisted on placating Bulgaria right up to her joining Germany—and, some people thought, even after she had done so. Delcasse, whose return to diplomatic life had been *via* the French Embassy at St. Petersburg, had been too uncritically loyal to Russia to be a really good French Foreign Minister, and his career ended with the revelation of the duplicity and adroitness of King Ferdinand of Bulgaria.[1] The greatest and only triumph of Allied diplomacy in the first year of the war was the accession of Italy. In bidding for her support, the Allies had the great advantage of being able to offer as much Austrian territory as they thought fit, while Germany could only offer as much as Austria could be induced to surrender. Russia and Serbia were, indeed, obstacles to a complete fulfilment of Italian wishes, and it was French diplomacy which found a way round the obstacle. But Italian intervention came too late to save Russia from her great defeats, and Serbia sulkily refused to aid the Italian offensive by an attack. The failure of the Dardanelles campaign and the entry of the Bulgarians into the war on the German side put an end to the hopes of Greek support which had been entertained since the very beginning of the war. France was an eager bidder for that support, pressing Britain to give Cyprus to Greece, as she pressed Russia to give Northern

[1] The Republic made use of the fallen dynasties in its Balkan diplomacy. The Duc de Guise was sent on a semi-official mission to Sofia to win his cousin, the King, over to the French side, and Prince George of Greece was relied on, because of his Bonaparte wife, to influence his brother, King Constantine, who had married the Kaiser's sister.

Sakhalin to Japan. The Salonika expedition was almost as much a French diversion as the Dardanelles expedition had been a British, and it involved the Allies in increasingly drastic interference with Greek sovereignty, in fomenting a revolution and, after the fall of the Tsardom, in the deposition of King Constantine.[1] That monarch became, in French eyes, a villain as despicable as his brother-in-law the Kaiser; on the other hand, his enemy, M. Venizelos, was not so much a hero to the French as he was to the British, a difference in the public opinion of the two countries that was to be very important.

Russian Pan-Slav policy had insisted on the detaching of Bohemia from the Austrian Empire, which not only made futile French dreams of driving a wedge between Germany and her partner, but threatened the break up of what was, from the traditional French point of view, an indispensable part of the European equilibrium. That danger was increased by the high price put by Rumania on her intervention, a price that not merely included Transylvania, to the bitter anger of the Magyar minority, but the Banat, which threatened the interests of the Serbians. When Greece was at last coaxed or forced into joining the Allies, *her* price was Smyrna, which made making terms with Turkey even more difficult. By the time of the Russian Revolution, the skin of the Central Powers had been largely allotted to their assailants and, as the Treaty of Brest-Litovsk showed, those powers in their turn had far-reaching designs on the territories of their neighbours. Victory for either side meant great territorial changes.

The first and second Russian revolutions relieved the Western Allies (at great cost) of a most exigent partner, and it is possible that had the German military rulers been more prudent, they could have made a permanently victorious peace in the East at the price of a few concessions in the West. But Ludendorff was resolved to play double or quits, and that forced the Allies, with whatever misgivings, to do the same.

But the higher diplomatic direction of the war had now passed out of European hands. It was not merely that Wilson was the head of the freshest and most powerful state of all those arrayed against Germany; war weariness and the Russian Revolution made some more positive ideal than mere victory necessary to the combatant nations. So it was that their rulers had to accept the lead from Washington, with mental reservations of course, but with fewer than is commonly supposed, for Wilson's terms to Germany, however sincerely based on general principles, were the terms of a victor. Only defeat could make the rulers or the people of Germany think them tolerable. As that defeat grew nearer, and more obvious, the direction of Allied policy passed openly into Wilson's hands. He laid down political terms

---

[1] The Russian Provisional Government objected to the deposition although not on dynastic grounds.

which were the price of German escape from disastrous military defeat and invasion. The technical security for those terms was a matter to be decided by that severe but sincerely Christian soldier, Foch.

In all the armistice negotiations the attitude of Foch was simple. War was fought to impose the will of one power or group of powers on the other; victory came when it was impossible for one side to resist. The Armistice terms would be designed to make impossible any armed resistance by the Germans. To continue fighting to make this complete triumph obvious to all would be a criminal waste of blood. There were differences to be settled, of course. The French, who were not interested in the German Fleet, were willing to make concessions over the naval terms that would induce the Germans to sign. The British wished to insist on the most rigorous naval terms, but were willing to go comparatively easy on military questions (their country had not been invaded). But the Germans were beyond any power or will to haggle. They signed in Foch's railway coach in the forest, and at eleven o'clock on the morning of November 11th, fighting ended. It was a year to a day since Ludendorff had decided on the great gamble.

CHAPTER II

THE REAR

I

IT had been a calculation of some enemies and a fear of some friends of France that the bitterness of her party quarrels, the apparent weakness of her government, would make her as disunited and as unfit for war in 1914 as in 1870. The comparison with 1870, whatever validity it may have had on the technical side, had none on the psychological. No sooner had the menace of war and invasion become obvious to the country, than there was an immediate rallying to the formal legal authority, a whole-hearted acceptance of the necessities of the case that restored shaken faith in the national destiny. In 1914 was proved the wisdom of Thiers, for it was shown that the Republic did, in fact, divide Frenchmen the least. The country awaited the news from the front with a calm and resignation that astonished the frivolous observer. There were occasional popular outbursts. The great dairy company of Paris, 'Maggi', had some of its shops attacked by crowds anxious to show their detestation of everything German, but in the main it was a sober country that went about its business, or as much business as was possible in face of a general mobilization that smoothly and efficiently took away from factory, farm and office, most of the most useful workers.

The Chamber met only to manifest its unity, a unity as well exemplified by the exchange of greetings between Albert de Mun and Édouard Vaillant, as by any other demonstration, for the old *communard* had never before consented to speak to his colleague. In 1871 they had been on different sides of the barricade. Now they were on the same side and on the other was the enemy of France. Voting all that the Government asked, Parliament was prorogued and deputies, like lesser people, waited for news. Indeed, it was not only the deputies who waited for news, for the Government itself was, if not in darkness, at least in a very dim light, the amount of light that the Commander-in-Chief allowed to be seen. From the moment mobilization began, civilian authority began to ebb and the fate of France was left in the hands of the soldiers.

So long as the military machine worked smoothly (as it did during mobilization) or successfully as it appeared to do during the early days of the campaign in Alsace, there was no disposition in the minds of the Ministers to interfere. But when it became evident, in the last week of August, that France had suffered a great defeat, a defeat that had the appearance of being worse than any suffered in the same time in 1870, the Government was stirred to action,—to panic action, captious critics have asserted, long after the event. The Minister of War, Messimy, had been a regular soldier before becoming a Radical politician, and his early blind confidence in the talents and character of Joffre was shaken by the bad news. That was natural enough, but the attempts of the Minister to interfere in detail and in general were dangerous, or would have been had he remained Minister much longer. But the frontier defeats not only meant the end of M. Messimy as War Minister, they meant the end of the Radical Government. On August 28th the Cabinet was replaced by the Government of 'Sacred Union'. Viviani was still Prime Minister, but his Cabinet was replaced by one representing all the forces of the nation. The Catholic leader, Denys Cochin, sat beside Combes and the Socialists Guesde and Sembat,[1] as 'Ministers of State' without any departmental duties. More important was the transfer of three most important departments to leaders of the political groups so decisively defeated at the elections. Ribot became Minister of Finance, Millerand of War, and Delcassé of Foreign Affairs. The Radicals (and the Left in general) were represented by the Prime Minister and by a young politician, a protégé of M. Caillaux—M. Malvy. He kept the Interior, a department whose great political importance had been, if anything, enhanced by the war.

The reconstruction of the Ministry was followed by a measure which, although fully justified, turned out to be unnecessary and therefore unfortunate. On the evening of September 2nd, the Government left Paris. It was the forty-fourth anniversary of Sedan, and the public of the capital, increasingly alarmed during the past week by the news that France was invaded, was naturally embittered by what appeared to be a flight. In less than a fortnight from the beginning of the great frontier battles, the Germans were at the gates of the capital. Joffre and the Governor of Paris, Galliéni, had no wish to have their hands tied by the immuring of the Government in what might soon be a besieged city. The precedents of 1870 all suggested the danger of allowing the Government to be cut off from France. If there was a Gambetta in the Government, he had better be saved any necessity for imitating the dictator's escape by balloon. But Parisian anger, despair, or resignation, did not dull Parisian wits. The *Marseillaise* was parodied:

> 'Aux gares, citoyens!
> Montez dans les wagons!' [2]

[1] Cf. p. 443.
[2] 'To the stations, citizens, get into the trains.' The fugitives were also known as 'francs-fileurs'.

With the Government to Bordeaux went most deputies (although Parliament was still prorogued) and officials and newspapermen, with many hangers-on of all three classes. The victory of the Marne proved the retreat to have been unnecessary and thereby justified Poincaré's extreme reluctance to take the advice of the soldiers and leave, but the Government stayed at Bordeaux until December 9th, long after it seemed to the optimists that it might have returned to Paris. Round this Bordeaux period of the war many legends grew up; all of them hostile. Galliéni's proclamation which announced the withdrawal of the Government had given as a reason their desire to 'give a new vigour to the national defence', but according to rumour, Bordeaux was more like Capua than like Sparta. Famous for its food and wine, the capital of Guyenne was, so the average Frenchman came to believe, a paradise for shirkers. At the famous restaurant ' the Chapon fin' these rascals ate and drank and amused themselves while their betters, the soldiers and the inhabitants of the invaded regions, above all the Parisians, showed the real heroism of France. Some of the discredit into which politicians fell during the war dated from this episode and there was a risk that the charge 'You were at Bordeaux' would be as dangerous as the charge 'You were at Coblence' or 'at Ghent' was under the monarchy of July.[1]

The politicians had enough to contend against without the shame of Bordeaux being imputed to them. The outbreak of war inevitably discredited (whether reasonably or not) many members of the majority who, a few weeks before, had been publicly and profitably scornful of the alarmists. The alarmists seemed to have been right, even such violent and uncritical alarmists as the pugnacious editors of the extreme Royalist daily, *L'Action Française.* If Léon Daudet was thus justified by the event, how much were the Radicals condemned? And the Radicals were deprived of their usual weapons. Parliament did not meet from August 5th until December 22nd and, during that time, it was difficult to persuade the country that anything that any politician had done mattered very much.

The press was effectively muzzled. There was, indeed, no formal censorship, but profiting by the lesson of 1870, it was provided that any newspaper publishing false news could be suppressed. This weapon was quite enough. The only way to avoid the risk of publishing false news was to publish only news approved of by the Government, and an effective preliminary censorship was thus made possible. Of course, the limitations of the freedom of the press designed to prevent the dissemination of false news were not intended to apply to false news that suited the policy of the Government. As the Government, rightly,

---

[1] Coblence was the German centre of the emigrés during the Revolution, who there plotted the invasion of France by foreign armies. Louis XVIII took refuge at Ghent from Napoleon during the Hundred Days and his supporters assembled there during the campaign.

was deeply concerned to keep up the spirits of the people, to avoid any panic, newspapers were allowed to publish any cheerful fables that they thought fit. From this arose the great campaign of 'bourrage de crâne', of patriotic 'ballyhoo'. The French reader of the newspapers was told not to worry about the German advance, the invader's supply system had broken down so badly that the enemy surrendered to any soldier who could offer them a buttered bun. In any case what did it matter? The Cossacks were only five days' march from Berlin!

The first effect of these fictions was no doubt useful, but very soon they bred a general scepticism that was very harmful. It was not that the French were told more lies than the people of any other country, but that their national temperament made them less willing to forgive their deceivers than, for example, the English proved to be.

The censorship soon developed other sides of its activities. Despite promises from Ministers and from officials, it was used to stifle political criticism. The prestige of the Government was an asset of France, to criticize that Government was to dissipate the asset, and it followed that it was the duty of the censors to prevent such waste. It was on questions like these that the most violent fights took place between successive Governments and the formidable Clemenceau. He changed the name of his paper from *L'Homme Libre* to *L'Homme Enchaîné* (from the 'Free Man' to the 'Shackled Man') but the trumps were in the hands of the censors.[1] It followed that, since nothing could be printed of which the Government did not approve, it was natural to assume that the Government approved of all that it allowed to be printed, and many of the difficulties in which M. Malvy, the Minister of the Interior, later found himself, arose from an application of this principle by his critics.[2]

Yet there was plenty of ground for legitimate criticism. The faults in army organization and equipment so soon and so disastrously revealed were of course clearly seen by the soldiers and, being French soldiers, they were ready to give up their lives but not their right to criticize and grumble. When Parliament did at last reassemble, the deputies had plenty to say, apart from the obligatory patriotic manifestations. It is true that at first their criticisms were held in check by the belief that the war would soon be over and by a hesitation arising from the fact that a good many deputies were also soldiers. These deputies were naturally those who had best reason to know what was wrong with the Army; on the other hand, they could only criticize the Army by staying away from the front. And despite brave words about it being as noble and more useful to serve France on the benches of the Palais Bourbon than in the trenches, there was a natural fear that the country might not see it that way. When Parliament was

---

[1] When Clemenceau at last became Prime Minister he remembered enough of his own principles in opposition to permit attacks on himself. 'The right to slander the members of the Government should be beyond all restriction,' he declared.

[2] See p. 535.

called together it was decided that it would be useful, as well as in the tradition of the Convention, to sit permanently, and as deputies who were soldiers were given leave as long as Parliament was sitting, it was left entirely to the individual member to decide how much or how little fighting he would do. Senators and deputies became the only Frenchmen, in fact, exempt from military service *ex officio*.

It was easy to sneer at this odd example of Republican equality, yet there was a good deal more to be said for the preservation of parliamentary control (even if it meant preserving parliamentarians from the risks of the average Frenchman) than the critics of the Right allowed. It was easy to list the dead deputies and assert that far more members from the Right were killed than from the Left, but even if this were true, it did not affect the main question: was parliamentary control worth having?

The professional soldiers, of course, opposed it for good and bad reasons. The coming and going of soldier politicians from the front lines to Paris and back again was inevitably bad for discipline. It was difficult to know how to handle a subordinate who was also a deputy. If it was unlikely that the deputy would avenge the soldier, it was not impossible, for there was always the example of General Sarrail to show that it paid to have political friends, even such lowly political friends as county councillors; and, of course, Sarrail had other and more powerful friends as well. It was natural, and in some ways wise for Joffre to attempt to cut communications between the Army and the Parliament. Whether mere self-seeking, or delusions that it was the duty of deputies to recreate the glories of the 'representatives on mission' of the Revolution was the greater nuisance, was hard to say, but both were nuisances. On the other hand, there were plenty of legitimate complaints that were made not only by deputies, but by most combatant soldiers that did not seem as important at General Headquarters as they did in Parliament—or in the trenches. Yet Joffre, with Gascon cunning and obstinacy, tried to stop all parliamentary inspection, one might almost say knowledge of the Army. A general who accepted an invitation to visit Clemenceau, at that time chairman of the Army Committee of the Senate, learned after his visit, in which he, a Catholic and Conservative, was treated with the greatest courtesy by the old priest-eater, that he was no longer *persona grata* at Chantilly.

Yet, despite Joffre, the deputies found themselves able to exercise their inspecting functions, their functions as voicers of grievances and finally their function (usurped though this was) as the makers and un-makers of Commanders-in-Chief. Joffre, in fact, could only have continued to exercise his uncontrolled dictatorship by being far more uniformly successful than he was. He was able to get rid of Sarrail, to inflict him on the Allies in Salonika instead of on the French armies at home ; but with the fall of the Viviani ministry at the end of 1915 he

515

lost his chief protector, Millerand, and he had soon to fight for his immunity from criticism against a public opinion which, in Parliament at least, blamed him for the early disasters at Verdun. He was forced to try to meet the politicians on their own ground and was beaten. Had he been more reasonable, less self-satisfied at the end of 1915, he might not have been dismissed at the end of 1916.

II

Economically, as well as militarily, all preparations in France, as in Germany, had been based on a belief that the war would be short. The financial and economic problems presented by a war lasting, not a few months but four years, had not been foreseen, and the solutions that were improvised had most of the faults of improvisation, though it should be remembered that those faults are less marked in French improvisation than in that of any other people.

To this widespread national talent for muddling through, to this successful reliance on 'System D', there was one great exception.[1] A commentator on French war finance[2] has sorrowfully quoted Léon Say's judgment: 'public intelligence, in economic questions, has made far less progress in France than anywhere else.' The experience of the war in the main justified this pessimistic view. Of all the major European belligerents, France managed her finances with the least skill, foresight and resolution. For this there were two classes of reasons: one accidental and temporary, another permanent. The first of the accidental reasons was, of course, the invasion which occupied or devastated one of the richest regions of France.[3] Not only was there a corresponding loss of revenue, but the economic damage done involved very serious further losses. Had the area occupied been mainly devoted to producing wine, for example, its loss would not have had the important secondary results that followed on the occupation of Lorraine and Flanders by the Germans. For these regions were the main French producers of the sinews of modern war, of steel and iron and coal and textiles. The resources thus destroyed, or in the hands of the enemy, were replaced by imports from Britain, from America, from Japan, from the whole world, and these imports had to be paid for, or borrowed for, with consequent loss of wealth or credit. The completeness of the military mobilization at the beginning of the war emptied French factories and so made further imports necessary and, a minor but not unimportant result, it completely disorganized the financial side of the bureaucracy. After the war began, it was soon

---

[1] From the verb 'se débrouiller' ('to muddle through somehow') the French have invented a 'système D' to which, in all emergencies, recourse is had. The result is often brilliant.

[2] M. Jèze.　　　　　　　　　　　　[3] Cf. p. 524.

impossible to learn what had been spent, or how, or on what, or even what had been borrowed, and the arrears of accounting were not over-taken until long after the war, when the damage had been done.[1]

A secondary cause of confusion arose from the arrival of the war at a moment when French public finance was just beginning to be re-formed. The first serious breach in the Napoleonic and revolutionary system (which themselves owed more to the *ancien régime* than it was politic to admit) had been made. The principle of income tax had been accepted and the beginnings of a system of collecting set up. The reform, long disputed and still in a very embryonic form, served ad-mirably as an excuse for a short-sighted financial policy.

The parties of the Left, faced with reasonable demands for an increase in the old direct taxes, replied, truthfully but largely irrele-vantly, that it was politically improper to increase taxes which were on the way to abolition. The parties of the Right were full of scorn for this argument; they pointed out that Britain had vastly increased her taxation. They failed to point out, or to realize, that if Britain was able to manage her finances better, it was due to the long existence and well-tried machinery of income tax in that country. The sections of French opinion which had fought bitterly the not very vigorous attempts of the Left to impose an income tax, showed no desire to remedy their fault; nor, indeed, did the Left. Borrowing was largely done through anonymous bonds which were sold over the counter with no questions asked, and a commentator was later forced to admit that 'the State did little more than legalize a *de facto* situation' when it exempted the bonds from the general tax on income.[2]

Farmers were legally as well as practically exempted from the excess profits tax, and such of them as made large profits during the war (and some wine growers, for instance, made very large profits) escaped from the curiosity and rapacity of the Treasury in a way that would have aroused envy in other lands. Not until the war had lasted over two years did the Government and Parliament make any serious attempt to raise new revenue, and on this side of public finance the most striking comment is that, during the war, the Government of France did not raise in taxes enough to pay for its normal *peace-time* expenditure. All war costs were borrowed. Internal borrowing was directed to tapping (and tapping successfully) the economies of the nation, not merely by great war loans as in most other countries, but by selling Treasury bonds, and not until November 1915 was the first war-loan launched.

A feature of French war-loans was the attempt to stabilize the rate of interest. The French investor, in such circumstances, expected to

[1] One of the oddest accounting mistakes was discovered in 1922, when it was found that the total of National Defence bonds had been *overestimated* by 7,000,000,000 francs.
[2] M. Truchy.

get 5 per cent. on his nominal investment. It was, of course, only possible to maintain this traditional rate of interest by selling *rentes* under par, and, when interest was reduced to 4 per cent., as it was for the last two loans, at far under par. (The last was issued at 70·80 per cent.) This feature, combined with a long period of inconvertibility, might have imposed an even more intolerable burden on the next generation had not successive devaluations of the currency saved the State from the consequences of its rashness.

For foreign borrowing, the French Government, like the British, tried to mobilize the securities held by its citizens. But it was much less successful than was its ally; it only managed to mobilize 2,000,000,000 francs.[1] This was much less than the nominal French holdings abroad, but those holdings were largely in Russian, Rumanian and other unmarketable securities and, in addition, the French Treasury had not the information which would have enabled it to stimulate lagging patriots (if such there were) who were hesitating to lay down their bonds for their country.

It followed, then, that a great deal of French foreign financing had to be done through Great Britain, that country advancing money to France, generally on condition that the sums thus lent should be spent either in America or Britain. In addition, loans were floated on the American market, though less successfully than is often believed, and when Federal Reserve regulations made it impossible for the French Government to borrow more in its own name, cities like Bordeaux and banks like the Crédit Lyonnais lent their names to transactions that formally at least met the rules.[2] By the spring of 1917 the credit of France, like that of Great Britain, was exhausted in the country that was supplying most of the war materials imported. No system of public finance could have altered this, although a more rigorous system of internal taxation would have kept down luxury imports and thus helped the French exchange. With the entry of the United States into the war, these difficulties disappeared; for the moment, all that America could give was financial aid, and that was lent lavishly, until by the end of the war the external debt of France alone had reached, in francs, almost double the total pre-war debt—which was, in 1914, the highest in the world.[3]

One last form of borrowing was lavishly employed from the beginning of the war, the use of the printing press. At the outbreak of war, the note circulation was 5,900,000,000 francs, by the end of 1919 it was 37,000,000,000 and, most devastating comment on this side of

---

[1] At then par of exchange £80,000,000 or $400,000,000.

[2] The law forbade any Federal Reserve Bank to discount loans made to any one borrower that exceeded 10 per cent. of the unimpaired capital and surplus of the lending bank.

[3] The national debt in 1914 was about 27,000,000,000 francs. The foreign debt in 1918 was 43,000,000,000. The debt owed to America was just short of $3,000,000,000 and the debt owed to Britain was just short of £620,000,000.

governmental policy, it was in 1919 that the biggest increase in the note issue took place. That year was the worst of all from the point of view of the financial purist; extravagance and optimism unaccompanied by any sense of the importance of getting in heavy taxes and lightening the paper burdens made the responsibility for the financial policy of the first year of peace more than any one reputation could stand. But the French parliamentary system is designed for emergencies like these, ·since no financial responsibility is ever laid on one pair of shoulders. During the war, indeed, the control of finance by the Chambers largely lapsed. Presented with accounts that neither Minister nor Committee could understand, the Chambers could only complain and hope for better things, or sometimes show their teeth at inopportune moments, as when the Finance Committees of both Houses expressed their dismay at finding that nearly ten million francs had been spent on protective caps and on trench helmets. 'The helmet', said the Senate report severely, 'is a new item of equipment which, legally, may not be introduced without legislation.' But such vigilance, even had it been more frequent, would have been of little avail in stemming the flood of expenditure. The real remedy of increasing the revenue side was, as has been suggested, too heroic to appeal to many members of either House or of any party.

It must not be thought that parliamentary control, if inadequate, was useless. That some order was observed, that accounts, even if incomplete accounts, were rendered, was largely due to the vigilance of the senators and deputies. What might have happened had that vigilance not been exercised, is suggested by the history of advances to munition makers. When it became evident that the regular sources of munition supply were hopelessly inadequate, all sorts of factories had to be called on to tender for the War Department. As a moratorium had been proclaimed at the outbreak of war, normal banking facilities were suspended and the factories could obtain no credit. In these circumstances, the Government found itself forced to advance the capital required by its own contractors. Not only were these advances made lavishly, not only with too little investigation of the economic status of the borrowers, but without sufficient security that the money lent would, in fact, go to equipping munition factories. And the funds thus advanced were not burdened with any interest charges! The Government, that is to say, borrowed on its own credit and lent part of what it had borrowed on sufficiently onerous terms, *free*, to its own contractors, who, with this capital, were able to fulfil their contracts usefully for the country—and at a considerable profit to themselves. It was not until Parliament insisted on a minimum of business method that this paradise of the *entrepreneur* was spoiled by the insistence of the politicians that, if the Government continued to lend money, it should at least charge the borrowers with the cost of borrowing it. But such useful interventions of politicians against the extravagance of officials and soldiers were not enough to repair the damage of the general fmancial policy for which the politicians were responsible.[1]

III

All over the world, the economic life of nations was disturbed by the war, but inevitably France suffered more changes than almost any other land. Despite her growing industrialization, France, in general, was in 1914 a country of small factories, of little businesses, and the regions where great industrial agglomerations were common were almost all occupied by the enemy. The character of the war, with its demand for vast quantities of machine-made goods ensured (once it was realized that the war was not going to end in a few months) that the industrialization of France would be immensely accelerated. For the first few weeks of the war this result was not foreseen. The disaster caused a great economic crisis, especially in the luxury trades of Paris; wages were reduced and many employees put out of work. So little was the character of the war realized that the Renault motor works in Paris were shut down, except for a small section that made stretchers and other small articles! By the end of the war, the factory was making tanks and aeroplanes, trucks and cars, and instead of its peace-time 5,000 workers, was employing 25,000. Bourges, which was the seat of one of the great arsenals, saw its population jump in about a year from 45,000 to 110,000 and the average output of its munitions works multiplied twelve-fold. The replacement of individual artisans by machine-tenders serving the needs of mass production was greatly accelerated. So, too, was the admission of women into industries where they had been unknown before the war. The invasion sent hordes of refugees into the safer parts of France, many to be a burden on charity and the Government; others, like the cotton and woollen manufacturers of Belgium and the north to stimulate the stagnant textile industries of Normandy; others, like the 200 prostitutes shipped from the fortress city of Toul to Marseilles, to disorganize completely the local market for a time.

The industry that suffered most from the war was the greatest of all—agriculture. In peace-time there were 5,200,000 male workers on the land; by 1918, 3,700,000 of them were in the Army and, despite the use of women, prisoners and immigrants, agricultural production fell

---

[1] In France, as in all belligerent countries, there were many real and more rumoured scandals connected with war contracts. In France, however, the long life of national traditions was well exemplified by various projects to make the profiteers disgorge by a 'revision' of all big contracts. But although there was much talk and trouble taken and given, the methods used by the Monarchy to make Fouquet and his like disgorge were found to be impracticable under the Republic.

off very badly. Even the vineyards, few of which were in the war zone, reduced their production by 20 per cent.

The two crops most seriously affected were wheat and sugar. A fifth of the 1913 wheat crop came from the invaded area, and France, which after consuming 700,000 tons of sugar, had an export surplus in peace-time, saw her production fall to 136,000 tons. The national stock of cattle suffered as much or more. In the first two months of war, more than half the cattle in the department of Indre et Loire had been sent to the Army and, as the stocks fell while the Army demand continued, serious privations were suffered by a population which was finally forced to eat frozen meat—when it could get it.[1] By 1918, Paris had three meatless days a week and the number of dishes which could be eaten at one meal was severely regulated. As supplies grew shorter, queues began to appear, and there were soon disturbances provoked by the shortage of such necessities as tobacco.

Bit by bit a rationing system was introduced for bread, sugar, tobacco, chocolate, and although the system was not as rigorous as that used in England, and was only slowly applied over the whole country and to most necessities, it was practically complete by 1918. The most serious shortage of all was in coal. Despite rationing and limitation of the use of coal, French imports of fuel rose from 17,000,000 tons a year to over 20,000,000 tons, a reflection of the fact that the most important coal-fields were in German hands. As the submarine war got worse, supplies were both limited and erratic. A port like Marseilles, which could only be reached from England by a long and dangerous voyage, could not compete with Le Havre or Rouen; it saw freight rates increase ten-fold and then saw the practical cessation of supplies. This forced the Midi on to that substitution of water power for coal power that had begun before the war, but for the moment it meant very serious hardship. The vast profits made by British coal interests and by shippers were forgotten much sooner in Cardiff than they were in Marseilles. Even Paris suffered from a shortage and on one occasion from a complete cessation of supplies.

Inevitably connected with the shortage of supplies was the rise in prices. Inevitably, but not obviously, to a nation which has preserved from the old régime a conviction that prices are fixed or should be fixed by law. Shortage of supplies and inflation, with its depressing effect on the foreign exchanges of a country whose imports had increased nearly four times (in francs) by 1918 and whose exports had fallen by a third, had their consequences. Needless to say, prices rose faster than wages, and for the large classes of the community for which wages did not rise at all, life became extremely difficult. The rise was naturally

---

[1] Parisian consumption of frozen meat rose from 15 tons to five to six thousand tons a month. It must be admitted, however, that the aversion of the Parisians to this food was at first stimulated by the refusal of butchers to sell it.

attributed to all kinds of maleficent agencies. In Rouen it was the presence of thousands of lavish British soldiers that was responsible. In Paris, one chronicler seriously [1] assures us, it was only when the even more lavish Americans 'with their pockets stuffed with dollars arrived' that prices really rose.

To meet this discontent, the Government took traditional measures. Since the Second Empire, indeed since Louis XVI, the cost of bread in Paris had been kept stable by various governmental devices. During the war, bread alone of the staples hardly rose in price at all, thanks to Government subsidies, with a consequent calming of the tempers of the greatest bread-eating nation of the world and the practical exclusion of the bakers from the fantastic profits that made the war so tolerable to many other classes of shopkeepers. But all other prices soared.

The official solution was the fixation of prices by the prefects. This system had two drawbacks: it was not uniform and it could not be enforced. If a prefect in one part of the country raised his prices, supplies flowed into his department from other regions; by the time the other prefects had followed suit, new discrepancies appeared. This could have been remedied by a uniform price-fixing for the whole country, but what could not be remedied was the growth of 'black', unofficial markets. The peasant who found the price of milk too low made cheese; when cheese was regulated, he ceased bringing supplies to the official markets and sold privately. The urban population was indignant and sometimes raided the markets and forced down the prices by threats; but, of course, the victims of this rough justice did not return to these markets and the universal shortage saved them from any risks. It was a permanent seller's market and no amount of decrees could alter this fact.

More hopeful was the encouragement of co-operatives or the establishment of municipal butcher shops or the 'baraques Vilgrain' of Paris where foodstuffs were sold at cost price. These shops helped to provide an element of competition at the retail stage. But the co-operative movement in general did not rise to its opportunity. It failed to offer the facilities of the great chain shops like the 'Docks du Centre'. The trading activities of the local authorities, taking place on a perpetually rising market, were generally profitable, although Paris suffered vast losses, written off as 'insurance against public disorder'. Legal restriction was much more successfully applied to rents, although in the great munition centres suddenly flooded with extra workers, in Le Creusot for example, the owners of houses did as well as if they had owned valuable farming land,—perhaps better, since they had no labour troubles.

In Paris, short of food and warmth, the war was more dramatically

---

[1] M. Bertaux. Another consequence was amorous, 'du coup, les plus beaux Australiens et les plus mâles Portugais furent éclipsés par les guerriers d'outre-Atlantique'.

evident than in any town not in the actual war zone, and Paris after all was partly in the zone.[1] When war was declared, all theatres were shut, restaurants closed at half-past eight, the trams and underground railways were put on limited schedules. The Comédie Française did not reopen until two days before the Government returned (December 6th, 1914) and the Opera remained closed until the beginning of 1916, and even then, evening dress was forbidden. Air raids had forced the darkening of the whole city, but although it was dark its social life revived. Moralists deplored the rage for dancing and musical comedy and the intrusion of foreign ideas and customs. By 1916 the Parisians had settled down to the war; it was part of their normal lives, sometimes comparatively quiet, sometimes too active, as in the spring of 1918 when the bombardment by Big Bertha, combined with the German advance, again sent floods of refugees away from the threatened city. But at each end of the social scale, Paris was alive. She was the centre of the Allied resistance, and if her position was onerous and dangerous, it was, after all, a price almost worth paying for the glory of being the cynosure of the world.

The workers, when at the end of 1916 wages began to rise, were flattered by the Government as indispensable and had a fictitious if not real sense of well-being. In Paris, as all over France, it was the middle classes that suffered, although until the imposition of uniform rates of pay by the munitions department in 1916, there were remarkable variations in the wage-level of the working classes in different parts of the country. But the weakening of the position of the professional classes which began during the war was one of the most striking results of the war in French society. The official, envied by his fellows in 1913, was pitied by them, if noticed at all, by 1917. Almost the only gain of the clerical classes was a shortening of the inordinately long hours of office-work.

The recognition by the Government of the claims of regular mistresses of soldiers on their country's generosity was an inevitable and just acceptance of a social fact, but the old-fashioned French family structure was badly shaken by the inflation, loss of savings in Russian bonds and by the new opportunities offered to women by the war. Nursing, office work, even factory work became a duty and often a necessity for many daughters of bourgeois families, a state of affairs that it was easier to deplore than remedy.[2]

To make up the shortage of labour, there was an importation of Spaniards and Italians, then of Chinese, and many Frenchmen first got

---

[1] Paris was officially classed as in the war zone in June 1918, after the German advance of the previous month.

[2] A historian of the life of Marseilles during the war reports with indignation cases of women who misconducted themselves 'attirées par une curiosité malsaine vers les Britanniques, les Hindous, les Africains du Nord, les Sénégalais, les Annamites'. No indication is given of whether this order is ascending or descending.

an idea of the size and variety of their empire when they saw men from Madagascar, Indo-China, Algeria and Morocco, and even some Kana-kas from New Caledonia, replacing the men of the ruling nation who were in the trenches. They may even have had some scepticism of the merits of imperialism implanted in them by comparing the sober Moroccans, but lately rescued from barbarism, with the Algerians who had added drunkenness to their native vices.

IV

During the first years of the war, the slogan of Clemenceau, the fact which he used to show up the failures of the Government, was the simple statement, 'the Germans are at Noyon'. But nobody on the French side of the trenches can have had a clear idea of the sufferings of their compatriots who were in the occupied territories. The destruc-tion of all life in the actual battle-line; the ruin extending over a much wider area on each side of the line—these could be understood. But the sufferings of the population of the areas which, from October 1914 to October 1918, were securely held by the invaders, were of a less obvious but very bitter kind. The normal population of the perma-nently occupied region was a little over two millions; by the end of the war it had fallen to about sixteen hundred thousand; the differences representing soldiers and refugees and, to a minor degree, movements of population into Belgium or Germany, some nominally voluntary, some openly forced. For four years this population was controlled entirely in the interests of the invaders. The north of France, said an American who had every means of knowing,[1] was a 'great concentra-tion camp'. It suffered from all the hardships that fell on Germany and most of those that fell on France. Some of the most odious mea-sures taken by the Germans; the stripping of the region of almost all its economic resources and the deportation of many of its inhabitants, were blamed by the invaders on the rigours of the British blockade. When it was thought worth while to conciliate the inhabitants, the official propaganda organ, the Gazette des Ardennes, the only newspaper written in French that the average inhabitant saw, blamed the obstinacy of the Allies and, above all, of England for continuing a hopeless war. But there was no determined attempt in France to build up a pro-German party like the Flemish party in Belgium. There was no raw material for such a party and, except in the region of Maubeuge which was for a long time attached to the German administration of Belgium and the iron fields of Lorraine which were earmarked for annexation, there was little effort wasted on conciliating a population which, in the mass, never modified its hostility.

Many of the sufferings of the inhabitants were simple incidents of

[1] Mr. Hoover.

war. The Germans shot soldiers who were found hiding and women who helped any of the anti-German activities that seemed to endanger German security, and, in general, imposed their authority by savage reprisals; but it should be remembered that the Allies had, in fact, an excellent intelligence service behind the lines, and many of the Frenchmen who were executed died as patriots but were no more martyrs than Schlageter, Major André or Nathan Hale. It was in less serious matters that the occupation showed the less admirable sides of the German character. Coming from a country in which, even in peace time, the officer was a privileged person not bound to waste politeness on civilians, the German officials were bound to be harsh in dealing with a people which had not been so thoroughly brought to heel. And in a few years, rigorous and humiliating punishment had done a good deal to tame the inhabitants of northern France. French officials returning in 1918 were astonished to find the inhabitants getting out of their way with profound bows! Petty annoyances like naming streets after the Kaiser and Hindenburg, enforcement of formal saluting, occasionally a perverse delight in humiliating what was too easily assumed to be a conquered people, kept the flame of hatred alight, if it was very necessary to hide the flame.

Life could be made tolerable by a humane or indifferent officer; intolerable by a brute or a fool. Appeals to high quarters, for example to the Imperial Crown Prince, sometimes had good effects, and selfishness was at times an ally of the French. One town escaped billeting for two years, thanks to the foresight of two German colonels who did not want their lavish accommodation lessened. A good many local despots had local mistresses, and these sometimes played the rôle of Esther and got the lot of their countrymen alleviated, although there were one or two cases of loose women revenging themselves on their respectable sisters who had despised them.

In four years of strain and of uncontrolled authority there were bound to be grave abuses. It seemed to the French that the German passion for beating was sometimes given rein to. Women were, from time to time, beaten with rubber truncheons, and men had to fear blows from the riding-whips that were the favourite German symbol of authority. Rigorous regulations designed to prevent espionage and to secure control of the economic resources of the country gave abundant opportunity for delation, and many a village feud was carried on with the more or less unconscious collaboration of the invaders.

The problem of feeding the population was never completely solved. The American Relief Organization alone stood between the population and starvation, but at the best the diet was short in meat and vegetables. The occupied territory was the richest part of France, but in four years of war it was thoroughly and skilfully skinned. At first it was a question of temporary requisitions. A colonel, for instance, demanded a down-quilt and a cook. But it soon became a systematic assessment, and removal of all that could be useful to the invader, raw materials, machines, cattle, manufactured goods. Cases of personal plundering, though common enough, did far less harm to the economic life of the country than the carefully organized exploitation of its capital resources. There were great financial levies too. Roubaix, in four years of occupation, paid 82,000,000 francs in levies, the pre-war annual taxes being about 5,000,000. The needs of the constantly moving troops could only be met at the expense of the inhabitants. One town of 12,000 inhabitants had to house 20,000 soldiers.

Worse still were the levies on the inhabitants for service. Although coercion was officially frowned on, in fact many thousands of the inhabitants were forced into labour gangs, a practice disliked when it was applied to men and detested when it was applied to women. Any resistance was severely punished—and in ways that seemed designed to insult as well as to intimidate.

The extreme centralization of French Government made the difficulties of the occupied area even greater. Only one prefect (of the Nord) stayed behind and he was ultimately deported. Thus there fell on the mayors and councillors a responsibility for local government for which they were not prepared and from which they were not allowed to escape. The moral health of a community often depended as much on the courage of the mayor as on the humanity of the German commandant. Some mayors were servile; some were too tactless to be of any use to their fellows; some were heroes; most deserved well of their communities.

As the war went on, something like despair fell on the occupied region. In no country had war weariness more material to feed on. Communication with France, where tens of thousands of their fellow-citizens were fighting, was extremely dangerous. Spreading good news of the Allied cause was punished—and for long there was so little to spread! There were gallant efforts made to keep up the morale of the people. The drunkenness of German officers was taken as a sign of the inferiority of the conquering nation; their occasional 'sexual eccentricities' were regarded as typical of a debased people. But the conquerors were the conquerors all the same; and, in the spring of 1918, the hearts of many thousands in Lille and Roubaix must have sunk near to despair at the news from the front. But as summer drew on things changed. By the autumn, the front was cracking; troops were heard to shout down their officers; there was an air of anxiety and then of alarm visible. The requisitions went on, but by October the end was in sight. The invaders were in retreat. On November 2nd, the *Gazette des Ardennes* appeared for the last time, and in the next two weeks the last of the invaders had crossed the frontier, and close on their heels came the delivering armies on their way to occupy western Germany. . . .

V

Among the greatest worries of a French Government faced with a great war was the possible attitude of the leaders and politically active members of the working-classes. In the years immediately preceding 1914, Jaurès, leader of the Socialist party and towering above all his rivals by prestige and personality, had concentrated more and more on military and diplomatic questions. He had attacked the army administration as being inefficient and wasteful as well as undemocratic; he had attacked the foreign policy of the Republic as opening an era of imperialism by its Moroccan policy and by its subservience to Russia. An alliance binding France to the Tsardom against the Germany that had given the world the Reformation was odious to him. Anti-militarism was not Jaurès' preoccupation only. It was largely by its campaign against the three-years service law that the Left had won the elections of May 1914. In June, the party congress of the Seine had heard a German Socialist leader remind it that Bebel had said that mobilization might mean revolution. So moderate a leader as Albert Thomas had asked that the party should declare itself in favour of stopping a war by a general strike.[1]

At the National Congress which opened on July 14th, the question was no longer remote; the cloud on the horizon was now bigger than a man's hand and Jaurès had to defend the strike as a peace weapon against Jules Guesde, who said it merely meant delivering over the more advanced to the less advanced countries. Even the once uncontrollable anti-militarist, Gustave Hervé, had recanted his former violence. When he had talked that way he had believed there was a body of real revolutionaries ready to follow him but now he knew there was not. But Jaurès consoled the audience by reminding them of the achievements of the strike in other countries: in Spain in the Moroccan affair; in Russia during the Japanese war; in Italy at the time of the war in Tripoli.[2] 'We must prepare to be worthy of the destiny which awaits us'. And on July 25th, in a campaign speech at a by-election to the Chamber, Jaurès again tried to induce his audience to keep calm, to remember how guilty France was over Morocco and how untrustworthy imperial Russia was. There was wrong on the other side too. Germany's diplomatic manner was bad, and the troubles in Bosnia-Herzegovina were due (it was an election speech) to Austrian clericalism which had tried to convert the inhabitants of the provinces to Catholicism by force. The one hope of peace was that the workers of all the nations should react, that all these thousands should unite 'that the

---

[1] One of the opponents of the general strike asked ironically how it could be supported by Thomas, who was in favour of taking part in the Government and might be a Minister of War.

[2] The chief opponent of Italian imperialism and militarism at that time was, of course, Comrade Benito Mussolini.

very beating of their hearts may avert the horrible nightmare'. It was the last speech Jaurès made in France.[1]

The permanent committee of the International had its headquarters in Brussels and, on the 28th, Jaurès, Guesde, Vaillant, Longuet went there to meet the other delegates. Guesde was sceptical of the reality of the crisis; he had said and believed that the day of great European wars was over. And in the atmosphere of Brussels, hope revived. The Austrian and Czech delegates, it is true, said that it was impossible to hold the annual Congress of the International at Vienna on August 23rd, but the committee was not in despair. The Congress was summoned to Paris for August 9th and the committee voted that the 'German and French proletariats would bring even more vigorous pressure than ever to bear on their governments'.

Jaurès returned to Paris to carry out his part of the bargain. He believed that the crisis would pass and, in any case, that there would be no sudden breakdown; the diplomatic battle, like any modern battle, was bound to be a long drawn out affair, so he told pessimists. And he repeated that the German leader Haase had told him that the German Emperor didn't want war—and he knew that the French Ministry did not want war. He had come from interviewing the Government when the news reached the Chamber of Deputies that Germany had declared a state of 'Kriegsgefahrzustand'. Jaurès, who was very proud of his German scholarship, insisted that this did not mean war but was merely a state of preparation for war. He sent for dictionaries and made his point while his colleagues marvelled at his optimism. According to one story he told a Minister who asked him what he was going to do, 'continue our campaign against the war'. 'You'll be shot down,' said the Minister. He went off to a favourite restaurant of his, and, while looking at the photograph of the little daughter of an editor of the *Bonnet Rouge*, was shot from the street. His murderer was an unbalanced Nationalist fanatic who thought that he was saving his country. He might well have ruined her. At a moment when unity was the one necessity, the most trusted leader of the workers had been murdered. Even if the story that he had planned to write a leading article denouncing all the governments, his own included, is true, the article would have been less of a blow to France than the murder. All sections of public opinion recognized this, even the *Action Française*, which had been the bitterest assailant of the orator. The Prime Minister issued a proclamation of homage which was also an appeal for calm. He promised that the assassin would be punished.[2] The appeal was heeded.

War was now certain ; the unfortunate phrase of Poincaré, 'mobili-

---

[1] When the war fever had reached its height, friends of Jaurès anxious to clear his name of charges of treasonable views denied the authenticity of the report of the Vaise speech, but there is abundant proof of its accuracy.

[2] The murderer was kept in prison for so long that the shock of his crime was forgotten; he was then tried and acquitted.

zation is not war', deceived no one; but even before mobilization was ordered, the trade-union leader, Jouhaux, speaking in memory of Jaurès, had declared that the French workers would punish 'the bloody despots who had made the war'. The leaders of the Left and the Government were faced with a common dilemma. How seriously were they to take the hot and bold words uttered at so many congresses? Had the French workers been so won over to revolution that they would not fight? Had they in fact nothing to lose but their chains? Workers, leaders and Government all came to the same conclusion and by the time the great meeting in the Salle Wagram which Jaurès had called for Sunday 2nd had met, mobilization had begun.

Leaders and led alike were all over France facing a very real problem. They had not, like English and American leaders, time to think the matter over. To refuse to answer the mobilization order meant, if the refusal was not general, suicide; if it was general, revolution—and this in face of a Germany which showed no signs of internal dissidence. Hermann Müller, a Reichstag Socialist, had been on his way to Paris when he heard of the murder of Jaurès, and when he arrived he promised (through his interpreter, the young Belgian Henry de Man) [1] that the Social Democrats would never vote war credits. But such vague (and unkept) promises were not enough. Each reservist had to decide for himself what might mean life or death for him or for France. And there was no hesitation. A left-wing leader was later to complain that the anti-militarists had been deceived by their own noisy propaganda. It was the same handful in a dozen different guises who shouted 'down with the Army' and alarmed the Government of France while misleading the Governments of other countries. Behind the façade of Marxism a deeper French revolutionary tradition was hidden, and it was the spirit of 1793, of Blanqui and the Commune of 1871, that now sprang to life. The mobilization not only took place with technical but with spiritual smoothness; for a moment there were only Frenchmen.

To this end the Government contributed by a decision which fully justified itself. There was in existence a police list of dangerous persons, of radical agitators who were to be arrested the moment mobilization was ordered lest they should, in their revolutionary fervour, sabotage the military machine. This was the famous 'Carnet B'. It contained 2,501 names, the names of the most dangerous revolutionaries in France; the names of trade-union leaders who might organize the general strike; and of revolutionary politicians, like Pierre Laval, who might incite them to it.[2] The Government was terrified either to use Carnet B or not to. They were advised by M. Clemenceau to use it

---

[1] Since chief planner for Belgian Socialism and Cabinet Minister.

[2] Later, when the pacifist section of the trade unions and of the Socialist party had recovered from the shock, it was asserted that the leaders had betrayed the workers to escape Carnet B. But there is no ground for this view. As a trade-union leader told the critics who talked of what they would have done, 'I should have liked to see you try. The Paris workers . . . wouldn't have waited for the police, they would have shot us on the spot.'

and the Prefect of Police agreed. But the advice of the Chief of the Sûrété was taken. He laughed at the fears expressed about the attitude of the workers. 'They will follow the regimental bands,' he said, and they did.

This patriotic unanimity was not broken for months. It is true that the veteran leader, Vaillant, representing the Blanqui tradition, was furious when the Government went to Bordeaux. This was 1870 over again. Paris, capital of the Revolution, was being betrayed, but the Marne calmed the old *communard*, although his patriotic vehemence soon became too much for the directors of *L'Humanité*. When the Viviani Government was re-organized at the end of August, the Socialist party sent two representatives into it, Jules Guesde, the inflexible opponent of participation in bourgeois governments, and Marcel Sembat, who had written a book to show that a republic could not wage a successful war. It was Minister Guesde who appointed trade-union leaders 'delegates to the nation', a vague reminiscence of 1793 and 1848. The main result of this move was that the leaders had to explain their motives in accepting such appointments when opposition revived and, above all, to refute (as they did) the charge that they had not only fled to Bordeaux, but had gone first class in the train!

The first rift in the unanimity of the country came on May 1st, 1915. The metal workers' federation, whose leader, Merrheim, was Jouhaux's only rival in prestige among the workers and which was very revolutionary in temper, announced that 'this war is not our war'. Socialist unity lasted a little longer and the national committee on July 14th was able to resolve unanimously that the only hope of freedom from fear of war was the defeat of German imperialism. It was the last unanimous vote the party was to pass.

The war had lasted a year and already the first enthusiasm had gone; the weariness, under which all European nations almost collapsed before the end came, was beginning to appear. The war and its consequences had greatly weakened at first both the political and industrial side of the workers' movement. Mobilization took away thousands of militants and made much of the peace-time propaganda out of place. The unions recovered fastest; not only did they recover lost ground, they made new conquests. There were new federations of unions formed, like the federation of railwaymen; and the growth of the munitions industry helped the militant metal-workers whose membership was 7,500 in 1912, 18,000 in 1916 and 204,000 in 1918. Financial resources rose, too, though characteristically not in proportion. Regions that had not been seriously unionized at all were now won over. After some resistance, women were welcomed to the unions if with a hope that they would go back to the home when the war was over.[1]

---

[1] The law permitting a wife or a minor to join a union without the consent of husband or guardian was not passed until 1920. Even then, these members in tutelary state could not become officials of the unions.

Such a growth was inevitable. If the unions had not existed, they would have had to be invented; indeed, in some regions and industries they were practically invented. The small groups of militants found themselves merged in a mass of newcomers with no real notion either of union discipline or union aims. But the union leaders were necessarily forced into close collaboration with the Government, which at once increased their prestige with the mass and made them an object of suspicion with the militants. As the demand for munitions grew, it was necessary to send many expert workmen back from the front—and it was necessary to call on the unions to help in the selection of these soldiers, both to avoid the release of incompetents and to avoid the demoralization of both the Army and the factories had the choice of men been left wholly to the employers or to the War Office.

The unions had to fight to protect the rights of their members who were working under military orders: to preserve their claim to compensation for injuries, for instance. As the war dragged on and as the need for labour and for soldiers grew greater than France could meet, the unions had to protect the French worker against the competition of Chinese labour. When it was proposed to bring 100,000 Italian workers to France, the unions protested bitterly that it was a device to get 100,000 Frenchmen from the factories to the trenches, while their places were to be taken by Italians who should go to the front themselves, and however flattering to the military pride of Frenchmen such a system was, it wou d not be endured. Even the elaborate preparations which marked the first year of American activity in France were not regarded with approval. There were, it was asserted, more American workers than soldiers in France, and as usual, the fighting would be done by Frenchmen while their Allies made shells, roads and money.

But although there was an increasing number of strikes, they were, until 1917, fought over wages and over conditions of labour, and compulsory arbitration of strikes was imposed at the beginning of 1917 without meeting much more than formal protests from the unions. The necessities of the times forced the Government to impose on factories a system of workers' delegates (or shop stewards as they were called in Britain). This innovation was strongly opposed by many employers and was regarded with some suspicion by the unions. Many of the shop stewards were, indeed, good union members,—so good that they made reports to the unions (which had officially nothing to do with them) as well as to their fellow-workers in the factories. But others, placed in authority, developed more or less reasonable ambitions of their own and became rivals rather than allies of the regular leaders. But for all the friction and all the oratory, French labour gave its Government very little to worry about for the first two and a half years of war.

More concern was felt at the rising pacifist protest that began to shake the Socialist party. In the autumn of 1915 took place the first conference between the representatives of the Socialist parties of the warring nations. At Zimmerwald in Switzerland a little group representing the left wing of the national parties met and, largely under the influence of the exiled Russian leader, Lenin, a joint Franco-German declaration was issued. 'This war is not our war.' The chief French delegate was Merrheim of the left-wing and formally pacifist metalworkers, but there were many militants in France who, although not at the Zimmerwald conference, sympathized with its leaders. To the pacifist cause symbolized by Zimmerwald and, next year by the Kienthal congress, rallied an increasing number of local Socialist parties, in the Haute-Vienne, in the Isère, in the Seine, where the revolutionary tradition was most lively. By December 1916, the majority of the party which supported the war was within sight of being a minority, and Jules Guesde noted bitterly that 'it's for that I have given so many years of my life', to which the minority might have answered, 'it is, indeed, for we are where you were'. Illegal pacifist tracts began to appear, including reprints of the speech of Jaurès at Vaise.

The vast majority of French workers were still untouched by doctrinal opposition to the war, but more and more the militants had begun to regret their adherence to the sacred union. The circulation of *L'Humanité* under the highly patriotic direction of Renaudel had fallen to 9,000. A rival paper, *Le Populaire*, was founded and, although only a weekly, it was more powerful with the Paris workers than the daily.[1] There was plenty of fuel; only a match was wanted, and that was provided when the news of the Russian Revolution came.

It was inevitable that the Russian Revolution should have an immense effect in France. Hostility to the Tsardom had always been a powerful force on the French Left (and for a time on the Right too). Victor Hugo and Montalembert were united in their detestation of Imperial Russia, and even the diplomatic necessities that led to the alliance did not destroy this tradition, which, indeed, the imbecile and bloody reign of Nicholas II had done nothing to weaken. Now the Tsar was gone and, more important still, the French workers who had been told about revolutions ever since 1871, who had been fed with violent words, taught to await the great day when the rifle and the barricade would replace the ballot box and the Parliament, had now before their dazzled eyes the spectacle of the great day coming. What had been, for over a generation, mere rhetoric in Paris had become reality in St. Petersburg. The wind from the steppes, like the wind from the sierra in Hugo's poem, took away the senses of most active members of the French working classes. What had been done in the

---

[1] It might be noted that *L'Humanité* subsequently became the Communist and *Le Populaire* the Socialist daily.

capital of the Tsars could and should be done in the capital of the Revolution.

This inspiration from the east became far more powerful after the October Revolution. Here was a real revolution; here was the way to peace. There was now no easy way of harmonizing the views of the two sections of the party. If the main interest of the French workers was victory for France, then the Bolsheviks were villains and intervention against them necessary and just. But if the workers of the world had nothing to lose but their chains, the Bolsheviks were heroes. How could the nation of the *Marseillaise* attack the Revolution?

The Painlevé Government of September 1917 was the first to have no Socialist representative in it; and all French Socialists were now in favour of a general Socialist Congress at Stockholm which, as it involved meeting German delegates, was strongly opposed by the Army leaders. In the general uneasiness that was provoked by the defeatist wave, by the campaign against M. Malvy, by the gloomy news from Russia, soon to be followed by the almost equally gloomy news from Italy, the nature of the decision to be made by France was becoming clearer. She could turn to the Socialists and liquidate the war on the best terms possible— or she could decide to fight to a finish—and that meant Clemenceau. The idea of a Clemenceau Ministry was abhorrent to almost all Socialists, but to many of them it was as preposterous as it was abhorrent. But the impossible came about and, although Clemenceau tried to get Socialist collaboration after the disasters of the spring of 1918, it was refused him. Merrheim might talk of saving France from a Peace of Brest-Litovsk, but by 1918 the only way to save France was to win the war and the resolution to win the war was incarnate in Clemenceau.

The Socialists and the trade unions were thrust into the background. The arrest of M. Malvy evoked protests from the 'Confédération Générale du Travail', for the Minister of the Interior was regarded by the trade-union leaders as a barrier to reaction. The great strike in the Paris munition works in March 1918 widened the gulf between the Government and the organized labour movement. The motives for the strike were various; it was not organized or led by responsible leaders, but as it was in part a protest against a calling of munition-workers to the colours and as it came at the moment of the great German offensive, the genuine grievances of the workers were, for the country, less important than the risks the strike made the country run. As a trade-union leader said, 'they have struck in good faith at a moment when they should not have struck'.

In the Socialist party, the revolutionary and pacifist wave continued to mount. In July the party congress was controlled by the Zimmerwaldian section. Renaudel had been ejected from the control of *L'Humanité*, and more extreme leaders like Cachin and Frossard [1] were

[1] Since expelled from the party as a moderate in the company of Renaudel.

coming to the top. The party, that is to say, was in the hands of a section that had despaired of the war and to an increasing degree had put its faith in the methods of the Russian Revolution, at a moment when the tide of war was turning suddenly and decisively in favour of France. They were excluded from a quasi-dictatorial government in whose power and duration they had refused to believe. In the last months of 1918, the leaders of the workers (for so they saw their rôle) were more powerless in their own country than they had been since the beginning of the century. They could only pass resolutions and develop their organizations. But the number of party members was still trifling (although it had risen from 28,000 in 1917 to 34,000 in 1918). There was an increasing gap between many of the old leaders and the militant rank and file. A conservative group had founded *La France Libre* to fight pacifism, and the sponsors of this paper were soon to be expelled from the party. As one of them wrote next year: 'the events in Russia represented to the French proletariat as a successful application of Socialism have made them so fanatical that all argument is impossible'. What was true of this Paris suburban constituency (Sceaux), was true of all the Paris industrial region. And Clemenceau, with victory in his grasp, had no notion of arguing with these fanatics. Inevitably, the leaders and the rank and file, powerless for the moment in France, turned for help and leadership to abroad, to Woodrow Wilson and to Lenin.

VI

The internal politics of France during the war were simple in their outlines. Only in the ranks of Labour and among the Socialists was there anything like a doctrinal development or conflict. And that development was more important for the future than for the war period itself. There was no party in favour of making peace on terms that the Germans would have welcomed. There was only a party, bred by the disappointments of 1915 and 1916, which began to despair of defeating the Central Powers as long as they stayed united. This party hoped to detach Austria from her ally, a hope that led to the secret negotiations with the brother-in-law of the Emperor Charles, but the hold of Germany over the Austrian Government was too strong to be shaken off by Charles and Prince Sixte of Bourbon. Other secret peace negotiations were proposed by various intermediaries, and Briand was willing, if permitted, to negotiate with unofficial German agents. He was not permitted: and wisely, for France had to resolve either to endure to the end, or to make peace openly with the invader. It was a main object of German policy to weaken the will to war of her greatest military antagonist. So there were spread absurd stories of British designs on Calais and less pointless jokes about England's willingness to fight to the last Frenchman, jokes that began to tell in 1916 and 1917 when they were rapidly losing all plausibility. But Germany had more than jokes to rely on; she had been able to subsidize pacifist propaganda in France with the aid of the French Government.

In all the changes of government, from Viviani to Briand and Briand to Ribot, one Ministry remained unaltered. M. Malvy kept the Interior. M. Malvy was young, popular, a left-wing Radical Socialist, representative in the Government of the Caillaux section of the party, and Caillaux, debarred from office by his wife's hasty action, was still not negligible. M. Malvy thought, and rightly thought, that national union should be preserved; some of his decisions early in the war for which he was most bitterly reproached were fully justified. But as the war went on, M. Malvy's fitness for his office lessened very rapidly. He was a typical product of the 'république des camarades'. He had friends in all sections and all classes. Among them were some shabby crooks of the type of Bolo Pasha, dangerous political adventurers like Vigo (known as Almeyreda) and reckless political zealots like Duval, editor of the *Bonnet Rouge*, a left-wing paper subsidized, like many others, by the French Government, even when it began to preach, more or less openly, against that policy of war until victory which was the formal policy of all the governments of which M. Malvy was a member. And when finally French subsidies ceased, German subsidies took their place.

There are still many dark places in the history of the *Bonnet Rouge* and the associated scandals. But enough is known to make astonishing reading. Agents of the German Secret Service were able to pay money to Frenchmen whose conduct was highly suspicious, but who assumed, and made others assume, that they would be protected by the Minister of the Interior. As war weariness increased, the importance of pacifist propaganda increased with it, and there began to spread, in Paris at least, a demoralizing impression that at a time when all French efforts were supposed to be concentrated on victory, there were certain well-known if not generally respected Parisian figures whose conduct it was difficult to reconcile with any enthusiasm for the cause. And these individuals had powerful friends, or, what was the same thing, were believed to have them. The crisis came in the summer of 1917. The disasters of the spring, the Russian Revolution, the mutinies, had brought France to the cross-roads. She could sacrifice everything to winning the war; she could decide to make peace on what terms she could get; she could not continue in the state of growing indecision and pessimism. The mutinies were decisive. How was it possible to shoot soldiers, to suspend their legal rights, to submit them to the hated system of 'cours martiales' while the men of the *Bonnet Rouge* were left alone and when their friend was a Minister? [1]

---

[1] French military law has two kinds of courts-martial, 'conseils de guerre', whose procedure is slow and which give special protection to the accused, and 'cours martiales',

The attack on Malvy came from many sides. Some of his Cabinet colleagues thought, kindly, that his health required him to rest, but he held his ground protesting, no doubt sincerely, that all that he had done was 'in a general honest thought and common good to all'. But two attackers especially got through the guard. Léon Daudet, in the *Action Française*, with a great literary talent and a complete absence of scruples, accused the Minister of treason, above all of being the instrument of betrayal of the plans for the attack on the Chemin des Dames. The reiteration of these charges (as far as the censor would allow) had its effect. And naturally, for though the specific charges were false, the general political charge was true. The continuance of Malvy in the Government was quite incompatible with a war to the bitter end. The Minister was now a symbol, and a symbol of slackness.

To the press polemics was added a most powerful parliamentary assault. The most formidable of orators, Clemenceau, roused to all his patriotic bitterness by the complacent toleration of 'defeatism', told the Minister to his face, 'You have betrayed the interests of France'. [1] The blow told. It was delivered on July 22nd; Malvy took his much-needed holiday and on August 31st he resigned. But that was only the beginning of a political revolution. The Ribot Ministry fell; and the Painlevé Government that followed failed to give the impression of energy that was needed. There was only one man left if France was to continue fighting. But Clemenceau was feared and detested by the majority of his colleagues. He was on the worst of terms with the President; he was more than anyone else the enemy of the Socialists. He had steadily refused to join any of the war Governments since in them he would be a subordinate. All politicians knew that if Clemenceau was called on, Parliament was accepting a dictator. There were manœuvres and rumours. Albert Thomas, the very capable Socialist Minister of Munitions, had his ambitions and one of his friends had the ear of Poincaré. But the President and Clemenceau had one thing in common: they both remembered 1870, and Poincaré detested lukewarmness more than he detested Clemenceau. On November 13th the Painlevé Government was defeated amid shouts of 'Down with Clemenceau' from the Left. It was a German saying, that Clemenceau was France's last card. It was now played and it was trumps.

A few days less than a year elapsed between the appointment of Clemenceau and victory. And as far as France was concerned that victory was the work of a man of seventy-six. [2] From the beginning of the war Clemenceau had raged at his impotence, since he was convinced that peace should only be made by a man who 'had read the Treaty of Frankfort'. [3] His policy was simple 'Home policy? I wage war!

whose jurisdiction is summary. Since the Dreyfus case, the insistence on the most strict procedural rules in military trials had been the mark of a good Republican.
[1] Altered in the official account to 'you have failed in all your duties'.
[2] The next oldest war leader, Hindenburg, was six years younger.   [3] Of 1871.

Foreign policy? I wage war! All the time I wage war.' His method of doing so was in the true Jacobin tradition, however painful such an admission would be to the self-styled heirs of the Jacobins. He had their fanatical patriotism; he had their ruthless vigour. He had never been an amiable man and he had now so many enemies he cared little how many more he made. The acceptance of him by the Chamber was as much an abdication as the creation by the Convention, in 1793, of the Committee of Public Safety. He was a one-man committee. He had no colleagues, only useful subordinates like General Mordacq, M. Tardieu, M. Mandel, less useful ones like M. Klotz. He took for his own Ministry the War Office. Even during the war, no Prime Minister had dared to run the political risk of not having a department of his own. A Prime Minister without a department of his own would soon have ceased to be a Prime Minister. But Clemenceau did not take the War Office for that reason; he wanted to keep an eye on the Army, to keep an eye on General Pétain, whom he trusted as far as he trusted anyone. That was not far, and the Minister sometimes interfered in matters that should have been left to the Commander-in-Chief; for example, he forced Pétain to alter (for the worse) the kind of training given the troops in the winter of 1917–18. But that was a trifle compared with the effect of his spirit on the Army and the country. He was an indefatigable visitor to the Army. His curious Mongolian face, his deer-stalker cap, his short robust figure were soon familiar all over the front. He seemed to soften, to be more hopeful of human nature when talking to the private soldier than when dealing with a general or a politician.

Behind the lines the campaign against defeatism was carried to its logical conclusion. Painlevé had begun the job by arresting the leaders of the *Bonnet Rouge* and their kin. Bolo Pasha was shot and so was the ambiguous female who called herself Mata Hari, the shots that killed her having since echoed round the world. Almeyreda was found dead in his cell, strangled with his own bootlace. He killed himself because his drug supply was cut off, said the Government; he was murdered, said Léon Daudet.

Far more dramatic was the trial of Malvy. That ex-Minister had rashly asked to be tried and he was taken at his word. He was charged before the Senate (sitting as a High Court) with treason. The Upper House, with a disregard for law that shocked jurists, disregarded the charge of treason, which could not be proved, and convicted Malvy of malfeasance in office with which he had not been charged, but of which he was, politically, if not morally, guilty. He was sentenced to five years' banishment on August 5th, 1918.[1] But a bolder step was the arrest of M. Caillaux. That politician had suffered, all during the war, the agony of being excluded from power and the knowledge, which he

---

[1] On the same day Foch was made a Marshal of France.

537

managed to convey to his friends, that no one in France was as fit as he for that burden. Against the charges of lukewarm patriotism, M. Caillaux had a right to indignation, but a self-esteem bordering on the morbid, the ill-luck of having, like so many parliamentarians, some very odd friends, and the misfortune of an indiscreet tongue and pen made him vulnerable. His arrest was in the best Jacobin traditions; so was the adroit mixing of political and moral charges against him, and his arrest was, like so much done by the Jacobins, necessary for the safety of France—if France were really determined to win the war. Like General McClellan whom the Democrats nominated against Lincoln in 1864, M. Caillaux was an able and patriotic man whose defeat was a national necessity.[1]

In the great military crisis of 1918, the Chamber almost revolted against its tyrant, but who was to replace him? By the middle of the summer a revolt was out of the question, and by the autumn, the Prime Minister was in a position to ignore President, Parliament and Commander-in-Chief. For most of France and for all of the world he was the nation incarnate. On November 4th he read to an enthusiastic assembly the terms of the Austrian armistice and reminded the Chamber that he was the sole survivor of the deputies who, at Bordeaux in 1871, had protested against the cession of Alsace-Lorraine.

On November 11th, all Paris waited for the great news. Foch had come to the capital and was recognized by the delirious crowds. At the War Office the two men, forgetting their rivalry, fell into each other's arms. At half-past two, the Prime Minister appeared in the Chamber and, raising his hand for silence, read the terms of the Armistice, and then calling for gratitude to the soldiers of France, he spoke in the terms of the revolutionaries of his childhood. 'Thanks to them, France, yesterday the soldier of God, to-day soldier of humanity, will be for ever the soldier of the ideal.' Then Parliament voted its order of the day to be placarded all over the territories of the Republic, 'Citizen Clemenceau and Marshal Foch have deserved well of their country'. That night, for the first time for years, the lamps of Paris could be seen from the sky. Frenzied mobs dragged the German guns from the Place de la Concorde and left them in ditches. An immense crowd gathered outside the War Office where it knew that the Prime Minister had gone. 'Clemenceau', they roared. He opened his window and, for a moment, looked on the triumphant people. Then he shouted 'Vive la France', and sat down in his room.

One of the Prime Minister's oldest friends was the great painter, Claude Monet, and during the darkest days of the past year, Clemenceau had often gone to repose his spirit in Monet's famous garden. He went this time, so the story runs, to tell his friend of the end of the war

---

[1] It is perhaps worth adding that these martyrs, whose rehabilitation was one of the first tasks of the victorious Left in 1924, have since bitten the hands that applauded them.

and of the triumph of France. 'Yes,' said Monet, 'now we have time to get on with the monument to Cézanne.'

In a few days, the last retreating Germans had crossed the frontier and behind them came the French and their Allies. At the head of his army, Mangin rode into Metz, having distributed to the troops copies of Verlaine's patriotic lamentation on the enslavement of his native city. And after Metz came Strasbourg, the city where the *Marseillaise* had first been sung. The 'day of glory' had at last come. It had cost France fifteen hundred thousand lives, a little less than the total population of Alsace-Lorraine.

BOOK X

BETWEEN TWO WARS

O cease! must hate and death return?
Cease! must men kill and die?
Cease! drain not to its dregs the urn
Of bitter prophecy!
The world is weary of the past—
O might it die or rest at last!

SHELLEY.

CHAPTER I

THE TREATY OF VERSAILLES

I

IT was the habit of Madame Letizia Bonaparte (who had known what it was to be the wife and widow of a shiftless minor Corsican noble-man), when she was asked to contemplate the latest example of the astonishing fortune of her son, Emperor of the French, King of Italy, Protector of the Confederation of the Rhine, to remark, 'It's all right as long as it lasts'. The scepticism of Madame Mère underlay what-ever Napoleonic illusions covered the surface of the French mind in the first intoxication of victory. The position of France was unique. She was a victor, but she had in many ways the psychology of a defeated nation. If her attitude had any parallel in past history, it was best represented by the attitude of Metternich in 1815. The rulers of France, like the rulers of Austria, knew that the conjunction of circum-stances that had brought them safely through the ordeal was unlikely to recur. What was not achieved in the way of security now, would not be secured later. And security was what France wanted above all else.

The ruler of France in 1919, in his years of bitter impotence between 1914 and 1917, had made his battle-cry of one phrase, 'the Germans are at Noyon'. For France, the primary fact underlying victory was invasion; the first and greatest result of the victory was the deliverance of the sacred soil of France from pollution. It was not irrelevant that a line of the *Marseillaise* had talked of impure blood soaking into French soil. When that song was written, France was on the eve of the first of five invasions from the east which had marked the history of the previous century and a half. Those invasions were not always unprovoked or unreturned, but a patient suffering from a dreadful disease is not to be simply comforted, or cured of his fear of its recurrence, by his doctor's pointing out that the first infection was due to his own fault. France, the victor, had suffered for four years of war all the agonies that normally accompany defeat, whereas her chief allies, even Italy, had not known them at all, or only for a brief period.

Then, in France, the peasant mentality was dominant. France was not a country like England, where the overwhelming majority of the people, in all classes, regarded the land as something to be looked at, or played on. Even a doctor like Clemenceau, and a lawyer like Poincaré, had close relations with the soil, each in his own province, La Vendée, and Lorraine. The occupation and the destruction of the soil of France was far more easily understood by them than was damage to any highly artificial system of economic organization. The peasant mentality had other results. The war had been a great lawsuit of a kind familiar enough; one side had won, it was entitled not merely to the verdict, but to the assets in dispute, and, for the peasant, these assets were tangible. The international world of credit and trade was a new thing; the old permanent world had not altered much since Joan of Arc had ridden west from Lorraine, confident in divine aid to drive the English out of France where they had no right to be. The Germans were trespassers and bandits of a kind well known to a country where history had toughened the minds as well as the bodies of men. And history taught, or seemed to teach, that arms —and the fortunes of war—were realities more permanent than paper bargains or paper debts.

For the French, the primary fact of Europe in 1919 was that in its centre lay a people more numerous than any of its neighbours, more warlike than any save one, more aggressive than that older and more chastened nation, France. Germany, by herself, was more than a match, thanks to her position, her population, and her military and technical talents, for any one of her neighbours, indeed than for several of them combined. Her social and political organization was primarily conditioned by her military needs. France and Prussia had taught each other too many lessons in this department of life for the French to be deluded into thinking that Hohenzollern Germany had been simply a slightly belated parliamentary state whose political evolution had been accelerated by a defeat in war which the German people would soon come to regard as a blessing in disguise.

These were illusions proper to nations that had not known defeat. France knew better. She had known what a great conscript army involved in the way of political problems; what defeat meant in the distortion of political life; what a real revolution was; what, on one side, the consciousness of invasion and, on the other, the consciousness of immunity from invasion meant. The way in which France and Germany and all the European nations were integrated was perceived by the critic, who, more than any one man, made the opinion of the English-speaking world on the Treaty of Versailles. 'England still stands outside Europe,' wrote Mr. Keynes. 'Europe's voiceless tremors do not reach her. Europe is apart and England is not of her flesh and body.' Still less was America, for although the chief American delegate had been born in the midst of a great civil war and had grown up in a defeated community and so could not share the optimistic English illusion that 'war never settles anything', America was even farther from Europe than was England, even more inclined to regard as of little importance the petty concerns of the Lilliputians seen through the eyes of the King of Brobdingnag.

Another cause of discord between the victors was the location of the Peace Conference in Paris. It was not merely that the French capital was feverish or hysterical. So great an event as the peace settlement, so pregnant with good and evil fortune for such mighty nations, would have awakened Philadelphia. But in Paris, the easy belief in the necessity of restoring a mechanical balance of power, easy fears of French political domination of the new Europe were evoked by the very splendour of the scene. It was, after all, at Versailles that peace was signed; and if that was dramatic reparation for 1871, it made it easy to think of Louis XIV as well as of Bismarck, to forget which nation it was in modern times which had shown itself 'nec pluribus impar'.[1] It was no longer the Germans of La Fontaine who could say truthfully,

> Nous cultivions en paix d'heureux champs, et nos mains
> Étaient propres aux arts ainsi qu'au labourage.

They had learned the lesson of cupidity and violence and their French teachers had wearied of their lesson more than had the pupils.

One last French prepossession was human, natural and unfortunate. Because France had made more sacrifices for victory than any of the 'Allied and Associated Powers' and had suffered more in her soil and in her blood than had any other of the great powers,[2] it was natural that she should imagine that her wishes had a special claim to recognition. Had her rulers been more familiar with the New Testament, they might have reflected on the parable of the labourers in the vineyard and realized that the very greatness of the French effort weakened her position in 1919. Bled white, stripped of so great a part of her capital equipment, she was incapable of resisting the demands of her less exhausted friends. And this was bitter news, for the French, like all the other peoples of the victorious coalition, the English, the Americans, even the Italians, considered that victory was primarily their achievement. It was a sign of Clemenceau's sagacity that he, at least, never forgot that a victory won by four nations could not be used according to the simple wishes of one of them.

The lines of the territorial settlement had been laid down by Wilson in the Fourteen Points and in the supplementary points. Faced with defeat, the rulers of Germany, that is the Army leaders, had surrendered on terms which were extremely onerous and whose character they did not realize. That Ludendorff had not read the Fourteen Points was

---

[1] See p. 54. [2] Serbia probably lost more men proportionately to population.

bad enough, but neither had Clemenceau. Wilson had in his hands some, though not all, of the trump cards, and the greatest of these was the political and financial disinterestedness of the United States. She had none but ideal axes to grind, which was not true of any other power, no truer of England than of France, and her representative in Paris was willing to take great political risks for ideal ends.

It was, perhaps, a pity that Wilson *was* in Paris. His position was unique; he was the sole head of the State, his own Prime Minister and practically his own Foreign Minister. But his political position at. home had been weakened by the results of the Congressional elections. He had not got the Democratic Congress he had asked for, and it was not certain that what he promised in Paris he could deliver in Washington. Yet his power was immense. It was, in effect, on his terms that the Germans had surrendered. He had great negative power over his associates; above all, economic power, which he was prepared to use. And he was not much in sympathy with the realist, sceptical French Prime Minister, or, indeed, with any of his European colleagues.

The effective power at the Conference was taken into the hands of the five great nations, but of these, Japan was only moderately concerned, Italy was weak and was for a time unrepresented, after Wilson had appealed over the head of Orlando to the Italian people. The real decisions were made by Clemenceau (who presided), Lloyd George and Wilson. Clemenceau had the advantage over the other two of speaking English[1] while they did not speak French.

The most important difference between French and 'Anglo-Saxon' ideas of territorial settlement arose over the Rhineland. Not only was the acquisition of the left bank of the Rhine an old traditional French policy, at least as old as the Revolution, but from the Rhineland bridge-heads and bases had come the invading armies of 1914. On the eve of the Russian Revolution, France and the Tsar's Government had agreed to the establishment of a separate Rhineland state, but the British Government had not been a party to this negotiation and the agreement was of merely historical importance. It remained so. Clemenceau had to be content with securing a military occupation of the Rhineland for fifteen years and the permanent demilitarization of both banks. To the security afforded by the fact that a new German invasion would have to start behind the river barriers and that France had fifteen years in which to prepare her defences, was added the decisive consideration of a joint Anglo-American guarantee of the French frontier.

This was the greatest triumph of French diplomacy; it relieved the

---

[1] To the indignation of some French patriots, the Treaty of Versailles was the first great international agreement not exclusively written in French or Latin. English was put on terms of equality with the great diplomatic language.

mind of the average Frenchman of his nightmare of another invasion by his over-strong neighbour. Foch protested that no agreement was worth actual military security, such as a separation of the left bank from the Reich or the setting up of a buffer state would give. But Clemenceau put Foch in his place; these were matters for statesmen not for soldiers, however eminent. France had got (on the word of her Allies) the greatest positive gain she could hope for from a joint victory and, in addition to security, she was to get reparation.

The idea of political reparation was plainly evident in the treatment of Alsace-Lorraine. The period between the Peace of Frankfort and the armistice was treated as a mere interregnum. Germany ceded the territory, as from November 11th, 1918, and all the State property in the former Reichsland was transferred, without any payment, to France. Included in the property were the railways, which had been nationalized by the Germans. The shareholders of the French company in 1871 had been compensated by Germany, but it was argued that this had been done out of the profits of the indemnity. It was a belated recognition of justice to take over the profits of the victors of 1871 in favour of the victors of 1919. And, as Germany had not made any allowance for the share of Alsace-Lorraine in the French debt in 1871, none was made now. In the last convulsions of the falling German Empire, Alsace-Lorraine had been granted the rank of a Federal State, but the French Government refused to recognize the claims of the leaders of this State to authority. The rule of the one and indivisible Republic was alone legal in the recovered provinces.

The Saar settlement, too, was a matter of reparation, but of economic reparation. French negotiators at the Conference put forward a case for outright annexation. The territory had been left to France in 1814. It was only as punishment for the 'Hundred Days' that it had been taken away in 1815. But only a small portion of it had been under French rule for more than a generation; only one commune was French-speaking and, whatever was the case in 1815, the Saar valley was indubitably German in 1919. It is true that a good military case could be made for annexation, for the Saar basin endangered the security of Lorraine; but since France had been made safe by the demilitarization of the Rhineland and by the Anglo-American joint guarantee, this argument was dismissed by the non-French negotiators as worthless.

There remained a last claim. The destruction of the coal-fields of northern France by the Germans had been deliberate; it should be expiated. The 17,000,000 tons a year of the Saar field would be both immediate compensation and a lesson to wreckers. So France was given absolute property in the mines, subject to a right of repurchase open to Germany after fifteen years, on terms to be settled by arbitration. The area of the coal-fields was carved out of Prussian and

Bavarian territory and erected into a new governmental unit ruled by a commission appointed by the League of Nations. German law, German language, German local government were all preserved. After fifteen years, the final fate of the territory was to be settled by a plebiscite which could vote for annexation to France or return to Germany or the *status quo*, which, as the Saarlanders were to be a privileged people, exempt from French conscription and Germany's reparations liabilities, might be expected, by people who underestimated the force of nationalism, to appeal to the majority.

The whole Saar settlement, with its careful balancing of the right of France to specific and exemplary reparation and the political right of German people to be German, showed a tenderness for those claims of the conquered people which the victors admitted to be based on the general principles on which the new Europe was being created, which had not many precedents in past peace-making. One last example of this spirit was the leaving in its artificial neutrality of the little state of Luxemburg, of immense strategic importance, as it was. The French and the Luxemburgers wanted a customs union, but it was Belgium that had its way and the Grand Duchy passed from the German to the Belgian economic system.[1]

There was one glaring exception to the application of the principle of self-determination and the reconstruction of Europe on a basis of the rights of nations. One consequence of the war was that the political, economic, and military position of Germany—if she were to be left immune from special restrictions—would be actually strengthened. On her eastern and southern borders, she no longer had two great powers but a large number of small nations, of which the largest and strongest, Poland and Czechoslovakia, were far weaker than their great neighbour. The disappearance of the Russian and Austrian Empires had created a political and military vacuum which Germany would fill if she were left unshackled. France would have on her frontiers a neighbour far stronger, relatively, than in 1914.

From the British point of view, anything that diverted German attention away from the sea to eastern Europe was to be welcomed, but for France such a result would be paradoxical indeed. That fear of Germany which had dominated French foreign policy since 1870 might well be increased, not diminished, by the war: and apart from the important improvement in the military frontier that resulted from the recovery of Alsace-Lorraine, the French position would be worse: a state of affairs that might not matter if a new Europe pacific and law-abiding was being born; but such a Europe was not yet conceived. If the German parts of Austria were to be added to the Reich, as both

[1] The restoration of the *status quo* of 1870 was not quite complete. The frontier of 1871 cut across the old departmental boundaries in Lorraine and the territory of Belfort remained the only portion of Alsace in French hands. The Lorraine boundaries were left intact and the 'Territory of Belfort' preserved its status as a miniature department.

Germans and Austrians wanted, the new German state would be as superior to France in population as the old had been and far more homogeneous. What Bismarck had not dared to do after Sadowa would have been done for his defeated heirs by the victors. It was resolved to defy the principle of nationality; and the minor but not unimportant cases in which it had been allowed to work to Germany's advantage were forgotten in the natural indignation aroused by this flagrant breach of the spirit of the new European order. It is possible that the situation might have been tolerable for a generation, or until the passions of 1919 had calmed, had the new Austria been immediately helped economically and given economic privileges to make up for her political disfranchisement, had she been excused from all indemnities like the other succession states of the old Dual Monarchy (except Hungary). But the new Austria was not given enough interest in her new status to make up for the absence of an adequate sentimental basis.[1]

Apart from the Austrian exception, the territorial terms of the Treaty kept remarkably close to the Fourteen Points and to the new political basis of Europe, the self-determination of nations. With the exception of Ireland, all the traditionally oppressed nations of Europe, including some whose national consciousness was even newer than that of the Germans or Italians, were given an opportunity for national life. The result was quickly damned as 'the Balkanization of Europe', an odd term of condemnation for anyone who reflected on the state of the Balkans before and after the Christian nations were freed from Turkish rule. Yet the application of the principle of nationality could not but hit Germany hard. The Prussian state had prospered and grown by conquest, and the fruits of over a hundred years of power politics were now lost. Danes, Alsatians, Poles, all escaped from an iron rule imposed by force and maintained by force. The section of the Treaty to which the Germans objected most, the Polish corridor, was not only in the Fourteen Points but no one had doubted, until 1919, that the inhabitants of the corridor were Poles. But the German objections to the Treaty as set out at Versailles showed that the German conviction of superiority in civilization and in political virtue over the neighbouring Slavs had not been shaken by defeat. The German liberals who had thought of the partition of Poland as a crime were apparently an extinct race.

If Europe was not to be reconstituted on a pure power-basis, there was nothing but the principle of nationality, the most powerful of all living religious dogmas, to build upon, and that principle meant that Germany had to disgorge. Nor was it true that the principle was

[1] According to one school of thought, it was the anti-Catholic bias of Clemenceau which kept Austria out of the Reich. Had this union been allowed, the new federation would have been dominated by the Catholic and civilized western and southern Germans. Hitler, Himmler and Goebbels come from these Catholic regions.

always used to her disadvantage. It secured for her the right to have the fate of Upper Silesia and the frontiers of East Prussia settled by a plebiscite. It secured the unity of the Reich and the eschewing by the victors of the annexation of indubitably German populations. What could be said by the Germans was that the system was not allowed to work against the victors. If France had no subject peoples in Europe, that was not true of Britain, and even the United States had no intention of allowing any general system of political morality to be applied in the Western World to, say, Puerto Rico.

As a European territorial settlement, the Treaties of Versailles, Trianon and the rest applied with moderation a principle that alone had seemed to justify fighting the war at all. Nor was the principle of self-determination left to work in a vacuum. The rights of national minorities were provided for, at least in the case of the smaller countries. The new League of Nations was to prevent the recurrence of the petty meanness that had marked Prussian rule in Posen for instance, or Magyar rule over more than half the Kingdom of Hungary. Mistakes were made; but fewer than it soon became fashionable in the victorious nations to pretend, and profitable in the defeated countries to assert.

Nor should it be forgotten that the makers of the new world at Versailles felt themselves bound to work with speed. The reconstruction policy of the North, after the American Civil War, could be spread over several years and change its character several times, usually for the worse, without the power of the North to impose its will ever being in doubt. But in the spring of 1919, it was not certain that the Allies would long preserve their superiority in power, for their troops were clamouring for demobilization and, by what were really mutinies, were achieving their object. More serious still was the revolutionary fever spreading over a great part of Europe. It was present even in Paris where a Left fanatic shot Clemenceau without killing the tough old man. It was epidemic in Munich, capital of the Catholic and conservative Bavarians, and it took a virulent form with the formal establishment of Bolshevism in Hungary.

The plan of quickly imposing military and territorial terms on Germany and postponing all fundamental questions until a preliminary Treaty of Peace had been concluded had had to be abandoned. Wilson was determined to incorporate the League of Nations in the Treaty, not merely formally but fundamentally; that is, decisions as to particular points would be made in light of the fact that a new world-order was being set up. In 1814–15, the conquerors of France had been able to impose terms on France and then to take time to reconstruct Europe because they did not

hear
Time's wingèd chariot hurrying near

—and also because the greater part of the peace settlement of 1815

550

hardly concerned France at all. But the central geographical position of Germany made the fate of Hungary, Lithuania and the other old and nascent nations which lay all around the central colossus, of the greatest importance to Germany and to her late enemies. Then the financial problem of reparation made it necessary to link up all the territorial settlements for, as the Germans rightly argued, their capacity to pay was limited by the resources of the territory left to Germany, a Germany with Upper Silesian coal could pay more than a Germany deprived of those resources. A quick 'business' settlement was in fact impossible; what was 'business' depended on the kind of Europe that was emerging. The Treaty had to be made in a hurry in face of a Europe that seemed to be collapsing, and it was necessary to trust to the unborn League to remedy what mistakes there were—and there were sure to be some.

II

The preamble of the Covenant of the League of Nations laid it down that the High Contracting Parties accepted the Covenant 'in order to promote international co-operation and to achieve international peace and security'. The emphasis of the British policy at Versailles and later was on the first aspect of the League. From the habit of international co-operation would grow the habit of peace. Too rigorous a definition of obligations, too ambitious an attempt to stabilize the territorial structure of Europe was to be avoided; it ran counter to British traditions and methods. French logic was the enemy of true progress.

This attitude seemed to the French both less wise and less candid than it seemed to the British. They saw no signs that Britain was abandoning anything she really valued or needed. Whether accidentally or not, the British Empire had emerged from the war greatly increased in territory and Britain herself had secured the destruction of that German fleet whose existence, at the side of the strongest army in Europe, had more than anything else forced her on the opposite side to Germany in the pre-war balance of power. With the High Seas Fleet at the bottom of Scapa Flow, Britain was not merely secure against German naval power, but the conduct of the Germans in sinking their own fleet had solved the problem of dividing up that part of the spoils of war.

The island kingdom was secure, or thought she was. France would have liked to be equally secure. But her problem was harder. It was impossible to create a fleet surreptitiously or to seize command of the sea by a surprise. But the collapse of the other great empires had left Germany in a position where, if her military power was to be anything like proportionate to the strength she drew from her geographical position, her population, and her industrial resources, she would be in a position to dominate the Continent. The peace of Europe must be secured by making it impossible for Germany to wage a successful war. The second objective set out in the Covenant, 'international peace and security', would not simply grow out of the first, that is out of international co-operation. International co-operation involved a common interest; Germany had not a common interest with Poland in the survival of the Polish state. She had an interest in its destruction or mutilation. She had not a common interest with the new Danubian states in their effective independence. Britain might be indifferent to the survival of either Poland or Czechoslovakia, but France was not an island. Debarred by her Allies from taking the territorial securities customary in such cases, forced to take a treaty of guarantee instead, France had to have a substitute. Marshal Foch would rather have had some Rhine fortresses than a limited German Army, but he was over-ruled.

The German Army was to consist of 100,000 long-service troops; there was to be no General Staff, or system of reserves, or tanks, or military air force—this system was a continuation of the terms of the Armistice. Like those terms it was designed to make it impossible for Germany to resort to arms. It would have been more candid and less dangerous to have admitted as much, to have pointed out that a limitation on their freedom of arming was the price the Germans were paying for the ultimate withdrawal of Allied garrisons from Mainz and Ehrenbreitstein. But as a tribute to the moral principles of the Allies, this simple precaution (one from the German point of view infinitely preferable to the probable alternative of territorial mutilation), was introduced by a very ambiguous preamble, 'In order to render possible the initiation of a general limitation of the armaments of all nations.' There was a sense in which this motive was genuine. There was no hope at all of a limitation of armaments as long as there was a possibility of a German war of revenge. To remove that danger was to make possible, not equality of armaments between the victors and vanquished (no one proposed that the British or American navies were to be limited as the German had been), but a serious reduction of armaments, at least in Europe. And as it is too often forgotten, one important result *was* the general reduction of the term of service with the colours of the conscript troops of all European powers, a gain that would have been warmly welcomed before 1914. Nevertheless, the preamble was a mistake, for it allowed German leaders to persuade their own and other peoples, that there was a contractual relation between German disarmament and the disarmament of France and the other military powers of Europe. It was an argument that was to prove especially potent in countries like England and America, which were absolved by their geographical position from taking seriously the problems of land power.

The same mixture of practical and sentimental motives was apparent in the one part of the Treaty of Versailles that deserves all, or almost all, the criticism that has been heaped upon it. It is highly probable that, had either side won quickly, indemnities in the strict sense would have been exacted by the victors. The precedent of 1870 was there; victory was then rewarded by an actual cash profit to the victorious state, if not to the victorious nation's economy. But as the war dragged on it became evident to all but the most credulous, that no one power could pay its costs. The Fourteen Points did not talk of 'indemnities' but of 'reparations', and there was justice in the distinction. The man in the street, even the German man in the street, could see the case for the restoration of France and Belgium, perhaps by a joint effort of all the powers. After a complete victory of one side, it was natural that the victors should insist on the reconstruction by the vanquished of the battle-ground. If it was the fortune of war that France and Belgium had been invaded and not Germany, it was the fortune of war that Germany, having lost, should pay for the damage her troops had done. It was felt impossible to state these simple truths and so the claim for reparation was based on the aggression of Germany; it was associated in the public mind with the 'war guilt' clause to which, from the beginning, the Germans reasonably attached no moral significance and which, as the years went by, became a millstone round the necks of the Allies.

It was not on a dubious, but on a certain point of history that the claim to reparation was based. It was Germany which *had* done the damage and it was Germany which *had* lost the war. But the reluctance to admit that the decisive fact was not the justice of the Allied claims, but the ability to impose them, prevented the Allies from putting those claims on a permanently defensible basis. It had other effects, for the victors soon forgot how decisive was the fact that they had won and began to think that, in international affairs, justice was all. The Germans, who had been defeated and who thought their cause as just as that of the victors, knew better. The prudery of the victors was really not the main cause of the linking up of the reparations clauses with the question of the guilt of Germany in causing the war. If Germany was not to be subject to a mere indemnity, there had to be some moral basis for the Allies' financial claims, or, which was politically unthinkable, the peoples of the victorious nations would have to be told the truth, that, guilty or not guilty, Germany could not pay for the war.

It was of course obvious to any competent and honest economist, that the astronomical figures of what Germany could pay and must pay if the burden of victory was not to fall on the victors, were mere magic. Yet a Governor of the Bank of England was ready to lend himself to this game of hocus pocus. Lord Cunliffe talked of £20,000,000,000; Loucheur of twice that amount, although at these levels it mattered very little what figures were used. Germany could have paid for the actual war damage to Northern France, Belgium, Italy and Poland. She could have borne the seizure of her merchant fleet and overseas investments. Even the most pessimistic estimate of 1919, that of Mr. Keynes, was adequate for such war costs. But although Mr. Keynes was backed up by a few economists, even in France, by M. Gide for instance, the half-mad world of 1919 would not listen. From the heights of Olympus the wisest course of action would have been to have fixed at a possible figure the German liability and to have given Germany an inducement, political or economic, to pay it off as fast as possible.

Even then, the problems of transfer would have been very serious. The economic clauses of the Treaty by imposing a five-year limitation on German tariff autonomy without any reciprocal obligation on the victors not to raise duties against Germany, was absurd in the case of nations which were insisting on receiving large quantities of German goods (for that was involved in making Germany pay for the war). One of the French experts employed to see that she *did* pay for it,[1] was moved to wonder if the authors of this provision had ever read the reparations clauses of the Treaty. It is true that Britain, by admitting German goods duty free, and France by receiving immigrants on a great scale, did not go to the paradoxical length of the greatest creditor power, the United States, which both returned to high tariffs and put what was practically a complete ban on immigration. But not much more can be said of their wisdom than that.

Nor was only their wisdom at fault. The device which, by counting pensions (an evasion of the Fourteen Points which is to the discredit of both France and Britain), allowed war costs other than damage to civilian property to be charged to Germany, weakened the morally educational effects of the Treaty on German opinion. Germany had not known invasion, and it was not unwise or unjust to show her that it is not everything to win the first round. A belief in the invincibility of the Prussian Army and in the inviolability of German soil was one of the superstitions of modern Europe that needed extirpation. But the extension of war claims to cover belligerents who had suffered no more from invasion than had Germany herself, weakened the moral basis of the Treaty. What was an act of justice came to seem a form of robbery: and by making it possible for Portugal, Australia and the rest to claim a share in the war indemnity, the reparation due to the sufferers with good title was diminished. No country had more reason than France to restrict the meaning of 'reparation', for Germany,

[1] M. Jacques Seydoux.

at best, could only pay the real war damages. But in 1919 such wisdom would have been more than human.

The hands of the victors were tied. All of the rulers of the victorious powers were wiser than their peoples who were exhausted, mentally as well as physically, by the ordeal they had come through. For four years victory had been talked of as old-fashioned novelists had written of marriage; it was a blessed state in which, once attained, all trouble ceased. The peoples of Europe in 1919 wanted and expected to live happily ever after, and no one dared wake them from their dreams.

In Wilson's mind, if not in that of his chief colleagues, the League of Nations was to take over the task of waking the sleeper gently. Every member was to respect the territorial integrity of the other and each member was to guarantee and to be guaranteed by every other member. If these guarantees were to prove effective, then the nightmare of insecurity that had ended in the war of 1914 would give way to a happier and more confident day. In that brave new world, risks might be taken and the more dangerous forms of national pride and ambition might die.

What chances the League had of developing as its founder dreamed it might, were lost by the refusal of the United States to enter it. That left France and Britain face to face with no mediator of equal power in the League beside them. More immediately important was the failure of ratification of the Treaty of Guarantee. With the withdrawal of the United States, Britain also withdrew and France was not only suddenly deprived of a political advantage of the greatest importance, but she felt that she had been cheated. In using the American withdrawal to escape an inconvenient obligation, Britain was very short-sighted. For she thereby lost her chance of stilling the French fear, that the danger of an ordeal like 1914 was not for ever past. Deprived of the support that she had been promised, France was forced to turn to the lesser powers—to Poland, to Czechoslovakia, to Jugoslavia—and to build up that system of loans and alliances which made the British public suspect a country, which was revolted by the very thought of war, of harbouring Napoleonic dreams.

Of course, the French attitude to the new states was not solely based on resentment and fear caused by the British withdrawal of the guarantee. French political doctrine was sympathetic to the principle of self-determination on which the new nations were based. The 'principle of nationalities' was an extension of the principles of 1789. In any case, in the collapse of the old empires, there was nothing else to build on in eastern and central Europe—except Communism. It was idle to talk of breaking up the Austrian Empire; it had broken itself up and it could have been restored only by force of arms. The disorder in eastern Europe, in the years that immediately followed the war, was winked at by France, because there was nothing else to be done.

In any case France had less interest in the restoration of the pre-war economic structure of Europe than had Britain. Once the German fleet was out of the way, Britain could afford to think hope-fully of the reconstruction of the old economic system out of which had come such wealth. France had reason to fear the reconstruction of the old political system out of which had come such disaster. Britain had regarded the unification of Germany under Prussia (once it was achieved) with approval; it spread Protestant civilization over a wider area and was in tune with the spirit of the age. It was; but that spirit was already different from what the optimistic Victorians thought. As John Stuart Mill saw, the victory of Prussia was no matter for rejoicing among Liberals. But the illusions of 1866 were still lively in 1919. That even a rich, parliamentary Germany would still present problems of power to her neighbours, was ignored by the British public, as the desirability of making Germany a partner in some of the benefits of the new European order was ignored by the French public. Both ignored the fact that there could be no one-sided solution of the European problem: and this meant both that Germany had to be included in a new society and that her inclusion must not mean the exclusion of other nations for whom her defeat had meant life.

By the summer the Treaty was made. It had been presented to the Germans, who had been reduced to discussing it, not by word of mouth, but in writing; and although some alterations were made in response to German arguments, it was certainly, like many or most treaties in the past, imposed on the conquered. But since the Treaty claimed (and with some justice) to be based on a more idealistic basis than victory, it suffered from this character of a decree handed down from above.

Already the fruits of victory were turning sour. The fear of Bolshevism was being added to the fear of the Germans and, in a country with hundreds of thousands of holders of Russian securities, the greatest crime of the Bolsheviks for many was defaulting on the Tsarist loans. The mutiny of the Black Sea squadron, the revival of revolutionary enthusiasm among the industrial workers, the troubles of demobilization, the belief, common to friends and enemies of the bourgeois order, that it was in grave danger, all spread alarm. M. Millerand, in a speech at the Ba-Ta-Clan dance-hall in Paris, denounced the Bolshevik danger and called for a 'Bloc National,' the union of all the parties which were free from the taint of internationalism. The greatest of economic 'lobbies', the 'Union of Economic Interests', launched the famous poster of the savage Bolshevik with the bloody knife between his teeth. All this might not have succeeded but for the added help of a new electoral law, a parody of that proportional representation which had been voted on the eve of the war.

According to this system, the single-member constituency was abolished; each department returned a group of deputies in proportion to the votes cast, but if any list of candidates got a majority of the votes, it got *all* the seats. Proportional representation worked only when there was no clear majority. The result was to put a premium on electoral discipline; and, for once, that was not on the side of the Left. The great Communist crisis which was soon to split the party made it impossible for the Socialists to combine on joint lists with the Radicals, and, in many cases, the Radicals did not want such compromising company. The elections were a landslide for the 'Bloc National', for the parties which were terrified of Bolshevism and for the parties which thought the Treaty of Versailles too mild. It is true that real proportional representation would have given the 'Bloc National' less than half the seats in the Chamber, but to the superficial observer—and to the practical politician concerned only with the legal authority—the result was decisive. For the first time since 1871, the French Chamber was openly to the Right. Who knew, the hopeful victors thought, perhaps war has cured the nation of its follies? Alas, there was evidence that among the workers at least the old ferments were at work!

CHAPTER II

THE FRUITS OF VICTORY

I

THE Armistice had hardly been declared when the organ of the trade
unions of Bourges announced, 'The War is dead. Long live the
War.' The sacred union was over; the class war was resumed. It was
inevitable that the French working class in 1919 should have felt optimistic about its prospects. Its indispensable rôle in the war had
created the illusion that it would be equally indispensable in peace,
equally able to make terms. The difference between a buyer's and a
seller's market was no better appreciated by labour than by many
businessmen. The great growth of the trade union movement, too, had
bred extravagant hopes. The fears of the old militants before the war,
their scepticism of the value of mass enlistments in the unions were forgotten. In Tours, for instance, the number of trade-unionists rose
from 2,000 in 1914 to 10,000 in 1920. The total number of trade-
unionists had by 1920 risen to over 2,000,000. Demobilization brought
back to the union ranks many militants; and the rise in the cost of living,
as well as the general effervescence, was reflected in a series of strikes,
many of which were successful. There were other successes: the adoption by the Clemenceau Government of an eight-hours law and the
spread of the 'English week' (the abolition of Sunday work and the
general adoption of the Saturday half-holiday). Many of the strikes
were run in defiance of the prudent leaders of the C.G.T., and the
opposition to the rule of prudent leaders like Jouhaux which had
grown during the war, could now come into the open.

It was the Russian Revolution, with its deceptive suggestion that the
bourgeois state was no very formidable obstacle to a class-conscious and
well-organized proletariat, that went to the worker's head. The illusions of the French General Staff in 1914 were now the illusions of
many of the leaders of the French workers. Allied intervention in
Russia was especially offensive to the revolutionary tradition of France.
Was the country of the *Marseillaise* to aid the Russian equivalent of the
Army of Condé? Were French soldiers and sailors to be kept under
arms in the service of the counter-revolution? The mutiny in the
French Black Sea fleet led by André Marty was direct action against

such a plot. A riot on May 1st, 1919, in Paris resulted in the death of several manifestants at the hands of the police and provided further material for revolutionary propaganda. The new rulers of Russia were busy organizing the Third International and the Communist International Federation of Trade Unions. There was now a proletarian Vatican with an infallible Pope, and a Congregation of the Propaganda which tried hard to make of France the eldest daughter of the new·Church.

The dispute over the methods and the promise of the Bolshevik Revolution was, if anything, more acute in the ranks of the Socialist party than in the ranks of the unions. The C.G.T. had continued in close collaboration with the Government even after the Socialists ceased to be represented in it. The union leaders could not merely ignore and condemn Clemenceau as long as he was, in fact, the representative of the chief employer of the French workers, the State. The policy of collaboration—on terms—with the Government and with the bourgeoisie as practised by Jouhaux had its attractions for the great mass of new recruits to the unions who wanted adjustments of wages and hours and for whom the legalization of the eight-hour day was a tangible victory of the policy of bargaining. But the Socialist party was not in that position. It had lost by the secession of the right-wing patriotic deputies who had founded *La France Libre* [1] an important moderating element. Its leaders, less involved in day-to-day business with the workers, the employers and the State, were more likely to take the optimistic view of syndicalist leaders like Monatte that the only obstacle to a successful assault on the frightened and demoralized bourgeoisie was the leaders' 'lack of faith in the destinies of the working class', than the pessimistic view of Merrheim that the obstacle was the conjunction of a revolutionary moment with a non-revolutionary proletariat.

The old illusions about the general strike had been revived. It was boldly asserted that the Russian revolution of February had been the achievement of a general strike which, it was added rather as an afterthought, had been followed by the winning over of the garrison of Petrograd. Even if the French workers were not as militant as they ought to be, the revolution was spreading elsewhere: and when it was in flame in Germany and Italy, as it soon would be, France in her turn would catch fire. The whole continent would soon be swept by the fire started in Russia, and the French Socialists and trade-unionists must be ready to add fuel to the flame and burn the old bourgeois fabric to the ground. These illusions were shared, it must be remembered, by Lenin as well as Monatte and, until the defeat of Tukachevsky in front of Warsaw in August 1920, they were not obviously silly, even though it was obvious that, if left unaided, the revolutions in Germany and Italy were going to fail and that Marshal Foch who had said that

[1] See p. 534.

559

Bolshevism was a disease of defeated nations was more right than Lenin.

That the French Socialist party consented, even briefly, to rejoin the discredited Second International which had collapsed in 1914 was more surprising than that the decision was bitterly opposed. At the Strasbourg conference of February 1920, the decision of 1919 was easily reversed, thanks to the lead of the old Guesdist 'Fédération du Nord'; and a delegation was sent to Moscow to learn on what terms the French party could hope for corporate reunion with the true Church. The delegates were Marcel Cachin and L.-O. Frossard who were made to undergo a rigorous cross-examination by four leading Bolsheviks then of the purest orthodoxy—Radek, Zinoviev, Bukharin, Kamenev.[1] The delegates stood the ordeal well, giving satisfaction to the Russians and to such visiting revolutionaries as John Reed, and returned to France ready to recommend complete submission to the Third International.

The degree of submission demanded was a shock to many who were ready to accept a great deal from the leaders of the only party that had, in fact, made a Socialist Revolution. For many of the French Socialist leaders, and even for rank-and-file militants, the desirable solution was a treaty between equals. But the Moscow Vatican, like its Roman prototype, did not wish to make terms with heretics. Indeed, it was more rigorous than Rome, for it did not propose to admit Uniat churches to communion. If France had been ripe for a revolution, many of the Russian conditions imposed then and later would have been superfluous. It *was* absurd for leaders of a revolutionary party, determined to overthrow the whole of bourgeois society, to remain members of such bodies as the Freemasons and the League of the Rights of Man. On the other hand, if the revolution was not imminent, it was absurd to expect the French Socialists to abandon their bourgeois allies, to put the *Dépêche de Toulouse* on the index along with the *Action Française* or the *Echo de Paris*, to see no difference between M. Clemenceau and M. Caillaux and to abandon the old tradition of Jaurès which insisted that the French worker had more to lose than his chains and that there were important differences between one bourgeois state and another. As a Communist leader was to put it, after the sheep had been separated from the goats, the moderate French Socialists were ready for a revolution when the time was ripe for it. But, Amédée Dunois went on, 'who will decide when the right moment has come? Lenin's right moment is not Blum's.'

It was not indeed. The clash between the actively and the merely theoretically revolutionary politician could hardly have been made more dramatic than by the contrast between such new militant

---

[1] Cachin had been one of the agents employed to convert that paladin of revolutionary Socialism, Benito Mussolini, to the Allied cause. His experience of dealing with 'Social-Traitors' is thus almost unrivalled.

workers' leaders as Jacques Doriot and the bourgeois intellectual who had stepped into the place of Jean Jaurès. A brilliant young man of letters, a dramatic critic, an important official of the Council of State, very soon to be a successful member of the Paris bar, Léon Blum was very far from being the kind of man who overthrows states. He was no

daring Pilot in extremity—

but a brilliant dialectician who brought to the writing of leading articles for the Socialist press the talents which had attracted the attention of Maurice Barrès over twenty years before and who brought to the platform of Socialist meetings or the tribune of the Chamber that debating skill which made him so successful in the courts. Blum, indeed, was even less of a revolutionary than Jaurès, for he lacked the great tribune's warmth of language, his living relation with his audience. It was possible to conceive Jaurès, like a new Camille Desmoulins, stirring up a mob to storm the Bastille and, swept along by his own eloquence, leading them to action. Blum was more of the type of Ledru-Rollin; if he was to be found with his followers in some forlorn hope it would be because, being their leader, he had to follow them.

If France in 1919 and 1920 was ripe for a revolution, if the 'great day' of two generations of Socialist oratory had dawned, the case for joining the Third International (then it must be remembered an active and optimistic revolutionary body) was very strong. But the Strasbourg Congress had been muddled. It had tried to make the best of both worlds, to water down the fierce and exclusive discipline of the Bolsheviks; but the party could not stay long in the *via media*.

Moscow did its best to clear the issue; it handed down a list of twenty-one conditions denouncing 'Social-Patriots' and 'Social-Patriotism' and insisting on the subordination of the local Communist parties to the rulers of the Third International in Moscow. In addition to the articles of the creed to be believed and the list of doctrines to be held anathema, there was a vigorous homily attacking the Socialist leaders and the Socialist press, both *L Humanité* and *Le Populaire*. The peasants had been neglected, it was asserted, and such propaganda as was undertaken among them was merely reformist and was entrusted to 'the Social-Traitor, Compère-Morel'.

At Tours, in December 1920, came the Congress which, like a new Synod of Whitby, separated the adherents of the œcumenical revolutionary church from the local sectaries. The debate again contrasted those of great with those of little faith. Sembat in 1920, like Sembat in 1913, threw cold water with great skill. He attacked the illusions about the possibility of winning over the peasants to a programme of immediate and violent revolution. 'I fear that the peasants are more concerned to keep the great profits they make now selling pigs and chickens and that you will find them to-morrow combating you at the polling-booths with their votes and in the streets with their rifles.' To encourage the workers to believe in an easy and immediate revolution was to deliver them over to a greater defeat and a more savage repression than the Commune had produced.

It was at first sight odd that in the rural districts the party was far more enthusiastic for the Third International than was the case in the urban areas, except in those urban areas where Guesdism had been strong. Even the objection of the peasant proprietor to the collectivization of the land was rather lightly explained away, which was just as well, for many of the regions most vociferously Bolshevik were full of Left militants who were, economically, *kulaks*.

The prospects of a revolutionary party so ambiguously constituted were not as bright as the zealots thought, but there was no restraining the majority. It accepted the bitter Zinoviev letter in which the grand-son of Karl Marx [1] was denounced as a traitor; the minority, including in its ranks most of the old leaders, left the party; the union of French Socialists was dead. Being the majority, the Communists got control of the assets of the old united party, most important of them being the daily paper, *L'Humanité*. No greater or less candid tribute to the memory of a great man was ever paid than that paid by the new owners of *L'Humanité*, for the paper still bore the legend, 'Founded by Jean Jaurès , but the new party was completely un-Jaurèsian. Its violence in controversy; its complete contempt for the old bourgeois virtue of truth; its slavish following of whatever orders or counter-orders came from Moscow; these set it poles apart from the generous, humanitarian, vague Socialism of Jaurès. If any past Socialist leader was the inspirer of the new course, it was Jules Guesde.

It was natural that, in the euphoria of the post-war boom, the trade unions should have been tempted to try their old weapon of the general strike. So many particular strikes had succeeded that it was hard to believe that a general strike could fail. The victimization of a union member on the P.L.M. railway [2] was followed by a localized strike that was settled on fairly favourable terms, but during the course of the strike some militants who had been trying to induce soldiers not to obey orders were arrested.

What began as a movement to rescue these martyrs, spread into a great strike whose ostensible object was the enforcement of the nationalization of the railways, the reinstatement of discharged militants and the recognition of full union rights. The date fixed was May 1st 1920; and, in addition to the railwaymen, miners, dockers and other transport workers were called out. But the Prime Minister was Millerand, an old Socialist, and an old colleague of Briand's. He was able to out-manœuvre the C.G.T. leaders in appeals to public opinion; the workers on the Nord and Est lines did not come out; the bourgeoisie helped to

[1] Jean Longuet.   [2] Chemin de Fer de Paris à Lyon et à la Mediterranée.

break the strike. The reply of the C.G.T. was to call out more trades; the reply of the Government was to seize the headquarters of the C.G.T. and dissolve it. The strike fizzled out; Governments were not to be overthrown by merely negative action. The defeat of the C.G.T. was complete; its new members rapidly left it; militants were victimized everywhere; co-operative societies which had extended credit generously, lost both their advances and many of their members. With its numbers down from 2,000,000 to 600,000, the C.G.T. had to face the ordeal of schism.

The leaders of the Revolution in Moscow naturally determined to add the control of the French trade unions to the control of the French Socialist party. This task was more difficult, since the C.G.T. was officially faithful to the policy of the Charter of Amiens which forbade any alliance with a political party and was officially animated by the deepest suspicion of political leaders who tried to use the unions for any but union ends. But, in fact if not in theory, the C.G.T. had been closely associated with the S.F.I.O. and it might equally well be united with the nascent Communist party, the legal heir of the old S.F.I.O. of Jaurès. It was harder to have to swallow the description of the old International Federation of Unions as being composed of blackleg, scab unions; and the C.G.T. refused to accept, at the Congress of Orleans, the terms laid down by Moscow. Merrheim argued against the dangers of preaching a doctrine of civil war and the subordination of trade union activities to political leadership. Jouhaux was equally firm: and the old union leaders, unlike the old Socialist leaders, had their way. They had not had to lament the loss of a Jaurès, the loss which no Renaudel or Blum could compensate for in the ranks of the S.F.I.O.

Moscow was not very nice in its methods of controversy, and a general excommunication against the non-Communist unions, above all the French unions, was issued by the then mouthpiece of Muscovite orthodoxy, Zinoviev. 'The hucksters of labour will not long be able to deceive the masses. Howl, bay against the Communist International, you dwarfs.' The attempt to take over the C.G.T. in bulk having failed, the 'cells' were called on to do their part. In many unions the Communists got control of the executive with resultant splits, notably among the railwaymen.

At Lille, in July 1921, came the formal schism; the delegates were almost equally divided and after less than twenty years, the French trade-union movement lost that unity it had so painfully achieved. In most trades there were now rival unions, more concerned to fight each other than to fight the employers. Soon there was to be seen what would have been, before 1914, the blasphemous paradox of Christian and Communist unions in temporary alliances against both employers and the old unions of the C.G.T., alliances which were not admitted by either party, but which had the same results as if they had been open and formal. In any case, the Christian unions, free at last from domination by the employers, could not help gaining some ground in face of a divided secular trade-union movement which, were one to believe half of what was said by the old union leaders, or a tenth of what was said by the new union leaders, against their rivals, was unworthy of any trust. Having successfully split the working-class organization, the Communist unions proudly took the title of Unitary and denied that they were subject to any political party, a claim which was truer than its authors thought, for within the Communist unions, the old independent leaven was at work and the first schism was not to be the last.

II

Even had the internal and external political and economic situation been less critical, more like the picture that the victors of the elections of 1919 had made for themselves, the 'Bloc National' would have been doomed to discomfiture. Like all parliamentary majorities in all countries, the victors of 1919 greatly exaggerated the confidence that the country had put in them. A real system of proportional representation would, in fact, have deprived them of a majority; the ordeal of the war had not shaken the average French elector in his political loyalties nearly as much as might have been expected. The bogus system of proportional representation produced a Chamber not really representative and naturally weak in cohesion. It was said, with plausibility, that more than half the members of the new Chamber were practising Catholics: this involved the consequence that a great part of the new Chamber was composed of political amateurs with no real backing in the permanent political organization of the country.

The result was not, indeed, a Chamber that had any reason to fear comparison from the point of view of character or ability with the British Parliament elected a year before, or with the Harding Administration that the Republican triumph of 1920 was to give the United States; but it was a Chamber full of illusions and prejudices and short of leaders. The long exile of the 'notables' from political authority in France was now to be paid for, for the 'Bloc National' was forced to fall back on the political personnel provided by leaders of the old parties who had left the Radicals or Socialists.

The elections of 1919 gave the leaders of the 'Fédération des Gauches' the chance they had been refused in 1914, but those leaders, Millerand, Briand, even Poincaré, had not in the new Chamber the intelligent body of supporters which could have made a new system viable. In the 'Bloc National' were men of all parties still impressed by the lessons or what they took to be the lessons of the war, men afraid of the internationalism of the Socialists and of the sectarianism of the

Radicals, men really scared out of their Left complacency by the menace of Bolshevism. Allied with these were the old Conservatives, saved just on the point of extinction, the younger Catholics pursuing their design of a Catholic 'Centre party' on good terms with the Republic and some uncompromising enemies of the régime of whom Léon Daudet was the symbol. If the other candidates of the *Action Française* had humiliatingly failed, among the victors were to be found men who were not removed by much more than a label from the extreme Royalist position.

To this last school, vigour and rigour were all that was needed. With that talent for drawing attractive conclusions from incredible premises with which a dissenter from their orthodoxy has reproached them,[1] the extreme Right blamed it all on the *Ralliement:* but for that criminal error, the Chamber would have been 'perhaps a Chamber of Conservative Union, as was the imposing minority of 1885'. But the author of this daydream [2] did not note the real bearing of what he said. For the minority of 1885 was a minority; and any electoral combination like that alliance of Orleanists, Legitimists, and Bonapartists was not only out of the question in 1919, but any purely Catholic, Conservative and Nationalist combination of 1919 could only have been a minority too. Indeed, a strong minority of the Right would have been better for everybody than a rootless majority. The job of liquidating the legacy of the war would have been undertaken by the real governing party, the Radicals; their policy would have been less likely to be repudiated as soon as political normality was restored and their illusions would have been less dangerous than those of the 'Bloc National'.

The financial illusions of the 'Bloc National' are part of the subject of French post-war finance.[3] They were genuine and natural; and, unlike Lord Cunliffe and other British sayers of smooth things, the most misguided talkers of nonsense in the Chamber were not saying what they knew to be untrue.

Less defensible were the political illusions. The unity of Germany, that is the resolution of the German people to remain united inside one fairly centralized state and not to go back to the pre-Bismarckian era, was now 'given' by history. It may have been foolish of the Germans to prefer the unified régime to the old loose confederation of independent states which had been, for foreigners at least, the glory and the charm of the Germany of Goethe. But the Germans were as determined as the French—or the English—to know the expensive pleasures of being members of a great state, and even the heavy bill presented at Versailles had not shaken this determination. It was hard for persons who could remember how new the Bismarckian Reich was, who knew from recent tradition how strong local patriotism, how powerful French

[1] M. Georges Bernanos. [2] M. Robert Havard de la Montagne.
[3] See p. 589.

influence had been in the Rhineland, to accept the fact that those days were gone for ever. Germany did not envy, nor did any section of Germany, any federal state or region envy, the happy life of Switzerland. As M. Albert Thibaudet reminded Frenchmen, a German Switzerland created under French auspices would be a country whose hero would be Gessler not William Tell. No genuine, dignified, worthy resistance to Prussianism, no anti-Bismarckian movement in Germany, could survive under French patronage. Its leaders could only be blacklegs, scabs.

This evident truth was hidden from many of the French politicians and publicists by memories of Napoleon and by day-dreaming about the possibilities of a return to the system of the Peace of Westphalia, by childish denials of the fact that German unity had been increased, not diminished by the war. The intellectual emptiness of this school was shown in their persistent refusal to realize that the days when the department of the Mont-Tonnerre was part of the French Empire, like the days when Louis XIV could patronize M. de Brandebourg, were for ever past. Maurice Barrès, in a course of lectures given at Strasbourg and called the 'Problem of the Rhine', revealed the poverty of this theme even in the hands of a man of genius; and, if such illusions were no sillier than those of Arthur Balfour on the subject of Ireland, they were of greater importance to the world.[1]

For there *was* a problem of the Rhine, a problem of the relation of Europe to the great central people whose numbers, resources, talents, docility, all made her a source of anxiety to her neighbours. It was the psychological unity of this nation that made her formidable, and that unity was not to be shattered by petty plots or undermined by the bribery of sections or persons. The fact of German unity had to be accepted and, if necessary, provided against. It could not be undone except by a partition on a greater scale than the partition of Poland: and that solution was impossible, since neither France nor her Allies were ready for the perpetual resolution to maintain partition, at all costs, which had marked the Prussian state. So great a violation of the principle of nationalities as a partition of Germany would have been, required far more resolution in power policy than a democratic state could muster.

It was natural that the French generals in command of the Army of Occupation should have overestimated the possibilities of encouraging a Separatist movement in the Rhineland. The occupied territory was full of memories for a French soldier. There was above all the memory of the twenty years when this land had been part of France, an era commemorated in the monument erected by Kléber to Marceau beside the citadel of Coblence. Mangin, not much better disciplined than his old chief Marchand, began at once to encourage the growth of a

[1] An English apologist for this school insisted for years on writing 'the Germanies'.

Separatist movement, an activity which helped to sow distrust in the minds of Wilson and Lloyd George. Clemenceau, who was not only resolved to keep on good terms with Britain and America but who detested political generals, called Mangin to order. Yet there was a sense in which there was a genuine Separatist movement in the Rhineland: but it was a movement away from Prussia, not away from Germany. The Weimar constitution provided for breaking up Prussia if its inhabitants so desired, but that was very far from breaking up the Reich. That the desire for an autonomous Rhineland was one for autonomy 'preferably in the Reich' has been admitted by one of the chief French officials [1] concerned with the occupied territories. The leaders of this movement were compromised by the existence of a small band of complete Separatists, led by a kind of Captain of Kopenick, Dr. Dorten. This party, whatever its motives, was important only so far as it was protected by French authority, and the vacillations of local French commanders did nothing to encourage any trust in the firmness of French policy and were yet enough to alienate the British Government, for whom the unity of Germany was now not merely a fact to be taken into consideration but a most desirable fact, since it was an offset to alleged imperialistic French dreams.

Apart from any question of political interference, the rôle of an occupying army is always ungrateful. The Rhineland was an integral part of Germany; only troops were barred from it, but what were troops? Was it a breach of the Treaty, for Nazi formations to organize field days? On what occasions could 'Deutschland über Alles' be sung in public? It was ruled, for a time, that the German national anthem was only to be sung on special ceremonial occasions, a ban which moved French soldiers, always delighted to score off their superiors, to learn the song and sing it on all possible occasions. But once the Ruhr affair was liquidated, the hardships and abuses of occupation were reduced to a minimum and the German grievance reduced to a genuine one of *amour propre*.

If the French unofficial support for Separatism was one cause of distrust in British breasts, the conduct of the plebiscite in Upper Silesia was another. In 1921 the vote showed a majority for Germany, but a very large localized minority for Poland. On the Bohemian analogy, the unity of the province might have been preserved and Germany left in possession. But that would have meant handing over nearly half a million Poles to German rule; and a violent outbreak of the Poles, favoured by the French garrison, showed what might follow such a decision. The province was divided with elaborate provisions for minority protection on both sides; and in the circumstances any victory for Poland was considered a victory for France in eastern Europe, as any victory for Germany was considered as a triumph for England. For

---

[1] M. Tirard.

within a year of the Armistice, the two Allies were regarding each other with deep suspicion; and the 'Horizon Blue' Chamber was drifting towards a policy one of whose chief merits was that it was not the policy of England.

III

The term of office of President Poincaré was to end on February 18th, 1920, and the question of the succession was one of the first political problems facing the new Chamber and the partially new Senate. There was one obvious candidate, the Prime Minister, and although Clemenceau refused to present himself, he admitted that he would serve if his friends elected him. The election took place a month before the expiry of Poincaré's term and on January 16th, at the unofficial preliminary meeting, Clemenceau was beaten by the elegant President of the Chamber, Deschanel. The traditional ingratitude of republics was displayed: and it was again made evident that the French politician did not want to see too great a man, too strong a personality at the head of the State. In addition to this general bar, few politicians had more enemies than had Clemenceau. The Left disliked the dictator, the Catholics the unbending anti-clerical, the extreme Nationalists the author of the Treaty of Versailles. In a brief letter, Clemenceau resigned and his successor was not chosen by Poincaré but by the President-elect. He chose M. Millerand and the Tiger retired to an impecunious old age.[1]

If Parliament had not shown a magnanimous spirit towards its greatest member, he was soon avenged. The new President began to display what was at first thought to be high-spirited eccentricity, but was soon seen to be madness; and seven months after his election, he 'resigned'. He was succeeded by the Prime Minister, M. Millerand, whose election was a triumph for the Nationalists and also, it was thought, a means of restoring the prestige of an office which had suffered almost equally from the rejection of Clemenceau and the election of Deschanel. M. Millerand, it was believed, would not be a mere figure-head, but would exercise the legal powers of his office, especially to secure the faithful execution of the Treaty of Versailles.

In his brief ministry, M. Millerand had done much to win the confidence of the new Chamber. Faced with the great strike movement launched with excessive optimism by the C.G.T., he had dared to dissolve the once potent Federation. In the summer of 1920 the French Government struck a more important blow at the forces of revolution, for they despatched General Weygand to Poland and, at the great

[1] According to the anecdote, Clemenceau's leading supporters had hastened to condole with him and assure him of the loyal energy they had devoted to his cause. The old man put a hand to his ear and asked, 'Did I hear a cock crow?'

battle of Warsaw, the Bolshevik armies were defeated and the chance of carrying the revolution into western Europe by force of arms was lost. France would not be faced with a Bolshevized Germany. In what, if more than an attempt at a diversion, was a folly, M. Millerand's Government recognized General Wrangel's Government, although it was doomed from the moment the Red Armies were turned south instead of west. It was a sign of the authoritarian view taken of his functions by the new President, that he retained in office the Cabinet he had led, merely giving it a new head in the person of M. Georges Leygues. The new Prime Minister was obviously much more the choice of President Millerand than the politically natural successor of Prime Minister Millerand. Even a 'Horizon Blue' Chamber was a Chamber, and it disliked any usurpation of its powers. Then it was alarmed by a sign of the times, the election of a Socialist Deputy, M. Renaud Jean (since a Communist leader), at a by-election; and, like the National Assembly in similar circumstances, it was ready to make a scapegoat of M. Leygues. The Ministry collapsed in January, after an overwhelming defeat in the Chamber. The attempt at presidential government —if it was one—had failed almost as soon as it was tried.

Even in revolt, the 'Bloc National' could not produce its own leaders and it was Briand who succeeded Leygues. Becoming Prime Minister for the seventh time, Briand needed all his great diplomatic and political talents. On one side he had a suspicious Chamber, putting only very limited confidence in the Prime Minister, on the other a situation in which it was almost or quite impossible to secure for France what most Frenchmen thought of as her incontestable rights.

The contrast between what France thought she deserved and what the outside world thought was adequate for her, was made manifest at the Washington naval conference of 1921. From the point of view of British, American and Japanese interests, this conference was a great success. None of the great naval powers concerned could be coerced and they had therefore to meet each other on reasonable terms. At Washington, France could not but appear to the English-speaking world in an unfavourable light. When the chief British delegate, Mr. Balfour, proposed the abolition in the name of humanity of the most formidable enemy of British sea-power, the submarine, it was France which made unidealistic objections and was chiefly responsible for killing the project. When Mr. Hughes, chief representative of the United States whose action over the Guarantee Treaty had had such unfortunate results, raised the question of reducing land armaments, it was France, neither an island nor a continent, which objected.

Britain returned from Washington with the right to a battleship tonnage more than twice that of the two next European naval powers, France and Italy, combined. It was a margin of British security undreamed of in the past two generations. Yet France appeared in

American and, what was more important, in British eyes as narrow and selfish. The French, noticing the curious identity between justice and humanity, and American and British interests, took such criticism ill. It was not that such identifications were confined to 'Anglo-Saxon' countries, but the refusal to notice the identity was. It was all right, according to Labouchère, for Mr. Gladstone to have the ace of trumps up his sleeve. What was intolerable was his pretending that God had put it there. Many Frenchmen felt much like Labouchère when they were lectured (as they increasingly were) by Englishmen on their duties as good Europeans. These duties seemed to be closely connected with the restoration of a Europe as nearly as possible moulded to English patterns and conforming to English interests. This belief seemed to colour the whole attitude of the majority of the Chamber to the reparations question, and colour it most unfortunately, for it did not really follow that what was to Britain's interest was not to France's, nor that there was no good sense in even the smuggest sermon.

IV

The question of reparations, like other parts of the settlement, suffered from the confusion of more or less genuine ethical considerations with the practicable possibilities of the case. It was obviously of the greatest importance to settle three questions quickly. For what was Germany liable? In what proportions were German payments to be allocated among the victors? To what extent could Germany bear the burdens imposed on her? It would have been more prudent to take all three questions together, or to have postponed the first two until the possibilities of German payments had been fixed, for it was obvious to all competent persons that, whatever variation in the estimate of German resources was permissible, the highest possible estimate of Germany's capacity to pay would be far below the most moderate estimate of her liability under the Treaty of Versailles. But what was eminently desirable was not politically possible; to disillusion the victorious peoples as to the 'limitations of victory', to use M. Fabre Luce's term, was out of the question. Its only result would have been the replacement of Mr. Lloyd George by some British politician more representative of the British Parliament elected in 1918 and M. Clemenceau by some French politician more representative of the views of M. Poincaré and the French Parliament to be elected in 1919.

It was not, therefore, until April 1921 that the Reparations Committee set up by the Treaty finally settled the question of Germany's legal liability. That was assessed at 132,000,000,000 gold marks,[1] and that fantastic sum was only a little over half what had been claimed. The distribution of this total had been fixed at Spa, the year before.

[1] £6,600,000,000 or $33,000,000,000.

France, as was right, got the largest share, 58 per cent. of the total, the British Empire got 22 per cent., Italy got 10 per cent., and Belgium got 8 per cent. with a prior claim on the first 2,000,000,000 marks.[1] On paper all was clear, what Germany owed and what each of the victors was to get, even down to the modest shares allotted to Portugal and Japan. All that remained to be done was to collect it.

While the negotiations between the Allies were going on, the Germans and the Allies were engaged in a long debate as to the amount Germany could pay and, as payments in kind began to be made, as to how much she had paid. The costs of the Army of Occupation were the first charge on German payments and one initial cause of friction between the victorious powers was French resentment of the fact that the cost of the Army of Occupation was very unequally distributed. It cost a great deal more to keep an American or British soldier in the Rhineland than it did to keep a French one. When, in May 1921, the Reparations Commission announced its decision that the payments made by Germany up to that date, which the Germans had asserted were equivalent to 21,000,000,000 marks,[2] were in fact a good deal less than half that amount; indeed were just enough to pay for the Army of Occupation; the conviction that was spreading among Frenchmen, that something was very far wrong and that not only the Germans but France's quondam comrades in arms were to blame, grew rapidly.

The differences of opinion between Britain and France were now visible to the world. Very naturally, the Germans made efforts to exploit them, but whether from a lack of judgment or from the political impossibility for German, as well as for Allied statesmen, of ignoring an inflamed public opinion, the German offers were so much below what even the most bold British negotiator thought possible and reasonable, that France and Britain were forced together, not apart, by such tactics. It was possible, as at Spa, to make adjustments on minor points like coal deliveries as part of payment in kind, but that was all, although this was not unimportant from the French point of view, where freedom from dependence on what had been, in war-time, the extremely onerous British coal monopoly was warmly desired.

The open clash between Germany and the victors came after a series of projects of which the January 1921 scheme put forward by the Allies not only showed a willingness to scale down payments, but a willingness to admit two classes of payments, from which it was only a step to making a distinction between the really recoverable and the very problematically recoverable part of the German obligations. But the German reply not only made a much smaller offer than even the British Government (now well on the way to sanity) could accept, but attempted to attach political conditions, notably the retention by Germany of the whole of Upper Silesia. The Allies retorted by an occupa-

---

[1] £100,000,000 or $500,000,000. [2] £1,050,000,000 or $5,250,000,000.

tion of some German towns, and Germany submitted to a demand for an immediate payment of 1,000,000,000 gold marks.[1] Force seemed to have succeeded.

The success was only apparent. Germany had only provided the milliard of gold marks by borrowing and that loan had to be repaid. The postponements of a final determination of German effective liabilities made all calculations extremely difficult and, as long as the total sum to be paid was in dispute, it was asking a great deal of human nature to expect German budgetary methods to be rigorous. The mark, which had naturally depreciated with the resumption of world trade in which Germany, at the beginning, was bound to be a greater importer than exporter, now began to suffer violent oscillations and to settle down after each crisis at a lower level. The increasingly rapid depreciation of the German currency improved the competitive power of German trade, and that distressed Britain. It also ruined the financial position of the German Government; and that was a new complication added to the reparations question. But whereas both British and French public opinion deplored the fall of the mark, the man in the street in each country gave a different explanation of it. In Britain, it was soon believed by most right-thinking people that the collapse of the mark was due entirely to the exorbitant reparations claims of the French. In France, the same type of person believed that the fall in the mark was deliberately planned by Germany to evade reparations obligations. Both views were wrong, but each had quite enough truth in it to justify a theory to a public opinion which wished to believe it.

The failure to settle the reparations question, the failure to reduce German liabilities to practicable figures rendered the position of the German currency shaky. And in Germany there were very powerful interests with their own profit to be made by the fall of the mark (as well as with ingenious if fallacious economic theories to support such a policy). Their pressure on a weak Government was one of the chief causes, perhaps the chief cause, of the rapid impoverishment of the German middle-classes that now began. To the British man in the street, the French did not care what economic ruin was wrought in Germany (and indirectly in Germany's trade partner, Britain), so long as the defeated nation could be kept helpless. To the French man in the street, the British Government did not care what happened to the French devastated regions, so long as British trade revived. Business was to triumph over justice.[2] This view was strengthened by the fact that France got none of the milliard marks paid over by Germany; there were good technical reasons why she did not, but politically this fact

[1] £50,000,000 or $250,000,000.
[2] To this, it was at that time replied that Britain had her devastated areas, too, the regions ruined by the collapse of international trade. But this argument has lost its force since the world has seen the resignation with which successive British Governments have left those regions devastated.

was unfortunate. The Chamber was increasingly anxious and angry as its illusions were increasingly subject to pressure from reality. They had so far withstood the strain, but something had to give. Briand knew that his position was undermined. He had to produce some success or go. He was not unwilling to go, to leave to others the responsibility of finding a new policy that would gratify the Chamber. 'If anyone thinks that a Government ought to be turned out, they should turn it out at once.' 'Anyone' was the new leader of the Nationalist majority, Poincaré, who had escaped from the prison of the Élysée where, for seven years, he had been condemned to silence and docility and who, as head of the Foreign Affairs Committee of the Senate, was now the acknowledged leader of the party that wished, whatever England thought, to force Germany to pay, to 'take her by the collar' as Briand himself had once put it.

At Cannes, Briand made his last effort. In the matter of reparations it was recognized that a limited moratorium was necessary; on the other hand, Britain was ready to renew the military guarantee. The Chamber and the Senate had both watched the meeting at Cannes with the utmost suspicion. Politicians from Ribot to Léon Daudet expressed their apprehension, which was not diminished when it became rumoured that, under the tuition of Mr. Lloyd George, Briand had played golf. What must be the domination of his mind by the British Minister if he was willing to go as far as that! Briand returned to Paris [1] and after attacking his enemies, who were firing on him from the rear, he resigned. It was the turn of Poincaré.

The fall of Briand meant the end of Franco-British collaboration. In rejecting the Cannes compromise, the Chamber expressed its conviction that enough had now been sacrificed to secure British support. The project of guarantee was not a sufficient make-weight, for it evaded the fundamental question from the French point of view. It guaranteed the French frontier, but it did not recognize as a *casus belli*, a German attack on any of the eastern allies or protégés of France. It did not even recognize the violation of the demilitarized Rhineland zone by Germany as bringing the treaty obligation into effect. Britain would only come to the aid of France to fight a war, likely to be long and costly, on French soil. What France wanted was the guarantee that, if war came, it would be on German soil—confident that if the Germans had to fight in their own demilitarized zone, they would not fight at all.

The new Prime Minister, Poincaré, had no doubts of the rightness of his policy. He was a lawyer and he saw the case in simple legal terms. Germany was a defaulter on her obligations, a situation for which the law provided. He did not propose to be talked out of doing his utmost

---

[1] It was later asserted that M. Millerand recalled Briand from Cannes. This M. Millerand has always denied, and Briand never openly affirmed it. Briand's position was obviously undermined and it would have been absurd to complete a settlement at Cannes if it was to be rejected at once by the Chamber. He did right to return.

for his client by personal contact with British statesmen. When the next great conference met at Genoa, M. Poincaré stayed away and had the satisfaction of seeing the conference destroyed by the revelation of the German-Russian alliance made at Rapallo. The object of German diplomacy, Poincaré held, was revealed. It aimed at calling in the Bolsheviks to destroy the balance of power so recently created in eastern and central Europe. France could only rejoice in the revelation of German policy in its true light.

In another field of post-war diplomacy, French policy had run counter to British and seemed to be fully justified by the event. The policy pursued by Mr. Lloyd George in the Near East was ending in disaster. A clash between British and French policy in the Near East was natural, indeed inevitable. To Mr. Lloyd George and to the British political and military representatives, Turkey was British spoil of war. The French point of view was candidly and naïvely put nearly six years later, after both the victorious powers of 1918 had learned that victories do not keep. 'France, whose victory made possible these things, who had lost 1,500,000 killed and had gained incomparable glory, is . . . despoiled, particularly by England, of her age-old pre-eminence in the East.' The war, that is, had been a joint enterprise; its gains should be divided in proportion to the sacrifices made to secure victory. It was a plausible point of view for a moralist but nonsense for a politician.

Unfortunately, in the years of conflict, Britain had had to make various promises to various interests. She had had to discuss the partition of Turkey while Turkey was still very much alive, and so had had to agree to share the spoil with her Allies. Russia had to get the lions' share; and not only had France her own claims, but she was useful too, for, by giving her Mosul, Russia and Britain could be kept from having an awkward common frontier when one had acquired Armenia and the other Mesopotamia. By the time peace came, the collapse of Russia had rendered France's rôle as a buffer state superfluous and other Allies had been promised shares in Turkish territory. The Arabs had been promised (or thought they had) the freeing of all Arab territories of Turkey from foreign rule, and the Jews had been promised a privileged position in what the Arabs thought of as part of their *Arabia Irridenta*, Palestine.

The special sphere of French interest in this region was traditionally Syria. The tradition was old and genuine, but it was oddly argued by an anti-clerical Government, for it was religious. To assert a claim to Syria on the grounds that, since the Crusades, the Eldest Daughter of the Church had special interests there, was slightly ludicrous in 1919. Mr. Lloyd George's zeal for the Holy Places was less suspect than this! The simplest solution would have been for Britain to recognize the authority of the leader of the Arab army, Feisal, son of the Sherif of

Mecca, over all Syria. But that cut across war-time promises to the Jews and to the French and across British public opinion, which was sentimentally interested in the Holy Land much more than anybody in France was interested in Syria—and across British policy which wanted to be quite sure that the flank of the Suez Canal was in safe, that is in British hands.

It was convenient for British purposes to insist on the unity and independence of Syria (omitting Palestine) and for France to insist on its unity and ignore its independence. As it was impossible for Britain to ignore French claims altogether, it was natural to limit them to the smallest possible area, the narrow coastal plain and the Lebanon where dwelt the Maronites, the traditional Christian protégés of France—and their traditional enemies, the Moslem heretics, the Druses. But the great Arab towns, Aleppo and Damascus, should go to Feisal, to the new Syrian kingdom. For France (and for Feisal) the best solution would have been the acceptance of some form of French protection in return for the unification of all Syria (save Palestine) under his rule. But neither France nor Feisal saw this soon enough; and Feisal, relying too much on the support of Britain, was driven out of Damascus without much difficulty by General Gouraud. There was to be no Syrian kingdom; there was, instead, to be a French mandated territory rather like Palestine and Iraq.[1]

In making all these arrangements, Britain and France, however much they resented each other's actions, had acted on the assumption that when they could agree, Arabs and Turks would have to accept the results of that agreement. The two great powers were not far wrong in the case of the Arabs; they were profoundly wrong in the case of the Turks, and the French were the first to see it. The disappearance of Russia as an ally had been a great disaster, but it had some agreeable aspects for British policy. She had no longer to reconcile herself to a Russian occupation of Constantinople. A Turkey under British control, kept in her place by an aggrandized Greece, was now the policy of the British Prime Minister, if not of the British Government. Greece, rapidly growing in power and wealth, would be an invaluable and grateful ally to Britain. Who knew? 'One day the mouse may gnaw the cords that bind the lion.'

The Turks had no mind to let Æsop prove true once more, and in the interior of Asia Minor, far away from the British fleet that found it so easy to command Constantinople, a new Turkey was being created by a soldier of genius, Mustafa Kemal. The resurgence of Turkish strength was rapidly felt by the French who were occupying Cilicia, and France was forced to consider not merely what paper rights she had in the former Turkish Empire, but how much in men and money she was willing to pay to make them real. Exhausted by the war, with her

[1] Iraq was not strictly speaking a mandated territory, but that was a fine legal point.

hands full in Europe and with a great discrepancy appearing between her real and her formal ambitions in the Levant, it was natural and prudent of France to liquidate her position in Cilicia, although that meant dealing with the new Turkish leader whom Mr. Balfour, while Kemal was still climbing, called a 'bandit'. Bandit or not, he could give France peace on her Syrian frontier at a price. France was willing to pay that price: which was tacit recognition of the 'rebel' Turkish Government and an abandonment of even formal good relations in the Near East with Great Britain.

Great Britain, in all but name, was allied with Greece in a war to deliver the Greeks of Ionia from Turkish rule. France had no interest in such a policy; but she had an interest in limiting her commitments in the Near East. So M. Franklin-Bouillon, with no official status, went off to the 'rebel' Turkish capital of Angora and laid the foundations of a pro-Turkish policy that, to the simple minds of the Levantine peoples, made France as much the backer of the Turks as Britain was of the Greeks. When, in December 1920, the Greeks imitated the French and overthrew their organizer of victory, Venizelos, such French consciences as needed quieting were soothed, for the return of King Constantine was particularly offensive to the French, who had managed to remain remarkably indignant at the loss of French lives in Athens in that fight between a French landing party and Greek troops which M. Maurras had called 'the Athenian vespers'. Constantine was less tolerable than Kemal.

When the Greek offensive of the summer of 1921 failed, a second Franklin-Bouillon visit resulted in the signing of an agreement between France and the resurgent Turkey that amounted to an open breach between France and Britain in Asia Minor. On a matter of form, the British grievance was genuine. It was idle sophistry for France to pretend that the agreement was not a treaty, or that it was compatible with the joint settlement of the Eastern Question. It was substantially the right policy nevertheless, and Britain would have been wise had she effected a retreat in good order that would have enabled her to save something for her luckless Greek protégés. But Mr. Lloyd George encouraged the Greeks in their obstinacy and irritated the Turks into an offensive in which the Greek Army was destroyed and the Greeks uprooted from the country of Homer.

The very completeness of the Greek disaster (followed as it was by the overthrow of Mr. Lloyd George) made the British diplomatic position much easier. It was not really surprising that, in making peace at Lausanne, Britain and not France should take the lead. France had already given Turkey all that Turkey needed from France and had obviously discarded from weakness. Britain, on the other hand, could no longer waste time protecting the Greeks, even had the new British Government wanted to do so, and she was ready and willing to look after her own substantial interests. That France, out of all the kaleidoscopic changes of the years between 1916 and 1923, got no more than Syria, was not surprising; what was surprising was that she got so much, for at no time was she ready to spend the men or money required to gain more. Indeed, as the event proved, the control of Syria was almost more than she was fit for, not because of material weakness, but because of lack of serious resolution to develop an imperial policy in yet another region of the world.

V

The autumn of 1922 was marked by the fall of Mr. Lloyd George, the last of the great war leaders to remain in power. His fall was in part caused by a revolt of his Conservative supporters, very like that which overthrew Briand, although the occasion was concessions to Ireland instead of concessions to Germany. The new Prime Minister, Mr. Bonar Law, had been out of office during the most embittered phase of Anglo-French relations and, faced with the French threat to take individual action against Germany, he made a very serious effort to meet the French demands and avoid what he thought would be a disastrous blow to European stability. Reparations had been divided into three classes, A, B and C. C represented the most remote payments, those spread over the longest period of time and were obviously, by now, like very ill-secured third mortgages. The British scheme proposed the cancellation of these liabilities and a funding of A and B obligations. In return it offered the complete cancellation of the French war debt to Britain in return for surrender of French debt claims on Belgium and on the French gold in the Bank of England. This last transaction would have shown a paper profit of nearly £500,000,000 for France, but Poincaré took only a day to reject the scheme which had, from his point of view, the fatal fault of giving Germany another extension in time. The German will to pay must be encouraged by sanctions. And it was obvious to him that France would get her rights only by taking 'productive pledges'. That meant the occupation of the Ruhr.

The occupation of the Ruhr was not a novel idea. In addition to the zone occupied by the Allied Armies, temporary occupations of German territory outside that zone had already occurred. Nor was the idea of extending an occupation to the exploitation of German assets a new one. It had been threatened by the Allies before this. It was on the surface a plausible idea. If the Germans would not pay because, as they asserted, the problem of transfer was beyond them, the French should go and get what was owing, as a creditor sends a bailiff to take the defaulter's cattle or household goods. It was, from a legalistic point of view, a natural enough procedure. And France was a country dominated by legalistic, and rural legalistic ideas at that, as M. Francis Delaisi pointed out. To carry out the scheme, it was, for a man like Poincaré, indispensable to have the law on his side. By a majority, the Reparations Commission decided that Germany was in default on some deliveries in kind; the occupation was decided on.[1]

The British Government contented itself with announcing that its lawyers denied the legal validity of the occupation and left France and Germany to their struggle. Belgium supported the French, and Belgian troops formed part of the expeditionary force that occupied the Ruhr in January. Italy merely sent some engineers to look after her interests. The new Fascist Government had been in power for only a few months and was still feeling its way; but, of course, if the expedition succeeded, Italy wanted her share of the profits.

The troops which accompanied the technicians were merely an armed guard, and as the occupation was envisaged at the beginning, it was to be quite a simple affair. But the German Government organized and subsidized passive resistance and almost every activity in the Ruhr basin ceased. Mine- and factory-owners, as well as workers, were compensated for the cost of passive resistance. The hopes of 'productive pledges' were dead. All that remained was the punitive aspect; an immense daily loss was being inflicted on Germany. Its most productive industrial area was cut off from the rest of the country, and the cost of subsidizing the strike of employers and workers was the last blow to the German currency. As far as wiping out the savings of the middle-classes was concerned, that had already been done by the inflation of 1919–22 and that inflation was very largely the work of the German Government. The inflation of 1923 did not destroy savings; it made any rational economic calculations impossible for all classes of Germans, not merely over a long period of time but from day to day. Of course, the astronomical inflation brought profits to some speculators and to the great industrial magnates, but for most Germans it was an unrelieved nightmare.

This first result of the occupation was not displeasing to some sections of French opinion. They would rather have a weak Germany unable to pay than a strong Germany able to pay. This was roughly the position of the *Action Française*, still powerful with the extreme Right in the Chamber. From the collapse of the German currency might come the collapse of German unity, a great positive gain from the war. If a coherent policy of bribing sections of Germany to escape from the Reich and its troubles had been undertaken, it might just

---

[1] It has been pointed out that the Reparations Commission as originally designed had five members, one of them American. Thus there would never be a deadlock, it was hoped. American withdrawal reduced the membership to four and the French Chairman assumed a casting vote. He did not need to use it, as the Italian Government backed up the French and Belgians; but, it is argued, Italian policy might have been different had the Commission been at its full strength.

possibly have succeeded. By the end of the summer, passive resistance was collapsing, to the surprise of some British observers who had let their wishes colour their judgment. The German Government was at the end of its tether and the French had, to a remarkable degree, succeeded in restarting economic activity in the occupied area. German despair revealed itself in sabotage; and in Schlageter the Germans were provided with a martyr, though the occupation was not rigorous by modern standards. There were attempted revolutions by Communists and by the political party run by the Reichswehr, the National Socialists, but both failed. There was a revival of Separatism, but it was only supported in a half-hearted way by the French authorities, and its chances, never good, were destroyed. So far as the occupation was a test of strength between France and Germany, the contest was over by September 1923. The German Government abandoned passive resistance. France had her 'productive pledges'.

From the beginning of the occupation, Poincaré had been supported by the Chamber. When all allowances are made for the pressure to show national unanimity in face of the foe, it still seems probable that the Chamber really believed that the occupation was necessary to put an end to German tergiversation and to British toleration of it. In every vote, the Government had an overwhelming majority. Only the Communists and Socialists opposed the policy; the Radicals either supported it, or more commonly abstained from voting like the prudent politicians they were. In the parliamentary debates over the occupation, the new leader of the Socialists, M. Léon Blum, showed his mettle. The intellectual, new to the Chamber, with a trying voice and irritating mannerisms, imposed himself on his party and on Parliament by the lucidity of his thought and the elegance of his language.

The Socialist opposition was sometimes based on improbable hypotheses; it was hard to believe that the real villains of the piece were the steel magnates of the 'Comité des Forges'. They presumably knew on what side their bread was buttered; and however tempting the idea of an armed raid into the Ruhr to fetch coal was to the simple-minded economists of the *Action Française*, the steel millionaires knew better than that, the more that passive resistance had for a short time revived the hated British coal monopoly. But Socialist opposition greatly increased the prestige of the party, especially as the effects of the exhausting struggle began to be felt in France in a franc that depreciated, not indeed like the mark, but with an alarming speed. What was missing in that opposition was not brains or courage; it was Jaurès. There was now no one to rise to the heights of the great argument and appeal from the narrow, honest and largely irrelevant logic of the lawyer to the spirit of the community of men, including Germans. It was in the years that followed the Armistice that the loss of the great tribune was most felt. Perhaps it would have needed a German Jaurès, too, to make true peace between the neighbouring nations. But a French Jaurès would have been a beginning.

Despite the collapse of German resistance, the enthusiasm of France for Poincaré's policy (if there ever was much outside the Chamber) rapidly diminished. The defeat of the Baldwin Government, in the elections of 1923, at least saved European economy from the blow of a sudden adoption of protection by the great European creditor; and the German Government was now ready to give any conceivable proof of its willingness to submit to payment of any reparations that could be demanded from a shattered economy. The new British Government was not as passive as its predecessor, and the negotiations that led to the Dawes Plan were begun. Long before the Ruhr was evacuated, France was disillusioned about the worth of military action; the troops called up resented having to serve in what was nominally peace-time; and French politicians were made permanently reluctant to use that military supremacy which they had gained at Versailles. Germany was still open to French invasion, but the will to invade was dead.

CHAPTER III

THE PRICE OF VICTORY

I

EVEN before disillusionment with the results of the occupation of the Ruhr weakened the authority of the Poincaré Ministry and of the majority which had supported the Prime Minister's policy, the political basis of the 'Bloc National' was being destroyed. It had no general uniting idea or even uniting interest, apart from a rapidly obsolescent stock of simple patriotic ideas and emotions. The Radicals, who had prudently not committed themselves on any great matter of policy, were rapidly recovering their old ascendancy. Everywhere they had the old 'cadres', the local machines, the local government units, controlled by the veteran politicians whom only the accident of war had thrust temporarily into the background. The disorganized amateurs of the majority were no match for the political Old Guard.

That majority, too, had made many enemies. It had attacked as parasites on the budget the great body of civil servants, who were injured in their pride and pocket, treated as bloodsuckers and deprived of their right to organize. The schoolmasters were even more alarmed than other government employees. The renewed diplomatic relations with the Vatican, the toleration of illegal religious orders, the parliamentary pleas for grants to Church schools, none of them very serious in themselves, were to the suspicious teachers signs of ill-will towards the lay laws. And if the Government could prevent open opposition from the employees of the State who were still in its service, it could not control those who had retired on pension and who were free to act as zealous electoral agents of the opposition.

The collapse of passive resistance made both Germany more anxious to negotiate a settlement, and Britain, and (discreetly) the United States, more ready to collaborate in bringing the French and German Governments together. In France, the claim, true as far as it went, that the occupation now more than paid its way, did not conceal from the public, or even from Poincaré, that mere affirmations of France's treaty rights were not enough. Germany must pay all that she could, but how much was that? Two committees were set up, one under Mr. Reginald McKenna to deal with the technical problem of the return of capital exported from Germany, the second under the chairmanship of an American, General Dawes, to deal with the wider problem of enabling Germany to meet any obligations at all and to determine what payments, once she was restored to something like economic health, she could make.

The Dawes Plan, as it was called, deliberately ignored all political questions. It laid it down that Germany must be provided with the means of becoming solvent and so must recover economic control of all her territory; and that meant, in effect, the withdrawal of the French troops from the Ruhr. Germany must be given enough credits to enable her to establish a stable currency and, to secure that stability, some independent body or official must be given authority to determine when payments of reparations were endangering it. It was thought to be impossible to fix the total of reparations to be paid. No estimate that could be made in 1924 could be anything but a reckless guess. But it was possible quite soon to fix what annual payments Germany could make; although, until a total reparations debt had been fixed, it was impossible to decide how long they would go on. They might, in theory, go on for ever, payments towards an unknown total. Despite, or rather because of, these deliberate refusals to attempt to answer fundamental and unanswerable questions, the Dawes Plan was admirably suited to the moment. Leaving all the long-term questions still to be settled, it promised some immediate gain to everybody; an end of the Ruhr occupation and currency stabilization to the Germans; some tangible cash results from the occupation to the French; an increase in European stability and, so it was hoped, in British prosperity to Britain; and an improved chance of collecting the war debts to the United States.

The payments were to rise over a period of five years to a standard annuity of 2,500,000,000 gold marks,[1] of which, when the scheme was fully working, France would get over half. Even leaving out all question of war debts, the income from the Plan was far below the dreams of 1919. It would just about have covered the debt charges for the restoration of the devastated areas. But, even burdened as they were with an unsettled liability to Britain and the United States, the Dawes Plan annuities were an improvement on any previous receipts from Germany. They promised an end of the endless political complications and, as far as it was believed in France that neither Germany nor Britain would have acted as they had done but for the occupation, it was held to justify the Ruhr and that in turn justified acceptance of the Plan, though not its formal ratification, by the Poincaré Government.

Not only were reparations removed from the political agenda, but the acceptance of the principle of the economic unity of Germany meant an end of flirtations with Rhineland separatism. The unity of the

[1] £125,000,000 ($625,000,000).

Reich was preserved and its economic prospects greatly improved. French officials and soldiers who had tolerated or encouraged the separatist movement were now forced to observe a real neutrality and the whole bogus business collapsed. The German population, once the protecting hand of the French officers was withdrawn, ended the Rhineland republic in a series of bloody riots in which the *Action Française* saw not merely the revival of Prussia, but the treachery of England. But in France there was, less than ever, any real will to pursue a policy of dismembering Germany. Unobserved by the outside world, the French people had wearied of the atmosphere of war; the elections were at hand and the nation was about to be given a chance to express its opinion of the policy of the 'Bloc National'.

The elections of 1924 were not, of course, fought exclusively or mainly on the question of foreign policy. Many motives revived and strengthened the dominant political tradition of the French political system, a tradition which had not really been repudiated even in the hysterical election of 1919. It was not only the superior tactics and superior discipline of the Radicals that made them so formidable. The elections of 1924 in France revealed the same desire to return to the easy ways of life of the good old days before the war, that the election of Harding in 1920 and the return to power of Bonar Law in 1922 had revealed in America and England. The doubtful success of the Ruhr was made manifest by the necessity of raising taxes, a necessity which the Poincaré Government had to admit on the eve of the elections.[1] Mere political routine and irritation at seeing the promises to make the Germans pay translated into higher taxes for Frenchmen, did not alone account for the crushing nature of Poincaré's defeat. The opposition to the foreign policy of the 'Bloc National' had spread from the small groups like the 'League of the Rights of Man' and the organized Socialists to the masses. A genuine horror of war, a revival of the old optimistic dreams of international understanding, a natural revulsion against the extravagant nationalism that had been preached and to some extent practised of recent years, revived the enthusiasm of the parties of the old Left.

As in the hopeful years at the beginning of the century, this enthusiasm had its newspaper, not the now dogmatically Communist *Humanité* or the struggling Socialist *Populaire*, but the *Quotidien*, which was the real if not the formal heir of the *Petite République* and the *Humanité* of Jaurès. The *Quotidien* was designed to be the reply of the masses of the Left to the dominance of the newspaper world by the great financial interests. All the great Paris newspapers with national circulations were either openly or covertly papers of the Right. In the provinces, there were important Left papers, chief of them all the keeper of the Radical conscience, the *Dépêche de Toulouse*, property, pride and source of the

[1] Cf. p. 591.

power of the Sarraut family. But that was not enough, and the *Quotidien* was started in 1923. Its founder, Henri Dumay, appealed to the militants everywhere to provide the funds for a Left newspaper which would display 'rigorous probity and ferocious independence'. Twenty million francs was raised from petty officials, local party leaders and the like who wanted to help the good cause and who, though to a less degree, were also moved by hope of a good investment. With this capital, the *Quotidien* was able to produce a paper fit to rival the great commercial papers on their own ground and the Left benefited greatly in the election of 1924.[1]

The emotional appeal of the 'Bloc National' had lost its power; the emotional appeal of the parties fighting it, the 'Cartel des Gauches', as they came to be called, was increasing in power. Europe learned with astonishment that on May 11th the French electors had voted against the policy of the formidable Prime Minister. Poincaré at once took the election as a condemnation, and the leader of the successful coalition, M. Herriot, prepared to take office. Before the month was out he had given an interview to the great German Socialist paper *Vorwärts*. It would be the greatest honour of his life, he said, to bring peace to all peoples.

If the outside world had paid most attention to the defeat of Poincaré, the victors of the Left had an even greater animus against the President of the Republic. For one thing, M. Millerand was one of their own who had gone wrong. Then as President, M. Millerand had stepped down from his high place, so it was asserted, and by his speeches and attitude had taken sides in party battles. Whether he had done more than Poincaré had done in the early months of his presidency was doubtful, but the precedent was, in any case, not one likely to placate the Left. Their general attitude had been summed up by the militant old Socialist, Pierre Renaudel, 'all the jobs and quick about it', and the Left meant to begin at the top.

On June 1st, 307 deputies passed a resolution declaring that 'the maintenance of M. Millerand at the Elysée would wound the Republican conscience, would be the source of endless conflicts between the Government and the Chief of the State and a constant danger for the régime itself'. M. Millerand fell back on his legal rights and duties. As he told M. Herriot, he had been elected for seven years and it was his duty to carry out his mandate, but he was really helpless. The noisier deputies enjoyed themselves. It was the duty of the Chamber to sit all the time to watch a 'Président de coup d'état', or so M. Berthon asserted. But the real weapon of the Left was a Ministerial strike.

---

[1] The later history of the paper was unfortunate. The original subscribers found their interests inadequately protected, and after a series of bitter controversies, the great liberating organ of the Left disappeared and its place was very inadequately filled by papers like the *Populaire* and the *Œuvre*, whose small circulations limited the effect of their brilliant editorial pages.

M. François-Marsal, the Prime Minister chosen to attempt the hopeless task of defending the President, could not command a majority and the Chamber refused to have anything to do with him. On June 11th, M. Millerand abandoned the battle and resigned. Another President of the Republic had been taught his place and the office was further weakened, or, at any rate, prevented from being strengthened. Full powers were again in the hands of the 'delegates of universal suffrage'. It remained to see what that meant.

France was politically weary; she wished to return to the good old pre-war days and she naturally turned on the political representatives of the unpleasant new post-war world. If the Left had been in office, and had thus acquired the political liabilities that destroyed Wilson and Lloyd George, Venizelos and William Morris Hughes, the swing of the pendulum might not have been so violent: but a swing to the Left was bound to be violent, since the Left were the best organized and most rapidly growing political coalition in France. The very name of the Left was symbolic of political victory; a movement in that direction had the inevitability of a glacier. Indeed, so much was the name a mascot that it was taken by parties which the country refused to regard as politically sound, in a vain endeavour to escape defeat.[1] That the 'Cartel' should triumph was inevitable, so far as the elections were concerned. Its troubles only began with victory.

The alliance between Socialists and Radicals was the most natural thing in the world at election times, but it was increasingly artificial once the election was over. For the Radicals disbelieved in the Socialist remedy for the main ills of the world. 'Socialist' in the title of their party (Radical and Socialist Radical) was no more than a sentimental intensification of the 'Radical'. It did not mean that the Radicals were really in favour of the extension of the economic rôle of the State, or the limitation of the rights of property. No doubt the party was opposed to selling the State monopolies to private companies and righteously indignant at such 'lobbies' as the Union of Economic Interests which spent money on behalf of reactionary candidates and thus interfered with the party's campaign. But there was a great deal in common between many eminent Radicals and Senator Billiet, the head of the Union, between Radical and Reactionary bourgeoisie. In most of the small towns and rural regions of France, you voted for or against the parish priest, for or against the local landlord, less no doubt if the priest was personally amiable or the landlord winked at poaching, but fundamentally to show that the Revolution had not been in vain.

You did not vote *for* much. The old Jacobin authoritarian tradition was weak in the modern Radical party. Clemenceau had been one of its last representatives and his name was now anathema to most

---

[1] One paradoxical result of this continual shift was that all the parties which still had the word 'Left' in their titles were classed with the 'Right'.

militants. Far more representative of the attitude of the party were the writings of its chief, almost its only eminent intellectual defender, Alain. 'The Citizen against the Powers that Be'—that was political life as Alain saw it. The unending audacities of elected persons in betraying their electors moved him less to the indignation of Whitman than to an ironical resignation and to a resolve to reduce, as far as possible, their power for evil, as it was impossible to increase their power for good. But the deputies, bad as they were, easily seduced by flattery and by the social poison of Paris, were not as bad as the bureaucrats, the 'Tite-Barnacles' (for Alain had read Dickens).

The State was a dangerous machine, almost certain to get into the wrong hands, and it should, therefore, be provided with brakes. Indeed it seemed as if some Radicals wanted far more brakes than the feeble engine power of the French State machine made at all necessary. The Radical was the man who wished to keep to the ideas and practices of 1789; to defend the Rights of Man as interpreted in the pre-machine age; and to ignore the fundamental difficulties of applying the methods of the age of diligences in the age of motor-cars. Just as the capitals of French departments were located by a calculation of a day's ride on horseback, so with the organization of the central government. For the Radical feared that, if the State were strengthened and modernized, the beneficiaries would not be the little men whose interests it was the business of the party to foster, but the powerful lords of business and finance, already far too potent for the peace of mind of believers in equality.

The Socialist leaders and militants, if not the Socialist voters, were contemptuous of the simplicity and superficiality of the Radical analysis. It was to them a cause of deep intellectual indignation that an intelligent people like the French should still be talking in purely political and uneconomic terms. How could the Socialists work profitably with such representatives of an obsolete technology and ideology? It was this contempt for the Radicals and this fear of their crippling alliance that justified, if it did not wholly account for, the revival of Guesdism, and for the hostility to any alliance with the Radicals, or to a compromising policy which, the Socialist party resolved, was condemned both by theory and practice. But as the elections of 1924 approached, it had proved harder to hold the party line: it was natural to think of returning to the pre-war tacit alliance—at least for electoral purposes—with the Radicals.

It was even more desirable to find allies than it had been in 1914, for the system of bastard proportional representation under which the election would be fought, made the lot of the isolated minority very hard. The purists, Bracke and his friends, would have no compromise, but local Socialist Federations were allowed to make their own arrangements and, in the non-industrial departments, they fought with the

Radicals. In the industrial areas alone could they afford the luxury of independence. The result was a return to the golden day of 1914. The election of over a hundred Socialist Deputies justified these tactics.

The election won, it was impossible to attack the Radicals at once, and it was, indeed, necessary to promise loyal support to M. Herriot, the new Prime Minister. It was all very well for the party to resolve in its Congress that it was a party 'necessarily distinct from all others' and, next year, to refuse to base new theories on the difficult experiment of support for the Herriot Government, theories which would be contrary to 'the doctrinal virtues of traditional Socialism'. But, in fact, the policy of 1924 and 1925 was a return to the policy of 1899–1905, to the practice of Jaurès, and away from the theories of Guesde. A new Millerand would not be given leave to enter a Ministry, but that was the only difference—and the party produced Millerands who, without leave, followed in his footsteps.

The dilemma in which the Socialists involved themselves, by supporting a government debarred by its own doctrine from providing the necessary remedies for the sickness of French society, was not painfully obvious as long as the Left Government was mainly concerned with political questions. On external and internal politics the Socialists and the Radicals were pretty well agreed and both were anxious to liquidate the Ruhr, whose failure the Socialists had prophesied and the Radicals had profited by.

The Radicals, it is true, were ready to get what profit they could from Poincaré's mistake. They wished to make French withdrawal a bargaining matter, not with Germany but with Britain. But there was nothing to bargain with. It was obvious that France was tired of the occupation and unwilling to prolong it. It was certain that even if Poincaré had stayed in office, he would have accepted the Dawes Plan, so the new British Prime Minister, Mr. Ramsay MacDonald, was safe in refusing to give fresh guarantees, financial or political, to M. Herriot. Negotiations could only be over details, and M. Herriot brought nothing back from his visit to Chequers that he could not have got by normal diplomatic methods. The conjunction of Left Governments, in France as well as in Britain, was an opportunity not to be lost, but the fate of the 'protocol',[1] though distressing, did not lead to a breach.

There was no disagreement over the attempt to fulfil some of the anti-clerical promises of the Radical campaign. It is true that Socialists smiled a little at the importance attached by their Radical friends to the clerical question, but attempts to withdraw the French ambassador from the Vatican and thus undo a crime of the 'Bloc National' and to introduce the lay laws into Alsace were approved. The policy of restoring their jobs to the militants who had been victimized after the great strikes of 1920 and of restoring their right of organization to the

[1] See p. 611.

officials was equally popular with Socialist and Radical Deputies and with their electors. After all, it was often a mere matter of accident of electoral law whether the victorious candidate of the Left was a Radical or a Socialist. However much the parties might differ in their organized form, the inchoate mass of Left electors, from which the deputies drew their ultimate authority, had a fairly unified outlook on current problems and no outlook at all on non-current problems.

Of course, in the victorious alliance of 1924, just as on the Left there were Socialists constantly tempted to go Communist, there were, on the Right, Radicals and others tempted by the safety and respectability of 'an alliance of the Centres'. These lukewarm 'Cartellists' were (with the overwhelmingly Radical Senate) responsible for the defeat of the Left candidate for the presidency. Paul Painlevé, eminent mathematician and mediocre politician, was defeated by the mediocre politician, Gaston Doumergue. Even in the Chamber, Paul-Boncour, who regarded himself in appearance and doctrine as a new Robespierre, was defeated in the election for the Chairmanship of the Army Committee by Poincaré's former War Minister, André Maginot. But it was the financial crisis that revealed the fundamental differences between the Socialists and their allies and that proved too much for the policy of support.

It was unfortunate that the Prime Minister, who had to deal with the financial crisis, should have been temperamentally so little fitted for the drab and unpleasant job of putting in order a very badly managed household. Years later, when the educational experience of 1924–26 should have chastened him, M. Herriot was still taking financial problems too lightly; France would 'muddle through'. But figures had a way of resisting all eloquence, and within a few months of its formation the Herriot Government was too busy trying to salvage the Treasury and the franc, to worry any more about ambassadors in Rome or nuncios in Paris.

Yet the troubles that beset the Government of the 'Cartel' were not really of its making. As it had had the good luck to escape the dangerous responsibility for the political liquidation, it had the bad luck to be faced with the problem of the financial liquidation of the war, a problem incapable of solution until the time was politically ripe. That ripeness coincided with the disillusionment over the Ruhr which was one great factor in the 'Cartel's' triumph. It was the main cause of its downfall. For it presented the allies of 1924 with a problem that made it impossible to evade the issues which divided them; on one side were the Socialist leaders, committed to the doctrine that the only solution of the financial problem was bound up with a complete economic reconstruction of French society, on the other were the Radicals, fundamentally sceptical of the need or desirability of such a reconstruction and loath to increase the authority of the State which alone could make the

Socialist programme practicable. In an economic choice the Radicals were certain to choose the old order, even if they accompanied that choice with noisy protests.

II

The political difficulties facing any reformer of French finance in the years immediately following the Armistice had been perfectly illustrated during a speech by Clemenceau's Finance Minister, Klotz.[1] He spoke, as was natural, of the heroism of France during her ordeal and, as was less justifiable, suggested that France had been as enduring in pocket as in person. Yet, despite this heroism, the finances of the victor nation were not in a good state. A voice from the Left declared that 'the rich must be made to pay'; a voice from the Right replied 'Germany must be made to pay'; and the Finance Minister satisfied both. 'It is not the rich who shall pay first; the first to pay shall be the enemy.' (Loud cheers.)

During four terrible years France had been steeled to her ordeal by the thought that victory would compensate her for her sacrifices. Firmly convinced that she had been the victim of a planned aggression; fully conscious (which was less disputable) that she had suffered far more than had the defeated nation; not at all sure that her allies were not ready to be extremely generous, at her expense, to the nation that had ravaged her soil, that had been as intolerable in victory as self-pitying in defeat, France could not bring herself to face the sad fact that, guilty or not guilty, Germany could not pay for the war.

The lack of respect for economic principles which was partly a fault of French higher education made the arguments of the few technicians who understood the problem seem mere logic-chopping to an intelligent but ill-informed nation. Those parties on the Left which were most exempt from mere emotional hatred of all things German were, as the past and the future alike showed, as incapable as the Right of accepting unpleasant facts in a financial world in which rhetoric was impotent. On the Right, the politicians and their electors thought, and rightly thought, that the advice given them from London and New York was not entirely disinterested. So it was natural to reply to all councils of prudence, to all policies based on that 'sense of possibilities' which Cavour thought the greatest of statesmanlike qualities, with slogans not much less childish than the famous dictum of Calvin Coolidge. 'They owe the money, don't they?' was how the average French elector might have answered scepticism as to the possibility of making Germany pay

---

[1] M. Clemenceau is reported to have said of M. Klotz that 'it was his bad luck to have as Finance Minister the only Jew who couldn't count'. The later career of M. Klotz cast a good deal of doubt on his financial ability.

for the war. France, as legally-minded as the United States, took the parchment of the Treaty of Versailles too seriously.

Nor was the illusion that Germany would pay all war costs the only trouble. The majority of the 'Bloc National' represented interests and sentiments which had never accepted the principle of the income tax. It is possible that some of them really thought it would be possible to undo the evil deed of the traitor Caillaux. So there was a reluctance to apply rigorously the only system of taxation that could have met the needs of the time. That the result was inflation was not at once perceived, nor was the fall in the franc proof of anything but the lack of co-operation of France's allies.[1] It was easy, therefore, for complacent Ministers to stress the great rise in revenue and great increase in taxation, while ignoring the debasement of the franc, so that it was not until 1921 that the tax revenue equalled that of the last pre-war year in gold francs. Even so, that revenue was, of course, grossly inadequate for the needs of a devastated country.

It was very natural to hide the unpleasant truth that the French State was going to need far more money than it had needed before the war behind the fiction of an 'ordinary' budget, an 'extraordinary' budget and a 'German' budget. The first was what its name signified and was solvent. The second was to receive special sources of revenue, liquidation of war assets, etc., and loans for special expenditure. The 'German' budget was to pay the costs of reconstructing the devastated areas and other charges which the Treaty had managed to classify as reparations, such as war pensions, and to be recouped by the sums paid by Germany—when Germany paid. Meantime, as in the case of the extraordinary budget, the deficit was to be met by loans, and in the case of the 'German' budget there were hardly any other receipts. Until the 'Boche' was made to pay up, the French investor was asked to trust the French State. His faith in the State was still great, but it was not indestructible. Even if it had been, the investor was not merely anxious to be sure that his investment was safe but that it was good. So, in boom times, the Treasury found it hard to borrow in competition with business, while in times of depression, it was easy to borrow, but slackness in business was reflected in the lower tax yield.

Klotz went out of office with Clemenceau, and his successor was François-Marsal. Both Ministers realized that something had to be done and, after various alterations in detail consequent on a Cabinet change and others arising from differences between the Chamber and the Senate, the budget of 1920 was voted. Its main novelty was a turnover tax which was to be the great standby of successive Ministers of France. Yet even these reforms left the real deficit untouched and

[1] Exactly the same reaction was perceptible among people in Britain in 1931, who, knowing that a National Government could not default, were convinced that the British departure from gold was the fault of the French and Americans. In the same way it was the wicked Europeans who prevented Mr. Hoover from turning the corner.

it was out of the question, it was asserted, to try to raise more by taxes. Next year it fell to Doumer to produce the budget and he was a severe critic of his predecessors, but his attempt to raise the turnover tax was bitterly opposed in the Chamber and, despite a fall in expenditure and the ending of the 'extraordinary' budget, it was necessary to borrow that year 17,400,000,000 francs.

In 1922 the Poincaré Ministry was formed to make Germany pay, and it was perhaps fitting that in such an atmosphere of optimism the Finance Minister should be even more optimistic than the rest of the Cabinet. The new Minister was a nobleman and resembled in some ways that eminent noble financier of the years before the Revolution, M. de Calonne. The dictum of the Comte de Lasteyrie that the deficit was due, not to excessive expenditure, but to insufficient revenue, was pure Calonne. Some time or other the budget would have to be balanced, say in three or four years' time. If it turned out then that the tax yield had not risen enough to end the ordinary deficit, 'one should not hesitate to ask for further sacrifices'. Apart from this hoping for the best, the rest of M. de Lasteyrie's policy was summed up in 'making Germany pay'. Who knew if, in that happy day, the income tax could not be abolished? For M. de Lasteyrie hankered after the good old days of non-inquisitorial finance. It took him almost a year to come out of his golden dreams; he did so on the eve of the occupation of the Ruhr, proposing a 20 per cent. increase in the existing taxes. The Chamber was not so open-minded as the Minister and there was no increase in the tax-rate, although there were minor adjustments. But the Chamber had now to listen to arguments more powerful than those of M. de Lasteyrie.

At last the lenders were going on strike. Loans were less and less successful and, by January 1924, a loan yielding 6·29 per cent. failed. The French State could no longer borrow in the long-term market and the franc was beginning to slide rapidly. By vigorous action on the exchanges, the Poincaré Government was able to rout the mere speculators who were selling the franc short, but the fundamental problem remained. It was obvious that, no matter how successful the occupation of the Ruhr might be in helping the Germans to make up their minds to pay, they could not pay all the costs of reconstructing the devastated areas and the other charges put to the account of the 'German' budget. Lasteyrie fell back on his 20 per cent. increase, combined with cuts in salaries and with attempts to make tax evasion more difficult. It was a suicidal programme on the eve of a general election, and among the more rash promises made by Left candidates were not only the repeal of the 20 per cent. increase but the abolition of the turnover tax. The 'rich will pay' replaced the 'Germans will pay'.

To make France solvent, drastic measures were necessary, and one that appealed to the Socialists was a capital levy. But this taxation of property holders in general to pay off debt holders in particular was bitterly opposed by the property holders, who were, in most cases, also debt holders. A forced conversion was really a bankruptcy, and for the State to announce a change in the formal value of its obligations was almost as bad as not to meet them; to cut down the *rente*, or not to pay it, was a far more serious blow at public confidence, in France at least, than to debase the currency. In any case there was no chance that an Auvergnat businessman like M. Clémentel would consent to be the sponsor of a capital levy. The last straw had been a revelation by the Finance Committee of the Senate that the figures of the Bank of France balances had been doctored or made, if you like, less depressing than they might have been. To make matters worse, the new Finance Minister, M. de Monzie, had tried something very like a forced loan.

The Herriot Government was out; the Senate was not disposed to tolerate much longer any serious attempt to meet the financial difficulties of the day by 'Cartellist' methods. M. Painlevé was the new Prime Minister and he summoned the one great Left financier from Mamers, where M. Caillaux was, like another Cincinnatus, if not at his plough at least busy mending his fences. The appointment of the recently disgraced politician was less daring than it seemed. To have been a victim of Clemenceau was by now a passport to the trust of the Left, and Messrs. Caillaux, Malvy and Sarrail were martyrs whom the victors of 1924 delighted to honour. But for all that, there was a wide difference in outlook between M. Caillaux and his Socialist friends. M. Caillaux had no use for the merely sentimental attitude to public finance that marked so many deputies of the Left. The economic theories of the new Minister were not those which had triumphed in 1924. To create a real budget, that is one in which all the separate accounts were fused, to avoid any such threat to the investor's confidence as a capital levy and to raise fresh funds to enable the Treasury to meet its obligations, were M. Caillaux's main and unrevolutionary proposals. The most ingenious of them was a loan whose interest was payable in francs, but at a rate which varied with the foreign exchanges; this should have tempted far-sighted investors who felt like being bears of the national currency, but unless the franc fell, the yield was only about 4 per cent. Not enough French investors combined confidence in the Government with fears for the franc to justify the experiment. But apart from this failure, M. Caillaux differed from the left of the 'Cartel' on the question of lowering the turnover tax. He could get support only from the Right, and that was uncertain. No government so based could carry through profound reforms and so France drifted nearer inflation. The pilot had to be dropped, and the second Painlevé Cabinet entrusted its financial salvation to the Prime Minister, aided by M. Georges Bonnet.[1] The remedy

[1] As 'Minister of the Budget'.

chosen was another capital levy and a moratorium on certain maturing debts. This was intolerable to many good Radicals; the formal solvency of the Republic was not to be jeopardized.

Briand at last managed to form a Ministry and his miracle-worker was the most eminent and richest of businessmen-politicians in France, M. Loucheur. His remedy was most drastic taxation and collection of taxes; the seven months' delay in voting the budget was suddenly to be made up for by intolerable pressure on the taxpayers, most of whom, not through their fault, were in arrears. In turn Loucheur went down; then came Doumer, who proposed to add a tax on payments to the turnover tax. It was no wonder that M. Bedouce, one of the finance experts of the Socialists, protested against such a betrayal of the electoral programme of 1924! Doumer went. He was succeeded by Raoul Péret, the main ingredient of whose panacea was an increase of the turnover tax, a pill made a little more palatable to the Left by the imposition of some irritating but not very useful formalities on income-tax payers.

So far the Chamber had had its way. The game had been played according to the rules; an attempt had been made to avoid too open a betrayal of the optimistic programme of 1924, although amiable masters of the game like M. Raoul Péret had secured concessions to sound finance which less skilled parliamentarians like M. Doumer had failed to get. But power was passing out of the hands of the deputies; what had been said in 1924 was of less and less interest. The franc was beginning to fall, and fall with increasing rapidity: and that fall was no longer mainly an affair of speculators, for the cost of living was beginning to rise in an alarming fashion. From Caillaux to Péret, the cost of living index rose from 512 to 697. Very many of the Left voters were worried by the fall in the franc; all were worried by the rise in prices. Briand, who, after all, was familiar with the device in foreign affairs, fell back on a well-tried remedy or diversion, a 'Committee of Experts'. It was a betrayal of a darling dogma of the Left, for the experts were, of course, financially orthodox. The Chamber was full of left-wing experts, but 'expert' meant, in fact, someone the investor or the anxious creditor would recognize as more concerned with his interests than with those of 'fiscal justice' or loyalty to the elector's mandate. Directors of banks, even eminent professors of Economics, were much more likely to restore confidence than were M. Vincent Auriol, M. Bedouce, M. Nogaro or any other political financier. But it was politically necessary to make some concessions to the *amour propre* of the Chamber and to the honest suspicion of many of its members. So M. Raoul Péret was replaced by M. Caillaux, who was still the one politician of the Left who had a reputation as a financier, a reputation that made it necessary for Briand to forget that Caillaux was his one personal enemy in politics and to accept him as the mediator between the experts and the deputies.

There were more reasons than one why Caillaux could not effectively mediate between the politicians and the lenders, great and small. His name, for many of the potential lenders, was the symbol of predatory taxation. Horror of the income-tax, or, at least, reluctance to permit that intrusion into private finances which was needed to make it effective, was widespread. It was all very well for the Left to talk as if the only opponents of income-tax were the great magnates. The small lawyers and the country doctors who were too devoted to the ethical code of their professions (which imposed secrecy) to permit inspection of their books—if they kept any—were numerous in the ranks of the Radicals and by no means unknown in the ranks of the Socialists. These sections of the majority might reinforce the angry minority, backed as they were by the odd view of the incidence of direct taxation expressed by the experts. For they asserted that direct taxes 'will eventually be incorporated in prices, and, in many cases, in a proportion higher than their real amount'. This doctrine was considered at least doubtful in other lands by economists of equal eminence. But truth may differ on one side of the Pyrenees from truth on the other, and millions of Frenchmen trusted the experts who told them what they wanted to believe.

It is possible that M. Caillaux might have succeeded had he adopted the experts' scheme at once and without serious alteration. The report was detailed, thorough, and was designed to meet the views of that important body of persons to whom the French State owed money. By the summer of 1926, France either had to go bankrupt and alienate the millions of public creditors among whom were hundreds of thousands of Socialist and, it may be suspected, not a few Communist voters, or it could pay them, which meant meeting the wishes of all the persons who could supply the funds, from the Governors of the Bank of France down to the village shopkeeper who had been hoarding banknotes but might soon be stricken with panic distrust even of the notes. Against this fact the Left could declaim in vain; if it had been true that the great majority of Frenchmen had nothing to lose but their chains, the creditors might have been coerced or defied. It was not true; they might have less to lose than they had to gain, but the loss was certain, the gain problematic. There was the example of the German collapse to frighten them and only academic doctrines of Left economics to comfort them.

Some of Caillaux's measures were timely; the settlement of the British war debt; the preparations for settling the American war debt; but the real problem of confidence was in Paris and in towns like Mamers, not in London or New York. What was needed, according to the new Minister, was a law giving him full powers, the very remedy attacked as dangerous by the Left when asked for by Right Finance Ministers. M. Léon Blum, now as always a brilliant dialectician, pointed out the dangers of such a step. More serious was the opposition of Right leaders, for it was in the main their supporters whose confidence had to be won. The past of the Minister rose to plague him. It had, as M. Louis Marin reminded the House, 'the inconvenience of dividing Frenchmen, and that is a serious consideration when one is trying to restore confidence'. M. Tardieu, heir of Clemenceau, read the famous 'Rubicon' document which revealed, it was alleged, the dictatorial ambitions of the man who asked for full powers. But the dagger stroke came from M. Herriot who, abandoning his place as President of the Chamber, attacked the Minister. The second Caillaux Ministry was dead; the franc fell to 235 to the pound, less than one-ninth of its nominal value.

M. Herriot could get no support from the Socialists unless he tried a capital levy, and M. de Monzie, the Finance Minister in the new Herriot Government, was no improvement as a maker of confidence on M. Caillaux. The franc still fell; and the Paris mob, or that section of it which was ready for a row (which was not a negligible section), was beginning to turn ugly. There was only one remedy left. The Chamber of 1924 would have to submit to the financial dictatorship of a Government of 'National Union' presided over by Poincaré The return of Caillaux had been one startling reversal of recent history, but it was not as startling as the return of 'Poincaré la Guerre, Poincaré la Ruhr'.

In a later financial crisis, the greatest of French political cartoonists, Sennep, showed M. Léon Blum trying to inspire confidence by dressing in the costume of a bourgeois of the time of Louis Philippe under the busts of the Citizen King and of the great banker, Lafitte. But it was not necessary for M. Poincaré to dress the part; he *was* a bourgeois of the time of Louis Philippe, or, at latest, of the time and ideas of Léon Say. He had no new economic ideas or financial specifics. None would have succeeded unless they had been revolutionary, and France, in 1926, was not revolutionary. What was needed was evidence that the Government at last was *serious*. Poincaré was and looked like an upright, unimaginative, industrious and intelligent village notary. The country was tired of professors and noblemen and semi-noblemen and orators and the rest. It needed the services of a good attorney. It got them.

There was nothing that was novel in Poincaré's programme. Most of it was borrowed from the Committee of Experts. He increased taxation of all kinds most rigorously, except on the higher income-tax brackets; there he lowered the rates to restore confidence and because the very high rates were almost totally unproductive. He greatly improved the system of tax collection; his own undoubted probity and his prodigious industry were well employed here; he made some serious economies in administrative details; he completed the process, which his immediate predecessors had begun, of producing a unified budget. He was, however, fortunate in some ways, for the Germans under the Dawes Plan were now paying substantial sums, enough to cover the cost of what rebuilding was still to be done. But the real secret was the impression made on the investor by the firmness of the Prime Minister and the docility of the Chamber. Whatever was to be done had to be done quickly and without any hesitation. It was. This explains the success of such transparent devices as the creation of the independent sinking fund and the transfer to it of the profits of the tobacco monopoly. Put into the Constitution by a special session of the National Assembly, the new institution could obviously only preserve its autonomy while the Chamber and the Senate permitted. But the solemn character of the legislation impressed the man in the street—or the man in the cottage—if it did not impress the deputies. The franc was saved; that is, it was possible to let it rise to a rate about a fifth of its nominal value. It may be that the Prime Minister had dreams of revaluing it completely, but they were put aside.

The triumph of Poincaré was not altogether pleasing to the Left; he had got Parliament out of a very ugly mess, but it had been done by methods very unlike those preached in the hopeful days of 1924. Another assault on the 'wall of money' had been repelled with heavy loss. It is true that the leader of the Radicals, M. Herriot, was in the Government, but it was also true that the Radicals were represented on the joint committee in Parliament which controlled the tactics of the parties of the moribund Cartel. They had a foot in each camp. But as long as the franc was not legally stabilized, it would be highly dangerous to upset the Ministry, for the lender was still timid and a return of any of the previous Finance Ministers, even of the great technician, M. Caillaux, might cause a panic.

If it was to the advantage of the prudent Radical to wait until after the formal stabilization of the franc before breaking with the Government of National Union, it was to the advantage of the Government to postpone the stabilization *de jure* if not *de facto* until after the elections. For, as M. Seignobos noted, the Poincaré Government was a political novelty of great interest—and of great menace—to serious politicians. It was a Government based on that union of the Centre parties in the Chamber which had been the dream of the more intelligent Conservatives since the agony of the National Assembly. It was not, like the Poincaré Government of 1922-4, dependent on the Right, and it was not, like the various Governments of 1924-6, dependent on the Socialists. The success of such a Government was anomalous in a Chamber with a strong Left majority, even though that majority was weakened by the refusal of the Communists to make any distinction between class-enemies, except to regard 'Social-Fascists' like M. Blum as worse, because less obvious, enemies of the workers, than open reactionaries like M. Tardieu. Poincaré did make some concessions to his Left allies. In Briand there were both a symbol and a policy, and he was maintained at the Foreign Office by the Man of the Ruhr. There was no danger to laicity to be expected from the heir of Waldeck-Rousseau; and all but the professional priest-baiters had reconciled themselves to the retention of the French Embassy at the Vatican and to the refusal of the Alsatians to be liberated from the clerical yoke.

It was hard to find campaign slogans or even hints. Of course the Communists had theirs; they were a revolutionary party pouring contempt (until further orders) on bourgeois democracy. The position of the Socialists was more difficult; they were bound to proclaim themselves revolutionary, or be even better targets for Communist gibes, but to be in favour of a revolutionary change *some time* or other was not incompatible with being elected at Narbonne, whereas any serious threat of a revolution *now* was.[1] The Communist proposal of a common *revolutionary* front had to be repulsed, for the Communists meant it. A not very well hidden alliance with the Radicals, believers in private property and strongly opposed to any 'holiday of legality', was accepted. 'We know,' said M. Blum, 'what reaction means. We trust our local parties to recognize it whether it shows its face or a mask.' In short, Republican discipline would work. It was the more important to do this since the Chamber had gone back to single-member constituencies with no nonsense about proportional representation. To fight for a lone hand would be electorally disastrous. As for the Radicals they would, in the country, fight on the side of the enemies of the Government which they supported in the Chamber. And to the traditional and rather shop-worn stock of slogans, they added the 'single school system'.[2]

The result was an election strongly in favour of the Poincaré policy of peace, retrenchment, and not very much reform. The results, inevitably, exaggerated this tendency, for the Communist party, by refusing any electoral compromise and running their candidates at both ballots, cost the 'Left' 36 seats and saw its own deputies reduced from 28 to 14, although it had increased its total poll by 200,000. The Socialists made little progress and suffered badly at the hands of the Communists in the real proletarian regions. The S.F.I.O. was in danger of becoming

---

[1] M. Léon Blum had found it easier to get elected on a revolutionary programme with no immediate content in Narbonne, than in the industrial areas of Paris.

[2] 'École unique.' This meant that all places in the *lycées* should be free, that the *lycées* should give up their elementary school departments and that all French children, at any rate all those who went to the State schools, should receive the same education. To avoid swamping the *lycées*, entrance would be by an examination which could not fail to be competitive. However democratic this system, it had the disadvantage of alienating bourgeois members of the party who feared that their sons might not get to a *lycée* at all if the ability to pay the fees was to cease to be a claim to admission. One fatal consequence would be, greatly to increase the numbers in Church schools, which filled the old partisans of the University with horror, and the only remedy for that, the suppression of all Church schools, was politically impossible, a daydream of schoolmasters at party congresses.

a workers' party with few workers among its members. The real victors were the Centre groups, for the Radicals, too, barely held their ground. Ideologies were at a discount: the Government could now stabilize the franc and let the political system return to normal. On June 25th, 1928, the franc was defined as containing '65·5 milligrams of gold, nine-tenths fine'. It was a reduction from the pre-war parity of four-fifths.

The wits on the Left might add to their list of epithets, 'Poincaré of the four-sous franc'. But the people who in this matter really counted, the small investors, the pensioners, the owners of woollen stockings now filled with banknotes instead of gold, were grateful that even four sous out of twenty had been saved. That the French middle-class had been rescued from complete ruin; that its faith in the workings of the system had not been completely destroyed; was a far better safeguard against fascism than the jokes of the bright young men of the *Canard Enchaîné*. It was, from the point of view of the little man, so great a thing that it concealed from him the fact that France had at last paid for the war by a capricious and unjust capital levy. M. Klotz' successor had avoided both horns of his dilemma; neither the rich nor the Germans paid, but the classes whose interests and sentiments the politicians of the Left were for ever and sincerely promising to protect without having the will or the political means to do so.

CHAPTER IV

RECONSTRUCTION

I

THE area over which the Allied Armies advanced in the late autumn of 1918 had been either stripped or devastated. In what was to be called the 'red zone', covering 4 per cent. of the area of the occupied territory, the soil had been so torn up by shell fire, poisoned by chemicals, gashed by trenches, that it was thought that the cost of restoring it to fertility would be greater than it was worth. This estimate was pessimistic, for it overlooked the irrational courage and tenacity of the French peasant; but even to-day there runs all across France a great scar, in the chalk country, visible to the naked eye, and everywhere marked by memorials, cemeteries and little woods; there on French soil, Germany was kept unscathed.

The ten northern departments, which had a population of 4,700,000 in 1914, had only 2,075,000 at the Armistice. Livestock in 1918 had been reduced to 174,000, about a tenth of the normal. Over 800,000 houses or farm buildings had been destroyed or damaged. In the richest of the occupied departments, the Nord, over 50,000 houses had been completely destroyed; nearly 5,000 miles of roads were seriously damaged; nearly 600 miles of main railway line had been completely destroyed; nearly 600,000 acres of farmland damaged. So it was in other departments and, by 1925, a sum of 80,000,000,000 francs had been spent on reconstruction.[1]

The reconstruction of the devastated areas was the greatest economic achievement of post-war Europe. It involved far greater difficulties than did better-advertised programmes in more fortunate lands like Italy and Germany. It was carried out, too, in specially difficult conditions. It would have been more economical to use German labour as a method of payment in kind, but the objection that it was intolerable that the invaders should return to work beside their recent victims had some emotional force, although it should be noted

---

[1] As this sum was spent over a period of five to six years with the gold value of the franc varying a great deal, it is hard to estimate its value in other currencies. But taking the deadweight debt it imposed at the value of the Poincaré franc, it represented a little under £700,000,000.

that it was an emotion much more warmly expressed by French contractors than by French workmen.   Then the stern individualism of
the French peasant stood in the way of a completely scientific re-
building of the ruined farms and villages.   The owners of the heaps
of rubble and water-logged foundations often insisted on building
again on exactly the same site and in the same style.   Some of the
dreariest villages of northern France had been reduced to ruins between
1914 and 1918, but when the time came to rebuild, they appeared
again in all their nineteenth-century hideousness.   In the devastation
of war, boundaries were often removed, and it was made legally easier
to concentrate land holdings, to assemble scattered strips.   But peasant
conservatism was still strong; in Picardy, the engineers whose business
it was to re-allot the land were sometimes driven off with stones,
although some progress was made.

Economic pressure did more than the law to change the character
of farming in the devastated areas.   The compensation paid for damage
to the land and buildings could legally be spent within a circle of 50
kilometres around the original site of the property, and a good many
peasants took the opportunity of this windfall to settle in the little towns,
further emptying the countryside of the marginal producers.   From
the point of view of agriculture the devastated areas, by 1925, had got
back to their pre-war position.   They were again the richest producers
of crops in France; of the great cash crop of beetroot, of wheat and,
to a less extent, of flax.

Like the rest of rural France, they continued to lose their native
population.   By 1926, the year in which reconstruction may be said
to have been virtually completed, the rural population of France
had declined to 50·9 per cent.   Over 3,700,000 agricultural workers
had been mobilized and of these over 600,000 had been killed.   Nor
was it merely the war losses that emptied the countryside; the old drift
to the towns continued.   Above all, the number of farm labourers fell
off.   The peasant holding, if it was not the divine thing it had been
to earlier generations, was still sacred enough to escape the full effect
of cash computation.   The family holding, worked without any hired
labour, or with only seasonal hired labour, could survive where the
farmer who had to pay high wages went under.   And, of course, the
great war losses among the peasant class, when coupled with the
limitation of the size of families, meant in many cases that the only
son for whom the holding had been destined had been killed.   In the
poorer regions land went out of cultivation and, if it was very poor, it
was not always possible even to find the owner, but it was not only in
the poorer regions that the plough and the spade were less and less
common.   Between 1913 and 1921, 7,500,000 acres went out of cultivation; nearly 6 per cent. of the total of arable land.   In the south-west,
Tarn-et-Garonne, Lot-et-Garonne, Dordogne were still in the bad

way they had been in before the war. In the Gers there were 2,500 abandoned farms.

One important social consequence was that the value of the land did not benefit by the general rise in prices that followed inflation. A pessimistic expert [1] thought that, as late as 1924, the value of land had risen by only one-half, while nearly all other values had risen to three or four times their pre-war value in francs. Although farmland did benefit by the boom years from 1926 to 1930, its value did not, except in the rarest cases, rise proportionately to general costs and, as was already the case before 1914, arable land did not gain as much as pasture. The social consequences in a country where landowning [2] was so widespread were not unimportant and, when taken in conjunction with the general results of inflation, the fall in the real value of *rentes* and other sources of fixed incomes, and the loss of three-quarters of the pre-war foreign investment, [3] it greatly weakened the position of the middle classes.

The generally high prices for agricultural products during the war and the great prosperity of the home market from 1920 to 1930 made the lot of a great part of the French agricultural population economically more tolerable than it had been in the pre-war years. It is true that in the rise of prices that followed the stabilization of the franc, the products of the land got a smaller share of the nominal increase than did the products of the factory. And the gains were most marked in the case of cattle raisers, especially for the peasants who had taken over stock from the proprietor of the land at a fixed valuation and, when their leases fell in, were often able to pay off the whole indebtedness for the price of one cow.

The fortune of the cereal producer was less agreeable. Despite prohibitive tariffs, the good years in which France produced all or almost all she needed were years of what the peasant regarded as unjustly low prices. For him, to produce wheat was more than a mere economic activity. To permit land that could produce crops to produce only cattle was, in the eyes of many Frenchmen, to commit a kind of treason, and M. Daniel Halévy has told us of the scorn with which a friend of his saw his neighbours go over to the lazy life of cattle raising. Even the old ferocious industry of the peasant seemed to be shaken. One of the best-informed observers of French rural life [4] saw, with pain, the neglect of the soil in Périgord and Gascony. Technically backward, living coarsely, the peasants seemed to his critical eye un-

---

[1] M. Caziot.

[2] The magic of property had not lost all its power. It has been noted that in rural regions where the Communist party is strong, many of its loyal members would yet be insulted if it were suggested that they should enter themselves on the census forms as farmers (*agriculteurs*) instead of as landowners (*propriétaires*). But there were cases where the son of a man who proudly insisted on his status as a 'propriétaire', was equally insistent that he was not a peasant but a mechanic.

[3] M. Colson's estimate. [4] M. Émile Guillaumin.

worthy of their opportunities. 'Middling workers, the peasants were above all too fond of shooting and going to fairs. And the heather spread over the fertile slopes where once there grew vines, plum trees, apple trees, fig trees.'

Some of this severe criticism was merited, but some of it represented resentment at inevitable change. The peasant was no longer so economical; he spent more on himself and on his family; he had more and newer if not better clothes; his wife and daughter dressed like 'bourgeoises'; he had better and more varied food. Encouraged by the Government, rural electrification made great progress, making the life of the village or the farm less dull. The motor-bus completed what the bicycle had begun; it tied up the life of the villages to the towns. The peasant was no longer a strange animal, seen in a favourable light by George Sand, in a gloomier light by Zola. He dressed, talked, and lived largely as the townspeople did. He preserved a certain degree of contempt mixed with envy for the townspeople; but improved transport, general literacy, improved economic status, all diminished the importance of local traditions and of peasant folk-ways. It also diminished the influence of local culture; many valuable things were lost in the spread of a uniform material and, largely, a uniform spiritual equipment: but not all was loss.

The changes in the peasant's attitude affected his farming methods. Shortage of labour, when it did not drive him to abandon arable farming altogether, induced him to risk his capital on agricultural machinery which, before the war, had been used mainly by the rich capitalist farmer. In its turn, the use of machinery imposed co-operation on the peasant, at any rate as far as purchasing was concerned. More chemical manure, better seed, a greater willingness to try new methods, enabled France, despite her falling rural population, to be more nearly self-sufficient than any other great nation of western Europe.

II

It was in French industry, not in French agriculture, that the war and its aftermath had the most striking results. The ruin of the invaded areas was even more complete in industry than in agriculture. The land, where it was not the scene of actual fighting, merely suffered from neglect; but all industrial plant had suffered from pillage and the mines from actual destruction by flooding. In the Nord there were nearly 10,000 factories and workshops, employing ten men or more, which had been damaged or destroyed.

To restore the most highly industrialized area of France to its old activity was a task to frighten any nation, but by the end of 1925 it had been done. Once it was done certain advantages appeared, for France had now an entirely new industrial equipment in her most industrialized areas. It was an old ground of complaint that French industrialists had been too niggardly in their expenditure on new capital equipment. Now they had to start from scratch, and every one of the major French industries (except silk) was of necessity provided with the most modern plant. The woollen and cotton factories of the Nord, the steel mills of Lorraine and the main coal-mines were now on a technical level with any industries in the world.

This development was not confined to the devastated areas, for the war had greatly accelerated the growth of heavy industry and of mass production in the uninvaded parts of France. The needs of the war had created new substitute industries in the centre and south; the motor and other engineering works had had their growth immensely accelerated; and the great profits of the war years enabled the *entrepreneurs* to expand in the post-war boom years.

The most striking change in the French industrial situation was a result of the Treaty of Versailles. By the return of the annexed half of Lorraine to France, she got complete control of the second greatest iron-field in the world. The ore deposits of German Lorraine nearly equalled those of French Lorraine. United, they made France one of the greatest industrial powers in the world, although, in the years immediately following the war, the natural marriage of Lorraine ore to Westphalian coal was interrupted by tariff and political disputes, and the chief French market was Belgium-Luxemburg. The recovery of eastern Lorraine not only increased French ore supplies, it greatly increased French steel output. France, in fact, became a very considerable steel exporter, in a position to make terms with the German industry. As competition of the old type grew less and less popular in the great integrated industries, the competition of French and German steel in the same markets was ended by a joint-selling agreement to which Belgium was made a partner.

The increase in French steel production was not solely due to the recovery of German Lorraine. Contrary to a general belief, many French steel mills in Lorraine were destroyed in the war and were rebuilt with all the latest technical equipment. But the basic difficulty of the French steel industry, the shortage of good coking coal, remained. German Lorraine had an important coal-field, and until 1935 the mines of the Saar were French property, but it was still necessary to import 15,000,000 metric tons of coal a year—and a great deal of French coal was not suitable for coking. So France had to be a great exporter of iron ore, not only from the metropolis but from Algeria, and a quarter of the 50,000,000 metric tons of iron produced at the height of the post-war boom of 1929 was exported.

In addition to a privileged position as the possessor of the greatest European iron-field, France was the possessor of the greatest European source of bauxite, and consequently in a position to develop a great aluminium industry. This was not her only advantage, for she was well provided with water-power and it was near her sources of hydro-electric power that her aluminium works were established. This industry was important before the war and its growth was one of the causes of the attention paid to the development of water-power, a development pushed ahead under the influence of high coal prices during and after the war of 1914–18. France and Italy ranked together as the two largest European countries with the most highly-developed hydro-electric systems, but by 1926, the most easily developed sources of water-power had all been tapped, while a fall in the price of coal and a great increase in the efficiency of coal-driven electricity plants had made much further exploitation of 'white coal' uneconomic.

Recovered Alsace was not so great an economic asset as recovered Lorraine, but the addition of the Alsatian spindles to the French cotton industry made it the third largest in the world, just ahead of Germany, though a long way behind England and the United States. Another Alsatian asset was the great potash field which enabled France to compete with the German industry and to force her way into the selling cartel. In Alsace, too, was France's only oil-field, but at best it only produced 3 per cent. of her annual consumption. Like all the great industrial countries, except the United States, France was dependent on imports for the most important of the new sources of power.

Despite the growth of her heavy industry, her increased production of steel and the rapid expansion of her motor industry, which, with an annual production of 200,000 cars, was for some time the leader in the cheap car market in Europe, and with the Panhard, Hispano-Suiza and Bugatti factories a leader in the luxury market, France was still mainly an exporter of luxuries and semi-luxuries. Her exports, as their great increase in mere bulk showed, were less purely luxury goods than they had been before 1914; but even in the boom years nearly half of their value was represented by textiles, and the most valuable textile export was still silk. It was characteristic, too, that although the artificial silk industry, like the heavy industries, was in the hands of a few firms, the textile industries were still dominated by family concerns and, in the case of real silk, by very numerous family concerns. French export industry still catered for the trades that put a premium on taste; that were highly susceptible to changes in fashion; that could not profitably be controlled by bankers and great international consortiums.

Beside the new names of Renault and Citroën, beside the growth of the Schneider-Creusot interests in Poland, Czechoslovakia and elsewhere, the names of the great French vineyards, the names of the great dressmaking houses, old ones like Paquin, new ones like Molyneux, Chanel and Mainbocher, reminded the world of the special rôle of France.

In her balance of payments, the profits drawn from her being an agreeable place to visit or to live in were greater than ever. The rise of the summer season on the Riviera was an important economic development. Despite short-lived periods of popularity for the Lido or Brioni, France was more than ever the playground of Europe. In 1925, nearly 500,000 British and nearly 200,000 American tourists entered France, and the development of motor traffic was accompanied by a great growth in the capital invested in the hotel industry. If there was a falling-off in the popularity of all but the smartest inland spas, it was more than covered by an immense growth in the prosperity, if a decline in the exclusiveness, of the sea-side resorts.

Yet it might be argued that France was less in command of the situation than she had been. If she was flooded by Americans, she was also influenced by them. The adopted city of Offenbach saw her light musical stage dominated by the unsophisticated lyrics and simple plot of *Rose Marie*. Where, a hundred years before, Anglomania had provided the English players with a glorious reception and Hector Berlioz with a wife, and, on the eve of 1914, the Russian ballet of Serge Diaghilev had given French artistic life a new dose of exoticism, it was now the turn of America or of Afro-America. Josephine Baker and Duke Ellington with, in a few years' time, the learned study of 'swing', were to be the rage of the city that had refused to tolerate Wagner. In the film industry the American influence was even stronger, and it might have been thought that France was not producing enough that was new *and* French to keep the affections of the multitudes who poured in each year to improve their minds, to enjoy themselves and to help the French balance of trade.

The growth of the tourist industry helped the position of the French ports. Now that the main source of the profits of the great liners was no longer the hundreds of thousands of emigrants who poured into North and South America each year, the competitive position of France was improved. For the new tourist traffic she was admirably placed, and the port of Cherbourg benefited by the change. But the French port that grew fastest was Marseilles. At last she had overtaken her great rival, Genoa, but her natural difficulties were considerable. Some minor parts of her old commerce, like that in sesame, had deserted her, but they had been more than compensated for by the great increase in the trade in ground-nuts for the manufacture of soap and oils. Marseilles, however, is cut off from her hinterland by hills, and her harbour is now almost entirely artificial. Not content with building new quays into the Mediterranean, the bold Massiliots planned to develop the great salt-water lagoon, the Etang de Berre, which lies behind the hills. A new ship-canal was made into the lagoon, and the greatest navigation tunnel in the world (nearly 5 miles long) rendered it possible for barges up to 1,500 tons to go from Marseilles to the oil refineries and other port facilities on the Etang de Berre.

If the Rove tunnel was the most original of French engineering works in the great years of reconstruction, it was not the only one. Communications between Alsace and France were greatly improved by a tunnel that reduced the distance between Saint-Dié and Strasbourg by nearly 50 miles. The Canal du Nord, unfinished in 1914, was completed; the river port of Strasbourg was greatly improved and given economic privileges not relished elsewhere in France. Dunkirk, Cherbourg, Le Havre, La Pallice were all made better fitted to compete with their rivals. But the fundamental limitations on French maritime commerce remained. Only a little over a quarter of the shipping entering and leaving French ports was French and the proportion did not rise; it fell.

As happened in all belligerent countries, the railways suffered severely in the war, from excessive traffic and from neglect of repairs. In addition to these common evils, a great part of the lines of the most prosperous French companies, the Nord and the Est, had been destroyed. There was a great deal of reconstruction to be done and there were serious financial problems to be faced. The solution adopted was not an amalgamation of the companies, as was suggested, but the creation of a common pool of earnings. The strong lines were to help the weak. The separate lines were to manage their own affairs as they thought fit, but were to be rewarded for efficiency by premiums, while the State was to bear the losses, if any resulted from the pooling. Such losses were to be recouped by an increase of rates. It was an attempt to combine the social advantages of nationalization, the provision of adequate services for regions unable to pay for them, with the initiative of private enterprise. But even had the scheme been more carefully planned from an accountant's point of view, it could hardly have come at a more unfortunate time. Rapidly rising costs ate into revenue faster than freight or passenger rates could be raised, and the growth of motor-bus services hit especially hard a railway system which, for political reasons, had been saddled with so many unprofitable local passenger lines. As a result there were hardly any years when a profit was shown by which the State could recoup the cost of years in which the losses of the system had to be underwritten. One of the permanent troubles of the French budget came to be the railway deficit, and it seemed that the settlement combined the worst features of nationalization with the worst features of private ownership.

On the other hand, the technical administration of the railways was greatly improved. The State lines no longer suffered in comparison with the private lines; French locomotive engineers had long been famous for their skill in design and they were still worthy of the fame of Nancy. The main development was the electrification of the Paris suburban lines and of many of the main lines, especially in the south-west. There were still considerable differences in efficiency in the lines; it was easy to tell when one left the P.L.M. for the Midi, but on the main lines, at any rate, the French railways provided a good passenger service which was speedy not merely by American or German, but by British standards.

One last object of capital expenditure during these years must be mentioned. Like all other countries, France suffered badly from a housing shortage. It is true that her population had fallen by 2,000,000 in the war years, but there had been a great destruction of property as well as a complete cessation of building. In the devastated areas, rebuilding was usually done by private persons borrowing from special credit institutions on the anticipated compensation for war damage. But the great industries, especially the railways and mining companies, built a great many houses for their employees with a resultant raising of the general standard of working-class housing. Other industries imitated them; rapidly growing towns like Clermont-Ferrand were surrounded by 'cités ouvrières' built by the great firms, Michelin and the like, as part of their policy of social works. Special privileges for numerous families, or rather remedial measures directed to making a numerous family less of a housing handicap than usual, were features of these settlements, especially where the employers were zealous Catholics.

In addition, there was an exodus from the cities to the country. New suburbs sprang up round all the great cities. Paris was at last freed from the constricting girdle of her obsolete fortifications. The underground railway was permitted to pass beyond the old wall and the population of Paris actually began to fall, as her inhabitants moved out to the recently rural communes of the neighbouring departments. In Paris itself there was a building boom; modern apartments took the place of the old severe blocks which, even in the fairly rich sections of the city, had very defective sanitary arrangements, as one of the most famous of British residents of Paris has pointed out.[1]

The desertion of the crowded centre of the cities was only one sign of important changes in French urban life. Although still socially conservative to a remarkable degree, war, inflation, the spirit of the age, all had their effect on French life. The war had impoverished many of the middle-class and had given young women an unprecedented opportunity to enter business. Clerical work was now open to them on a far greater scale, especially in banks and Government offices, and it was a necessary recognition of a new social order to open all examinations to girls on the same terms as to boys.

In other ways the change in the actual, if not the legal, position of women was striking. For some years the most famous woman in France was not an actress (though there were some actresses of talent), or a writer (though there was one of genius), or a scientist (though

[1] Mr. Robert Dell.

607

there was also one of genius). Suzanne Lenglen was known to millions who had never heard of Colette or of Madame Curie. '

Mademoiselle Lenglen was not the only gift of France to the world of sport. She was unique, but there was Borotra and there was Carpentier and there was Ladoumègue. Indeed, considering that it was still the case that few Frenchmen and still fewer Frenchwomen took part in sport, the proportion of French stars in most sports was abnormally high. But sport was spreading. For the workers, it is true, the real sporting event of the year was still the bicycle race round France, but in the north Association football was increasingly popular, and Rugby was firmly rooted in the Midi, if the *furia francese* with which it was played proved too much for the Scottish Rugby Union and caused the disappearance of France from the international list. There were still some signs of the old prejudice against organized sport that had been entertained on the Left. To the old-fashioned Radical intellectual, sport might be brutal, its teaching might inculcate those false ideas of physical prowess and unintelligent achievement which it was the business of education to destroy. From that point of view, sport was thought of as too often merely a means of clerical propaganda. Had it not been fostered in the past by persons like Dr. Paul Michaux who was not only a zealous Catholic but openly advocated physical training as a means of making better soldiers? In a town where the local 'Reactionary' magnates subsidized sport, it might be desirable for a Left municipality to provide public facilities for games to counter the seductions of the Right, but the average French worker's idea of spending his spare time was bicycle-racing when he was young and fishing when he was older, unless, indeed, as was too often the case for the peace of mind of zealous trade-unionists, he spent his spare time working.[1]

If he did, he had more time to spend, for the eight-hour day had been conceded by Clemenceau in 1919. It is true that the eight-hour day, as the worker understood it, was soon eaten into by provision for overtime, rush work and the like. But even so it meant a very considerable reduction in the hours of work. With it went the general adoption of the 'English week', that is a Saturday half holiday as well as a Sunday holiday.[2] This important social change was soon general in all the great shops, offices and factories.

If any one class in France gained by the war, it was the workers. As long as the reconstruction boom lasted they were free from the danger of unemployment. In France as in the United States there were no accurate employment figures, but on the basis of the demands

---

[1] That typical Left intellectual, M. Charles Seignobos, expressed in 1921 his indignation at the interest taken by the students of the Sorbonne in the approaching Dempsey-Carpentier fight. However, M. Seignobos, unlike Mr. Bernard Shaw, had the prudence to refrain from absurd prophecy.

[2] Sometimes it was found more convenient to take the half-holiday on Monday.

on the poor-relief organizations of the towns, unemployment at the worst period after 1920 was less than 100,000, and on several occasions it sank below a thousand! Wages were, by French standards, good; the worker was getting a larger share of the national income than ever before; and, if prices rose fast, the economies of mass production meant an increase in real wages. Between 1926 and 1930 the workers, more than any other section in France, had comparative reason to rejoice.

But what was the worker? He was now to an increasing extent a foreigner. France had for long been hospitable to foreigners, but in the years after the war she replaced the United States as the main recipient of immigrants. American law, by debarring immigration, made life more intolerable even than usual in Italy, Spain, Poland. France was the one refuge and she was soon host to 3,000,000 foreigners, most of them workers. Some went on the land, especially Spaniards and Italians in the Midi, but for the most part they were a source of heavy industrial labour. Poles manned the coal-mines and to some extent the iron works of Lorraine. Italians were to be found in all trades. There was a more or less temporary migration of Belgians and Germans over the northern and eastern frontiers. From North Africa came Kabyles from the poverty-stricken mountain villages, to which they returned with their hoarded wages and, too often, with a taste for alcohol and the seeds of tuberculosis. Like the migration of Negro labour from the southern states during and after the last war, this emigration was not approved of by the ruling class in the regions whence the emigrants came. The colonists in Algeria did all they could to keep their labour force at home, content with lower wages and worse conditions than they got in France; but the difficulties of interposing a barrier between what were, in theory, parts of France, were very great. Stiff regulations as to health and solvency did something to meet the wishes of the colonists, but Algeria came to be considered as part of the French labour market. In opening her gates to immigration on this great scale, France was no doubt acting wisely, but it is not customary for a country to-day to be wise; and France deserved more gratitude than she got for providing a new safety valve for that so vigorously screwed down by the United States.

The immigrants had, of course, many faults. The Poles drank too much; the Kabyles were given to crimes of violence; the politics of Marseilles were made even more confused than usual by an immense half-digested population of miscellaneous foreigners. But French confidence in the attractive power of French civilization and French ideas was not baseless. In face of the rising tide of racial mysticism, France asserted that being French is a state of mind, not a mystical inheritance. And she united faith and works.

It would have been excessively optimistic in 1919 to have foreseen that, less than ten years later, France would have recovered so completely from her ordeal and have recovered almost entirely by her own efforts. The fairy gold of the German reparations account had been long in materializing and had not been a serious addition to French resources. Nevertheless, the north was rebuilt. The arrears of capital equipment of the war years were more than made up. The budgetary situation was sound. The balance of trade was flourishing, despite the great remittances sent abroad by the immigrants, remittances more than compensated for by the fact that, thanks to that immigration, the population of France was now greater than it had been in 1914, and the great predominance of young males among the immigrants was just what was needed to fill the dreadful gap made by the war.

Old-fashioned people might lament many things, from the short skirts to cocktails. American songs, American technology, in general 'Anglo-Saxon' ideas seemed to be conquering the world. The most that a competent French observer [1] could offer in the way of choice was Mr. Henry Ford or Mahatma Gandhi. France, if forced to make so unpleasant a decision, would choose Mr. Ford. It was therefore with mixed feelings that the news was received of the collapse of the great American boom in 1929, followed as it was by the financial discomfiture of the complacent English. France had earned her immunity, earned her security: for her surely had come at last the enjoyment of

'le vierge, le vivace, et le bel aujourd'hui' ?

III

The withdrawal of the United States from the League and the consequent collapse of the guarantee treaty had made it imperative from the French point of view to provide a substitute. What Britain and the United States would not provide must be sought elsewhere, in the new states of eastern and central Europe; in this way a balance of power would be created in favour of peace.[2] But these obligations must be mutual; France obviously had to guarantee the Vistula if Poland was to guarantee the Rhine. Moreover, it was obvious, after the first year or two of peace, that the non-European members of the League were, for all practical purposes, to be considered as contracting out of any possible military obligation under the League Covenant. The British Government could and did use the reluctance of the Dominions to undertake any serious commitments as a reason or excuse for its own withdrawal from any general pact of guarantee, whether that guarantee was based on a strict interpretation of the Covenant or on a new treaty or treaties within the framework of the League. It

---

[1] M. André Siegfried.
[2] In its old British sense of an overwhelming weight of power on one side.

was Dominion opposition that justified, in British eyes, the rejection of the pact of mutual assistance drafted in 1923. In the meantime, the situation caused by the occupation of the Ruhr had increased British readiness to take some risks for peace, and the return of two Left Governments, the first Labour Government in England and the first Herriot Government in France, made for better understanding. It was, in fact, the only time that both countries moved in the same political direction at the same moment.

The result was the adoption of the Geneva 'protocol' which made easier the identification of an aggressor, made compulsory the acceptance of arbitration and provided for the application of sanctions, as indeed the Covenant did. War was no longer a permissible remedy for League members, as it might be argued it had been while the Covenant failed to provide for the compulsory arbitration of all disputes. But the first Labour Government was short-lived; and the new Conservative Government, again stressing the unwillingness of the Dominions to undertake such serious obligations, refused its assent. Another attempt at providing general security had failed.

The next move came from Germany; she wanted a mutual non-aggression pact in which a third party, Britain, should be a guarantor. This proposal, first made in 1922, had many attractions from a German point of view. It would tie the hands of France as against Germany, and, at the moment, that was an unmixed good, as Germany was too weak to attack France. It was not until the drawn contest of the Ruhr had convinced Germany that she needed security even more than she had thought, and France that the 'right' to invade Germany was a two-edged weapon, that the proposal became viable. The Germans made the first move but then drew back, and the initiative fell to Austen Chamberlain and to Briand, who now took over the control of French foreign policy.

Briand's qualifications for diplomacy were personal. He was not learned, he was not, normally, industrious, but he was a born negotiator. It was said of him that while Poincaré knew everything and understood nothing, Briand knew nothing and understood everything. He had an unrivalled gift for making friends which his curious political career had allowed him to utilize. His oratory was unreadable in print, barely correct, full of repetitions and unnecessary verbiage. But listened to, it was quite another matter; something was heard that could not be transferred to the page. Briand's auditors could say to those who criticized him from the bare record of the printed page, as Pitt said of Fox, 'they had not been under the wand of the magician'.

In appearance, 1925 was not a good year for a new departure in French foreign policy. The sudden death of Ebert had been followed by the election of Hindenburg as President of the Reich, an event interpreted by many Frenchmen as a sign of the incorrigible militarism of the German people. There was a reaction to the Right in Germany, and that made the position of the German negotiator difficult, too. He was bound to ask for substantial concessions, not merely entry to the League and a seat on the Council, but evacuation of the first Rhineland zone of occupation. At Locarno the difficulties were smoothed over by the triumvirate, Austen Chamberlain, Briand and Stresemann. The frontiers between France and Germany were mutually guaranteed and so were the provisions for the demilitarization of the Rhineland. The Germans were allowed to interpret the League Covenant in a fashion that did not bind them to help Poland against Russia, and although no guarantee was given for the eastern frontiers, Germany signed arbitration treaties with Poland and Czechoslovakia and, to make assurance doubly sure, France signed a treaty of mutual assistance with Czechoslovakia. But for both France and Germany, the great feature of the treaty was the British and Italian guarantee, at the moment of greater value to Germany than to France, but bound to be of increasing value to the latter. It was not an absurdity for the preamble to justify the treaty with a reference to 'the desire for security and protection which animates the peoples upon whom fell the scourge of the war of 1914–18'.

For the moment the tension on France's eastern frontier was at an end; and Briand, in 1925, attained what he had tried to attain in 1922, a British guarantee of French security. He turned his attention to France's southern frontier, where the Italian Fascist Government was embarking on its own vigorous foreign policy, building up its own client states in the neighbourhood of France's allies and beginning to make of the question of Italian claims in Tunis a source of pressure on the elder 'Latin nation'. When an agreement was made, it bore the true but unsatisfactory name of a *modus vivendi*; the real questions of power and interest were left unsettled. But relations with Italy were, after all, of minor importance if the problem of relations with Germany was on the way to solution.

After some delays, Germany had been admitted to the League and to the Council, and Briand and Stresemann seemed to the outside world harmonious partners. They were that in many ways, but there were reservations on both sides. Briand wanted an organization of Europe on peaceful lines which would preserve the chief result of Versailles, the impotence of Germany in a military sense to exert that power which was hers by her position. It was his wish to give Germany everything that could be given without enabling her to return to the position of 1914, which would mean, in fact, attaining a position of predominance she had not known in 1914. If the experience of war had cured Stresemann of some of the illusions of his fervently nationalist days, he was still a National Liberal, ready to 'finesse' while Germany was weak, but with a permanent reserve in his mind as to the acceptance of the territorial *status quo*. He knew, better than most outsiders, how weak was the position of Liberalism in Germany, how rickety the democratic structure, and he was ever insistent that the only way to avoid a violent reaction against his policy of 'fulfilment' was to make generous concessions to Germany while she was yet weak. Mere gains of prestige, like a seat on the League Council, were not enough. She must have tangible benefits from her collaboration in the reconstruction of a peaceful Europe. What the ultimate aims of Stresemann's policy were, can only be guessed at, but he scored some great successes for Germany, and these concessions were made possible only because they were recommended to France by Briand. Briand's enemies assured France that each concession would be followed, not by an improvement in the relations between France and Germany, but by a deterioration. 'The way to treat a Prussian is to stamp on his toes until he apologizes' was their maxim of policy. But the French people trusted Briand in foreign policy as they trusted Poincaré in finance, and concessions were made.

The Dawes Plan had never pretended to be final, and it was time, the Germans said, that something more permanent was put in its place. The result was the setting up of a new Committee presided over by Mr. Owen D. Young, who had been second American expert on the Dawes Committee. On this new Committee Germany was now represented as an equal. Like Locarno, the Young Plan was not a 'Diktat' but a freely accepted bargain. The Young Plan was naturally more tender of German sovereignty than the Dawes Plan had been. Control of German finance ceased and with it the responsibility of the transfer problem passed from Allied to German shoulders. There was a considerable reduction in the total amount due, and in the new Bank of International Settlements, Europe was provided with yet another example of the smooth working of international organizations. With the financial settlement went a political concession, the area of occupation of the Rhineland was to be cut down and the final evacuation to be put forward to 1930.

In France, these adjustments were, inevitably, criticized. Any reduction in reparations payments was attacked. The great building boom in Germany, made possible mainly by American loans, was irritating to many French people, especially as so much of it was the result of lavish municipal expenditure obnoxious to French ideas of what local governments should do. The premature evacuation of the Rhineland, too, was bitterly attacked. Once the French troops were gone, it would be seen what German gratitude was like! As long as the Allied garrisons were there the Germans would be on their best behaviour, but once free from their supervision, the old military arrogance would be revealed. Events did not, on the surface, belie this view. But the real contest over the Young Plan was not with Germany but with Britain. It was necessary to allot new percentages of the reparations payments among the recipients, and at the Hague conference, called to do this, Mr. Snowden, the Labour Chancellor of the Exchequer, denounced the attitude of M. Chéron, his French colleague, as 'grotesque and ridiculous'. The zeal with which British interests in the share-out were defended by a Labour Government was a gratifying surprise to the City of London, but Mr. Snowden's manners did not endear him to the French Government, which was soon to be in a position where it had to be coaxed, not bullied.

The last great financial question of the war period, the war debts, was, if not settled, at least temporarily evaded by the Caillaux-Churchill and Mellon-Berenger agreements with Britain and the United States. Although the financial terms of these settlements were not rigorous, they did not tie up the war-debt payments to the reparations settlement; thus ignoring, in the opinion of many Frenchmen, the very elements of justice. But the French Government, although it did not for the moment dare to ask Parliament to ratify the agreements, acted on them and began to pay.[1]

One last promise of the peace settlement remained to be dealt with. A general project of disarmament had been on the League agenda ever since Locarno. But a general disarmament treaty without Soviet Russia would have been absurd, and it was difficult to induce Russia to co-operate and then hard to know how to handle her proposals when she did. The French position was simple; security must precede disarmament. Only if they were certain that they would not be overwhelmed by a dangerous neighbour would states take the risk of trusting to a general disarmament treaty and, even then, only if the provisions of that treaty were enforced by inspection. To British statesmen this insistence on security and inspection seemed to be too cynical, too mechanical. To French politicians, British trust in the good faith of her neighbours was due to the fact that they were not close neighbours.

Then in British opinion, conscription was an evil, if only because it permitted the powers of eastern Europe excessively large armies which they could not have afforded had they been on a voluntary basis. In all negotiations Germany had every interest in making the standard of armaments in Europe comparable to her own. When Soviet Russia finally came to announce her programme, she startled the world by asserting that the way to disarm was to disarm, a bold measure that was in line with the interest of the most secure of continental states: a state which had, in every country, its own troops: the local Communist party. Britain and France, after the Zinoviev letter and the

---

[1] They were finally ratified after a bitter campaign in which the Opposition plastered the walls of France with the reminder that the statesmen who were accepting this burden for the next two generations of Frenchmen were nearly all childless.

revolutionary activities of the Soviet ambassador in Paris, were alarmed at this kind of peace offer. Indeed, the first practical steps to meet the German case were not measures of disarmament but the removal of the Allied Commission which had the duty of keeping Germany to her treaty limits in arms. It was easier to begin to level up than level down. But in France, apart from the Socialists, whose leader, Léon Blum, made a bold policy of disarmament as a means to, not a consequence of, security, the main theme of his polemics, security before disarmament was an axiom.

There were other differences between the continental and the insular points of view. France argued that there were more elements in military strength than open armaments; in modern industrial society, war potential had to be borne in mind. A second Labour Government in Britain meant a new effort, and the League made the Labour Foreign Secretary Chairman of the Disarmament Conference whose work was just beginning when Europe was shaken by the economic storm, one of whose victims was the Labour Government itself. There was, on one side, not enough confidence in the future peace of Europe to induce the threatened powers to give up their own armour unless they could be sure that, on the other side, less immediately threatened powers would contribute—at once and effectually—to replace it if occasion arose. And the less immediately endangered powers for that very reason were unwilling to take on extra obligations. Who knew, they might have to be fulfilled one day? Naval armaments were a simpler matter. Germany and Russia were not at the moment active in this department of military diplomacy; and there was the precedent of the Washington Treaty. But France and Italy refused to agree that the problem could be solved in isolation from military problems in general and they did not take part in the abortive naval conference of 1927. An attempt by Britain and France to secure the acceptance of their own points of view led to an agreement by which France accepted the British views of the proper method of limiting naval competition in the cruiser class (which annoyed the United States), while Britain accepted the French view that trained reserves should not be counted in computing military strength (which annoyed the Germans). The agreement had to be abandoned. When the 1930 naval conference was held, the dispute was between France and Italy. Italy was ready to accept any naval limitation which gave her parity with France, but France maintained that formal parity between a country with a coast line on three seas as well as an immense Empire and a country with naval responsibilities on only one sea was, in fact, not parity but the imposition of intolerable and dangerous inferiority on the former country.

Before it was obvious that disarmament on sea or land by general agreement involved a degree of mutual trust that the world could not yet supply, Briand had achieved his most spectacular, if not his greatest triumph.   On the tenth anniversary of the entry of America into the war, he suggested to the United States a joint renunciation of war as an instrument of policy, an idea he had got from Professor Shotwell. Mr. Kellogg, the American Secretary of State, replied by suggesting a general renunciation of war open to all the world.   The idea was bound to appeal to the spirit of the age.   It was believed that the lesson of 1914 had been learned and that the evil thing was condemned by the conscience of the world, and that what that conscience condemned, died.   It was a great triumph of optimism, of that belief in the reasonableness and humanity of man of which Briand was the greatest exponent.   He had apparent reason for his faith.   He had had checks. A bold scheme drawn up with Stresemann at Thoiry, which not only provided for the evacuation of the Rhine before the treaty date, but for the settling of the Saar question, had had to be withdrawn. Not all his (or Stresemann's) countrymen were so trusting.   But the ratification of the Kellogg Pact by that vigilant body, the Senate of the United States, in January 1929, seemed to be one final proof that all was at last right with the world.

IV

In some ways the greatest cause of French disillusionment with victory was caused by Alsace.   By 1914, the pain that France had felt at being mutilated in 1871 had become much less acute.   The Vosges was on the way to being a spiritual as well as a political and physical frontier.   The generation whose feelings Déroulède had expressed, if in an exaggerated form, was passing away.   The wreaths on the Strasbourg statue in the Place de la Concorde meant less and less to the average Frenchman, and if the French protest against the crime of 1871 was less purely artificial than the clerical protest over the loss of the temporal power of the Pope, it was acquiring something of the same character.

The rising generations of Frenchmen neither talked nor thought of Alsace as their fathers had done.   There was even an attempt to reconcile France to her loss.   Alsace was to serve as a link between France and Germany, to become a bond of union instead of a cause of hate.   It was evident, too, to all but the most uncritically patriotic Frenchmen that Alsace no longer reacted against its conqueror with the old energy.   As decade after decade passed and the hope of an armed deliverance from German rule grew fainter, the Alsatians necessarily adjusted themselves to their new situation; their political ambition became not a return to France, but a better status within the Reich. The federal character of the German State made it fairly easy for Alsatian claims to be met; and the constitution of 1911, if it did not make the Reichsland a Federal State, did give it a high degree of internal autonomy.

Those sections of French opinion which attempted to keep alive the old interest in the lost provinces watched this evolution with distress. What in these circumstances was the duty of the Alsatians still loyal to France? The question was debated in two books; one by Maurice Barrès defended the Alsatian notables who stayed on in Alsace and tried to preserve their local influence, even though that meant accepting German rule; while the older, more sentimental doctrine was represented by René Bazin, whose hero, faced with the choice of becoming a German officer or going into exile in France, goes into exile; thus saving his honour, said one school; thus abandoning the position in which he could have continued to fight for French ideals, said the other.

The outbreak of war revived the old interest in Alsace. It was a dramatic gesture to send the frontier posts uprooted in the first disastrous invasion of Alsace to be laid on the grave of Déroulede, for the prophet of the 'revanche' had died a few months before the opening of that war of which he had dreamed. General Joffre issued a proclamation to the Alsatians welcoming them back to France and promising them that their local privileges would be respected. But the failure of the campaign of August meant that only a small fragment of Alsace remained in French hands: and there was, for long, no occasion to think of the problem of what should be done with Alsace when and if it was recovered.

The German collapse made the question suddenly urgent. It was easy enough to hold military parades in Metz and Strasbourg and to expel, overnight, the German professors of the university which had been made the instrument of Germanization in the province, a natural if regrettable action that evoked an astonishing amount of moral indignation in some circles outside France. But what was next to be done was not so clear. In some ways the Germans had made the French task easier. The loyalty of the Alsatians to their new masters was naturally suspect and, during the war, German rule had been rigorous and had undone much of the good that, from the German point of view, had been achieved before 1914. Then one great source of attraction for Alsatians had been the prestige of German arms and power—and that power of attraction was, for the moment, destroyed.

The Alsatians, in 1919 as in 1871, had the material advantage of being taken over by the victors. They were able, for example, to escape the great losses that befell the other parts of the old Reich as a result of the collapse of the mark, for the French changed Alsatian holdings of marks into francs at a high rate. The first few months after the Armistice were a kind of honeymoon; it did not last long. The problem was well put, years later, by the Senator (Canon) Muller of

Strasbourg, priest and politician. He rebuked the folly of the simple souls in France whose only thought was that the interregnum of 1870–1918 was over. To ignore these years and 'to bring back to France Alsace just as she had been when she was lost, is this not to suppress the very problem of Alsace and to escape any need or duty to understand and solve it? . . . Neither France nor Alsace has found each other as they were at the moment of separation. It is not merely two or three departments which have added themselves to other administrative units, it is the living and vibrating soul of Alsace which has returned to France, the soul of an Alsace which had become more conscious of her personality, which she had learned to defend against all attempts at oppression, strengthened in the struggle, jealous of the liberties she had conquered, accustoming herself to take into her own hands the care of her own business.' This Alsace, modified by German rule, accustomed to far greater local freedom than the French system permitted, provided with far more elaborate social legislation, with a far less prudent not to say stingy attitude to local expenditure, could not, without great political tact, be assimilated to the French system.

The French Government, to some extent, realized the existence of the problem. Instead of an immediate imposition of the French system, instead of the division of the Reichsland into the three quite separate departments that had existed in 1870, a High Commissioner was sent to Strasbourg to govern the two recovered provinces. The delicate task of governing Alsace was given to M. Alexandre Millerand, now a most staunch Nationalist, but not by that evolution deprived of those political talents, of that practical good sense which, in his Socialist past, had justified the choice of Waldeck-Rousseau. M. Millerand was not a doctrinaire, but a practical lawyer and administrator. He set up a consultative committee which, though it had no legal powers and consequently was no effective substitute for the Diet of the Reichsland, at least made it certain that Alsatian opinion was listened to and that decisions would not be made on a false assumption of complete identity between Alsace and the rest of France. But the work of adjusting Alsatian and French points of view required patience on both sides and in 1924 the French supply of patience was abruptly cut off.

One survival of German rule that was bound to attract the attention of French politicians was the continuation of the Concordat. Whether that agreement had any legal validity after the cession of Alsace to Germany was doubtful, but it had continued to be observed both by the Germans and by the French, after 1918. The Catholic, Protestant, and Jewish clergy were paid by the State, and the lay laws affecting education were not applied. To the Radicals, anxious to return to the political normality of pre-war days, this anomaly was intolerable— and the attack on it politically attractive. So in preparation for the electoral campaign of 1924, they denounced the clerical danger in general and the survival of clerical privileges in Alsace in particular. As all State schools in Alsace were 'confessional', this was equivalent to exclusion of the Republican teacher of the standard French type; and it was impossible to unify the educational systems, so long as this state of affairs lasted.

The new Prime Minister was M. Herriot, himself a member of 'the University', who was sympathetic to the complaints of his former colleagues and he profoundly offended the Catholics of Alsace by preparing to denounce the Concordat and to laicize the schools. The protest was not confined to the Catholics, for all the Alsatians who were opposed to the assimilationist policy of the French Government, evident enough even under the 'Bloc National', rallied round the clergy. The abolition of the office of High Commissioner and the transference of the central administration from Strasbourg to Paris were further proofs of the intention of the new Government to ignore the realities of the Alsatian scene.

The Radical error was natural enough. Alsace, before 1870, had been, if anything, an anti-clerical province; and before 1914, Left writers, like M. Maxime Leroy, saw in the Republican tradition of Alsace the best guarantee that France had left a permanent mark on the lost province. But under German rule, the clergy had been one of the main forces of organized opposition; and the spirit that, in Alsace before 1870, was Republican and anti-clerical, expressed itself after 1870 in opposition to German rule. The leaders in that opposition were often priests: and the Alsatians, like all other minority parties in the German Empire, were in something like a permanent alliance with the great minority party, the Catholic Centre. Then Alsace had not known the Sixteenth of May, or the failure of the *Ralliement*, or the Dreyfus case. The Alsatian equivalent of these crises was a series of contests with the German authorities in which the Catholic clergy had been on the popular side.

In Alsace, the priest was more in the position of a Polish or Irish than of a French priest; he was a natural leader of a predominantly peasant population. It was easy for Left doctrinaires, like the Alsatian Charles Andler, to put all the blame on the greed with which the Alsatian clergy clung to their stipends. That did not explain why the people followed the clergy in their opposition to the extension of the benefits of the lay laws to Alsace. The Governments of the 'Cartel des Gauches' were too weak to conquer determined resistance, and as they could not even withdraw the embassy from the Vatican, they could not annul the Concordat in Alsace or laicize the schools. The dictum attributed to Gambetta that 'anti-clericalism was not for export' had to be applied to the recovered provinces.

Peace on the religious front was not all that was required to restore good relations between the Government in Paris and the independent citizens of Alsace. The linguistic problem remained. Before 1870, the absence of compulsory education had meant that the language problem did not become acute. Yet even under the Second Empire there were signs in both Alsace and Lorraine of special difficulties. The Education Ministry was insistent that all instruction should be in French; the clergy who controlled the elementary schools were insistent that part, at least, of the school instruction should be in the mother tongue of the children: and that, in almost all Alsace, and in a considerable part of Lorraine, was some kind of German.

German rule had greatly complicated the situation. Before 1870, French had been the language of administration; it was spoken by all officials and by all the bourgeoisie, and learned by all conscripts. The commercial connections between Alsace and the rest of France fostered its use. Under German rule, except in a few communes, all instruction was in German and education was compulsory. All the prestige of the administration was now on the side of High German, which was closely linked with the Allemanic dialect of Alsace. Moreover, the emigration of so many of the leading families of the bourgeoisie was a loss to French speech and culture, the more seriously felt that there was a corresponding immigration of Germans. Alsace, in 1870, was a province in which all the upper- and middle-classes were bi-lingual, but with a preference for French, and in which the peasantry spoke a Germanic dialect. In 1918, it was a province in which everybody had a fair knowledge of High German in addition to the local dialect and in which French was, for most of the population, a foreign tongue. There was more of a sentimental attachment to it than there was actual knowledge of it.

At first sight, the policy adopted by France was not absurd. There were other regions of France where the mother tongue was not French; there were Breton and Flemish and Basque, all remote from French, as well as kindred Romance languages like Provençal. In school only French was taught, a policy that had justified itself by results; France was more linguistically united than any other great European power. But in Alsace the case was different. Across an open frontier or across the Rhine, German was the mother tongue and official tongue of the nearest neighbours of the Alsatians. It had been fostered for over a generation, whereas the other minority languages in France had never had patrons. More than that, German still had in the Reich a patron which saw in the linguistic patriotism of Alsace a way of keeping the 'Alsatian question' open, while southern Alsace was linked, historically and linguistically, to German Switzerland. It was childish to pretend that in such circumstances German could be treated like Basque or Breton.

Yet the French educational administrators were very reluctant to admit this truth. They saw that the main instrument of German penetration in Alsace was linguistic; by no means all Alsatians who habitually spoke German were disloyal to France, but all who were disloyal habitually spoke German. There were educational arguments too. The Alsatian dialect was not a highly developed literary language, and Alsatian High German suffered from dialectal impurities. Whereas, in Lorraine, everybody spoke good German or good French or both, in Alsace the beneficiary of the attack on French was not the language of Goethe but the language of Hans Snockeloch. Yet, despite these arguments, only an authoritarian government careless of its popularity could have enforced the linguistic uniformity aimed at by the school policy.

France in Alsace has not been willing to adopt the methods of Prussia in Poland. But neither has she been willing to abandon the view that has been the official doctrine since the time of the Convention, that in the Republic, one and indivisible, the language shall be an expression of that unity. German is taught in all schools but only for limited periods and it is not the language in which instruction in non-linguistic studies is given. But although the language question has been a source of irritation, its importance has been exaggerated. Alsatians who habitually speak the local dialect are not always willing to speak correct German even when they know it. Twenty years of French education have produced a class literate in French and therefore not disqualified from promotion in the French services. The ending in 1925 of the free market in Germany, provided for at Versailles, has shifted economic interests from the Reich to France, and communications between France and the recovered provinces have been greatly improved.

The faults of tact, to put it kindly, that marked the policy of the 'Cartel des Gauches' was one, but not the only, cause of the growth of the Autonomist movement in Alsace. With the recovery of Germany after the adoption of the Dawes plan, the Reich presented a more attractive spectacle than it had done in the years following the collapse of 1918. Curious political alliances between Alsatian Catholics and Communists angered both the Left and the Right in France, and a movement that tried to promote a federal solution of the Alsatian question was in French eyes suspect of merely being a blind for German-fostered sedition. The trial of the Autonomist leaders at Colmar in 1928 resulted in a few convictions, but the election of the martyrs to the Chamber resulted in their speedy pardon.[1] The Poincaré Government, although it undid some of the more offensive acts of the Herriot Government, was 'laic' and encouraged laicization of the

[1] Since the outbreak of the present war, one of the defendants at the 1928 trials has been executed for espionage.

schools; moreover, so rigorous a Lorraine patriot as Poincaré was not likely to be sympathetic to the demands of the Autonomists.

The rise of the Nazis complicated matters. On the one hand it encouraged the small party that wanted the re-annexation of Alsace to Germany; on the other, some sections which had been in violent or noisy opposition to the French Government, the Communists for instance, saw new merits in French rule. The 'Front Populaire' dallied with the idea of further laicization; and as the danger of war grew, Alsace suffered from its frontier character, since businessmen were reluctant to invest in so dangerous an area and the province pleaded, with good reason, for special economic help. The threat of war resulted in an increase of anti-Semitism, since the numerous Alsatian Jews were accused of wishing for a war against the oppressors of their race across the Rhine. Uncontrolled Communist agitation against the implacable enemy of the workers, Herr Hitler, was considered by the French Government to be too dangerous a luxury for a frontier, and, much to the indignation of the party, their freedom of anti-Nazi propaganda was limited.

When war at last came, Alsace was largely evacuated. Five hundred thousand of its people, scattered over France, especially in the south-west, represented an opportunity for mutual understanding that had not been known before. The exile of the children of the Rhine to the banks of the Garonne was yet another proof of the special hardships that befall a frontier folk. It was no new story for Alsace, in whose capital Rouget de Lisle had first sung the *Marseillaise*. That was not the only memory of Franco-German relations in Alsace. A few years before 1792 Goethe had been a student there; in the next century, the two greatest glories of the University of Strasbourg had been the Frenchman, Pasteur, and the German (for Jews could then be Germans), Ehrlich. To be a link between France and Germany was the true destiny of Alsace: a destiny which she may again be allowed to fulfil.

CHAPTER V

THE EMPIRE

I

IT was natural that post-war France should be more conscious of her Empire than pre-war France had been. The Empire had provided men and supplies on a great scale. The inferiority of French population to German had been dramatically illustrated, and it was comforting to talk of a France of 'one hundred million people', however far from reality such language was. The strain of the war had been badly felt, but the drain of troops (pushed to extremes that alarmed colonial officials like Van Vollenhoven) did mean that hundreds of thousands of French subjects saw France, and the demand for raw materials fostered a rapid, if not always a healthy growth. In the fervour of war, too, promises were made of political advance which it was difficult if not impossible to fulfil in peace-time, and if the French Empire did not suffer as much from post-war nationalism as the British, it did not escape altogether.

As was natural, it was in Indo-China that the political authority of France was most directly challenged. Closely connected economically and psychologically with South China, the States of the Union, especially Tonkin, were caught up in the revolutionary fervour of the Chinese. Not only were Chinese immigrants extremely powerful in the economic life of the Union and treated by t e Administration with the circum-spection their powerful and uncontrollable organizations made prudent, but it was easy for the young Tonkinese Nationalists to read very encouraging lessons in the Japanese victory of 1905, the Chinese revolution of 1912 and the Russian revolution of 1917. Canton was the centre of all these movements, so far as they affected Chinese nationalism. It was in Canton that the alliance of the heirs of Sun Yet Sen and Lenin had its headquarters, and from Canton to Hanoi was not far in space or spirit.

Some concessions were made to the new age. In the Federal Government and in the States, native representation in the consultative councils was increased; but not only were the powers of the councils limited, in all of them there were still French majorities. M. Albert Sarraut, who had been sent back to the great colony as Governor-General, found that it was harder to satisfy native aspirations than it had been before the war. The new University of Hanoi was only a limited success, as far as breeding a generation of natives, French in spirit as well as in formal training, was its object. The eager imitators of Chiang Kai Shek and Borodin were not to be put off by mere constitutional window-dressing.

One real grievance of the native intellectuals was to a large degree met. The improvement in the quality of the civil service that had been one of the most valuable reforms of the pre-war Sarraut régime, was maintained; and a Socialist Governor-General, Alexandre Varenne, greatly increased the range of posts open to native ambition. In Annam, a young Emperor who had been largely educated in France, was the formal and, to some extent, the real initiator of reforms in his Empire. But there had been at least one great scandal in war-time, which was not only disgraceful in itself but whose inadequate punishment showed that the ideal of equal justice between the races was still far from being realized. If there was no blood barrier between rulers and ruled like that raised by the Amritsar massacre in India, there was not enough kinship of spirit and mutual trust to inoculate Indo-China against propaganda from across the frontier.

There were not merely literary and political demonstrations of nationalist discontent, there were outbreaks of violence beginning in 1930 and attacking each of the three eastern States in turn. There was even the very dangerous symptom of an army mutiny which was rigorously suppressed. The envy which the Indo-Chinese Nationalists experienced at the sight of the triumphs of their kinsmen in China was diminished by the feud between the Communists and their allies of the Kuomintang; and the inability of the Kuomintang to resist Japanese aggression effectively made French protection less intolerable to the most ardent spirits. Peasant discontent was, of course, largely a matter of good or bad crops and prices; and the world depression was a great blow to the hitherto flourishing Union. With the decision of the rulers of Russia to support an allied government, Communism became less of a menace to French authority in Indo-China [1] than it had been; it was external aggression from Japan, irritated at the use of French roads and railways as a means of supplying the Chinese armies, that the French Government had now most to fear.

In North Africa, the war and its aftermath brought new problems. France had drawn more heavily on North Africa for troops than on any other part of the Empire; there was a far more frequent movement of population across the Mediterranean than was possible between France and any other colony ; and if the transitory immigrants from North Africa to France learned French in their exile and were, in many ways, modernized, they also learned modern political ideas which

---

[1] One of the leaders of the Fourth (Trotskyite) International is a municipal councillor of Saigon.

were inconvenient for the French Administration when the labourers returned home.

It was in Tunis that the Nationalist movement took deepest root, and this was natural enough. Tunis was purely Arab speaking; it was influenced by the course of events in Egypt, by the successful escape of that country from direct British tutelage; and there was a marked and depressing difference between the consultative assemblies, local and central, set up by the new Bey in 1922 and the full-fledged Egyptian Parliament controlled by the Wafd. French rule, from the point of view of the young educated Tunisians, petrified Tunisian political life. But for French support, the Bey could not have resisted the political demands of his subjects. Tunis, from this point of view, was worse off than if she had been in the position of Algeria. For the direct representation of Algeria in the French Parliament meant that, where the economic interests of both colonists and natives were alike (as they often were), they were represented in the sovereign assembly.

The Tunisian 'Constitutional' parties, the old and the new 'Destour', were simply milder and less mild examples of the Nationalist parties that were active all over the colonial world in the post-war era. For a brief time, the régime of the dying liberal governments of Italy made Libya seem more attractive to politically minded Arabs than Tunisia; but Fascism soon removed this temptation to disloyalty to France, and the rigorous methods of Italian conquest and colonization made Tunisians less anxious for a change of masters which, it seemed likely in an age more and more dominated by power politics, was the only choice open to a naturally pacific people.

Italy had, however, her own reasons for encouraging Tunisian discontent. Although the number of French citizens in Tunis first equalled and then surpassed the number of Italians, the increase was due more to the naturalization of Italians than to the increase of genuine French settlement. In the Regency, the Italians still supplied most of the labour force, the French most of the capital and technical skill. If the French counted, with reason, on the dislike of the not very industrious Tunisians for the severe competition of the Italian immigrant labourers, the Italians counted on the strong anti-Jewish feeling that it was easy to rouse. It was significant that the Jews provided more pupils for the *lycée* of Tunis than did the vastly greater native population, and they were far more numerous in the professions and official classes than their numbers suggested as likely. That the fault was that of the Tunisian Moslems, who would not abandon their ancestral ways of life and learning, was no effective political answer. But the simple fact that under French rule in Tunis the native population doubled while under Italian rule in Libya it halved could be understood, especially as the frontier between the two countries was easily crossed, even although the increasing population did not benefit, proportionately, by the great growth in wealth in the Protectorate. And to the old disease of typhus (which the French fought with great skill, so far as native social habits allowed them), was added the new vice of tea-drinking, more deadly than the religiously banned alcohol would have been.

In Algeria, the war promises were peculiarly hard to fulfil. To extend the franchise indiscriminately to all the male population, or even to a considerable part of it, would be to swamp the colonists. The continued insistence on the abandonment of their personal status by the Moslems was a complete barrier, in fact, to political assimilation. The old grievance of the automatic naturalization of the Jews still rankled and the wider representation of the native population on the local government bodies was no substitute for complete political equality. Only a few thousand Arabs were naturalized after the war. But in Algeria the thoroughness of French conquest had its advantages. The new native bourgeoisie was the product of French rule and French education. Real equality was open to the few who chose to pay the price. French was the language even of Arab discontent; literacy in French was rapidly increasing, as far as the male population was concerned; and, with the coming of wireless, for the first time the French Administration had an opportunity to penetrate to the hitherto closed world of Moslem women. Within Islam in Algeria, modern ideas were telling, if only because of the penetration of the natural leaders of the people by French culture. The dream of a mere extension of France across the Mediterranean was an illusion, but in Algeria, at least, France had made a new Arab society beside the colonial society. Their fusion was still an aspiration, not an achievement.

French North Africa had been cut off from the rest of French Africa by a more effective barrier than the sea, the Sahara, but the formidable character of that barrier was rapidly reduced in the post-war years by the development of motor and air transport. Journeys that, by camel, took weeks, were done by car in days and by aeroplane in hours. The remote and inaccessible mountains of the Hoggar in the heart of the great desert were turned, overnight, into a mere post on the trans-Saharan bus lines and the formidable Tuaregs, the veiled warriors of the desert, were tamed and turned into valuable tourist assets like the Sioux or Hopis, but what took a generation in the American West took only a few years in the Sahara. It was dramatically fitting that the great master of the old Sahara, General Laperrine, should have been killed making an aeroplane reconnaissance of the desert that till then had only known the camel caravan. Soon after his death, the special desert bus and the aeroplane made the long projected trans-Saharan railway no longer necessary and Timbuctu no longer mysterious.

If the desert was in one sense conquered, in another it went on conquering, for it continued to encroach on the fertile lands of the coastal hinterland, Lake Tchad continued to shrink and the great French West African domain every year lost on its inner edge more habitable land to the advancing sand. The post-war settlement had rounded off that great colony by the acquisition of Togoland and most of the Cameroons, as well as by restoring to France the Congo territories ceded to Germany after the crisis of 1911. Of these acquisitions, the most valuable was the Cameroons. This colony was held under mandate, but the vigilance of the League was not enough to prevent the French (as in Syria) from evading the prohibition of forced labour and, at great immediate cost, the old German colony was transformed. The new roads and bridges, paid for in the sweat of one generation, were of the greatest benefit to the next and in the Cameroons a tyrannical system of sanitary control wrought a miraculous improvement in public health.

After as before the war of 1914, the French Congo was the weakest of the African colonies and its stagnation and the survival of some of the old abuses of the company system made it the least creditable part of the French Empire. The contrast with the Belgian Congo was humiliating, and a brilliant man of letters, André Gide, called the attention of his countrymen to the seamy side of their rule in Africa, to the delight of the most severe critics of the régime, the Communists.[1]

It was in Negro Africa that the policy of making over native society in a French fashion achieved most success. The comparative absence of colour-prejudice continued to be politically profitable, and when the agitation for the return of the colonies to the Third Reich became serious, it was a stroke of genius to translate and circulate the relevant passages of *Mein Kampf* among such natives as might have thought—if any did—that a return to German rule was likely to be to their advantage.

The neglected parts of the Empire were still the old colonies. The French West Indies, like the British, were stagnating; the attempt to colonize Guiana by time-expired convicts was less hopeful than it had ever been, since no one even pretended to retain any of the faith in the beneficent social effects of the system that had been proclaimed by Joseph Reinach and the young Gambettists. The Pacific islands suffered from the great loss of population that civilization had brought, and attempts to use Indo-Chinese labour had merely provided the politicians of the Union with further materials for inflammatory oratory. The fishing islands of the St. Lawrence knew a brief period of boom as long as American prohibition lasted, but like the Bahamas after 1865 when blockade running ceased, the golden day of Saint-Pierre and Miquelon came to an end with the experiment noble in

[1] When M. Gide applied the same critical standards, the same refusal to be taken in by the official façade, to Soviet Russia, the Communists had reason to deplore their thoughtless praise of his honesty and intelligence.

purpose. It seemed, indeed, that what the Republic had not founded it could not develop. The real difficulties of the old colonies came from their age; they were relics of an earlier economic system, survivals of a time when the sugar islands were the great prize of war. In the modern world they were the equivalent of the ghost towns of a mining area, only these ghost towns had still a large, indeed an unduly large population. What to do with that population was a question not perhaps insoluble if thought and energy had been devoted to it; but neither was.

II

In 1914, France had only secured the recognition by the great powers of her right to endeavour to control Morocco; the control itself was still to be achieved. Legally France, in Morocco as in Tunis, had all the authority of the native ruler, but not only was the authority of the Bey much more real than the authority of the Sultan, the problem of making his nominal rule effective was far less complicated. Morocco was much larger, its mountains much more difficult to control than were the Tunisian plains, and its peoples were far more warlike than the docile inhabitants of the Regency. By the outbreak of war in 1914, French authority was confined to the coast and a few easily accessible regions, but the Resident, General Lyautey, was skilfully supplementing the threat of the 60,000 men of his army with the tact and political ingenuity he had learned in Indo-China and Madagascar. The outbreak of war made it fortunate that he had not merely relied on force, for he was deprived of the force. Most of his best troops, French and native, were sent off to fight in France: and, for four years, Lyautey had to rely on bluff and on persuading the Moroccans that the newcomers were not so intolerable a menace to their life and traditions as they had feared. When peace came the area of French authority had not shrunk, it had grown.

The Moroccan problem, as Lyautey saw it, was three-fold. French peace and order was to be established over all the regions where the Sultan nominally ruled (except the Spanish enclave). Not merely in form, but in fact, native rights and prejudices were to be respected; only so could French authority spread peacefully over the land. Lastly, Morocco was to be opened to European development only as rapidly as was compatible with the first two objectives.

For this delicate task, Lyautey was admirably equipped. He had lived most of his life in the colonies and if, as his brief and unfortunate experience as Minister of War in 1916 showed, that had unfitted him for life in France, the converse was that he was really sympathetic to the ways and prejudices of backward peoples. His own aristocratic manner, his aloofness from the standards of the day, his æsthetic

appreciation of the life of his subjects made him fit to cajole as well as
to coerce. He was a great European ruler, more than a little de-
Europeanized. In his palace at Rabat he was not merely in form a
Grand Vizier of the Sultan. There were none of those mistakes in tact
that had weakened what might have been the useful authority of the
crown, in Annam and Cambodia. The authority of the Descendant
of the Prophet was made manifest in all outward show, to the great
advantage of the real beneficiary of that authority. Lyautey had been
brought up in Legitimist circles; he could use the divinity that hedged
a king because he had once believed in it. He had been brought up,
too, in Catholic circles and he could understand the place religion
played in Moroccan life, in this last western outpost of Islam on the
Atlantic. Respect for the religion and traditions of the country came
easily to him and was imposed on his subordinates. There were no
profanations of sanctuaries such as had occurred, as lately as the conquest of Tunis, in the most holy city of Kairouan.

Lyautey knew Islam too well, however, to wish it to have an un-
checked authority, and in Morocco it was possible to do something to
counterbalance it. Morocco was the extreme edge of the Arab-speak-
ing world and Arabic grew thinner the farther west one went. It was
the universal tongue in Tunis, almost so in eastern Algeria, less and less
so as one moved south from the coast and west to the ocean. With
Arabic went the Koran and Islamic theology, the literary and linguistic
links that bound together all the peoples which looked to the university
of El Azhar in Cairo for sacred learning and political inspiration.

In Morocco there were many regions where Arabic, the Koran and,
except in a formal sense, Islam were unknown. There the Berbers,
without a written tongue of their own, should be taught French; there
France would get in first and surround the Arabic-speaking coastal
plain and nearer hills with a Berberia modernized by French language
and civilization. That this should be done successfully meant that
war had to be avoided. French ways and speech were not to be taught
in Morocco, any more than in Madagascar, at the point of the bayonet.
The great Kaids of the Atlas in their mountain castles were to be won
over, by kindness and by fair dealing, to accept French rule and then,
slowly, to accept French ways. If they resisted they were to be crushed;
but it was hoped that few would resist, and if only one or two did,
crushing them would not be an unduly difficult or long business.

The Moors of the cities, the officials, the priests, would dislike all
this and, in fact, like the Orthodox Hindus, they developed a novel
missionary spirit when their control of their neglected brethren in the
faith was threatened, but the Moors of the towns were no great military
threat. And short of allowing them to interfere in the Berber country,
all their susceptibilities were carefully considered, even pandered to.

It was fortunate for Lyautey that, in addition to many other great qualities, he was a good advertiser. For his policy cost vast sums of money and a great deal of political patience. It involved a frank admission that, over a great part of Morocco, France did not exercise effective authority and a refusal to try to hasten the day when her writ would run over all her nominal territory. The policy of conciliating the Moors meant that in Morocco (unlike Algeria and unlike even Tunisia) great areas of fertile land had to be left in native hands to be badly farmed or not farmed at all when, if the natives could be induced to sell or lease, modern methods would immensely increase the yield. But Lyautey knew, if the eager colonists did not, that the lands they held or claimed in the plains at the foot of their hill fortresses were hostages which the Kaids had given to French rule. To rebel meant to lose their chief source of income. A rapid exploitation of the plains that involved a great war in the hills would be a very bad bargain.

It was only in certain areas then that, apart from modern roads and good order, modern civilization in the usual sense of the term was evident, as it was in Algeria or Tunisia. But if most of Morocco was left to its old barbaric ways, there were enough miracles of modern development to stifle criticism, as long as all went well. The mud-huts of the miserable little town of Casablanca gave way in less than twenty years to a magnificent modern city and port. All over the coastal regions, new European towns grew up beside the old Arab towns. But Lyautey was careful not to let the new cities crush the old or reduce them to mere slums imbedded in the new European cities as had happened in Algiers and Tunis. The old and new cities were kept separate. The twelfth century lived complete and intact a mile or so from the twentieth, and at Casablanca a new native city was built in native style. It must be admitted that the new towns gave a false impression of what had been achieved, for the tenderness for native land rights had made large-scale colonization practically impossible, to the indignation of some of the Algerian colonists who had an American frontiersman's attitude to a policy that kept land untilled out of exaggerated respect for legal rights that the Moroccans hardly understood. But Morocco had many sources of wealth: and even with the immobilization of so much of the land, it was able to borrow cheaply and pay for all but the purely military costs of its Government. In ten years wonders had been done and it was with general consent that the great ruler was known as 'Lyautey Africanus'.

Although a soldier by profession and one of the Marshals created after the war, Lyautey was not a soldier in the narrow sense of the term. He was not perhaps soldier enough, for he neglected the military risks of his political policy. He was not altogether to blame, for the risks were not of his making. They arose from the diplomatic compromise by which Delcassé had bought off Spanish opposition to his schemes. Spain was given a share in the booty; a strip of Morocco opposite Gibraltar behind her garrison town of Tetuan. Tetuan was a name dear to the Spanish Army, for it commemorated one of the few victories won by that army in the nineteenth century in other than civil war. With the expulsion of the Spaniards from Cuba, Morocco became the only place where Spanish officers could be kept busy and a series of generally disastrous campaigns served, though very expensively, to justify promotions and titles. In 1921, however, came the disaster of Anual; the greatest defeat suffered by a European army at native hands since Adowa. The victor was a chieftain of the Riff, Abd el Krim, whose fame naturally spread through all North Africa. The Moslem world was triumphing in the west as well as in the east (if we can count Kemal as a Moslem). The defeat of the Spaniards was awkward for the peace of French Morocco, but the victor of Anual had still a good deal to do in the way of expelling the Spaniards from their garrisons. Among the repercussions of his victory was a military *pronunciamento* in Spain; and the new dictator, Primo de Rivera, had the courage to cut the losses and to withdraw, slowly and with difficulty, to the coast.

Meantime, the French advance had impinged on what the Riffs deemed to be their territory. Flushed with victory, Abd el Krim launched an attack that nearly carried him to the gates of Fez. Lyautey was not prepared for war on this scale, and the greatest compliment that was paid the Kaid was the hurried despatch of no less a person than Marshal Pétain to redress the fortune of war. The Riffs found that Pétain and the French were very different opponents from Primo de Rivera and the Spaniards. Worse still, they had given the Spaniards an opportunity, and a joint campaign in 1926 ended the career of the new Abd el Kader. As was right, it was to the French that he surrendered, and they exiled him to Réunion in the Indian Ocean.

The Riff war gave the enemies of Lyautey their chance. He was blamed for its outbreak and for its early disasters; the junction in one hand of military and political authority was attacked, and a civilian Resident General, the eminent Left politician, M. Steeg, was sent to replace him.[1]

The Marshal had made mistakes as well as enemies. There was native resentment in Morocco, despite all his tact, for the impact of modern economic life on the Protectorate often found the Moroccans ill-prepared for the shock. The large Jewish population was a further problem, for it was regarded not as part of the ruling race, but as an inferior branch of the ruled; yet the Jews were far more easily Europeanized than were the Arabs, who, themselves refusing to abandon their old ways, regarded with a jealous eye the progress of more adaptable

---

[1] As Morocco has continued to be an international storm centre, France has fallen back on soldiers to rule for her in this very debatable land.

Jews. Economically a new country, Morocco suffered from boom and slump as speculative waves rose and fell and, as a primary producer, she, like all primary producers, gained less in the fat years, and suffered more in the lean than did industrialized countries. But by the time of the official conclusion of 'pacification' in 1934, Morocco had been transformed. And that transformation, on the whole so peaceful and so successful, was mainly the work of one man who, with his political and religious views, would have found it hard to be a deputy and impossible (in peace-time) to be a Minister of the Republic. Fortunately for France, in the Army there was a perpetual *Ralliement* going on.

In Syria, France had to face a problem more complicated than any facing her in North Africa. In North Africa, she had been the dominant power for a century; modern civilization and modern ideas had come to the Maghreb in French dress; no outside power, except Egypt and the common feeling of Islam, exercised much attraction upon native opinion. But in Syria, France was a new-comer and an unwelcome new-comer, except in the Christian part of the Lebanon where the delivery from the extremes of Turkish misrule by the troops of Napoleon III was gratefully remembered. There was, of course, an old and real intellectual relation between all Syria and France, but in modern times the American missionaries had been potent rivals of the Jesuits at Beyrouth, and nascent Arab nationalism preferred the infidels with no political axe to grind to the infidels who were, and thought themselves to be, in some degree the advance guard of French influence. It was an American investigation that, in 1919, had produced the best evidence of Syrian hostility to French rule.

More important, however, was the contagion of Arab nationalism from the surrounding lands. Jewish immigration into Palestine irritated Arabs all over Syria, of which Palestine, in Arab eyes, was only a wrongfully detached fragment. In Egypt and in Iraq, Arab nationalism was in constant effervescence against British rule and it was inevitable that France should have to face the same problem. It was true that, as the French maintained, Syrian unity was not a reality as yet; and the division of the French territory into four autonomous states by General Gouraud was defensible—on paper. But except in the Lebanon it worked badly, if only by artificially dividing the most irreconcilable sections into the two states of Aleppo and Damascus. General Weygand undid Gouraud's work, and although the union of Aleppo and Damascus and the abolition of the top-heavy federal system were probably necessary, they gave to the rule of the protecting power an air of impermanence that it could not afford.

The Weygand system was not given a chance to prove its worth, for after the triumph of the Left in 1924 it was considered out of the question to leave a reactionary Catholic in charge of an area where the religious question was so important. But the exposed situation of Syria seemed to demand a soldier ruler. And who more deserving than the martyred Sarrail? So he was given a third chance to show what a good Radical soldier could do.

It did not take Sarrail long to decide that Weygand had unduly favoured the Christians of the Lebanon, but despite their freedom from Jesuit influence the other tribes did not display the proper spirit. In Syria, as in the Cameroons, the French passion for public works had been pushed to what were politically speaking, dangerous extremes. Syria was to be provided with roads, bridges, tunnels, irrigation, all of them things she needed, but she was given them in a hurry and largely by forced labour. These Russian methods caused discontent in the towns and plains; they caused more than discontent in the mountains. Sarrail, having invited some Druse chiefs to consult with him about their grievances, promptly arrested them on their arrival at Damascus and found himself with a rebellion on his hands.

The rebellion spread and Sarrail was attacked in his own stronghold of Damascus, a threat to his authority which forced him, in his opinion, to bombard the city. A government which has to destroy considerable parts of cities it professes to rule is not likely to be loved or respected, as the British authorities could have told Sarrail, after their experiences in Cork. Even if the first fine fervour of electoral enthusiasm of 1924 had lasted until 1926, General Sarrail's friends might have felt that, whatever his merits, he had one unpardonable fault, he was unlucky. But the Radicals had, by 1926, more to worry about than the reputation of their General. Sarrail, like Lyautey, was recalled and a more tactful civilian, the aristocratic Left politician, Henri de Jouvenel, was sent to replace him.

It was possible by force and tact to put down the rebellion; it was harder to quiet the Syrian nationalists who clung to two simple beliefs; that Syria was a unit (and included Palestine) and that neither France nor Britain had any right to be there at all. The old ill-feeling between the British and French officials had not wholly died down; each saw the recurrent troubles of the other with a moderately distressed eye and each believed that the other did less than he should in the way of preventing the use of Transjordania—or Syria—or Palestine—as a base for intrigue or open war against the authority of the other mandatory.

The Syrians had been promised a constitution, but between what they claimed and what the French were willing to grant there remained a great difference. The Syrians looked to Iraq and Egypt with envy, but they ought, thought the French, to be looking to Palestine with gratitude that their fate was better than that of their brethren. In 1930, France granted a constitution much in the manner of Louis XVIII granting a charter and, despite protests, the Syrians had to accept the fact or risk another rebellion. As in all the Moslem territories of France, land tenure was an almost insoluble problem, for the great absentee landlords kept the peasantry so poor as to make it hard for any Administration (not prepared for revolutionary measures) to do much for them. And Syria in the twentieth century was a poor, underpopulated land, a shadow of what it was reported to have been in classical times. It had far fewer natural resources than had French North Africa, and the mandatory power had not that sense of personal interest and permanent authority which had made France willing to ignore narrow bookkeeping considerations and make the great capital investment which had transformed her North African territories.

CHAPTER VI

BACK TO POLITICS

I

THE disillusionment bred in Socialist ranks by the failure of the 'Cartel des Gauches' to overcome the resistance of the money power, followed as it was, by the unsatisfactory character of the elections of 1928, might have revived the revolutionary fervour of the first post-war years. But the general prosperity, the absence of unemployment, the fact that a great part of the true proletariat, with little or nothing to lose but their chains, was foreign, voteless and resident in France only on sufferance, made the prospects of that 'holiday from legality', of which even Socialist leaders had found it necessary to talk, very far from bright. If in the elections of 1928, the official revolutionary party, the Communists, had gained 200,000 votes, they had won only fourteen seats—and not one of these, even in the reddest areas, had been won on the first ballot. Nowhere, that is to say, was there a mass of revolutionary-minded workers from which a great mass movement could come. The Communist deputies, for all their verbal intransigence, were elected in part by bourgeois voters who discounted the verbal violence of their representatives as they had discounted, for two generations past, all Left oratory. The electors liked a good show of ideological purity, but they expected it to be translated into tangible favours like better local roads, petty local patronage, minor adjustments of the administrative machine.

In a rural department, Communism often had an odd appearance; its leaders might be leaders of a local faction rather than agents of a world conspiracy. Peasants had always voted, in some departments, for the reddest candidate and they still did. But they were not voting for the immediate expropriation of all private property since they were nearly all proprietors and, in many cases, *kulaks* at that. The rural Communist leader learned to wear his red with a difference, except at election meetings, just as the officials of the Ministry of Agriculture learned to suspend the pursuit of the Colorado beetle at election times where an influential voter was concerned. In rural France, all political doctrines had to be translated and the sense of property was regrettably strong. The Socialists recognized this; and their rural expert, M.

Compère-Morel, had assured the peasant that only the lazy, non-working landowner had anything to fear from Socialism. The peasant proprietors would be left to cultivate their own land until, educated by co-operatives and syndicates, in good time that land became 'by their own will, the collective property of the whole world of labour'. But that good time was far off, as candidates very well knew. Until it was nearer, Socialists could replace Radicals, especially in the traditionally red departments of the Midi.

With the recognition of Soviet Russia by France (October 1924), the relations of the two countries were formally put on the usual basis. But they were in reality bound to remain highly unusual as long as France had a powerful Communist party which, whatever its pretensions to autonomy, was known to be effectually under the control of the Comintern whose own permanent harmony of views with those current in the Kremlin was miraculous, if spontaneous. It had long been customary to accuse various parties in France of taking a lead from foreign powers; the Conservatives had been abused as the mere agents of the Vatican, the Socialists as mere agents of Germany. But these charges had been largely electoral and, although not ineffective propaganda at elections, were not taken too seriously after the ballots had been counted. The case of the Communists was very different. They were directly influenced by a government whose policy was directed either to the aggrandizement of Russia or to the spread of world revolution.

The French Communists could not and, at that time, did not pretend to accept the doctrine that the security of the French State was a first charge on any political policy. From the old slogan that the workers had no country, they had moved to the position that they had a country, the 'Workers' Fatherland', the Union of Socialist, Soviet Republics. Much of what they said could have been paralleled from past Socialist speeches and manifestoes, but the Communist leaders meant it. They were not likely to follow the slippery path that had led Guesde, for all his formal Marxism, to joining a government of National Defence in 1914. They were not content to reproach the governing parties in France with their imperialism; they took active steps in Indo-China, in Morocco, wherever the French Empire was assailed, to aid the assailants. How was it possible in these circumstances to admit the Communist deputies to all the rights of the other parliamentarians, to admit them to the Committees of the Chamber, to make available to them the confidential information that was given the ordinary deputy?

To a degree unknown to the Guesdists, the Communists were an immediately revolutionary party, not waiting for a parliamentary majority or tainted with the patriotic sentimentalism of the Blanquists. They dreamed of a speedy repetition of the great days of 1917. More than that, as the revolutionary tide moved at different levels in different countries, as the Comintern, having launched a disastrously ineffective campaign in one country, turned to another to try out its well-tested recipes for defeat, the issues and slogans had to vary. French workers, alarmed at local wage-cuts or sore over unsuccessful strikes, were called on to debate theses of great immediate interest in Moscow but somewhat remote from Lille or Saint-Denis. Local campaigns were started and stopped on distant orders from the Comintern, conducting the revolutionary war with all the pedantic complacency of an Austrian Aulic Council combating General Bonaparte.

Apparently adopting as their principle that it was not in mortals to command success and that it was quite enough to deserve it, the Communist press had to chronicle a long series of gallant fights against hopeless odds whose failure was always due to some subordinate, never to the distant Commander-in-Chief. Trusting in the shortness of memory of the workers and still more of the sentimental intellectuals, regretting the existence of files of *Humanité* not safely under party control, but ever faithful (apart from the steady loss of traitors expelled or disillusioned leaders who resigned) to the *mot d'ordre* from Moscow, the French Communists went on their way. Their chief enemy was not the openly capitalist leaders, the Tardieus or Poincarés, but the 'Socialist-Fascists', the 'Socialist-cops', the Blums, Faures, Salengros. French political controversy was never tender of private lives, but a new record of abuse was set up: the finances, the love-affairs, the war records of Socialist leaders, all were attacked with the use of all the arts of scurrility, to the delight of Right controversialists who now needed to go no further to find ammunition against the leaders of the growing Socialist party, than to the columns of the paper which bore the name of Jaurès on its front page.

It was easy to be intransigent in the Chamber, or at great public meetings; it was harder, when the party got control of a municipality, to avoid all collaboration with the bourgeois order. For one thing, the mayor of a French commune is an officer of the Central Government, although elected by the local council. If a Communist mayor refused to carry out his duties to the Central Administration, that did not mean that the bourgeois state was seriously handicapped, it merely meant that an official took the place of the mayor. Communal autonomy was too valuable an asset for the party for it to be prudent to risk its loss merely to annoy the Administration. There were, of course, frequent conflicts between Communist municipalities and the Central Government. But they were usually, on the surface at any rate, over such mundane matters as inadequate book-keeping at Alès or Villeurbanne or bonuses rashly paid in a Mediterranean village for the capture of what, Paris asserted, were mythical sharks.

The Communist-controlled municipality was more likely to be distinguished by its reformist activities than by its doctrinal rigour. French local government had one characteristic common to nearly every part of France: thriftiness. The local tax-payers did not tolerate in their local government the lavishness that was reproached to the Central Government by Conservative critics. As long as the taxes were kept low, very meagre social services contented a thrifty and independent population. This thriftiness was, by some, attributed to the powers of financial veto that the law gave to the prefect, but when it is remembered that the mayor of every important town was an important politician, it is difficult to believe that this veto could not have been got round, or over, had the mayor wanted to do so. The obsolete taxing system of the *octroi*,[1] provided very inelastic revenue, but enterprising mayors, like M. Herriot in Lyons, could abolish the *octroi*. The French citizen got from his local government as much as he was willing to pay for. That was not much, and he was as reluctant to borrow as to tax. No great country had a less debt-burdened system of local government than France.

Even before the rise of the Communist party there were cities, Lyons was one, where a bolder local policy was attempted. But Communist municipalities did, as a matter of principle, spend as lavishly as the law allowed. It was their only chance to control the distribution of the national wealth and they took it. Sometimes the results were comic, like the building of a lavish modern lavatory in a mountain village; sometimes impressive, like the ultra-modern housing schemes of Villeurbanne near Lyons. But it was around Paris that the party was strongest and its municipal policy most profitable, politically and socially. After the war, the rapid outpouring of the population of central Paris into the semi-rural communes of the Seine and Seine-et-Oise presented problems for which the old-fashioned communal council was ill-prepared. The new-comers were often victims of ingenious real estate dealers; they were still more often victims of the post-war housing shortage and they soon found themselves in the majority in the surrounding communes. They had plenty of grievances; there were no decent roads or drains or street lights. The timid Radical politicians of the old order shuddered at the thought of the cost of the necessary improvements. The Communists, in any case strong in a population largely recruited from Paris workers of the old revolutionary quarters, took their chance. They would provide what the 'badly-housed' party wanted. They did and, regardless of financial prudence, the electors got roads, drains, lights; the swamps where they were forced to dwell were made more habitable, and many a district was firmly welded to the party by methods that recall Joseph Chamberlain in Birmingham more than Lenin in Petrograd.

Nor was it only in local government that the Communists found themselves forced to make concessions to the world they lived in. They

[1] A tax on consumption goods entering the commune.

were far more purely a proletarian party than were the Socialists, and that was revealed in the social origin of their candidates, but it was revealed more in the candidates than in the deputies, since for some reason or other, the Communist candidate who got elected tended to be much less proletarian than the run of the members of the party. After all, every bourgeois Communist deputy owed something to bourgeois electors, even if it was only changing the cap of the workers for the hat of the bourgeois once he had been elected! The difference between the social composition of the two workers' parties was reflected in the trade-union movements that represented their industrial side. The old Federation of Unions, the C.G.T., was in fact closely linked with the Socialist party ; it represented the reformist tendencies that had developed during the war. It was far more ready to trust the capitalist state than was its Communist rival, the 'Unified' Federation, and this was natural, as a far higher proportion of its members were State employees who could benefit by political pressure and could double political with industrial action. It even dallied with the idea of compulsory arbitration, again not unnaturally, for, as the employers' 'Union of the Metallurgical and Mining Industries' pointed out, compulsory arbitration would greatly strengthen the position of the unions. 'It would give them a rôle out of all proportion to their numerical strength; this is far less than is thought.' The Communist unions were bitterly opposed to such an organization in the capitalist state, though even they had to swallow their principles when there was a chance of making tangible gains for a body of strikers through state action. The C.G.T. was ready to work within the framework of the capitalist state, even to accept compulsory insurance, though it meant workers' contributions. The Communists attempted to preserve an attitude of complete non-coöperation with the bourgeois state, but in trade union as in municipal politics, they had to make concessions to the realism of the rank and file. Neither party in the golden days of the boom was, or looked like, a menace to the established order of things which had made such a miraculous recovery from the ordeal of war.

II

'I never saw, heard, nor read that the clergy were beloved in any nation where Christianity was the religion of the country. Nothing can render them popular but some degree of persecution.' This was the opinion of Jonathan Swift; and that he was right seemed to be suggested by the greater popular favour enjoyed by the Church in France since her disestablishment and since the way to power in the State had become more easily open to her enemies than to her friends. Catholicism was no longer 'the religion of the majority of Frenchmen,' although its rites were still important in the life of the great majority. Even in the red zone round Paris, in the new Communist municipalities, most people were married in church (although only the civil ceremony had any legal effect); most children were baptized; and an overwhelming majority had religious funerals.

As an eminent French Protestant [1] reminded his non-Catholic countrymen, it was always risky for Protestants and Jews to mix too openly in the quarrels between zealous Catholics and anti-clericals of Catholic origin. There were few of the last class in whose family archives was not preserved a photograph of a scourge of the priests wearing the white arm-band of the first communicant. The priest was 'part of the furniture' of traditional French life, and the anti-clerical fight was in some degree a family quarrel. Whatever chance M. Herriot had had, in 1924, of quietly and quickly breaking off diplomatic relations with the Vatican and abrogating the Concordat in Alsace-Lorraine had been diminished by his tactlessness in making his intentions first public in a letter beginning 'My dear Blum'. It was not only in Alsace (where anti-Semitism was always ready to be awakened), but in most parts of France that the letter had been regarded as a gaffe.

In any case it was increasingly hard to whip up enthusiasm for campaigns against the Church. Catholics attributed this change too much to the realization that the clergy had produced good soldiers, that the religion of Foch, Pétain, Guynemer was not necessarily contemptible. It was due even more to the practical acceptance by French Catholics of their position as a religious minority. The Church was no longer a menace to the State. Publicists like M. Maurice Charny, politicians like M. Maurice Allard might sound the alarm at clerical designs. The cynical, on both sides, might comment on the fact that the family whose paper was the Bible of Radicalism married a daughter in the Cathedral of Toulouse and not merely at the Capitol, which was all the law demanded, but M. Sarraut was only doing what all good bourgeois and most working-class families did. The anti-clericalism of a Left comic paper like the *Canard Enchaîné* was almost as much a standard and stale joke as adultery was in *La Vie Parisienne*.

In most regions of France, the Church was not a centre of regular interest for more than a minority of the population. In general, the regions where the Church was strong were Conservative in politics, although some politically Conservative regions, like Normandy, were far from being deeply religious. But even in very Catholic districts the old identification between the presbytery and the château was no longer universally true. The younger clergy were often affected (their rich parishioners thought tainted) by Left social doctrines. More than social doctrine put a barrier between the gentry and the clergy, for young priests were often hostile to traditional Nationalism and, in an

[1] M. André Siegfried.

age where the question of peace and war was more important to many Frenchmen than the old staple topics of economics and politics, this ranged some Catholics more definitely on the Left than any mere social programme might have done.

The clergy, in general, recognized, as Canon Dimnet has pointed out, that the old Virgilian country curé, busy with his garden and his bees, was no longer adequate. The French priest had to be a missionary in France as much, almost, as outside. In the red zone round Paris he had to start almost at the beginning: he had to establish 'cells' of Catholics, as the Communists themselves had established cells in factories and regiments. The old rural Bobigny had gone, and the new Bobigny had to be treated like a mission field. What would have astonished both friends and enemies of the Church at the time of the separation, was the immense growth of church building all round Paris and, while the State was still bound to the formal, official architecture, some of the most brilliant examples of modernity were the new Paris churches. In other ways, the Church moved with the times. It was now far more active in social work of the kind that, in France, was thought of as 'Anglo-Saxon'. The scout movement was highly developed (despite suspicious Catholics of the old school who saw in it a foreign idea, not improbably part of a conspiracy connected with Theosophy or other kindred evils). These activities were what an anti-clerical called 'the trumps of the clergy', and it was not very easy to over-trump them. The established clergy of the Republic, the school-teachers, were not as zealous as their dissenting rivals. It was easier, as was done in one city, to invite the Salvation Army in to compete, than to compete oneself. Only the Communist party could show comparable vigour in winning and serving the young.

The old political shibboleths, too, were less profitable. It was easier to threaten a Radical mayor with masonic censure for permitting a religious procession in his city, than to apply political sanctions to him in his capacity either as mayor or as deputy. M. Georges de La Fouchardière, as much the official humourist of the Radical party as Alain was the philosopher, laughed at the curate who cultivated his hero's mother-in-law in a much more kindly spirit than would have been safe a generation before, and even 'Alain' preferred the Church to the Army as a corporation. One, like Saul, had slain its thousands, but the other, like David, its tens of thousands.

A new generation of Catholic politicians who did not so much accept the *Ralliement* as not conceive its not being accepted, appeared, and M. Champetier de Ribes was not regarded with the permanent suspicion that hampered the work of Eugène Lamy and Marc Sangnier. Within the Church, the prelates of the school of Cardinal Liénart of Lille and of M. Verdier, head of Saint-Sulpice and soon to be Cardinal-Arch-bishop of Paris, replaced such survivals of the old régime as Cardinal de

Cabrières or the nominees of Pius X. It was suspected, too, that the old Left tradition which the French Dominicans had inherited from Lacordaire was reviving, and even the Jesuits were less authoritarian in their politics than they had been a generation before.

These tendencies were suddenly brought to public and scandalous notice by the breach between the most vehement defenders of the political rights of the Church and the authorities of the Church. On the eve of the war of 1914, the Roman authorities had put on the Index of prohibited books several of the works of M. Maurras, books which were certainly not edifying to the average Christian. But Pius X was unwilling to condemn so warm an enemy of his enemies and the condemnation was kept secret. Nevertheless, the numerous enemies of the 'Action Française' among the French clergy and laity were ready to attack and, when the death of Pius X ended the rule of the intransigent Cardinal Merry del Val, their hopes were given some justification by the choice of a Secretary of State made by Benedict XV. He chose the former Nuncio of Leo XIII in Paris, the promoter of the Ralliement, Cardinal Ferrata. Cardinal Ferrata only lived a few months, but the attitude of the new Pope was noted; he was more a disciple of Leo XIII than of Pius X. The war had brought about a détente in the relations between France and the Vatican; the renewal of diplomatic relations was an augury of better times; and, although the 'Cartel des Gauches' made some anti-clerical gestures, it soon found, as has been shown, that it had more serious dangers to worry over than the aggressions of the clergy.

Among the younger clergy, the old dogmatic monarchist tradition was very weak; there were more disciples of Marc Sangnier among the young priests and seminarists, in some regions at least, than were disciples of M. Maurras. Indeed, in provinces like Brittany, it was a complaint of the local gentry that their political power was weakened by the action of demagogic priests bent on creating in France a Left political party modelled on the German Centre.

The defeat of the Right, in 1924, led to recriminations, and the attempt of M. Daudet to get back to Parliament by entering the Senate from La Vendée failed; largely, it was believed, through the opposition of the clergy, some of whom felt that the author of L'Entremetteuse [1] was hardly a fit representative for the traditional home of Conservatism in morals as well as politics. In the west, the powerful Catholic daily, the Ouest-Eclair, was hostile to the Action Française, and what the Ouest-Eclair thought was highly important in the region where Catholicism and Conservatism had their traditional stronghold. A series of feuds within the movement had deprived it of two of its leading members, Georges Valois and Louis Dimnet, both of whom wrote damaging

[1] A remarkably 'frank' novel that M. Daudet somewhat belatedly withdrew from circulation at the request of the Archbishop of Paris.

attacks on their old leaders, and the mysterious affair of the death of M. Daudet's young son, Philippe, entailed for the readers of the paper almost daily doses of violent abuse of the police which, however just and however natural in a distressed father, grew monotonous.

The battle really opened with an attack on the doctrine of the movement made by Cardinal Andrieu, Archbishop of Bordeaux, an attack which was not very much more fair than the attacks made by the *Action Française* itself. The leaders of the movement attacked Cardinal Andrieu and his supporters with such vehemence that Pope Pius XI was forced to come to the rescue. Although the Pope supported the bishops who were involved in a struggle with what was a powerful and unscrupulous organization, his policy was implicitly criticized by the attitude of many eminent ecclesiastics, chief of them one of the most eminent theologians, the Jesuit Cardinal Billot. But Pius XI, on one side, was as authoritarian as Pius X or Pius IX on the other. He demanded the resignation of Cardinal Billot and the world was treated to the almost unprecedented spectacle of a prince of the Church retiring to a house of his order as a simple priest. It was not the only innovation, for the Pope had not only put the works of M. Maurras on the Index, publishing the decree of 1914, but he put the newspaper, both for the past *and* the future, on the Index too.

The result was a permanent weakening of the movement. Many of its supporters defied ecclesiastical authority and supported it, but most Catholic supporters submitted, although there were some death-bed scenes that recalled the fight over the bull *Unigenitus* in the early eighteenth century, with the disciples of M. Maurras in the place of the Jansenist followers of Arnauld and Pâris. Such a rôle won approval for the victims of papal authority in the most unexpected places.

Yet no amount of sympathy from old enemies of Rome could compensate for the loss of Catholic support. Nor was this all. The movement which had been new and daring twenty years before, was a little out of date by 1926. It had argued in the good old days that a violent overthrow of the odious system was possible; but it had not seriously attempted to bring that overthrow about; it had not found a Monk. Still worse, the possibility of a revolution on the Right had been demonstrated, not by an orthodox disciple of Maurras, but by a former disciple of Georges Sorel. Fascism promised more than the improbable restoration of the monarchy ; and movements like the 'Jeunesses Patriotiques' of M. Taittinger won many recruits who, ten years before, would have become 'Camelots du Roi'. Like the old orthodox Socialists faced with the Russian revolution, the *Action Française* faced with Fascism seemed academic and ineffective.

The newspaper *Action Française* was to know one later moment of importance, but whatever chances and hopes of overthrowing the

Republic its devotees may have had, were dead long before the papal condemnation.[1]

III

The degree to which the victory of the Centre parties in 1928 had been due to the general feeling that the maintenance of the Poincaré Government was necessary for the financial stability of the country, was revealed in the revived militancy of the Radicals which followed the stabilization of the franc. At the Angers Congress, the party insisted on demonstrating its recovered doctrinal vigour ; M. Herriot and his Radical colleagues had to leave the Cabinet. Nor were the relations between the Prime Minister and the great Republican party improved when he defied their most profitable political doctrine and introduced a bill authorizing the opening of establishments for recruiting religious orders which were active in the mission field. So great an affront to the lay tradition not only rallied all the Left against the Ministry, but even split the Centre. The Government majority fell perilously low.

The leader of the opposition to Poincaré was the young Deputy, Édouard Daladier, who was now the chief Radical rival of Édouard Herriot (who had been his schoolmaster). M. Daladier was anxious to wean the party away from its compromising association with the Centre and from the excessive demonstrations of detestation of Communism which were the political line of M. Albert Sarraut and which were quite incompatible with the old safe rule of political war, as understood by the Radicals, 'no enemies on the Left'. In the Socialist party itself, a dispute of the same kind was going on between M. Blum and some younger men like M. Marquet, M. Déat and M. Montagnon who were increasingly irritated by what they deemed the barren intellectualism of M. Blum, a defect in the leader which one of them, a little later, publicly asserted was explicable in terms of M. Blum's racial origin. But M. Blum, M. Vincent Auriol and M. Paul Faure were more than a match for the dissidents and, apart from any other obstacles to a reunion of the Left as dreamed of by M. Daladier, the terms asked by the leaders of the Socialists were too high to be met.

The Prime Minister's health, which was increasingly bad, forced his resignation, since he refused to remain on as a figure-head; and a short-lived Briand Ministry fell, appropriately a few weeks after the death of Stresemann. It was the turn of M. André Tardieu who, despite his old connection with Clemenceau, now best represented the Poincaré spirit. The new Prime Minister, in his internal policy, was resolved to recreate something of the atmosphere of the good days of the 'Bloc National'.

[1] In 1937, the Pretender announced that neither the methods nor the teaching of the movement represented the true royal tradition. The position of a Catholic and Royalist party denounced both by Pope and King was ludicrous and, in 1939, after submission, the papal ban was raised from the newspaper but maintained for the works of M. Maurras.

One method was to attack the Communists with all the rigour of the law, forcing the timid Radicals and the Centre parties to proclaim too much tenderness for the revolutionaries or, on the other hand, to alienate potential allies on the Left. The budget surpluses which had accumulated made a programme of great public works apparently feasible. France was to have a new 'national equipment'. It was a more magnificent version of the Freycinet programme of the 'eighties and a reward to the country for the stoicism which it had displayed in accepting the bitter medicine of orthodox finance. The devastated areas had been restored; now the rest of the country had a right to improve its material equipment.

It was a policy of 'good humour', and that France was in such a flourishing condition was all the more gratifying since her highly critical friends in England and America were revealing that, as had been suspected, these economic physicians, so lavish with advice in the past years, were finding it hard to cure themselves. A minor budget defeat brought about the resignation of the Ministry, but M. Camille Chautemps found that even a moderate Radical Government could not live in that Chamber. M. Tardieu came back to office with, at the Ministry of Labour, the ex-Socialist, M. Pierre Laval. Fifteen years before, M. Laval had been thought worthy of a place on Carnet B, but despite many personal friends on the Left, he was now definitely reassuring to the admirers of sound finance. Like the majority of the 'Bloc National', the Tardieu Government was anxious to show that it was not opposed to social reform and, at long last, it was this coalition of the Centre and Right which passed into law a system of social insurance.

It was notable, however, that despite the 'reactionary' general character of the Government, Briand stayed on at the Foreign Office. He had now become a symbol. His declaration that so long as he was in office there would be no war, made his continuance in office of the greatest political value to any Cabinet. The Left, fully conscious of this fact, stressed the obvious difference in temperament and attitude between the Prime Minister and the Foreign Minister, but M. Tardieu refused to admit that the policy of M. Briand was a thing apart from the general policy of the Government. He took over the direct negotiations with Britain on the reparations question, but few Frenchmen really regretted that the pugnacious Mr. Snowden had now to deal with the combative M. Tardieu. The more idealistic side of foreign policy, the proposals for a United States of Europe above all, were the work of Briand who found that his old political friends were voting against him and his old enemies for him. The Right might make fun of the 'Pilgrim of Peace', their great cartoonist, Sennep, make of the cigarette gummed to the pendant lip an emblem of semi-treasonable weakness, but the vast majority of Frenchmen trusted Briand to reconcile security with peace.

The rise of Hitler weakened Briand more than it did the Government, but it was a financial scandal affecting a leading Minister that brought it down. The collapse of the Oustric bank [1] not only made it necessary for M. Raoul Péret to stand trial before the Senate (he was acquitted) and exposed the Government to the attacks of the indignant Left; it was one of the first signs of the ending of that golden day when the main duty of the Government was to decide what to do with its surplus. M. Steeg found, as M. Chautemps had found, that a Radical Ministry could survive in this Chamber only on conditions that would fatally alienate either Left or Centre, and his brief Ministry, although it lasted over the New Year, was replaced on January 27th, 1931, by the first Government of M. Pierre Laval.

With the rise of M. Laval came the decline of the man whose early career, in many ways, so much resembled his own, the militant spokesman of the extreme Left who had become for a time a leader of the Right. But Briand, in his old age, had recovered the esteem and affection of his former associates. Despite the rise of Hitler, the death of Stresemann, the threatening affair of the Austro-German customs union, his prestige was still high ; and it was confidently expected, at least by everyone outside the close corporation of politicians, that he would be rewarded by being elected to succeed M. Doumergue as President of the Republic. The extreme Right was in a fury; not merely was Briand a betrayer of the dead who had won the victory of 1918, but as the *Action Française* took pains to make widely known, he had been criminal enough in his youth to be caught in an amorous adventure, a fact which moved M. Daudet to an unwonted display of shocked moral indignation. When the election came, whether it was as a punishment for his early indiscretion, or merely another example of the political law that the candidate of the Left could not hope to win a presidential election, Briand was narrowly beaten. The result was such a surprise that one unfortunate newspaper appeared with a doctored photograph of the President-elect's triumphal return from Versailles. The victor was Paul Doumer, who had been a candidate against Fallières a quarter of a century before! Briand, like Clemenceau and Ferry, had learned that it was possible to be too great a man for the Élysée.

Briand had pride but he had no vanity, and he was induced to stay on at the Foreign Ministry where his work was crumbling round him in the critical summer of 1931. The dream of a peacefully united Europe was only a dream. It was a world of power politics that was being revealed, and France, for the moment, had power, the power of her great gold reserve. A series of foreign statesmen came to Paris, to negotiate or plead, Mr. Mellon, Mr. Stimson, Mr. Henderson, Dr. Luther, Dr. Curtis, Dr. Brüning. M. Laval and Briand returned Dr.

[1] See p. 678.

Brüning's visit in Berlin, but no country was willing to make the sacrifices that were necessary to restore mutual trust among the nations of the world. From being a question of helping Germany, it soon became a question of helping England, and the Bank of France and the Federal Reserve Bank of New York strove in vain to save the most famous of all banks from the humiliating results of the improvident optimism of the great men of the City of London. England went off gold. The death of André Maginot, whose reply to the evacuation of the Rhineland by the French Army had been not pacts, but a great fortified line, gave M. Laval a chance to rearrange his Cabinet and Briand resigned.

In March 1932 Briand died, but before that release came, the Laval Cabinet had been overthrown by the vigilant Senate and a new Tardieu Government formed. The combative Prime Minister prepared to fight the elections with a modernized version of the tactics of 1919; Communism was the enemy. The results of the first ballot showed that 1919 had not come again, the tide was running to the Left; but before the second ballot could be taken, the President of the Republic was assassinated by a mad Russian exile and, in a hasty and unopposed election, the President of the Senate, M. Lebrun, was chosen. In an hour when the news from Germany was getting more and more ominous, it was not irrelevant that the new President had been born in Lorraine in 1871. The second ballot merely confirmed the indications of the first. The parties of the Right were reduced to around 250 in a house of 605. It was a decisive repudiation of the policy of the heirs of Poincaré, or of their bad luck, for the world depression from which France had for so long thought herself secure had struck her with full force by 1932.

The shock with which the French learned that they were not immune from the economic troubles of the world was less profound than the shock given to American complacency by the collapse of 1929. There had never been wanting, even in the days of the most complete euphoria, critics to point out that France had gone to the devil or was going and that many unpleasant features of the situation were being neglected in the reign of good humour as typified, with different degrees of success, by M. Chéron and M. Tardieu. The national habit of denigration had never been wholly abandoned. But the suddenness of the blow, in France as in other countries, was violent enough to make almost any remedy seem palatable.

In 1930 there had begun a fall in the total trade of France that was significant of things to come. Her foreign customers were less and less able to buy her exports, which were largely luxuries, and the tourist traffic was beginning to fall off rapidly. Moreover, these customers were in desperate need of markets and willing to sell at almost any price, so that although the cost of imports fell, their bulk increased and, so far as they were competitive with French products, they demoralized the internal market. With the fall in value of imports went a greater fall, in the value of exports: that is, the unfavourable balance of trade grew while total trade declined. Thus the balance of trade with Germany, which had been favourable up to 1928, was now rapidly moving in favour of Germany as that country fought desperately for foreign exchange. With exchange control in some countries and with open inflation following the British example after 1931, the international price structure was hopelessly distorted.

At any rate the old simple remedy of a high tariff was no longer thought adequate. No duties, it was asserted, could prevent a sudden flooding of the few remaining markets. France ever since the war had trusted to high protection, which meant repeated manipulations of the tariff imposed by the fluctuations of the currency. All that protection could do had been done.

The new remedy was the allocation of a quota for classes of imports. In theory, the quota made available in the French market only what could not be supplied from home sources, at any rate at the proper, i.e. the current, price. It was an instrument of price stabilization; and French economic policy in this period was directed to permitting French prices to stay as they were in a world in which prices were falling rapidly. If it was desirable to insulate the French price structure, the quota system had something to be said for it. But, unless the allocation of a quota to one country or class of imports was accompanied by a system of licensing, it was hard to avoid breakdowns, for who was to import and when? If, in addition to the general quota, specific licences to import were given, favouritism was bound to be suspected, even if it did not occur. Then the rigidity of the quota system had absurd results in the case of agricultural products. If the French production of a certain crop was low (which was the fault of the weather), high prices would, under a tariff system, provide the necessary imports. But under the quota system France had simply to go short, and if, as was often the case, France was an exporter of finished agricultural goods, jams, or sweets, or candied fruits or vegetables, a valuable export market was lost.

But the resolution to maintain the internal price structure of France was unshaken, above all as it affected agricultural prices. Whatever exporting industries might say (and some of them were themselves agricultural in character), the right of the French peasant to get a just price for his wheat and wine (which meant, in effect, the prices he had been getting in the good years) was a political datum. All parties must promise to maintain these just prices, and woe to those that failed to keep the promise; that is to those in power as world prices cascaded downwards. For there were limits to what could be done by tariffs, quotas, internal restrictions on the planting of new vines or on the marketing of wheat. It was possible to cut down foreign trade but not to abolish it altogether (for France after all was a creditor country). It was possible, by quotas, to divert more trade to and from the colonial empire than had been possible under a mere tariff system. But so long as the disparity between French and world prices continued great, the French balance of trade would get steadily worse on a much smaller total. France would increasingly export less than she imported, though she both exported and imported less and less. That is, a declining trade structure would have to bear the weight of a growing unfavourable balance of payments, which meant diminished customs revenue and, internally, less and less business activity, with consequently less and less revenue from indirect and direct taxation.

That, in turn, meant an end of the days of budget surpluses, the beginning of a series of deficits and of danger to the franc. Nor was the last scourge of depressions spared France. Unemployment began to appear, though on a scale that was trifling compared with the figures of Germany, Britain and the United States in 1931-2. The chief sufferers, indeed, were the immigrants. No longer did France welcome Poles and Czechs and Italians. Governmental pressure not merely put an end to immigration but encouraged repatriation. There was a loss of hundreds of thousands of the young, vigorous males who had filled the gaps in the French post-war population. It was one of the most serious losses of the depression for a country in France's deplorable demographic position.

M. Herriot in 1932, like M. Herriot in 1924, was the predestined Prime Minister; and he was again unlucky in that his main problem was financial, while his main talent was political. Leader of what was a veiled coalition of the Left, he was faced with a situation very like that which had ruined the last successful Left coalition, a financial problem whose solution was certain to bring to the surface the usually hidden differences between Radicals and Socialists. In many ways (apart, even, from the threatening external situation) the situation was worse than it had been in 1924, for there was now an economic problem added to the financial, or, rather, the financial problem was merely the fiscal aspect of the economic problem. The Socialists stressed this point in their speeches and their policy. No mere fiscal soundness would suffice. To increase taxes and diminish expenditure in a state of declining production was folly; consumption must be increased, not decreased. It was a prescription abhorrent to the prudent, old-fashioned, bourgeois financier.

Even in the Chamber of 1932, old-fashioned views had a great many defenders, though not all of them were vocal. For the Centre parties were still strong enough, in alliance with a majority of the Radicals, to produce a majority of moderates, free from dependence on the Right or the extreme Left. But it was out of the question for the Radicals, so soon after the election, to think of separating themselves from the other indubitable Left parties. Not to speak of the Communists, who were a mere handful of 12, there were 129 members of the Socialist party in the Chamber; their leaders were insisting on a very high price for their support. Before the election, M. Blum had professed his willingness to take office if his party were the largest in the new Chamber and if a minimum programme, disarmament and nationalization of railways and insurance companies, were accepted by the Radicals. The Socialists had not become the biggest party, but their terms for support were as high as ever and M. Herriot could not meet them. One eminent Socialist had broken away from party discipline: M. Paul-Boncour became Minister of War, a post where he could plan those elaborate mobilizations of men, women, children and wealth which made war seem a preliminary to Socialism and alarmed the older Radicals who disliked both Socialism and war. But although the international situation deteriorated with a speed that made M. Paul-Boncour's plans seem more terrifyingly relevant than could have been dreamed of two or three years before, the financial situation perplexed the Government more than did the political convulsions in Germany. The deficit was growing with fantastic speed, all the economic troubles that had helped to win the election for the Left remained to plague the victors. The problem of keeping France solvent was too much for the Radical party and its leaders, if they had to remain on reasonably good terms with their Socialist friends.

At Lausanne, reparations had been buried with all the necessary face-saving formalities. The pessimists who thought that the Hoover moratorium was the end of making Germany pay anything had been right. Would they also prove right in their belief that the author of the moratorium would fail to see the link between reparations and war debts that was obvious to all Frenchmen? It did not matter very much, for Mr. Hoover, obviously, was not going to be re-elected. But, even defeated, he was still President and on December 15th, 1932, France owed another instalment of $19,000,000 to the United States. The President in office and the President-elect could do nothing to alter the letter of the bond. The United States would neither abate nor postpone, and M. Herriot appealed in vain to the Chamber to honour France's word. He failed and he resigned, nor could he be induced to withdraw his resignation. His successor was M. Paul-Boncour, who strove to balance the budget by reducing official salaries; and M. Chéron simply stopped all entry into the civil service for a year as some aid to a distressed treasury. The Ministry gave way to another, headed by M. Daladier: who at least was younger, less oratorical, less tied to the past than M. Paul-Boncour and, therefore, better fitted to deal with the problem of the deficit which was now nearly 10,000,000,000 francs.[1]

[1] In gold pounds, about £80,000,000 ($400,000,000).

CHAPTER VII

AND KNAVISH TRICKS

I

As it was in large part to the impact of the world depression on France that the Left had owed the apparently decisive character of their victory in 1932, it was inevitable that, unless the crisis took a turn for the better, they would suffer for it. The pressure on the treasury did not lessen, for falling national income was reflected in falling revenue; and extra taxes and ordinary economies could not be made effective fast enough to overtake the deficit. It was inevitable, then, that the Government would be forced to take more drastic measures, and, very reluctantly, M. Daladier had to decide to cut the salaries of officials.

This step was not necessarily unpopular in the country. Small shopkeepers, workers on short time or, in some cases, out of work, clerical employees whose salaries had been drastically cut, all bore with comparative equanimity the attack on the salaries of that privileged class, the civil servants. But the proposed cut put the Socialist party in a peculiarly difficult position. They were, above all, the party of the *fonctionnaire*, as the Radicals were the party of the small business and professional man, and the Communists the party of the proletarians. To accept a cut in the salaries of their own supporters was to risk a great deal. The militants were already angry. They had condemned at the party Congress of 1933 the alliance between the parliamentary party and the Radicals, an exhibition of doctrinal rigour that had been enough to drive to the edge of secession some of the most vigorous Socialist deputies, the able Mayor of Bordeaux, M. Marquet, the Auvergnat apostle of 'planning', M. Déat, and the veteran friend of Jaurès, the living emblem of the heroic past, M. Renaudel.

M. Daladier tried to make things easier for the Socialists by putting a good deal of jam on the pill; or rather, promising that jam would follow the pill. There was to be control of private manufacture of arms; there was a vague promise of the ultimate nationalization of armament factories and of insurance companies; as well as of the introduction of a forty-hour week. But the harsh reality of the moment was the threatened 6 per cent. cut in official salaries. In private, the

Socialists pointed out how dangerous it would be for them as a party to accept the cut; in public they pointed out, through the voice of M. Blum, how unwise any such measure would be, for the remedy for the crisis was not economy of this narrow type but the restoration of economic health by Government action, by restoring demand. Secure in this political and economic ivory tower, M. Blum condemned the Government to death. In vain, M. Renaudel, a neglected Cassandra, warned his party of the dangers they were making imminent. 'We must defend parliamentary government and democracy.'

The danger invoked by M. Renaudel seemed imaginary to M. Blum. Fascist threats in France were mere noise! The majority of the Socialists followed M. Blum and the party line; the minority was to form its own party, the 'Néos' as they were to be known in a few weeks' time. But for the moment the Chamber had to provide a new Government. The choice of the President fell on M. Albert Sarraut, who lasted three weeks and who was succeeded by M. Chautemps. It was not a good method of impressing the nation with the seriousness of the deputies, for the successive Ministries differed only in their heads; the Socialists, who had forced M. Daladier out of office rather than accept the salary cuts, accepted them from M. Chautemps. It is true they did not vote for them; when the vote came, they stalked out of the Chamber in great indignation, thus avoiding the overthrow of the Government and yet keeping their record clean. It was a childish evasion and hardly even funny.

Faced with increasingly difficult financial problems and with the impact of Hitler on French security, the Chamber seemed incapable of following one line of policy or one man or group of men. It was playing a kind of musical chairs of its own, and this at the best was an innocent game for quiet times. The times were not quiet and there was a violent campaign under way to convince the nation that the game was not innocent.

The leader of the campaign was the vivacious expert of the personalities columns of the *Action Française*, M. Léon Daudet. The moral turpitude of the rulers of the Republic was an old story to the readers of his newspaper, but in addition to the old scandals and the old names, M. Daudet was busy in these months calling the attention of all good Frenchmen to the activities of a group of politicians and friends of politicians. There was the prominent Radical Minister, M. Dalimier, the well-known but not generally respected lobbyist-journalist, M. Dubarry, and other prominent figures in the corridors of the Chamber, men little known to the outside world, but conspicuous in the twilight zone where politics, business, journalism, sport and the theatre met on a common and low level of interest.

The campaign might have fizzled out but for the sudden collapse of a financial scheme which was the last coup of a prominent member of the underworld, Serge Stavisky. His activities had been brought to the attention of the police and, indeed, to the attention of the whole investing world by the officials of the Ministry of Finance, who had vetoed an ingenious scheme of M. Stavisky for marketing bonds issued to compensate Hungarians resident in what was now Rumanian territory. But the good friend of M. Dubarry—who edited *Volonté*, a paper which took a very kind view of Germany and especially of Herr Hitler, a kind view that, it was suspected, was paid for—and of M. Darius of the *Midi*, and of so many politicians and lawyers, had many irons in the fire. The one that finally burnt him was an issue of bonds based on the assets of the Bayonne pawnshop, a scheme that might have collapsed, only much later, but for the failure of the Hungarian issue. However that may be, it was at Bayonne that the first effective police action against him was taken and that the man in the street for the first time heard his name.

On December 30th, 1933, the *Echo de Paris* mentioned the issue of a warrant by the public prosecutor of Bayonne against 'Serge Alexandre Stavisky'. Within a week, the name was to be the best-known in France, but at the moment it conveyed little, outside the fairly large circle of people in Paris who lived on their wits and the other large circle of lawyers, journalists and politicians who lived on the people who lived on their wits. To these classes, Stavisky was an ingenious and bold if vain crook, with a police record and with charges hanging over him since 1927. That the charges were still merely hanging, showed that Stavisky (or Alexandre as he called himself in his more elegant moments) had secured powerful protection, no doubt at a price. Son of a Russian-Jewish dentist, the young Serge Stavisky was a fine specimen of the 'métèques' who were, or so the *Action Française* asserted, the ruin of France. He had dabbled in most forms of petty graft, he was well known to the police, but he was apparently immune from any police interference. He had lots of money to spend, and although, as the current Duc d'Audiffret-Pasquier noted with pride in the Chamber, he had been kept off the turf by its vigilant and aristocratic guardians, he had shone at Deauville and the other resorts of the rich and their parasites.

His last *coup* was the issuing of many millions of bonds on behalf of the Bayonne pawnshop; the extraordinary amount of capital required for the working of the pawnshop of a small country town attracted attention in the long run. The victims were mainly insurance companies, and the discovery of the fraud was postponed by the venerable device of two sets of books. The first Stavisky mystery was how he had been able to carry out his fraud? The answer seemed to involve the Mayor of Bayonne, who was also a Radical deputy. But M. Garat was not big game. The second question was how Stavisky had managed to avoid defending himself from the charges first brought against him in 1927. How had he managed to get his trial postponed and his bail renewed nineteen times? Who had protected him? Then, how had the not very subtle fraud at Bayonne been so successful with the insurance companies? The answer to this question was supplied by the *Action Française*, which published, on January 3rd, facsimiles of two letters by the eminent Radical deputy, M. Dalimier, who was at the moment a Minister in the Chautemps Government, letters recommending the Bayonne bonds. They had been written in 1932. For what motives, in return for what services, had M. Dalimier helped to quiet the suspicions of the insurance companies? For payments to the party funds of the Radical party, suggested the *Action Française*. Last and, from the man in the street's point of view, most important question of all, where was Stavisky?

While the readers of the *Action Française*, a body very rapidly growing more numerous, thought this over, the last question was answered. Stavisky was at Chamonix, slain by his own hand as the police burst into the house where he was hiding with his mistress. There was now death added to thievery and corruption. The death of Stavisky was to his case what the death of the Baron de Reinach was to Panama. Alas, it was just this simple truth that the Prime Minister, M. Chautemps, failed to recognize. And that failure was especially disastrous because the Prime Minister's brother-in-law, M. Pressard, was head of the Paris *parquet*, the body entrusted with the duty of prosecuting people like M. Stavisky. The situation was delicate; only great political skill could prevent an ugly scandal, and M. Chautemps did not display that skill. He was a brilliant debater, a capable administrator, a hereditary politician, a member of the Republican aristocracy, well and agreeably known in many circles, but none of these qualifications for high office compensated for the absence of the Cavourian 'sense of the possible'. What was not possible was to take the line of Méline in the Dreyfus case, to pretend that there was no Stavisky case. M. Chautemps had won Socialist support and so he was sure of a parliamentary majority in face of the traditional tactic of the Right, the attempt to discredit the Republic by throwing mud at Republicans. M. Chautemps had his majority; not a very enthusiastic majority, yet a majority. But that was no longer enough, for the decision was passing from the hands of the deputies into the hands of the Paris mob or mobs.

As has been pointed out, the idea of a revolution from the Right, of the organization of the counter-revolutionary forces for a *coup d'état*, was, in its modern form, a French invention. But the *Camelots du Roi* of the Royalist party were never very numerous and, if they were militant enough to share with the police the task of keeping central Paris free from Left violence, they were never a menace to the Republic. M. Maurras had asked, in the optimistic years before the war of 1914, if a violent overthrow of the hated and despised régime was possible, and he had demonstrated that it was. But that demonstration was purely intellectual. The proof of the theorem on the practical plane was the work of the *Fascisti* in Italy.[1] The success of the armed bands of Signor Mussolini naturally won admiration and imitation in France. It was not, however, the intellectual force of the Fascist creed that won admiration, but its success; and the 'Patriotic Youth' of M. Taittinger [2] were recruited largely from people who would earlier have been *Camelots du Roi*. Then M. Coty, when he turned from perfumes to politics, had his own combatant organization, a semi-Bonapartist body calling itself the *Solidarité Française*. This body was lavishly subsidized but, like all the other political activities of M. Coty, was treated with an irreverence astonishing to an English reader who reflects that, for most though not for all of this time, M. Coty was very rich. His storm troopers were suspected of being mainly mercenaries, and on the Left they were always known as the *Sidilarité Française*.[3] Then there were the *Francistes*, who dressed in a uniform rather like that of Hitler's storm troopers and who took their name from the two-headed axe of the ancient Franks, but although French politics are highly historical, they were not historical enough for a party of ancient Franks to get very far.

In the agitation which was coming to a head in the first months of 1934, the various Fascist bands were reinforced, morally if not materially, by various ex-servicemen's associations which, like Bonaparte on his return from Egypt in 1799, asked the rulers of France what they had done with the victorious nation of 1919. The unions of old soldiers were politically divided, though the National Union grouped most of them. But a minor society of this kind was coming into the limelight, the *Croix de Feu*. Originally the *Croix de Feu* was an organization of war heroes who had been decorated for courage on active service. Then it added a branch composed of what were, in Germany, called 'front-line soldiers' and to these it added sympathizers, sons of heroes and so on. Not all or nearly all front-line soldiers were members. M. Daladier was not, for example. But the *Croix de Feu* did group a body of Frenchmen who were, in popular esteem, entitled to special respect. They were mainly a bourgeois body and their chief was a nobleman, Colonel de la Rocque; proletarian members of the league were rare, but then France was not a proletarian country.

It was these bodies which, each in its own way, made the parlia-

---

[1] The Italian Nationalists, who had their own blue-shirted bands, were allies of the Fascisti in 1922 and were absorbed with the Black Shirts in the Fascist militia in 1923. The Nationalists owed a good deal to M. Maurras in the matter of doctrine.

[2] An exaggerated admiration for Youth marked all these movements. Even the Radicals had their *Jeunesses*. This worship of 'Giovinezza' was both natural and comic in France, where, as the German gibe had it, the country was ruled by men of seventy-five 'because the men of eighty are dead'.

[3] The members were largely recruited from unemployed Algerians, known in Paris by the generic name of 'Sidis'.

mentary dexterity of M. Chautemps irrelevant. The war cries came from the *Action Française*, the campaign of abuse was the main contribution of M. Henri de Kerillis of the *Echo de Paris*, but all sections contributed something. The peace of central Paris was disturbed by nightly riots in which the *Camelots du Roi* showed their ingenuity. It was they who discomfited the mounted police by strewing the streets with marbles and were most ingenious in causing short-circuits in the street transport system. But all the combatant bodies did their bit; the police treated the rioters kindly, with suspicious kindness the Left asserted; but behind every debate, behind every parliamentary move, was the noise of the rioters, the shouts of 'Down with the Thieves' mixed at times with the 'Up the Soviets' of the Communists.

The refusal of M. Chautemps, backed by the most eminent of Radicals, M. Herriot, to authorize a parliamentary inquiry might have been pardoned in more normal times. After all, as Panama had shown, a parliamentary inquiry was not necessarily a very good way of getting at the truth. But these were not ordinary times. The national sense of the fitness of things was outraged. The Stavisky case was no worse than the Oustric case, than the Hanau case: granted; but the general boom atmosphere that secured pardon for the allies of Oustric or of 'la Presidente' was missing.[1]

M. Chautemps, not content with refusing an inquiry, proposed to strengthen the law of libel and remove such cases from the jurisdiction of a jury! Not being able to prevent the vigilant press from showing up Stavisky, he was guaranteeing immunity to future Staviskys, so his critics put it. Even the Socialists, who loyally backed him up, did not do so with any enthusiasm. Despite his majority, he resigned.

Unless M. Lebrun ignored all the rules of the game, he was forced to appeal to a Radical leader; and it was to M. Daladier that the task of clearing up the mess fell. M. Daladier, at the start, showed far more sense of realities than M. Chautemps had done; he tried to form a Cabinet on a wide basis, to win over the leader of the Néo-Socialists, M. Marquet, and to reassure the suspicious elements of the Right by including M. Ybernégaray. But his negotiations fell through, and it was a dull Radical Cabinet that was formed, with a few novelties like the presence of the energetic and young M. Frot at the Interior. Putting off meeting the Chamber for a week, M. Daladier got time to deal with the increasingly complicated Stavisky business. It was necessary to do something that would make a good impression, if only because, since the split between Radicals and Socialists that had brought about the fall of the first Daladier Government, the parties of the Right had been anticipating a National Government which would ignore the electoral bargains and promises of 1932. The former President of the Republic,

---

[1] This attitude is not peculiarly French. It is certain that the genial tolerance, by the American people, of the Teapot Dome scandals in 1924 was due to the general prosperity.

M. Doumergue, had been talked of as a saviour of the situation, but he had told a reporter that he was too old.

When, at last, M. Daladier acted, the expectations of all Paris, if not all France, were ludicrously disappointed. M. Pressard, the hitherto untouchable brother-in-law of M. Chautemps, was moved from the *parquet* to a high judicial office; this kicking upstairs was not well received. But the transfer of the head of the detective-service, the *Sûreté*, to the *Comédie Française* was too comic to be wise in such an atmosphere, and it was universally believed that it was done, not merely to placate the dismissed detective, but to punish the head of the national theatre whose great success of the past season had been a production of Shakespeare's *Coriolanus*. *Coriolanus* is a play that may fairly be described as undemocratic: and the *Thermidor* affair[1] had shown that the Radicals were very sensitive to theatrical attacks on their creed. But it was one thing to ban Sardou and another to ban Shakespeare; and to put a detective at the head of the 'Maison de Molière' was to create a situation to which only Molière could have done justice.

The most serious step taken was the dismissal of M. Chiappe from the Prefecture of Police. The lively little Corsican was a great Paris figure. He knew 'everybody' in Paris (including the late M. Stavisky). He had improved the traffic control. It was no longer dangerous to life to cross the street. And he had exercised what was, for Paris, a rigorous control of morals, so that it was no longer impossible to walk through certain quarters without being the object of improper proposals. But M. Chiappe had courted and earned the enmity of the Communists, whom he had harried even more than he had harried pimps and prostitutes, and his comparative kindness to rioters of the Right made him highly suspect to the Left. But like Schober in Vienna, Grzesinski in Berlin, Yagoda in Moscow, M. Chiappe was thought, by the credulous, to be an autonomous power, to be too dangerous to touch. Even M. Daladier, when he decided to remove him and replace him by the Prefect of Seine-et-Oise, M. Bonnefoy-Sibour, offered to make him Resident-General in Morocco. This was another mistake, for if M. Chiappe was not to be trusted in Paris, he was not to be trusted in Rabat. According to M. Daladier, the Prefect's reply was to threaten a riot; according to M. Chiappe, it was to point out that after years of faithful service, the Prefect would leave office a poorer man than he had entered it.[2]

The riots had stopped while M. Daladier was thinking out what was to be done. The informal truce would last only so long as the genuinely disgusted Parisian petty bourgeois was convinced that he was not being

---

[1] Forty years before, the Radicals, led by Clemenceau, had forced the withdrawal of *Thermidor* from the *Comédie Française*, as 'counter-Revolutionary'.

[2] According to M. Daladier, M. Chiappe had said (over the telephone) that he would be 'dans la rue' (e.g. rioting); according to M. Chiappe, he had said he would be 'à la rue', that is, broke.

put off with yet another of those ingenious parliamentary dodges in which M. Chautemps was so fertile. He wanted assurances that no respect of persons would prevent justice at last taking her course; he was presented with a game of administrative musical chairs in which officials were removed from the jobs they held, and for which they, presumably, had proved unfit, only to be transferred to equally good jobs for which their only evident qualification was their failure in the posts they had hitherto occupied. Better things had been expected of M. Daladier, who was not one of the Republican smart set, not a Freemason, not an orator. The system had been too much for him. It was time to make an end of the system, to let some fresh air into the Chamber where these preposterous tricks still found defenders.

The dismissal of M. Chiappe was the match that fired the powder. The ex-Prefect's letter to the Prime Minister revealed that, for an official, M. Chiappe had curiously monarchical ideas of his function. He would not, by accepting any other job, 'sacrifice to you my personal reputation and the prestige which I had succeeded in giving to my post and my title'. However, he added magnanimously, 'giving all my collaborators a proof of good citizenship and of republican discipline I ask of them, no matter how keenly they feel the injustice done to their chief, to stay at their posts'. The implication was that, had he chosen, M. Chiappe could have induced the Paris police to follow him and not the legal government. Whatever the faults and follies of the Ministry, the country was well rid of a Prefect of Police with such ideas.

With him into retirement went the Prefect of the Seine,[1] M. Edouard Renard. The resignations provoked vigorous protests. Thirty deputies of the Seine signed a joint manifesto [2] charging the Prime Minister with sacrificing Chiappe to his need of a majority, and of being blackmailed by *Humanité* and by the *Populaire*. 'The head of the army of order has been sacrificed to the forces of disorder.'

It was the dismissal of Chiappe, it was generally believed, that was the price of Socialist support for M. Daladier; and by it he secured a parliamentary majority that was adequate for ordinary times. But these were no more ordinary times than 1848 had been, and M. Daladier was making the same mistake as Guizot had made then. The indecisive character of the new Government's policy, the inconsistent not to say farcical nature of its removals and promotions, all this seemed to the man in the street to be a crowning example of the unteachableness of the politicians. The *Action Française*, the *Ami du Peuple*, *Humanité* all rubbed in the lesson and thousands who were neither Royalists, Fascists

---

[1] The executive authority of the City of Paris and of the Department of the Seine is divided between two prefects, the Prefect of Police and the Prefect of the Seine. Paris, unlike other cities, has no elected mayor; the nearest equivalent is the President of the Municipal Council.

[2] Among them M. Paul Reynaud.

nor Communists found themselves echoing the 'Down with the Thieves' slogans of the extremists.

On February 6th, the new Government was to make its first parliamentary appearance; it was sure of a majority, so now was the time or never to show the deputies that the game was up. All the reactionary organizations summoned their members to demonstrations, some of them to combat. The Communist ex-servicemen were also called out to protest against the thieves and against pension cuts. The deputies were complacent; there had been so many demonstrations and the police always had the best of it.

In the Chamber, veteran connoisseurs of parliamentary disorder admitted they had never known such a din as greeted the unavailing efforts of the new Prime Minister to make himself heard. The Right howled, the Communists sang the *Internationale*, the Ministerial declaration had to be suspended in the middle to allow something like order to be restored. An attempt to limit the debate to a few selected speakers was another of the blunders of the harassed Prime Minister, and, all the while, a great crowd was pouring into the Place de la Concorde, across the river from the Chamber.

Jacques Bainville, the Royalist historian, was accustomed to illustrate the feebleness of the Government of Louis XVI by the fact that the bridge of Suresnes, which had been wisely kept in wood so that it might be destroyed if a mob tried to advance on Versailles from Paris, was not destroyed on the fatal 5th of October, 1789. The Republic seemed to have surpassed the Monarchy, for the Pont de la Concorde had been widened a year or two before and the hard-pressed police and mobile guards were trying to keep the demonstrators on the right bank of the river. The demonstration was soon a riot, and soon again an *émeute*. There were a few revolvers on the side of the rioters, but they were mostly equipped with weapons that recall the battles in the *Napoleon of Notting Hill*; they had as pikes the iron railings plucked up from around the trees, they had bottles and stones and, most formidable of all, razor blades on the end of sticks, very effective in use against horses. The police charged and charged again; a bus was set on fire and the stink of burning rubber filled the air. The police were forced to fire—and all the time the debate went on, lifelessly, futilely timid deputies slipped away; indignant deputies shouted that men were being killed outside; a wit among the newspapermen put a notice on the press gallery addressed to the rioters. 'Gentlemen, there are no deputies here.' At last the Government got its majority, a handsome one, and the flight from the Chamber began.

Outside in the darkness, they were singing the *Marseillaise*. A mob burst into the Ministry of Marine and tried to set it on fire, but a naval officer in full uniform so impressed the incendiaries that they left the building. There were attacks on the firemen as well as on the police. A procession of ex-servicemen singing the *Marseillaise* was joined by a procession of Communist ex-servicemen singing the *Internationale*: if a deputy was spotted he was lucky to get away unhurt.[1] By midnight, the last attack on the bridge had been repulsed. The Chamber had been saved; it was not 1848 or 1870 over again. But the authority of the Government was too greatly shaken for it to survive. M. Frot might thank the police and M. Blum preach the necessity of resisting by force the attempt of Fascist bands to overthrow the Republic, but the blood on the streets was too fresh a comment on parliamentary manœuvres for M. Daladier to ignore it. It was said that another demonstration was planned for the next day; this time it was to be led by the aged Marshal Lyautey. If he were shot down, would a mere majority in the Chamber be enough to save the authority of the State that had not managed to arrest Stavisky alive?

The reason for the collapse of the Government was well put by M. Gaston Bergery. When he was a soldier, he had been told by his sergeant never to touch a machine-gun if his hands were dirty. The hands of the Daladier Government were not dirty in the ordinary sense, but the whole parliamentary system seemed a little dingy. The 'Republic of Pals' meant that rigorously honest men were on good terms with fairly honest men who were on good terms with shady men who were on good terms with despicable crooks. Aymard, Dubarry, Dalimier, Raynaldy, Chautemps, Daladier; the chain for the moment was no stronger than its weakest link; Aymard and Dubarry were weak links indeed.

Then, in addition to the moral weakness, there was a material weakness: the police were worn out. They had been under strain for a month now; there had been riots nearly every day culminating in something like a great Paris 'day'. And if they were not bitterly indignant at the loss of M. Chiappe, they were not very enthusiastic at the thought that they were killing and wounding, being wounded and being killed, for so confused an issue as the correct way of looking into the scandalous affairs of a notorious crook and his political friends and protectors. If the police failed, there was the Army, but even if it could be relied on, a Government maintained by military force was a novelty for the Republic. So despite all the bold or timid critics who saw in such a surrender the end of parliamentary government, M. Daladier resigned and M. Doumergue, the ex-President of the Republic, was called on to form a National Government to liquidate the ugly business.

It was time, for there was serious rioting on February 7th; this time it was a demonstration by and not against thieves. The scum of Paris

---

[1] M. Herriot, Mayor of Lyons, was threatened with being thrown into the river. He was naturally indignant that a mayor whose city boasted two such rivers as the Rhône and the Saône should have been in danger of being thrown into the Seine.

turned out to take advantage of the disorder to pillage shops and individuals in the providential darkness. The police had another nasty night of it and they were threatened with yet another.

True to their policy of showing up the crooked bourgeois politicians, the Communists had made common cause with the Right in the press campaign against the Chautemps and Daladier Governments. Some Communists had done more than that and had taken part in the demonstrations of the 6th, and the party leaders had refused all collaboration with the Socialists in defence of the Republic against Fascism. On the morning of February 7th, they denounced Daladier and Frot and called for a demonstration in the Place de la République. This forced the Socialists to postpone their demonstration and to concentrate on a general strike for the next Monday. Even the most party-ridden Communist militant could see that the real victors of the 6th of February had been the Fascist organizations and, with the German example under their eyes, they decided to join in the general strike. But the leaders still insisted on having their own demonstration, despite the pleadings of the new Prefect of Police, M. Bonnefoy-Sibour, with the Communist leader, M. Doriot. So the 9th saw rioting almost as bloody as the 6th, but as it took place in the poor quarters of the East End and as the victims were mostly workers, the press was less worried about police brutality.

On February 12th came the strike. It was only a demonstration but it was a successful demonstration. Like the demonstration that followed the attack on Loubet, it showed that the Paris worker, if not the Paris bourgeois, was determined to defend the Republic if not the Republican politicians—and it showed, too, that the Paris Communist was no more willing to believe that the Republic didn't matter one way or the other than his father had been.

II

If the Republic was to be saved, M. Doumergue seemed to be the man to do it. If Poincaré had not been so ill, he might have been called in again, but he was unavailable. M. Doumergue would have to repeat in 1934 the Poincaré miracle of 1926. But the miracle was much harder to repeat than to perform for the first time. Moreover, the problem set Poincaré in 1926 was comparatively simple: how to ensure that the Government got its share of the abounding national wealth. But the Government in 1934 was no poorer than the nation was, and more than financial health had to be restored. Lastly and most important, M. Doumergue was not M. Poincaré.

Not many people had liked the dour Lorrainer, but most people had respected him; his industry, his integrity, his courage were all admired. M. Doumergue was no Lorrainer; he was a cheerful, expansive man, despite a Calvinist education. It was not unimportant that the cheap tailors had used him as a model for the fat jolly man on whom to put their louder suits. It was the business of a President of the Republic to smile, but M. Doumergue during his seven years of office smiled with an ease and conviction that were half his battle. He was not smiling now. He was called on to form a National Government and he contrived to get representatives of all parties except the Socialists and Communists to join. M. Herriot and M. Tardieu were both brought in—but without offices. M. Chéron, whose fatness and good-humour made him a Norman version of the Prime Minister, was made Minister of Justice. M. Sarraut was put at the great Radical Ministry of the Interior and, greatest ornament of the Cabinet, Marshal Pétain became Minister of War. Not very much noticed was the most important appointment of all: General Denain was made Minister of Air. To him fell the job of seeing that France kept that lead in military aviation she had had for so many years.

The duty of the Doumergue Government seemed simple. It had to discover why Stavisky had been so long immune from due process of law and why the demonstration of February 6th had ended, to take one version, in a bloody massacre of innocent citizens by the police, or, to take another, why it had been possible to organize a conspiracy to overthrow the Republic. The first committee was known as the 'Thieves' Committee', the second as the 'Murderers' Committee'.

The Committees worked hard and worked candidly, but in the nature of things, their reports left a great deal in darkness. The Committee on the riots was unable to prove or disprove either of the rival theories, although the small body of Frenchmen who kept their heads decided that there was no planned revolt and no planned massacre either. The 'Thieves' Committee' had no difficulty in showing that there was a great deal wrong, but less than the more virulent critics had asserted. A number of deputies, Garat, Bonnaure, Dalimier, Hesse were shown up in a displeasing light. To the content of the historically minded, there was a Proust in this scandal (though innocently) as there had been a Proust in Panama. Some of the worst scandals of the Paris blackmailing press were made public; and the dangers of the habit of subsidizing newspapers were again made evident as they had been in the case of the *Bonnet Rouge*.

A great deal of the mud thrown by the expert hands of M. Léon Daudet was scraped off. M. Georges Bonnet, for example, had been represented as an ally of Stavisky; had he not lunched with him at Stresa? At Stresa the oddest things had happened and it was possible that M. Bonnet and Stavisky had both been present at a great lunch, together with scores of other persons. But, as was pointed out by an acute critic of the system,[1] if the other departments had been half as

_____
[1] Mr. Alexander Werth.

vigilant as M. Bonnet's Ministry of Finance, there would have been no Stavisky scandal—or not one on anything like the same scale.

The real sinners were the detective police and the judiciary. The police were divided into two rival organizations: the *Sûreté*, which covered all France, and the Paris detective force under the *Préfecture*. These organizations did not merely not collaborate, but actively opposed each other. This clash of jurisdictions accounted for some of the immunity accorded to Stavisky and to others. But there was more in it than that. Stavisky had actually been a police spy for the *Sûreté*—and he was paid not in kind but in privileges. The nation was treated to an inside view of the gambling world in which Stavisky had moved, from the internationally famed Zographos syndicate to the petty bookmakers of the Paris region. In that world, police toleration was, if not indispensable, valuable. How was it got? By connections, above all by political connections. Police officials learned to go easy with certain gamblers and groups of gamblers because they had political friends.

These connections were the explanation of the failure of the judicial officials to put a stop to the career of Stavisky and of other crooks of the same type. True, the inefficiency of the system was partly due to inadequate staffing. The *parquet* of Paris, whose duty it was to investigate complaints and decide if there was ground for a prosecution, was hopelessly overworked. With all the good will, integrity and independence in the world, it could only decide by a crude rule-of-thumb. And if its good will and integrity were not in doubt, its independence was. For, by the side of Stavisky, there was always the deputy. That it was a help to a practising lawyer to be a deputy was an old story. But there was a difference between M. Léon Blum and M. Bonnaure, the Radical deputy who was Stavisky's mouthpiece. Without his parliamentary connections, Bonnaure would have been impotent. With them, he was able to make legal officials see the advisability of going slow. And no wonder, for if M. Bonnaure was not likely to be a Minister of Justice, his political allies included men who might well be. And from the Minister of Justice came those promotions which crowned a legal career with honour. To defy a Minister who, for any reason, wanted certain things done or undone, was risky.

Magistrates could remember Rochette, whose political sponsor was that eminent elder statesman, M. Caillaux. They might even remember the rôle of M. Doumergue in the matter. No doubt these interventions were rare, but they were possible. How was an examining magistrate to know that behind Bonnaure there was not some more formidable political figure? And the Stavisky case did little to shake the belief of the average Frenchman that there was a superior type of judicial administration at the disposal of those persons who could pull political wires.

It was a theory that it was impossible to refute completely. To argue that political morality was better now than it had been under the First Empire was merely silly. Napoleon I had Austerlitz and the Code to cover his tolerance of Ouvrard. The Republic had the Place de la Concorde and the holes in the Code. Nor was the statistical argument much better. Even if one takes M. Tardieu's figure of seventeen deputies as the maximum number of those involved in the case, it does not follow, as has been ingeniously argued, that this shows an improvement in parliamentary ethics since Panama. For if a hundred or more deputies were involved in Panama, that was because a law was needed to keep Leviathan afloat. Stavisky needed not a law but dispensation from existing law. And Stavisky was no Reinach, not even a Herz. That so shabby and petty a crook should have had seventeen deputies in his train was more disconcerting than that so great an effort should have been made to buy salvation for the greatest enterprise of modern French industry. How much wiser was the line taken by the 'Socialist Youth' before the *émeute*. They were against the thieves, of course. 'But we will not permit the exploitation of the scandals against the régime.' They fell back, that is to say, on what M. Ribot had said in 1892 and, politically speaking, they could not have done better!

The real clue to the scandals was to be found in the lack of responsibility. Ministries came and went; authorizations were given and refused; in the perpetual flux, the Bonnaures had their little share of authority. The horror of trusting to one man, or a group of men, any real power of coercion or control over the State, meant that the authority of the State was parcelled out among the mass of politicians and their hangers-on. Most of these politicians were honest, but they were not and could not be critical. A horror of State power was the Radical philosophy; the sale of their share of this divided power was the practice of such Radical Deputies as MM. Garat, Bonnaure and Hesse.

It had long been a complaint against French administration that it was burdened by too much paper, by too much *paperasserie*. An event that almost wiped out the memory of February 6th, showed that it sometimes suffered from too little. On the morning of February 21st, there was found on the railway line near Dijon, the horribly mutilated body of Albert Prince, a high legal official of the Paris *parquet*. He was fastened to the line, he had been drugged; it was easy to conclude that he had been murdered. And if he had been murdered, by whom? That was easy to answer! By those who had reason to silence a man who could really explain why Stavisky had been let alone. And who were they? Why, M. Camille Chautemps and his brother-in-law, M. Pressard! It was assumed that M. Prince had inside knowledge of the case, that he had documents proving that M. Pressard had prevented justice taking its course, and that these documents had been in the possession of Prince when he had been murdered at Dijon. Prince, himself, had dropped hints of this kind before his wife had received a mysterious telephone call, instructing her husband to come at once to Dijon where his mother was dangerously ill. He had gone off to Dijon; he had arrived; he had next been seen cut into three pieces on the line.

It was a story beating all but the most improbable inventions of detective fiction.[1] The Minister of the Interior, M. Sarraut, immediately caught the public attention with denunciations of a 'Mafia' which had murdered Prince, but at whose orders? A newspaper, suspicious of the official police, hired retired members of Scotland Yard to make their own investigation, and various highly deplorable characters were arrested, but they could not be connected with the mystery of the Fairy Dell.[2]

The criminal mystery was not solved then or since. Prince may have been murdered, but it is equally likely that he committed suicide, as others implicated in the Stavisky case did. Nor, if he had decisive evidence of the complicity of M. Pressard in the protection of Stavisky, was it obvious why he should take it off to Dijon with him—or why all should turn on one document in a country where so large a part of the population was employed in writing reports. But for the moment, public credulity was naturally impatient of these refinements. M. Chautemps and M. Pressard were both eminent Masons, and their Masonic ranks and titles were spread on the pages of all the hostile journals; to some they were comic, to others they were sinister. In the origins of the case, M. Chautemps had been disastrously incompetent. He was now subjected to an ordeal which seemed, to those who think that a democratic leader need only mean well, an excessive punishment.

The storm died down. M. Chautemps took refuge in the Senate (or was rewarded by the loyalty of those who knew him best, the political leaders of his department); the Stavisky-Prince case remained with a fair share of mystery still attaching to it. But politically there was no doubt what was its lesson. Only an Executive far stronger than that provided by the French parliamentary system could protect the authority of the State and the integrity of the administration of justice against the recurrence of scandal of the same kind. The diffusion of authority in the French Chamber bred crooks, as the concentration of it in the House of Commons breeds yes-men.

M. Doumergue was convinced that a restoration of the independent authority of the Executive was necessary, and by that he meant an increase in the authority of the Prime Minister. He proposed changes

[1] To add to the mental confusion, there had travelled to Dijon in the same carriage, the son of Rasputin's secretary! He was off on his honeymoon, but for the moment his rôle was thought to be most sinister.
[2] *La Combe aux Fées.*

which would increase the power of the Cabinet and decrease the power of the Chamber. The deputies were to renounce their right to propose specific expenditures. To the existence of this right, critics attributed both the inordinately long time it took to vote the budget and the unbalanced character of the budget when it was voted. The deputies were organized in loose groups of interests as well as in formal parties. There were groups formed to look after the interests of the railwaymen, of the wine-growers, of farmers in general. It was a feebly organized special interest which had not its accredited protectors in Parliament—and protection almost always took the form of expenditure. By the time the Minister of Finance and the Finance Committee had bought off these groups, the original shape of the budget was lost. But, if no deputy could move a vote involving expenditure, the first and last word on that side of the accounts would be with the Minister. Such was the rule of the House of Commons, and the excellence of British methods was as much a French Conservative commonplace in 1934 as their badness had been in 1931. But it was realized that there was little point in reinforcing the authority of the Minister, if the Minister was insecure in his position.

To cure the Chamber of its weakness for overthrowing, on frivolous grounds, the Ministry of the day, M. Doumergue asked that the power of dissolution should be given to the President of the Republic on the recommendation of the Prime Minister, without the consent of the Senate being necessary. This proposal was, in the eyes of most good Republicans, outrageous. Senators pointed out that they had never refused to grant a dissolution; since 1877 they had never been asked. Deputies were infuriated at the thought that one of their number should have the power to intimidate them by threatening to send them before their master, universal suffrage, while the sacred mandate of four years of power was still unexhausted. It was pointed out that the position of a British Prime Minister, the choice of a semi-plebiscitary election, was very different from that of a French Prime Minister chosen by a President from a number of possible candidates of equal weight. The President, by his choice, would be able to affect the powers of Parliament very seriously; with the formidable weapon of dissolution at his disposal, the real centre of power would shift, not from the Chamber to the Prime Minister, but to the Élysée. In the long run, the right of dissolution might build up a tradition of party discipline and party unity that would approximate to the British system, but in the short run it would only cause confusion and the exaltation of the presidential prerogatives.

The idea of dissolution was in the air. After less than two years' life, the Chamber elected in 1932 had been coerced by rioters into deserting its own principles and leaders. The mandatories of universal suffrage, even apart from those of their number who were in jail, were neither respected nor self-confident in the spring of 1934. It was a reactionary joke to wear in the buttonhole a little plaque, 'I am not a deputy', but it was a joke that appealed to many who were not normally reactionaries.

Faced with the collapse of the Radicals, to whose support they had belatedly rallied, the Socialists had themselves asked for a dissolution of the Chamber. They did not get their way, and the Right, which had clamoured for it while the Chamber of 1932 was still supporting the Left, was content to leave well alone when it had been bullied into accepting the Doumergue Government. One deputy took the obvious step which was open to the Socialists but which they had failed to notice. M. Gaston Bergery resigned his seat and was very narrowly beaten after a bitterly fought election.

There was to be no electoral appeal to Cæsar. But there was another. As the Doumergue Government had been forced on the Chamber by the street, its chief took upon himself to report not to the Chamber but to the nation by wireless speeches. Once, perhaps, was tolerable, but when the Prime Minister made it evident that he intended to repeat his 'reports to the nation', the politicians were angered and alarmed. As the first panic subsided, the old party lines had begun to re-form. The Left tried to involve M. Tardieu in the Stavisky scandal on the very inadequate evidence of a semi-legible cheque counterfoil. M. Tardieu broke the party truce by attacking M. Chautemps with great virulence, and the Government of which M. Tardieu was a member nearly collapsed. There was more to do than to liquidate the Stavisky affair, and the Prime Minister had more to report than projects of Constitutional reform. He had to attempt to balance the budget by cutting salaries and war pensions. The ex-servicemen's organizations talked as if they were the American Legion and seemed disposed to treat with the State on terms of equality.

As his task grew more disagreeable and as the first panic wore off, M. Doumergue showed signs of resenting criticism, fair or unfair ; and a great deal of it was unfair. That he was a well-paid director of the Suez Canal Company was made a subject of reproach to M. Doumergue, and he was irritated into making an acid comparison between himself and some of his critics. Although he was a lawyer, he had never practised while he was a deputy, contenting himself with paying his annual fee to keep nominal membership of the Paris Bar. Such self-denial was not usual among lawyer-politicians, a palpable hit not merely at the deputy-lawyers of the Bonnaure type, but at such eminent practitioners as M. Blum.

There was in these speeches over the air something of the manner of a king addressing his good people; there was manifested an increasing anger against the Left, especially against the Socialists and Communists, and there was, in any case, a breach of the convention whereby, except at election times, the sovereign rights of universal suffrage were put in commission. The deputies who were, they believed, the only authorized representatives of the sovereign people, were recovering courage, and they were increasingly tired of hearing M. Doumergue call himself 'the Just'. The unwilling submission to the necessity of constitutional reform which had been general in March soon evaporated. The Radicals in the Ministry were now more disposed to resist the victors of February 6th than to make concessions to them, and, without Radical support or tolerance, the Ministry was doomed. The Fascist peril, real or imaginary, was imposing new political combinations on the parties: and Stavisky was forgotten in the threat of Colonel de la Rocque. In November the end came; M. Doumergue returned to Languedoc; his place was taken by M. Pierre-Étienne Flandin; and the real interest of the nation shifted from the Government to the Fascist leagues and the organs of resistance to them.

CHAPTER VIII

THE RISE OF THE PEOPLE'S FRONT

I

THE overthrow of a Left Ministry with a safe majority in the Chamber by riotous bands of the Right was a great shock to the political complacency of the nominally dominant party. Even without the lesson of Germany, the menace of a new February 6th would have angered the Radicals. They had, it is true, their representatives in the Governments that were formed after the resignation of M. Daladier, but the younger members of the party, M. Daladier himself, M. Cot, M. Chautemps and the others, resented the odium heaped on them by the reactionary press and the attempt to veto the entrance of any of the 'murderers of February 6th' into the Government. These Radicals were naturally thrown back on the support of other Left parties, and in the 'Délégation des Gauches', the steering committee of the nominal majority, they were active and critical. From the point of view of the Radical party, there was a great deal to be said for having M. Edouard Herriot in the Cabinet and M. Édouard Daladier in the ranks of the critics of the Cabinet.

The fear of a new February 6th was not confined to the Radicals. The Communists had learned their lesson for the time being. The folly that had led them to rejoice in the discomfiture of the 'assassins', that is in the overthrow of M. Daladier and M. Frot, was, for the moment, done with, though of course neither acknowledged nor repented of. Then the lesson of the triumph of Fascism in Germany with the consequent danger to the Soviet State was being mastered. The real leaders of the party in Moscow had, for the moment, an interest in keeping France out of any close association with the Fascist powers; and as a beginning it was necessary to keep France from going Fascist herself.

M. Gaston Bergery had been preaching the necessity of a 'common front', and his idea was taken up both by Radicals and Communists. The rank-and-file of the Socialists were soon won over to the idea, but the leaders remained sceptical. On the one hand, they distrusted the Communist leaders and feared that an alliance with them could only result in giving new opportunities for that destruction of the Socialist party which had for so long been the main aim of the Communists. Then the sudden patriotic fervour of the Communists was too much for many of the Socialists; less versatile than their proletarian rivals, they could not suddenly appear as the champions of a re-armed and militant, if unaggressive France, after a lifetime of denouncing militarism and the commoner forms of patriotism as bourgeois traps. The appeal to the old Jacobin tradition (which was soon to include an appeal to Joan of Arc) was easy enough for the rising young mouthpiece of the new Communist policy, Maurice Thorez, but harder for the Socialist leaders.

A common front with the Communists involved a common front with the Radicals, and the Socialist party was divided between the militant optimists, the Zyromskis and Piverts who wanted a revolutionary overthrow of the capitalist order, and the more cautious school led by Bracke, who wanted to transform society by legal means, after acquiring an independent parliamentary majority. Neither method was in the least likely to succeed for a long time to come, and, while waiting for the miracle in whichever form it was to take, the party could continue its old policy of highly critical if negative parliamentary action. It could draw up programmes like the Huyghens programme of 1932 and then content itself with austere criticism of the doctrinal incoherence of the Radicals. In 1932, M. Pierre Cot had ironically complimented the Socialists on the popularity they derived from the fact that they had never been in power. He wished, but obviously did not believe, that they would retain—if in power—'the prestige they had known how to acquire in the ante-room of power'. A good many Socialists still preferred to stay in the ante-room.

An alliance with the Radicals had its special dangers, for the Socialist party's position was constantly being undermined by the Communists, and the left wing of the party was not anxious to compromise itself by a deal with such incorrigible bourgeois as the Radicals. It is true that the Communists themselves were in favour of such a deal, but it did not follow, whatever formal logic might suggest, that the Socialists would not suddenly appear as class-traitors for doing reluctantly what the Communists were doing with enthusiasm.

The necessary stimulus to the common front was supplied by the militant organizations of the Right. Although the real begetters of the 6th of February were the *Camelots du Roi*, the glory of that day was seized by the *Croix de Feu*. That organization was growing very fast. Its original character as a veterans' society was now almost destroyed by a flood of young recruits. Its leader, Colonel de la Rocque, was a power in the land. He was good looking, he was reputed honest; his very lack of obvious political talents won support from many disillusioned members of the bourgeoisie. Even the clotted meaninglessness of his literary style was not, at the moment, a great handicap, a remarkable fact in a country where muddleheadness and literary incompetence bordering on illiteracy are not merely not political assets, but actual handicaps. 'Public service', as he called his doctrine, was an odd mixture of noble sentiments and incoherent proposals. It was a sign of the confusion of the times that it was taken more or less seriously by intelligent people.

The legend of the 6th of February was a useful asset. The belief that an innocent and harmless procession of ex-soldiers had been massacred by the orders of a set of rascally politicians was firmly implanted in the minds of hundreds of thousands of well-meaning and honest people, whose consciences had been very properly shocked by the solemn frivolity of M. Chautemps and the vacillation of M. Daladier.[1] Colonel de la Rocque talked of vigour and of action. As long as he talked, all was more or less well, but a good many young men in his organization really wanted action and expected to be shown vigour. The great rallies in the grounds of châteaux, the mobilization of the faithful by squads of cars, in one case by a squadron of private planes, were pleasing demonstrations of organizing power, of material resources and of numbers, but what did they lead to? When some militants went so far as to raid a Socialist party office, they were disowned by the Colonel, which was reassuring for the devotees of legality but a sad disappointment for the potential storm troopers.

Whatever the irritation of fire-eaters like M. de Maud'huy at the timidity of M. de la Rocque, the Colonel was active enough to provide useful campaign material for the Left. The alleged threat to the existence of the Republic was a timely bond of union between Radicals, Socialists and Communists. The public was reminded that 'Casimir' (as the Left press insisted on calling the Colonel) was an aristocrat. Was not his brother a member of the household of that rather torpid Pretender to the throne of France, the Duc de Guise? In the columns of the *Populaire*, the more credulous of the Socialist faithful were treated to wonderful and hair-raising stories of *Croix de Feu* plots against the Republic, plots that really flattered M. de la Rocque by treating him as a Hitler or Mussolini when he was not even a Déroulède.

The Communists played up nobly. If they had a weakness, it was a tendency to display a belligerent nationalism that distressed the Socialists. Their pride in Valmy and in Joan of Arc, their insistence on a 'free, happy, and strong France' was almost overdone. When the term of service in the Army was raised from one to two years, against the noisy opposition of the Socialists, it was disconcerting to find that the Communists swallowed it when Moscow approved. But whatever

---

[1] The growth of the legend was not accidental. At least one of the victims of February 6th, listed as a war veteran, was not a war veteran and not a demonstrator, but an innocent businessman going home from his office and killed by a stray bullet. Attempts by his widow to rectify the error and to have the name removed from the list of martyred demonstrators were unavailing.

ironical suspicions may have been entertained by Socialists who remembered the old days of Communist slander and who could recall the stories of plots against the Workers' Fatherland, when leading French statesmen carried on conspiracies against Russia in cafés on the boulevards, the movement for a common front was too strong to be resisted. So long as the Fascist organizations lay low, the Socialists hesitated to burn their boats, but in the late spring of 1935, the *Croix de Feu* were more noisy and conspicuous than ever. It was time to develop the common action of the Left parties, to concentrate on a common minimum programme ranging from mobilization of the 'entire working-class population against the Fascist organizations' to a 'struggle against the Fascist terror in Germany and Austria'.

The failure to induce the Government to suppress the Fascist organizations, the victory of the Left in a Paris by-election, the rising tide of anti-Fascist feeling, all led to the formation of a common front by the Communists, Socialists and Radicals, a front which was given its religious consecration by the demonstration of the 14th of July, 1935. It was an attempt to recapture the national holiday from the reactionaries. In the west-end of Paris, the Army review, the great rally of the *Croix de Feu*, the arrival (late) of Colonel de la Rocque at the Arc de Triomphe might recall the great days of the previous year. But the real national festival was celebrated, as was fitting, much further east.

July 14th, 1935, was a magnificent day. In the east-end of Paris the very names of the streets were anti-Fascist demonstrations. From the Faubourg Saint-Antoine the crowds poured east towards the Place de la Bastille; they poured down from Belleville and in from the new industrial suburbs. The historical associations that, in other capitals, evoked memories of royal triumphs and national glories, here recalled the days

> When Death was on thy drums, Democracy,
> And with one rush of slaves, the world was free.

If, a few miles away, the possessing classes were complacently celebrating their power, here they were reminded (as Morel reminded M. de Charlus) that the ancestors of the workers had cut off the heads of the ancestors of the nobles. This was not Berlin, or Vienna, or Rome, but Paris.

The very disorganization of the procession was a sign of strength. What did it mattter that a richly over-dressed Negro found himself leading the section whose banner bore the names of 'Alain-Langevin' and was supposed to represent the embattled intellectuals? The mothers of victims of the last war had, in their ranks, obvious mothers of victims of the next war. There were officers in the procession, and at least one duchess—and writers—and politicians. It is true that the hurried change of front of the Communist party had come too recently to affect all the rank-and-file. The police, who were to have been welcomed as defenders of the Republic, were greeted with shouts of 'Assassins' as usual, and, despite attempts to get the crowds to sing the *Carmagnole* or the *Marseillaise*, the only song that was really sung with heart and knowledge was the *Internationale*. The 'damned ones of the earth', 'the conscripts of hunger' looked both cheerful and robust that day. Red flags and tricolours waved over crowds shouting 'Up the Soviets', 'De la Rocque to the gallows'. Few spectators noted that a great and hastily stitched tricolour flag, floating over a group of Communist, Socialist and Radical leaders, ripped in two, the blue and white on one side, the red on the other. Only the most cynical murmured '*absit omen*'. When the night came and, with it, the dancing and the fireworks, such fears seemed more out of place than ever. The sovereign people, in its good city of Paris, had bidden defiance to the heirs of the émigrés and the enemies of the one and indivisible Republic.

By the time of the great manifestation of July 14th, 1935, the parliamentary situation had become too paradoxical to be tolerable; it would have to be ended one way or the other, by a sweeping victory of the Left or of the Right. If M. Doumergue saw himself as Cincinnatus-Poincaré, M. Flandin saw himself as Waldeck-Rousseau, saving the Republic from the menaces of the armed leagues. M. Flandin was not, however, Waldeck-Rousseau; he was simply a tall, vain, dull politician of moderate ability, if of great ambition. He was industrious, less hide-bound by mere traditional phrases than was M. Doumergue, more in touch with the needs and ideas of the age. But he was, among other defects, unlucky. In his economic policy he discounted a convalescence of world economy that was coming, but did not come fast enough for M. Flandin's plans. He needed, too, external peace and confidence, and he was confronted with the increasingly obvious imperial demands of Signor Mussolini and the rapid increase in the power and in the ambitions of Herr Hitler.

Within France, the main trouble of the Ministry was the fall of prices and the stagnation of industry and trade. The peasants were, at last, bearing the full burden of the catastrophic fall of world prices. Fairly good harvests had produced heavy unsold stocks of wheat, wine and other farm products. A law fixing a minimum price for wheat had merely served to irritate the peasant. Since the Government did not offer to buy wheat at the minimum price, the legal prohibition of sale below the fixed price was a mere political gesture which served to justify a high price of bread, but did the producer of wheat no good. He could sell his wheat at an illegal price or not at all. He chose to break the law; and to blame the great grain merchants, the millers, and the importers for the gap between the legal and the real price of wheat. Believing as most Frenchmen did, that prices could be controlled by merely making a law about it, he was convinced that he was the victim of a conspiracy of commercial thieves and their Government allies.

It was, for a moment, touch and go who should benefit by peasant discontent. A 'Peasant Front' was formed by a vigorous Conservative demagogue, M. Dorgères, who threatened a tax strike and frightened the rural politicians of the Left as much as Colonel de la Rocque frightened the urban. But the suspicion with which the French peasant regards his betters was fatal to the rural Fascism of M. Dorgères. The fiction of a legal price for wheat was abandoned; the Government bought up stocks to keep them off the market; the price of bread was reduced; the production of wine curtailed. By 1936, the worst of the rural crisis was over, but the improvement came too late to diminish peasant resentment against the rulers of the land, especially the economic rulers of the land.

The discrepancy between world prices and French prices had been greatly increased by the retention of the gold standard in France, and the export industries saw in devaluation the only way out. After the abandonment of the gold standard by the United States in 1933, as the Economic Conference showed, the 'Gold Bloc', of which France was the chief, was fighting a losing battle. In a town like Calais, complete paralysis seemed to have settled over the local industries, Lyons was hardly better off, and even Paris suffered severely from the decline of tourist traffic and luxury buying. The tourist mark and the tourist lira benefited German and Italian rivals of Paris and the Riviera. It was not surprising that the most determined advocate of devaluation of the franc should represent a Paris district terribly hard hit by the high cost of a good time in the former capital of world extravagance. But M. Paul Reynaud failed to convince M. Flandin, who asserted that the gap between world prices and French prices was exaggerated and, in any case, was decreasing every day.

To M. Flandin, devaluation was unnecessary and it was immoral; it prepared the way for future difficulties and it threatened social disorder. 'Terribly shaken by the war and by the first devaluation of 1928', the middle classes had to be defended, for if they were not, the result might be 'to expose France to the worst risks: for the middle classes are the backbone of the republican régime'. Instead of devaluation, there was to be a reduction of the interest rates and a further lowering of French prices which would soon be overtaken by the rise of the price level in Britain and the United States. In the meantime, confidence had to be preserved and republican institutions defended. The individual deputies gave up their right to propose expenditure, but there was no more talk of dissolution or of constitutional reform. The Dictator was back in the Midi, soured by the ingratitude of republics and little consoled by the praise of Colonel de la Rocque or the lamentations of M. Henri de Kerillis. He had come in because the Chamber was afraid of new riots; it was not afraid any longer, so M. Doumergue retired for good.

The problem of the power of finance in the Republic was no new one. The great banks had been too much for Gambetta, and the most successful Finance Ministers, since his time, had been men who, like Rouvier, were themselves in the closest touch with the banking world. Criticism of the great banks was often ill-informed and, when it was well-informed, was often less the result of public spirit than of a high estimate of the potential value of silence. No great issue was floated without a proportion of the overhead being earmarked for publicity, publicity often meaning the very opposite of what the word usually suggests. Even when it was publicity in the ordinary sense, what was bought was not straight advertising but highly optimistic comment.[1]

Apart from the degree to which the investor was well or ill-advised, the concentration of power in the hands of a few banks was very much disliked by the Left. Even before the war, that concentration had gone far; although there were still a good many local banks, some of which financed local industries. But the *Crédit Lyonnais*, the *Société Générale*, the *Comptoir d'Escompte*, with the two great bankers' banks, the *Banque de Paris et des Pays-Bas* and the *Union Parisienne*, were overwhelmingly powerful in the stock market. There were minor establishments, but the big five either controlled the mass of French investment or were closely linked with its controllers.

They were especially closely linked with the only possible rival of the private banks, the Bank of France. The Bank of France was not a state bank, as was often hastily assumed. It was a private corporation which, in return for certain privileges, the most important being the right of note issue, stood in a special relation to the Government. But it was the property of its shareholders; who elected the Regents, and, although the State appointed the Governor, he had to possess a minimum number of shares, a provision that limited the choice of the Minister of Finance to such competent persons as had the shares or could acquire temporary title to them,—that is, to important financiers or to friends of important financiers. The Regents survived Ministers and Governors; they were drawn from the great banking and business families, Rothschilds, Wendels and the rest, the same small class that provided the directors of the railway companies, of insurance companies, the rulers of the *Comité des Forges* and of the other great industrial trusts. A very strong Government might have kept this oligarchy in its place, but the French political system was not designed to produce strong Governments.

Pessimistic political philosophers like Alain were more or less

---

[1] One of the critics of the Paris money market ('Lysis') asserted that as soon as the Russo-Japanese War broke out, the great banks doubled their monthly publicity budgets.

reconciled to this state of affairs. He thought it less remarkable that in a state dedicated to political equality there should be such economic inequality, than that in a society marked by such economic inequality there should be any political equality. Kind words and small favours for the weak: harsh words and great favours for the strong: that was the most one could expect. Such resignation was not common, and other Radical doctrinaires saw in the power of the banks and of the financiers one of the chief obstacles to the realization of the party programme. To M. Jammy-Schmidt things had not greatly changed since the days of Garnier-Pagés and Renouvier, if, indeed, since the days of Cambon. The Third Republic was faced with the same hydra-headed monster as the First and Second. To another Radical thinker, M. Albert Bayet, the problem was one of post-war immorality in politics and private life.[1] On the one hand, there was the sovereign people, or that depository of its sovereignty, the Chamber, and on the other a mere handful of magnates. Yet in conflicts between the representatives of universal suffrage and the bankers, how few and brief were the victories of the politicians! Somehow this defiance of the laws of politics and morals must be put an end to.

As an electoral cry, attacks on the bankers were highly profitable. In 1924 they were described as the 'economic religious orders', thus enabling those numerous Radicals who could recognize an enemy only if he wore a cassock, to rally to the good cause. But however useful as an electoral cry, the disguising of the banks and bankers as monasteries and monks was a source of illusion. It suggested that it would be as easy to uproot the *Société Générale* as the Society of Jesus, that the *Banque de Paris et des Pays-Bas* could be put in its place as easily as the Sulpicians. This was an error. M. Émile Combes, the model Radical statesman, had only to risk the hostility of his political enemies when he made and enforced the law against the orders. Few of his own supporters had a secret weakness for the Carthusians or the Dominicans.

It was very different when it came to attacking the temples of the money-changers. The Radicals might have read *Erewhon* with profit and pondered the history of the musical banks. The religious orders had, in their lay branches, in the 'third order' of St. Francis or of St. Dominic, very zealous friends, but there were few religious tertiaries in the ranks of the Left. Very different was the situation of the banks, the issue houses, the great industrial companies. They had their tertiaries, in hundreds of thousands, in all parties, including all parties of the Left, including even the Communist party. That there was no real identity of interest between M. de Wendel or M. Finaly and the thrifty militant with 50,000 francs in mixed securities was easy to

---

[1] Writing before the Stavisky explosion, M. Bayet was able to imply, without running the risk of being laughed out of court, that all or almost all the sinners were on the Right.

affirm, but harder to get believed. From top to bottom, the investing public had in common a passionate desire not to lose its capital or its interest by inflation or repudiation. A thoroughly solvent State could have defied the 'congrégations économiques' as a securely established State had defied the 'congrégations religieuses', but the French State, since 1914, was seldom thoroughly solvent. It could not command, it could only beg, and when it tried to command, the threatened financiers were able to

> . . . put on the weeds of Dominic
> Or in Franciscan think to pass disguised.

The disguise always worked; the alarmed faithful rallied to the cause of financial safety and prudence, and the mortified deputy, taking all too seriously the applause which had greeted his rhetorical defiance of the 'wall of money' at election times, found that the wall still stood and that, on the other side of it, were enough of his own supporters to make it impregnable.

It was the constantly recurring financial stress of the French State that made the chief difference between the political problem of the money power before 1914 and after. It was not Panama, or Russia, or Serbia, who now needed free access to the French investor's savings but the French Republic. The solvency of the Republic was what was in question; and that solvency was repeatedly in danger as great masses of short-term bonds became mature, or as an unbridgeable deficit put the Government in the position of having to borrow, or print banknotes, or default. It always chose to borrow, and that meant it was at the mercy of the lenders. It was not only the rich who organized, in these circumstances, what M. Bayet picturesquely called a 'Vendée of Money' or proved more ready to sacrifice their sons than their savings for France.[1]

In these circumstances the position of the Bank of France was decisive. For one thing it was playing a greater part in the general banking life of the nation than it had done in the past. Before 1914, the Government had had to force the Bank to set up provincial branches in order to make its discount facilities available in every department. Before 1914, the great French deposit banks, the *Crédit Lyonnais*, the *Société Générale*, were comparable in size with the great English joint-stock banks: that is, were among the largest banks in the world. But they did not grow at the same rate as their English sisters, faced as they were by the competition of Government-favoured institutions like the *Banques Populaires*. These, starting out to be 'People's Banks' to make cheap credit available to small shopkeepers

---

[1] M. Bayet might have remembered his *Quatre-vingt-treize*. As Victor Hugo pointed out, the peasants were more ready to sacrifice their sons than their horses. It is a noble thing to die for one's country, but as for being bankrupted for it, the theme still awaits its Horace. *Carent quia vate sacro.*

and small craftsmen, found it easier and more profitable to deal with the more prosperous sections of the middle-class. Other special banks were set up after the war to liquidate war damages, or to lend to creditors of the State, or for other special purposes. But the chief competitor of the great commercial banks was now the Bank of France.

The Bank of France had no longer to be coerced into financing the needs of local business. It went after it, with what its rivals thought indecent eagerness. Its branch managers were encouraged to approach local business men and to undercut the local banks. More than that, by re-discounting commercial paper up to nine months and then, after a period in which the bill was in the hands of a commercial house long enough to recover a legal virginity, re-discounting it, the Bank became a source of long-term capital as well as of current needs.

It was difficult for a small local bank to compete with this octopus, and the Bank was accused, with some plausibility, of using its special position to crush out opposition in cases where a local bank could have competed successfully, given anything like equal conditions. The local bank, often serving local industries, was, in any case, doomed to decline in importance, but the decline was hastened by the action of the Bank of France as well as by the growth of great holding companies which financed whole industries from their own reserves and raised the capital directly from the investing public.

The local bank did not always die peacefully, absorbed in the larger communion of the great financial trusts. It was sometimes killed, and in one of these murders, the Bank of France played a rôle that revealed how difficult it was for it to do so many different kinds of banking business at the same time.

A bold, speculative financier, M. Oustric, by a series of ingenious coups got control of some important provincial banks which he used in his complicated juggling in the stock market. When the crash came, it was revealed that the funds used by Oustric for his campaign came largely from the Bank of France, which had allowed this obscure financier over a hundred million francs of credit. Worse still, the paper discounted was only formally good, for it consisted of bills drawn by one Oustric company on another Oustric company. The gullibility of great banks in all countries was no great secret by 1930, but for the great national controller of the French money market to be caught out as a sleeping partner in a vulgar fraud which wrecked several important local banks did not increase its prestige. The press, it may be added, did not stress the rôle of the Bank of France in the matter unduly—nor as some people thought, enough.

Criticism of the Bank was increasingly widespread. There were markedly oligarchic characteristics about its organization. Although there were 40,000 shareholders, only the 200 with the largest holdings could vote at the annual meeting. The result was to create a banking aristocracy; seats on the board of directors, that is the Council of Regents, were in many cases hereditary. There had been a member of the Mallet family among the Regents ever since the Bank was founded; there were several other dynasties among the Regents, and it was pointed out that the great industries represented on the board were the sheltered industries. It was the directors of railways, shipping companies and other subsidized industries, the directors of steel and armament works whose chief customer was the State, the directors of insurance companies fearful of State competition, who ruled the Bank. That is, interests wholly or in great part dependent for solvency on State action were in a condition to dictate the monetary and budgetary policy of the nation. It was not to be wondered at that the policy of the Bank often seemed to be opposed to that of the Government and of great branches of industry not represented among the Regents.

The currency position added to the difficulties of the relationship. The Bank thought that it had a duty to guard the franc against the improvidence of the politicians. After the devaluation of the dollar and the pound, the franc remained the one great currency attached t) gold; the Bank's action could make speculation against the franc highly dangerous or comparatively safe. As the agitation for devaluation grew, it became more and more important to secure harmony between the Ministry of Finance and the Bank, and that harmony was not always evident.

The money market was saturated with short-term Treasury bonds; there was no chance of a successful flotation of long-term obligations; there was a recurrent deficit. How was this situation to be dealt with? By rigorous economy, by cutting salaries and expenses of all kinds, even war pensions: so, the orthodox bankers insisted, and only so, could devaluation with all its risks be avoided. M. Flandin was opposed to devaluation, but he was also opposed to the policy of mere deflation preached by the Bank to his very orthodox Finance Minister, M. Germain Martin. But the rumours of devaluation produced a run on the franc and the Bank did not seem very anxious to defend the currency by the usual means. It was discovered how vain it was merely to put a new Governor in, for M. Flandin's nominee, like a good Republican priest made a bishop in the old days of the Concordat, soon absorbed the point of view of his Regents. A bad motor-accident crippled the Prime Minister, and when he finally gave way and asked the Chamber for full powers to carry out the economy programme insisted on by orthodox finance, he failed to secure support.

To replace M. Flandin was not easy. The first aspirant was the President of the Chamber, M. Bouisson. He was an excellent presiding officer, but he learned even more quickly than Addington had, the limitations of an excellent presiding officer. His Minister of Finance was no less a person than M. Caillaux, but M. Caillaux was no longer either a martyr or a miracle worker. The Bouisson-Caillaux Cabinet fell the first day it presented itself to the Chamber. M. Bouisson tried to bully ·the deputies, and they were no longer to be bullied. They could be led but not driven, and the task of leading them fell to M. Flandin's Foreign Minister, M. Pierre Laval. As M. Flandin noted, the Chamber which had refused to trust him with full powers made no difficulty about trusting them to M. Laval. The Bank had won; France was to try another dose of deflation.

It was an expensive victory for the Bank. The politicians, humiliated by the mobs of 1934, were bitterly resentful of further humiliation at the hands of the Regents of the Bank of France. The anger of the Left was no longer concentrated on M. de la Rocque, but on the ruling oligarchy. It was the hold of the '200 families' over the economic life of France that was the theme of indignant oratory and of acute polemics from the pen of left-wing economists like M. Francis Delaisi. With another of those historical parallels so stimu-lating to oratory, so crippling to thought, the Bank was thought of as 'another Bastille to be taken'. What France needed was the abolition of the new feudalism; there was in the offing a new 4th of August in which the new nobility would surrender its privileges—whether willingly or not did not matter.

For the moment, the Bank and its allies had their way. M. Laval, empowered to issue decree-laws to redress the financial position, used his powers most lavishly. Aspects of the national life, as remote from budgetary importance as the control of carrier pigeons, were regulated along with salaries, wages, the rents of houses and the terms of leases. Purists were angered by the compulsory reduction of rents; and economists pained by the assumption that prices could be controlled by law. But deflation was applied all along the line: and if France was to stay on gold, there was no other remedy. Nor was the attempt to control prices by law (window-dressing as it largely was) entirely fruitless. Already prices were very rigid over great areas of the national economy; trusts, import quotas, price lists approved by cartels, had all sheltered so much of the price structure from the free play of the market, that administrative pressure had more chances of reducing costs than at first sight seemed likely. The general upturn in world production and price-levels helped M. Laval, as it might have helped M. Flandin had his Government survived.

The reductions in salary, in pensions, in interest yields were more obvious than the general improvement in the economic position of France. The cleavage between the interests of the civil servants and the other employees was greatly diminished now, since all suffered more from the rapid fall in cash incomes than they were conscious of benefit-ing by the maintenance of their real wages by a fall in prices. Many persons who had thought of themselves as secure members of the bourgeoisie, among them the employees of the banks, were embittered by a fall in their standard of living that did not drive them (as it might have done earlier) to the Right but to the Left. The demonstrations against the 'decree-laws' were more noisy than violent, but they helped to swell the tide of popular resentment against a system that seemed to be descending an endless spiral of increasing poverty. The Right promised health at the end of an unpleasant treatment. The Left promised health and the abolition of the treatment—and both at once.

The formation of the Laval Ministry seemed to revive the hopes of the militants of the Right, and as the foreign crisis grew more acute,[1] the *Croix de Feu* and the other Fascist or semi-Fascist organizations took the field, while the Peasant Front of Dorgères launched its tax-strike. The Left press was full of the most alarming stories of the designs of La Rocque and of the guilty complicity of M. Laval. The Radical leaders, even so conservative a Radical as M. Herriot, refused to tolerate the patronage by M. Laval of the *Croix de Feu*, and when he denied, as he did, that he patronized the movement, they demanded proof of that love for and loyalty to Republican liberties of which the Prime Minister boasted. The Radicals, indeed, were so angered or frightened by the menace of the Fascist leagues that they at last empowered their leaders to enter into a close alliance with the Socialists and Communists. Meantime they demanded guarantees from the Government.

They got them. They had asked for dissolution of the Fascist leagues. They got the word of honour of M. Ybarnégaray that his friend, Colonel de la Rocque, was not a conspirator against the Republic or liberty—and in the Chamber, M. Ybarnégaray's word counted for a great deal. M. Blum and M. Thorez wanted more; they wanted an assurance that the military side of the *Croix de Feu* would be done away with. M. Ybarnégaray agreed to this condition and, as it was assumed that he was speaking in the name of the Colonel, the Chamber was delighted to have the threat of conflict (however unlikely it was) thus removed by a gentleman's agreement that all semi-military organizations should be disbanded. But it was not certain that M. Ybarnégaray had been speaking for the *Croix de Feu*, and it was quite certain that he had not been speaking for the more militant organizations on the Right. Despite the angry protests of the *Solidarité Française* and the *Jeunesses Patriotes*, Parliament went ahead with making para-military organizations illegal, entrusting the right to dissolve them not to the courts but to the Government, restraining the sale of arms and making incitement to murder or lesser crimes a misdemeanour.[2]

By the end of 1935, any danger of a Fascist coup (and the danger

[1] See p. 687.   [2] The first application of the law was to M. Maurras, see p. 683.

had always been greatly exaggerated by journalists and politicians who took Paris too seriously) was over. The *Croix de Feu* had become merely an electoral organization of the Right, like the *Ligue de la Patrie Française*. On the other side, the Left had at last got together in an electoral alliance of all the important parties. On January 11th, 1936, the *Rassemblement Populaire* published its programme. It was inevitably vague and compromising, since it had to cover the common minimum demands of Radicals who were what in most countries would have been regarded as really Conservatives, and of Communists who, only a few years before, had been denouncing their present allies as the worst enemies of the workers.

There were safe generalities. The oath of July 14th, 1935, was repeated. Everybody was ready to defend 'democratic freedom, give bread to the workers, work to the young and a great human peace to the world.' To achieve this end without 'abandoning either their own principles, doctrines or ultimate objectives' the parties to the pact made some specific proposals.

They were mainly political laws against the Fascist leagues and in favour of publicity about the ownership of the press; with a plea for collective security and the strengthening of the League of Nations. But there were some economic proposals. There was to be a national unemployment fund; a reduction of the working week without any reduction of wages; a revaluation of agricultural prices (the last to be accompanied by vigilance as to the cost of living). It was implied that the middleman was the cause of low prices to the farmer and high prices to the consumer, a generality that, in some cases, resulted in the same candidate being able to promise, with a clear conscience, a high price for wheat in the rural part of his constituency and a low price for bread in the urban part of it. A central Wheat Board was to put an end to speculation and the stock market was to be reformed. The tax system was to be reformed, too, and evasion by the rich to be made difficult by the old panacea of a 'fiscal identity card'. It was a programme that had great political appeal and it was launched on a flowing tide.

The chances of the Left were greatly increased by an event which made the Socialist leader more of a hero to his followers than he had ever been before. The death of Jacques Bainville had removed one of the members of the trinity of the *Action Française*. Distressed adherents of the movement, waiting for the funeral procession to start, noticed M. Blum with a colleague and his wife in a car. The zealots of the movement had been for months inflamed by the rhetoric of M. Maurras; here was the chief *métèque*, the enemy of Italy, the dispenser of sophisms and *saboteur* of the true French policy. The Royalists postponed their mourning and attacked the Socialist leader. M. Blum was badly beaten. The police were in time to save him from what might have been worse than a beating, and the cold, distant intellectual became a martyr.

The news of the attack did for the Left what the assault on Loubet had done. It angered them and discredited their enemies, for in France, gang assaults on elderly and defenceless victims were not regarded as signs of dynamism but of cowardly brutality. The Royalists might defend the assault (as his constituents defended the beating by Preston Brooks of Senator Sumner before the American Civil War), but the danger of action in the street against the politicians, so serious a year or so before, was now negligible. M. Maurras was sent to prison for incitement to violence [1] and the cause of the *Front Populaire* was even more certain of victory.

The Right entered the electoral battle of 1936 in more than its customary disorder and depression. The refusal of the *Croix de Feu* to run candidates meant that the body which had diverted to itself so much of the energy and money of the Conservative forces would neither play the regular political game nor really play the alternative game of revolution.

On the other side the enthusiasm with which the Communists threw themselves into their new rôle of the patriotic party was funny but electorally profitable. Their picture of Hitler with a blood-stained knife between his teeth was an ingenious turning of the Right's cannon against it, for it recalled the Bolshevik with the bloody knife between his teeth who had done such good service in 1919. That the knife was marked 'Krupp-Wendel' made the picture even more effective, for it reminded the French workers that French capitalists were ready to do business with the enemy of the German workers, the enemy of all workers, the Nazi régime whose intolerable criminality was such that, beside it, the French bourgeois Republic was worth fighting for. After the past years of ingenious devices, financial, diplomatic, political, there was something new in the air.

The electors responded nobly. Of course (as was occasionally forgotten), 1932 had been a great Left triumph, too, so there was not room for a great shift of seats in the Chamber. The parties supporting the People's Front gained about 30 seats, but the significant shift was within the Left coalition.

The Radicals lost about as many seats as the Left gained as a whole. The Socialists became the biggest party, though they polled only about the same number of votes as in 1932; but the Communists doubled their votes, and, thanks to the working of their alliances, for the first time they got seats in the Chamber in rough proportion to their strength. A million and a half Communist voters, 72 Communist Deputies

---

[1] Defenders of the right of French political journalists to say what they please, dug up from the files of the Communist press examples of attacks on M. Blum as violent as any made by the *Action Française*.

instead of 10! That was the most striking aspect of the election and the greatest political justification of the *volte face* in Communist policy. There was almost as much attention paid to the young Communist leader, Maurice Thorez, the vigorous and convincing preacher of the new patriotic, not to say jingo, doctrine, as there was to Léon Blum. The election was a victory over the friends of Mussolini and of Hitler, as much as over the French capitalists. In the Paris region, where the Communists polled more votes than the Radicals and Socialists put together, and were by far the strongest party, the schism in the nation seemed to be healed. The old Jacobin tradition was renewed; the cries of 'Up the Soviets' and 'Up France' were no longer contradictory.

II

In 1930, the neglected and electorally contemptible German National Socialists suddenly became one of the greatest parties in the Reichstag; the number of Nazi voters rose from 800,000 in 1928 to 6,500,000, and the world was brought face to face with a sudden revival of extreme German nationalism. The impact of the depression on Germany had given an opportunity to the party that had denounced the 'system', that had opposed both the Dawes Plan and Young Plan, and whose main programme was the restoration of the glory of Germany which had been lost by the crimes of the Socialists, Liberals and other traitors of 1918. In no European country was the rise of Hitler more deserving of calm study than in France, since it was against France that his most violent diatribes had been directed, and since it was the position of France in Europe and her security that were most directly menaced.

France had two policies open to her, either of which might have succeeded. One was the policy of using her present military and economic strength to make a triumph of Hitler too expensive for Germany to contemplate. She could have treated the Führer, while he was still an Austrian agitator, as Bismarck was prepared to treat Boulanger. The ruling politicians in Germany might have been coerced or encouraged into really vigorous resistance—or France could have attempted to make the economic conditions which had helped to bring about the startling growth of the Nazi party less intolerable. The second policy was not incompatible with the first, but to adopt either, or both, required vigilance—and continuity.

In a sense there was plenty of vigilance. The incorrigible militarism of the German people, their unending wish for revenge on France, were asserted and stressed by the leaders of the extreme Right. Had not the premature evacuation of the Rhineland been followed, not by the improvement of the relations between France and Germany, but by the rise of Hitler? Would the Germans have rallied in such numbers to the cause of the man who had planned the annihilation of France if the bridgeheads of the Rhine had still been garrisoned by French troops? *Oderint dum metuant*: the Germans might have squirmed but they could not have fought. On the other side there were to be found optimists to whom the alarm over Hitler was simply an invention of the Right. 'What the Nationalists are once again trying to revive is the state of mind, or rather, the passions of 1912–13. . . . Hitler to-day is miles away from power. He may be a little nearer it than, say, Franklin-Bouillon, but he is infinitely farther away from it than General Boulanger on the night of 27th January, 1889, or than Paul Déroulède on the day of Félix Faure's funeral.' The author of this optimistic view was M. Léon Blum; and the main ground for his optimism was the traditional trust in the German Socialists which M. Blum had learned from Jaurès. What was to be feared from a country in which the Prussian citadel of democracy was guarded by Herren Braun and Severing?

These were the illusions of the early spring of 1931 and they did not long survive. In March, came the sudden and dramatic announcement of the customs union between Germany and Austria. It was sprung on the world in a fashion that made it very unlikely that the powers immediately interested would believe that only a financial arrangement was in question. France, Italy, Czechoslovakia protested, and if the partners to the union had any notion of defying the League, the great Austrian banking crisis which began with the failure of the *Credit-Anstalt* made both Germany and Austria more docile. A decision of the Permanent Court of International Justice that the union was contrary to the obligations assumed by the Austrian Government was highly political in its character. The judges voted along the lines of the policies of their respective Governments which, it was assumed rather easily in England, showed that the French and other judges of the majority were influenced by non-judicial considerations; the minority, of course, were not.

The rapid spread of the banking panic made the Austrian question less important than it had been, for if the world had been recovering from the Wall Street panic of 1929, that recovery was soon stopped. From Vienna, the panic spread to Germany, and it was, from the point of view of orthodox finance, a necessary and desperate last remedy when President Hoover issued on June 20th an appeal for a general moratorium on reparations and war debts. Mr. Hoover was in a hurry and he had neglected to secure the consent of the most important financial power at that moment—France. Nor could he do anything to reassure the French, who believed that once reparations were stopped they would never be resumed, and who wondered if, in that event, the American people would forgive their debtors with anything like the resignation that the French were expected to display in forgiving theirs.

France was unwilling to take any serious financial risks to support the tottering German banking structure and, within a few weeks, the crisis had spread to England, whose bankers had been engaged in borrowing French money and lending it, at a profit, to the now congealed banking system of Central Europe.

In December, the first formal recognition of the end of reparations was made, but the link to the war debt question, which all Europeans could see, was invisible in Washington. It was invisible despite a visit to Washington made by M. Pierre Laval, since the French, for the moment masters of the situation, were not accommodating, and since no American politician, on the eve of a presidential election, could give France the guarantee she wanted, that what she did not get from Germany she should not be expected to pay America. By the time the American presidential election was over, French public opinion was resolved that the escape of Germany from paying what she had undertaken to pay should not be made more intolerable still by France's having to pay the country whose President had first launched the idea of a suspension of payments.

In vain M. Herriot pleaded with the Chamber to honour its bond. It was politically as impossible in France to pay anything to America, as it was politically impossible in America to admit any connection between the war-debt payments and reparations. But by the time that the debt question ended M. Herriot's Ministry, France had much more to worry about. The re-election of Hindenburg over the newly naturalized Hitler reassured most of the timid, but the Marshal, once safe in office, got rid of Brüning; and the Chancellor's fall was followed by the expulsion from the stronghold of republicanism in Germany, the Prussian Ministry, of those Social-Democratic leaders in whose energy and vigilance M. Blum had put such excessive trust. There was, as yet, less alarm than might have been expected. The Socialists were still inclined to criticize M. Herriot for being too obsessed with security; and those who thought of a German menace to peace, rather rejoiced. Hitler was still out of office, and von Papen and the Barons were less of a danger than Hitler would have been. When Schleicher followed Papen, there was a revival of hope. Had not the Nazis lost a great part of their support at the new elections? Had not the recognition of the German right to arms equality, tempered by verbal reassurances to France, shown the Germans that they could hope for justice and friendship from the Western powers? But in January the last hope of that kind had gone. Hitler came into office, and in a few weeks the Reichstag fire, and the Nazi terror that followed it, destroyed the last shreds of French belief in the power of the greatest of Socialist parties. Whatever hopes of peace and security France could still cherish could not be based on the power and goodwill of the organized workers of Germany.

French opinion had its own special difficulties in making up its mind about the nature of the German Revolution. It was free from some of the more foolish illusions of British opinion. Having known the pangs of defeat, it could understand the emotion and motives of the young Germans who wished to wipe out the disgrace of 1918, as young Frenchmen had wished to wipe out the disgrace of 1870, although André .Gide was no doubt more understanding than the average Frenchman when he noted that 'Hitlerism is a successful Boulangism'. That behind the Nazi movement were merely emotional resentments of injustices, and that these once remedied, all the fever of the new order would die down, was a view that not many Frenchmen could sincerely hold. But, on the other hand, the French intelligence was peculiarly unfitted to sympathize with the limitless mysticism of the Nazi movement; the passion for the absurd, the exaltation of unreason were phenomena whose power the countrymen of Voltaire and Molière were prone to underestimate. 'What is not clear is not French', Rivarol had written in the French revolutionary epoch, and that what was not French was unimportant was a natural illusion of an insular people.

If the very nature of the Nazi Revolution, its mystical brutality, its romantic and hysterical doctrines were calculated to perplex the French spectator, his bewilderment was not entirely the result of his own mental limitations. It was fostered by the new rulers of Germany with a skill that was underestimated by people who failed to realize that the Nazi leaders were capable of suiting their tunes to the audience, providing the Wagnerian warlike motifs for the home market and humane and reasonable Mozart for sale abroad.

Herr Hitler's great diplomatic problem, how to lull to sleep the suspicions of his potential enemies while Germany was still militarily impotent, was more difficult of solution in France than in Britain. There was that too famous text in *Mein Kampf* laying down the annihilation of France as one of the objectives of true German policy, while the same sacred book made peace with England a necessary preliminary to the destruction of France.

It was difficult to explain away these things, but there were ways and means. The journalistic favour that, in England, was secured by mere social politeness, was often on sale for more tangible gratification in France. But no amount of venality would have greatly affected French public opinion, if what Herr Hitler wanted the French people to believe had not been something which they profoundly wanted to believe, that, despite all that he and his associates had said, he was devoted to peace and that, with a few minor adjustments, especially after the return of the Saar to Germany, Germany would settle down. What if Pertinax doubted? Had not Mr. Ward Price expressed his conviction that France and Britain could count on the moderation of the Chancellor? It is true that the apologist who gave France this comforting assurance [1] suffered, like so many of his Communist enemies, from a lack of prophetic power, for he chose as a mouthpiece of the pacific sentiments of the Third Reich, and worthy exponent of the ideas of the Führer, Herr Röhm, shortly before that leader paid with his life for his political treason and sexual eccentricity.

Other apologists were less unlucky than M. de Brinon. M. Alphonse de Chateaubriant, as was natural in a romantic literary nobleman, saw (and not altogether wrongly) in the energy and passionate faith of the Hitler youth, something that was not abundant enough in France, while others saw in Nazi Germany a bulwark against Bolshevism. So with each new advance, new claim, new threat, the voices of the timid, the deceived, the morbidly anti-Bolshevik, mingled with those of the bought, in a common chorus of praise and explanation. Stout Nationalists like M. Louis Bertrand moved from defences of Louis XIV to defences of Herr Hitler, a historical progression not without its plausibility seen from another age or another continent, but a little odd in a defender of the true French national tradition. [2]

In addition to the admirers of dynamism and to the Nationalists with a natural admiration for the man who had succeeded in doing in Germany what no one had succeeded in doing in France, making national pride and national glory the main staple of politics, there were, on the Left, convinced pacifists who were willing to close their eyes to some of the more disagreeable methods of the new Germany in the hope that they would be reserved for internal use. This selfish, or prudent, view of French duty must not be too severely condemned, for France, on the other hand, was far more generous in the admission of refugees than was Britain, and it was Paris, not London, that received the mass of fugitives from the Gestapo.

One last source of reassurance to the alarmed French was directly fostered by Germany, by the old traditional method of buying praise and suppressing criticism. In a country where being a dupe is as great a sin as being a knave, the disinterested Nazi propagandist was harder to find than was the case in Britain. But too much should not be made of this. There was a genuine and honest willingness to end the Franco-German feud. Believing that one-sided history was a menace, a group of French and German scholars drew up a common statement on the origins of the war of 1914, revealing a large measure of agreement and a candid willingness to discuss points of disagreement. That the

---

[1] M. Fernand de Brinon.

[2] The high-water mark of this nonsense was reached by a gentleman calling himself by the almost too Proustian name of Séramidal de Saint-Georges d'Ardenay. Having rather hastily to interrupt a denunciation of the spreaders of false news of German aggression to note the occupation of Vienna, he described that untoward event as 'the reaction against the shady plebiscite improvised by the "Patriotic Front" Chancellor, Schuschnigg, which ended in a National-Socialist revolution'. Like M. Flandin, M. de Saint-Georges d'Ardenay came from the pacific Yonne.

resulting memorandum was not (except in one unimportant period-ical) published in Germany was of some significance.

Yet the triumph of Hitler in Germany had immediately raised a diplomatic problem of the first importance for France. Would she stand by her ally, Poland, whose very existence was menaced by the revival of a Nationalist Germany in which the traditional Prussian hostility to Poland would, in all probability, be dominant? Signor Mussolini was willing to try to find out; and he launched, in March 1933, the idea of a four-power pact between France, Britain, Italy and Germany which would enable the great powers to 'revise' the Treaty, in this case placate Germany at the expense of Poland, while preserving the Italian gains of 1919, the South Tyrol and the independence of Austria.

The succession states were at once alarmed and, at that stage of German military weakness, they could not be coerced, so the project of revision was dropped. But the passivity of France in face of the revival of a Germany which was obviously bent on escaping from the shackles of Versailles was not lost on Poland, and in January 1934, Hitler and Pilsudski signed a non-aggression pact and the intolerable wrongs of the German people were put in cold storage, so far as Poland was concerned. The Polish example was catching. If she could trust Nazi Germany, why should not others?

The powers of the 'Little Entente' which had an interest in pre-serving the *status quo* in the Danubian basin, began to draw apart from each other—and from France. Only Czechoslovakia affirmed its complete trust in France. The Foreign Minister of the Doumergue Government was Louis Barthou, Poincaré's closest political ally, and he was determined not to be lulled into inertia by the most profuse German promises. He would only go as far as offering a general system of non-aggression pacts in eastern Europe, open to Germany as well as to all the other powers. But Germany was no longer interested in general pacts of the Locarno type. She did not expect to be attacked; and what she wanted was a system of bi-lateral treaties which would enable her, when the time came, to isolate her enemies one by one. Poland, too, was for the moment hostile to any system that diminished the value of the immunity from German aggression that had been assured her.

In the Danubian basin, the problem was complicated by the dis-like for Italy felt by Jugoslavia; and France was still anxious to stay on good terms with Italy. The royal dictator, King Alexander, came to France to clear up the matter, and he and Barthou were assassinated in the streets of Marseilles by a Croatian terrorist. The Jugoslav Government was convinced that the assassination was the work of bands harboured by Hungary and Italy, and the situation of 1914 was almost reversed. But the awkward question of what interests benefited by the murder was glossed over. The death of King Alexander was for

France the loss of a trump card. The new rulers of Jugoslavia were much less securely in the saddle than Alexander had been. The Prince Regent, in particular, was believed to be violently opposed to any rapprochement with Soviet Russia, and it had been Barthou's policy to call in Russia to redress the balance upset by the defection of Poland.

In France, such a policy had been for some time advocated by such respectable leaders of the Left as M. Herriot, and it was soon to be advocated by such realist leaders of the Right as M. de Kerillis. Russia, the argument ran, was a satisfied power. She had an interest in the territorial *status quo* far greater than her theoretical interest in world revolution. So France backed up Russia in her claim to a seat on the Council of the League of Nations in 1934 and began negotiations for that treaty of mutual assistance which was to bring Russian weight down on the side of stability in Europe.

But while these questions were still unsettled, France had to make up her mind how far she would think herself bound, in the face of the new Germany, by the Treaty of Versailles. The time for the Saar plebiscite was at hand.

III

Long before 1935, when the Saar plebiscite fell due, few people in France still retained any illusions about the outcome. But for the Hundred Days, the provisions of the first Treaty of Paris in 1814 might have stood and the Saar have been made French in spirit. Over a century of German rule had made the territory as German as Franconia or Brandenburg, and before the rise of Hitler the outcome of the plebiscite was never thought to be in doubt. The Saarlanders would, of course, be making economic sacrifices by leaving the French customs union which permitted the entry of their products, from coal to the excellent Walsheim beer, without any tariff duties. But what were such losses compared with the gain of return to the Fatherland?

The Nazi Revolution seemed to alter things. For one thing, it was notorious that Germany was breaking the disarmament clauses of the Treaty of Versailles. Should she be allowed to benefit by the territorial clauses? The Prussian precedent of Bismarck's refusal to carry out the Schleswig plebiscite might be turned against his heirs. Nobody in France seriously proposed to take so bold a course, but there was surely a possibility that a region so full of Socialists, Catholics and Communists would refuse to vote to put itself under its class and creed enemies? If the plebiscite was safeguarded, it was conceivable that the Saarlanders would vote for the *status quo*, on the understanding that, when Hitler fell, they would be allowed to join a liberated Germany. The security of the plebiscite was, in fact, safeguarded by an international force mainly British, which was impartial, with—French observers thought—a kindly tolerance of the Nazi leaders which might mislead timid Saarlanders. The efforts of the Socialists, the Communists and a few Catholics to secure votes for the *status quo* were not looked on very sympathetically by many Frenchmen; they were not taken much more seriously than were the efforts of a handful of Frenchmen to secure votes for France. If it was true, as the hopeful believed, that Hitler was sincere in his promises of peace and amity after the Saar question was settled, it was to the advantage of France that it should be settled and settled quickly.

The result was decisive enough. Less than 10 per cent. voted for the *status quo*, less than 1 per cent. for annexation to France. In a predominantly proletarian region, an overwhelming majority had voted for the nation, not for the class. When all allowances had been made for the influence of the Bishop of Trier on the Catholics and for intimidation by the Nazis, the result was, or should have been, of the greatest significance for the leaders of Left parties in France who were still doped with illusions about the artificiality and transitoriness of national divisions. Whatever might be the case in France, it was not true in other countries that more than a handful of the workers were free of the national superstition and conscious only, or mainly, of their common interests as proletarians. And if this was true, the degree to which France had many truly class-conscious proletarians was of the utmost importance.

The question involved was of some urgency for, in France, the effect of the abnormally low birth rate of the war years was now being felt. In face of a rearming Germany what was to be done? Raising the period of army service from one to two years was the Government's solution, a solution opposed with the greatest bitterness by M. Blum and the Socialists. The alleged need for a stronger army, he argued, was the invention of the generals who wanted an aggressive army. The true policy was to agree with the other powers on disarmament and to force the programme of disarmament on Germany. It was an argument directly in line with the Jaurès tradition and it was likely to be electorally profitable (which was not quite out of line with the Jaurès tradition either). For a brief moment the Socialist protest was supported by the Communists. But the Communists had a master who was alive, not in the Panthéon; and on orders from Moscow they withdrew their opposition to a measure which strengthened the military power of a State which, however bourgeois, was about to become an ally of Russia.

Before the Communists had been given their orders, Herr Hitler had taken the occasion to announce openly that he was disregarding the arms limitations of Versailles. That Germany was rearming was no secret. An agreement for mutual air assistance between France and Britain, though not directed against Germany, was not unconnected with the success with which the Nazi Government was restoring the military might of the Reich. The official revelation that Germany had, in fact, created an illegal air force was no news in March 1935, and the further announcement that she was establishing an army whose peace strength was about twice that of the French home strength was alarming, but not unexpected. These unilateral denunciations of treaty obligations were, as the British Government solemnly pointed out, likely to destroy the chances of a 'comprehensive agreement'. But the German Government was wisely not taking British verbal denunciations at more than their paper value.

The rapid rise of an armed Germany was of interest to more countries than France and Britain. In July 1934, after the blood purge of his party, Herr Hitler's Austrian agents attempted a *coup d'état* which, although successful in removing the obstacle of Chancellor Dollfuss, was otherwise a failure and a failure largely because of the firm resolution of the Duce to oppose, by arms if necessary, so great a menace to Italian security as the establishment of a militant Germany on Italy's northern frontier. The threat to Austria (despite lavish promises and professions of good intentions from Herr Hitler) was driving Italy over to the side of the *status quo* powers. The new director of French foreign policy, M. Pierre Laval, was resolved to keep her there. With Italian support, France could hope to impress on Germany the fact that a new general war and a new defeat would follow a German attempt to undo the territorial settlement of Versailles. If the rulers of Germany were convinced that this was so, there would be no war.

The first steps to winning over Italy had been taken in January when M. Laval had visited Rome. There he believed that he had bought Italian support, or friendly neutrality, by some territorial cessions of not very valuable desert soil, by the transfer of some shares in the Addis-Ababa railway, and by extending until 1965 the right of the Italians of Tunis to have their children regarded as Italian, not as French subjects. It was a good bargain for France, if Italy had indeed been won. But the price was in fact a good deal higher: and the form the price would take was already evident.

In 1934 there had been a frontier fight between Italian and Abyssinian troops at a spot in the debatable land which was probably inside the Abyssinian frontier. The rights and wrongs of the case had been disputed, and Abyssinia which, under Italian patronage, had been admitted to the League of Nations, appealed to Geneva. Various forms of procedure were tried, but the Abyssinians paid less attention to Italian words than to Italian deeds; they noted the increase in Italian military strength on their borders and assumed, rightly, that Italy meant war.

War between two League members was an outrage on all the painfully accumulated post-war hopeful optimism. The French official reaction was to regret that a semi-barbarous state was a member of the

League, but even if she were, China had been a member too, and much good had that done her when her fellow-member, Japan, attacked her. The League was not really fit to keep peace all over the world, but it could keep peace where it was most menaced—in Europe. Even if it came to war in Abyssinia, what was at issue? The Abyssinian Empire's independence was almost as much a fiction as the independence of Morocco or Egypt. Alternatively it was by no means certain that its independence *was* menaced, for the Italians had once before found that it was easier to plan the conquest of Abyssinia than to achieve it. The Left, which of all sections in France had the greatest dislike of Mussolini, had also the greatest contempt for the military prowess of the Duce's armies, and it was content to leave the punishment of his temerity to the people immediately concerned—the Abyssinians. M. Laval, at any rate, was very reluctant to lose the fruits of his diplomacy, the separation of Italy and Germany, for such trivial reasons. He asked no awkward questions and it was unnecessary to tell him any lies; to deny, for instance, that war was decided on.

When the British and French Ministers met Signor Mussolini at Stresa, this tactful silence was not broken. The conference was agreed on the necessity of maintaining the integrity of Austria (which meant, if it meant anything, military action by Italy and France) and collective security was to be studied in order to 'maintain peace in Europe'. There was no mention of peace in Africa; the alarm of the French at the reported views of the British Chancellor of the Exchequer [1] was quieted. All was very satisfactory on paper; preparations were made for a mutual withdrawal of troops from the Franco-Italian border, and M. Laval could regard himself as another Camille Barrère. Italy had been won over. Nor was that all, for on May 2nd the Franco-Soviet pact was signed, and its form having been adjusted to the League system, London had approved. Germany, the treaty-breaker, the menace to the peace of Europe, was indeed encircled. She would not now be subjected to the temptation to use her new armaments to which the chance of a limited war would have exposed her. As Germany was not to be coaxed and cajoled into good behaviour, she must be politely but firmly intimidated.

The apparently sudden interest of the British Government in the Abyssinian question was a shock to M. Laval. He believed that to risk the loss of so important a stabilizing force in Europe as Italy, merely because of formal obligations to Abyssinia, was absurd. Britain had been right when she opposed the entry of Abyssinia into the League, and right when, in 1925, she negotiated with Italy over spheres of influence in Abyssinia in a fashion that showed little respect for the formal sovereignty of the Negus. The sudden British regard for legality, for the sacredness of frontiers, for the sanctity of treaties (which

[1] Mr. Neville Chamberlain.

693

France would have welcomed a few years before) was now suspect. Had it not been imposed on the British Government by the informal plebiscite of the 'peace ballot', by those sentimental 'clergymen' who, in the eyes of so many Frenchmen, were a danger to the peace of Europe, with their muddled and almost always ill-timed moralization of fundamentally non-ethical problems? M. Laval, too, was peculiarly ill-fitted to understand the British feeling for the small nation attacked by the great, since he, unlike his predecessor M. Barthou, had no great opinion of the smaller allies of France. Europe was ruled by the great powers; that was a fact to be acted on and not a problem in moral philosophy to be debated over.

These were the considerations that, it is assumed, were the basis of the policy of M. Laval. That these considerations were not only those of M. Laval was obviously true. To many, if not to all Frenchmen of the Right, the sacrifice of the new-won friendship of Italy on what they genuinely thought a frivolous or hypocritical pretext, was absurd. To the numerous Fascist sympathizers it was a crime. And to the Frenchmen with a predisposition to admire Italian policy and to covet Italian support, were suddenly added many Frenchmen whose suspicion of the candour of British policy had been aroused by a series of minor pinpricks. Again and again, since Hitler had come into power, the policy of the British Government had seemed to be one of verbal reproof followed by condonation. The Berlin visit of Sir John Simon after the announcement of German rearmament was not forgotten and it suddenly acquired a sinister appearance when it was announced that, without consulting the other signatories of the Stresa agreements, Britain had concluded a naval treaty with Germany, waiving the restrictions of Versailles and limiting, instead, German surface tonnage to 35 per cent. of the British. France felt more than wounded; she felt betrayed. After all the ridicule of French preoccupation with security, Britain had gone behind the back of her former ally and made what was, from her point of view, an excellent bargain, giving her a far greater margin of security than she had had in 1914. France remembered, too, that a deal with Britain as a preliminary to the annihilation of France was a part of the plan of campaign laid down in *Mein Kampf*. The last touch was added by the signing of the treaty on June 18th, the anniversary of Waterloo. Was this a new 'Belle Alliance' at the expense of France?

All through the summer of 1935, France, profoundly alarmed and irritated, hoped that she would not have to choose between Britain and Italy, that some face-saving device would be found, but the speech on September 11th of the new British Foreign Secretary, Sir Samuel Hoare, made it plain that France would have to choose, that is, if Britain were *really* going to throw all her strength in support of the League. The British Minister's speech was, indeed, so definite, so positive a commitment of Britain to the principle of collective security, that acute observers in France could hardly believe their ears. A Britain so devoted to the obligations of 'full acceptance of League membership' was worth the price of the alienation of Italy. A few years before a French writer on disarmament [1] had pointed out to his countrymen the great merits, from a French point of view, of the obligations of the League system. 'The provisions of the Covenant ought to be sacred to us Frenchmen: first of all we reject the theory of "scraps of paper"—and that means the Treaty of Versailles—then the Covenant makes a comprehensive effort to put an end to the present chaos of international relations by a methodical organization which is both political and juridical. We are attached to peace and the author of the *Discourse on Method* is one of us.' But there was little Cartesian rationalism displayed in the last months of 1935.

The cleavage over the Abyssinian question ran through all sections of the country. Despite the outward enthusiasm of the Left for the League and for sanctions, there were many enemies of the internal policy of the Laval Government who privately wished him well in his attempt to avoid estranging either Britain or Italy. The despatch of the British Home Fleet into the Mediterranean encouraged those Frenchmen who were willing to incur risks if Britain were really serious. They told their countrymen that, when she really made up her mind, Britain was unshakable and unbeatable: had she not 'had the hide of Napoleon'? On the other hand, if Britain meant business, and that meant war, the timid, the pacific, the prudent and the pro-Italian parties all found themselves united in a common hatred and fear of drastic action. Among the students, the appearance of Professor Jèze of the University of Paris, who had been the counsel for the Emperor of Abyssinia at Geneva, was the occasion of a series of riots which prevented one of the most eminent of French law teachers from lecturing.[2] Among the French Catholics a violent dispute ranged on one side the supporters of the Duce and on the other the critics of Italian political morality led by M. Paul Claudel, M. François Mauriac and M. Jacques Maritain, a division that was to reappear a few months later in a more profound form over Spain.

The fear of war was the chief argument, the chief emotion to be utilized by Signor Mussolini and his French partisans and employees to weaken the party in favour of the full League policy. The Italian régime was dictatorial; it could not afford to retreat, and its chief had better go down fighting in face of the great powers than be quietly squeezed out of existence by sanctions. Slow sanctions he could ignore for the time being, counting on speedy victory to deliver him from the mild boycott organized from Geneva. Real sanctions, the imposition

[1] M. André D. Toledano.
[2] Too much attention was paid to this student demonstration. Law students in France contain a much higher proportion of idle and rich young men than is the case with the student body of the other faculties.

of impotence on his mechanized troops by holding up the oil supply, that, he gave to understand, meant war. Was France willing to fight a war on which the immediate burden would fall on her (she had a frontier bordering Italy as well as one bordering Germany) for such sentimental reasons as the British Government gave to cover their realist political jealousy of the appearance of a great power on the borders of Egypt?

The newspapers that defended the Italian case and spread the Italian threats went to extremes of abuse that startled even old readers. *Gringoire*, the weekly organ run by M. de Carbuccia (a Corsican clansman—associate of M. Chiappe) was perhaps the most virulent of all the pro-Italian and anti-English journals, but it was a hot race and M. Beraud, the chief mud-slinger of *Gringoire*, only won by a short head.

Mixed up with the question of foreign policy was a question of internal policy. The semi-Fascist parties in France were on the downgrade politically; the approaching elections would inevitably mean a triumph for the Left, unless the Right could pin on its opponents the deadly charge of war-mongering. And the philosophical Fascists could not afford to see the régime in Italy collapse; its strength, efficiency, and vigour had been the pride of the *Action Française* for over a decade. In Italy, the revolution which M. Maurras had preached was practised.

The great victory of the Baldwin Government in a general election in which the matter of dispute was which side would support the League and the Negus more vigorously, further forced M. Laval's hand, for his opponents, attacking him for many other reasons, could also attack him for his failure to collaborate more warmly with a Government so representative of British sentiment. Indeed, however reluctantly, M. Laval was bound to follow a strong British lead, unless he could induce Britain to adopt his policy of a compromise that would give the Duce enough to justify a slight retreat on his part. M. Laval thought that such an arrangement was necessary unless Britain was ready to fight, and he asserted that Sir Samuel Hoare from the first had assured him that Britain would not push economic sanctions anywhere near the edge of war.

M. Laval had his way. The world learned through the indiscretion or indiscipline of *Pertinax*, who had consistently opposed the Laval policy of trying to run with the hare and hunt with the hounds, that the brave words of September were being swallowed, that by war and the threat of war, the Duce was getting a great deal of the territory of his fellow-member of the League and of the *Annunziata*. If the Duce had at once accepted the Hoare-Laval plan, the faces of the League and of France and Britain might have been saved. But he waited and British public opinion, less plastic than was necessary, killed the scheme.

All now depended on the prophetic talents of the military experts in

France and Britain who calculated on a long and exhausting war in whose course the mild sanctions adopted would, perhaps, be decisive. As the experts were wrong, the defeat of the League and of the two chief powers in it, was made manifest to all the world in the first months of 1936. M. Laval's policy had failed. Italy had been neither conciliated nor intimidated. Britain had not been won over to collective security (the willingness of the Baldwin Government to accept the Hoare-Laval pact, like the failure to impose effective sanctions, showed that); and the British people, whose heart and pride had more been deeply involved than their Government's, were angered at what they thought was a betrayal by France. Even if M. Laval had not failed, elections were near at hand and it was time that the Radicals were back in power, so the Radical Ministers resigned from the Cabinet, which meant that it fell and M. Pierre Laval gave way to a Government headed by M. Albert Sarraut, whose business was to do nothing until the elections in May.

M. Sarraut and his Foreign Minister, M. Flandin, had, however, some current business to do. They had to keep their eyes open for a chance to liquidate the Abyssinian question, which Italian victory was making so desirable. They had also to ratify the treaty with Russia which M. Laval had ostentatiously neglected to do. The ratification was opposed mainly on the ground that it would irritate Germany and give her an excuse, however bad, for new treaty violations. It was also opposed (it was an election year) by many politicians who feared the French Cómmunist Party and who believed the ex-Communist, M. Doriot, when he assured them that the only object of Russian foreign policy was to get France into a war with Germany—and leave her to fight it alone. These predictions were warmly attacked both by friends of the Soviet Union and by practical politicians, some of whom appealed to the precedent of the alliance of Francis I and the Sultan against the Emperor Charles V. A deputy of the Right, M. Vallat, denied the validity of this parallel. Soleiman the Magnificent, he said, did not keep a Moslem party in France to overthrow his ally's Government and replace the Bible by the Koran! But the Chamber ratified the treaty and sent it to the Senate where it was still being debated when France was suddenly faced with the greatest decision of her post-war history. On March 7th, the people of Paris learned that Herr Hitler, who so shortly before had accepted, freely, the obligations of the Locarno Pact, had sent his troops into the demilitarized area of the Rhineland.

With the occupation of the Rhineland, a question that most Frenchmen thought of subordinate importance suddenly became primary. What was the strength of the French Army? So long as Germany was more or less limited in her military organization by the Treaty of Versailles, the strength of the French Army could be allowed to decline. It is true that, apart from serious doubts as to the efficacy of the disarmament clauses of the Treaty, the highly disciplined and trained Reichswehr was a formidable force and, as it consisted entirely of long-service troops, it provided an admirable nucleus that could grow very rapidly. Nevertheless, the disparity in force was too great for Germany to be ready to risk the arbitrament of arms, unless backed up by another country that could supply arms and men. That country was, for a long time, Russia; or so French military opinion feared. But even after the escape of Germany from the military strait-jacket of Versailles, the military position of France was secured by the demilitarization of the Rhineland. Guarded from sudden invasion by the great fortress line called after the War Minister, André Maginot, France was in a position to make sure that war, when and if it came, would be fought in Germany, and the prestige of Prussian methods in Germany was largely due to the justifiable boast that, since 1815, the Prussian Army had saved the lands it served from invasion. With the Rhineland demilitarized it would be impossible to give such a guarantee and the French, obsessed with their own memories of invasion, attached great importance to the fact that in a new war it would be Cologne and Coblence, not Rheims and Lille, that would suffer. 'To each one his turn', as a candid deputy had put it at the time of the Ruhr invasion. It was this belief that encouraged the Left to demand and the Right to concede a great reduction in the term of military service. From three years it was first reduced to eighteen months and then, in 1930, to one year. From the point of view of many Frenchmen this was the most tangible fruit of victory and a sufficient reply to the not always well-informed foreign critics who talked of French militarism and the French refusal to reduce armaments.

The reduction in the length of service did not, of course, reduce the strength of the Army by two-thirds. It was in the first place an inseparable part of the scheme to increase to around 100,000, that is to about the legal strength of the Reichswehr, the long-service professional troops who were to be the backbone of the new army. But it was hard to recruit so many in a country that had next to no unemployment, especially as the terms offered recruits were not financially very tempting and as, in the general expectation of peace, there was not much to attract the ambitious soldier. It was, indeed, hard enough to recruit even officers. The pay was bad; captains with around £11 and commandants with around £16 a month were in a desperate situation, if they had no private means, and although these starvation rates were raised, officers believed, with more or less justice, that since they had no votes and were not allowed to organize, they suffered in comparison with the electorally powerful bureaucracy.

A more effective method of making up for the fall in peace-strength of the Army was the system of treating the conscripts who had served one year, not as free from their military obligations except for their annual reserve training, but as being 'en disponsibilité'. The men who had had an intensive training for one year were, in legal theory, sent off on long leave, but were still liable to recall at any moment. To recall them was not to order general mobilization, it was merely to stop their conditional leave. This system had been tried before, under the Second Empire and in the early years of the Republic. It had been found, however, that the conscripts on long leave regarded being called back to the colours as a grievance; and it remained doubtful down to 1936, how far the distinction between being on conditional leave and being released from active service was sufficiently appreciated to make the recall politically any more feasible than a mobilization would have been.

The illusions about the possibilities of a great colonial army making up for the stagnation of French population had survived the war in a few breasts. Mangin was as enthusiastic as he had been in 1913, but the colonial officials disliked conscription, which Lyautey had kept from being applied to Morocco; even where it was applied, in Algeria, Tunis, West Africa, it was on a very limited scale and the mass of native troops were volunteers. Not only was conscription generally unpopular, but the military value of Malagasies and Congo Negroes was found to be small. The French Native Army was, as in the past, drawn from the fighting stocks, Senegalese, Moroccans, Algerians, and even these regions contributed comparatively small contingents. Indeed, the necessity of stationing highly-paid professional French troops in the colonies made it a matter of debate whether the metropolis gained very much in a military sense from its Empire, although, as the Foreign Legion recovered from its low post-war establishment, the necessary police work was largely entrusted to it. That recovery of the Legion had its awkward side, however, for the Legion's efficiency grew as the post-war White Russian and other flotsam and jetsam of the war were replaced by Germans who, as was the case before 1914, were the main element in the Legion. Again, as before 1914, a large proportion of the recruits were Frenchmen, usually enlisted as Belgians, but the conditions and pay of the Legion compared unfavourably with those in the Colonial Army: the Frenchman of an adventurous and military turn of mind found it more natural to enlist openly in the colonial troops than clandestinely in the Legion.[1]

Expectation of a long peace and necessary economy made the French Army depend on its immense war stocks of equipment, with a consequent high and increasing degree of obsolescence that was evident as early as the war with Abd el Krim. In the post-war years, too, the proportion of cavalry that had fallen very low by 1918 rose again, until

---

[1] Contrary to general belief, there are few Americans or Englishmen in the Legion. But a very high proportion of these few write books; a very high proportion also desert; some do both.

the spread of mechanization led to the transforming of horsemen into tank drivers.[1]

At a time, that is, when the militarism of France was a subject of attack from politicians and theorists inside and outside the country, the French Army was actually a very cumbrous organization, powerful in defence but not readily prepared for the aggressive design attributed to it by critics like M. Blum. Hostility to the profession of arms, the assertion that conscription was the greatest of evils beside which the evils of capitalism were negligible, was a theme of which Alain, the Radical philosopher, never tired. But despite all the unpleasant memories of the last war, it was hard to arouse suspicion of a hard-worked and ill-paid professional body like the French officers. They were largely of lower middle-class origin, not the haughty aristocrats of the Radical tradition and, although attempts were made to chill the blood of electors with the dark designs of the Royalist and Catholic Commander-in-Chief, General Weygand, it was hard to believe that any army whose leaders, like Foch, had been so docile in the moment of victory, were going to turn into so many Spanish or Spanish-American generals many years later. The French Army was a faithful, even a docile servant of the State.

When the Locarno treaties had been signed, some soldiers had criticized them on the ground that they bound France to respect the neutrality of the Rhineland; which meant that Germany could prepare for war in peace, secure from a French invasion. But the advantages of the treaty—for a non-aggressive power—were manifest; and France was decidedly non-aggressive. So long as the Rhineland frontier was open, the French Army could carry the war into Germany, thus protecting France and effectively. aiding her eastern Allies. In these circumstances it was confidently believed that Germany would not fight. European peace was secured by the imposition of a limitation on German sovereignty that was both a punishment for her destructive prowess in the last war and a guarantee that she would not again enjoy the pleasures of victories won on foreign soil. 'Qu'un sang impur abreuve *leurs* sillons' was now the French motto.

It was this guarantee of peace, bought with nearly a million and a half lives, that France saw slipping away from her in the second week of March. What was to be done? M. Sarraut proclaimed that it was intolerable that Strasbourg should lie under German guns: but either Strasbourg or Stuttgart had to be endangered. It was a France prepared for a defensive war which was faced with the crisis of March 7th. The first and obvious retort to Hitler's breach of faith was for the French to occupy the territory. She was still much stronger than Germany;

---

[1] It is said that cavalry officers trained in the æsthetic tradition of the famous *Cadre Noir* of the Saumur cavalry school, took this transformation ill. 'Oil is dirty, dung is not', was how one critic summed up their attitude.

Hitler probably did not dare to fight; if he did he would be soon and thoroughly defeated. But to move at all meant to call up the troops on 'long leave', and if there was a real fight, even a brief one, it meant a general mobilization. It was a dreadful decision for a caretaker government to have to take.

When the news came to Paris, the man in the street had asked 'What will the English do?' On paper there was no doubt what they would do; they were bound as tightly as a country can be bound by the Locarno treaty, but the reaction in London to the German advance was not comforting to the French. There was a widespread measure of agreement that the German claim for equality was quite reasonable, that French worry over security was unnecessary, even disgracefully timid. The papers of the Left intelligentsia were particularly positive on these points. To point to the flagrant breach of faith, to appeal to the dangers of the future, was to be 'unconstructive'—and often to be unprinted. Then many in England were glad to pay back France for her lack of energy in the Abyssinian crisis, as many in France had been glad to pay back England for the naval treaty. Whether a French Government of the Sarraut type would have dared to do anything is hard to say, but its indecision was made a decision by the British attitude. Germany got away with the boldest and most essential of her early manœuvres. She was now ready to move on to conquest: and Europe passed into the shadow of war.

It is possible that the Government would have liked to have its hand forced by the General Staff and to be compelled to order a French counter-occupation that we now know would not have been opposed; but the generals of the Republic had been for long servants not masters. There was nothing to be done but to prepare for a dark future.[1] The immediate problems of the situation were left to the incoming Prime Minister, that veteran critic of French militarism, M. Blum.

[1] One result of this crisis was the recasting of the French mobilization system. Instead of calling up troops by classes consisting of year groups, the reservists were sub-divided into various specialist categories and called up by these categories. This made for more flexibility and more secrecy.

CHAPTER IX

THE FATE OF THE PEOPLE'S FRONT

I

WHEN it became evident that the electoral victory of the 'Front Populaire' had surpassed the most optimistic previsions and that the Socialist party had been the greatest beneficiary of the tidal wave, M. Léon Blum addressed, on May 10th, 1936 the National Council of the party.   He reminded them of the meeting at the Salle Huyghens, four years before, and of the regrets he had then expressed that the Socialists had not been the strongest of the Left parties.   Had they been so, 'it would have been a fine thing to see some men trying to serve the interests of their country while remaining faithful to the doctrine of their party'.   It was not without boldness that such memories could be evoked, for in the exultation of the victors there was a risk that a very high standard of fidelity to party doctrine would be demanded.   It was soon necessary to remind the Congress which had authorized the Socialist leaders to form a Government that, not only had the Socialists not won a majority at the last elections, 'but the proletarian parties did not win one either.   There is no Socialist majority, there is no proletarian majority, there is a People's Front majority. . . .   It will be the object of our experiment, and the real problem that this experiment is going to set us, to discover whether it is possible to get out of this social system, the amount of order, well-being, security, justice that it can produce for the mass of workers and producers.'   If the hopes now held were falsified, 'I should be the first to come to tell you; it was a chimera, it was an empty dream, there is nothing to be done with society as at present constituted'.

In those early hopeful days, there was not much worrying about such unpleasant eventualities.   There was a great parliamentary majority supported by a great wave of popular enthusiasm; there was office at hand and the support of that band of practised politicians, the Radicals.   The Right was in ruins; there was only one cloud on the political sky, the action of the Communists.

That party had benefited more than any other from the electoral bargain; its organizations had been in the forefront of the fight and, since the fusion of the two trade-union federations, many of its leaders were colleagues of the faithful allies of the Socialist party. All seemed to be well, but the refusal of the Communist party to take office was alarming. It meant that there was always present a Left party, which was not involved in the immediate responsibilities of government. It would be able to profit from any hitch, any weakness of the Government, any of those adjustments of programmes to the hard necessities of the times which were inevitable as seen from the Minister's desk, but which could be made to seem like treason in the workshop or the meeting. Only complete trust in the good faith of their recently-acquired allies could have prevented the Socialists from being uneasy, as they took office with the Communists outside.

'We should doubtless be more powerful,' said M. Blum, 'better equipped to persuade the workers, if there was nothing to allow us to envisage or to contemplate, even as a hypothesis, a difference of views of any kind, between the different forms, the different organs of the working class, whether in its political or trade-union character.' To translate this cryptic language, the new Ministers would have felt safer if they could have had their Communist friends more closely under their eye. As it was, they would have to keep one eye on the defeated Right and one on the auxiliaries of the extreme Left, allies who might ruin all by their exigencies and their tactics. It was not to the Right, which had compared him to Kerensky, but to the Communists that M. Blum next addressed his warning. 'I really hope that the Government which the Socialist party is going to form, will not be the Kerensky Government. But, if it were to be so, believe me, in the France of to-day it is not Lenin who would replace it.'

The warning was not superfluous, for it was necessary for the new Government to reassure the possessors of capital that they were not to be expropriated. It was also necessary to calm the fears of the frightened bourgeois who were exchanging francs for dollars or sterling and thus causing a strain on the currency, which might develop into a panic and which was causing a serious export of gold. Such reassurances, such negotiations were not what the militants expected. M. Blum was parleying at the gate of the Wall of Money instead of storming it. This feeling of betrayal was the price that had to be paid for over-simplification. As an English Communist writer pointed out,[1] 'it is a simplification of things to imagine that an attack on the privileges of the Bank of France might bring such swift results as the storming of the Bastille by the people of Paris in 1789'.

Although, as was their wont, the Communist leaders afterwards talked as if the stay-in strikes were their doing, they, like everybody else, were surprised by the decision of the workers in some great Paris factories to exploit, industrially, the electoral victory and, by occupying the factories, bring a special form of pressure to bear on their employers,

[1] Ralph Fox.

a pressure that could only be countered if the power of the State were used to expel them—and they were rightly confident that the power of the State would not be used against them in May 1936!

The first strikes took place on May 26th, but it was the second wave of the first week in June that impressed the Government, the employers, the workers, and simple spectators with the conviction that something had changed in France, that this was more than a revolt, if not yet a revolution. The demands of the strikers ranged from better lavatory accommodation to paid holidays, but more significant than any specific claim were the discipline and self-confidence of the workers. Although it pleased the writers in the popular press and, no doubt, titillated their readers to hint at a general let-down of all discipline, the turning of factories into Abbeys of Thelema or Islands of Cythera, the holiday-spirit of the strike never degenerated into riot. The popular song of the moment, *Tout va bien, Madame la Marquise* ran the *Internationale* a good second in popularity, and its temper fitted the mood of the strikers well enough. They were willing to take a tolerant and optimistic view of the situation, if they got their way in fundamentals.

It should be remembered that very few of the strikers were members of any trade-union, or had any recognized leaders, although the Communists at once set about filling the gap. A complication that added to the danger of panic was the spreading of the strike to Hachette's, the distributors of newspapers, so that on the morning after the Blum Government was formed there were only three papers on sale on the streets to announce the news; the *Populaire, Humanité*—and the *Action Française*.

There followed a race between the Government and the official trade-union organizations on the one hand, and the spontaneous efforts of the workers on the other. The workers were full of resentment at the policy of deflation; they were full of hope as a result of the electoral victory; they were not full of faith in the new Government. It meant well, no doubt, but it needed pushing. Had there been no stay-in strikes, would the Blum Government have been willing or able to coerce the employers or the Senate? The workers thought it very doubtful—and they were right. On the other hand, the Government was afraid of alienating a large part of its middle-class supporters by toleration of illegal violence. Even the Communists were apprehensive of a reaction. Had not the futile occupation of the Italian factories in 1920 been the preliminary to Fascism? Who knew whether the most unmanageable factory crowds were not the victims of Fascist *agents provocateurs* [1] or 'Trotzkyites'? At any rate, the Government thought it prudent to drop hints of possible activities of *saboteurs* and thought it safe to promise condign punishment, if any of these mysterious agitators were caught.

[1] Some may have remembered that Signor Mussolini, at the time, approved of the seizure of the factories.

The basic fact was, that the stay-in strikes could be ended only by violence, or by the acceptance of the main demands of the strikers. It was necessary to end, at once, such dangerous strikes as that of the butchers, and it was desirable to get the workers out of the factories as quickly as possible—and peacefully. That meant winking at illegality; but it was impossible, as M. Blum told the Chamber on June 7th, for his Government to appear to disavow 'a part of the working-class which to-day is struggling to improve its conditions of life'. It was necessary, indeed, for the Government to defend itself against charges of having talked and thought too much of 'order'. No one in the Chamber, except the discredited minority, could object to these sentiments, and M. Blum scored a great success when he imposed on the employers the Matignon agreements.[1] Imposed, for the employers had very little choice and even if those employers who were represented by the 'General Confederation of French Production' freely consented, their consent did not bind, morally even if it did legally, the numerous small employers who were not represented. The C.G.T. itself still did not represent more than a minority of the strikers. For the moment, the discontent of the smaller employers mattered little; what was more serious was the ignoring of the authority of the C.G.T. by many strikers. The agreements provided their own remedy for this last danger; by making collective bargaining compulsory, they gave an immense fillip to the C.G.T., which more than recovered the ground that it had lost in 1920-1. Its membership rose to 5,000,000 and in it the French working-class had again an effective and accredited mouthpiece.

The enforcing of collective bargaining was easier to lay down in general terms than to enforce in law. There were soon to be plenty of conflicts over the true meaning to be given to the law, but the great employers could no longer ignore the unions or safely blacklist the leaders; the united trade-union movement was no longer largely a lobby of minor Civil Servants, an instrument of electoral rather than of industrial pressure.

Of more immediate interest to the strikers was a rise in wages of from 12 to 15 per cent., and the institution of paid holidays. Special excursions were organized by road and rail: and in the sudden outpouring of the workers and their families, brought about by reduced rates in hotels and for transport, optimists saw the French reply to the recreational facilities of Fascism.

Most dramatic of all the reforms was the adoption of a forty-hour week in industry. This had been part of the Socialist programme and had been vaguely promised in the platform of the People's Front, but, in all probability, the Government looked forward to long and leisurely negotiations with other countries before doing much or anything about

[1] From the name of the new office of the Prime Minister, the Hôtel Matignon.

it. The strikes put an end to the hopes of postponement, and the forty-hour law had to be passed. It may be surmised that the Blum Cabinet had its own doubts about the advisability of this reform. In addition to increasing the leisure of the workers, it was supposed to reduce unemployment; and the leaders of the Government, then and later, were forced to make astonishingly naïve pronouncements on this topic which it would be insulting their intelligence to profess to think that they really believed. So long as there was any unemployment in France, it was argued, reduction of hours was a good thing; until the unemployed were all absorbed, there could be no reason for altering the law. This was not true and, in any case, the main trouble of the French working-class in the past few years had been not unemployment but very low wages. The main burden of unemployment, which was less in France than in any other country, had fallen on the foreign immigrants. It was the main economîc thesis of the new Ministry, as set out by M. Blum to a critical Senate, that the basic cause of trouble was insufficient demand. An increase of purchasing power was to stimulate production, and, by increasing the amount of business done, make it easy for the *entrepreneur* to bear the burden of increased wages. This theory was to be repeated again and again by apologists for the new policy and backed-up by citations, more or less relevant, from economists ranging from Quesnay to Mr. Durbin. But the application of the forty-hour week did not increase the purchasing power of the masses and it could hardly fail to diminish production and so raise comparative costs. This, in turn, made it harder for France to compete in world markets, increased the unfavourable balance of trade and so made for further pressure on the franc which M. Blum and his Finance Minister, M. Vincent Auriol, were promising to defend.

The real argument for the forty-hour week was political. As M. Blum told the Senate, it was a free body but it was a political body. He asked it to remember 'the state of the country a fortnight ago. I ask you to think of the fact that the voting of these laws which we have put before you is most certainly one of the parts of the task of conciliation and of concord that we have attempted.' The Senate in 1936, like the Chamber in 1934, could take a hint. It accepted the Government's programme without enthusiasm, but it accepted it.

The new Government had to do something for the peasants, since it had done so much for the workers. Above all, it had to do something for the producers of the noble crop, wheat. The remedy was drastic enough. A Wheat Board, an 'Office du Blé', was set up which was to fix annually a price that would both be remunerative to the producer and avoid the recent fantastic ups-and-downs. To this end, free dealing in wheat was to stop. The millers who were, in the eyes of many peasants, the villains of the piece, were no longer to have anything to say about the price of wheat. That was to be fixed by the Office, a board on which producers, consumers and the State were all represented. All wheat, in the original plan, was to be sold by the producers at the fixed price and exclusively to co-operatives who would store it, and after paying the producer, sell it as required to the millers. There would be no possibility of evasion. Like Joseph in Egypt, the Office would have a complete corner on the wheat supply. To enable the Office to fix the price, the producers had to make rather elaborate returns, of acreage sown, of the crop harvested, of the amount of earlier years' crops in store. The critics of the scheme expressed doubts as to the ability of the Office to protect the consumer against the temptation to price wheat too high, and there were complaints of the amount of bookkeeping imposed on the peasants. Then the Senate struck at the elimination of the grain-merchant. He was allowed to remain, although his utility in a system of fixed prices was not obvious. Some co-operators objected to the flooding of their societies with new members and the turning over of their organization to extraneous purposes. In some regions it became a political paradox that the wheat policy of the 'Front Populaire' had greatly increased the resources and importance of co-operatives almost exclusively run by 'Reactionaries'. The new legislation was very complicated and it had to be altered and amended by innumerable new rules, but, helped by a rather poor harvest in 1936, the Office was able to give the peasant a better price than he had had for some years. Needless to say, some perennial grumblers asserted that without the Office, prices would have been higher! But the Government received as much gratitude as it is wise to expect from farmers.

The Blum Government had survived its first ordeals and survived them well. The new Prime Minister had, in an anonymous tract, written just before his entry into active politics in 1919, preached a reform of governmental method, a reinforcement and rationalization of the executive machinery. He now carried out some of his own ideas, grouping ministries in a more coherent fashion and, startling novelty, taking three women into his Government as Under-Secretaries, so presenting Parliament with the paradoxical sight of members of the Government who, by reason of sexual disqualification, could neither vote nor be elected to the meanest office. Madame Juliot-Curie and her colleagues were only one of the signs that the new Government, full of people who, like the Prime Minister, were taking office for the first time, was not to be as hidebound as the Cabinets of the past. France expected more from the peaceful revolution of 1936 than a mere ministerial reshuffling.

The Blum Government, like other French Governments, found its hands tied by financial shackles. A loan was issued that appealed directly to the small investor and that was intended to show that the Government was not wholly dependent on the banks, on the money power. It had some success as a demonstration, but to secure that success, M. Vincent Auriol had to promise not to devalue the franc. It was a serious commitment of the moral authority of the Government and it did not prevent a constant ebbing of the gold stock of the Bank; 20,000,000,000 francs of gold were exported between May and September, more than a quarter of the total reserve.[1] The men-in-the-know had less confidence than had M. Vincent Auriol in the ability of the new Government to evade the consequences of its own policy.

Abruptly reversing the deflationary policy of M. Laval, the new Ministry had launched forth on a programme that was sure to cost a great deal of money and it had, willy-nilly, accepted a programme of limited hours of work that could not help the adverse balance of trade and, indeed, was certain to make it worse. In its electoral campaign it had denounced as slanderous any suggestion that France under a People's Front Government would go off gold. Those clear-sighted deputies, of whom Paul Reynaud was the chief, who had preached that France would *have* to go off gold and that the only questions were when and whether the departure would be made with the maximum of advantages and the minimum of disadvantages, were treated as ill-informed pessimists or as agents of reaction.

The conviction in financial circles, both abroad and at home, that the day of the gold standard was over was so widespread that there grew up rumours, when it became obvious that the People's Front was sure to win, that what had been really hoped for was that the outgoing Cabinet should take the decisive step. M. Sarraut would take the discredit and leave the cash to M. Blum. Whether this was so or not is still unknown. What was undeniable was that the flow of gold outwards steadily diminished the assets of the Bank of France and so diminished the profits to be made by the State if (or when) it bowed to the inevitable.

It was hard to bow. The reputation of the Left as a 'killer of currencies' was thought to be dangerous, and the old jokes against the Poincaré franc would be repeated against the Blum franc. To give way to the pressure of the speculators was very irritating, and some members of the Ministry dallied with the idea of exchange control. But with exchange control so many other things were bound up: and exchange control would frighten more supporters in all parties than would a devaluation of the franc in terms of gold. Worse still, exchange control would put France into the company of the dictatorial nations and cut her off from the monetary communion of the great democracies. The decision was reached, and after an agreement had been made with Britain and the United States not to enter into competitive devaluation, the franc was 'revalued' on September 25th at 113 to the pound. An exchange equalization fund was set up; some

[1] About £250,000,000 ($1,250,000,000) at the current rate of exchange.

debts owing to the Bank of France were paid off; and the remaining profits of the revaluation of the gold stock of the Bank were taken by a needy Treasury. It was not quite a defeat for the financial policy of the Government, but it was very far from being a victory; and the captious pointed to Belgium as a country where these retreats were made in better order, and compared the technical skill of M. Van Zeeland to that of M. Vincent Auriol, to the disadvantage of the latter.

Connected with the devaluation of the franc and the general inflationary effects of the social policy of the Government, was a rise in the cost of living which was combated in the traditional fashion by the appointment of committees of vigilance and threats of punishment for unwarranted increases. Prices were not much affected by these measures, and the critics of the Government were able to point out that real wages were lower under M. Blum than they had been under M. Laval. This was not the only disconcerting revelation of the difficulties of translating the wishes of 'our judge and master', as the Prime Minister had called universal suffrage, into tangible economic improvements. The Treasury was still in deficit and it was necessary to tempt lenders with some special sauces on the old dishes of loans. Worse still from the point of view of the rigorous enemy of the 'wall of money', attempts to force the holders of gold to sell to the State at a price which would give it the profits of devaluation, failed. There had to be a fiscal amnesty; and the prudent, if unpatriotic Frenchman who had kept his gold to himself, was allowed to sell it at the market price. At the end of the first year of the People's Front, the real strength, if not of the two hundred families, at least of the two million families who had money to lend and who would only lend it on their own terms, was realized. And, as it had been advisable to call in the clergy to aid in the great loan campaign (to the disgust of the true-blue Radicals), it was now necessary to soothe the alarmed or irritated investor whose political stronghold was the Senate.

In the days of Tardieu and Laval, the Senate had been rather popular with the Left, but those days were gone, for the French Senate was unique among the Upper Houses of the world: it did really redress the balance, leaning to the Left when the Chamber was to the Right and to the Right when the Chamber was to the Left. Now the Senate was decidedly to the Right. Its action merely made evident a political truth that was ignored by enthusiasts in the heady days of May. The People's Front was a negative conception; it was against something rather than for anything, at any rate for anything more concrete than the 'defence of democracy'. At election times it was inevitable, given the political history of France since 1870, perhaps since 1789, that there should be alliances of parties which had a common enemy but not a common policy. The Left consisted of people who opposed the Right. It ranged therefore from the Communists to the Radicals.

Once the election was over and once purely political questions had been replaced by economic questions, it was the most natural thing in the world that the Radicals who believed in the right of private property, in old-fashioned patriotism, and in many other bourgeois ideals or superstitions, especially in the desirability of the continued existence of the *bourgeoisie*, should find themselves involved in more or less open alliance with other bourgeois who, perhaps, were not sound on the Church, but who had far more in common in other matters with their Radical enemies, than the latter had with their Communist or with their Socialist friends. Even in the landslide of 1936, the electors had not wholly forgotten these truths; and some Radical Deputies owed their election to Right voters who had preferred them to more dangerous candidates.

In the Senate the chief critic of the Government was M. Caillaux. The mishandling of the devaluation problem gave him plenty of excuse for the display of his confidence in his own unequalled financial virtuosity, but he objected to all the economic theories of the Blum Ministry. He especially objected to the assertion that France was in the position of the United States in 1933 and that what it needed was a New Deal in the manner of Mr. Roosevelt. Whatever the merits or demerits of Mr. Roosevelt's methods, they were not, he believed, applicable to France. France had no vast borrowing power France had no immense continental resources; the Blum policy was Rooseveltism for Lilliputians. M. Blum did not agree. He even contrived to discover that France was better prepared for economic experiment than the United States had been, since her main trouble was currency hoarding, the very opposite of the troubles that beset America during the bank holiday.

Abstract discussions on points of economic theory were unimportant. What mattered was the obvious determination of the Senate to keep a firm grip on the Government's collar. Within a few months of its coming into office, the Senate taught it a lesson. The old arguments against devaluation were revived by the Communists and, to placate its supporters, the Government proposed to adopt a sliding scale of wages to indemnify the workers against a rise in prices following on the fall in value of the franc. But the Senate would have none of this; was not one of the objects of devaluation to get round the exaggerated rises in wages and so in costs that had marked the summer of 1936? The Senate stood firm and M. Blum had to retreat.

The Radical party was, by itself, in command of a majority in the Senate, but it was a majority of Radicals who had succeeded in politics, who had been Senators before the People's Front was formed and might well be Senators after it had gone the way of the 'Cartel des Gauches'. Nor was this all; over four million Frenchmen had voted, even in 1936, for the parties opposed to the People's Front, as against over five millions for the candidates of the People's Front. In the ranks of the majority were hundreds of thousands of electors who, if confronted with another series of financial disasters like those of 1925 and 1926, or with continued disorders, might say, like the Bonapartist peasants in 1871, 'we did not vote for this'. It was the duty of the Senate, so the Senators thought, to oppose the resistance of the elder statesmen to the pressure exerted on the Government by strikers, by party meetings and by irresponsible and dangerous allies, that is the Communists.

If the first months of the Blum Government saw the achievement of some positive improvements of the condition of the workers, they also saw the punishment, or at least the restriction of the power, of some of the enemies of the victors. In the first rank of the enemies of the people the Bank of France, or the Regents of the Bank, had been classed. The day when they could dictate to Parliament was over; no financial oligarchy would, in the future, be able to thwart the will of the delegates of the sovereign people. The old Board of Regents was abolished and a new one representing the Government, the trade unions, the co-operatives, business, the employees of the bank and the shareholders was set up. The shareholders were left with their private commercial rights and they were all, the whole 40,000 of them, free to attend the annual meeting if they chose. But the real control was in the hands of the Board and of the Governor. The latter was no longer required to own shares; his income was no longer voted by Regents and, if he ceased to be Governor, he still drew his salary for three years, during which time he was forbidden to take a post in any business. As far as the financial troubles of the Government had been due to the Bank, there was no reason to fear that they would recur.

Another unpopular section of the economic masters of France was the armament manufacturers. They were profiteers; they were unpatriotic; they were as bad as Krupps. Indeed, the greatest of them were worse than Krupps, for the founder of Krupps was a real workman while the first Schneider to come to Le Creusot was a mere financier! So with due caution, the Government proposed to nationalize the armament industry, separating the military from the civil side of mixed firms like Renault works. For the aeroplane manufacturers, a more ingenious system of buying control of the companies and thus preserving the flexibility of private enterprise was preferred. M. Pierre Cot was convinced that the results, from every point of view, would be excellent. French military aviation would soon recover its pristine glory.

Within a few weeks of the election, the Blum Government had dissolved the *Croix de Feu* and the other Right leagues, forcing Colonel de la Rocque to reconstitute his troops as a mere political party, the 'French Social Party'.[1] For a time it seemed that the interest of the Right had moved from the luckless Colonel, who had not run candidates in

[1]Parti Social Français.

1936 (and, better prophet than his critics, refused to take any interest in the elections of 1940), to the combative Mayor of Saint-Denis, M. Doriot, late leader of the Communist party in the Chamber.

M. Doriot had been one of the first preachers of the necessity for a People's Front, but he had preached it too early ; by the time he saw his policy adopted, he was outside the party. He still held his own in his bailiwick of Saint-Denis and, plentifully provided with ammunition from his knowledge of the inner history of the party he had left and briefed by such enemies of Stalin as M. Boris Souvarine, he was able to infuriate his late comrades. He was an especially vehement critic of their foreign policy, sneering at their new-found patriotism and asserting that its sole object was to embroil France and Germany in a war for the benefit of Soviet Russia. He, too, founded a new party, the 'French People's Party' [1] ; it might have obtained more success had its leader been more discreet.

It was not only that M. Doriot had shady supporters from Marseilles (all parties had shady supporters from Marseilles), but that he was too openly allied with reactionary elements. There was, perhaps, a place for a native Left party assailing the official Communists on their weak side, which was their docility to Russian leadership. But there was no place for such a party if its leader was obviously on good terms with people like M. Philippe Henriot. Then M. Doriot, harassed in his rôle as mayor by the Blum Government, resigned his seat in Parliament and was not re-elected. He had been before his time in advocating reconciliation with Germany and an end of trust in Soviet Russia. Neither of the new parties made any serious progress ; and from the Right and its auxiliaries, the new Government had nothing for the moment to fear.

M. Blum, however, had his troubles and they were serious enough. The apprehension he had politely expressed when he learned that his Communist allies preferred to support the Government from outside was not without justification. In every crisis, the Communists were able to make the best of both worlds, to get credit for whatever gains were made by the workers and to put on the shoulders of the Socialists and Radicals the blame for any disappointments. They made political capital out of the devaluation of the franc, and it was notorious that the most important Socialist leader after M. Blum, M. Paul Faure, trusted the Communists as far as he could see them and no farther. Old trade-union leaders, especially among the miners, were loud in their lamentations at the undermining of their position by the Communists. The unification of the unions had in many cases not put an end to the old conflict. It had merely brought the Communists, like the garrison of a new Trojan horse, inside the old unions. Nor was that all; for the Communists got into street rows with the disbanded *Croix de Feu* which

[1] Parti Populaire Français.

did not always end to their advantage and helped to perpetuate an atmosphere of effervescence that the Government deplored.

II

The really serious problem of the Government was in foreign affairs. It had come into office prepared with slogans that were not very relevant to the situation. Sanctions had failed and it was a question of how best to get out of the undignified mess. It was obvious that Italy, victorious in Abyssinia, was nöt likely to surrender to the pressure that had been so inadequate when the new empire was still being conquered. Would it not be best to recognize facts, to abandon sanctions and win back Italy to the Stresa front? Despite Communist disapproval this was attempted, but the Duce was now hard to woo. He showed no signs of any willingness to rebuild the Stresa front : and all such dreams were made impossible by the outbreak of civil war in Spain.

As soon as it was evident that the *pronunciamento* had neither completely succeeded nor completely failed, the war south of the Pyrenees became of the greatest importance to France. She alone of the great powers had a common frontier with Spain; the problems of neutrality were more acute for her than for any other country. She had more to lose by a mistake than had more remote countries which should, had times been what was, less and less plausibly, called normal, have had no concern in the matter at all. No country had better reason than the victim of the trap of 1870 to know that the internal politics of Spain could be of the greatest importance to Spain's northern neighbour.

For the 'Front Populaire', the Spanish war was the Spanish ulcer. It was not only because of the new international complications it involved, not merely that to the menaced frontiers of the Rhine and the Alps, it threatened to add the Pyrenees. But the military revolt in Spain shocked the political mysticism of the victors of May. The Spanish Government, against whom the *pronunciamento* had been directed, was itself the product of a People's Front. The military rebels were rebels against the delegates of popular sovereignty. It was not for being rebels, as such, that they were to be condemned. M. Blum had to guard himself against any doctrine that equated right with legality. That would have absolved the Second Empire, the Restoration, all those Governments which French Republican tradition regarded as legal but not legitimate, as criminal usurpers or, at best, at caretakers for the sovereign people, for the Comte de Chambord himself did not hold the doctrine of his legitimate authority more strongly than the French parliamentarians held the doctrine of theirs. They received the news of the Spanish crime as Nicholas I had received the news of the overthrow of Charles X. The forces which were in revolt in Spain seemed to be the forces that had threatened the Republic in France. Men who had been frightened by Colonel de la Rocque had reason to be frightened by men like those makers of the Spanish Republic, Sanjurjo, Queipo de Llano and Franco, who had now turned against their creation. For the Communists it was worse. It was in the name of the common front against Fascism that they had surrendered many of their old doctrines and practices. A series of defeats on the international front had been halted by the electoral victories in France and Spain. In face of the Fascist International, in face of the evident collusion of Mussolini and the Spanish Nationalists, was the Government which they had helped to bring into power not to help its friends?

The answer was 'no'. The French Government would not only do nothing out of the way to help the Spanish Government; it would deliberately not permit the Spanish Government to buy arms, although the Spanish Government had the money to pay for them, had the means of importing them and, by all international precedent, had every right to buy them. It was a decision very hard for any French Ministry to justify. It was especially hard for the Blum Ministry; the danger of alienation of the Government from its supporters was greatly increased by its decision to accept the British policy of insulating the Spanish conflict, the policy, as it was technically called, of 'non-intervention'. The foreign policy of M. Laval had been to do as little to humour Britain as was necessary to avoid a rupture. It was based on a correct belief that the British Government would not, in fact, tug at the French leash very hard. The policy of M. Blum was to allow Britain to put the leash on the neck of France.

It was soon discovered that however weak Britain might have been in the defence of her Abyssinian policy, she could be firm enough in defence of her Spanish policy. Rather than offend Britain, the Blum and almost all subsequent French Governments were forced to do as Downing Street wanted. The final justification of this policy was 'orders from London'. It could not be put that way, too openly, but the hints were not lost on the deputies, nor on the public. Madrid was not worth London.

Not all supporters of the 'Front Populaire' could be put off by this hinted defence, especially the workers of the Paris region could not be so put off. Their own tradition was too militant for them not to see in the defenders of Irun, and later of Madrid, heirs of the Revolution. It was necessary for M. Blum to explain his policy to them and to defend it—and he succeeded. He succeeded because he played on what was genuine in himself and, in most of his hearers, horror of war. Just before he took office, M. Blum, in a speech to the American Club in Paris, had renounced the militant warlike tradition of the French Left.

'We do not even think as our ancestors of 1792 or 1848 did, that war can have its good, its liberating and revolutionary side. It's a good many years since a great man called Jaurès cured us of that illusion.' It was to this new tradition that he appealed in his speech at Luna Park to the Socialist Federation of the Seine. To give the Spanish Government its legal rights, was to risk a great war. If there was to be no ultimatum to the intervening powers, what was to be done? In a competition of supplying resources for war, what advantages lay on the side of the dictatorships! So professing to believe, perhaps really believing in the honesty of the signatories of the non-intervention agreement, and threatening war as the consequence if his policy were abandoned, M. Blum had his way. When, in December, he had to defend himself in the Chamber against the belligerent M. Thorez, he insisted that only a government can really arm another government with men and munitions, that, in effect, to denounce the non-intervention agreement meant, if it was to mean anything, that France was to intervene—and as he pointed out, M. Thorez dared not admit that that was what he advocated.

So it was with each tightening of the blockade of Government Spain. What was the alternative? A breach with Britain? War with Italy? War with Germany? When furious crowds (not all of their members being French) assailed the luckless M. Delbos, the Radical Foreign Minister, with shouts of 'arms for Spain', politically there was one answer. The peasants would not risk a world war for the Spanish Republic, and their leaders told them that from Spain war might come. And there was, too, the old grievance of the peasants against the sheltered munition workers. The Paris crowds, so some said, would make the guns for Spain—at a price; the peasants would have to fire them.

Yet despite the prudential arguments, perhaps the conclusive prudential arguments, that justified the Spanish policy begun by M. Blum and carried on by his successors till Madrid fell, that policy took the life out of the 'Front Populaire'. In another of his references to the sacred authority of Jaurès, M. Blum told how he had once asked him whether Lamartine had not been wrong in refusing to help the Poles and Italians in the early critical months of 1848 when the great adventure of the Revolution seemed to be succeeding instead of saving the lives then, that were to be lost on the barricades of June? And Jaurès had replied, 'No! No! it would not have been any better. Every time that you can avoid war, you must avoid war. . . . It is not war but peace which is revolutionary.' Perhaps Jaurès was right, but if he was, were the defenders of Madrid, the men of the Commune wrong? These were questions that no Socialist Government in France could afford, spiritually at least, to allow to be raised.

The Spanish War continued and made deeper a rift in French

society that had become obvious with the Abyssinian War. When the civil war, which was largely if not entirely an affair between Spaniards, developed its natural savagery, it provided ample raw materials for each side in France to accuse the other of being a friend of barbarism. Members of the victorious Left parties saw, or professed to see in their opponents, so many French Francos and Molas. Members of the defeated side saw in their opponents mere dupes of Moscow. Had not the Communists in Spain, in unholy alliance with the Liberals and Socialists, made the elections of 1936 an ingenious device for introducing their hellish poison? Had not too candid friends seen in Spain the next Soviet State, just before the military saviours had taken the field? To pious Catholics, even if they did not believe a tithe of the atrocity stories, there was one startling and horrifying fact about the non-Basque territories of the Spanish Republic. Everywhere it was impossible to say Mass. They were not to be put off by the vague promises that, some time or other, permission would be given again for Mass to be said publicly in the country of St. Theresa, of St. Dominic, of St. Ignatius. It was a sign to them that a main, perhaps the main aim of the Spanish revolutionaries, was to uproot the Catholic faith. It was not surprising that many Catholics saw in Franco and his allies, crusaders, or at least (in the case of the Moors) unconscious allies of the Faith.

Especially was it natural in the Royalists to see the Spanish War as another round in the campaign against the errors of the Revolution. Not only did the *Action Française* exalt the defenders of the Alcazar of Toledo and, excommunicate as its own leaders were, exalt in the victories of the Catholic armies,[1] but many conservative Catholics, like Cardinal Baudrillart, were uncritical supporters of the cause of the Nationalists.

It was not surprising that so many eminent Catholics took the side of Franco. What was surprising was that so many did not. M. François Mauriac was horrified at the savagery of the bourgeois society to which he belonged, and expressed his horror. The young Catholic reformers of '*L'Aube*' refused to see in General Franco a new Godefroy de Bouillon; and M. Jacques Maritain analysed the idea of a holy war with a care and critical power that was much disliked by the friends of the new Spanish renaissance. All these Catholics felt, in some degree, the reflection on the life of the Spanish Church that was made by the savage hate it had managed to inspire in the workers and peasants of a country that, a century before, had been so devoted to its ancient faith. And though more prudence was naturally observed by them, it was suspected that some of the most eminent of the French clergy, beginning with the Cardinal Archbishop of Paris,

---

[1] It might be noted that the most successful Catholic *exposé* of the Catholic crusade was the work of a former member of the *Action Française*, M. Georges Bernanos.

were reluctant to see the cause of the Church identified too closely with the cause of General Franco.

The doubts and hesitation were not all on one side. On the Left, if, in public, there was nothing but admiration for the defenders of parliamentary legality in Spain, there was plenty of criticism in private. The torpor of the Catalans in the early part of the war was adversely commented on. The French belief that there were only two serious races of soldiers in Europe—themselves and the Germans—was reinforced by the apparently amateurish character of the war in Spain. A Socialist deputy who was asked in private whether the local army corps of his home town could end the whole business in a month and replied indignantly, 'in a fortnight', was not, perhaps, representative of his party but he was representative of a large body of public opinion on the Left.

Among the Radicals there was a good deal of irritation at both sides. They were nuisances, with their savage feuds and their common inheritance of incompetence. They menaced the peace of France and the solidity of the governing coalition. The stubborn Spanish valour evoked too little admiration, and the political friends of M. Delbos did him an injustice by behaving, at times, as if the whole Spanish business was just one of those nuisances that had been interfering with the smooth running of politics ever since 1914. Was one of their leaders not being shouted down by Communist mobs? Did not the Communist party refuse to vote for the Government on questions of foreign policy? Were they, perhaps, bent on forcing France into war?

Although it was not convenient to dwell on it, was it not the Communists who had begun the campaign against the Socialist Minister of the Interior, Roger Salengro, which had ended with his suicide? M. Blum, M. Herriot, eminent politicians, eminent journalists native and foreign, might attack (as they had every reason to do) the infamous scurrilities of the Chiappe press. But was there really much to choose between the tactics of *Gringoire* and the tactics of *Humanité*? Was Henri Beraud any more dishonest, really, than the Communist leaders who swallowed every new order from Moscow, denounced their old leaders as traitors and rallied to the defence of men whom, in February 1934, they had treated as thieves and murderers? The 'Front Populaire' was formed to save the Republic. Well, the Republic was now safe, safe at any rate from its Fascist enemies. Was it safe from its new-found friends? Many Radicals and some Socialists had begun to wonder.

III

It was a sign of the increased tempo of the age that the retreat that every Left majority in the Chamber made about two years after its

717

election was made by the Blum Government in less than a year. On February 24th at Saint-Nazaire, the Prime Minister announced a 'pause'; it was not, of course, a retreat, it was merely 'in order to consolidate the ground we have conquered'. The Right, which could interpret political and military communiqués as well as anybody else, decided that the 'Front Populaire' would soon be on the run. M. Vincent Auriol might hanker after exchange control, there might be talk of strong government, but strong government and Left government were almost philosophically contradictory terms. M. Blum decided to placate the owners of capital. There was to be retrenchment on the ordinary budget (and that meant an end of the public works programme which was dear to the trade unions). There was to be a loan guaranteed against loss caused by a fall in the franc exchange —a device that had been tried before—and just as in the last great financial crisis, there were to be experts in charge, MM. Rist and Baudoin.

It was not only the exultant Right which could see that it was a retreat, the disillusioned Left could do so too, and the 'pause' was followed in a few days by the 'Clichy massacre'. A Left mob, stirred up by two rival demagogues, one Communist, one Socialist, attacked a cinema where a *Croix de Feu* show was being held. The police defending the cinema, like the police defending the Chamber, had to fire; there were six deaths, and the Government which had surrendered to the banks had now 'the blood of the workers' on its hands. There was a new wave of strikes, and these were especially important since 1937 was to be the year of the Great Exhibition. Traditionally, exhibitions always open unfinished, but the Paris Exhibition of 1937 set a new record for lateness. The French saying 'when the building trade is flourishing, all's well' was shown to be true when inverted. The builders, terrified of ending the only big job in Paris, went slow to an unprecedented degree.

When the formal opening day came, only three of the great powers had their pavilions ready: they were the three dictatorial powers, Germany, Italy, Russia. Across the avenue from the hammer and sickle flag of the Soviets rose the swastika-adorned pavilion of the Third Reich. The French sections were still almost all flags, hiding foundations and frames. The delays in the completion of the Exhibition increased the anger felt by many of the petty *bourgeoisie* against the Socialists and Communists, an anger noted and acted on by the observant Radicals. Paris, central Paris anyway, lived by the tourist trade. The Exhibition, in its unfinished state, was a bad advertisement.

It was not the only one. The application of the forty-hour law to hotels and restaurants caused especial difficulties, and in a year in which the tourist trade (as much because of the devaluation of the franc as because of the Exhibition) was expected to be highly profitable, it was maddening to have tourists irritated by bad service and, worse still, to have them frightened by strikes and violence. Armed police guarding some of the most famous cafés at the very height of the season was a sight that destroyed the mystical Republican faith of many who had voted for the 'Front Populaire' fourteen months before. Justly or unjustly, disorder, strikes in the conspicuous industries, transport, food supplies, amusements, are always certain causes of unpopularity to the section blamed for causing them. This time the blame fell on the workers.

In any case, the rigid application of the 'five eights', that is a working week of five days of eight hours, was crippling to many industries. That it hurt the great chain stores was all to the good in the eyes of the little shopkeepers whom the law largely spared. But it was not so good for the employees of the stores who lost their jobs, or found their earnings inadequate. Then there were superior critics like M. Jules Romains who complained that, instead of using their now abundant leisure in some great cultural improvement, the French workers spent their spare time fishing. More serious was the case of the workmen who spent their spare time working. The unions had to organize a campaign against 'black work', against the men who held two jobs or did odd jobs in odd moments. And whatever may have been the case in the great industrial agglomerations, in provincial France the idea that exceptional industry was a crime was a novelty—an unpopular novelty.

It is probable that the Government felt these qualms about the forty-hour week as much as did its critics. But as prices rose faster than wages, the forty-hours became the chief tangible victory of the great year of 1936. The eight-hour day, the great victory of 1919, had in practice been whittled away. Labour was resolved that the same trick should not be played on the forty-hour week. It is possible that a Government in which the organized workers had complete confidence might have persuaded them to accept 'the pause' and to permit what had become really necessary adjustments of the hours question. But the Blum Government, with Spain and Clichy on its record, could not successfully make the appeal. And it was compelled to return a firm 'no' to the demand of M. Jouhaux that it should find money for a great public works programme as well as for armaments. France could not, in fact, afford both unless she adopted totalitarian methods. She could not do that; or if she did, M. Blum was not likely to be the dictator.

In June came a new financial strain which was made a crisis by the resignation of the two experts. They had been put in to reassure the timid investor, so their departure could not but frighten him. The pause would have to become an open retreat or M. Blum would have to become a semi-dictator. He appealed to Parliament for 'plenary powers', for that abdication of parliamentary control over finance which was the remedy that all French statesmen tried in office after denouncing its dangers in opposition. The Chamber gave him the powers, but the Senate's time had come. It refused to trust a government, which M. Caillaux, quoting a poem of Jean Richepin, compared to a drunk woman. There were the usual attacks on the Senate in the name of universal suffrage, but as usual the Senate had shown great tactical sagacity. M. Blum resigned.

The head of the new Government was M. Chautemps, but the real novelty was the Finance Minister. M. Georges Bonnet was called back from the Washington embassy to save the finances of France. He was to be the new Caillaux. Like M. Caillaux he had been a high official; like M. Caillaux he had ancestral connections with politics, though his came not through a reactionary father, but through having married the niece of Camille Pelletan, the modern Cato, the Radical who, morally if not physically, had incarnated the unstained orthodoxy of Republicanism. M. Bonnet's appointment was a sign that the comedy was over. Socialist finance, it was said, had had its day, which was not quite true, for Socialist finance had not been tried. What had been tried was capitalist finance worked by hands made incompetent by little knowledge and less faith.

M. Blum had persuaded the Socialist party to allow him to serve under M. Chautemps. It was a People's Front Government, Number 2. That the Front was cracked was denied by everybody, but cracked it was. The Communists had only rallied to the parliamentary support of the Blum Government at the last moment. Their old enemy and now very lukewarm friend, M. Paul Faure, facetiously attributed their change of front to the execution, between two telephone calls to Moscow, of their Comintern mentor. For the Russian trials, culminating in the Army purge, had enabled the Socialists and Radicals to get their own back. The rubric in the *Populaire* which, day after day, listed new executions under the title, 'The Russian Crisis', was in itself enough to infuriate the directors of *l'Humanité*, which regarded the same events as eighteenth-century doctors did gout, as a most reassuring sign of physical and mental vigour. The execution of Marshal Tukachevsky especially startled a country with a conscript army which, it was realized, might have found itself taking the field in alliance with a power whose high command was conspiring with the common enemy. It was suggested that the failure to implement the Franco-Soviet pact with a military convention was not an unmixed disaster, and visitors to the Exhibition made a new game of counting how many of the originals of the portraits of Soviet leaders clustered round Stalin had turned out to be traitors!

If there were traitors in Russia (and there were some, somewhere in Russia), there were conspirators in France. A leading Italian refugee, Carlo Roselli, was found murdered in circumstances that suggested that the Matteotti technique was not obsolete. There were explosions at the headquarters of the French industrialists which, first of all, suggested an outrage by the Left—and then suggested a crime by the Right. For the country was alarmed at the discovery of a grotesque but startling Fascist society, the Cagoulards, the 'Hooded Men', that was something of a joke but enough of a reality to frighten the voters and the deputies back to the 'Front Populaire'; and, in turn, the move to the Left was halted by further strikes which the Government had to help to break.

The year had seen a steady decline in French confidence and moral energy. M. Bonnet, for all his technical skill, had had to devalue the franc again, and this time there could be no pretence that it was a question of a voluntary 'alignment'. The franc was allowed to 'float' around 130 to the pound, that is below the Poincaré parity. This was the reward of orthodoxy! It was no wonder that, on the 14th of July, the marching crowds consigned M. Bonnet as well as M. de la Rocque, to the gallows. It was not the only change in the celebration of the national holiday. The atmosphere of the great popular festival was grim and gloomy. The union and optimism of 1935 and 1936 were missing. Instead, a predominantly Communist procession marched through back streets, past indifferent crowds, shouting for Spain. For Spain was still being torn to pieces by war; German non-intervention was now second only to Italian non-intervention. If an end had been put to what was euphemistically called 'piracy', that is a blockade of Government Spain by Italian submarines, by the Franco-British declaration at Nyon, the comedy of non-intervention was otherwise played as before.

Tempers in the ranks of the allied parties were naturally frayed, and M. Chautemps, it seemed to many, deliberately took the chance of driving the Socialists out of his government at the beginning of 1938. He then formed a new and purely Radical Government. This was considered particularly shabby of M. Chautemps, since the Socialists had defended him so warmly in 1934; but the Socialists ought to have been warned by the conduct of MM. Caillaux and Malvy. In any case there are enough proverbs in all languages about the danger of doing a good turn to make Socialist indignation seem a little naïve. Once he had got them out, M. Chautemps did nothing in particular until, at the beginning of March, he found an excuse to resign, so that when Herr Hitler marched into Austria to deliver the Germans of that country from the tyranny of being allowed to vote on their destiny, France had no government at all.

The shock of the invasion of Austria was profoundly felt, for in this case Germany was not breaking treaties and agreements affecting her own territory, but crossing an international frontier. Moreover, the resignation of Mr. Eden and the speeches of Mr. Chamberlain had seemed to threaten a British policy that would, from the French point of view, be highly dangerous. So much had been sacrificed to the British alliance: was it to prove worthless after all?

It was true that, in the long run, if it came to a show-down, Britain could not desert France; but if the British Government did not realize this, it might come to its senses too late. The dangers of the situation were keenly felt by M. Blum, who was called on to follow M. Chautemps. He had already tried to rally support for a true national government, 'from Thorez to Reynaud'. He now tried a bolder scheme, 'from Thorez to Marin', but the Right parties would not agree to let their leaders serve. So M. Blum had to form a government of Radicals and Socialists and to carry on in face of a new series of strikes, including one that tied up the aeroplane industry. When he asked the Senate for plenary powers, he was defeated; and even more clearly than a year before the Senate proved to have gauged public opinion rightly. There was no wave of indignation at the impudence of the delegates of restricted suffrage.

M. Blum fell and with him fell the new Foreign Minister, M. Paul-Boncour, who in his few weeks of office had dared one novelty. He had refused to follow the lead of London and he had called a halt to the non-intervention joke by opening the frontier and letting the Spanish Government buy arms. Now that Mr. Eden was gone, the common policy of France and Britain had gone too. But this rebellion of France was short lived. Only a united country and a stable government could have resisted British pressure; the third Blum Government did not last a month, and the country was profoundly divided. The 'Front Populaire', except as a piece of electoral window-dressing, was dead. To its original reforms of 1936 it had added an amalgamation of the railway companies into a semi-nationalized system. It was all—and it was not much. There were many faults, faults in all the partners to it, as well as in its enemies, to account for its comparative failure. But the real shackles on its freedom had been riveted when the Rhineland was occupied. France was no longer free to decide her own destiny.

EPILOGUE

'Tis true there's better booze than brine, but he that drowns must drink it :
And oh my lass, the news is news that men have heard before.
A. E. HOUSMAN.

WHEN M. Daladier presented himself before the Chamber on April 13th, 1938, the very name he gave his Government not only made evident the death of the old 'Front Populaire', but made the fundamental cause of that death evident. 'A great free country can be saved only by herself. The Government of National Defence which presents itself before you has decided to be the expression of this will to be saved.' It was an appeal to the Jacobin tradition, for whatever the optimists might say, the country was in danger. But that danger, which all admitted and which had led M. Blum to plead (with some response from the extreme Right) for a truly national government, was to be faced by a Ministry based mainly on the real governing party, the Radicals, which, with all its many weaknesses, is the best judge of what the average Frenchman will stand for—if necessary in the trenches.

The foreign policy of the Daladier Government was a Radical policy; there was no place for bold initiative, or for long-term planning. Radicalism meant prudence and tenacity—when pushed to the wall and not before. That meant, in turn, that French foreign policy was bound to be passive, that it would be a series of reactions to German and Italian policy, or that it would be simply a following of British policy.

When the British Government made its treaty with Signor Mussolini which involved, among other things, the open abandonment of the Spanish Republic to Italian arms, the removal of the last fig-leaf from the implausible lay figure called non-intervention, the French Government, despite the anger of Communists and of Socialists and of some alarmed patriots of the Right, had to follow suit.

When it became evident (as it became evident very soon) that having solved the 'Austrian question' had only whetted the appetite of the ruler of Germany, France, although bound by the most sacred ties of treaties to Czechoslovakia, allowed her policy to be controlled from London. From the sending of the Runciman mission it was evident to all but the most blind optimists that the existence of the Czechoslovak state was in question, that the fortress on which so much of French security was based was in the gravest danger. Legal sophists like M. Joseph Barthélemy might explain that the treaties no longer bound France, but the French Government made no such pretences. Nor were the French really duped by the words of persons like Herr Henlein, who assured credulous Englishmen and English-women that he was not an agent of Hitler.

The Czechoslovak 'problem', the Spanish 'problem', were either of these worth the risk of a war in which Italy and Germany would be on one side, in which the chance of saving the Czechs would depend on the efficiency of a Russian Army just purged of most of its com-manders and in which the burden of the war would fall on the French Army while Britain, as before, slowly prepared to move from the passive and comparatively bloodless war of blockade to the ordeal of war on land? On this question, M. Bonnet, the Foreign Minister, had few doubts. Following the footsteps of the British Prime Minister, he tried to win over Italy. How could he do otherwise? The success of the British royal visit to Paris showed how much importance the French people attached to the alliance with Britain. Of course, if the Germans actually invaded Czechoslovakia, France would march, and if France marched, Britain would have to follow. But could France march for the remote and debatable question of the exact military frontier of Bohemia, when she had not marched in 1936 for the safety of her own frontier? Could the British Government wage a war in such a cause, after having by a most determined refusal to notice anything odd about Nazi Germany, made it impossible to raise the war to a higher plane than that of mere security? What the 'freeing of Germans' meant, the infamies of the occupation of Vienna had shown, but the new English and French converts to the ideal of self-determination, ignoring any awkward consequences of the blind acceptance of the principle for great imperial powers, went far beyond the wildest Wilsonian dreams.

The most vigorous critics of these doctrines were the Communists, but M. Daladier did not regret this opposition of the Communists, for he believed and asserted—and the country did not wholly disbelieve him—that that party was only too ready 'to waste the blood of French-men for interests which are not those of France'. What if M. Thorez had accused the rulers of France of ignoring the fact that Herr Hitler was resuming against France 'the old designs of Charles V'? It was no business of a Radical Minister to play the part of a Francis I or Richelieu—or of Ollivier and Gramont.

During the critical months, only the extreme Right and the Communists were prepared to take any risk of war to put an end to the German menace. The immense lassitude bred by the last war, the sincere horror of another massacre, the human hope that things could not be as bad as they seemed, irritation that remote and un-intelligible quarrels of distant peoples should involve the destiny of France, all combined to prepare France for Munich.

Internally, too, the opposition of the Communists did the Government no harm. The franc had again been devalued to around 175 to the pound; the Government had been given 'full powers' and it used them to attack the rigid forty-hour week. France could not (with Mexico) be 'the only country with two Sundays'. M. Paul Reynaud was only Minister of Justice as yet, but he was in the offing, the new Poincaré who would restore the economic balance when the time came. M. Daladier had no doubts that, at least, he could and should attack the Communists who were at the bottom of the endless agitation which resulted in the dreadful fact that alone among the countries of Europe, French production had fallen, not risen; France must work more or accept a lower standard of living.

The feeling that France, technically and economically, could not risk a war was very widespread. In the golden days of the 'Front Populaire', M. Léon Jouhaux had affirmed his belief that the technicians of the *bourgeoisie* would rally to the unions since they promised a way out of the system which was stifling production. It was not, perhaps, the fault of the C.G.T., but that 'indispensable common feeling and contact between the proletariat and the urban middle classes' had not lasted, if it ever existed. Repeated strikes irritated the bourgeois population, which did not blame the Government for the third change in the value of the franc in two years and which was not won over to a belief in the merits of a controlled exchange.

If the nationalization of armaments had been one of the most popular reforms of the 'Front Populaire' in 1936, its results, or what could be interpreted as its results, were highly unpopular in 1938. For in the air, France was completely outclassed. The Denain programme of 1934[1] had resulted in a great increase in the French air force just at the wrong time, for the planes were obsolete as soon as they were finished. The great technical advances came too late to be incorporated in the French designs. But not only were French planes too slow, there were far too few of them. While Germany was producing 500 or 1,000 a month, France hardly produced 50. And in the spring and summer of 1938, it was being made evident, as the German and Italian aviators blasted the way for Franco's troops to cut the territories of the Spanish Republic in half, how important air power was.

By the time September came, it was obvious that whatever the convenient pretences of earlier months, what was afoot was a controversy between Germany and Czechoslovakia. Czech concessions to the Sudetens were useless unless they were accepted in Berlin. And if they were not accepted? If the Germans invaded a country guaranteed by France? Despite the sophists, despite the pro-Fascists whose patriotism was so curiously blinded when it came in conflict with their party interests, France could not retreat.

[1] See p. 662.

There came the three visits to Hitler: Berchtesgaden, Godesberg, Munich. Only in the last conference had France a say. In none of them had the Czechs a say. In none of them had the French Parliament a say, until all was over. Then the Chamber, with some abstentions, ratified the Munich agreements against the vote of the Communists and of M. Henri de Kerillis. He and M. Gabriel Péri of *Humanité* were the main, almost the only critics of Munich. Even the view hinted at by Communist intellectuals like M. Paul Nizan, that the whole war danger was worked up to frighten the people into swallowing the mutilation of Czechoslovakia was not distasteful to some French defenders of Munich who thought that such stage-management, if it had occurred, was a credit to the ingenuity of its authors.

Before the May crisis of 1938, M. Daladier had complained that France was too often represented abroad as a 'drab country, frightened about her future, concerned only with material interests'. In the months that followed Munich, it did not seem a bad description. The days when Jules Grévy was rebuking those foolish persons who thought France would ever emerge from the second rank of powers, seemed to have returned. It is true there were signs that French resignation had limits. M. Flandin found that out when some enemy published the telegram of approval that had been sent him, after Munich, by the Führer. It was going too far to talk of 'Gauleiter' Flandin, but most Frenchmen felt that however innocent M. Flandin had been, his public utility was seriously diminished.

Whatever chances existed of a true *détente* in the relations of Germany and the Western powers were seriously diminished when the murder of an attaché in the German embassy in Paris by a Jew was followed by an outburst of disciplined savagery in Germany which only the strongest stomachs could support. This was the Nazi State whose accessions of territory and power had been so complacently accepted by the rulers of France and Britain!

Among the aspects of Munich that had worried even the most pacific of the French had been the private peace treaty between Herr Hitler and Mr. Chamberlain, a treaty that M. Daladier had not been given a chance to sign. M. Bonnet remedied that, but by the time Herr von Ribbentrop came to Paris to sign the Franco-German treaty of peace, Munich was too clearly, at best, the lesser of two great evils, and it was more and more doubtful if it was more than the purchase of a postponement of war by what was—certainly, for France, if not so certainly for Britain—an evasion of an obligation of honour. Herr von Ribbentrop was received with only formal cordiality and in an atmosphere of pessimistic distrust that he had not been used to in London or Rome—or was to know in Moscow. Mr. Chamberlain's document had its few days of popularity; what Herr von Ribbentrop and M. Georges Bonnet signed seemed to concern only themselves.

The financial position of France was made still more difficult by the expenses of the September mobilization; M. Daladier turned at last to M. Paul Reynaud, whose orthodox methods of restoring the situation were a denial of all the economic doctrines of 1936. M. Jouhaux rashly threatened a general strike and, when he tried to escape from using the supreme weapon (whose dangers he had good reason to remember), his Communist associates would not let him. The Government was prepared; it took over the railways and the strike was a complete failure. If its main consequence was to strengthen the authority of M. Daladier and of the State, a secondary one was further to embitter the relations between Socialists and Communists; for, according to the former, the Communists had insisted on striking although it was obvious the Government was ready and anxious to break the strike—and when the great day came, it was the unions which, like the miners, were dominated by Socialists that had struck, while the Communist-controlled unions had docilely gone to work. As M. Jouhaux had feared, 1920 was repeated; over a million members left the C.G.T. and, for the first time since May 1936, the employers felt strong enough to take the offensive. They had no longer to face the danger of a sit-down strike, for the Daladier Government had expelled the strikers from the Renault works with a vigour that made a repetition of the expulsion unnecessary.

France at last had a Government with the resources of a government. It was time, for if Germany was officially pacific, Italy, the other end of the axis, staged a demonstration that revealed how low France had sunk in the eyes of her neighbour. That *Italian* deputies should dare to shout 'Nice, Savoy, Tunis', that *Italy* should dare to claim portions of French territory, even in so indirect a fashion, was intolerable. French self-esteem was profoundly shocked.

The attempts of M. Bonnet to minimize Italian insolence did not in the long run help matters, and it was M. Daladier who provided the answer by visiting Corsica, Tunisia and Algeria and affirming that not an inch of these lands would be given up. The Spanish Republic was dying; Signor Mussolini had had his way there; but whatever might happen in other lands, the soil of France (and of her territories) was sacred. That was an argument that the peasants, for whom M. Daladier claimed more and more to speak, could understand. Despite some absurd examples of journalistic optimism almost reaching the British level of folly, the occupation of Prague was less of a shock to French public opinion than to British. But again the nature of the reaction was left to Britain to determine. She led the way in guaranteeing Poland and in the effective if not the formal recognition of Franco's (and Mussolini's) triumph in Spain.

France was no longer worried at an Italian military menace to Tunisia. The Mareth line made the narrow band joining the French

North African 'island' to Libya impassable. In Tunisia itself, the threat of Italian conquest rallied most natives to the protecting power and the Duce had obligingly decapitated the local Italian colony, since nearly all its economically and socially prominent leaders were Leghorn Jews. The economic position of France and, with it, her powers of aerial defence improved; and even the professional patriots of the Right were no longer such uncritical lovers of Italy as to forget their duty to France. There were changes for the worse, too. The Germans had got immense stores of the instruments of war in Bohemia; every day that passed meant that the Siegfried line cement was hardening, the forts getting nearer completion.

France was neither elated nor terrified at the ordeal which all but the most optimistic saw was coming. Politicians might squabble over the beauties or dangers of proportional representation and the Socialists make a silly pretence of constitutional indignation, when M. Lebrun was persuaded to remain at the Élysée for another presidential term. There were not, of course, wanting genuine pacifists or men whose hatred of Bolshevism blinded them to more immediate dangers. It was, as Jacques Maritain was to point out, one of the tragic difficulties of the times that men seemed to be forced to choose between greater or lesser evils, the support of the tyranny of Hitler or the tyranny of Stalin. But the slow negotiations in Moscow, conducted by the various British agents, seemed to promise a united front against territorial aggression. In France the patriotism of the Communists was, in 1939, as it had been for years, almost too vehement, too unconditional, but patriots like Henri de Kerillis rejoiced that the chosen leaders of so great a part of the French workers were now so reliable a barrier against another Munich.

The crisis at last came. From the moment that the Russo-German treaty was announced, it was obvious that war was at hand. Taken unawares, the French Communists could only issue desperate last-minute apologies. But the Government suppressed *Humanité* and the formally non-Communist evening paper, *Ce Soir*. The Communist leaders protested that they were misunderstood, and when at last France declared war on Germany, they, like all the Chamber, rallied in defence of their country, the more easily that that country was fighting the man and the system they had denounced so vehemently ever since the Nazi revolution. 'Il faut en finir', said the average man wearied by repeated mobilizations, by repeated calls to arms, followed by truces of a few months that lasted until the ruler of Germany decided what engagement it would be most easy and profitable to break next. France in September 1939 (as in September 1938) answered the call to arms with stoical calm and resolution. It was time.

In the days after Munich when, with varying degrees of candour, the escape from the ordeal was being celebrated, Georges Duhamel had bitterly noted that France, in withdrawing behind the Maginot line, had lost the Descartes line, that intellectual tradition of being the European home and friend of liberty of the body and liberty of the mind. It had now been discovered that such a retreat was impossible for France: that the Descartes line and the Maginot line were one. An unknown soldier in September 1938 had known that. Across the Rhine the Germans had hoisted a placard, 'Ein Reich, Ein Volk, Ein Führer'. He, in reply, put up his board. On it was written 'Liberté, Égalité, Fraternité'. The battle between these two ideals has begun.

CHRONOLOGICAL TABLE OF MAIN EVENTS IN FRENCH HISTORY FROM THE REVOLUTION TO 1870

1789 July 14th. Fall of the Bastille.
August 4th. Abolition of feudal rights.
1791 June 20th. Flight of Louis XVI to Varennes.
1792 August 10th. Fall of the Monarchy.
September 22nd. Establishment of the First Republic.
1794 July 7th (9th Thermidor). Overthrow of Robespierre and the Jacobins.
1799 November 9th (18th Brumaire). Bonaparte makes himself First Consul.
1804 May 18th. Establishment of the First Empire.
1814 April 6th. First abdication of Napoleon I. Restoration of Louis XVIII.
1815 June 18th. Waterloo : second abdication of Napoleon I ; the second Restoration.
1830 'Revolution of July' : abdication of Charles X : accession of the Duke of Orleans as 'King of the French'.
1848 February 24th. Overthrow of the 'July Monarchy'. The Second Republic.
June 24th–26th. Defeat of the Paris workers.
December 10th. Prince Louis Napoleon Bonaparte elected President.
1851 December 2nd. 'The *coup d'état*': Louis Napoleon makes himself Dictator.
1852 December 2nd. Establishment of the Second Empire under 'Napoleon III'.[1]
1870 September 4th. Establishment of the Third Republic.

[1] 'Napoleon II' was the King of Rome who was deemed to have succeeded on the abdication of Napoleon I.

INDEX